MAJOR SOCIAL PROBLEMS

Major Social Problems

EARL RAAB

President, California Association for Mental Health

GERTRUDE JAEGER SELZNICK

Survey Research Center, University of California, Berkeley

ROW, PETERSON AND COMPANY
Evanston, Illinois   White Plains, New York

1959

Copyright © 1959 by Row, Peterson and Company
All rights reserved for all countries,
including the right of translation.
5692

Manufactured in the United States of America

*For Earl Benjamin and Elizabeth
and for Meg*

Acknowledgments

We should like to thank those authors who graciously gave us permission to abridge and adapt their writings. Pauline Lehrman's administrative assistance was invaluable throughout, and Christine Hoffmann, Maryan Lebell, Betty Jean Miller, and Walter Phillips helped us in essential ways. We are glad of this opportunity to express our gratitude. We are also especially indebted to Leonard Broom and Philip Selznick for help and encouragement.

EARL RAAB

GERTRUDE J. SELZNICK

Table of Contents

ACKNOWLEDGMENTS vii

LIST OF ADAPTATIONS xiv

A NOTE TO THE STUDENT 1

CHAPTER 1. SOCIAL PROBLEMS: A CITIZEN'S APPROACH 3

    I. WHAT ARE SOCIAL PROBLEMS? 3

    II. MEASURING A SOCIAL PROBLEM 6

        Objective Measurement. Subjective Measurement.

    III. CAUSATION 9

        Major Social Changes. Social Disorganization. Psychological Factors. Specific Risk Conditions.

    IV. MEETING THE PROBLEM 23

        Citizens' Associations. Channels of Action. The Role of the Citizen. Conclusion.

CHAPTER 2. JUVENILE DELINQUENCY: ANALYZING THE PROBLEM . . . 31

    I. WHAT IS THE PROBLEM? 31

        The Legal Concept. The Legal Concept Questioned. The New Problem of Delinquency.

    II. PORTRAIT OF DELINQUENCY—WHO AND HOW MANY? 37

        The Statistics of Delinquency. The Limitations of Delinquency Statistics.

III. WHY? THEORIES OF CAUSATION 40

Basic Causal Theories: Heredity; Personality Factors; Learning Factor; Group-Control Factors.

Specific Risk Conditions: The Delinquent Society; The Mass Media; Delinquency Areas; Underprivilege; Peer Groups; The Family.

IV. SUMMARY 60

CHAPTER 3. JUVENILE DELINQUENCY: MEETING THE PROBLEM 91

I. PROGRAMS FOR PREVENTION 92

Group-Work Agencies and Organized Recreation. "Big Brother" Activities. Child Guidance. Programs for Early Detection. Gang Direction. Neighborhood Area Projects.

II. TREATMENT OF DELINQUENTS 104

Arrest. Detention. The Juvenile Court. Correctional Institutions. Probation.

III. SUMMARY 115

CHAPTER 4. CRIME 135

I. WHAT IS THE PROBLEM? 135

II. THE FACES OF CRIME 137

Predatory Crime. Organized "Service" Crime. White-Collar Crime. Special Crime Problems: Sex Offenses and Narcotics.

III. MEETING THE PROBLEM 148

Prevention. Treatment.

CHAPTER 5. GROUP PREJUDICE: ANALYZING THE PROBLEM 173

I. WHAT IS THE PROBLEM? 173

II. MANIFESTATIONS OF PREJUDICE 176

Kinds of Prejudiced Behavior. A Chart of Prejudiced Behavior. Kinds of Prejudiced Attitudes.

CONTENTS xi

    III. EFFECTS OF PREJUDICE 184

        Social and Political Effects. Economic Effects. Psychological Effects: On the Targets of Prejudice. Psychological Effects: On the Prejudiced.

    IV. THE OBJECTS OF PREJUDICE 186

        The American Negro: Background History; Patterns of Prejudice.

        The American Jew: Background History; The Pattern of Prejudice.

        Other Targets of Prejudice

    V. WHY? THE CAUSES OF PREJUDICE 209

        Basic Causal Theories: Personality Factors; Social Factors.

        Risk Conditions: The Prejudiced Community; The Family; Economic and Political Tensions.

    VI. SUMMARY 221

CHAPTER 6. GROUP PREJUDICE: MEETING THE PROBLEM 239

    I. THE LAW 241

        Constitutional Questions. Law and Private Discrimination. Law and Public Discrimination.

    II. DIRECT ACTION 258

        Negotiation. Public Exposure. Boycott.

    III. EDUCATION 261

        The Schools. The Mass Media.

    IV. COMMUNITY ORGANIZATION 268

        Patterns of Influence. Aims of Community Organization. Who Are Key Forces? Involvement of Key Forces.

    V. THE STRATEGY OF APPROACH 276

        Differences in Agencies. Differences in Issues.

    VI. SUMMARY 277

CHAPTER 7. IMMIGRATION 311

    I. WHAT IS THE PROBLEM? 311

II. THE GROWTH OF THE PROBLEM 313

Stage I: Early Immigration (1607–1830). Stage II: The "Old" Immigrants (1830–80). Stage III: The "New" Immigrants (1880–1920). Stage IV: Controlled Immigration (1921–52). Stage V: The Present—Renewed Control.

III. IMMIGRANT ADJUSTMENT 326

Stages of Adjustment. Theories of Satisfactory Adjustment. Aids to Adjustment. The Record of Adjustment.

IV. MEETING THE PROBLEM 339

CHAPTER 8. THE FAMILY 355

I. WHAT IS THE PROBLEM? 355

II. DIVORCE 360

The Divorce Rate. Who Gets Divorced? Divorce as a Social Problem. Why Divorce?

III. THE FAMILY, SOCIETY, AND THE CHILD 383

Loss of Function. Sharing Socialization.

IV. MEETING THE PROBLEM 391

Influences toward Family Unity. Social Services.

CHAPTER 9. THE SCHOOLS 413

I. WHAT IS THE PROBLEM? 413

Recent Social Issues and the Schools.

II. EDUCATIONAL PURPOSES—FOR WHOM AND FOR WHAT? . . . 416

Background. The Current Issues.

III. THE EDUCATIONAL INSTRUMENT—PUBLIC OR PRIVATE? . . . 418

Background. The Current Issues.

IV. THE EDUCATIONAL METHOD—CURRICULUM 429

Background. The Current Issues.

CONTENTS xiii

    V. MEETING THE PROBLEM 441

        Making the Decisions. Staffing the Schools. Financing the Schools.

CHAPTER 10. DEPENDENCY 471

    I. WHAT IS THE PROBLEM? 471

        Changes in Family Responsibility. Changes in the Concept of Dependency. Insurance *vs.* Dole.

    II. DEPENDENCY BECAUSE OF PHYSICAL DISABILITY 476

        Extent and Nature of the Problem.

        Meeting the Problem: Prevention and Treatment; Meeting the Family Medical Bill; Rehabilitation; Supporting the Disabled.

    III. DEPENDENCY BECAUSE OF EMOTIONAL OR MENTAL DISABILITY . 488

        Extent and Nature of the Problem: Mental Retardation; Clinical Emotional Disorders; Personality Disorders; Causes of Mental Illness.

        Meeting the Problem: Mental Retardation; Emotional Disorders.

    IV. THE DEPENDENCY OF OLD AGE 502

        Extent and Nature of the Problem: Diminution of Physical Powers and Health; Loss of Economic Function; Loss of Family Life; Loss of Status and Social Isolation.

        Meeting the Problem: Employment; Economic Support; Leisure-Time Activities.

CHAPTER 11. THE INDIVIDUAL AND SOCIETY 535

        Government and the Individual. The Individual and His Work. The Individual and His Leisure. An Evaluation: The Loss of Individuality. An Evaluation: Loss of Social Organization.

NAME INDEX 573

SUBJECT INDEX 577

List of Adaptations

1. SOCIAL DISORGANIZATION AND DELINQUENCY 62

   From Bernard Lander, *Towards an Understanding of Juvenile Delinquency.*

2. UNRAVELING JUVENILE DELINQUENCY 71

   From Sheldon and Eleanor Glueck, *Unraveling Juvenile Delinquency.*

3. AN EXPERIMENT IN PREVENTION OF DELINQUENCY 116

   From Edwin Powers, "An Experiment in Prevention of Delinquency," *Annals of the American Academy of Political and Social Science.*

4. WORKING WITH STREET GANGS 122

   From James R. Dumpson, "An Approach to Anti-Social Street Gangs," *Federal Probation.*

5. THE PSYCHIATRIC TREATMENT OF CHILDREN 127

   From H. Whitman Newell, "Principles and Practices Used in Child Psychiatric Clinics," *Mental Hygiene.*

6. PREDICTING PAROLE SUCCESS AND FAILURE 158

   From Lloyd E. Ohlin, *Selection for Parole.*

7. FALLACIES CONCERNING THE SEX OFFENDER 166

   From Paul W. Tappan, *The Habitual Sex Offender.*

8. THE SEMANTICS OF PREJUDICE 222

   From Felix S. Cohen, "The Reconstruction of Hidden Value Judgments: Word Choices as Value Indicators," in Lyman Bryson et al. (eds.), *Symbols and Values: An Initial Study.*

9. THE "MINORITY" CULTURE OF THE AMERICAN NEGRO 226

   From Gunnar Myrdal, *An American Dilemma.*

LIST OF ADAPTATIONS

10. INTERRACIAL HOUSING 279

    From Morton Deutsch and Mary Evans Collins, "Intergroup Relations in Interracial Public Housing: Occupancy Patterns and Racial Attitudes," *Journal of Housing*.

11. PHILADELPHIA RACE RIOT 286

    From Hannah Lees, "How Philadelphia Stopped a Race Riot," *The Reporter*.

12. PROMISING PRACTICES IN INTERGROUP EDUCATION 292

    From Marion Edman and Laurentine Collins, *Promising Practices in Intergroup Education*.

13. A SOUTHERNER'S VIEW OF DESEGREGATION 300

    From Thomas R. Waring, "The Southern Case against Desegregation," *Harper's Magazine*.

14. THE SUPREME COURT ON SCHOOL DESEGREGATION 304

    The Court's decision in *Brown* v. *Board of Education*.

15. WHOM WE SHALL WELCOME 342

    From the President's Commission on Immigration and Naturalization, *Whom We Shall Welcome*.

16. IN DEFENSE OF NATIONALITY 344

    From Henry Pratt Fairchild, *Race and Nationality*.

17. THE ASSIMILATION OF MINORITY GROUPS 347

    From Louis Wirth, "The Problem of Minority Groups," in Ralph Linton (ed.), *The Science of Man in the Modern World*.

18. MARRIAGE—A CULTURAL PERSPECTIVE 397

    From M. F. Ashley Montagu, "Marriage—A Cultural Perspective," in Victor W. Eisenstein, M.D., *Neurotic Interaction in Marriage*.

19. DIVORCE—A CATHOLIC VIEW 400

    From chapters by Clement S. Mihanovich and John L. Thomas in Clement S. Mihanovich (ed.), *Marriage and the Family*.

20. THE ADOLESCENT 404

    From Nathan W. Ackerman, M.D., "The Adaptive Problems of the Adolescent Personality," in *The Family in the Democratic Society*.

LIST OF ADAPTATIONS

21. PUTSCH IN PASADENA 450

    From Milton A. Senn, "Putsch in Pasadena," *Frontier*.

22. EDUCATIONAL WASTELANDS 458

    From Arthur E. Bestor, *Educational Wastelands*.

23. PAROCHIAL SCHOOLS AND THE FIRST AMENDMENT 464

    From the decision of the Supreme Court in *Everson v. Board of Education*.

24. THE FIGHT FOR FUNDS 511

    From Marguerite Shepard, "The Battle for Health . . . and Dollars," *St. Louis Globe-Democrat*.

25. POLITICAL PANACEAS AND THE AGED 517

    From John J. Corson and John W. McConnell, *Economic Needs of Older People*.

26. MENTAL HEALTH AREAS THAT PROMISE PROGRESS 523

    From Paul V. Lemkau, M.D., "Toward Mental Health Areas That Promise Progress," *Mental Hygiene*.

27. ALCOHOLISM AND GROUP THERAPY: ALCOHOLICS ANONYMOUS . . . 529

    From Robert F. Bales, "Social Therapy for a Social Disorder—Compulsive Drinking," *Journal of Social Issues*.

28. PARTICIPATION AND MASS APATHY IN ASSOCIATIONS 547

    From Bernard Barber, "Participation and Mass Apathy in Associations," in Alvin W. Gouldner (ed.), *Studies in Leadership*.

29. WORK AND ITS DISCONTENTS 552

    From Daniel Bell, "Notes on Work," *Encounter*.

30. THE ALIENATED INDIVIDUAL 562

    From Rollo May, "A Psychologist Looks at Mental Health in Today's World," *Mental Hygiene*.

31. SOCIETY AS THE PATIENT 566

    From Lawrence K. Frank, "Society as the Patient," *American Journal of Sociology*.

32. COMMENT ON "SOCIETY AS THE PATIENT" 568

    From L. Guy Brown, "Society as the Patient—A Communication," *American Journal of Sociology*.

A Note to the Student

SOCIAL PROBLEMS AND COMMUNITY ACTION

Social problems provide laboratory materials for students of society. At the same time, they are living problems with which the practicing members of society must somehow cope. In this book, social problems are first analyzed in the light of modern sociological and psychological research and theory. Each such analysis of the nature, dimensions, and causes of a given social problem is then followed by a section on "Meeting the Problem." In this section, the earlier theoretical analysis is related to the patterns of deliberate social action in which the community is engaged, or could be engaged, toward mitigation of the problem.

ADAPTATIONS

Following the textual material in each chapter, except Chapter 1, there are adaptations of selected works by various authors. In some cases, these adaptations represent précis and summaries of basic pieces of research reported in books, monographs, or articles in scholarly journals. In other cases, they are selections representing expressions of opinion on issues having a strong controversial flavor. These latter adaptations are included because of their representative character and do not necessarily mirror the opinions of the authors of this book.

E. R.

G. J. S.

GOV. BLAIR CALLS HOUSE SLASH IN CHILD AID FUNDS 'DISHEARTENING'

He Speaks Out Against Committee Action in Cutting $346,896 From Needs to End of Fiscal Year.

By EDWARD H. THORNTON
A Staff Correspondent of the Post-Dispatch.

JEFFERSON CITY — A cut of $346,896 in House Appropriations Committee in funds to provide dependent children for of the current fiscal year termed "most disheartening today by Gov. James T...

"If allowed to stand declared, "it will mean ship, suffering and hardship more than 76,000 children mothers who depends aid for their livelihood...

The reduction was in a strongly worded statement issued by the Governor diately after the committee commended to the House statute bill providing mentary appropriations...

The East Bergen Picture
School Population Up

When school bells ring in East Bergen next month, some 13,066 youngsters will answer the first call of the year to take up readin', 'ritin' and 'rithmetic.

This represents 395 over the 12,6 rolled in schools of Bergen towns las...

A major increa in Ridgefield, ough's new $2,000 will open its do, semester, bringin back from neigh schools.

Leonia and show slight decre other municipal...

Park to attend the high school here.

No significant changes are expected in enrollment from last...

FAIRVIEW

Problems of Growing Old Will Be Studied

The University of California at Berkeley is planning an extensive study of the physiological and psychological changes which take place throughout the life span of the human being. President Clark Kerr has announced... Dr. Harold E. Jones, professor of psychology, will continue as director of the institute. Dr. Hardin B...

persons. It will be concerned with providing better services and facilities for this portion of our population.

Negroes Appeal Bus Decision

Negro attorneys have filed formal notice of appeal in the Memphis bus desegregation case.

The appeal is being made to both the Appellate Court and the Supreme Court.

H. K. Lockard, negro Memphis attorney, is representing a negro postal employe, O. Z. Evers, who charges he was put off a Memphis Street Railway bus when he sat in the front of it in 1956.

A three-judge court, sitting in phis, threw the case out on ds Evers had created the nt—that there was no rea... The court did not discuss question of bus segregation decision.

GLORIOUS TEXAS?

West Dallas Area Ripe for Renewal

By DON FREEMAN

What is the meaning of all this?

A family is living in a greyed shack the size of a shed — 10x10 feet, hardly room to walk in.

broke into a private gara took fishing tackle and cycle. The owner of the who said his wife and had been terrorized by the age group, was arrested fo charging a firearm at the intruders.

Juvenile delinquency ha increasing since the June ing of the school district 18 program for trouble youths, Mr. Kane said. The gram was dropped becau criticism from some facti the community.

The civic groups propo a similar program be in tuted by the state, coun town.

To others, West Dallas is the problem and conscience of the whole city. A social problem, a dust cost-of-city-services and tax prob...

CHARGE MOM BEAT GIRL, 4

(Special Dispatch to The Register)

MOLINE, ILL. — Mrs. Genevieve Vrombaut, 25, Moline, Saturday was charged with assault after police said she admitted beating her 4-year-old daughter with a one-inch thick piece of lumber.

The daughter Susan, was in good condition in a hospital here with two fractured bones of the right hand and cuts and bruises on her back, forehead and legs.

Police Called

Police were called Friday...

undergo psychiatric examination.

The Vrombauts have three other children, a daughter, 6, and sons, 18 years old and 8 months old.

GAMBLING RING SOLICITED FOR BETS BY PHONE

Clients Tell How They Were Called at Home

Indianapolis, Aug. 13 [Special]—The 5th amendment to the United States Constitution first appearance y in the three day grand jury inquiry

needed, particularly if industry is to be attracted. Only full scale renewal, with replatting, could achieve that pattern.

code enforcement and patient encouragement.

A reporter, accompanying two city officials last week, saw the West improvements. He also saw blight that could be regarded as beyond

Security Tightened At Juvenile Court

Rash of Escapes and Attempted Break-Out Brings Crackdown on Way Youths Handle

A rash of escapes and attempted break-outs at Juvenile Court has brought a crackdown in securit measures.

Judge Elizabeth McCain said prefects at the cour have been trying to accommodate the youngsters—

LEVITTOWN TO ACT ON UNRULY YOUTH

Violence Prompts 2 Civic Groups to Call Meeting Wednesday Night

By ROY R. SILVER
Special to The New York Times

LEVITTOWN, L.I., Sept. 13 — An effort to combat juvenile delinquency in this community will be made by two of its largest civic groups...

Little Rock Schools
Ike Troop Hint---
'Integration Rulin Must Be Obeyed

WASHINGTON, Aug. 20 (AP)—President Eisenhower indicated today he would again call out Federal troops if he felt a State failed to suppress unlawful opposition to school integration ordered by the Federal courts.

Anarchy will result if persons, communities States continue to defy court decrees, the President said.

Mayors Urge More Aid On Airports and Slums

MIAMI BEACH, Fla., Sept. 13 (AP)—The Nation's mayors called today for speedy enactment by Congress next January of a 400-million-dollar Federal aid for airports program and a 350-million-dollar a-year urban redevelopment program.

President Eisenhower in vetoing the bill felt Congress were asked to cooperate in getting out the two programs without delay.

Resolutions urging the ac...

vening to block passage of slum-clearance legislation.

One resolution said state and local government are unable to finance needed airport construction and Congress should provide $100 million a year for the next to lion a year for the next to years as grants-in-aid.

While Mr. Eisenhower was time for the Federal G ernment to begin withdraw from the airport grant p gram, the Conference said a...

Negro Youths Win 'Sit-Down' Strike

OKLAHOMA CITY, Aug. 21 — (UPI) — Store officials at Katz Drug Co., today gave in to Negro youths who went on a "sit-down" strike for fountain service, and began to serve the Negroes.

The youths had occupied all ats of the store's soda counter for several hours today, otesting the store's policy serving Negroes only when ey want food to be taken away for consumption elsewhere.

The store's manager, J. B. Masoner, had no comment on

they wish, but served."

But at 5:15 p. who had stood de arms under ins to take the food working again, daes, sodas, and to the Negro cus

The protest tion jumped 25 per cent from said they wou other stores ton

A brief bom firemen and pol the sto cision anonym employ in the who sign o Poli crowde day, b report The ganized Youth Associ

Number of Mentally Ill Rises in State

HARTFORD (UPI)—Acting State Mental Health Commissioner Elias J. Marsh reported yesterday that the percentage of persons admitted to state mental hospitals is growing twice as fast as the population of the state.

Marsh said the state population from 1946 to the present, but at the same time the number of first admissions to the state's three hospitals jumped 50 per cent. In addition, the mental

ation measures were out by the committee took prepared copies

Inter Club Council to hear expert on alcoholism cure

The Inter Club Council, at its Monday noon meeting, at the YMCA, will hear Percy Sessions discuss the treatment of alcoholics at the outpatient clinic here.

Sessions, chief cial worker at the Center of Alcoholic tensive training in work.

He is a graduate versity of Tennessee work. He attended State University at cial welfare, then mer school at studies on alcoholi

SESSIONS HAS the faculty of the Social Work, Unive ington, and has be eastern Louisiana tal. Almost nine devoted to work v

Reservations fo meeting should b Mrs. Melba

ident to reconsider his p posal to reduce Federal under the urban redevelo ment program. It urged C

Unsavory Pair Admit Breakin at Ced Bluffs Service Station Early on May 1

The fate of two Lincoln youths who confessed to a breakin in Cedar Bluffs last week rested in the hands of District Court Judge H. Emerson Kokjer following their appearance before him Monday morning of this week.

The two, along with another youth, were apprehended for questioning

y Harlan?
A (By the defendant, Percy Harlan). Yes, sir.
Q How far did you go in school, Percy?
A Twelfth grade.
Q You graduated?
A
lfth grade.
go to school? Lincoln, Nebraska
liquor.
Q In Lincoln?
A Mmhmm. (Meaning yes).
Q You understand what this ceeding is all about?
A Yes.
Q And the possible results?
A Yes, sir.

Rogers Says Crime Costs U.S. $20-Billion Annually

Chicago Tribune Press Service

CHICAGO, June 11 — Crime costs the United States $20-billion a year, an amount second only to expenditures for national defense, Atty. Gen. William P. Rogers said here tonight.

Rogers warned a meeting of state attorneys general that the public must be made aware of the destructive force organized crime represents to this country.

Charging that professional gangsters are disproving the adage that crime does not pay, Rogers told the closing session of

with little risk by exerting remote control over those types of criminal activities that yield the most profits — gambling, narcotics, and extortion—and they pay only a small portion of their taxes on ities."

Several state attacked public organized crime erans and social to get unofficial thorities to oper Rogers expres

Three Domestic Relation Officers Named by Daly

HARTFORD (AP) — Three domestic relations officers for the state's largest counties have been appointed by Chief Justice Edward J. Daly of the

alimony and support and custody of children. They will start Sept. 1.

Former Sheriff

Cary is a graduate of La Sa...

ticut probation and parole assn.

Polvani, who resides in Meriden, attended Meriden High School and the University of

Q Have you ever been ch with a felony before?
A No, sir.
Q Have you ever been in before?
A No, sir.
Q Outside of the Army?
A In '55. Minor in possessi

CHAPTER 1

Social Problems:
A Citizen's Approach

Section I: What Are Social Problems?

The newspaper headlines in the montage on the facing page are typical of those that appear every day in communities across the nation. Each of them reflects a disturbing phenomenon, affecting many people, which is usually called a "social problem." Other headlines reflect other problems which affect many people and yet are not considered social problems. Why do we regard some problems but not others as *social* problems?

First of all, *social problems are primarily problems in relationships among people.* All community problems are not social problems. An agricultural area may be severely stricken by drought. The farmers have a serious problem, but the drought does not in itself constitute a social problem. When the question is raised as to how the more fortunate members of the community should assist those stricken, *then* the problem acquires a social dimension. It becomes a matter of the kind of relationships which members of the community have established or should establish among themselves.

Whenever people live together, they must establish firm relationships so that they will know what is expected of them and what they can expect from others. In our society one man is expected not to hit another except for certain well-defined reasons. People are expected not to steal from one another. Every man is expected to assume certain responsibilities in the presence of community danger. Parents are expected to support their minor children. Negroes are or are not expected to sit next to white people in restaurants or to apply for clerical jobs. These are the rules of relationship that guide the behavior of individuals toward one another. These rules are intimately related to prevailing values; if the subordination of Negroes is an accepted value in the community, the day-to-day relationships between whites and Negroes will shape themselves accordingly. Some rules are simply part of the norms, or common ways, of the community; for example, we are expected to be respectful to the aged. Other rules, however, are formalized as law; theft is a crime against the state.

Social problems are distinctively those problems that concern the rules of relationship, formal or informal, which the people of a society establish among themselves. However, not all problems in relationship are elevated to the order of social problems. Traffic congestion in downtown metropolitan areas is an abiding problem that often involves certain questions of relationship, e.g., between downtown and suburban merchants, but is not generally considered a social problem in itself. *A social problem exists (1) where prevailing relationships among people frustrate the important personal goals of a substantial number of people; or (2) where organized society appears to be seriously threatened by an inability to order relationships among people.* In other words, a social problem is a problem in human relationships which seriously threatens society itself or impedes the *important* aspirations of *many* people.

1. *Social problems concern the basic aspirations of many people.* A community has a social problem when relationships among people fail to meet, or interfere with, the important personal goals and aspirations of a substantial number of its members. This is not a matter of what these aspirations should be but of what they are in fact. Until an impelling aspiration for freedom has been kindled among slaves, slavery is not an active social problem, although it may indeed be considered a moral problem and may be recognized to be a potential social problem. A better case in point might be the situation in some of the underdeveloped areas in the world. The foremost aspirations of the people in these areas are for food, shelter, medical care, and freedom from foreign domination. These are the most immediately perceived details of their degradation. As a rule, the refinements of democracy, such as full freedom of expression, do not yet rank as prime personal goals, and censorship, for example, is not perceived as an acute social problem. In time, however, it may become an active social problem.

Shipwreck: Deck scene of the sinking S.S. "Vestris," 1928. Panic is one response, solidarity another, in the face of common danger.

It is apparent that the absence of social problems is not necessarily the mark of an ideal society, at least not as measured by our prevailing moral values. Nor does the intensification of social problems necessarily signify that a society is moving in a backward direction. The contrary may indeed be true. A society which permits no change and no progress tends almost by definition to have fewer social problems. In a changing society, such as America, some social problems may be symptoms of a change for the better.

The problem of group prejudice in this country is an example. This problem was not in sharp focus until aspirations for equal opportunity emerged and developed. At one time the desire to strike the chains of slavery seemed to be the primary concern of the Negro people and of those who had aspirations for the Negro people. There was no serious expression of concern, for example, about a housing discrimination that would have prevented Negroes from renting or buying houses in more desirable neighborhoods. As long as Negroes were enslaved or, as free men, were trapped in the lowest economic and cultural level, this was not a realistic problem. As the economic and educational condition of the Negro population improved, both the aspiration for and the possibility of better housing became real, and this aspect of the social problem was, in a sense, created.

2. *Social problems concern the basic order of society.* A social problem exists when organized society's ability to order relationships among people seems to be failing: when its institutions are faltering, its laws are being flouted, the transmission of its values from one generation to the next is breaking down, the framework of social expectations is being shaken. The widespread contemporary concern with juvenile delinquency, for example, is only partly that delinquency is the doorway to crime or is a threat to personal safety and property. It is also a fear that society is failing to transmit positive social values to its youth. This failure is seen as a symptom of society's increasing inability to impose an orderly pattern of relationships upon its members; it is seen, in other words, as a breakdown in society itself.

The breakdown of the social order and the frustration of individual aspirations are not unrelated. If individuals are continually frustrated, they feel themselves in conflict with the prevailing rules and exert pressure upon the traditional order of things. This is at present occurring most dramatically in the South. On the other hand, the failure of society to transmit positive values often results in individual unhappiness and disorientation, as in delinquency. Nevertheless, the difference is significant. In the one case, the existence of the social problem is measured by the extent of personal dissatisfaction involved. In the other case, the existence of the social problem is measured by the breakdown of the rules and machinery of society.

Section II: Measuring a Social Problem

A social problem, then, is any social situation which makes a substantial number of people unhappy or which seems to threaten society's ability to keep house. But it is not easy to measure either condition precisely. Facts and figures are often not available; and even when they are, they require careful assessment.

OBJECTIVE MEASUREMENT

The most obvious technique for measuring the seriousness of a social problem would seem to be a numerical count of the number of people who are affected. How many juvenile delinquents are there? How many criminals? How many people are in mental hospitals? How many incidents of racial or religious discrimination occur? How many immigrants fail to integrate themselves into American life? But statistical measurement is only a tool, and sometimes a treacherous tool. The mere use of numbers often gives the dangerous impression of mathematical precision where none exists.

First of all, the reliability of statistical data is often questionable. In measuring social behavior, any presumption of precision usually breaks down at the first step: the collection of data. How many juvenile delinquents are there? The semiannual *Uniform Crime Reports* of the Federal Bureau of Investigation has been a main source of statistics on this subject. These statistics rely on reports of arrests by police chiefs around the nation, but many communities are not included in these reports, and among those that are included there are widely varying reporting procedures. In addition, legal criteria of delinquency vary from state to state. In some states a child may be adjudged delinquent because he habitually plays on railroad tracks, while in other states this is not a violation of delinquency law. In some states no one over the age of sixteen can be categorized as delinquent; in other states, under certain circumstances, any offender under twenty-one is classified as a delinquent. No compilation of statistics brought together under such conditions can be considered precise. Many other social problems are even more difficult to measure accurately because data-collecting procedures are even less uniformly organized.

In any effort to evaluate the seriousness of a social problem, the interpretation of raw statistical data must be further qualified by a careful definition of terms. How many delinquents are there? There are habitual delinquents, and there are those who commit one or two delinquent acts and no more. Both kinds of delinquents are usually included in the over-all statistics, but their significance for the social problem of delinquency may be quite different.

Where an attempt is made to measure attitudes—for example, attitudes toward Negroes—pitfalls to accuracy are multiplied. One of the difficulties is that no attitude test can with assurance estimate the difference between what a person says he will do and what he actually will do or the difference between what a person says he thinks and what he does think. One study found that a number of people who said they would not purchase from a Negro clerk in fact did so, both before and after answering the question.

These cautions by no means exhaust the hazards that lie in the use of statistics; they merely demonstrate the initial problems of measurement. Statistics, even when soundly gathered, may still be put to mischievous, inappropriate, or mistaken use. By themselves, figures tell very little; statistical data must always be interpreted in the light of other knowledge. For example, more men than women tend to be admitted to mental hospitals. We cannot legitimately conclude from this that more men than women are mentally ill; from what we know of the different occupational roles of men and women in our society, it is plausible that a woman who is mentally ill is more likely than a man to be taken care of in the home. Delinquency statistics indicate that girls are more often adjudged delinquent for sexual dereliction than for theft, while for boys the opposite is true. We cannot therefore conclude that girls are more prone than boys to engage in prohibited sexual activity. On the basis of what we know about prevailing morality, we are better advised to assume that different standards of delinquency are applied to girls than to boys.

However, to the extent that statistics have been procured by unbiased and sound technical methods, they are useful and can serve as important cues. Although they do not in themselves define the nature or seriousness of the problem, the over-all statistics on delinquency, for example, indicate the probable existence of a problem. If available juvenile court statistics indicate that a half-million boys and girls are brought to the attention of the courts each year, this may not tell us much about these boys and girls or how many children really are "out of social control." But we can be assured that there is here *some* problem or set of problems affecting enough people to be worthy of further and careful investigation.

SUBJECTIVE MEASUREMENT

More often, the critical measurement of the seriousness of a social problem is based on value judgments rather than statistics. Even though they involve relatively few people, homicide and deviant sexual behavior are nevertheless often considered especially serious social problems because their very existence is an affront and a threat to some of our society's most hallowed rules. The sheer numbers of people whose fundamental aspirations are involved are enough to make prejudice a major social problem, but recognition of prejudice as a social problem is also shaped by the feeling that a critical value of our society is at stake. At issue is the ability of our society to create a social order which will realize and fulfill its ideals of equality. Similar considerations apply in the case of the aged. What is presently making old age a social problem is not only the sheer number of people involved but the conviction that the loneliness and indigence of some of our aging population represent a moral failure of industrial urban society.

Though the number of people directly affected is always a factor, it is not always the ultimate criterion by which the seriousness of a social problem is measured. A social problem is also a serious one if it represents a failure on the part of the social order to realize the values to which it is committed.

Section III: Causation

What causes a given social problem? Every parlor sociologist seems to have an answer, and most of them are probably right in one degree or another. Even a relatively simple public health problem such as malaria has a multiplicity of "causes": the bite of a malaria-carrying mosquito; the number of open-water breeding places for mosquitoes in the area; the fact that the people do not live in screened houses; the ignorance which tolerates the breeding places; the poverty which maintains the breeding places and the ignorance; the failure of government to do something about these conditions. All of these answers to the problem of malaria are correct as far as they go. Although medical science has isolated a germ as the specific and immediate cause of malaria, the germ does not result in malaria unless other conditions are operative. Without mosquito bites, the germs do not find their victims; without breeding places, there are no mosquitoes. The malaria germ is just the final link in the long causal chain of which malaria is the end product.

However, the analogy between physical disease and social problems breaks down at one important point. There is no single, isolable factor in the genesis of social problems corresponding to the malaria germ. In social problems, the causative factors appear to be many and diverse, and the relations among them are often unclear and unpredictable. In understanding social problems, we do not concentrate upon a single, specific cause but investigate instead the broad causal context in which a particular problem arises. The analogy to malaria is useful only to the extent that it dramatizes the fact that *many* causal conditions bear upon each other in the genesis of social problems.

In the following chapters, detailed analysis of causal factors is made in each case. However, there are three major avenues of approach to the understanding of social problems: (1) the historical, which emphasizes the broad social changes that have occurred and are occurring in modern society; (2) the sociological, which usually emphasizes the social disorganization accompanying these changes; and (3) the psychological, which emphasizes the personality factors in social problems.

MAJOR SOCIAL CHANGES

The nature of our major social problems is inexorably tied to the changes that have been occurring in Western society for the past century. These changes have unsettled old and traditional social patterns and have altered the perspectives and aspirations of many people.

Industrialization

Men once made their livelihood with their hands and with hand tools, largely in the fields and sometimes in small shops. On the farms and even in the handicrafts the family tended to be a working unity. Power machinery created increasingly new dimensions of manufactured goods and wealth, formerly undreamed of by the people of the world. Holding the value of the dollar constant, both gross national product and consumption expenditure per capita have almost doubled since 1900.[1]

At the same time, industrialization led to the mass migration of men from farm and shop to large industry or to large-scale commercial enterprises attached to industry. Farm population dropped, the decrease being accelerated by the mechanization of the farm itself, and the significance of the family as a productive economic unit diminished.

Urbanization

Industry concentrated in the cities, where power, transportation, and an ample supply of labor were available. From the farms and from the small towns streamed more and more people to fill the needs of industry

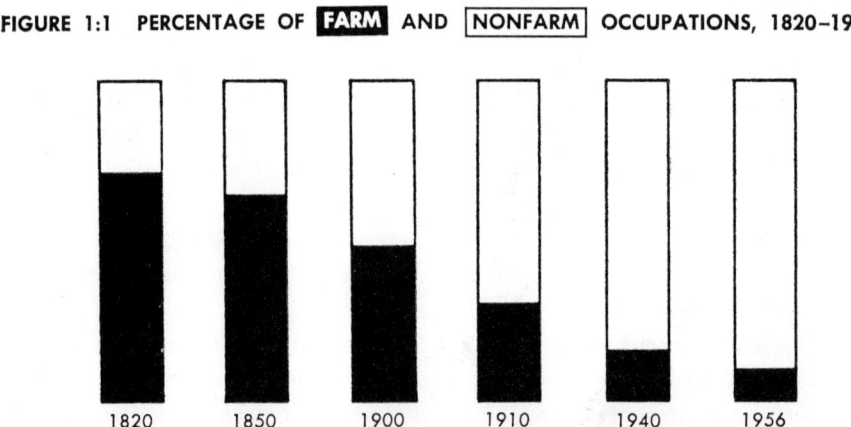

FIGURE 1:1 PERCENTAGE OF FARM AND NONFARM OCCUPATIONS, 1820–1956

Adapted from U.S. Bureau of the Census, *Statistical Abstract of the United States, 1957* (Washington, D.C.: U.S. Government Printing Office, 1957), pp. 195 and 199.

---

[1] U.S. Department of Labor, *Economic Forces in the U.S.A. in Facts and Figures* (Washington, D.C.: U.S. Department of Labor, 1955), p. 47.

The Metropolis: The borough of Queens, adjoining Manhattan. This is part of an unbroken stretch of concentrated city life spreading from New York to Northeastern New Jersey and containing over 13 million people.

and commerce. This movement increased with the declining need for manpower on the farms.

In 1790 only about 5 per cent of the American people lived in areas defined by the Bureau of the Census as "urban," that is, in incorporated cities having a population of 2,500 or more. By the middle of the nineteenth century about 15 per cent of our people lived in urban areas. At the turn of the century about 40 per cent, and by mid-century some 59 per cent, of the people were urban dwellers by this definition.[2]

In the 1950 census, official note was taken for the first time of the concept of the "metropolitan area." This was done in order to classify as "urban" those populations living in densely settled areas on the borders of cities of 50,000 or more inhabitants. In 1950 more than half the population of the country was living in such metropolitan areas, and four-fifths of the population growth was taking place in such areas. Taking these people into account, as well as those who were living in unincorporated urban areas, the urban population at mid-century could be counted as 64 per cent of the total population.

[2] U.S. Bureau of the Census, *Statistical Abstract of the United States, 1957* (Washington, D.C.: U.S. Government Printing Office, 1957), p. 20.

Not only did the number of urban places increase from about 200 to about 4,000 between the middle of the nineteenth and the middle of the twentieth century, but the size of individual cities grew apace. In 1850 there were no cities in the country with a population of a million; in 1950 there were five. In 1850 there was only one city with more than a

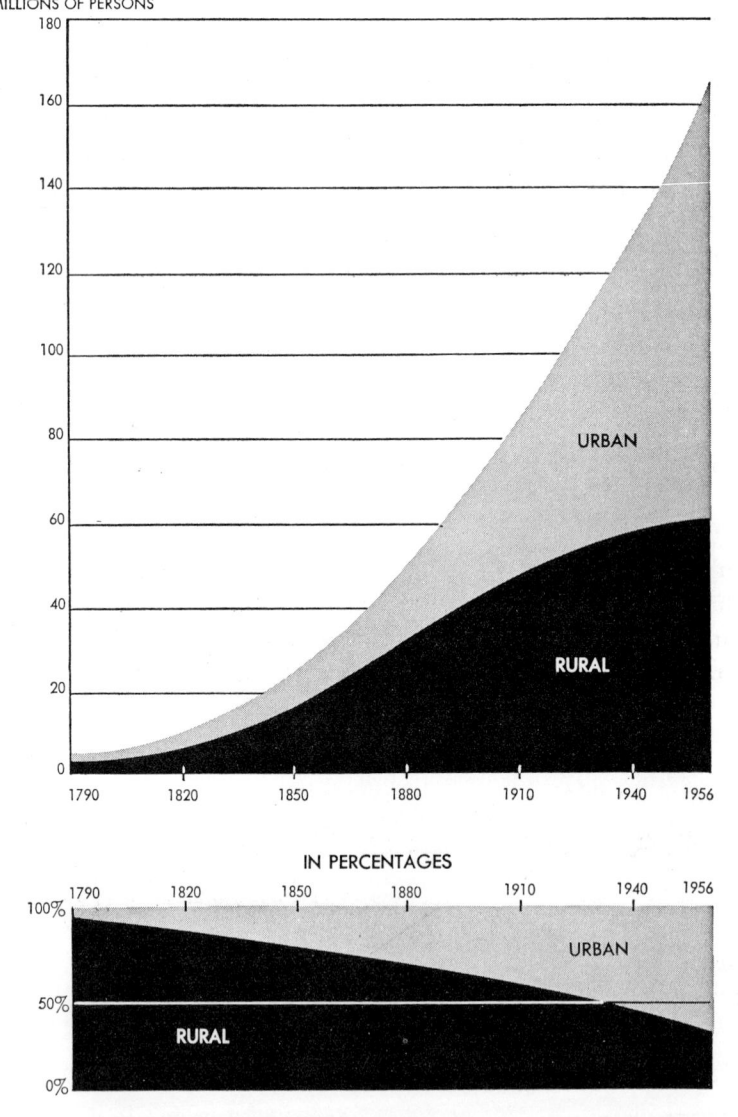

FIGURE 1:2   U.S. POPULATION BY URBAN AND RURAL RESIDENCE, 1790–1956

Adapted from U.S. Bureau of the Census, *Statistical Abstract of the United States, 1957* (Washington, D.C.: U.S. Government Printing Office, 1957), pp. 21 and 24.

quarter of a million people; in 1950 there were 41. During the same period, the number of cities with 100,000 people or more increased from 9 to 106.[3] If the metropolitan-area concept is applied, the increase in the size of urban places is even more dramatic. For example, the New York–Northeastern New Jersey metropolitan area contained over 12 million people in 1950, although only about $8\frac{1}{2}$ million of these lived in formally incorporated cities of 2,500 or more. The several million others were nevertheless living in a highly urbanized area.

Mobility

With the advent of industrialization and urbanization came an increase in mobility. Many people do not live out their lives in the town or region where they were born, near their families and with friends and neighbors with whom they have been reared and where their families have lived for generations before them. The American population has always been on the move—from abroad to America, from one section of the country to another, from farm and town to city. But in the cities themselves people move even more freely, if only from one district to another, often pressed by new waves of migration to the city. New modes of transportation have accelerated this mobility, and it has become easier to move from coast to coast. The automobile has become a staple of the American family, and there is less need to have friends, church, recreation, or other interests in the neighborhood in which one lives.

Heterogeneity

Modern urban life is characterized not only by mass aggregations of people but also by the heterogeneity of their backgrounds and traditions. To begin with, the United States is an immigrant country. The 1950 census indicated that almost one quarter of the American population,

FIGURE 1:3 PASSENGER MILES TRAVELED PER CAPITA, 1916 AND 1952

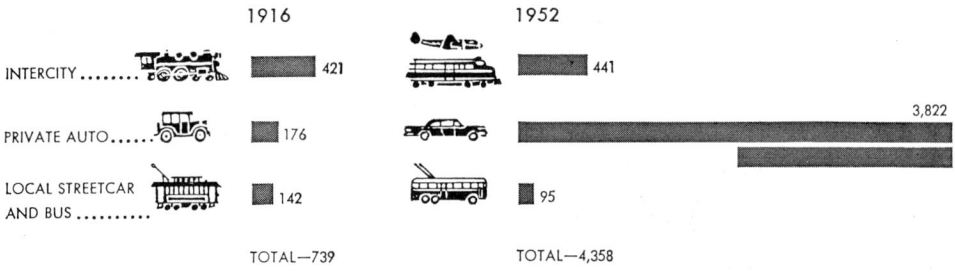

Adapted from J. Frederic Dewhurst and Associates, *America's Needs and Resources* (New York: Twentieth Century Fund, 1955), p. 261.

---

[3] *Ibid.*, p. 19.

or almost 34 million people, were either foreign-born or of foreign parentage. Ten different European countries each accounted for over a million of these.[4] Immigrants brought with them a variety of ethnic and religious backgrounds. American mobility has also increased heterogeneous contacts; between April, 1955, and April, 1956, 5 million Americans moved from one state to another.[5] Finally, a significant result of the increasing concentration of population in the cities has been a corresponding multiplication of contact among people of different ethnic, religious, racial, and cultural backgrounds. In the school, in the community, often in the neighborhood, the child is more likely to brush up against ideas, customs, and traditions which differ from those in his own home. The modern city is an open market place of traditions.

Acceptance of Change

The experience of rapid and visible change brought with it a sense of change and an expectation of change. The breaking of tradition became less and less of a shock. The rapid advances of technology and science, creating new frontiers of knowledge, buttressed this expectancy of change and new ideas. The modern population fully expects with each morning's newspaper the discovery of new ideas which will set old ideas aside. The concentration of people in urban areas has been a factor in this changing outlook, as has their mobility. Never before have men made so many different contacts with so many different kinds of people, different traditions, and different ideas and customs. Never has there been such open competition among ways of life.

These are the historical changes that have taken place within the last century. As defined earlier, social problems exist when society is seriously threatened by an inability to order relationships among people or when it frustrates the important aspirations of many. How have these historical changes operated to create these conditions in modern society?

SOCIAL DISORGANIZATION

Society's inability to order relationships among people is often explained as the result of social disorganization. The word "society" connotes "organization." A society is more than a mass of individuals; it is the organization of these individuals into some order. This order depends not on police power but on the common acceptance of certain rules of relationship among people. There are two major ways in which acceptance of prevailing rules of relationship is undermined: through the breakdown of tradi-

---

[4] U.S. Bureau of the Census, *Nativity and Parentage,* 1950 Population Census Reports, Series P-E, No. 3A (Washington, D.C.: U.S. Government Printing Office, 1954), p. 75.
[5] U.S. Bureau of the Census, *Statistical Abstract of the United States, 1957,* p. 38.

LIFE Photo by Nina Leen; © 1955, Time, Inc.

A Sense of Family: In contemporary America, this identification with family ancestry is unusual.

tional social groups, such as the family, and through a developing conflict between rules and aspirations.

Breakdown of Traditional Groups

People tend to absorb the values, the aspirations, and the rules of social behavior of those groups and institutions to which they belong. The ability of these groups and institutions to transmit their values and traditions depends directly on their ability to command respect and allegiance. Social disorganization refers primarily to the weakening of the groups and institutions in society which traditionally transmit its official values, such as the family, the school, the church, the community, and the law. The family, for example, is no longer the cohesive unit that it once was. The urban family is not tied together in a common economic enterprise, as was the traditional farm family. The members of the family are not as dependent on one another for entertainment or social companionship.

These institutions have lost some of their functional importance for their members and therefore some of their ability to bind their members together. They no longer claim the same allegiance and loyalty or sense of identification. As a result, they are no longer as effective means of social control, of transmitting social values, as they once were.

If, hypothetically, all the traditional sources of value in society are becoming weaker and are without adequate substitutes, then society's transmission of its official or dominant values is no longer organized but rather is becoming chaotic and haphazard. "Social disorganization," the descriptive term primarily applied to the breakdown of these traditional groups and institutions in society at large or in some particular area of society, is a basic causal approach to many social problems, such as delinquency and crime.

Conflict of Rules and Aspirations

When the traditional groups in society begin to lose their function for, and the allegiance of, group members, their ability to transmit their values is impaired. Conversely, however, when the values which reside in these groups are somehow questioned or weakened for group members, the ability of the groups to hold that allegiance is presumably impaired. Changing aspirations may subject some of the old rules of society to strain. Society is faced with the necessity of *maintaining* some of its basic rules of conduct in the face of these new aspirations; the child who has a heightened desire for material gain will still not steal if he has effectively absorbed the values which keep such a desire under social control. But society is also faced with the necessity of *changing* some of its rules of relationship to fit new aspirations. The growing desire of older people to have independent financial support in their retirement years from the government as a "right" is not only the result of the growing inability of the family to support its older members; it also stems from the fact that the desire for financial independence in these years has become more firm and widespread. An adjustment between traditional rules of responsibility for older citizens and the modern aspirations of these older citizens becomes necessary. The absence of such an adjustment on a substantial scale constitutes a social problem.

Society's need to adjust its rules to changing aspirations is most clear and dramatic when the changing aspirations of one group in society come into conflict with the aspirations of another group. This occurs, for example, when a traditionally subordinate group in society begins actively to aspire to the values of the traditionally and determinedly dominant group. Take the case of a Negro girl who enters a restaurant where the only available seat is next to a white girl. If both girls have learned well the traditional rules that have prevailed in parts of our society, then the Negro girl will not expect to sit next to the white girl and will not attempt to. However, if the aspirations of the Negro girl have advanced beyond this traditional rule, to which the white girl still subscribes, then there will be trouble or at least tension, uneasiness, and dissatisfaction.

The social problems which flow from changing aspirations have a different quality from those which flow from society's failure to transmit values. The conflict between traditional rules and new aspirations is often a normal and healthy concomitant of change. For example, during World War II, millions of Negroes found unprecedented opportunities for economic advancement because of the need for their services. For the first time, many of them saw the realistic possibility of achieving equal status with other Americans. Aspirations sharpened, as did dissatisfaction with existing relationships.

Heightened intergroup tension, in its current phase, can be compared better to the fever that accompanies a battle against disease than to the disease itself. It is a challenge to society rather than a threat in itself; it does not stem basically from the internal disorganization of society, although it may contribute to such disorganization and take sustenance from it.

PSYCHOLOGICAL FACTORS

Two brothers reared in the same family and cultural environment may manifest widely differing needs for personal recognition and support from those around them. One brother, as a consequence, may be more susceptible to the blandishments of a delinquent gang where he can find the recognition that he needs. Or one brother may have a special emotional need which lends itself readily to intergroup hostility. Because of distinctive emotional needs, one person may be generally more aggressive than another, more fearful, more suspicious, less capable of dealing with the frustrations of daily life. Such special emotional needs may comprise a special individual susceptibility to involvement in a given social problem.

The cause of individual differences in emotional character and needs is still the subject of much speculation and conflicting theory. The constitutional factor is not ignored in modern psychological speculation. An individual's constitution, in this sense, is a result not only of hereditary influences but of all physical influences before and after birth, whether they be glandular imbalance, evolutionary deviation, brain damage, or conditions which have not yet been isolated. Against the background of the constitutional qualities of the individual, however, we know that psychological history plays some role in the production of special emotional needs.

There is a mass and even a maze of theory on this subject, but present evidence indicates that much of the individual's basic emotional development normally takes place within the framework of an early give-and-take between him and society. Every child must be shaped within the confines of his own society. But since he is not pliant clay, this shaping involves a constant struggle. The exact nature of this struggle is subject to a wide range of theoretical interpretation, but psychologists and parents attest that the struggle takes place. Society in general and the family in particular are most successful insofar as they succeed in transmitting their values rather than imposing them by force or fear. The manner in which this is done is often critical in the development of basic emotional security.

For example, in making his way with such difficulty into the society of man, the child should, it would seem, be supported by a proper balance of affection, on the one hand, and directive discipline, on the other. However, the proper balance may differ for each child as a result of differences in constitution, personal history, and cultural environment.

Special emotional needs, growing out of certain kinds of emotional development, often play a role in an individual's involvement in a given social problem; but, as direct explanations of most *social* problems, these psychological theories are incomplete.

The existence of certain emotional needs might explain why some children become delinquent under certain social conditions while others do not, and the examination of these individual needs is imperative in the investigation of any given child's delinquent behavior. These psychological theories do not, however, explain *widespread* and epidemic changes in the occurrence or form of delinquency. If it is indeed true that families *in general* are becoming less able to provide an early framework of emotional security for a child, then theories such as social disorganization are most likely to provide a reason.

Nevertheless, psychological theories of susceptibility, in their proper perspective, are a vital part of the total causal picture in most social problems. They often help to explain differential reactions to prevalent social conditions, thereby filling in part of the jigsaw puzzle of causation.

SPECIFIC RISK CONDITIONS

It is also necessary to understand exactly how the general social and psychological factors described above operate in the daily life of the community to produce social problems.

In other words, it is important to isolate the specific *places* where values are transmitted or fail to be transmitted, where aspirations are or are not learned, where personality deviations are or are not developed. It is necessary to examine the specific conditions in the family, the school, the community, which seem to make the production of any given social problem more likely. For example, do some children become illicit collectors of hub-caps because they have never really absorbed the value that it is wrong to steal? Then what is the role of family life, or neighborhood life, or of other separable aspects of a child's life in producing such a failure? What *kind* of family life is likely to produce this kind of failure or the other kinds of failures which seem to be associated with delinquency? These various conditions can best be understood in the light of the broader causal theories, such as social disorganization. On the other hand, basic causal theories acquire their substance and validity only after an examination of these specific conditions in community life.

To understand the bearing of social disorganization upon a social problem, it is imperative, therefore, to examine those places where values and aspirations are most significantly learned and personality traits are developed: the family, the neighborhood, the peer group, and the influences of society at large, which pervade all of these more intimate relationships. The risk conditions which prevail in each of these places do not in themselves fully explain the existence of any social problem; they are mutually dependent and are only artificially separated. These are slices of life in which the genesis of social problems can be brought into specific focus. Moreover, they help bring order to the question of where, when, and how remedial measures can most effectively be brought to bear.

Society at Large

1. *"Official" society.* Laws, the actions or statements of public officials, and the behavior of public institutions help to teach values. For example, public schools which are racially segregated by law are effective in transmitting certain attitudes about intergroup relations. Their very existence serves to suggest a value difference between whites and Negroes. Similarly, widespread lawbreaking by public officials depreciates the importance of obeying the law.

2. *Common customs.* Accepted and visible practices in community life, even when not enforced by law or official action, are just as effective in

transmitting values. For example, if it is a widespread custom of employers in a community to advertise for employees that are "white" or "Gentile," the young people growing up in that community will tend to regard such practices as normal and acceptable, just as they will accept without question the practice of eating mashed potatoes with a fork rather than a spoon. Similarly, the fact that certain neighborhoods are obviously "restricted" has somewhat the same effect as legally segregated schools. For another example, any widespread practice of illegal gambling or tax-cheating, of overcharging by businessmen or misuse of funds by union leaders, almost inevitably becomes an effective part of the culture.

3. *Mass media*. Radio, television, motion pictures, magazines, and newspapers are all part of the broad cultural environment. They can transmit values explicitly in their news reports and editorials. They can also transmit values in more subtle ways. For example, if gangsters in the motion pictures are always portrayed as Italians, if the heroes are generally Anglo-Saxon types, or if Negroes are more often than not depicted as comical and menial, the effect on prejudiced attitudes can be considerable; even more subtle may be the way in which aspiration values are affected. If the motion-picture screen constantly reflects homes which are opulent and characters who casually winter on the French Riviera, the ability of some youthful viewers to come to immediate terms with a less glamorous life may be impaired. As a matter of fact, it is through the mass media that the most comprehensive picture of community life is projected, whether accurately or not.

The Neighborhood

The neighborhood has no formal laws and no effective mass media, but it can bring potent subcultural influences to bear. The common customs of a neighborhood can either reinforce or clash with the common customs of the larger community in some respects. The unofficial spokesmen of the neighborhood can sometimes outrank in influence the official spokesmen of society at large. Furthermore, the neighborhood is often the *place* where certain kinds of families tend to concentrate, where gangs flourish, where a criminal subculture is established. It is therefore often a convenient examining ground for probing certain social problems.

Some of the most dramatic research in the field of juvenile delinquency has centered around the discovery of neighborhood areas in which there are typically high rates of delinquency. There are a number of qualifying factors that may apply to these comparative statistics, such as the possibility that the police are more active in certain neighborhoods and that families are less well equipped to intervene between erring children and the courts. Nonetheless, evidence seems to point to a higher rate of delin-

Social Action: A suffragette, outside Buckingham Palace, London, June, 1914. The suffragettes found that getting arrested was an effective technique for attracting public attention to their cause.

quency in those neighborhoods which notably bear the marks of social disorganization. Family ties are looser; or families themselves are more alienated from society at large—are out of the mainstream of society's aspirations and rules of social relationship.

The neighborhood does not necessarily *cause* these family conditions, but it is often the place where families which suffer from these conditions tend to congregate. It is also often the place where families with definite criminal values tend to concentrate. It is the place where children can learn criminal values from sources outside their families; or where, at least, they are most likely to participate in delinquent acts because of their association with delinquent gangs.

The Peer Group

Next to the family, an individual's close circle of friends often ranks as the most intimate sphere of influence. At some stages it is sometimes more important than the family. Many children, and teen-agers in particular, feel deep allegiance to "the gang." Sometimes these gangs are an expression of group alienation from the values of society at large. Often they serve functions for the individual child that the family has failed to serve. Some of them are prime breeding grounds for delinquent behavior, although it is not always clear how often they produce delinquents and how often they merely serve as convenient mechanisms for those who are already delinquent.

Other Associations

There are many formal groups to which individuals belong: churches, labor unions, trade associations, fraternal orders, clubs. The ability of these groups to transmit or support social values depends in each case on the relation of the individual to the group. In some cases, the church is for the individual a highly valued religious institution. In others, the church is most important as a place to meet people with whom the individual identifies. In many other cases, church membership is token, and the church does not seriously affect the values of the individual either as a sociability center or as a religious institution. Veterans' organizations provide another kind of example. For most, membership in veterans' organizations is a token gesture or is an expression of support for the goal of specific veterans' benefits; only for a small proportion do these organizations provide a cohesive social group which consistently claims allegiance. Similarly, membership in labor unions or businessmen's groups does not necessarily carry a commitment to the wide range of social values which such organizations sometimes espouse. Nevertheless, organizations help to shape attitudes, especially attitudes toward current social problems.

The Family

The family is the basic unit of society and always deserves special examination. It is the place where the child initially learns or can learn his most basic values, aspirations, and attitudes. It is from his family that a child can initially learn racial prejudice, or can fail to learn attitudes that would make him more resistant to racial prejudice. It is from the family that the child can most directly absorb criminal values, or can fail to absorb values which would make him more resistant to criminal activity. Because of its major role as transmission belt, there is concern not only with what the family does but with what it fails to do.

There are many kinds of conditions which can characterize the failure of a family's ability to transmit traditional values. The family may be physically broken by divorce or separation. It may be more subtly broken in the sense that meaningful ties among its members do not exist. It may be part of a culture conflict, e.g., between immigrant parents and their children. The contribution of such family conditions to the widespread existence of particular social problems has been the subject of much investigation. But once the relation of family life to a social problem has been established, it is also necessary to complete the causative circle by determining the circumstances under which these widespread family conditions arise. What is there in American society that leads to family instability and lack of cohesiveness? Finally, it is necessary to determine what remedy can be most effectively applied.

If value conflict is serious, it will be discovered most specifically at the level of the family, which is the value-transmission base of society. And it is in the family also that the basic psychological factors are created which shape the variable susceptibility of the individual to personal involvement in social problems. It is in the study of family life, therefore, that the basic causal theories in social problems can be supported and analyzed.

Section IV: Meeting the Problem

A full understanding of the causal picture tends to prevent oversimplification and the resultant misapplication of energies. It is valid to ascribe a prime causative role to the family *if* the nature of the family's role in any given social problem is understood, *if* the relationship of the family to certain historical factors is understood, and *if* the role of other risk conditions in society is understood. But understanding the general causes of a social problem does not necessarily tell us how to meet the problem most effectively.

Once the causal merry-go-round is understood, the trick, remedially speaking, is to know where to get on. Should we address ourselves to the matter of industrialization, which has apparently played its part in the creation of the modern problem we know as delinquency? Or to society at large and the value conflicts which it transmits? Or to the neighborhoods which seem to spawn the most delinquency? Or directly to family life, wherein lies the genesis of much individual delinquency?

There are at least two basic considerations: What are the sources of the social problem in which we are interested? And can we do something about them? It is futile to decide that some factor is the root cause of some social problem if there is at hand no practical way of influencing that factor. In that sense, the root cause, if it can be discovered, is not necessarily the most important cause.

If the control of any causative factor at any level promises to lead to a significant decline in the rate of delinquency, this must be accounted an important factor. In addition, the recognition that more than one factor may contribute to a social problem brings with it a recognition of the need for a multiple approach to the question of remedy. There is no panacea for social problems, and there is always more than one legitimate avenue of attack.

CITIZENS' ASSOCIATIONS

Democratic society has developed the phenomenon of the voluntary citizens' association as a normal expression of democratic life. Political parties are themselves forms of citizens' associations. In addition there have proliferated across the nation literally thousands of citizens' associations which have the purpose of altering social behavior and combating social problems. There are such country-wide associations, with local branches, as the American Civil Liberties Union, the National Association for the Advancement of Colored People, the National Education Association, the American Association for the United Nations, the Planned Parenthood Association, and the National Association for Mental Health, to mention just a few. These comprise citizens banded together for the accomplishment of certain prescribed kinds of social action. There are such groups as the AFL-CIO, the National Association of Manufacturers, the National Catholic Welfare Conference, the American Friends Service Committee, and the League of Women Voters, whose gamut of interest in the field of social action includes such matters as international affairs, education, delinquency, crime, welfare, immigration, and intergroup prejudice. Then there are countless local citizens' associations, committees, councils, conferences, and federations created in almost every community to meet local problems.

These are all, indeed, "pressure groups," a term which deserves opprobrium only when the kind of pressure involved itself deserves opprobrium. Such associations provide a significant and practical means by which the citizen can join with other like-minded citizens in exerting a proper influence on the course and shape of society.

CHANNELS OF ACTION

There are several principal ways in which these citizens' associations attempt deliberately to alter social behavior and thereby to modify any given social problem. They are not all equally effective for all social problems, nor can they be employed in all places and at all times. In addition, different citizens' groups, by their nature, are equipped to move in different remedial channels and to employ different methods.

The Law

Besides legislation, the category "law" includes the administration of law by government agencies and the interpretation of law by the courts. Law obviously affects social behavior by prohibiting certain kinds of behavior. More significantly, law alters the kind of social situations in which values are normally formed; for example, when public housing projects in New York City were racially integrated by law, the attitudes of the white residents of integrated housing projects became significantly more favorable toward Negroes in general. A law which states that it is against the public policy of a city or state for employers within that state to discriminate in their hiring practices becomes part of the cultural climate. Public health and housing laws can change the complexion of a city's slum neighborhoods and therefore some aspects of the environment in which a number of children will be raised. It is also, of course, through law that the government's responsibility in economic relationships and social welfare in general is established. Specific welfare facilities to be supported or supervised by the government must be authorized by law.

Social action in this field includes organized attempts to persuade legislators and public officials of a certain course of action, to rouse public opinion, to campaign for the inclusion of certain items in political platforms, to promote the election of certain officials, and to support the argument of cases before the courts.

Direct Action

Groups of citizens may privately take matters into their own hands when the application of law is impossible or seems inappropriate. In 1956 the Negro citizens of Montgomery, Alabama, instituted a boycott of the city's segregated buses. Normally the main support of the public transportation system, they walked to work or formed car pools. This boycott, coupled with a court case, ended segregation in the bus system in Montgomery. In this way, an important social condition was altered. Moreover, the boycott served to dramatize the cause of integration around the nation and to stimulate support for similar action elsewhere.

Education

Within the context of social action, education connotes any direct attempt to alter the social attitudes of people and, therefore, their social behavior. In this broad definition it includes both formal schools and the mass media of communication. With universal education, the schools now represent a formal training ground for society's future citizens. Educators often argue that the function of the schools is not to indoctrinate specific attitudes but rather to prepare students to arrive at their own attitudes out of a fully developed reasoning power and personality. It is clear, however, that any educational program and curriculum must be based on certain implicit values. The shaping of public school policies offers many of the same possibilities for social action as the shaping of public policy in general.

The mass media are the only organized channels, outside of the schools, for reaching the attitudes of the population en masse. Newspapers, magazines, radio, television, and motion pictures are, in America, private enterprises but are considered to have a public-service aspect. There is presumably the possibility of altering content by public pressure. There is also the possibility of placing material or buying space or time in the mass media. Many social-action groups have, for example, produced short motion pictures for distribution, and a great many have their own publications.

The distinction that is sometimes drawn between action, legislative or otherwise, and education does not bear close scrutiny. Presumably it is a distinction between attempting to change behavior and attempting to change attitudes. But it is now axiomatic that when social behavior is effectively changed, as in the planned integration of housing projects, social attitudes can be changed as a result. On the other hand, *some* shift in social attitudes must generally precede the passage of a law. Again the need for a multiple remedial approach is indicated.

THE ROLE OF THE CITIZEN

It is perhaps a cliché worth repeating that the citizen remains the key to the deliberate solution of social problems. At his most active, it is the citizen who campaigns for legislators and public officials and who participates in voluntary citizens' associations to further shape public policy or to create voluntary projects. Even when he is less active, it is the citizen who votes for legislators and public officials and who supports voluntary associations or voluntary projects with his sentiments and with his funds. Even at his most passive, it is still the citizen who shapes public policy by abdicating his social responsibility. The professional, whether politician, welfare worker, or educator, cannot launch remedial programs in the complex area of social problems without the social action which falls within the province of the citizenry at large.

This textbook is primarily directed to the citizen who faces or will face at least the minimal responsibility of having a point of view on the social problems of his community. It is obvious that such a citizen should understand the significance of specific social problems and should have the benefit of whatever valid information has been gathered about the causes and remedies of specific social problems. But, over and above this, he must come to certain understandings about social problems in general.

In the first place, he must be equipped to avoid the sentimentality of easy and total solutions and panaceas. He must come to some understanding of what *not* to expect in meeting social problems. Not only does sentimentality often lead to a misplaced use of community energy; more seriously, it may lead to frustration and immobility when the easy and single-approach attempt at solution fails to achieve significant results. For example, a favorite proposal for a project to combat delinquency is the construction of a recreation center or boys' club. These projects are certainly worth while in themselves, but they have typically failed to make any radical inroads into the problem of delinquency. An observer whose mind is trained, in even an elementary way, to analyze social problems will be suspicious of such an easy solution to begin with. He will suspect, if he does not know, that such a deep disturbance in social behavior as delinquency is caused by more than the existence of idle hands. He may even suspect, if he does not know, that such recreational facilities will be of more benefit to nondelinquents than to habitual delinquents, who will indeed tend to avoid such facilities. Similarly, he will doubt the proposition that laws to punish or fine parents of delinquent children will make a major contribution to the solution of delinquency, knowing that there are causative forces at work more fundamental than the willful negligence of parents.

In the second place, the citizen must be equipped to avoid cynicism about efforts to ameliorate social problems that fall short of striking at the "ultimate cause." Such cynicism commonly leads to immobility, since ultimate causes are fairly unapproachable through deliberate citizens' action. The informed citizen will know that it is less than useless to say that delinquency will not disappear until we have "reformed the moral fiber of society." Such reformation, he will know, cannot be achieved by blueprint or overnight, but must wait upon other changes. Similarly, he will suspect the futility of the proposal that any given social problem will not disappear short of an economic reformation of society. He will suspect this as an oversimplification, knowing the general nature of social problems. Rates of delinquency, for example, tend to rise in periods of economic prosperity and to decline in periods of economic depression; intergroup prejudice has been stimulated for economic reasons, but it has flourished long after these economic reasons have withered away. Moreover, he will recognize that any proposal to wait upon major changes in economic structure would amount to abdication of responsibility to do something about urgent social problems *now*. He will know that social problems *can* be diminished by sound and deliberate citizens' action.

Finally, the citizen must recognize the importance of short-range, piecemeal citizens' action against social problems over and above its immediate effect. Such action, where successful, is justified if only because it relieves a situation where otherwise there would be no relief. In dealing with social problems, we are dealing with human beings. But there is an additional factor which should give pause to the citizen who shrinks from a piecemeal approach. It is an educational axiom that people learn more by doing than by rhetorical exhortation or supplication.

There is perhaps no more effective and practical way of developing insight into the nature of the fundamental problems of our society than through specific community ventures intelligently designed to meet those problems. To put it another way, perhaps the only manner in which the citizenry will ever get to the root of a social problem is by addressing itself to the details of the problem and by attempting to deliberately alter the dimensions of the problem in as sound and informed a way as possible.

CONCLUSION

There has been no intent in the preceding pages to build a system of causal theories or remedial approaches which would apply uniformly or neatly to all social problems. "Social problem" is not that homogeneous a category. Delinquency, for example, is primarily a problem in social control and in the transmission of values which constitute social control. Prejudice is a problem which centers in the mass conflict of aspirations. The changing family is a more pervasive phenomenon, touching on many social problems. These problems and those involved in a discussion of crime, the schools, or dependency all satisfy the basic definition of a social problem. They are all concerned in some way with the failure of relationships among people to meet the personal goals of a substantial number of those people or with the weakening ability of society to order relationships among people. They all reflect, in one way or another, the basic and changing nature of our society. They are all major problems with which almost every community in the country is grappling. But they exist on different levels, are often produced by different causative factors, and usually require different remedial approaches.

SUGGESTIONS FOR FURTHER READING

General works helpful for an understanding of basic concepts:

Leonard Broom and Philip Selznick, *Sociology* (Evanston, Ill.: Row, Peterson and Company, 1958).

Kingsley Davis, *Human Society* (New York: The Macmillan Co., 1954).

Logan Wilson and William L. Kolb, *Sociological Analysis* (New York: Harcourt, Brace & Co., 1949).

Works stressing the concept of social disorganization:

Herbert A. Bloch, *Disorganization* (New York: Alfred A. Knopf, 1952).

Robert E. L. Faris, *Social Disorganization* (New York: Ronald Press Co., 1955).

Collections of readings relevant to various social problems, urbanization, and contemporary society:

Kingsley Davis, Harry C. Bredemeier, and Marion J. Levy, Jr. (eds.), *Modern American Society* (New York: Rinehart & Co., Inc., 1949).

Paul K. Hatt and Albert J. Reiss, Jr. (eds.), *Cities and Society* (Glencoe, Ill.: The Free Press, 1957).

John Eric Nordskog, Edward C. McDonagh, and Melvin J. Vincent, *Analyzing Social Problems* (New York: Dryden Press, 1956).

Guy E. Swanson, Theodore M. Newcomb, and Eugene L. Hartley (eds.), *Readings in Social Psychology* (New York: Henry Holt & Co., 1952).

T. Lynn Smith and C. A. McMahan (eds.), *Urban Life* (New York: Dryden Press, 1951).

Works helpful in clarifying the citizen's approach to social problems:

Joseph S. Himes, *Social Planning in America* (Garden City, N.Y.: Doubleday & Co., Inc., 1954).

Richard Waverly Poston, *Democracy Is You* (New York: Harper & Bros., 1953).

Roland L. Warren, *Studying Your Community* (New York: Russell Sage Foundation, 1955).

Girl's Teen-Age Kidnaper Is Captured at Gunpoint

FRAMINGHAM, Mass. (AP) — When Weston J. Babineau went to work yesterday as a car polisher at General Motors assembly plant, he thought his 16-year-old stepson Richard Gray was still asleep.

So did Mrs. Babineau, the boy's mother, when she left for work at no telephone exchange.

...er shoelaces and carrying her to a hiding place beneath a lilac bush between the two homes, less than 100 yards apart.

McCarthy said the boy held her beneath the bush for five hours until his parents went to work, then took her to a second-floor bedroom.

Ransom Note Found

A note left behind at the O'Connell home said the kidnaper would call in two-days and say where to put the money. "The typewritten note, unsigned, also demanded two rifles and ammunition.

Because Gray had been charged two years ago with kidnaping a 13-year-old girl but not molesting her, and because he was released from a state's correctional school two months ago, Juvenile decided...

Jurors Rap Police Over Youth Cases

By JAMES EWELL

Dallas County grand jurors oppose a new city police policy of charging teen-age offenders in automobile theft cases once they become eligible under state law to face criminal prosecution, The News learned Thursday.

Records on the ... jurors op... The po... seeking ... by juvenile ... the policy ... port of ... and Police ...

Two ... records ...

'Club' Taken From Pupil at School 37

An eighth-grade student at Public School 37, who Friday struck a teacher in the face and threatened him with a butcher knife, pleaded guilty yesterday in Youth Court to possessing a dangerous weapon.

Almost simultaneously, another in a series of disturbances...

It was learned the girl was looking for another student in the school who she maintained had bothered her. After she was questioned, the pupil left with an aunt who had been summoned to the school.

Because of her age, the girl was not identified.

The incident took place a half...

Youth Bound Over On Check Charges

David E. Olson, 19, of 10 Franklin St. was bound over to Superior Court on charges of fraudulent issue of checks. Disposition was made in Waterbury City Court by Judge Hugh J. McGill, who set bond for the youth at $1,000.

Olson was arrested Middletown Aug. 20 as he attempted to open an account the Middletown Savings Bank...

Disturbance Referred to Youth Unit

Police Monday handed county juvenile authorities the job of judging delinquency cases against four Park Cities boys, 13 to 15, who figured in a Saturday disturbance-shooting at a teacher's home.

Detective Capt. Frank M. who heads the police juvenile bureau, said after a meeting of parents or guardians of three of the boys that "We'll refer (four) of the cases to the county juvenile people."

He said no police action is planned against E. O. Rogers, 34-year-old Highland Park junior high school teacher who used pistol Saturday night to curb vandal raids at his home, 404 Chevy Chase.

After the third pistol slug struck another, 14, teacher and two other ordered before officers with the Names of the been published not been charged violation.

The teacher's words show, has several recent Rogers said caused about $... home, fence, a... Police said the of an insurance builder, a sales sale firm boys Rogers home tossed a dummy haunted Rogers places in the d...

The teacher "out the youth called police. T... a 13-year-old, d... treatment until his leg wound...

Captain Mart... ance with boys results of his l... detective W. 15 available to Hi... ficials, but added "they haven't contacted us for any information." to said county probation workers may contact school authorities.

Rogers declined to press charges or damage. Police were unable to nk any of the previous raids Rogers, a vet lassroom, tha chool authorit ess to exert oys' acts. Police booked r "investigat elinquency rbing the pe artin.

Schools May Outlaw 'Dyed Ducktails', Tight Pants

The city School Board may declare war on "dyed ducktails" and tight pants.

An official "personal appearance policy," discussed in an executive session by the board yesterday, outlines what constitutes "appropriate, decent shion for de eachers and d to deal wi policy.

Supt. E. C. Stimbert said the Board will consider adoption at its next meeting Aug. 22. He said possible examples of dress to be prohibited are skin-tight jeans, high- ... d er- tails. The board adopted a policy on until attendance and activities of married students. It outlines what corpo- has been in effect: au- 1. Married students may at...

thorized in Memphis schools but the policy will outline specifically just how and when the paddle may be used.

Mrs. Francis Coe, board member, wants a further check into the legal aspects of it.

tend city schools at the Board's discretion.
2. They may not attend the same school.
3. Continuance shall be based on good conduct, regular attendance and scholastic achievement.
4. Assignment of married students to schools will be made by the assistant superintendent working with the school principal.

Man Accused Of Using Son In Burglary Gets 3 Years

A modern-day Fagin accused of hoisting his pint-sized 7-year-old son through two windows during an apartment burglary on North Caroline street was sentenced yesterday to three years in the House of Correction by Judge Anselm Sodaro in Criminal Court.

Judge Sodaro directed that the accused, Calvin Payne, Sr.

other door, the court was told.

The defendant then stole $23 from a clothes cabinet and nine bullets from a dresser drawer, the prosecution charged. The bullets and $5 in cash were found on Payne when he was arrested.

He gave his son $1, told him to go to the movies and warned the boy not to say anything about the burglary, Mr. Romano said.

Pleads Guilty

Payne, a Ne... guilty to the cha... he contended he lection of the tenn the 300 block N... street. He said the been given him b...

The assistant p... the Court that Pa... committed to Cro... Hospital but had turn from a Than... last year. The ac... open an extended criminal...

Guy M. current lable for Nichols, bureau, the scrapping spite the jury se... quitting ly carry...

Cops Probe Teen Ring Of Forgers

Falls Barmen Are Warned

Courier-Express Niagara Falls Bureau

NIAGARA FALLS, July 31 — A warning was issued to area bartenders today as ice launched an investigation into a teen-age forgery ring here.

cting Detective Chief Hu- Collins disclosed at least orged-chauffeurs' and drivlicenses have been sold to juveniles at $5 to $10 each. purpose of the illegal transans is to enable under-age juveniles to purchase alcohol at

he ring was discovered as result of an auto theft investigation. Six teen-agers e been arrested in Court

heduled for arraignment in Court tomorrow are:

ctor Sutor, 17, of 6610 Buf- Ave., charged with alteration of car registratio nd degree forgery. ichard C. Waterstran 71st St., first degre ery.

enneth Wlock, 16, St., charged with l ssory to the larceny. rank Stamborski, 1 St., also charged ac ory to the larceny. wo other youths, Jos 17, of 426 74th s juvenile are bein out charge in con the forgery activiti cities said "several be arrested. The youths were picked up

Jailed Youth Woos Court Sympathy

NEW YORK, Sept. 6 (UPI) youth who first won the sympathy of the courts 10 years when his mother burned his h... to punish him and again last vember when he was accused using that crippled hand to stu was back in jail Saturday.

This time Philip Vetter, 19, in the limelight as a confes forger.

He pleaded guilty in fed court to stealing an $84.78 So check, forging its own d) getting his bro to cash it.

first appearance years ago, when Geraldine, was sentenc onths in prison becau his hand over a flam m for stealing a few

LAND was crippled, but the boy stood her. His father was possession of burg.

November, in his se pearance, young V used of stealing an a General Sessions J avidson took pity on of the maimed hand. had Vetter's one-yea arranged for an o restored partial fle crippled hand. Aid Society lawyer ers pleaded for lenie their "unfortunate and said Philip's ing a child and Ph intly became a moth

Girl's Kidnaper Held in $150,000

FRAMINGHAM, Mass. (UPI) — Richard J. Gray, 16, was held in $150,000 double surety today on charges of kidnaping a 4-year-old girl and attempting to extort money from her parents.

... youth was committed stboro State (Mental) for 35 days observa- N. Garley ordered him and innocent to the

y indicated that the uld be moved from the Court to the adult for a hearing Oct. 1, who once before kid-girl and served 14 in a boys' school, took arole O'Connell from be of her parents early day morning.

She was later found in his home, less than a 100 yards...

Counseling Termed Young Offender Aid

Courier-Express Albany Bureau

ALBANY, June 10 — Ninety per cent of Erie County's youthful offenders were rehabilitated during an 18-month trial of a teen-age counseling service, Richard V. Carnival reported today.

Carnival, executive director of the Buffalo Youth Board, spoke at a meeting of the Commission. He said interceded in 10 cases before a plea h tered in County Cou Judges were asked disposition of each ca months and release in custody of the Bo sentative of the You with the teen-ager his background and him a job if he did Carnival said the two grand jury citi been turned over t attorney's office.

Today's meeting tended by about 25 tives of county an youth service organ

Boy Escorting Girl Is Beaten

Robert Wood, 16, of 186 Brunswick Blvd., yesterday told police he was beaten by a gang of youths while walking his girl friend home Tuesday night. He suffered a head injury and multiple contusions. He was in good condition at Emergency Hospital.

Detectives Vincent Sherlock and Raymond Metzger of the Crime Prevention Bureau said they obtained the names of the youths involved. Two admitted beating Wood during an argument over the 15-year-old girl. The detectives said no arrests have been made pending the completion of the investigation.

Two Boys Confess Cigarette Theft

Theft of 50 cartons of cigarettes, valued at $116, was solved in short order yesterday afternoon by Detectives Joseph F. Luma and George Berescik of the Police Department's Youth Bureau.

The cigarettes were stolen from a truck on Camp street, police reported, and the first word of the theft came from a woman witness who said the theft had been committed by boys. They had run toward Walnut Hill Park, she reported. Shortly afterwards the truck driver, from Middletown, reported the theft.

Get Confessions

Luma and Berescick hurried to the park, rounded up six boys and drew a confession. they said. from Raymond Gorneault, 16, of 126 Sexton St., and another 14-year-old boy. Gorneault's case was continued in Police Court and the other youth was turned over to juvenile authorities.

The boys had hidden the cigarettes in a wooded section of the park, police said.

Police Break Up Zip-Gun Factory

NEW YORK, June 11 (UPI) — Police have dissolved a zip-gun manufacturing plant operated by two teen-age brothers for the benefit of Juvenile gangs.

A 16-year-old carrying a zip-gun led police to a Bronx apartment where they found the brothers, aged 14 and 15, working on an order of 12 guns for a Bronx gang.

Officials Give Up Hope of Curbing Juvenile Reign of Terror at Maxton

MAXTON, N.C. (UP) — Police and juvenile authorities admitted Thursday "we have reached the end of our rope" in efforts to curb a wave of juvenile robberies have netted the youths less than $160 in cash and merchandise, among young Negroes in this Robeson County community.

Police Chief Robert W. Fisher said a youthful gang of delinquents ranging in age from 9 to 13 years

pears to be the leader. The breakins, at residences, stores, concession stands and filling stations, Fisher said.

The mother and sister of one of the gang members were tried in

Recorder's Court on charges of contributing to the delinquency of a minor, growing out of an apparent neglect of the child. Judge Earley Bullard gave the two a week to get out of town.

"The mother's time is up tomorrow," said Fisher. "If she isn't out

of town by then, we'll go after her again. Something's got to be done."

McMillan and Fisher agreed that additional facilities for handling juveniles "must be provided in the immediate future, not only for our community but for other towns

and cities faced with the same problem."

McMillan said state law prohibits confining a child under 14 in the county or city jail for more than 24 hours. The Morrison Training School, where the gang members could be sent for rehabilita-

tion and training, is now handling about 300 boys in quarters originally planned for 160. Some new buildings are under construction there, but McMillan said these would not be sufficient to more than take care of a long waiting list.

CHAPTER 2

Juvenile Delinquency: Analyzing the Problem

Section I: What Is the Problem?

"There is no such thing as a bad boy," Father Flanagan of Boys Town has stated flatly. And a noted judge said of juvenile delinquents: "They are not bad, they never were bad. They are just victims, just neglected youngsters."

"Just victims . . . ?" According to the FBI, juveniles account for about half of all arrests for crimes against property, a fourth of all arrests for rape, and one out of every six arrests for murder. If *these* juvenile delinquents are victims, they are also victimizers. At least *some* delinquents commit serious offenses against the community.

What, then, is the juvenile delinquent? Is he just a neglected youngster, or is he, as the FBI figures seem to indicate, the young criminal?

THE LEGAL CONCEPT

By legal definition, the juvenile delinquent is neither a neglected youngster nor a young criminal but occupies instead some twilight zone between the two. According to the law, if a young lawbreaker is legally defined as a juvenile delinquent he cannot be charged with crime or treated as a criminal; like the neglected and dependent child, he becomes a ward of the state. Sometimes, as in the case of murder, the young lawbreaker *is* charged with a crime and is tried and punished in the regular courts. For most other offenses, however, the law requires that if the offender is under a certain age he must be adjudged delinquent and not criminal.

The distinction between delinquency and criminality was set up very plainly in the first formulation of the legal concept of juvenile delinquency. The intention of the historic Illinois Juvenile Court Act of 1899 that the young offender be treated not as a criminal but as a ward of the state was conveyed by the very title of the law: "An Act to Regulate the Treatment and Control of Dependent, Neglected and Delinquent Children." [1]

Historical Roots

The modern concept of delinquency is in part the product of our legal philosophy, which distinguishes between the youthful offender and the criminal. Special treatment of youth has roots deep in Anglo-Saxon legal tradition.

1. *Age and criminal accountability.* Anglo-Saxon law attaches great importance to the question of intent and, therefore, to the capacity of the accused to understand the consequences of his act and the difference between right and wrong. England early set age limits below which the child was automatically judged incapable of being guilty "in will," although the age was often set as low as seven years. If the child could not be charged with crime, he obviously could not be punished for it.

2. *The responsibility of the parent.* Our law recognizes the responsibility of the parent to insure the social obedience of the child. In support of this parental role our legal tradition has tended to take official cognizance of what it calls the "incorrigible" or habitually disobedient child. As late as 1819 the law of the state of Illinois provided for the imprisonment of disobedient children "until they shall be humbled" and for their punishment by whipping should they strike a parent.

3. *The guardianship of the state.* The right of the state to assume guardianship over children has long been acknowledged, though formerly that right was restricted to orphans or neglected children.

Trends in Social Philosophy

But the legal concept of delinquency as we know it today is also the product of fairly recent trends in social philosophy.

1. *Emphasis on environmental influences.* Public opinion has, over the years, come to emphasize the influence of environment on behavior and to

---

[1] Gilbert Cosulich, *Juvenile Court Laws of the United States* (New York: National Probation Association, 1939).

minimize individual responsibility in all areas. This has resulted in a universal tendency to raise the age at which the individual can be held accountable for having committed a crime. Most delinquency laws now place this age of legal responsibility at about eighteen years. In addition, it is now the child rather than the parent who is seen as the "victim," and incorrigibility is no longer legally punishable; rather, it is interpreted as symptomatic of a failure of parental guardianship and control for which the state's guardianship must be substituted.

This environmental emphasis has also led to greater faith in rehabilitation, especially in the case of the young. Care and protection rather than punishment or mere custody are stressed.

2. *Emphasis on prevention.* A further development consonant with modern social philosophy is the conviction that the state has the moral obligation to assume guardianship not only when parental control is absent but also when it is inadequate and irresponsible. What is more, the state is now conceived to have the responsibility to *seek out* such cases of parental failure. The concept of delinquency has thus become an instrument of detection, with the result that the legal definition of delinquency has expanded accordingly.

The Concept of Precriminality

A committee of the National Probation Association in defining the term "juvenile delinquent" has included not only the child who has violated any adult law and the child who, by reason of his being wayward or habitually disobedient, is uncontrolled by his parents but also the child who habitually so deports himself as to injure or endanger the morals of himself or others.[2] The states average eight or nine items of delinquency in addition to infraction of adult law and incorrigibility, e.g., immoral or indecent conduct; knowingly associating with vicious or immoral persons; habitually using vulgar language in a public place; habitual truancy; habitually wandering about railroad tracks. These are items which, like incorrigibility, are interpreted as foreboding future immorality and criminality and therefore as justifying the intervention of the state.

On the face of it, the concept of juvenile delinquency may be said to be one of "precriminality." (1) The youthful violator of adult law is regarded as precriminal, as someone not only in need of rehabilitation but likely to be amenable to it. (2) The "incorrigible" child, even though he violates no adult law, is also regarded as probably precriminal; the breakdown of parental authority is by itself considered ominous. (3) Specific items of behavior set forth by delinquency law, such as truancy or the

[2] National Society for the Study of Education, *Forty-Seventh Yearbook*, Part I (Chicago: University of Chicago Press, 1948), p. 9.

use of vulgar language, are regarded *when they occur in children* as signs of potential criminality justifying the guardianship of the state.

THE LEGAL CONCEPT QUESTIONED

Many people have raised questions about the legal concept of delinquency as it has developed under these influences.

1. The legal definition of delinquency has broadened beyond violations of adult law and even beyond incorrigibility. Parental failure in itself has become increasingly subject to state intervention. This development has been partly motivated by considerations which have nothing to do with precriminality. Crime aside, children who lack proper parental guidance are not being given the opportunity to become personally well-adjusted or productive individuals. Delinquent symptoms are clues to children whose behavior is potentially harmful to themselves as well as to the social order. By extension, therefore, the legal category of delinquency has in some minds become primarily an instrument for detecting personally maladjusted children who may be potentially criminal rather than for detecting potentially criminal youngsters who may be personally maladjusted.

The wisdom of employing crime-detection and law-enforcement agencies to deal with cases of maladjustment and parental failure can, however, be seriously questioned.

2. Does the concept of delinquency trap, along with others, a substantial number of youngsters who are only pseudodelinquent, who are expressing the temporary and transitional aggressions, tensions, and conflicts that may be normal for adolescence?

The single delinquent act, if it is brought to the attention of the law, makes a youth officially a juvenile delinquent. But this single act, especially if it is a minor infraction, does not necessarily mean that the youth is on the road to crime or is seriously out of social control. Polls reveal that most people would admit having committed some act during their youth which would have qualified under the law as a delinquent act. This is especially true since the infractions which are legally considered delinquent have multiplied, and many of them would not be considered seriously antisocial if committed by adults. Because of his earlier independence from family regimen, the adolescent is at present less of a child than the adolescent used to be. But because of his delay in becoming a member of the family economy or community work force, the adolescent is also less adult now than he used to be. Adolescence—or being a teen-ager—has tended to become a new social status or social category. Unfortunately, the community is often not geared to serve the special needs of this age group.

Ralph Crane; Black Star

Reckless: Overexuberant driving is a delinquent act, not necessarily committed by habitual delinquents.

The apparently increasing independence of the teen-ager from parental standards is doubtless a community problem in itself, but it is not necessarily a true problem in delinquency. Adolescents who commit a single delinquent act—or even several minor delinquent acts—cannot automatically be considered to be seriously out of social control. It is estimated that about 65 per cent of the children who appear in juvenile court statistics do not repeat their delinquencies. Most of them mature out of their minor delinquencies without attention or treatment from society. They do not have any confirmed disposition toward aggressive antisocial behavior. They do not represent a menace to society. In short, the pseudo-delinquent may temporarily stray from what is considered acceptable behavior, but he is basically committed to the values of society and to a life within those values. He is "in control" by society.

One unfortunate result of the development of the legal concept of delinquency is that it encourages the community to bring to official attention youthful behavior that might better be handled in informal and personal ways. This disadvantage is accentuated wherever delinquency is conceived as an instrument for the detection and treatment of maladjustment rather than precriminality. Despite the humane intent of the law, the category "juvenile delinquent" has become a stigma in the eyes of the ordinary citizen.

3. Under the concept of delinquency is still subsumed that segment of our juvenile population who are already integrated into criminal society, who accept criminal values, and who are, in all but legal name, professional criminals. The concept of juvenile delinquency automatically places the seventeen-year-old habitual committer of crime in the same legal category of responsibility with the ten-year-old child who steals a tire as an escapade. One danger is that the concept of juvenile delinquency will blur our perception of the distinction between delinquent youths and those who are, to all intents and purposes, youthful criminals.

THE NEW PROBLEM OF DELINQUENCY

The special importance which delinquency has in recent years acquired in the public mind does not appear to be attributable to the fact that it portends precriminality or a high adult crime rate. It seems traceable rather to a growing conviction, whether soundly based or not, that delinquent behavior patterns are spreading among young people formerly relatively immune to them. Although it is at present impossible to state whether delinquency is in fact on the increase among white middle-class youth, their parents appear to believe it is. The respectable community has in recent years begun to worry lest *its own* children become delinquent, and not merely children from the wrong side of the railroad tracks.

There are two reasons for this concern. One is the fear that with the decreasing geographical and social isolation of those groups among whom delinquency is most prevalent—the poor and those minorities which suffer discrimination—delinquent behavior and attitudes will spread throughout the adolescent community. The other is the fear that the rise in delinquency rates represents a general breakdown in adolescent-parent relations and the authority of the family. Juvenile delinquency is thus seen as more than just a part of the total crime picture. The rise in delinquency figures seems instead to signify to many that young people in general are "out of control."

Juveniles who are out of control may or may not be precriminal; they may or may not be habitually out of control. The current legal concept of delinquency has resulted in bringing to official and judicial notice many acts formerly left to the healing influence of developing maturity. The current common-sense concept of delinquency tends to equate the acute problems of the present-day teen-ager with the problems of the delinquent. Nevertheless, the concept of delinquency points to a reality that cannot be ignored: the habitual delinquent. There are many seriously and aggressively maladjusted and antisocial youngsters who come to the attention of the courts. Some of them may finally undertake criminal careers; others may not. But all of them need help. The question for these

WHO AND HOW MANY?

youngsters is how—if at all—the state in its guardianship will be able to provide this help.

Section II: Portrait of Delinquency—Who and How Many?

THE STATISTICS OF DELINQUENCY

The delinquency rate, as measured by court cases in relation to total juvenile population, increased steadily during World War II, slackened

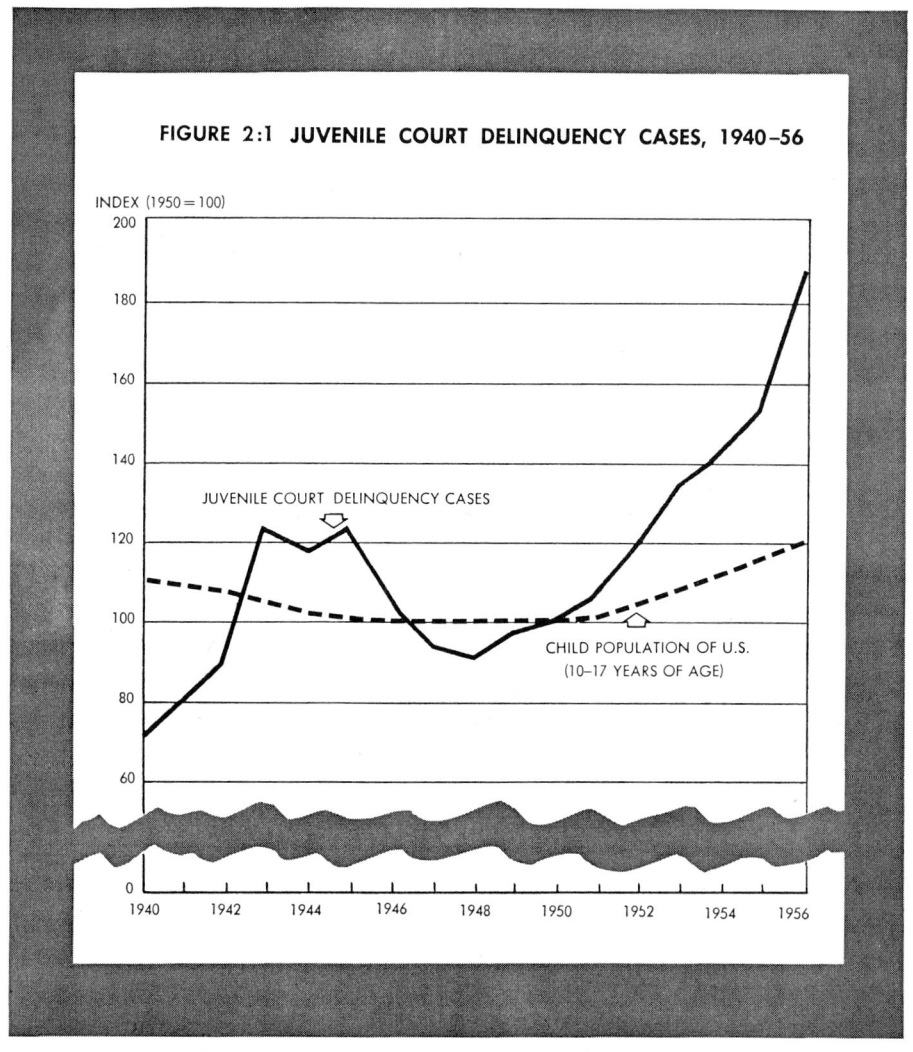

FIGURE 2:1 JUVENILE COURT DELINQUENCY CASES, 1940–56

Source: U.S. Children's Bureau, *Juvenile Court Statistics, 1956* (Washington, D.C.: U.S. Department of Health, Education, and Welfare, 1958), p. 7.

at the end of the war, and then started to rise again (see Figure 2:1). According to available juvenile court statistics, about 450,000 different boys and girls were brought to the attention of the juvenile courts in 1956.[3] In the same year, 1,551 cities, comprising about half of the total U.S. city population, reported[4] that about two million different people had been arrested during the year and that almost a quarter of a million of them

FIGURE 2:2 PERSONS ARRESTED UNDER 18 YEARS OF AGE, 1957

IN 1,473 SELECTED CITIES OVER 2,500 POPULATION

OFFENCE CHARGED	NUMBER OF JUVENILES ARRESTED	PERCENT OF TOTAL ARRESTS
CRIMINAL HOMICIDE	207	6.5
ROBBERY	3,124	26.4
AGGRAVATED ASSAULT	2,091	9.0
BURGLARY, BREAKING OR ENTERING	28,179	54.8
LARCENY—THEFT	52,550	51.3
AUTO THEFT	19,682	67.6
STOLEN PROPERTY; BUYING, RECEIVING, ETC.	1,249	32.3
FORGERY AND COUNTERFEITING	695	8.0
RAPE	932	19.5
NARCOTIC DRUG LAWS	219	3.0
WEAPONS; CARRYING, POSSESSING, ETC.	2,998	17.8
LIQUOR LAWS	7,125	16.4
DISORDERLY CONDUCT	26,029	10.8
GAMBLING	615	1.2

Based on selected figures from Federal Bureau of Investigation, *Uniform Crime Reports*, Vol. 28, No. 2 (Washington, D.C.: U.S. Government Printing Office, 1958), p. 115.

[3] U.S. Children's Bureau, *Juvenile Court Statistics, 1956*, Statistical Series, No. 47 (Washington, D.C.: U.S. Department of Health, Education, and Welfare, 1958).

[4] Federal Bureau of Investigation, *Uniform Crime Reports*, Annual Bulletin, 1957, **28**, No. 2 (Washington, D.C.: U.S. Government Printing Office, 1958).

were under eighteen years of age. Figure 2:2 shows the incidence of alleged offenses in these arrests. Arrests for alleged delinquency do not, of course, always result in an official judgment of delinquency.

In the juvenile courts, where delinquency is officially adjudged, disorderly conduct of one kind or another, including malicious mischief, usually runs a close second to crimes against property. Following closely are the delinquent offenses of ungovernability and running away from home. The character of these statistics is actually shaped by male delinquents. More than five times as many boys as girls are referred to the courts for delinquent offenses. Girls are adjudged delinquent most often for sex offenses and for running away from home.

THE LIMITATIONS OF DELINQUENCY STATISTICS

Available statistics can serve, at best, as only a rough guide to the nature and extent of delinquency because of these sharply limiting factors: inadequate sources, lack of uniform standards, hidden delinquency, and changing community attitudes.

1. *Inadequate sources.* The United States Children's Bureau has been a main source of delinquency statistics since 1926. It draws on juvenile court reports, but these reports have represented only about 500 of the approximately 3,000 courts that operate throughout the country. Furthermore, the reporting courts are heavily concentrated in the northeast and central portions of the country. Since 1946, the Children's Bureau has attempted to use state summaries based on reports of departments of welfare and other state bodies, but the coverage is still incomplete. The FBI has issued its *Uniform Crime Reports* semiannually since 1930, relying on reports of arrests by police chiefs around the nation. Many communities are not included in these reports, and reporting procedures vary widely.

2. *Lack of uniform standards.* State and local definitions of delinquency vary. One state may adjudge juveniles found habitually playing on the railroad tracks as delinquent. Another state may not. One jurisdiction may interpret the offense of "endangering the morals of oneself and others" in a manner different from that of the next jurisdiction. Even the upper age limit for delinquency varies from 16 to 21 in the different states.

3. *Hidden delinquency.* Many juveniles who commit delinquent acts are never brought to official court attention. This is partly the result of the fact that the juvenile court plays different roles in different communities. In New York's borough of Richmond, for example, the only referral agency for juveniles in trouble is the juvenile court. In the neighboring borough of Manhattan, where there are numerous social agencies, many children are referred to these agencies and never come to official attention. A Boston study showed that in 1946 of some 6,416 infractions of the law

by juveniles only 95 were brought to official action. Over 600 of these infractions were considered serious, but only 68 of them were prosecuted.[5] By this token it must be assumed that many delinquent acts are unreported in the statistics.

4. *Changing community attitudes.* A rising rate of delinquency may reflect an increase in the willingness of adults to place juveniles under court jurisdiction. Delinquency figures represent delinquency acts *reported*. Their increase may mean more delinquency, but it also may mean more avid reporting. For example, police, parent, and neighbor attitudes may influence the extent to which they are willing to report delinquent acts. As urban neighborhoods, especially in slum areas, become less cohesive, less homogeneous, and less marked by community feeling, we may expect people to be less indulgent and less protective.

Section III: Why? Theories of Causation

If a juvenile delinquent is a victim, of what forces is he a victim? Why does a juvenile become delinquent? The basic causal theories, discussed below, attempt to describe the fundamental disorders in the individual or in society that create delinquency. The later examination of specific risk conditions is an attempt to discover how these disorders operate in the daily life of the community to create delinquency.

Basic Causal Theories

There are four distinguishable approaches to understanding the problem of delinquency. The *hereditary* approach, which once naïvely proposed that criminal tendencies as such are inherited, now assumes a more scientifically sophisticated posture. The *personality* approach attempts to identify the emotional problems related to delinquency. The *learning* approach describes how delinquent values are transmitted. The *group-control* approach stresses the role of social disorganization.

HEREDITY

The argument: There is something in the (inherited) constitution of the individual which predisposes him to delinquency and crime.

The extreme statement of this approach is embodied in the Lombrosian theory of a "born criminal type." Cesare Lombroso, Italian physician of the nineteenth century, studied a number of prison inmates and con-

---

[5] Fred J. Murphy, Mary M. Shirley, and Helen L. Witmer, "The Incidence of Hidden Delinquency," *American Journal of Orthopsychiatry,* **16** (1946), 686–96.

cluded that the "typical criminal" could be identified by certain specific anatomical traits, such as slanting forehead, abnormal size of ears, or abnormal amounts of body hair. These characteristics were supposed to mark people who were throwbacks to a more savage state and therefore somehow predisposed to crime.

A more moderate theory attempts merely to establish a relationship between general body type and temperament, including antisocial temperament. William H. Sheldon studied 200 boys, all institutionalized as "problems," and most having been adjudged delinquent at one time or another. He first rated them on a scale of antisocial characteristics. Then he classified them according to three major body types: "endomorphs," who tended to be soft and fat; "mesomorphs," who tended to be muscular and of athletic build; and "ectomorphs," who tended to be thin and fragile. Sheldon concluded that delinquents are apt to be mesomorphic, a trait generally inherited from their parents.[6]

The Gluecks (see Adaptation 2, pp. 71 ff., below) also found a disproportionate number of their delinquents to be mesomorphic. A dominance of muscular and athletic characteristics was found in 60 per cent of the delinquents but in only 31 per cent of the nondelinquents.[7]

Another variation of the constitutional approach states that abnormally low intelligence is a prime cause of delinquency and crime. The psychologist Henry H. Goddard reported, in the early part of the century, that there was a feeble-mindedness rate of over 70 per cent in seven different institutions for delinquents.[8]

Evaluation: 1. The Lombrosian theory of anatomical criminal types has been flatly contradicted by scientifically conducted comparative studies. For example, Dr. Charles Goring spent twelve years studying 3,000 criminals and comparing them with other groups. He found no striking anatomical differences, Lombroso's "stigmata" occurring as frequently in the noncriminal as in the criminal population.[9]

2. Modern research findings are inconclusive with regard to the relation between either physique or intelligence and delinquency. Dr. William Healy and Augusta Bronner, matching delinquents with nondelinquents among more than 400 children, reported negative findings with respect to physical differences.[10] Maud Merrill matched 300 adjudged delinquents

[6] William H. Sheldon, Emil H. Hartl, and Eugene McDermott, *Varieties of Delinquent Behavior* (New York: Harper & Bros., 1949).

[7] Sheldon Glueck and Eleanor Glueck, *Unraveling Juvenile Delinquency* (Cambridge: Harvard University Press, 1950), pp. 281-82. This important work will be cited frequently in this chapter. Portions of it are abridged in Adaptation 2 (pp. 71 ff., below).

[8] Henry H. Goddard, *Feeblemindedness: Its Causes and Consequences* (New York: The Macmillan Co., 1914).

[9] Charles Goring, *The English Convict* (London: H.M. Stationery Office, 1913).

[10] William Healy, M.D., and Augusta F. Bronner, *New Light on Delinquency and Its Treatment* (New Haven: Yale University Press, 1936), pp. 39 ff.

with 300 controls living in the same neighborhood and attending the same school and found 39 per cent of the delinquents and 47 per cent of the nondelinquents of "normal average" intelligence.[11] William Wattenberg, studying over 2,000 boys, found 31 per cent of the delinquents and 21 per cent of the control group below average in tested intelligence. Though differences appear to exist, they are not striking.[12]

3. Even where a statistical relationship between low intelligence and delinquency seems to be established in a particular study, it is not necessarily indicative of a causal relationship. Many delinquents test high in intelligence. Besides, we now know that IQ can be raised or lowered by a favorable or unfavorable environment. The slight statistical inferiority in IQ that is often found in delinquent groups may be the result of their relatively inferior environments.

4. It would be hasty to assert that constitutional factors play no role in delinquency. However, the role would seem to be ancillary and indirect and would not support a belief in the hereditary transmission of criminality itself. Further research may, for example, confirm the relative dominance of mesomorphic traits among delinquents. Such a fact might be interpreted as follows: Mesomorphic individuals tend to be aggressive people. If a mesomorph has no legitimate and socially constructive avenue for the expression of his typically extraverted tendencies, he will more easily than other types be led to take the deviant path of delinquency.

PERSONALITY FACTORS

The argument: Delinquency is the expression of a delinquent personality.

This position does not hold that delinquents are necessarily mentally ill, in the clinical sense that they need or are threatened with the need for hospitalization, but merely that their personality structures are such that they normally react to their problems with antisocial behavior. The delinquent personality can be typified as follows:

1. *He suffers from extreme emotional deprivation.* A primary need for the child is affection, recognition, a sense of belonging. Not only is the withholding of love painful to the child; it also undercuts his sense of security and his estimate of himself and his competency.

This causal theory does not state that emotional problems or anxiety lead directly to delinquency. Rather it holds that extreme emotional deprivation robs the juvenile of the resources for handling his emotional problems or anxiety in a constructive way.

---

[11] Maud A. Merrill, *Problems of Child Delinquency* (Boston: Houghton Mifflin Co., 1947), pp. 173–74.
[12] William W. Wattenberg, "Boy Repeaters" (unpublished study, Wayne University, 1947).

2. He has failed for emotional reasons to internalize moral principles. The failure to develop a conscience is a critical characteristic of delinquency. It means, in effect, the inability to master immediate urges and needs for the sake of conforming to social standards. This failure may result from being raised in a moral vacuum, where social standards are weak or are ineffectively transmitted. But this failure may also result from an emotional incapacity to take on moral standards even when they are present. The child is usually willing to "be good" out of love for his parents and to identify with them as models of behavior; but where the parent is rejecting and neglectful, the child has no incentive to curb himself for the sake of approval, acceptance, and security.

3. He responds to his problems by aggression toward authority. Aggression toward authority is more a manifestation of delinquency than a cause. However, if only as a symptom of more basic emotional factors, aggression toward authority is an operating component of the delinquent personality. Aggression may be a weapon adopted by a child against the parents by whom he feels he has been rejected. The aggression against rejecting parents may then be turned against all authority. Indeed, the child may originally develop aggressive mechanisms in order to gain the attention of parents who would otherwise ignore him. Punishment is preferred to nonrecognition. Often, where moral standards are operative, a sense of guilt accompanies the misbehavior and compounds the aggressive tendencies.

It is possible, of course, that these three components of the delinquent personality may coincide with personality deterioration, with clinical neurotic symptoms. However, only an insignificant proportion of delinquent behavior is attributable to serious mental illness of a kind, for example, which requires hospitalization. The basic "delinquent personality," as described above, is not as a rule regarded as in itself a neurotic or psychotic or mentally ill personality but merely as a distinctive personality pattern, offered as one explanation of the persistent delinquent.

Evaluation: 1. The personality approach often lends itself to oversimplification; for example: "Delinquency is the result of anxiety." Actually, the Gluecks found the anxiety level to be high in both the delinquents and the nondelinquents studied. Although a general reduction of anxiety and emotional conflict would probably result in a reduction in delinquency, it would probably also result in a reduction of many other personal and social disorders. The distinction between the delinquent and the nondelinquent seems to reside not in a sharp difference in the nature of their emotional problems but in the different ways they respond to and "act out" these problems.

2. The delinquent-personality theory does not in itself fully explain why some maladjusted children react with antisocial and delinquent rather

than with some nondelinquent form of maladaptive behavior, such as overwithdrawal.

3. However, even where personality disturbance may not be the full answer to the cause of juvenile delinquency, psychiatric understanding is an important factor in the rehabilitation of individual delinquents. This is true even though juvenile delinquency is too widespread for individual psychiatric treatment to be a practicable approach to the mass problem.

4. The personality approach has the further advantage of bridging the gap between society and the delinquent individual by focusing attention upon the family relations of the child.

LEARNING FACTORS

The argument: The child learns delinquent behavior just as he learns other kinds of behavior. The learning approach to delinquency has several distinctive propositions, as epitomized by Sutherland's theory of "differential association": [13]

1. The child learns his values and behavior from those with whom he associates. Indeed, he has little choice but to do so. If he is chiefly in contact with attitudes and behavior that are antisocial and delinquent, then his own attitudes and behavior will be delinquent. He will take on the moral standards of those around him.

2. Anxiety and unmet needs characterize many nondelinquents as well as many delinquents. Delinquents are differentiated, then, not by their psychological needs but by the way they learn to meet them. A case in point might be the child whose immediate need for recognition is not provided by his family. One group of children might teach him vandalism as a means of securing recognition. If his exposure, however, is to a group of children whose pattern of behavior is nondelinquent, his own will also tend to be nondelinquent.

3. The process of learning delinquent values and behavior involves not only conscious imitation but all the mechanisms of learning. The child is quick to absorb attitudes implicitly favorable to violation of the law or antagonistic to the social order.

On this premise, all of the cultural influences which surround the child are presumably part of his learning environment. His attitudes toward gambling, for instance, might be influenced by what the mass media reveal about general community attitudes on this subject. However, the child's learning is primarily influenced by the personal association he has with groups and individuals that he values highly.

[13] Edwin H. Sutherland, *Principles of Criminology* (Philadelphia: J. B. Lippincott Co., 1947), Chap. I.

THEORIES OF CAUSATION

Evaluation: 1. The theory of differential association does not explain why, when alternative groups are available, some children choose the delinquent gang. Nor does the theory explain the original presence of delinquency in the environment or any epidemic rise in the rate of delinquency.

2. However, the theory of differential association does help to explain the spread of delinquency, and it seems to be most telling for areas where the juvenile delinquency rate is extraordinarily high. If there is nothing available to the child except gangs of delinquents, it is understandable that the child, with his need for group membership, will choose delinquency rather than isolation.

GROUP-CONTROL FACTORS

The argument: Juvenile delinquency is best understood as a breakdown in the machinery of social control.

According to the social-disorganization approach, there has been a weakening of our traditional groups and institutions, such as the family, the church, the local community. These have become less integrated, less cohesive, less unified in purpose. As a result, they are less able to control their members. This lack of control manifests itself primarily as a failure to transmit traditional moral standards and social values.

This view is clearly distinct from the learning approach, which claims that some children become delinquent because the essentially delinquent groups to which they belong *do* effectively transmit their criminalistic values. The social-control approach emphasizes instead the failure of *nondelinquent* groups to transmit their moral ideals and control their members.

Actually there are "two sides of the same coin" involved in the breakdown of group control. One side is the breakdown of the group itself; the other side is the breakdown of the values which the group holds. There is an unfissionable relationship between a group, such as the family, and the moral standards which it embraces. It is because of the ties among its members that the group evokes their loyalty and is able effectively to transmit its values. Ties and loyalties may be the result of many interlocking elements: mutual dependence, mutual affection, mutual interests. But a mutual system of values is itself one of the components that cement a group together. If a group member is somehow alienated from the values of his group, his ties to that group are apt to be less firm. Conversely, if its hold is loosened, the group is less capable of impressing its moral standards on him. Thus group ties and group values are bound together in the maintenance of group control.

What are some of the circumstances which make it easier or more difficult for a group to control its members and pass on its traditions?

1. *Loss of group function.* Moral standards and social control are more easily sustained when group life has a function for the individual, that is, when it is important for individual self-fulfillment. For example, one characteristic of the modern family is that it has become less and less a center of either work or play. It has partly lost its economic function. In cities, particularly, the father works outside the home as an employee, and neither the wife nor the children are engaged with him in a common family economic enterprise; in some agricultural areas, mechanization and large-scale farming have tended to produce the same result. Nor has the modern family retained its value as a center of sociability. Entertainment outside the home is easily accessible, especially to youth.

In short, being a member of a closely knit, integrated family and community no longer has the same value for the individual it once had. Since what was once available to youth only within the confines of family life is now readily available outside, obedience to parental authority is no longer essential to individual gratification. Though family life has in some ways been enriched, it tends to be limited to personal relations among its members. Where these are not satisfying and rewarding, the family is apt to lose control over the child.

2. *Conflict between sets of values.* Moral standards are more easily sustained when the influences upon the child are mutually reinforcing. When two sets of values impinge upon the individual, his acceptance of either is apt to be weak, ambivalent, and confused. Urbanization, physical and social mobility, the development of the mass media, have meant that the individual is subject not to one set of values but to many. Family standards of morality may be weakened as the child comes into contact with other attitudes and other ways of behaving. Neighborhoods that encompass culturally diverse groups, whether of national, regional, or socio-economic origin, are apt to demonstrate this conflict of values most sharply. Especially important is the fact that, where such conflict exists, parents may themselves become unsure of their beliefs and uneasy in their parental role.

3. *Conflict between values and goals.* It is difficult to instill moral standards when virtue goes unrewarded. In our society there is a tendency for emphasis on success to outweigh emphasis on legitimate means of achieving it. Dishonesty, breaking the law, and violence are often rewarded by power, prestige, and money. If winning the game becomes all important and those who cheat are rewarded in material and financial terms, the rules are apt to go by the board. In the light of the actualities, youth more easily takes the attitude that "anything goes."

4. *Conflict between goals and attainment.* It is difficult to instill moral

standards when the gap between socially prized goals and the possibility of achieving them is too great. This holds for groups against whom discrimination and segregation is practiced and for those of low socioeconomic status. When ideals seem forever unattainable, they easily atrophy; demoralization sets in. An attitude of "What's the use?" takes hold, often alternating with bursts of aggression against society as the source of deprivation.

These various debilitating circumstances are obviously interactive. Loss of group function and the consequent weakening of group ties sharpen value conflicts because the group is less effective in transmitting its own moral standards. The sharpening of value conflicts, on the other hand, potentially weakens group ties, which are partly based on a thorough acceptance of group values. This vicious spiral downward can lead to general deterioration of social control.

Evaluation: 1. There is sometimes a temptation to make a shibboleth of "social disorganization." Taken by itself, of course, the theory of social disorganization does not explain delinquency any more than other theories, taken by themselves, are able to explain it. In using the concept of social disorganization, it is especially important to distinguish between the social disorganization of society in general and the social disorganization of particular areas and neighborhoods. As a concept, it can be applied to a *general* tendency in society for traditional groups to break down in the wake of modern social change, or it can characterize merely a particular area or neighborhood where the ability of groups such as the family to transmit dominant values, or any values, is relatively weak. In the latter case, this value vacuum may indeed allow other groups, such as the delinquent gang, to be more strongly organized and to wield more influence than they otherwise could. Such neighborhoods do not necessarily bespeak a general disintegration of society; they often exist because they are the places where ineffective families tend to congregate, because such ineffectiveness has common social and economic consequences as well. Thus, while social disorganization can lead to personal demoralization, the reverse can also be true. In other words, while the theory of social disorganization describes the social process most pertinent to the creation of delinquency, it is still necessary to examine the various causes and effects of that process.

2. The apparent breakdown of traditional groups may too often be taken at face value. What may often be happening is not that these groups are inevitably losing all their functions but that they are reinforcing some of them in a different way. The fact, for example, that family members typically do not spend as much time together as before does not automatically indicate the breakdown of the family. The companion-

ship function of the family in the modern world might still be unique, even if manifested in different ways.

3. However, even with these possible limitations, the group-control approach offers the broadest understanding of the causation of epidemic delinquency.

Specific Risk Conditions

How do these causative factors actually *work?* Where are the areas in community life in which social disorganization, delinquent learning, and the development of the delinquent personality operate? What are the conditions in these places that make it more likely that these causative factors will prevail and therefore increase the risk that delinquency will be widespread? The following places and conditions have customarily been singled out: (*a*) the delinquent society, (*b*) the mass media, (*c*) delinquency areas, (*d*) underprivilege, (*e*) peer groups, and (*f*) the family.

THE DELINQUENT SOCIETY

The argument: Many of the values projected by society at large are delinquent values. In addition, emphasis on success makes many moral standards ineffective. On the community level, then, are spawned many of the value conflicts which slacken social control.

Antisocial values abound with either open or tacit approval in the adult world which surrounds the juvenile. On the most obvious level, this double standard is apparent in so-called "white-collar crime," i.e., adult behavior which is socially acceptable even though it is legally unacceptable. Violation of the antitrust laws is often cited as an example, and there seems to be generally a wide area where business shrewdness and antisocial conduct overlap. One pair of researchers went on a nationwide tour to put garages, radio shops, and watch-repair shops to the honesty test. Before going into a garage, they disconnected the coil wire of an automobile that was otherwise in perfect condition. Of the 347 garages they visited, 63 per cent overcharged or charged for work either unnecessary or actually not done. Of 304 radio shops, the majority similarly overcharged, did unnecessary work, or even replaced good parts with inferior parts. The watchmakers were the most honest, but 49 per cent of them lied or cheated in some way.[14] Most of these businessmen would have been shocked at the idea of robbing a bank, yet many were ready to

---

[14] Roger W. Riis, "The Repair Man Will Gyp You If You Don't Look Out," *Reader's Digest,* **39** (July, 1941), 1–6; "The Radio Repair Man Will Gyp You If You Don't Look Out," *Reader's Digest,* **39** (August, 1941), 6–10; "The Watch Repair Man Will Gyp You If You Don't Look Out," *Reader's Digest,* **39** (September, 1941), 10–12.

make a profit by cheating a customer. This is not to place a special burden on businessmen. "White cheating" is a common enough phenomenon among all segments of the community. The widespread violation of gambling laws is an example.

Society's projection of delinquent values is conceivably a factor in delinquent learning, especially where intimate personal associations do not act to set up strong nondelinquent standards. Moreover, when delinquent values "pay off," moral standards appear obsolete, and society's ability to control the individual is thereby reduced.

Society stresses individual success and judges it largely by financial and material standards. Officially we praise honesty; but it is the attainment of goals by almost any means that we often more solidly reward. Official values call for brotherhood and scrupulous fair play. Yet the art of "putting things over" on other members of society or on organized society itself is highly developed. As the stress on success begins to match and outweigh the emphasis on moral standards, the transmission of these moral standards becomes more difficult.

Coexistent with and aggravating this key situation is the fact that an image of material achievement is set up which large numbers of people cannot attain. There is a gap between the possibilities of success and riches held out by the mass media and the actual conditions with which the average juvenile is surrounded. This gap may prove a stimulant, a source of dissatisfaction, and a spur to the "short cut."

Indicated remedy: The moral reconstruction of society.

Evaluation: There is a tendency for some who place major blame on the delinquent society to take this indicated remedy at its face value and demand a reformation of moral values forthwith. This often leads to an emphasis on the mechanical and abstract teaching of moral values. Studies cited in the next chapter indicate that there is little relation between the extent of delinquency and the extent of knowledge *about* moral values. The delinquent society is a complex result of many social and historical factors rather than the arbitrarily perverse behavior of a number of people. The delinquent society is generally presented as a background factor in understanding the delinquent rather than as a guide to a specific preventive program, and its significance as such a background factor is generally unchallenged.

THE MASS MEDIA

The argument: Radio, television, movies, comic books, and newspapers contribute to delinquency by glorifying, overemphasizing, and giving instruction in crime.

It has been estimated that most children go to movies from four to eight times a month, listen to radio or television dramas practically every afternoon or evening for several hours, and read more than a dozen comic books per month. Several studies have found that delinquents attend movies more often than nondelinquents. Of 368 delinquent boys interviewed by Blumer and Hauser, 49 per cent said that movies gave them the desire to carry a gun, 28 per cent said that the movies taught them methods of stealing, and 45 per cent said that they had picked up the notion of "easy money" from the movies.[15]

This is one of the theories of delinquency-causation which have attracted the most popular support from the public. Among the charges against the mass media are: (a) they stimulate the juvenile appetite for adventure, excitement, and violence; (b) they stimulate an appetite for sexual adventure; (c) they glorify the criminal; (d) they impart knowledge of criminal techniques; and (e) they overemphasize the extent of criminal life in our society.

Indicated remedy: Voluntary or government censorship of the mass media.

Evaluation: 1. The evidence is inconclusive. Juvenile court Judge Camille Kelley of Memphis said that in some 50,000 cases that had come before her there were not even a half-dozen where the trouble could be attributed to motion pictures.[16]

2. The testimony of delinquents as to the source of their delinquency is unreliable. They share the human desire to place blame elsewhere.

3. It is plausible to conjecture that the delinquent youth interprets the mass media in delinquent ways. To the nondelinquent child a movie may be a lesson that "crime does not pay"; to the delinquent child it may be a lesson in crime techniques.

4. At most, the mass media seem to be a secondary factor, aggravating, rather than causing, already existing dispositions to delinquency. Researchers who offer evidence in support of some influence on the part of mass media generally concede that it is an auxiliary rather than a basic influence, the mass media making it easier for juveniles to find the stimulation and knowledge which they would probably manage in any case to find elsewhere.

5. Though partially successful efforts have been made to encourage voluntary censorship, especially by publishers of comic books, many oppose government censorship on the ground that it would establish a dangerous precedent in a democracy. They argue that the solution lies in developing high standards of taste and public responsibility in adult society.

[15] Herbert Blumer and Philip M. Hauser, *Movies, Delinquency and Crime* (New York: The Macmillan Co., 1933), p. 71.
[16] *New York Times*, May 4, 1947.

DELINQUENCY AREAS

The argument: Delinquency tends to be concentrated in certain areas of the community where the breakdown of social control is most marked.

In most cities there are areas adjoining the central business and warehouse districts which are characterized by physical deterioration and congestion. The rate of known delinquency has been found to decrease in proportion to distance of residence from this industrial center. This spatial principle has been corroborated in Chicago, Philadelphia, Richmond, Cleveland, Birmingham, Denver, and Seattle.[17]

These are, of course, the slum areas, marked by overcrowding, substandard housing, and poverty. However, the focus of the area theory is on the *social* rather than the merely *physical* characteristics of delinquency areas. These are the areas in which social disorganization is far advanced—where the conditions which make for the moral integration of the individual into society are absent.

To these areas come a disproportionate number of families with the most shallow roots in our society: migrants from foreign countries or different sections of the United States; minority groups suffering from segregation and discrimination; people on the economic fringes of society. These are families, however law-abiding themselves, in which parents are likely to find it difficult to maintain the respect of their children and to exercise adequate authority over them.

To these areas come also the already demoralized and disoriented: families with histories of drunkenness, criminality, unemployment, chronic dependency. These are families in which the parents are unfit to command respect or to exercise control.

These areas are, moreover, neighborhoods in flux. They attract transients and drifters. Residents quickly move out to better residential sections when their economic and social adjustment makes it possible, leaving behind a growing residue of the less successful. Personal relations among families and neighborhood organizations have little opportunity to develop. Children grow up in an atmosphere of adult indifference, impersonality, and lack of concern.

A number of tangential risk factors exist in these areas. Here the gap between actuality and the American image of material success is greatest. The breakdown of parental authority is often accentuated by the absence of working mothers from the home. In addition there is a cumulative tradition of delinquent behavior which creates a delinquent learning situation.

[17] Clifford R. Shaw and Henry D. McKay, *Juvenile Delinquency and Urban Areas* (Chicago: University of Chicago Press, 1942).

FIGURE 2:3 DELINQUENCY RATES BY ONE-MILE ZONES—BALTIMORE,—1939-42 PER THOUSAND POPULATION AGED 6-17

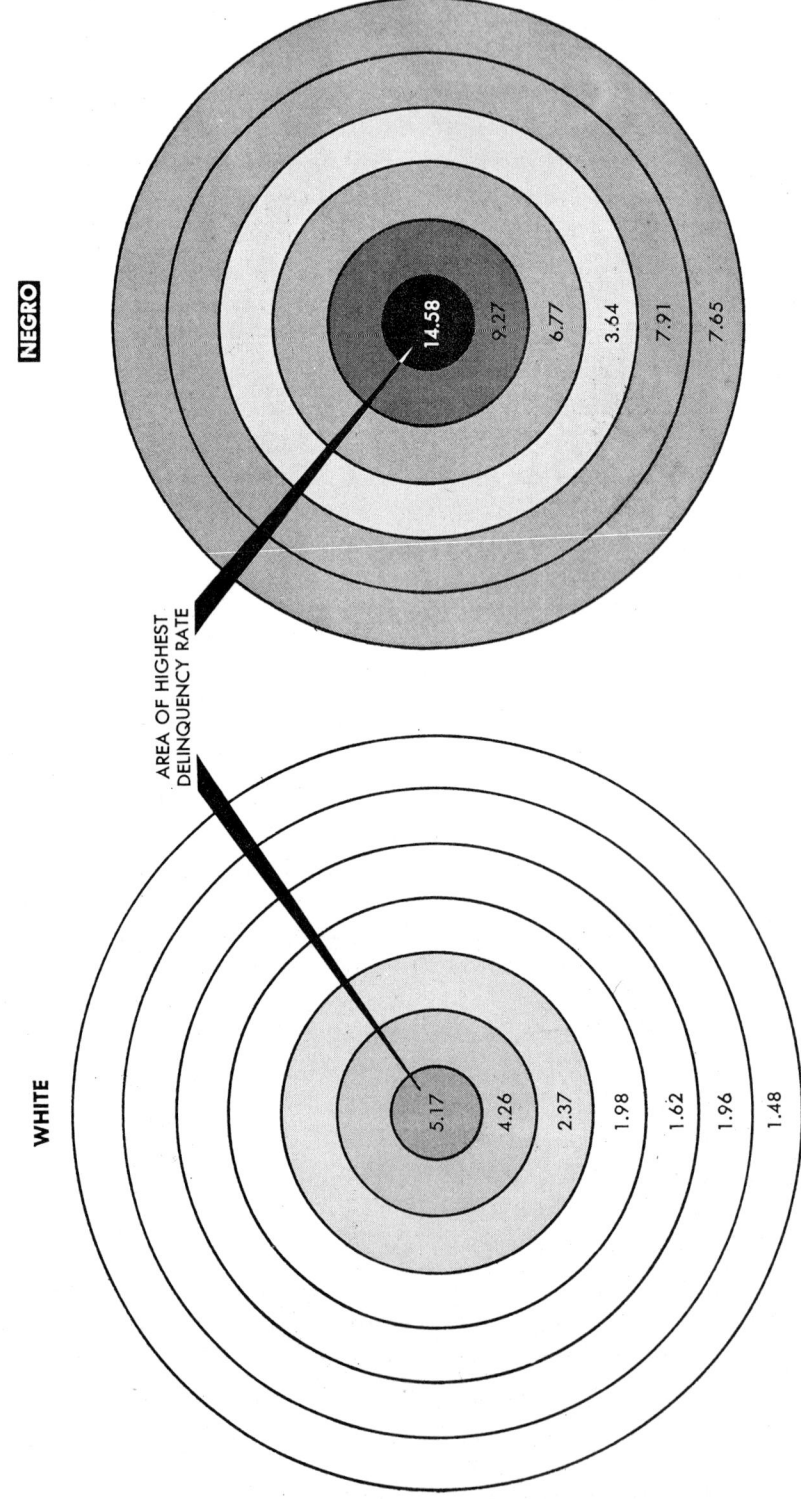

Based on Bernard Lander, *Towards an Understanding of Juvenile Delinquency* (New York: Columbia University Press, 1954), Table II, p. 24, and Table III, p. 25.

Indicated remedy: Organizing the disorganized community.

This effort may take place on one or both of the following levels: (1) Developing the organizational life of the adult community in order to create cohesiveness and neighborhood pride. This may mean strengthening a neighborhood church, or it may mean creating a neighborhood organization to deal with the problem of delinquency rather than relying upon outside community agencies. It may mean organizing a neighborhood politically or otherwise to combat its own slum conditions. (2) Organizing the youth in recreational clubs and settlement houses. In both cases, the emphasis is on providing a measure of social organization for the area.

Evaluation: 1. Statistics on area delinquency rates are probably somewhat distorted because delinquents from better residential areas are less likely to be brought to official attention.

2. Some high-delinquency areas contain "pockets" where delinquency is low.

3. The area approach may lead to an overemphasis on the relation between slums and social disorganization. Some of the same *social* conditions which mark many slum areas may characterize other areas as well. Impersonality, a transient population, adult indifference, the absence of the mother from the home, appear to be increasing in some neighborhoods relatively high on the socio-economic scale. As a matter of fact, recent evidence points to increasing delinquency rates in suburban areas.

4. Attempts to introduce meaningful social organization in areas where individual demoralization is high are likely to be fruitless. In any case it is necessary to distinguish between areas in which parents tend to be unfit to exercise control over their children and areas in which they are simply unsuccessful in doing so. The first kind is exemplified by deteriorated neighborhoods populated by individuals with criminal histories, alcoholics, prostitutes, and transients of all kinds. The second is exemplified by many Negro or Mexican-American neighborhoods where demoralization is present not so much at the adult as at the youth level.

5. Though delinquency areas lack meaningful social organization, this is fully achievable only through the integration of people, now marginal, into the larger life of society as a whole. Social organization is a natural and spontaneous result when people have a stake in society and therefore an interest in preserving and protecting those social institutions which provide them with satisfaction and self-fulfillment. Of course, as has been pointed out, delinquency areas are not necessarily devoid of organization. Delinquent gangs may be highly organized. Some of the delinquent youth may have a strong stake in the gang and in their delinquent subsociety. But social disorganization refers to the breakdown or absence of those

West Side, New York

Bob Towers; Black Star

THEY FIND THEIR PLAYGROUND ON THE STREETS

East Side, New York

U.S. Children's Bureau Photograph by Esther Bubley

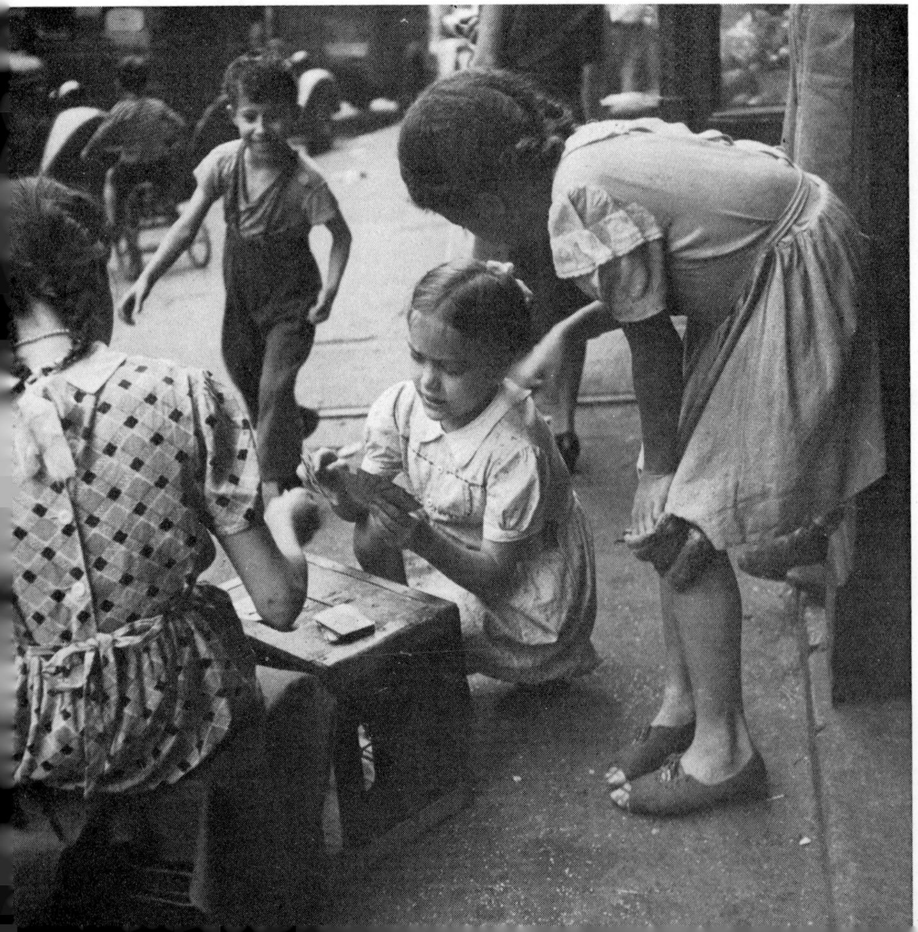

THEORIES OF CAUSATION

groups which can effectively transmit the dominant values of society at large. Where people lack a stake in *that* society, organization, when it is not indeed antisocial, is at best apt to be impermanent and formal rather than real.

UNDERPRIVILEGE

The argument: Economic deprivation breeds delinquency. Juvenile delinquency rates are highly correlated with low income, substandard housing, and residential overcrowding. Very few would, however, put forth the argument that poverty is a direct cause of juvenile delinquency. Many impoverished rural areas are free of the problem of juvenile delinquency, and the recent national economic prosperity has brought with it not a decrease but an increase in juvenile delinquency.

There are two important ways in which poverty enters as a risk factor in juvenile delinquency.

1. In modern industrial urban society poverty is intimately linked to social disorganization. (*a*) Poor families often have no choice but to move into low-rent areas with a criminalistic and amoral population. (*b*) Where material success is highly prized, poverty breeds demoralization and apathy. (*c*) Poverty and lack of integration into society often go hand in hand. Those who receive low wages, such as unskilled laborers or day workers, are often those with no fixed and secure place in the community of work and whose ties to the larger society are, by the same token, extremely tenuous.

2. The physical aspects of the slum conditions in which poor urban families often live cannot be dismissed as having no bearing on juvenile delinquency. (*a*) Inadequate housing, density of population, the large number of children and young people, all help to encourage the development of a "street society." The effective social life of the slum often centers on the streets, the front steps, the corner hangout. Life becomes street-centered, not home-centered. The sheer number of peers living within small areas makes the formation of gangs feasible and natural. In the streets the young people are exposed to influences from which middle-class children are often isolated. (*b*) Slums are also characterized by the absence of adequate recreational facilities. The theory is that many youths are deprived of the possibility of directing their energy into nondelinquent channels because of the lack of playgrounds and other recreational outlets.

Evaluation: 1. This approach sometimes leads to a popular overemphasis on the *physical* rehabilitation of slum areas. Slum clearance cannot knit the unstable families, heal the value conflicts, or fill the moral vacuum characteristic of delinquency areas.

2. Although in our success-oriented society poverty often breeds demoralization, it is also true that demoralization often results in poverty. The Gluecks found that though families of delinquents and nondelinquents both tended to be economically dependent on outside aid, it was for different reasons. The fathers of delinquents tended more often to be unwilling rather than unable to assume responsibility for the family.

3. Even where recreational facilities are available, there is differential use of them by delinquents and nondelinquents. In any case, in 1938–39 the Shanas and Dunning study found that boys, delinquent and nondelinquent, spent about twice as much time in the movies as in organized recreation.[18]

4. It seems doubtful that the importance of recreational facilities lies in their providing an outlet for excess youthful energy. Their absence can, however, be a sign of general adult indifference to its youth.

5. Nevertheless, slum clearance and the provision of public places of recreation are worthy ends in themselves and in all likelihood have some beneficial effect on a certain proportion of potentially delinquent youth.

PEER GROUPS

The argument: Juvenile gangs recruit, stimulate, and teach delinquents. Shaw and McKay, the Gluecks, Healy and Bronner, and others have concluded that delinquency is largely a gang operation. Of 5,480 offenders, Shaw found that only 18 per cent had committed their delinquency alone; 30 per cent had a single companion; 27 per cent had two companions; the remainder had three or more. Eighty nine per cent of those charged with theft had at least one accomplice.[19]

In June, 1950, the New York *Times* reported:

> There are in New York City between 150 and 180 active teen-age gangs composed of boys and girls who beat up victims, steal, commit sex crimes, smuggle and use narcotics and sometimes kill. . . . Most of these gangs are drawn from slum areas but one of the worst is recruited from upper-income schoolboys who specialize in crashing parties in wealthy homes, breaking up furniture and stealing.

The gang is charged with contributing to delinquency rates in several connected ways: (1) The adolescent tends to want to conform to the ways of his peers. Delinquent gangs, because they are organized groups, are in a particularly good position to exercise pressure for con-

---

[18] Ethel Shanas and Catherine E. Dunning, *Recreation and Delinquency* (Chicago: Chicago Recreation Commission, 1942).

[19] Clifford R. Shaw and Henry D. McKay, "Social Factors in Juvenile Delinquency," in National Commission on Law Observance and Enforcement, *Report on the Causes of Crime*, Vol. II (Washington, D.C.: U.S. Government Printing Office, 1931), pp. 195–96.

Police corral a street gang and search for illegal weapons.

formity. (2) Delinquent gangs provide a learning experience in delinquency not only for their own age group but for younger age groups. (3) Delinquent gangs provide ready antisocial channels for the energies and the normal and special personality needs of the adolescent. A gang can provide security, recognition, affection, and new experiences when these are not provided by the family or elsewhere in society.

Indicated remedy: Efforts to lead juvenile gangs and clubs into socially acceptable avenues of behavior.

Evaluation: 1. There is no clear indication of the extent to which delinquent gangs are a symptom rather than a cause of delinquency. To some extent delinquent gangs, instead of being agents for creating delinquents, may simply be cases of delinquent individuals flocking together.

2. However, the delinquent gang is probably the most important factor in maintaining and spreading delinquent behavior. The delinquent gang represents the place in society where delinquent behavior is accepted, approved, rewarded, and transmitted to others.

THE FAMILY

The argument: The most direct source of delinquency can be found in the family's failure to maintain social control: through its failure to effectively transmit the dominant values of society; through its successful transmission of delinquent values; or through its central role in the development of the delinquent personality.

1. *Personality factors.* Emotional deprivation begins at home. In the Gluecks' study it was reported that 71 per cent of the nondelinquents, as against 23 per cent of the delinquents, estimated their mothers' concern for their welfare as "good," while 65 per cent of the nondelinquents as against 19 per cent of the delinquents estimated their fathers' concern for their welfare as "good."

In 197 case records from the Institute of Child Guidance in New York City, Helen Witmer studied the factors that were associated with success or failure in treatment.[20] Such factors as intelligence, economic status of the home, and family size seemed to have little relation to the success of the clinic in treating the child, but the marital harmony of the parents and the attitudes of the parents toward the child had a striking relation to successful treatment.

The Healy and Bronner study found these symptoms most often among 91 per cent of 105 delinquents who were paired with nondelinquent siblings: rejection by family, insecurity, feelings of being misunderstood and unloved, feelings of discomfort with regard to family harmony, and jealousy of brothers and sisters. Only among 13 per cent of the nondelinquents were these symptoms prominent. The fact that these particular delinquents were in each case brother or sister to the nondelinquent studied pointed up the possibility that the family situation for two children in the same home may be far from the same.[21]

2. *Control factors.* The family's possible loss of function as a play and work center has already been discussed. Insofar as this occurs, family ties are presumably weakened, with a consequent weakening of the family's ability to transmit moral values. The absence of cohesiveness in the family and its resultant weakness as a control factor are most obvious in the case of the physically broken home. Statistical reports of the incidence of broken homes among delinquents vary. Shaw and McKay compared delinquent boys with nondelinquent boys of the same age and national origin and found that 42 per cent of the delinquent group and 36 per cent of the control group came from broken homes.[22] A similar study of delinquent girls in Chicago found that about 67 per cent of the delinquent group and 45 per cent of the control group were from broken homes.[23] In the Gluecks' study, parents were not living together in 34

---

[20] Helen L. Witmer *et al.,* "The Outcome of Treatment in a Child Guidance Clinic," *Smith College Studies in Social Work,* **3** (1933), 341–99.

[21] Healy and Bronner, *op. cit.*

[22] Shaw and McKay, "Social Factors in Juvenile Delinquency," pp. 261–84.

[23] Margaret Hodgkiss, "The Influence of Broken Homes and Working Mothers," *Smith College Studies in Social Work,* **3** (1933), 259–74.

per cent of the delinquent cases and in 16 per cent of the nondelinquent cases.

However, a home physically intact but psychologically broken is also lacking in real cohesiveness. The attitudes of parents toward the child, reported above, constitute one index of that lack of cohesiveness. The attitudes of the parents toward each other is another index. In the Gluecks' study, the relationship between the parents was reported as "good" in 37 per cent of the delinquent cases, 65 per cent of the nondelinquent cases.

Effective control and effective transmission of moral standards are also indicated by the state of discipline in the home. Merrill reports "good" discipline in 15 per cent of the delinquent homes, in 63 per cent of the nondelinquent homes. The Gluecks report "lax" discipline in 57 per cent of the delinquent cases, 12 per cent of the nondelinquent cases. In deeper analysis, the Gluecks found that the fathers typically used physical punishment as a method of control in 68 per cent of the delinquent cases, in 35 per cent of the nondelinquent cases; they used reasoning as a method of control in 11 per cent of the delinquent cases and in 24 per cent of the nondelinquent cases. The mothers' methods of control were statistically similar. Failure in discipline may be, in some cases, an individual failure in parenthood, but more often it would seem to reflect factors already discussed: a lack of concern for the child, a lack of affection for the child, or a product of the parents' own demoralization and lack of self-discipline.

Control factors and personality factors in family life often merge. The character of emotional relationships in the family certainly affects the family's ability to transmit moral values and to exercise control. But these emotional relationships themselves often depend on the cohesive quality of the family. A physically or psychologically broken home is one in which the child is most likely to be neglected and emotionally deprived.

Finally, it is through the family that the child most directly comes into contact with the value conflicts that exist in society. Not uncommon are the parents whose admonition to the child is that "money isn't everything" but whose own overwhelming drive for material success is all too obvious.

3. *Learning factors.* There are certainly some cases in which the theory of "differential association" might seem to apply directly. The Gluecks reported that 85 per cent of the young offenders released from the Massachusetts reformatory were from families in which other members were delinquent. The Gluecks also found that there was a criminal record for the mother in 45 per cent of the delinquent cases and in 15 per cent of the nondelinquent cases; for the father in 66 per cent of the delinquent cases and 32 per cent of the nondelinquent cases; for siblings in the same

family in 65 per cent of the delinquent cases and 32 per cent of the nondelinquent cases. The Merrill study reported delinquent siblings in 40 per cent of the delinquent cases and in 10 per cent of the nondelinquent cases.[24] These statistical relationships must be tempered by a consideration of the common control and personality factors in these delinquent homes.

Indicated remedy: Wider social service agency attention to family situations; parent education.

Evaluation: 1. The family is too often made the scapegoat for delinquency without attention to other community factors. In one sense, the family situation is often just a resultant of the delinquent society, a victim in its own right.

2. Even though much delinquency can be traced to inadequacies in the family situation, the family is difficult to reach directly by any extensive remedial program. In the following chapters it is pointed out, for example, that those very families which tend to produce the most serious delinquents are those most likely to resist remedial measures.

Section IV: Summary

Juvenile delinquency is an umbrella term covering a variety of phenomena. Delinquency statistics, for example, include all those juveniles who have been legally adjudged delinquents, but this total "catch" includes at least three types:

1. The pseudodelinquent, who may commit a delinquent act but is not seriously out of social control.

2. The criminal delinquent, who has absorbed criminal values and is merely the youthful reflection of the crime problem. In essence, he is the young criminal, who is counted a delinquent rather than a criminal because he is below the age of legal responsibility, and who is treated as a delinquent because his age calls for special modes of rehabilitation.

3. The amoral delinquent, who has somehow failed to internalize and fully accept the moral principles of his socially-oriented family and subculture. He may or may not become a criminal, if undeterred. But his criminality—a problem in itself—is only incidental to the central problem he represents: the failure of society at large to exercise control through the effective transmission of values. Herein lies the major concern with the apparent increase of modern delinquency.

There are three major causal approaches to the problem of delinquency: (1) the weakening of traditional control factors which characterizes our

[24] Merrill, *op. cit.*

modern industrial, urban, mobile, and changing society; (2) the learning of delinquent values from delinquent associations and subcultures; and (3) the development of delinquent personalities which are prone to aggression and resistant to authority for reasons, primarily, of emotional history.

These three approaches are not mutually exclusive but operate on different levels. There is obviously a tendency for delinquent youths to have personality characteristics, such as aggression toward authority, which make them relatively more susceptible to delinquent behavior. In the analysis of individual delinquents, the specific genesis of such characteristics can frequently be found in individual emotional history. However, there are many delinquent youths who do not evidence marked personality traits of this kind, just as there are many nondelinquent youths who do. The delinquent-personality approach is valuable in individual therapy and in filling out the causative map, *but it does not explain the rise or fall of the delinquency rate*. It is more useful in explaining a given delinquent than in explaining the social problem of delinquency.

Likewise, it is clear that many youths learn their delinquent values or participate in delinquent behavior because of their proximity to and association with a delinquent subculture. In some cases this is simply a reflection of "normal" criminal learning and apprenticeship. The child of a professional criminal who is not seriously exposed to contrary values may start stealing as a matter of course. But in many more cases the child *is* seriously exposed to nondelinquent values; he may come from a home which is essentially and sometimes vehemently law-abiding. This child may indeed learn his delinquent behavior from a delinquent gang. The "learning" approach is valuable in pinning down some of the important breeding places of delinquency, *but it does not explain the rise or fall of the delinquency rate*. It is again more useful in explaining a given delinquent, or a given delinquency area, than in explaining the social problem of delinquency.

It is within the framework of the social-control approach that the delinquent-personality and learning theories are most meaningful. It is the social-control factor—the effective transmission of dominant values—that normally prevents children with various emotional problems and aggressive tendencies from becoming delinquent. It is the social-control factor that normally prevents children from succumbing to delinquent influences to which they are exposed. The exceptions, of course, occur where the psychological disorders are unusually severe or where the control factor is itself delinquent. But these circumstances do not apply in the majority of delinquent cases.

In addition, it is the social-control approach that *can* best explain the rise or fall of delinquency rates. It is the social-control approach which provides a bridge to the historical circumstances that create more or less delinquency. If there are more delinquent gangs, if there are fewer families capable of providing emotionally satisfying relationships, the most satisfactory explanation can be found in theories of social disorganization. And if there are fewer children whose internalized values can immunize them against delinquent influences or deter them from delinquent reactions to their personality problems, then the fullest explanation will be found in the social-disorganization approach—in the breakdown of social control through the breakdown of traditional groups and the conflict and attenuation of values that ensue.

Establishing this kind of causal perspective, however, is not identical with establishing a remedial perspective. Regardless of how fully each of them may explain the social problem of delinquency, these causative factors are all to some degree operative, and some of them are more susceptible of remedy than others. It is still necessary to test specific programs of treatment and their relation to the actual reduction of delinquency.

---

adaptation 1   SOCIAL DISORGANIZATION AND DELINQUENCY

Abridged and adapted from Bernard Lander, Towards an Understanding of Juvenile Delinquency *(New York: Columbia University Press, 1954). Published in this form by permission of the author and the publisher.*

[Like crime, juvenile delinquency varies considerably according to geographical area. As a rule, cities have higher delinquency rates than do rural areas; but even in cities there are some sections in which the rate is negligible, others in which it is well above average. The following study of juvenile delinquency in Baltimore found that in the very heart of the worst delinquency area there were neighborhoods relatively free of delinquency. The author undertakes to explain this variation in delinquency rate in the light of the hypothesis that social and family disorganization underlie juvenile delinquency.

The author approaches his problem through statistical analysis. At first glance, the statistics seem to support the belief that poverty is the cause of juvenile delinquency; areas with high delinquency rates were, as a rule, impoverished areas. According to the author, however, more refined statistical methods show that poverty is not a fundamental factor in delinquency. His results indicate that juvenile delinquency is more basically related to (1) percentage of renters in an area and (2) percentage of Negro residents in an area. All other factors being equal, where these were high, the delinquency rate also tended to be high.

The author does not conclude that being a renter or being a Negro are causes of juvenile delinquency. He reasons that percentage of renters and percentage of Negroes are both fairly good indicators of the degree of family and social disorganization present in an urban neighborhood. He concludes that his study supports the belief that the fundamental cause of juvenile delinquency is social and family disorganization.]

DELINQUENCY RATES

From 1939 to 1942 there were 8,464 official hearings in the Baltimore Juvenile Court involving 7,193 individual children—about 4.5 per cent of the total juvenile population in the 6–17 age range. About 7 per cent of the white male population 10–13 years of age, and about 12 per cent of the 14–15 age group, were alleged delinquents. Of Negro boys in the 10–13 age range, about 26 per cent were registered in Juvenile Court on delinquency petitions; for Negro boys aged 14 and 15 the figure was 40 per cent.

DIFFERENTIAL DELINQUENCY RATES

Delinquency was far from evenly distributed over the city. Baltimore is divided into 157 small census tracts, which are subdivisions of city wards containing fairly homogeneous populations of approximately 5,000. In more than a dozen tracts there were no white delinquents. In over twenty, of white boys aged 14–15, 20 per cent were recorded as delinquent. In three tracts 50 per cent of this group were recorded.

The wide range of delinquency rates was even more marked for Negro boys. In two areas there were no Negro delinquents. In several areas 75 per cent of the 14–15-year group were in court on delinquency petitions. For one tract the figure was as high as 95 per cent.

JUVENILE DELINQUENCY AND CENSUS-TRACT VARIABLES

Many studies have been devoted to establishing correlations between juvenile delinquency and individual traits. They have asked questions of the following kind: What is the relation between a child's IQ and whether or not he is a juvenile delinquent? What is the relation between a father's occupation and whether or not his child is a juvenile delinquent?

In this study correlations were made between census-tract delinquency rates and a variety of other census-tract characteristics. Questions of the following kind were asked: What is the relation between the rate of juvenile delinquency in a census tract and the average educational level of a census tract? Between the rate of juvenile delinquency in a tract and its percentage of nonwhite residents? Attention was focused not on individual traits but on the traits of the neighborhoods in which juvenile delinquents lived.

The statistics obtained were examined in the light of some existing theories concerning the nature of juvenile delinquency.

THE CONCENTRIC-ZONE HYPOTHESIS

According to this theory, juvenile delinquency rates are highest in zones immediately surrounding the central business district of large cities and tend to drop rather steadily as the city radiates outward. This concentric distribution is attributed to the physical decay of residential areas as they give way to business and industrial encroachment and the consequent concentration of the poor, the underprivileged, the uprooted, and the criminal in these relatively low-rent sections. Table 2:1 gives the white and Negro delinquency rates for Baltimore according to one-mile zones measured from the central business district. In a general way it supports the concentric-zone hypothesis.

However, if census-tract figures are inspected, they reveal (1) that in zones close to the heart of the city there are pockets in which juvenile delinquency is low and (2) that juvenile delinquency extends to the periphery of the city. Though the innermost zones have a high average delin-

TABLE 2:1 NUMBER OF DELINQUENTS, POPULATION, AND DELINQUENCY RATE FOR BOTH SEXES, AGED 6–17, BY ONE-MILE ZONES—BALTIMORE: 1939–42

ZONE	WHITE			NEGRO		
	Number of Delinquents	Population 6–17	Delinquency Rate	Number of Delinquents	Population 6–17	Delinquency Rate
1	399	7,718	5.17	1270	8,709	14.58
2	1610	37,790	4.26	2038	21,996	9.27
3	843	35,550	2.37	198	2,925	6.77
4	343	17,327	1.98	11	302	3.64
5	227	14,045	1.62	22	278	7.91
6	188	9,602	1.96	13	170	7.65
7	31	2,089	1.48			
Total	3,641	124,121		3,552	34,380	

quency rate, this rate varies from one census tract to another, ranging downward from 20.8 per 100 persons 6–17 years old to only 1.1. When delinquency rates are calculated on the basis of relatively small geographical units such as census tracts, virtually the entire range for the city as a whole is represented within its high-delinquency zones.

JUVENILE DELINQUENCY AND SOCIO-ECONOMIC VARIABLES

One explanation of juvenile delinquency is that it stems from social and economic disadvantage. Table 2:2 recapitulates the correlations between juvenile delinquency and a number of variables customarily used to establish socio-economic status. The coefficients in the last column show us that overcrowding (.73), substandard housing (.69), and percentage of nonwhites (.70) are highly related to the incidence of juvenile delinquency in a census tract. The principal "deterrent" to juvenile delinquency appears to be home-ownership (−.80).

Nevertheless it should be noted that one tract ranking very low on the socio-economic scale had a much lower rate of juvenile delinquency than might be expected. Its median rental was second lowest in the city; it ranked fourth in percentage of substandard homes; it was the least educated section of Baltimore. It had fewer radios and fewer homes with central heating than any other section of the city, and 60 per cent of its homes had either outside or no toilet facilities. Yet it is not among the ranking juvenile delinquency areas. Nor were special agencies operating

TABLE 2:2 CORRELATIONS BETWEEN JUVENILE DELINQUENCY RATE AND SPECIFIED VARIABLES—BALTIMORE: 1939–42

	Education	Rent	Overcrowding	Nonwhite	Homes Owner-Occupied	Substandard Housing	Foreign-Born	Juvenile Delinquency
Education	—	+ .89	− .71	− .41	+ .39	− .76	− .12	− .51
Rent	+ .89	—	− .68	− .34	+ .47	− .73	− .13	− .53
Overcrowding	− .71	− .68	—	+ .69	− .72	+ .86	− .01	+ .73
Nonwhite	− .41	− .34	+ .69	—	− .76	+ .58	− .32	+ .70
Homes owner-occupied	+ .39	+ .47	− .72	− .76	—	− .67	+ .12	− .80
Substandard housing	− .76	− .73	+ .86	+ .58	− .67	—	+ .07	+ .69
Foreign-born	− .12	− .13	− .01	− .32	+ .12	+ .07	—	− .16

here to lower the delinquency rate "artificially." This area is but one of many examples which reveal the complexity of the problem of juvenile delinquency. It suggests that poverty, though often highly associated with factors that cause delinquency, is nevertheless not itself a direct cause of delinquency.

JUVENILE DELINQUENCY AMONG NEGROES

Negroes in Baltimore, as in many other cities, contribute a disproportionate number of delinquents. During the period under study, Negro children constituted only 20 per cent of the juvenile population. Yet they comprised 49 per cent of Baltimore's delinquents.

There is no reason, however, to impute causal significance to race per se. Table 2:2, above, indicates high positive correlations (1) between percentage of Negroes in a census tract and overcrowded, substandard housing and (2) between overcrowded, substandard housing and juvenile delinquency. Similarly, it shows a high negative correlation (1) between percentage of Negroes in a tract and percentage of homes owner-occupied and (2) between percentage of homes owner-occupied and juvenile delinquency. An area with substandard housing and absence of home-ownership is likely to be a juvenile delinquency area regardless of race, but it is also likely to be the kind of area in which Negroes live.

In any case simple correlations like those shown in Table 2:2 are often too "simple" to give us an accurate picture of the facts. For example, Table 2:2 shows a .70 correlation between juvenile delinquency and the percentage of Negroes in a census tract. *On the average,* juvenile delinquency tended to increase as the number of Negro residents in a tract increased. On the basis of this correlation, can we therefore say: The more Negroes, the more juvenile delinquents? By no means.

TABLE 2:3 NUMBER AND RATE OF NEGRO JUVENILE DELINQUENCY FOR AREAS GROUPED BY PERCENTAGE OF NEGROES—BALTIMORE: 1939–42

Percentage of Negroes	Negro Delinquency Rate	Number of Negro Delinquents	Negro Population (Aged 6–17)
0– 9.9	8.10	153	1,891
10– 29.9	13.39	439	3,277
30– 49.9	13.75	461	3,353
50– 69.9	10.42	688	6,601
70– 89.9	12.33	1,056	8,563
90–100.0	7.06	755	10,695
Total		3,552	34,380

TABLE 2:4 NUMBER AND RATE OF WHITE JUVENILE DELINQUENCY FOR AREAS GROUPED BY PERCENTAGE OF NEGROES—BALTIMORE: 1939–42

Percentage of Negroes	White Delinquency Rate	Number of White Delinquents	White Population (Aged 6–17)
0– 9.9	2.40	2,462	102,371
10– 29.9	5.36	663	12,375
30– 49.9	5.74	247	4,302
50– 69.9	5.15	162	3,146
70– 89.9	6.39	92	1,439
90–100.0	3.07	15	488
Total		3,641	124,121

Table 2:3 shows us that the juvenile delinquency rate did *not* rise steadily and constantly as the percentage of Negroes in an area rose. As the percentage of Negroes went from 9 to 50 per cent it did indeed rise. However, as the Negro population proportion increased beyond 50 per cent, the Negro delinquency rate tended to decrease. As a matter of fact, where the concentration of Negroes was as high as 90 per cent, the delinquency rate was at its lowest, and was well below the city-wide white average. Table 2:4, which shows the white delinquency rate measured against percentage of Negroes, indicates that there is a tendency for even white delinquency to drop off in areas of highest Negro concentration.

That there is no fundamental relation between race and delinquency is supported by immigrant experience. In 1903 the Federal Slum Survey found delinquency concentrated primarily in the foreign-born sections of Baltimore. In the present study, percentage of foreign-born in a census tract was insignificantly associated with delinquency. If anything, an inverse relationship was indicated.

THE CAUSES OF JUVENILE DELINQUENCY

How are we to interpret Table 2:2? Can we conclude that the correlations in the last column tell us about the basic causes of juvenile delinquency? Can we say that a high correlation between juvenile delinquency and some other variable points to a cause of juvenile delinquency? Are lack of education, low rents, overcrowding, substandard housing, percentage of nonwhites all independent causes of juvenile delinquency?

No such conclusion can be drawn if for no other reason than that the items in Table 2:2 are all highly interrelated. The best we can say is that Table 2:2 suggests the causal network in which juvenile delinquency is embedded; it does not single out independent causes. The only way to show that lack of education, for example, is a cause of juvenile delinquency is to show that, *all other things being equal,* juvenile delinquency increases as educational level decreases. We might approach the problem by comparing areas exactly alike in all respects except educational level. In actuality no such areas are likely to exist; therefore, statistical devices are used to hold constant all variables except those in which we are interested. In this way we can see whether educational level is correlated with juvenile delinquency even where poverty, for example, is not present.

When various statistical techniques were used to determine the independent effect on juvenile delinquency of each of the items in Table 2:2, only two factors were found to be basically related to the delinquency rate. These were (1) the percentage of homes owner-occupied and (2) the percentage of Negroes in a tract. Given knowledge of these two factors alone, it was possible to predict with a relatively high degree of accuracy census-tract delinquency rates. The other variables—such as rent, education, substandard housing, and overcrowding—were not by themselves good predictors of delinquency rates.

However, neither home-ownership or percentage of home-ownership in a tract nor being a Negro or percentage of Negroes in a tract can be interpreted as causes of juvenile delinquency. Their significance is to be found in the fact that both seem to point to something that is the underlying cause of juvenile delinquency. This fundamental cause is family and community disorganization.

SOCIAL DISORGANIZATION AND HOME-OWNERSHIP

As the percentage of owner-occupied homes in an area increased, there was a marked tendency for the delinquency rate to go down. Conversely, more renters meant, on the whole, more delinquency. As the proportion of home-ownership in an area increased from 20 to 40 per cent, the delinquency rate declined precipitously. From 40 to 50 per cent the rate continued to decrease, though more gradually. This decrease occurred regardless of the percentage of nonwhite residents.

It might be objected that home-ownership is a measure of economic status and that, if anything, the findings confirm the relation of poverty to juvenile delinquency. However, there is good reason to believe that, on the lower economic levels especially, and to some extent on the higher rungs of the economic ladder as well, home-ownership selects out the more stable families in the community. Home-ownership usually requires a measure of responsibility and sense of family unity. It implies permanence, steady employment, disciplined work habits, the existence of aspirations, the capacity to plan for the future. Among the relatively impoverished members of the community, home-ownership is probably one of the best indicators we have of social stability and family unity, cohesiveness, and discipline. As income goes up, home-ownership probably becomes less reliable as an indicator of family and social disorganization. This supposition finds a modicum of support in the present study. In areas where the percentage of homes owner-occupied went beyond 60 per cent and in which there was a presumption of fairly good economic status, there was a slight increase in delinquency rate.

Previous studies have found that more home-owners than renters are churchgoers, union members, and voters; home-ownership tends to select out families already fairly well integrated into society. It also gives individuals an additional stake in community life. Together with home-ownership and residential permanence often goes the desire to make the home a center of activity and recreation, the chance to make friends, and efforts to achieve respectability and social acceptance. In home-ownership areas, standards of conduct are apt to be higher than in rental areas. Children are likely to be more closely scrutinized and supervised by both parents and neighbors. Community approval and disapproval are probably readier and quicker to make themselves felt, and children are unlikely to live in an atmosphere of indifference.

We should expect all these things to hold even where homes are poor and substandard and the general economic level is relatively low. We should not be surprised to find rental areas with relatively high delinquency rates despite relatively good economic conditions and home-ownership areas with relatively low delinquency rates despite relatively bad economic conditions.

The high correlations in Table 2:2 between poverty and juvenile delinquency can be explained as the result of the high association in modern urban life between poverty and family and social disorganization. Rural experience and past history tell us that poverty by itself is a cause neither of social disorganization nor of juvenile delinquency. However, in cities the disintegrating effects of urban life—its impermanence, its aimlessness, its lack of strong communal bonds—bear down more heavily upon the poor than upon those who are better off.

SOCIAL DISORGANIZATION AND PERCENTAGE OF NEGROES

Family and social instability characterizes our Negro population even more radically than our white. A large proportion of Baltimore's Negro population, like that of many northern cities, is composed of migrants from the South. These people are uprooted from their former rural life and old community ties. In addition, the Negro family has historically been subjected to a series of disruptive and disintegrating influences. It is estimated that about a third of Negro families in cities are without a male head. Many Negro mothers work outside the home and are thus forced to neglect their children and leave them unsupervised most of the day.

The discrimination to which the Negro is subject is an important factor in creating the instability of the Negro family. Discrimination pares aspiration down to a bare minimum. When the future holds little promise, it is difficult to feel that discipline, hard work, and self-denial are worth the candle. Under such circumstances, it is hard for adults to develop a strong sense of parental responsibility, and it is equally difficult for their children to exercise a self-constraint and self-discipline which are very likely to go unrewarded.

Negroes also tend to reside in precisely those areas characterized by the most disorganization and instability. Because of prejudice, Negroes are forced to move into the worst white neighborhoods, neighborhoods already often marked by the relaxation of standards of behavior.

It is not race or poverty which by themselves account for the higher delinquency rates in areas of high Negro concentration. In this study, where there was evidence that both family and social stability existed in Negro areas, there delinquency also declined.

DEVIATIONS

Some tracts deviated from the predicted delinquency rate. In most cases where the actual rate was higher, the census tracts were even more disorganized and unstable than the statistics indicated. These were areas of transients, cheap hotels, prostitution, and the like. Where tracts had lower delinquency rates than might be expected, they turned out to be more stable than could be gathered from the statistics. In one such tract, for example, 90 per cent of the population was Jewish. During the period studied, fewer than 50 of the more than 7,000 registered delinquents were of Jewish background. The low incidence of delinquency among children of Jewish parentage seems to be explicable by the fact that the Jewish family tended, at least during this period, to be more stable and unified than the non-Jewish family. A similar explanation appears to account for the fact that not a single Chinese child was brought to Juvenile Court during the 1939–42 period.

Other downward deviations are explicable on the grounds that homeownership, while a good indicator of family stability, is not a perfect one, especially as economic level goes up. The Johns Hopkins University community is centered in one tract which has a high proportion of apartment buildings and resident hotels. Yet, it is not surprising that it has a relatively low delinquency rate despite its low proportion of owner-occupied homes.

CONCLUSIONS

1. Social and family disorganization is the most fundamental factor in juvenile delinquency.

2. Social and family disorganization is very likely to characterize racially mixed neighborhoods with a low percentage of homes owner-occupied.

3. Poverty is not a cause of juvenile delinquency. In cities it is highly associated with juvenile delinquency because it is highly associated with the disruption of social and family relations.

4. Race is not a cause of juvenile delinquency. The high rate of Negro delinquency is related to the high rate of family and social disorganization among Negroes.

5. Neither percentage of renters nor percentage of Negroes is an infallible sign of social disorganization. Some apartment-house areas where the economic, social, and cultural level is high are not characterized by juvenile delinquency. Furthermore, as the percentage of Negroes goes above 50 per cent, juvenile delinquency is apt to decline and, where a neighborhood is almost all Negro, it tends to settle down to "normal."

[*Comment:* Studies of the above kind, which correlate area attributes, need support from studies which correlate individual attributes. This study suggests that social and family disorganization is the basic cause of juvenile delinquency. This hypothesis would be more solidly established if a study of randomly selected juvenile delinquents showed that they actually came from families less unified and stable than families of nondelinquents.]

UNRAVELING JUVENILE DELINQUENCY   adaptation 2

Abridged and adapted from Sheldon and Eleanor Glueck, Unraveling Juvenile Delinquency *(Cambridge: Harvard University Press, 1950). Published in this form by permission of the authors, the publisher, and the Commonwealth Fund.*

[Many studies of juvenile delinquency have focused attention on differences between high- and low-delinquency *areas*. This study compares, not areas, but delinquent and nondelinquent *individuals*. The authors contend that the sociological attributes of a neighborhood are not sufficient to explain why some of its youths become delinquent while others do not. They reason that there must be something in the biologic makeup and childhood conditioning of delinquents which makes them more vulnerable than others to the pathology of their environment. Conversely, just as some people are immune or resistant to certain germs, so there are individuals who are able to withstand the disorganizing influences of a poor neighborhood. Therefore, the authors investigated not only the socioeconomic status of delinquents but their physical, emotional, and intellectual makeup and family life as well. The authors contend that delinquency results from the interaction of social processes with the biological and psychological makeup of individuals.]

THE PROBLEM

Urban area studies have discovered correlations between neighborhood and incidence of juvenile delinquency. The most frequently quoted finding is that delinquency rates are highest in core areas around central parts of cities and business districts and tend to drop in zones farther removed from the central section. From a physical standpoint, a delinquency area is likely to be adjacent to industry and commerce and to be a neighborhood of dilapidated houses, dirty alleys, low rents, much poverty and dependency, and inadequate recreational facilities. From a cultural standpoint, it is a place where the neighborhood has ceased to be an integrated and authoritative agency of sentiments, values, behavior standards, and social control; has drawn in peoples of differing and more or less conflicting standards of behavior; has to some extent developed a tradition of delinquency; and has largely failed to furnish unifying and edifying substitutes for the crumbling traditional patterns of behavior and authority.

This approach to the problem of delinquency, though useful, is of relatively little help in exploring the mechanisms of causation. These mechanisms are operative not in the external environment but in the mental life of the individual. Area studies establish that a region of economic and cultural disorganization tends to have a criminogenic effect on people residing therein; but the studies fail to emphasize that this influence affects only a selected group comprising a relatively small proportion of all the residents. They do not reveal why the deleterious influences of even the most extreme delinquency area fail to turn the great majority of its boys into persistent delinquents. They do not disclose whether children who do not succumb to disruptive neighborhood influences differ from those who become delinquents, and if so, in what respects.

It is necessary, therefore, to compare delinquents with nondelinquents from the same underprivileged neighborhoods in order to see in what ways they differ. In this study, 500 delinquent boys were compared with 500 nondelinquent boys. The individual boys were matched as closely as possible as to age, general intelligence, ethnic and racial origin, and residence in an underprivileged neighborhood.

Data were obtained on twelve aspects: (1) home conditions, (2) setting of family life, (3) quality of family life, (4) the boy in the family, (5) the boy in school, (6) the boy in the community, (7) physical condition, (8) bodily constitution, (9) verbal and performance intelligence, (10) qualitative and dynamic aspects of intelligence, (11) character and personality structure, and (12) dynamics of temperament.

HOME CONDITIONS

Table 2:5 is a summary of some of the findings in regard to home conditions; it includes only those items on which relatively sharp differences existed between delinquents and nondelinquents. It shows that, though subjects were chosen on the basis of residence in underprivileged neighborhoods, delinquents were in many respects less favorably situated than nondelinquents. More of their homes were in the worst slum areas, had incomplete sanitary facilities, and were neither clean nor physically adequate. Families of delinquents tended to move more and to be more often dependent on outside aid. The family income in delinquency cases

TABLE 2:5   HOME CONDITIONS OF 500 DELINQUENTS AND 500 NONDELINQUENTS *

	Delinquents	Nondelinquents	Difference
Lives in blighted slum area	55%	34%	21%
Lives in interstitial area	31	50	− 19
Less than 1 year at present address	34	15	19
Eight years or more at present address	11	26	− 15
Home normally neat and clean	49	66	− 17
Complete sanitary facilities	20	32	− 12
Home physically inadequate	34	20	14
Family economically dependent	29	12	17
Family income comes from illegitimate sources	23	9	14
Average weekly family income per person $2–$3	9	1	8
Average weekly family income per person $11 and over	18	31	− 13
Lives with both his own parents	50	71	− 21
Lives with his own mother	85	93	− 8
Lives with his own father	59	75	− 16
Parents living together	54	73	− 19

* Selected items from tables in Sheldon and Eleanor Glueck, *Unraveling Juvenile Delinquency* (Cambridge: Harvard University Press, 1950), Chapter VIII.

NOTE: In some cases percentages are based on totals of less than 500.

was more apt to come from other than legitimate sources; it was likely also to be less adequate. The nondelinquent was more apt to live with both or at least one of his own parents; it was also more probable that his parents were living together.

It is clear, therefore, that while both groups of boys resided in underprivileged neighborhoods and could be considered to be subject to the same general environmental influences, the household situation was significantly worse among delinquents than among nondelinquents.

SETTING OF FAMILY LIFE

Table 2:6 shows the close resemblance in ethnic origin between the parents of the two groups of boys which stemmed from matching the delinquents and the nondelinquents by national origin. Table 2:6 also shows that there is not much difference in the national composition of their families. A slightly larger percentage of delinquents came from nationally homogeneous homes where both parents were born in the same country, whether a foreign country or the United States.

The most important differences in the family histories of the subjects are to be found in the areas of physical and mental health. According to Table 2:7 mental retardation, emotional disturbance, drunkenness, and criminality were present in the maternal and paternal families of both delinquents and nondelinquents, but its incidence was higher in the families of delinquents, especially as regards their maternal families. These factors were also more prominent, together with serious physical ill health, in the parents of delinquent boys and among their sisters and brothers.

Ill health, mental retardation, and emotional disturbance undoubtedly make parents less capable of coping successfully with the problems of family life. This is evidenced more directly in the greater dependence of families of delinquents upon outside social agencies for help. Sixty-eight per cent of the families of delinquents had appealed to more than 9 differ-

TABLE 2:6   NATIVITY OF PARENTS OF 483 DELINQUENTS AND 494 NONDELINQUENTS *

	Delinquents	Nondelinquents	Difference
Both native	42%	39%	3%
One native, other foreign	21	27	− 6
Both same foreign country	35	30	5
Each different foreign country	2	4	− 2

* From Sheldon and Eleanor Glueck, *Unraveling Juvenile Delinquency* (Cambridge: Harvard University Press, 1950), p. 95.

ADAPTATION 2

TABLE 2:7 SETTING OF FAMILY LIFE OF 500 DELINQUENTS AND 500 NONDELINQUENTS *

	Delinquents	Nondelinquents	Difference
Mother's family:			
Mental retardation	26%	15%	11%
Emotional disturbance	36	20	16
Drunkenness	47	36	11
Criminality	55	36	19
Father's family:			
Mental retardation	12	9	3
Emotional disturbance	25	16	9
Drunkenness	37	31	6
Criminality	40	32	8
Mother:			
Serious physical ailments	49	33	16
Mental retardation	33	9	24
Emotional disturbances	40	18	22
Drunkenness	23	7	16
Criminality	45	15	30
Father:			
Serious physical ailments	40	29	11
Mental retardation	19	6	13
Emotional disturbances	44	18	26
Drunkenness	63	39	24
Criminality	66	32	34
Siblings:			
Serious physical ailments	41	24	17
Mental retardation	50	25	25
Emotional disturbances	37	11	26
Drunkenness	21	6	15
Criminality	65	26	39
No dependence on social agencies	0	6	− 6
Dependence on 1–8 social agencies	32	70	38
Dependence on 9 social agencies and more	68	24	44
Breadwinner unable to assume financial responsibility for family	16	16	0
Breadwinner able but unwilling to assume financial responsibility	45	25	20
Father's work habits good	38	71	− 33
Father's work habits poor	26	6	20

* Selected items from tables in Sheldon and Eleanor Glueck, *Unraveling Juvenile Delinquency* (Cambridge: Harvard University Press, 1950), Chapter IX.

NOTE: In some cases percentages are based on totals less than 500.

ent social agencies at one time or another; of these, over 13 per cent had appealed to more than 17 agencies. Among families of nondelinquents, though a majority had received help from at least 1 to 8 agencies, only 24 per cent had appealed to as many as 9 or more, while of these less than 2 per cent had appealed to more than 17.

Both sets of families were highly dependent upon outside financial aid, but their reasons for seeking assistance tended to be different. Unwillingness of the breadwinner to assume responsibility was the chief reason among families of delinquents for resorting to outside aid. In the majority of families of nondelinquents, sheer inadequacy of income stemming from economic depression and seasonal unemployment was the major reason for supplemental support. A further difference in the quality of the two sets of families is reflected in the far lower proportion of fathers of delinquents who had good work habits.

By these simple yet fundamental yardsticks, it is clear that the families in which delinquents were reared were more inadequate than those in which nondelinquents grew up. This basic finding is abundantly supported by additional data on the quality of family life.

QUALITY OF FAMILY LIFE

Table 2:8 discloses that a lower proportion of the families of delinquents were in the habit of planning their expenditures. More of these families lived from day to day, borrowing without thought of their ability to repay and showing little comprehension of the need to tailor their expenditures to a meager income.

Fewer families of delinquents had household routines according to which mealtimes, bedtimes, and hours for homework were specified. It is not surprising that among these low-income families few showed evidence of appreciation for the "finer things of life." However, where such evidence existed, it was more likely to be found in homes of nondelinquents.

In a further search for differences in the quality of the homes, differences in self-respect and ambition were sought out, as revealed in the attitude of parents toward protecting the family name, in their embarrassment about any irregularity in the behavior or status of members of the family, and in their preference for self-help as opposed to outside relief. In these respects the families of nondelinquents were considerably superior. The parents of nondelinquents were also more apt to get along well together. Which parent was the dominating influence in the family did not seem to matter, but mothers of delinquents were more likely to work outside the home. A sharp difference appears in the kind of supervision provided by the mother. Only 7 per cent of the mothers of delinquent children gave their children suitable care or provided for it; almost 64 per

TABLE 2:8   QUALITY OF FAMILY LIFE AMONG 500 DELINQUENTS AND 500 NONDELINQUENTS *

	Delinquents	Nondelinquents	Difference
Family income entirely planned	35%	56%	− 21%
Family income haphazardly planned	35	20	15
Household routine well planned	24	49	− 25
Routine of household haphazard	30	16	14
Slight cultural refinement of home	8	18	− 10
No cultural refinement of home	92	82	10
Self-respect of family marked	11	48	− 37
No self-respect of family	43	10	33
No family ambition	90	70	20
Parental relations good	37	65	− 28
Mother is housewife	53	67	− 14
Suitable supervision by mother	7	65	− 58
Unsuitable supervision by mother	64	13	51
No family group recreations	68	38	30
Warm toward children's friends	20	38	− 18
Inhospitable toward children's friends	37	22	15
Meager provisions for recreation in home	54	36	18
Marked family cohesiveness	16	61	− 45
No family cohesiveness	25	1	24

* Selected items from tables in Sheldon and Eleanor Glueck, *Unraveling Juvenile Delinquency* (Cambridge: Harvard University Press, 1950), Chapter X.
NOTE: In some cases percentages are based on totals less than 500.

cent were deemed to be remiss in their care. The evidence points also to striking differences in the cohesiveness of families of delinquents and nondelinquents. The former were more apt never to engage in family recreation, to be inhospitable to their children's friends, and to provide only meager provisions for recreation in the home. An evaluation of each family on the basis of data derived from social investigations and psychiatric interviews showed that the families of nondelinquents were very much more likely to be cohesive families, that is, to evince strong emotional ties among the members, joint interests, pride in their home, and a "we" feeling in general; less than 1 per cent treated home as "just a place to hang your hat."

Since the two sets of boys had been carefully matched at the outset, most notably with reference to residence in underprivileged neighborhoods, the above differences between their families are all the more impressive. Without consideration of the under-the-roof culture and the kind of family life the child leads, there can be no explanation of the differential influence of similar neighborhoods.

TABLE 2:9 FAMILY RELATIONSHIPS OF 500 DELINQUENTS AND 500 NONDELINQUENTS *

	Delinquents	Nondelinquents	Difference
With one or both parents since birth	54%	88%	− 34%
Home broken	60	34	26
Home broken when child was less than 5	56	47	9
Parents separated sporadically	27	9	18
Parents separated or divorced	22	13	9
One or both parents died †	20	14	6
One or both parents away at least a year ‡	14	6	8
Parents abandoned boy at birth §	5	1	4
Boy reared by parent substitutes	46	12	34
Father affectionate toward boy	40	81	− 41
Mother affectionate toward boy ‖	72	96	− 24
Boy attached to father	32	65	− 33
Father wholly acceptable to boy for emulation	17	52	− 35
Father unacceptable to boy	31	7	24
Boy attached to mother	65	90	− 25
Believes mother concerned for his welfare	23	71	− 48
Believes father concerned for his welfare	19	65	− 46
Parents' plans for boy's future definite	0	6	− 6
Parents' plans for boy's future vague	35	53	− 18
Parents' plans for boy's future absent	65	40	25
Parents knew of boy's bad habits	14	67	− 53
Mother's discipline:			
Lax	57	12	45
Overstrict	4	1	3
Erratic	35	21	14
Firm but kindly	4	66	− 62
Physical punishment	56	35	21
Deprivation of privileges	46	45	1
Threatening or scolding	47	37	10
Reasoning	16	28	− 12
Appeal to pride	9	9	0
Father's discipline:			
Lax	27	18	9
Overstrict	26	9	17
Erratic	42	18	24
Firm but kindly	5	55	− 50
Physical punishment	68	35	33
Deprivation of privileges	25	26	− 1
Threatening or scolding	32	31	1
Reasoning	11	24	− 13
Appeal to pride	4	6	− 2

THE BOY IN THE FAMILY

Despite the fact that culture conflict is frequently cited as a major cause of delinquency and crime, in this study there was no evidence that conflict with their foreign-born parents was greater for delinquents than for nondelinquents. Whether they were delinquent or not, a majority of the boys expressed embarrassment or rebellion over the exclusive use of a foreign language in the house, foreign cookery, customs, traditions, disciplinary practices, and so on.

It is often thought that only children, first children, and youngest children are especially vulnerable to behavior difficulties because they receive preferential treatment. Here, too, contrary to general expectation, there was a larger proportion of only children, first children, and youngest children among nondelinquents, while a larger proportion of delinquents were middle children (60 per cent as compared with 48 per cent).

According to Table 2:9, other differences in dynamic family relationships were apparent. Delinquents as a group were to a greater extent the victims not only of less stable households but of broken homes. While most of the nondelinquents had lived with one or both parents since birth, only half the delinquents had experienced an unbroken family relationship. To a far greater extent, delinquents had substitute parents, that is, they lived with relatives or had foster- or step-parents.

The delinquents were also more often the victims of the indifference or hostility of their parents and were in turn less attached to them. Their greater emotional deprivation is further reflected in a greater feeling on the part of the delinquent boys that their parents were not concerned about their welfare. They also tended more strongly not to identify themselves with their fathers and not to wish to emulate them.

Discipline in the homes of delinquents was in every respect inferior to that of nondelinquents. The parents of nondelinquents, though they used physical punishment, deprivation, and threats as methods of discipline, tended more often to use reasoning with a child. In interpreting these results, it should be kept in mind that the delinquent boys, being so continually involved in misbehavior, might have called forth more rigid and more erratic controls on the part of their parents. Nevertheless, the figures are a revealing commentary on the relative ineffectiveness of physical punishment in preventing delinquency.

---

* Selected items from tables in Sheldon and Eleanor Glueck, *Unraveling Juvenile Delinquency* (Cambridge: Harvard University Press, 1950), Chapter XI.
† Only 4 delinquents and 2 nondelinquents had lost both parents.
‡ Because of criminalism or illness.
§ Parents not married and did not live together after birth of boy either at all or for long.
‖ In this category 24.4% and 15.2% were overprotective.

NOTE: In some cases percentages are based on totals less than 500.

THE BOY IN SCHOOL

Despite original matching of the boys in age and general intelligence, delinquents were definitely more retarded educationally than were nondelinquents. Table 2:10 shows that to a much greater extent than nondelinquents, delinquents expressed violent dislike for school, resentment at its restrictions, and lack of interest in school work. The few nondelinquents who disliked school felt that they were unable to learn or were intellectually inferior.

A markedly higher proportion of delinquents expressed a desire to stop school at once, while many more nondelinquents planned to go on to high school, trade school, or beyond. A higher proportion of delinquents also expressed childish notions about what they wanted to do in life; they were inclined toward adventurous occupations or work requiring little training.

TABLE 2:10   SCHOOL BEHAVIOR OF 500 DELINQUENTS AND 500 NONDELINQUENTS *

	Delinquents	Nondelinquents	Difference
Attended from 2 to 4 schools	37%	66%	− 29%
Attended 5 or more schools	59	32	27
Repeated 2 grades or more	46	27	19
Retarded 1 year or more	69	44	25
In special class for retarded boys	21	10	11
Grades below "C"	41	8	33
Reading quotient below 80	54	36	18
Arithmetic quotient below 70	49	22	27
Markedly dislikes school	61	10	51
Dislikes school because unable to learn or feels inferior	47	78	− 31
Dislikes school because of restrictions and routine or lack of interest	46	15	31
Wants to go through high school, trade school, or beyond	32	79	− 47
Ambitions vague or wants adventurous or unskilled occupation	55	32	23
Seriously or persistently misbehaved in school	95	17	78
First school misbehavior before age 12	81	33	48
Occasional or persistent truancy	95	11	84
Truancy began before age 12	75	32	43

* Selected items from tables in Sheldon and Eleanor Glueck, *Unraveling Juvenile Delinquency* (Cambridge: Harvard University Press, 1950), Chapter XII.

NOTE: In some cases percentages are based on totals less than 500.

Most delinquents seriously or persistently misbehaved in school as compared with less than a fifth of the nondelinquents. Even more markedly they tended to truancy. They also tended to exhibit school misbehavior from the very beginning of their school careers, a fact which indicates the deep-rootedness of their emotional difficulties and maladaptation.

THE BOY IN THE COMMUNITY

To what extent did the boys have the opportunity to take root in a neighborhood? As we would expect, Table 2:11 shows that delinquents had far less opportunity to develop close neighborhood ties, a majority having moved from 5 to 13 times. Of these, almost a quarter moved 14 or more times.

TABLE 2:11 COMMUNITY RELATIONS OF 500 DELINQUENTS AND 500 NONDELINQUENTS *

	Delinquents	Nondelinquents	Difference
Five to 13 changes of residence	55%	36%	19%
Fourteen or more changes of residence	24	5	19
Prefers adventurous recreation	48	10	38
Stole rides or hopped trucks	92	24	68
Kept late hours	91	7	84
Smoked at early age	90	23	67
Sneaked into theaters	67	10	57
Destroyed property	62	4	58
Ran away from home	59	1	58
Bunked out	59	2	57
Gambled	53	9	44
Drank at early age	29	0	29
Set fires	13	0	13
Attended movies 3 or more times a week	45	11	34
Played on street corners	95	58	37
Played in distant neighborhoods	87	14	73
Played at home	42	93	— 51
Played at playgrounds	29	61	— 32
Member of a gang	56	1	55
Played with delinquents	98	7	91
Companions predominantly older	44	10	34
Attended boys' clubs on urging of adults	57	30	27
Attended boys' clubs on urging of companions	26	48	— 22
Only occasional or no church attendance	61	33	28

* Selected items from tables in Sheldon and Eleanor Glueck, *Unraveling Juvenile Delinquency* (Cambridge: Harvard University Press, 1950), Chapter XIII.

NOTE: In some cases percentages are based on totals less than 500.

As a group, delinquents inclined more to adventurous activities than nondelinquents did. Nondelinquents attended movies in moderation; they tended to play at home or in playgrounds rather than on street corners and in distant neighborhoods; they avoided gangs almost entirely and did not associate with delinquents. Almost all the delinquents chummed largely with other delinquents and gravitated toward older boys.

While almost all the boys had some contact with boys' clubs, settlement houses, and other agencies of supervised recreation, delinquents were more apt to attend on the urging of parole or probation officers, parents or other relatives, or teachers and other authoritative adults. Nondelinquents, on the other hand, were more apt to go on the advice of companions of their own age. Although few boys neglected religion entirely, delinquents tended to go to church only occasionally, nondelinquents to go regularly.

PHYSICAL CONDITION

The view that delinquents are in poorer health than nondelinquents receives no support from this study. Very little, if any, difference exists between the physical condition of the two groups as a whole.

A considerably higher proportion of delinquents are reported to be enuretic (bedwetters) and extremely restless. At the same time, fewer delinquents than nondelinquents have neurological handicaps. Slight or marked tics are slightly more prevalent among nondelinquents, while extreme nail-biting is slightly more prevalent among delinquents.

BODILY CONSTITUTION

In gross bodily size delinquents are superior to nondelinquents, especially in the shoulders, chest, waist, and upper extremities, and bodily disproportions are less frequent among delinquents than among nondelinquents. Delinquents are relatively more homogeneous in physique than are nondelinquents; they tend on the whole to be muscular, and both thin and plump types are decidedly less frequent among them. Nondelinquents as a group exhibited no heavy predominancy of any one type.

VERBAL AND PERFORMANCE INTELLIGENCE

Although delinquents and nondelinquents were matched as to over-all intelligence quotient (allowing not more than a ten-point difference), they varied in the extent to which their total score was based on verbal or on performance skill. On the whole, delinquents averaged less in verbal intelligence than did nondelinquents. Though delinquents appeared to have a slight advantage in tests based upon a direct approach to concrete reality, they were handicapped in areas where symbols and words were important.

QUALITATIVE AND DYNAMIC ASPECTS OF INTELLIGENCE

The Rorschach (or Inkblot) Test was administered to the subjects in an attempt to assess the qualitative and dynamic aspects of intelligence. As the subject interprets a set of different inkblot patterns, he is scored for such things as originality, creativity, banality, power of observation, unrealistic thinking, common sense, intuition, phantasy, methodical approach to the problem, objectivity, and so on.

Delinquents and nondelinquents resembled each other in many ways. However, delinquents had somewhat less power of observation and showed less potential capacity for objective interests, and more of them tended to be unrealistic in their thinking, to lack common sense, and to be unsystematic in their approach to the mastery of mental problems. Since these factors are closely interwoven with emotional dynamics, they seem to point to the relative handicap under which the delinquent operates, not only in intellectual matters but in the area of personal and social adjustment.

CHARACTER AND PERSONALITY STRUCTURE

The Rorschach Test was also used to compare the incidence of many personality and character traits among delinquents and nondelinquents. Delinquents as a group were to a much greater degree socially assertive, defiant, and ambivalent toward authority; they were more resentful of others and were far more hostile, suspicious, and destructive; they were more impulsive and vivacious and decidedly more extroversive in their behavior trends.

At the same time, delinquents as a group were far less submissive to authority than were nondelinquents. They suffered far less than nondelinquents did from fear of failure and defeat, and they were considerably less co-operative with and dependent on others. Delinquents were also markedly less conventional in their ideas, feelings, and behavior. Finally, delinquents were noticeably less masochistic than were nondelinquents, and less self-controlled.

However, the incidence of some psychological traits was surprisingly high in both groups. For example, both groups showed marked feelings of insecurity and/or anxiety (delinquents, 89.2%; nondelinquents, 95.7%) and of not being wanted or loved (84.3%:88.0%). Neither group manifested self-assertiveness (93.7%:97.8%) or highly competitive attitudes (94.0%:92.3%). Both groups lacked attitudes of kindliness and trust (95.8%:92.9%) and manifested little spontaneity (91.7%:94.5%). The absence of introversive trends (living within oneself) was uniformly high (72.7%:75.5%).

DYNAMICS OF TEMPERAMENT

A review of the findings that emerged from the psychiatric interview with each boy makes clear that delinquents as a group differ from nondelinquents in many aspects and manifestations of temperament. They are less efficient than the nondelinquents and have less emotional stability. On the other hand, they are more dynamic and energetic and much more aggressive, adventurous, and positively suggestible as well as stubborn. They are also more inclined toward impulsive and nonreflective expression of their energy drives.

Delinquents are more inclined to the immediate indulgence of their appetites; they are less sensitive aesthetically and more desirous of acquiring material things. They are far less conventional and not nearly so conscientious in connection with achieving their goals. They are less realistic in facing existing situations, less practical in considering the feasibility of a course of behavior, far less critical of themselves, and more self-centered than the nondelinquents. Finally, a basic difference between delinquents and nondelinquents has been found in the way they tend to resolve their conflicts; delinquents rather typically reacted to stress situations by extroversive expression (action), nondelinquents by introversion (withdrawal).

NONCAUSAL FACTORS IN DELINQUENCY

Some factors were demonstrated to be so similar for delinquents and nondelinquents that they may be regarded as of little or no significance in the causal dynamics of delinquency.

Background of parents. Size of families of mothers and fathers. Schooling of grandparents. Serious physical ailments among members of the maternal and paternal families. Proportion of native- and foreign-born parents. Age of parents at time of marriage. Difference in age of mothers and fathers. Age of parents at birth of boy. Economic condition of homes in which fathers were reared. Drunkenness and mental retardation in families of fathers.

Home background. Length of time boys lived in underprivileged areas. Rent paid by parents. Home furnishings. Average size of household of which boys were a part. Family domination by mother. Culture conflict.

School and recreation. Age at school entrance. Marked dislike of certain school subjects. Prior or present attendance at boys' clubs (this does not refer to frequency of attendance).

Health. Weight. Height. Genital pathology. Functional deviations. Glandular disturbances. Irregular reflexes. Irremediable defects.

Intelligence. Score on Similarities, Arithmetic Reasoning, and Memory

Span for Digits tests (in the verbal battery) and on Picture Completion and Picture Arrangement tests (in the performance battery) of the Wechsler-Bellevue Scale. Performance intelligence. Certain qualities of intelligence as revealed by the Rorschach Test: phantasy, originality, creativity, banality, intuition, and ororverbalizing intelligence.

Basic character traits, as revealed by the Rorschach Test. Feeling of not being taken seriously. Feeling of not being taken care of. Feeling of being unable to manage own life. Attitude of overcompetitiveness. Spontaneity. Introversive behavior trends.

Emotional stress, as revealed by the psychiatric interview. Stress resulting from school difficulties.

FACTORS WITH PROBABLE CAUSAL SIGNIFICANCE

We are now ready to focus attention on factors that may have causal significance. It is as yet too early to arrive at unassailable conclusions regarding the relative influence of biologic and social factors on human behavior in general, including juvenile delinquency. Nevertheless, our data do permit a rough division. There are, on the one hand, factors that are closer to the genetic than to the environmental end of the biosocial scale and, on the other, those that are closer to the "conditioned," cultural end of the scale.

Physique. The delinquents as a group tend toward the outline of a solid, closely-knit muscular type, one in which there is a relative predominance of muscle, bone, and connective tissue. Perhaps related to this is the fact that a much higher proportion of delinquents than nondelinquents were reported to have been extremely restless as young children in terms of energy output.

Temperamental traits and emotional dynamics. On the whole, the delinquents are more extroverted, vivacious, impulsive, and less self-controlled than the nondelinquents. They are more hostile, resentful, defiant, suspicious, and destructive. They are less fearful of failure or defeat than the nondelinquents. They are less concerned about meeting conventional expectations and are more ambivalent toward, or far less submissive to, authority. They are, as a group, more socially assertive. To a greater extent than the nondelinquents, they express feelings of not being recognized or appreciated.

Intellectual traits. The delinquents tend to express themselves intellectually in a direct, immediate, and concrete manner rather than through the use of intermediate symbols or abstractions. There seems also to be a somewhat greater emotional disharmony connected with their performance of intellectual tasks.

Behavior trends. In their recreational activities and companionships, the delinquents further evidence a craving for adventure and for opportunities to express aggressive energy output, with the added need of supportive companionship in such activities. In their poorer school achievement, delinquents again evidence restless energy, with accompanying difficulties in adapting and conforming to a regime of rules and discipline.

Sociocultural factors. The families of delinquent boys were on the whole less adequately equipped for the task of rearing children than were those of nondelinquents. As a group, families of delinquents showed more disorganization, mutual hostility, and lack of cohesiveness. To a far greater extent than nondelinquents, delinquents were raised in homes of little understanding, affection, stability, or moral fiber by parents usually unfit to be effective guides and protectors or desirable sources for emulation.

The exciting and stimulating but little-controlled and culturally inconsistent environment of the underprivileged areas in which they lived fostered the expression by delinquents of their untamed impulses and self-centered desires. These tendencies toward uninhibited energy expression seemed to have their source in the bodily constitution and temperament of delinquents and were further reinforced by malformations of character during the first few years of life.

PREDICTION OF DELINQUENCY

Having established resemblances and differences between delinquents and nondelinquents we turn to the possibility of devising a test by which potential delinquents may be recognized very early in life, preferably at school entrance. It is necessary, however, to construct a test which is not based on actual delinquent behavior. In the first place, the danger signals of delinquent behavior, such as truancy, running away, stealing, and lying, are found in many nondelinquent children; what separates the delinquent from the nondelinquent is not that he indulges in antisocial behavior but that he persists in it. Moreover, to wait for clear signs that a child is actually delinquent is to close the barn door after the horse has been stolen.

It was decided to use five factors that satisfied at least the following two conditions: (1) that the factors be present in the lives and makeup of children prior to school entrance and (2) that they be items which the study showed were *significantly* more prominent in delinquents than in nondelinquents.

The following are the five factors finally selected for inclusion in a prediction table constructed from the social background of the boys.

1. *Discipline of boy by father:*   Weighted Failure Score
    Overstrict or erratic   72.5
    Lax   59.8
    Firm but kindly   9.3

	Weighted Failure Score
2. *Supervision of boy by mother:*	
Unsuitable	83.2
Fair	57.5
Suitable	9.9
3. *Affection of father for boy:*	
Indifferent or hostile	75.9
Warm (including overprotective)	33.8
4. *Affection of mother for boy:*	
Indifferent or hostile	86.2
Warm (including overprotective)	43.1
5. *Cohesiveness of family:*	
Unintegrated	96.9
Some elements of cohesion	61.3
Cohesive	20.6

A method of scoring was devised which resulted in the figures shown above for each item. The highest possible score was 414; the lowest possible score, 116.7. On the basis of the present study, it was calculated that for a boy with a score under 250 the chances of becoming a delinquent are only sixteen out of a hundred, while for a boy with a score of 250 or over, they are as high as seventy-nine out of a hundred.

It must be emphasized that a potential juvenile delinquency score can never yield definitive knowledge concerning any particular child. A particular boy with a score over 250 may be one of the approximately twenty out of a hundred who do not become delinquent. At the same time, the test by itself does not enable us to pick out those sixteen boys who, despite scores of 250 and less, do turn out to be delinquent. Consequently, the score obtained by a boy on the five factors chosen must be supplemented by additional knowledge. Sometimes this knowledge can come from other tests, such as the Rorschach, or from psychiatric interviews.

SUGGESTIONS FOR FURTHER READING, CHAPTERS 2 AND 3

August Aichhorn, *Wayward Youth* (New York: Viking Press, 1935).
Bruno Bettelheim, *Love Is Not Enough* (Glencoe, Ill.: The Free Press, 1950).
Albert K. Cohen, *Delinquent Boys* (Glencoe, Ill.: The Free Press, 1955).
Paul L. Crawford, Daniel I. Malamud, and James R. Dumpson, *Working with Teen Age Gangs* (New York: Welfare Council of New York City, 1950).
John R. Ellingston, *Protecting Our Children from Criminal Careers* (New York: Prentice-Hall, Inc., 1948).

Kate Friedlander, M.D., *The Psycho-Analytical Approach to Juvenile Delinquency* (London: Routledge & Kegan Paul, Ltd., 1947).

Sheldon and Eleanor Glueck, *Delinquents in the Making* (New York: Harper & Bros., 1952).

Alfred J. Kahn, *A Court for Children* (New York: Columbia University Press, 1953).

William C. Kvaraceus, *The Community and the Delinquent* (Yonkers-on-Hudson, N.Y.: World Book Co., 1954).

F. Ivan Nye, *Family Relationships and Delinquent Behavior* (New York: John Wiley & Sons, Inc., 1958).

Fritz Redl and David Wineman, *Children Who Hate* (Glencoe, Ill.: The Free Press, 1951).

Clifford R. Shaw, *The Jack-Roller* (Chicago: University of Chicago Press, 1930).

Clifford R. Shaw and Henry D. McKay, *Juvenile Delinquency in Urban Areas* (Chicago: University of Chicago Press, 1942).

Paul W. Tappan, *Juvenile Delinquency* (New York: McGraw-Hill Book Co., Inc., 1949).

Clyde B. Vedder, *The Juvenile Offender* (Garden City, N.Y.: Doubleday & Co., Inc., 1954).

William Foote Whyte, *Street Corner Society* (Chicago: University of Chicago Press, 1943).

United Press International

CHAPTER 3

Juvenile Delinquency: Meeting The Problem

A delinquent, disorganized, and value-confused society is the background for many of the major risk factors of delinquency. The delinquent, disorganized, and value-confused family is at once the source and the reflection of that society. So is the neighborhood. So are the mass media. But these in turn are linked to social and historical changes: urbanization, mobility, industrialization, the development of a highly prosperous and competitive business economy. These are not changes that we can simply reverse nor would we perhaps want to. Would we want, for example, to forego the benefits of mass production because delinquency may be one of the by-products of urban, industrial society? There is, moreover, little reason to believe that the ills characterizing present-day society are inevitable or that the dislocations induced by a century of rapid and unparalleled social and technological change will remain forever unmitigated.

Nor does it seem feasible to get at the roots of the problem by attempting a rhetorical program of value reform for society. It has sometimes been proposed, for instance, that an organized program to emphasize religion, church attendance, and Bible-reading would serve to reduce delinquency. But there is no evidence that this isolated emphasis would serve such a purpose. Mursell, for example, compared boys in a state reform school with nondelinquent boys of similar background and concluded that "there is no significant relation between religious training and delinquent or nondelinquent behavior."[1] Hightower tested some 3,000 children and found that there was no significant relation between extent of Biblical information and lying, cheating, or deception.[2] Hartshorne and May found no significant difference in honesty between those who attended Sunday school and those who did not.[3]

These and similar results do not invalidate a possible relation between religious values and nondelinquency. They do serve, however, to throw doubt on the efficacy of a program which emphasizes mere participation in the external aspects of religion, often artificially imposed.

Similarly there is no indication that the family can be reconstructed by any specific program in isolation from the society in which it is shaped. Broad-scale parent education in classroom settings and specific attempts to reform the family by imposing penalties on parents in cases of delinquency have proved neither practicable nor productive.

However, even as it searches on all levels for answers to its long-range, "root" problems, society must seek some specific programs for combating or at least mitigating the immediate problem of the habitual delinquent.

Section I: Programs for Prevention

This section presents a description of some of the most common efforts to directly reduce the incidence of delinquency. Some remedial approaches seem to be squarely based on one or another of the causal theories already described. For example, the child-guidance movement seems to be tied to the delinquent-personality approach; the redirection of gangs to the delinquent-learning approach; and neighborhood area projects, at their best, to the theory of social disorganization. However, these programs are not usually conceived or applied along clear theoretical lines. Often they are directed toward obvious risk conditions and places in society: the family, the gang, the neighborhood. Nevertheless, in some cases, the relative failure of a program is largely the result of a failure to apply a cogent causal theory to the obvious risk conditions in society and thus

---

[1] George R. Mursell, "A Study of Religious Training as a Psychological Factor in Delinquency" (unpublished Ph.D. dissertation, Ohio State University, 1930).

[2] Pleasant R. Hightower, *Biblical Information in Relation to Character and Conduct* (Iowa City: University of Iowa, 1930).

[3] Hugh Hartshorne, Mark A. May, et al., *Studies in the Nature of Character* (3 vols.; New York: The Macmillan Co., 1928–30).

By Gertrude Samuels, The *New York Times*

Training for Citizenship: A YMCA club. Worth-while youth agency projects are not necessarily delinquency control programs.

to understand exactly *why* and *how* one family produces delinquents and another does not or *why* and *how* one neighborhood produces many more delinquents than another.

GROUP-WORK AGENCIES AND ORGANIZED RECREATION

Goal: To integrate children into supervised and nondelinquent group activity. This is a generalized program aimed broadside at all children.

Description: Group-work agencies include such well-known organizations as YMCA, YWCA, Girl Scouts, Boy Scouts, and Campfire Girls, as well as independent boys' and girls' clubs and neighborhood and community centers.

For the most part, these agencies are *not* set up as delinquency control programs but are designed to meet the activity needs of all children. This is also true of less comprehensive recreation activities provided by local government. But, according to the claims of some of these agencies, one of the by-products of these activities is delinquency control.

An increasing emphasis has been placed on providing trained professional group workers who, by supervising group activity, can develop living skills and positive values in children. The main targets naturally are children who have time on their hands, who would otherwise be unsupervised, and who might therefore not be integrated into or receive recognition from a nondelinquent group.

Ellery Reed's study of group-work agencies in Cincinnati in 1942 discovered that in only 28 per cent of the cases appearing before the juvenile court had the children been registered with a group-work agency during the previous three years.[4] But what did this mean? Did it mean that most agency children were being deterred from delinquency, or did it mean that group work was not reaching those children most likely to become delinquent? Further study supported the latter interpretation: group work tended not to reach those segments of the juvenile population most likely to have the highest rates of juvenile court appearance. In the first place, a higher proportion of accused delinquents than agency children came from economically underprivileged areas. Furthermore, agency children who did live in underprivileged neighborhoods tended to come from "more stable and fortunate" homes as measured by family registrations with the Social Service Exchange. Finally, agency children were more likely than were accused delinquents to be white, to be girls, and to be under fifteen years of age, that is, to be those children least likely to contribute to delinquency statistics. Reed concluded that

> group work agencies are not in general identified closely with the underprivileged and insecure elements in the population, nor with the age groups among which delinquency is most prevalent . . . . The findings of this study may suggest the question of whether some group work agencies by the nature of their programs, attitudes and methods do, in fact, screen out the boys and girls who are handicapped physically, mentally, economically or racially; or who are emotionally maladjusted; or who have an unfortunate and unhappy family background.[5]

The delinquency rate of 1,679 of these agency children was checked in court records. In 1942, the delinquency rate of agency children was 2.08 per 1,000 against a total city rate of 2.57. In 1943 the delinquency rate of agency children was 2.73 against a total city rate of 3.09. These somewhat lower rates must be evaluated, however, against the fact that group-work agencies were not reaching a proportionate number of children most likely to become delinquent. When this fact is taken into account, group work appeared to have little, if any, influence.

Frederic Thrasher evaluated the success of a boys' club in New York which had a cumulative membership of over 12,000 between 1927 and

---

[4] Ellery F. Reed, "How Effective Are Group Work Agencies in Preventing Delinquency?" *Focus,* 28 (November, 1949), 170–76.
[5] *Ibid.,* p. 170.

1931.⁶ This club was geared toward welcoming delinquent and predelinquent children as well as nondelinquent children. As a matter of fact, its enrollment included a disproportionate number of boys considered to be in "delinquency-prone" circumstances: low social and economic status, poor educational achievement, foreign parentage, and emotional instability. Of the total delinquent offenses committed by members of the club before, during, and after membership, 61 per cent took place while the boys were actively participating in club activities and another 28 per cent took place after participation. Further, the percentage of members brought to the juvenile court increased as the boys continued membership in the club. The club was apparently not effective in arresting the rate of increase in delinquency that normally would have been expected with the increasing age of the boys. It should be noted, however, that the boys' club program in question heavily emphasized recreational activity and provided very little skilled individual attention.

Thrasher studied in detail the cases of 60 problem boys who were members of the club and came to this conclusion:

> The acute behavior problems in these cases, precipitated by various combinations of family disorganization, dire poverty, school maladjustments, gang activities, association with older hoodlums and underworld characters, demoralizing experiences on the streets and in institutions of commercialized amusements and neighborhood hangouts—these influences for the most part were beyond the power of the Boys' Club to neutralize, particularly in the limited time each week which the average Boys' Club member spent in club activities involving, as they did, little real guidance from the Club personnel.⁷

A study of delinquency in relation to the recreational facilities of the Chicago Recreation Commission found that more nondelinquents than delinquents used the facilities.⁸ However, in the five areas studied, 35–61 per cent of the official delinquents *did* use the facilities, and they spent more time in them than did the nondelinquents. These delinquents, however, spent less time in the closely supervised activities than did the nondelinquents, preferring the game rooms and competitive sports and avoiding club activities. Finally, it was found that no child in the entire program spent more than an average of about an hour and a half a week in supervised play. Most spent less. And all of them spent about twice as much time in the movies.

Evaluation: 1. Recreational facilities which merely serve to fill in time,

⁶ Frederic Thrasher, "The Boys' Club and Juvenile Delinquency," *American Journal of Sociology,* 42 (1936), 66–80.
⁷ *Ibid.,* p. 78.
⁸ Ethel Shanas and Catherine E. Dunning, *Recreation and Delinquency* (Chicago: Chicago Recreation Commission, 1942).

TABLE 3:1 MUNICIPAL RECREATIONAL FACILITIES, 1930–50 *

	1930	1940	1950
Playgrounds—outdoor	7,316	9,921	14,747
Recreation buildings	642	1,750	2,987
Recreation centers—indoor	1,963	3,986	6,630
Paid recreation leaders	24,949	24,533	58,029
Volunteer recreation leaders	8,216	12,890	52,982

* Source: J. Frederic Dewhurst and Associates, *America's Needs and Resources* (New York: Twentieth Century Fund, 1955), p. 374. These figures cover only communities that sent reports to the National Recreation Association for the years cited and are not complete national totals.

without supervision or individual attention, show no significant potential for delinquency control.

2. As Table 3:1 indicates, recreational facilities have considerably increased during the past decades, but this period has also seen the sharpest rise in delinquency statistics.

3. Supervised club and group-work activities may reduce the over-all rate of delinquency, but at present there is no indication that they can deal successfully with more serious and habitual delinquents. Certain delinquents avoid supervised and club activity; in any case, the relatively small amount of time spent in such activity does not seem sufficient to balance serious and enveloping risk factors in home and neighborhood.

4. Group-work and recreational activities serve an important function for the youth of the community. If more intensive individual attention and child guidance are necessary for delinquency control, perhaps the answer is to be found in extending child guidance facilities rather than in converting group-work and recreational agencies into delinquency "clinics."

"BIG BROTHER" ACTIVITIES

Goal: To provide the child with a missing "control" factor in the form of a volunteer adult who can give him friendship and counsel. This program is mainly aimed at predelinquents, although it has also been used for children on parole or probation.

Description: There is a private nation-wide Big Brother and Big Sister movement, but similar programs have been established by local and state law-enforcement and welfare agencies. "Big Brothers" are as a rule not trained social workers but interested citizens. The adult attempts to build a friendship with the child he is sponsoring by showing an interest in his problems and perhaps engaging in common recreational activities. He gives the child advice and helps him to get whatever services he needs from the various social agencies.

The hope is that, through this activity, the adult will provide a model for the child, helping to instill in him positive social values and, at the same time, giving him some of the affection and attention he lacks.

The Cambridge-Somerville Youth Study was set up by Dr. Richard Cabot of Harvard to test the "Big Brother" hypothesis.[9] (See Adaptation 3, pp. 116 ff.) This eight-year experiment selected two groups of 325 boys, from 9 to 11 years old, each group matched as carefully as possible for age, social environment, and intelligence. One group of children were then provided with professional counselors, whose goal was to establish a friendly relationship with the child and maintain that relationship throughout the experimental years. Emphasis was placed on joint recreational activities, but counselors also attempted to be as generally helpful as possible by tutoring, giving counsel, finding needed services, and showing continuous interest.

After the program was over, the police and court records of the treatment and control groups were compared. They were almost identical. Independent observers estimated that the program had been "definitely beneficial" in 21 per cent of 234 cases studied. However, those that were benefited did not tend to be those who were most likely to become serious and habitual delinquents. Boys whose circumstances included various combinations of poor home life and parental care, delinquency area residence, and more serious emotional disturbance did not tend to respond to the program.

Evaluation: 1. Some delinquent children are so seriously damaged that they cannot accept adult love and guidance even when it is offered them. The difficulty of serious delinquents can lie not in their lack of an adequate adult model to emulate but in their psychological inability to overcome their mistrust of all parent-figures. When this is the case, only a personal relation with a skilled, professional worker can be of significant aid. Help by laymen, though well meaning, may prevent the youth from getting the professional care he needs.

2. Especially in slum areas, where many children need more adult attention and counseling, "Big Brother" sponsorship is worth while apart from delinquency control. Where family life has not been overly destructive, this substitute parenthood may be of some help in milder cases of delinquency.

CHILD GUIDANCE

Goals: "Child guidance" has become a specialized term generally denoting two steps: (*a*) making a thorough psychiatric study and diagnosis

---

[9] Edwin Powers, "An Experiment in Prevention of Delinquency," *Annals of the American Academy of Political and Social Science,* **261** (January, 1949), 77–88.

of the individual child's personality problems and (b) providing psychiatric treatment and prescribing the environmental changes indicated by the diagnosis. The growing child guidance movement is aimed at all "problem" children, including predelinquents. This technique has also been used by many juvenile courts in dealing with adjudged delinquents.

Description: A child guidance clinic typically operates through teams of psychiatrists, psychologists, and social workers. The social worker investigates the social history and environment of the child. The psychologist administers personality and intelligence tests. The psychiatrist interviews the child and his parents. The information and insights gathered are continuously pooled at staff conferences as both diagnosis and treatment progress.

In the early history of child guidance clinics the emphasis was on diagnosis and *social* treatment. Staff conferences culminated in a plan for the child which usually called for modifications in his social environment: foster-home placement, school changes, recreational changes, other provision of social service, or even some attempt by a social worker to improve the parents' understanding of the child's needs.

The Judge Baker Guidance Center in Boston initially provided this kind of diagnosis and recommendations for the Boston Juvenile Court. In 1934 Sheldon and Eleanor Glueck published their study of 1,000 boys referred to this guidance center by the court. Court records showed that 88 per cent of these boys had persisted in some form of delinquency, more than two-thirds had subsequently been convicted of serious crimes, and a third had been arrested at least four times. Finally, the court records were examined of 1,000 boys who had come to the attention of the court during the same years but had not been referred to the clinic. There was no significant difference between their records and the records of those who had been referred to the clinic. The Gluecks concluded that "the treatment carried on by the Clinic, Court and associated community facilities had very little effect in preventing recidivism." [10]

In recent years the emphasis of many child guidance clinics, including the Judge Baker Guidance Center, has shifted perceptibly. To diagnostic examination is added direct psychiatric treatment of children and parents by the clinic staff. Primarily this consists of continuous and intensive *therapeutic* interviews with both parents and children. This is more than an attempt to provide wise counsel. The broad object is to attempt, through professionally skilled interchanges, to lead both children and adults to a greater understanding of their personal problems and a more realistic assessment of their goals and resources. This may require an extended

---

[10] Sheldon Glueck and Eleanor Glueck, *One Thousand Juvenile Delinquents* (Cambridge: Harvard University Press, 1934), p. 167.

period of therapy, and some measure of co-operation from the subjects is required. In conjunction with this psychiatric treatment, the child guidance clinic tries to modify environmental conditions wherever possible through the use of existing community facilities: schools, community centers, foster homes, employment agencies, other social agencies.

In addition to child guidance clinics, which may be independent agencies or may be attached to public or private welfare institutions, there are other social agencies which include child guidance work in their programs. These include casework agencies of the Community Chest variety, as well as casework agencies attached to the welfare organizations of the various religious communities. These agencies are generally staffed by social workers with a psychiatric orientation and use psychiatrists only in a consulting capacity. The programs of many of these agencies include provision for intensive casework by trained social workers.

Dr. William Healy and Augusta Bronner set up a research project to determine the effectiveness of intensive psychiatric treatment in child guidance clinics.[11] The subjects were 105 habitual delinquents, 105 matched nondelinquents, and about 40 other unmatched pairs. Efforts were made to involve all delinquents and their parents in therapeutic treatment. Two years after treatment ended, the records of these delinquents were examined. About half of them had not been involved in delinquent behavior since the close of treatment.

It was further found that those who were *not* helped were preponderantly boys with more serious emotional disturbances and those living under more pathological social circumstances. Where seriously adverse family and neighborhood situations existed, clinical treatment tended to fail.

Sutherland and Cressey's review of the literature on child guidance clinic results indicates that from a fourth to a third of the children treated continue to be problems; and where family relationships are unsatisfactory, there is rarely any improvement.[12]

As a result of re-evaluation, the Judge Baker Guidance Center began to select and to concentrate on those cases which gave some promise of being able to respond to treatment. The potential co-operativeness of the parents was considered, and families in extremely adverse social circumstances were avoided.

Evaluation: 1. Child guidance clinics serve a *general* community need in the diagnosis and treatment of many emotionally disturbed children. Their effectiveness, however, is largely limited to problems stemming

---

[11] William Healy, M.D., and Augusta F. Bronner, *New Light on Delinquency and Its Treatment* (New Haven: Yale University Press, 1936).

[12] Edwin H. Sutherland and Donald R. Cressey, *Principles of Criminology* (Philadelphia: J. B. Lippincott Co., 1955).

from parent-child relationships where there are no severely adverse social circumstances and where the family is willing and able to co-operate in the effort.

2. The child guidance clinics tend to avoid the large core of predelinquents of lowest socio-economic status, those whose problems are severely aggravated by other factors besides strained relations with their parents, and those whose parents are not receptive to clinical aid. Like many other delinquency control programs, the child guidance approach fails to reach those most susceptible to serious delinquency.

3. The admitted value of the child guidance movement as a delinquency control program is further restricted by the sheer expense of providing the facilities and personnel for the thorough individual treatment required.

PROGRAMS FOR EARLY DETECTION

Goal: The early detection of predelinquents so that they may receive individual attention at an early age.

Description: The school has generally been considered to have the greatest potential for early detection of delinquency, since all children in the community come to its attention. In addition, a number of communities have set up special projects to co-ordinate the findings of all social agencies dealing with children.

A congressional subcommittee in 1956 reported these findings: "In all probability, even today, it is the rare delinquent child whose problems were not recognized by the teacher early in his or her school career."[13] The classroom teacher is indeed often the first to detect behavior problems, and in recent years much attention has been given to this facet of the teacher's job. Workshops have been held, and guidance material has been prepared to assist teachers in the recognition of disturbed behavior. However, some administrators feel that the teacher's job has become complex and encumbered enough without expecting him also to be an expert in identifying predelinquency. It has been recommended that more specialized school services be made available to which the teacher can refer a child. These services can take the form of trained counselors, school social workers, school psychologists, and psychological clinics. Where school systems have such services, they usually depend on other community agencies to provide therapeutic treatment.

In some cities a central exchange has been formally set up to provide for liaison between schools, police, and other social agencies. In New York City, "referral units" have been created in a number of elemen-

---

[13] *Education and Juvenile Delinquency,* Interim Report of the Subcommittee To Investigate Juvenile Delinquency to the Committee on the Judiciary, 84th Cong., 2nd Sess. (Washington, D.C.: U.S. Government Printing Office, 1956).

tary school districts to seek out predelinquent children. The New York City Youth Board has gone further by setting up a project to try to involve those families that have rejected referral to treatment agencies. This requires great skill and an unusual investment of time in the development of a relationship between such a family and the assigned social worker.

Evaluation: 1. Many of the important indications of probable future delinquency are subtle home factors not easily accessible to teacher observation.

2. Though it has been found that proportionately many more delinquents than nondelinquents engage in truancy before the age of twelve, the Gluecks report that truancy at an early age also occurred in about one-third of their nondelinquent subjects. This is a reminder that no one factor can be isolated as a sign of probable delinquency.

3. "Early" detection and diagnosis are often not early enough. By school age, irremediable damage is sometimes already done.

4. Nevertheless, the value of early diagnosis and treatment is uncontested. The probability that clinical therapy will be successful, for example, partly depends on the age at which the child is reached.

GANG DIRECTION

Goal: To redirect gang activities into socially approved constructive channels.

Description: Several projects in gang direction have been initiated in metropolitan areas around the country by youth welfare agencies. The key hurdle is for the professional worker to win the acceptance of the gang. One New York City project reported that this process took from three to seven months. (See Adaptation 4, pp. 122 ff., below.)

The working assumption behind this program is that predelinquent and delinquent gang members are not totally without the desire to live within a socially approved pattern. However, they are suspicious and afraid of adults and turn to the organized gang as their only source of security and approval. If the gang as a whole, without obvious manipulation from the "hostile" world, moves successfully in more socially acceptable directions, individual members are usually quite willing to move with it.

Both Los Angeles and New York report some initial successes with gang-direction projects. These successes have been measured mainly by the increasing redirection of gang activities rather than by the effect on individual delinquent records. For instance, the New York City projects report that intergang conflict has been lessened and that some gangs have successfully been diverted from destructive activities. But they also report that gang members' attitudes toward family, police, and school have apparently not been substantially changed. Nor do they pretend to have been able to deal with serious personality problems.

Evaluation: 1. By establishing relations with the leaders of gangs, it seems possible to redirect many gangs into less socially aggressive channels and thus to reduce the amount of delinquent behavior which flows directly from gang activity.

2. We do not know, however, whether this redirected gang activity has the effect of curbing the individual delinquency of gang members. While some delinquent conduct may be averted, there is as yet no indication that the habitual delinquent will be seriously affected, especially if the gang has served as outlet for, rather than prime mover of, his delinquent tendencies.

NEIGHBORHOOD AREA PROJECTS

Goal: To combat failure of control by creating a more cohesive neighborhood interested in the welfare and values of its children. This approach is aimed at high-delinquency areas where social disorganization is severe.

Description: The most notable attempt at an area approach is the Chicago Area Project, initiated in 1934 by Clifford Shaw and his associates and subsequently used in about ten slum neighborhoods in Chicago.[14] The first step is the formation of a neighborhood committee, using the natural leaders in the neighborhood. These may include merchants, barbers, truck-drivers, housewives. Some committee members may be ex-convicts or former delinquents. The area project helps initiate the program but allows the neighborhood to take over as much as possible, even to raising most of the money that is required. Trained outside leadership is kept to a minimum.

The neighborhood program is initially built around a neighborhood center with recreational facilities, but the recreational program is not considered an end in itself. As one neighborhood committee put it, a recreation program "serves to draw people together and thus to produce agreement with respect to standards of conduct among children." [15]

Neighborhood committees also sponsor summer camps, children's nurseries, mothers' clubs, sports tournaments, community forums, community newspapers, adult education programs, and employment centers. They also emphasize techniques for drawing delinquent and predelinquent youngsters into these programs, and in this connection much reliance is

---

[14] Ernest W. Burgess, Joseph D. Lohman, and Clifford R. Shaw, "The Chicago Area Project," in Marjorie Bell (ed.), *Coping with Crime* (New York: National Probation Association, 1937), 8–28.

[15] *Bright Shadows in Bronzetown* (Chicago: Southside Community Committee, 1949), p. 86.

By Gertrude Samuels, The *New York Times*

In the Neighborhood: A group leader of the Hudson Guild Neighborhood House talks to neighborhood youths on a Brooklyn Street.

placed on the development of personal relationships between interested neighborhood adults and the children who seem to need special attention. One neighborhood report asserts:

> The important thing is to give the predelinquent or delinquent boy an opportunity to form an attachment to, or come under the influence of, a person or persons from whom he will receive recognition for conforming to the conventional standards of conduct. In another sense this becomes the problem of substituting, for the delinquent boy's leaders, law abiding men and women who can come in time to mean as much to him as his delinquent leaders.
>
> The neighborhood organization is in an unusually favorable position to achieve this objective. It has the inestimable advantage of being able to draw upon the services of persons with whom the delinquent boy is likely in any case to develop a natural relationship—his neighbor, the corner grocer, the local social leader, the ward or precinct official. And it is in these relationships that attitudes are formed and life goals set.[16]

[16] *Ibid.*, p. 88.

The neighborhood projects are aimed, first of all, at the neighborhoods themselves. Through common and purposeful activity the adults of the neighborhood, and then adults and children, are drawn more closely together within the framework of socially acceptable values. The primary importance of the neighborhood recreation center, then, is not that it provides recreational facilities but that its creation provides a center for cohesive and socially desirable neighborhood activity.

Delinquency rates for the period 1930–42 showed a decline in three out of the four neighborhoods in which projects were then operating. However, there are many factors which make it difficult to evaluate the meaning of such statistics, particularly for the small areas concerned. Changes in delinquency definition and law-enforcement practices are possible factors in the decline. It has been suggested, for instance, that once the neighborhood project is well launched, the police trust it to handle some of its delinquents informally, thereby reducing delinquency statistics without necessarily reducing delinquency. There has been no attempt to evaluate the effect of the project on individual predelinquents or on habitual delinquents.

Evaluation: 1. The neighborhood project is often feasible with regard to its initial objectives: it can be conducted, administered, and financed successfully by the neighborhood residents themselves; it can serve to draw these residents together in common and purposeful welfare activity. However, it is likely that neighborhood projects will be least feasible in the highly disorganized areas that need them most.

2. Because of its relatively total approach, it provides the optimum environment in which other delinquency control techniques can be applied: gang direction, counseling of a "Big Brother" variety, recreational activity. It is also, by the same token, the only program which attempts a comprehensive counterattack on social disorganization. Theoretically, the neighborhood project would seem to have some potential for reducing the volume of delinquent acts.

3. However, without supporting evidence, it is impossible to assume that the neighborhood project can substantially reform those habitual delinquents who have serious personality problems and whose family lives reflect not just neglect and indifference but more serious emotional conflicts. In other words, the neighborhood project is less equipped to counteract the destructive family life than the simply neglectful family life.

Section II: Treatment of Delinquents

ARREST

Goal: The police are the referring source for about three out of every four cases that appear before the juvenile courts; many more children who never reach the courts come into contact with the police as alleged delinquents. The primary treatment goal at this stage is police handling that will not further corrode juvenile attitudes toward the law.

Program: A number of communities have established special juvenile bureaus in their police departments. Only members of the juvenile bureau are authorized to question a child after his arrest or to decide whether he should be detained. In some cases the juvenile bureau is authorized to adjust minor offenses without court action; the Juvenile Aid Bureau of the New York City Police Department settles about half its cases in this manner.

The success of these juvenile bureaus depends on the existence of trained and qualified personnel. At present many are inadequately and incompetently staffed. A number of universities have instituted special courses and workshops to which police departments may send trainees. The handling of juveniles has also become part of the standard training course for all policemen in many cities.

Special procedures for the arrest of juveniles have also been set up in certain communities. In Jersey City no child may normally be carried in a police wagon or taken to a police station. He is taken to his home by a police officer, and parents and child are then notified to appear before a special youth welfare board, which makes initial disposition. There is still some controversy around the question of whether juveniles should be fingerprinted. Many police officials maintain that fingerprinting is not only a deterrent but is also one means of protecting the innocent; others claim that fingerprinting has a stigmatizing effect.

DETENTION

Goal: As many as 300,000 children have been detained in one year pending investigation and court action. The primary concern of good detention practice is to provide the most favorable initial setting for the rehabilitation of the child, avoiding both undue stigmatization and association with adult or confirmed criminals.

Program: When should a juvenile be detained? The Standard Juvenile Court Act, adopted as a model by the National Probation and Parole Association, states that when a child is taken into custody the officer should notify the parent or guardian as soon as possible and that, whenever possible, the child should be released to the custody of the parent or other responsible adult upon the written promise of such a person to bring the child to court.

It is generally understood that detention may be necessary where children are so beyond control that their delinquency might be immediately repeated or where they seem to be in physical or moral danger at home.

In some communities policemen who are not trained to deal with juvenile cases make this decision out of hand. One recommendation has been made that no child be detained except by authority of the juvenile court or a specially designated and qualified representative of that court.

Where should a juvenile be detained? Between 50,000 and 100,000 juveniles are detained each year in regular local jails, often contrary to the intent of state laws prohibiting the placement of children in prisons with adults charged with or convicted of crime. In some cases these state laws are ambiguous, in other cases they are without enforcement procedures, and in still other cases they are simply violated. The results have been epitomized in these words by a report of the Federal Bureau of Prisons:

> Here in dismal, cheerless surroundings, in constant association with drunks, perverts and hardened offenders, and usually in complete idleness and under perfunctory supervision, they are given their first extensive education in the ways of crime. The experience is one that is seldom forgotten, and all too frequently it leaves emotional wounds and scars from which the victim never fully recovers.[17]

Several state laws require that local authorities provide special detention quarters for those juveniles who must be detained. These may take an institutional form, such as the Youth House in New York, which annually shelters several thousand juveniles and has a staff of ninety-two persons, including a psychiatrist, a physician, and six social workers. Communities sometimes lease or buy a residence, staff it with professionals, and use it as a detention home in order to reduce the institutional atmosphere. Or, in some cases, the community uses boarding homes, under the supervision of a married couple, placing only six or eight children in a home. Good detention practice requires that juveniles be quarantined not only from adult criminals but also from more habitual delinquents. Physical and psychiatric care and an activities program to avoid idleness are also recommended, although it is doubtful that detention should last longer than a week in any case.

THE JUVENILE COURT

Goal: The role of the juvenile court is to prescribe treatment after a diagnosis of the unique needs of each child. Disposition is made primarily on the basis of the child's problems rather than, as in the case of the criminal courts, on the basis of legal evidence and prescribed sentences.

Description: There are about 3,000 juvenile courts in the country. Some of them are administratively independent. Others are part of family or domestic relations courts which also deal with matters of family con-

---

[17] Federal Bureau of Prisons, *Handbook of Design and Construction of Correctional Institutions* (Washington, D.C.: U.S. Government Printing Office, 1949), p. 164.

Father and son in juvenile court.

flict, divorce, and separation. Others, especially in nonurban areas, are just special sessions of the regular court. Most cases are referred to the court by the police, but referrals are also made by parents, teachers, or social agencies.

The major characteristics which distinguish a juvenile court are usually these:

1. Prehearing investigations conducted by a probation officer. The probation officer is ideally a trained social worker who investigates and makes some assessment of the child and his environmental situation. Physical, intelligence, and personality tests are also often conducted.

2. Separate and private hearings and confidential court records.

3. Informal hearings not bound by the technical rules of procedure or evidence.

4. The normal absence of a district attorney or jury. The judge usually carries on the interrogation as well as makes disposition of the case. He

may designate a referee or authorize a probation officer to make disposition in the case of minor offenses.

Major Issues

1. *The court's jurisdiction.* A number of states except such offenses as murder and rape from the jurisdiction of the juvenile court. In at least forty states juvenile courts have concurrent jurisdiction with other courts at certain age levels or in certain offenses. A magistrate, a district attorney, or even the child himself can make the decision as to whether a case is to be heard before a criminal or a juvenile court.

This practice is often held to be inconsistent with the basic philosophy of the juvenile court. If a child cannot be held responsible for crime, he cannot be held responsible for murder any more than for vandalism. If his rehabilitation, rather than punishment by the criminal code, is to be the prime consideration, it is no less so when he commits rape than when he plays truant.

But this argument can, and has been, turned around. If an adolescent can be held responsible for murder, he can also be held responsible for theft. This converse argument holds that the age of responsibility has in general been set too high. A typical sentiment was expressed by an editorial in the *Chicago Tribune:*

> The criminal court should assert its constitutional jurisdiction over young offenders. The function of that court is to punish offenses against the law. The juvenile court does not inflict punishment. The present maximum age for juvenile delinquents is too high.[18]

However, it is not uncommon for a sophisticated adolescent, when he has the choice, to choose a criminal rather than a juvenile court to hear his case. The criminal court is bound to maximum sentences by the penal code. Not so the juvenile court, which can prescribe a longer period of probationary or institutionalized treatment for the same offense if it wishes. It has been argued not only that juvenile court decisions are often arbitrary but that they sometimes result in more severe punishment for juveniles than for adults. Loss of freedom, by whatever name, is a punitive experience.

2. *The court and civil liberties.* The juvenile offender does not customarily have the privilege of a jury trial. Some states provide that jury trial may be provided if demanded by child, parent, or court. But most state laws either exclude jury trials or make no provision for them. In addition, rules of evidence do not apply at a delinquency hearing. In practice a child's delinquency is often presumed, or at least the investigating

[18] *Chicago Tribune*, May, 1939.

officer's assessment is considered definitive. Finally, there is no criminal code to prescribe the outer limits of the disposition of juvenile cases. The judge is limited only by his own discretion.

It has sometimes been charged that juveniles are thus denied the "due process of law" guaranteed by the Constitution. State supreme courts have regularly held that juvenile court practices are not unconstitutional because the child, not having been charged with a crime, is not legally entitled to the constitutional rights granted accused criminals. Others contend that, despite the fine points of the law, much public opinion identifies official delinquency with criminality and that, furthermore, loss of freedom *is* punitive regardless of its legal designation. The Federal Juvenile Delinquency Act of 1938, which set up juvenile court procedures for cases involving violation of federal law, carefully stipulates that "due process" may be abdicated in federal cases only if the juvenile gives his written permission.

The right to appeal juvenile court decisions to a regular appellate court is generally recognized, although this appeal is often limited to technical matters of law or to matters affecting parental custody.

3. *The court as social agency.* Many juvenile courts have created their own child guidance clinics and foster-home placement services and have also established probationary practices which undertake treatment as well as prehearing investigations. On this count they have been accused by some of "coddling criminals." In addition, many social work agencies feel that these courts have embraced too many administrative functions. The question has been raised as to whether these services might not be more aptly and professionally administered by qualified social agencies. It is sometimes contended that courts should restrict themselves to their judicial role, leaving it to established social agencies to plan and conduct treatment. This is essentially a cautionary criticism, pointing to the limited qualifications of the average juvenile court to act as a social agency.

4. *Uniform court practices.* The various state laws are quite disparate in the matter of defining "delinquency." When, for example, is a juvenile "endangering himself morally"? Most laws allow for a wide area of interpretation by the individual court. There are, in fact, many differences in interpretation among the various courts. There is also much variation in disposition practices. Some courts dispose of as many as 90 per cent of their cases informally and unofficially, without an adjudgment of delinquency; other courts dispose of none of their cases in this fashion. Nor is there uniformity of decision—for example, on the question of whether the one-time juvenile offender should be officially tagged as delinquent. As long as adjudged delinquency carries with it a stigma in the mind of both the public and the child himself, some think that hasty court action may be a serious disservice to the child.

5. *Qualified court personnel.* Because of his wide discretionary powers, the individual qualifications of the juvenile court judge are of critical importance. His legal training is actually of minor relevance, but usually he has no special training in psychology, social welfare, or the social sciences. An interest in children, a willingness to draw on informed research, and a sympathy for juvenile court philosophy should be the least of his special qualifications. Yet the average juvenile court judge has been elected or appointed as a judge of the general court with no reference to possible service on the juvenile bench. Commonly, judges are rotated to the juvenile court regardless of their qualifications. Nor is it usually considered a top judicial post.

The Standard Juvenile Court Act suggests that judges of the juvenile court should be appointed by the governor from a list of three names submitted by a panel of seven persons, consisting of the presiding judge of the general court, two members of the local welfare department, two members of the local bar association, and two members of the local board of education. This plan has been substantially adopted in Missouri, although the governor's appointment must be confirmed by the voters after the judge has served for a year. It has further been recommended that juvenile court judges serve for at least six years.

There are only about 4,000 local probation officers in the country to assist juvenile court judges. Many of these probation officers must also serve adults and not only delinquent but dependent and neglected youngsters as well. There is an average of 1 probation officer for every 135 children coming to the attention of the courts; it is thus impossible for many probation officers to do the intensive work with each child that is required. Many juvenile courts, especially in nonurban areas, lack probation workers of any kind. In some jurisdictions probation work is the part-time function of the sheriff or court clerks. Because of low salaries, it is difficult to find trained probation officers. Involved here is not only a budgetary problem but a problem of raising the level of probation supervision in general. The National Probation Association recommends as a minimum qualification at least one year of special training in a graduate school, or equivalent experience.

Evaluation: 1. Juvenile courts have not as yet been able to operate under optimal circumstances. Many of them suffer from inadequate budgets and personnel. Many are not clear as to their purpose or the extent of their jurisdiction. Neither the public nor the judiciary itself always understands and accepts juvenile court philosophy.

2. Under these circumstances and because of wide variation in court practices, it has been impossible to measure accurately the success of the juvenile court as a delinquency control measure. Reports of progress in

averting recidivism have varied from court to court and have not been evaluated.

3. The efficacy of the juvenile court is in any case limited to the efficacy of the various treatment measures to which it can subject the delinquent. On the other hand, the juvenile court has both the authority and the procedure to enable other social agencies to reach a maximum number of those delinquents who can successfully respond to treatment.

4. The juvenile court has been lauded for bringing to the country a new *attitude* toward youth in trouble, which has been carried over to adults as well. Dr. William Healy writes: "The great achievement of the juvenile court so far has been, to my mind, the founding of a social institution which respects the dignity and potentialities of children and adolescents."[19] The idea of individualized attention and disposition, with rehabilitation as the goal, has been adopted in other settings. Adolescent and young-adult courts have been set up on this model, and an increasing number of general courts are initiating presentence investigations in adult cases. This is considered a tribute to the soundness of the juvenile court concept.

CORRECTIONAL INSTITUTIONS

Goal: The ideal purpose of the correctional institution is to provide rehabilitative services for the delinquent who must be withdrawn from the community.

Description: About 10 per cent of adjudged delinquents are committed to correctional institutions. Approximately 33,000 children were living in public institutions for delinquents at the end of 1956; this was 18 per cent more than in 1948. About 72,000 children had been in these institutions at one time or another during the year. Table 3:2 shows that the 14–15-year-old children constituted the largest age group. On the average, children released from these institutions had been there for 9.5 months; but the average for boys was 8.6, for girls, 12.2 months."[20]

These institutions have been soundly and regularly attacked on at least two grounds: brutality and failure to accomplish their rehabilitative purpose. In a survey of ten institutions in 1948, Albert Deutsch catalogued a grim list of brutal practices: disciplinary baths in ice water; disciplinary doses of laxative; head-shaving; deep knee-bending to the point of collapse.[21]

The Gluecks followed the careers of delinquents discharged from one correctional school and found that over 75 per cent of them subsequently

---

[19] William Healy, M.D., "Thoughts about Juvenile Courts," *Federal Probation,* **13** (September, 1949), 19.

[20] Children's Bureau, *Statistics on Public Institutions for Delinquent Children: 1956* (Washington, D.C.: U.S. Department of Health, Education, and Welfare, 1958), p. 1.

[21] Albert Deutsch, "Is This Reform?" *Woman's Home Companion,* March, 1948.

TABLE 3:2   AGE OF CHILDREN IN PUBLIC INSTITUTIONS FOR DELINQUENT CHILDREN, DECEMBER 31, 1956 *

Age	Number of Children
All ages	27,836
Under 10 years	61
10–11 years	464
12–13 years	2,698
14–15 years	9,413
16–17 years	8,666
18 years and over	1,589
Age not reported	4,945
Median age (years)	15.7

* Source: Children's Bureau, *Statistics on Public Institutions for Delinquent Children: 1956* (Washington, D.C.: U.S. Department of Health, Education, and Welfare, 1958), p. 26. These figures cover only reporting institutions; total number of children in public institutions at the end of 1956 was approximately 33,000.

engaged in delinquent or criminal behavior.[22] In 1956, correctional institutions reported that 15 per cent of admissions during that year had been at the same institution at some time or another and were returned because of parole violation or commitment of a new offense.[23]

Major Issues

1. *Security* vs. *rehabilitation*. Most students of delinquency are convinced that the only atmosphere in which rehabilitation is at all possible is one of friendliness, constructive discipline, and humanitarian concern. Authoritarianism, with its harsh discipline and punitive attitudes, can only serve to strengthen the roots of delinquency in most of those institutionalized. Somehow the suspicion and hostility felt by these youths against adults must be broken down if adult authority is ever to be accepted. For this reason, progressive administrators are anxious to maintain only minimal security measures and to remove the high walls from around their institutions. Inevitably there are occasional runaways. These escapes are publicity-catching and inevitably arouse criticism in the community. As a result, many walls stay up. Sometimes they are "invisible fences," but they are just as damaging to the atmosphere of the institution. Though obvious se-

[22] Sheldon Glueck and Eleanor Glueck, *Five Hundred Criminal Careers* (New York: A. A. Knopf, 1930).
[23] Children's Bureau, *op. cit.*, p. 1.

curity devices are at a minimum, the staff, in self-protection against the wrath of the community, often threaten and practice brutal discipline against both runaways and potential runaways.

2. *Personnel and facilities.* Brutal practices are also a symptom of the inadequacy of the staff members of many correctional institutions. The salaries are uncommonly low, and many of the jobs are obtained through political patronage. Few institutions have the professional staff to guide or conduct a genuine treatment program. More than half do not have the services of even a part-time psychiatrist. More than a third do not employ even a social worker.

Most of the schools are too large and too crowded. In 1956 half of them had capacities greater than the recommended maximum of 150 children. Furthermore, about a third of them were filled to overcapacity.[24] The recommended arrangement is to have rather small cottages, where homogeneous groups can be formed according to age and special need. Individualized treatment is scarcely possible in a mass setting. But even where physical facilities appear to be acceptable, individualized treatment is possible only when interested and qualified personnel is available to conduct it.

Evaluation: 1. The correctional institution has clearly failed as a delinquency control technique. Part of the failure can be ascribed to the fact that the correctional institution has been the most poorly managed of the various treatment measures.

2. Even where properly managed, however, the correctional institution is likely to remain ineffective, if for no other reason than that it is saddled with the hard core of delinquents with whom other treatment measures have failed.

3. The nature of institutionalization, even at its best, prevents it from being able to reform a significant proportion of delinquents. Even the most humane institution is a natural hazard against individualized attention and treatment. Nor is the institution, with its built-in need for a measure of regimentation, equipped to deal with or treat the seriously deviant personality.

4. While institutionalization has failed to demonstrate any substantial ability to rehabilitate delinquents, the possibility that its sheer "imprisonment" element has a deterrent effect cannot be dismissed. The discussion of the role of punishment in the next chapter suggests that, while imprisonment may not deter most habitual criminals from further crime, it may be the balancing factor in turning many other people from entering a career of habitual crime. However, here as elsewhere, the youth who is most seriously disposed to delinquency is not likely to be checked by the possibility of being sent to a correctional institution.

[24] *Ibid.*

PROBATION

Goal: The purpose of probation is to enable an adjudged delinquent to be rehabilitated within a normal home and community setting rather than in a correctional institution.

Description: Probation, like the suspended sentence, is dependent upon the continued good behavior of the juvenile. Its essential ingredient is the supervision of a probation officer who is, preferably, a trained social worker. About one-third of all delinquents are placed on probation by the court, being returned either to their own homes or to foster homes. Probation is primarily designed for the nonhabitual offender. Stigmatization is reduced to a minimum; so is contact with hardened delinquents. There is the possibility of individualized treatment through the probation officer. Furthermore, the general rehabilitative services of the community, whether psychiatric or recreational, are often more plentiful than those available in correctional institutions. There are auxiliary advantages as well. The cost to society is substantially reduced; and the offender on probation can, if he is old enough, work and even make restitution for damages he may have caused.

There is no clear statistical evaluation of the effects of probation. One study of 400 boys placed on probation in Boston recorded permanent success in 41 per cent of the cases, complete failure in 21 per cent of the cases, and "temporary success" in the other cases.[25] The Gluecks reported a success rate of less than 15 per cent.[26] However, Austin H. MacCormick summarized the actual experiences of a number of courts with this estimate:

> Based on actual performances over a term of years, a good juvenile court and probation service, operating in a community with adequate social resources and utilizing them fully, can put as high as 90 per cent of its juvenile delinquents on probation the first time around and 50 to 65 per cent the second or third time around, and get as high as 75 to 80 per cent successes.[27]

Much of the success of the probation system depends on the proficiency of the probation officer, whose effectiveness is almost universally hampered by an outsized case load. The National Probation Association has claimed that no probation officer can handle more than 75 cases and still do his job. In practice, probation case loads go as high as 250 to 300, and this is in addition to the many prehearing investigations which the worker conducts for the juvenile court.

Evaluation: It is generally acknowledged that the probation system is

---

[25] Belle Boone Beard, *Juvenile Probation* (New York: American Book Co., 1934), pp. 208–9.
[26] Sheldon Glueck and Eleanor Glueck, *One Thousand Juvenile Delinquents*, p. 173.
[27] Austin H. MacCormick, "The Community and the Correctional Process," *Focus*, **27** (May, 1948), 88.

preferable to institutionalization in the case of nonhabitual offenders whenever a proper home setting exists or can be found.

Section III: Summary

It cannot be assumed that every program which is beneficial to youth is therefore a significant delinquency control program.

Research evidence bears out this cautionary note. The mere provision of recreational facilities may reduce to some extent the incidence of delinquent behavior, but it probably does not have a great effect on the habitual delinquent. It is, indeed, the nondelinquent who tends to use these facilities, while the delinquent tends to avoid them. Psychiatric programs and guidance programs conducted by adult volunteers also tend to have their chief success with those who are least seriously delinquent and who are subject to the least damaging environment. Some effective work has been done by painstakingly reshaping the directions of juvenile gangs, although it is not clear to what extent the more serious delinquents are integrated in the new directions. Perhaps the most promising work has been done in "total-push" neighborhood projects, which are designed to restore some of the internal social controls and to reverse in some small measure the process of social disorganization. However, these projects are extremely difficult to initiate, and even the best of them cannot report sensational statistics of success.

The treatment and rehabilitation of those already adjudged delinquent is subject to somewhat the same factors of failure as the prevention programs. As a matter of fact, treatment of delinquency is most sensibly considered as a prevention program: the prevention of repeated delinquency. There is, however, the complicating consideration that the law-abiding members of society must be protected from the criminal acts of delinquents. The juvenile court system, where it has an effective probation system and access to community facilities, is perhaps the most significant development in the treatment of delinquency. There has been some progress in the treatment and detention of juveniles by police, and this can also be counted a significant advance. It is generally acknowledged that institutionalization has notably failed to provide any worth-while measure of delinquency control. This failure is partly the result of lack of proper facilities; but it can also be ascribed to the very nature of institutional life, which tends to run counter to the needs of delinquency control. Where facilities are available, probation has proved a more successful disposition for less habitual offenders.

To panacea-seekers this picture of delinquency control, and especially the relative failure of so-called "delinquency prevention" programs, may be frustrating. An overview of these measures, however, will reveal that a carefully designed and co-ordinated program of delinquency control can provide some limited measure of success. In the long run, frustration will be reduced if the limitations of any one element of that program are recognized and if it is understood that not even a total program will completely eradicate delinquency. Juvenile delinquency is in large measure a symptom of some of the basic characteristics of our changing society; it cannot be substantially modified by any one direct remedial program. Meanwhile, there remains the responsibility to reduce the delinquency rate to whatever extent possible. Finally, the mounting of even limited programs, if these are soundly conceived, may contribute toward the general insights that will be required by organized society before it can find a more satisfactory adjustment to its own changing nature and needs.

---

adaptation 3   **AN EXPERIMENT IN PREVENTION OF DELINQUENCY**

> *Abridged and adapted from Edwin Powers, "An Experiment in the Prevention of Delinquency,"* Annals of the American Academy of Political and Social Science, **261** *(January, 1949), 77–88. Published in this form by permission of the author and the* Annals. *For a detailed description and analysis of the Cambridge-Somerville Youth Study see Edwin Powers and Helen Witmer,* An Experiment in the Prevention of Delinquency *(New York: Columbia University Press, 1951).*

[The Cambridge-Somerville Youth Study, established by Dr. Richard C. Cabot, was perhaps the first research project in delinquency prevention to use a carefully constructed control group. To each of six men and four women trained in social work or allied professional fields were assigned a number of boys, usually 30 to 35, all under the age of 12, in the hope that by wise and friendly counsel, supplemented by social casework techniques, these young children might become useful, law-abiding citizens. About half the group were already showing definite signs that pointed to a delinquent career. The plan called for an evaluation by comparing 325 T (treatment) boys at the end of a contemplated ten-year program with a C (control) group similar in numbers and in all other relevant respects but receiving no help or guidance from the study. The hypothesis was that if the two groups were similar at the outset, then any significant behavioral differences between them at the end of the program could reasonably be attributed to the major variable in the picture—the counselors' treatment.

Work was started with 325 T boys between 1937 and 1939. After two or three experimental years, 65 boys were dropped from the program because they presented no special problems and were definitely nondelinquent. A number of the other T boys were lost to the program because of various factors. Close associations were maintained and casework was continued with 113 boys for an average period of four years and two months; with 72 boys for an average of five years and eleven months; and with 75 boys for an average of six years and nine months. When this report was written (1949), more than a decade had elapsed since the study's first acquaintance with these boys and their families. However, for none did the treatment period last more than eight years, although many of the counselors kept in touch with the boys assigned to them for a considerable period after the study closed.]

THE EXPERIMENTAL DESIGN

Teachers in the Cambridge and Somerville public schools and the Cambridge parochial schools submitted on request the names of many boys whom they regarded as "difficult" (in the study's scheme this meant "probably predelinquent") and many others whom they considered normal or "average" boys. Approximately 1,500 names of boys under 12 were submitted by the schools. Social agencies were also requested to submit names of "difficult" boys known to them. Court records were examined and police and probation officers were interviewed in order to include all boys in both cities who at an early age were considered troublesome or likely to become delinquent. From these supplementary sources 450 names were received.

A comprehensive picture of each boy, his family, and his social environment was obtained from a number of sources. Social workers were sent to the homes for interviews with one or both of the boys' parents. In three-fourths of the homes they were received in a very friendly spirit; in only 8 cases out of 839 homes visited did the parents definitely refuse to be interviewed in the first instance.

Extensive information was then obtained from each boy's teacher through long personal interviews conducted by a member of the staff. Staff psychologists gave each boy tests to measure his mental ability and school achievement. Physical examinations were also given. Official reports about delinquency or criminality of boys or parents were obtained from the State Board of Probation and from the courts and the police, all of whom were very cooperative. The neighborhoods in which the boys lived were studied and rated in terms of the probably good or bad influences on a boy living in each locality.

The plan called for 650 boys to be divided equally into an experimental and a control group. To determine which boys might reasonably be labeled delinquent and which nonpredelinquent, a committee of three individuals experienced in dealing with delinquents made a thorough study of the comprehensive data assembled in each case. This committee consisted of one psychiatrist and two prison caseworkers; they employed a diagnostic scale that ranged from plus five, indicating the greatest probability that a boy would *not* develop a delinquent career, through zero, the midpoint, to minus five, indicating the greatest probability that a boy *would* develop a delinquent career. They were able to classify the 782 boys who had survived the preliminary screening process.

Out of the 782 cases available, two psychologists created two matched groups consisting of 325 boys each. A method of matching boy with boy was devised by combining a statistical study of more than 100 relevant variables with a clinical interpretation of the personality as a whole; thus the 650 boys were divided into two similar groups. Two boys were considered a well-matched pair if the configurational pattern of the most important variables showed them to be psychologically similar. A coin was tossed to determine which boy of the given pair was to be placed in the treatment group and which in the control group. The most important variables in addition to age and prediction rating (which within each pair showed little, if any, variation) were health, intelligence, educational achievement, personality, family factors, and environment.

THE TREATMENT PROGRAM

The 325 T boys were then assigned to ten counselors. At no time were there more than ten counselors, but not all of the original ten remained throughout the entire program. For the last several years of the program, the services of a pediatrician, a psychiatrist, and a clinical psychologist were available. The younger boys were, as a rule, assigned to four women counselors. The treatment consisted of the application of whatever skills each counselor was capable of applying. The essence of the relationship between the boy and his counselor was personal intimacy and friendship. Each counselor was left largely to his own resources. The agency policies, instead of being predetermined, were gradually evolved during the course of treatment.

Although some counselors considered the job to be that of an orthodox social caseworker, others did not. One counselor, for example, believed that genuine personal friendship was of greater value to a boy than all the technical skills that a more objective social worker could bring to the case.

Attention was given to each boy individually. Many visits were made to his home and to his school. Group work was seldom used. Some boys were seen two or three times a week for long periods of time, but most of them were seen at less frequent intervals. An important feature of the program was the co-ordination with available resources and agencies in the community. Actually, treatment comprised a wide variety of activities.

A major emphasis was placed on the boy's adjustment to school. Counselors continually visited each school. Frequently it was important to interpret to the teachers the boys' difficulties. The staff also employed special tutors to give individual attention to 93 of the boys during or after school.

Another area of treatment constantly receiving the attention of the counselors was the boys' health. Many of them were taken to clinics or hospitals or treated by a staff pediatrician. For eight summers, camping was made available through local camp associations or other youth organizations. The counselors generally guided the boys to recreational opportunities. Boys were encouraged to develop their own religious ties. Much family casework was called for to gain the co-operation and understanding of the parents and to assist them in dealing with their own and their children's problems.

In brief, it can be said that the treatment program, utilizing some of the best professional advice obtainable, comprised an unusually wide diversity of special services to boys and their families, from removing nits from boys' heads to preparing them for higher education.

DID THE PROGRAM PREVENT DELINQUENCY?

The record at the end of the treatment program revealed the following results.

The Treatment Group

1. There were 70 T boys who were, at the time of evaluation, well past the age of 17, whose careers had been closely followed and who, as boys under 12, had appeared to the predictors to be more likely than not to develop delinquent careers; that is, they had been rated on the minus side of the prediction scale. After these boys had been through the treatment program, not more than one-third (23 boys) committed serious or repeated delinquent acts, while 31 of them proved not to be delinquent at all.

2. There were 163 T boys who, when under 12, were rated on the minus side of the prediction scale as probable predelinquents. How many of these boys in the ensuing years committed delinquent acts that led to their commitment to a correctional institution? Inspection of the registers of the two Massachusetts correctional institutions for juveniles—the reformatory for older offenders and the House of Correction for the county—showed that only 23 had been committed as of March 1, 1948. This rate of 14 per cent seems a surprisingly low figure in view of the fact that the study, it was believed, included practically all boys in the two cities, with a combined population of 213,000, who showed early signs of future delinquency.

3. Counselors' opinions were sought. Each counselor, during the middle period of the program, was asked on three or four different occasions to list all T boys who he or she thought had been "substantially benefited by their

contact with the study." Of the 255 boys then in the program, 166, or about two-thirds, were so listed.

4. The T boys themselves were consulted for evaluation. One hundred and twenty-five boys who in 1946 and 1947 were available for a personal interview were questioned by special (nonstaff) investigators who had had no prior information about the study. More than half of this large, unselected sample stated that the study had been of value to them. Jim's declaration, that "They helped me keep out of trouble," was typical of many of the replies.

By such evidence alone one might reasonably conclude that the study had been successful in preventing delinquency. Such an evaluation, however, is inconclusive.

The Control Group

The core of the plan was the control group. What had happened to the C boys, who had received no help at all from the study during the years in question?

1. The records of the Crime Prevention Bureau, established in 1938 by the Police Department in the city of Cambridge, revealed some interesting facts. Practically all boys who were reported by citizens or officials for minor offenses come to the attention of this Bureau. Without differentiating degrees of seriousness, the tabulation of offenses from 1938 to 1945 (while treatment was in progress) lists the names of 267 T boys but only 246 C boys. It appears at first sight that treatment was ineffectual.

2. Studying the records of the 68 C boys past the age of 17 who were characterized as predelinquents in their early years but who were not subjected to the study program, we find that an almost equal proportion had refrained from serious delinquency. The record showed that 27, or 40 per cent, of the older C boys had become more or less serious delinquents as compared to 23, or 33 per cent, of the comparable group of T boys. The difference of 7 per cent in favor of the T boys was obviously not great.

3. Taking the 165 C boys who had been predicted on the minus side (in the same manner as the 163 T boys above referred to), an inspection of the registers of the two correctional institutions revealed that 22, or 13 per cent, of the C boys had been committed for delinquent behavior—about 1 per cent less than the percentage of committed T boys.

4. A comparison was also made of the frequency of delinquent offenses that brought the T or the C boy to the attention of the court. The State Board of Probation disclosed the following facts: Of the 325 T boys, 76 were listed as having a court appearance for a relatively serious offense, as compared to 67 of the 325 C boys. If we include minor offenses along with the serious, the score stands: 90 T boys, 85 C boys.

First Conclusion

A T–C comparison of official records made within a few years after the termination of the treatment program shows that the special work of the counselors was no more effective than the usual forces in the community in preventing boys from committing delinquencies. The utilization of a control group thus casts a sharply revealing beam of light on the record. The effectiveness of the professional staff in preventing delinquency was clearly below anticipation.

Before we conclude, however, that the treatment program was completely ineffectual, let us look deeper. There is evidence to suggest that, given a further lapse of time, greater differences between the T and C groups in the seriousness of official offenses may appear in favor of the T boys. It begins to look as though the C boys are the more serious and the more persistent offenders. We find, for example, the following facts:

1. The Crime Prevention Bureau statistics showed that the C boys were more frequently brought in for repeated violations.

2. The records of correctional institutions showed that more C boys (8) had been sent to more than one institution than T boys (4).

3. Eight of the more serious offenders were committed to the Massachusetts Reformatory, an institution for older male criminals between the ages of 17 and 30. Seven of these were C boys.

4. Again, in comparing the number of boys who had committed more than four serious offenses, we find the names of five T boys and 9 C boys.

5. In a list of the 108 relatively serious offenses (arson, sex offenses, burglary, assault with a dangerous weapon, robbery, and manslaughter), 46 were committed by T boys, 62 by C boys.

Second Conclusion

Though the counselors were unable to stop the rapid advance of the young boys into delinquency with any greater success than the usual deterrent forces in the community, some of the boys were evidently deflected from delinquent careers, which without the counselors' help might have resulted in continued or more serious violations.

In other words, these facts based on group statistics do not necessarily imply that the counselors were not helpful in individual cases. Furthermore, delinquency was not the whole story. The making of good citizens—"social adjustment" in the language of the social workers—was the broader objective on which the study was based. An examination of the records and interviews with the boys themselves offer evidence that in many cases emotional conflicts were alleviated, practical problems were dealt with successfully, and boys were given greater confidence to face life's problems.

adaptation 4   WORKING WITH STREET GANGS

Abridged and adapted from James R. Dumpson, "An Approach to Anti-Social Street Gangs," Federal Probation, *13 (December, 1949), 22–29. Published in this form by permission of the author and* Federal Probation.

[Most efforts to reach the delinquent have been attempts to reach him as an individual and to break his ties with other delinquents. The following is a report of one effort, increasingly being adopted, to reach the individual delinquent through the gang of which he is a member. Attention is focused not on weaning the individual away from the gang but on working with the gang itself to redirect its activities into constructive channels.

This approach to delinquency is based on a realistic appraisal of the role of the street gang. (1) The street gang is here to stay, at least for the time being. (2) The street gang is an expression of the need of adolescents to emancipate themselves from adults. (3) Given the reality in which he lives, the street gang may be the only social group which gives the boy acceptance, attention, and security. The author implies that the street gang is a normal phenomenon of the urban slum. It cannot be destroyed, but its antisocial behavior can be significantly reduced.]

BACKGROUND

During 1945 and 1946 violence among "conflict gangs" reached an all-time high in New York City. From September 10 to September 19, 1946, three youngsters were killed in gang warfare in one neighborhood. At this juncture, the Prison Association of New York called on the Welfare Council of New York City to formulate a definite program of action for the amelioration of antisocial activity by gangs. The Welfare Council—as the central planning and co-ordinating social agency in the city—gathered together a committee of experts in the field of youth services to devise an experimental project. Lack of funds confined the final effort to one seriously affected area. This was in Harlem, the Negro residential district in Manhattan, and in the spring of 1947 the Central Harlem Street Clubs Project was set up.

The area chosen is one of the most depressed and underprivileged sections of the city, marked by overcrowding, poor housing, low economic status, and grossly inadequate health, educational, and recreational facilities. Its people, for the most part, react to the segregation and racial discrimination imposed upon them with hostile and tense feelings. These in turn underlie many of their attitudes toward the value system of the community at large. Violation of conduct norms by adults is an ever-present reality. Thus the setting for the average child is one not only of poverty, value conflict, bitterness, anxiety, and fear but of antisociality. However, there has been no evidence of sympathetic attitudes on the part of adults toward interclub warfare among teen-age groups, and as the boys have come to engage in constructive social activities, there has been an increasing measure of cooperation on the part of adults. Nevertheless, their mixed feelings about the conventional institutions and values of the larger community, and the ever-present realities of segregation and discrimination, continue to be obstacles to effective organization for local community action.

The recreation and leisure-time agencies in the area were not equipped to cope with the street-gang situation; not more than 10 per cent of the adolescents in the area were participating in adult-sponsored leisure-time activities. In any case these agencies had not been able to attract those autonomous street gangs which had already developed patterns of aggressive antisocial behavior. In addition, the cultural and socio-economic factors underlying the street-gang pattern are too deep and complex to be overcome by a recreation program. The prevention and treatment of delinquent behavior requires the utilization and co-ordination of every available and known resource in the community. It must be a total community approach.

Nor do punitive and repressive methods control the street gang. Such methods on the part of police and other community agents tend to heighten existing tensions and thus increase hostile activity. Authority has its proper place in treatment and control, but it must be part of a total plan geared to the individual and his needs. Brutality and ruthlessness on the part of the police merely strengthen the unity of the group and its felt need for protection and retaliation.

THE AREA-WORKER APPROACH

The approach devised by the committee was based upon the belief that the street gang is a normal expression of the needs of adolescents to emancipate themselves from adults and to establish themselves as independent individuals. By its very nature, the street gang has constructive potentialities. Through membership in the gang the adolescent gains the security that arises from acceptance by one's social group. Though as an individual he may be unapproachable, the adolescent may be reached through the medium of his gang. The primary object of the Street Clubs Project was, therefore, to redirect the antisocial behavior of the gang itself into socially constructive channels, that is, to transform the conflict gang into a club.

Five area workers were assigned to work directly with the various street gangs in the neighborhood. Their task was to make contact with the gangs, attain their confidence, and help the gangs both materially and psychologically to find satisfaction in socially acceptable club activities.

CHARACTERISTICS OF THE GANGS

During the two years of the project's existence, relations were established with four of the area's most aggressive and antisocial gangs. Each had a history of violent gang warfare, weapon-carrying, stealing, rape, and use of narcotics. Truancy, drinking, and tangles with the police were prevalent among the boys, who ranged in age from 11 to 23. Many of the boys had been in one or more correctional institutions.

Except during mobilization for gang warfare, the structure of gangs is generally loose. The largest gang had approximately one-hundred members, the smallest about thirty-five. However, the boys travel in groups of two or three, and it is unusual to see more than ten or fifteen members together at any one time or place. The gangs are basically autocratic and can be divided into two distinct groups; on the one hand there is the leader and a leadership clique of five or six boys, on the other, the ordinary members. The gangs also have different age divisions, each with its own organizational structure; in this way the gang assures its own perpetuation as a distinct unit. Titles of officers reflect the conflict-based organization of the gangs; besides the president and vice-president, there is usually a war counselor, an assistant war counselor, and occasionally a "light-up" man, whose function is to carry the pistols and initiate the war by "shooting up" the rival gangs.

Journalistic accounts of street gangs convey a distorted picture of the frequency of their participation in antisocial behavior. Sports, movies, parties, dances, "be-bop" sessions, and "bull sessions" take up the greater part of their time. Just "hanging around" and visiting their girl friends are important gang activities.

CONTACT WITH THE GANGS

The approach to the gangs was informal. After "hanging around" the stores and street corners where a particular gang congregated, drinking coffee and playing the juke box, the workers gradually became known as "one of the boys." A worker would in time be included in conversations, challenged to pitch pennies, or asked to play football. The area worker's purpose was frankly stated, though each worker had first to overcome the suspicion that he was a policeman or other representative of the law.

A worker saw the gang with which he had established contact almost every day, usually afternoons and evenings, spending from about fifteen to twenty-five hours a week with them. Usually a worker saw from four to twelve boys at a time; sometimes only one; sometimes as many as fifty. The contacts took place wherever the boys met, in the street, in a candy store or poolroom, at the boys' homes, and finally, as confidence was gained, with growing frequency at the project office.

THE ROLE OF THE AREA WORKER

The area worker's role varies with the needs of the group. A worker may arbitrate a dispute if asked to by the boys, give help in securing a job, or offer advice on personal problems, but it is important that the worker not reject the boys when they do not accept his opinion. In a discussion of antisocial behavior, the worker's role also varies. Frequently the worker simply listens without expressing approval or disapproval. Sometimes he asks questions to learn more about the boys' attitudes or behavior. At other times he will openly disapprove of their behavior and give his reasons. If the situation warrants, the worker may initiate a group discussion.

Sometimes the worker's attention and efforts are directed to some particular boy. Where antisocial behavior is involved, the worker must use great skill. He must make clear that his attitudes differ from the boy's and, at the same time, maintain a friendly and accepting relation with him. He must also recognize that his ability to aid the individual boy is limited and should help him make use of community services when the boy is ready to use them.

The area worker must also constantly intercede with schools, police, and other community agencies on the boys' behalf in order that constructive ways of meeting the needs, frustrations, and hostility of the boys may be devised. Very gradually he must help the boys make fullest use of the facilities in the community, but he must also help the agencies understand and accept the gang member. Many leisure-time agencies find it difficult to accept the hit-and-miss participation of the street-gang boy.

One of the most important club activities stimulated by the area workers was the running of block parties and dances. In the beginning the area worker assumed a large part of the responsibility for organizing the parties; later he transferred responsibilities to the boys. One area worker, in describing a second block party, writes as follows:

A significant change that is apparent is the contrast between the amount of responsibility that the boys took upon themselves at the first block party and this block party. At the first block party I had to get my hand into a great many things and the boys waited for me to do things before they would start. This time they took on responsibilities without waiting for me. I just had to carry out my duties as a member of the group rather than as the supervisor.

At this block party, Fred took the responsibility for running the record machine; Leon asked the fellows not to shoot fire crackers; he had signed the permit for the party and therefore felt a keen responsibility for conducting it without unhappy incident with the law. Harry took chief responsibility for drawing up a list of the refreshments to be purchased, making the purchases and supervising all of the boys who helped to prepare and sell the refreshments. Spike's feeling of responsibility was exhibited in his helping out where needed and checking up on all phases of the activity. Jim, an older boy, got a number of his friends to assist the boys in selling raffle tickets and took the responsibility for borrowing a large lamp from the owner of the barber shop and setting it up to provide light for the party.

EVALUATION

By its very nature the area-worker approach to the street gang is difficult to evaluate. Nevertheless, some tentative judgments may be made:

1. The boys are spending increasingly more time in constructive and satisfying club activities. Behind these activities are hours of joint planning and sharing. The boys have gained some status both in their own group and in the community.

2. Certain forms of antisocial behavior have decreased. Since the beginning of the project none of the clubs has engaged in interclub warfare, although there have been incidents in other sections of the city. Concomitantly, there has been a marked decrease in intergang warfare among the gangs occupying territory immediately adjacent to that of our clubs. There has been a less measurable decrease in the use of narcotics, sex activities, individual stealing, truancy, and drinking. It may be that these forms of antisocial behavior are symptomatic of deep personality disorders not amenable to the approach of the project. However, there is evidence that the boys have a greater awareness of a new value system and, in individual instances, are consciously striving to identify with the value system of the area worker.

3. The ability of these boys to establish a relationship with a mature, warm, accepting adult has been unquestionably established. This accomplishment augurs well for their future relations with helpful adults.

4. Relations within the groups have improved. The leaders are less autocratic, and the opinions of the club members are more consistently sought.

5. The boys have been helped to use community facilities and to test their acceptance by group-work and leisure-time agencies.

6. Here and there existing recreational agencies have been helped to accept these autonomous groups and to gear their programs to the boys' interests and needs. Considerable reorientation needs to be done in this area before the boys are ready to use the agencies and before the agencies are ready to accept the boys.

7. Finally, several agencies in the city have begun to adopt this project's approach in an effort to reach groups of boys similar to those in the project. In one instance, a group of extension workers from a group-work agency is working with street gangs in the immediate area of the agency. In another instance, two recreational workers in the public schools have been released from the after-school program to work with two street gangs that recently caused the death of one boy and seriously injured another. A project in still

another area of the city, under one of our regional councils, using the approach of the Central Harlem Project, has been completed successfully and the report is now being written. The program of the New York City Youth Board to prevent and control juvenile delinquency will include a group of workers who will use the approach of this project in working with street gangs in various parts of the city.

THE PSYCHIATRIC TREATMENT OF CHILDREN

adaptation 5

Abridged and adapted from H. Whitman Newell, "Principles and Practices Used in Child Psychiatric Clinics," Mental Hygiene, *35 (October, 1951), 571–80. Published in this form by permission of the National Association for Mental Health.*

[Child guidance clinics, or psychiatric clinics for children, deal, by and large, not with officially adjudged delinquents but with a larger class of children who exhibit behavior problems of one sort or another. The following account delineates the general character of psychiatric work with children. It also outlines the history of one small patient, aged four years, ten months, who exhibited some of the behavior often associated with delinquency, such as destructiveness, lying, and stealing.]

TEAMWORK IN THE PSYCHIATRIC CLINIC

The Psychiatric Clinic of the University of Maryland operates on the basis of the teamwork of three professions: psychiatry, psychology, and psychiatric social work. The psychiatric social worker, in a series of interviews with one or both parents, studies the child's history and environment, stressing particularly the emotional environment as evidenced by the attitudes of parents and other important people. This study enables the social worker to make a diagnosis of what disturbs the parent-child relationship and an estimate as to how well the parent can respond to, or make use of, clinic treatment. The clinical psychologist gives the child a group of tests which throw light on the child's assets and reveal any unevenness in intellectual development and any psychological blocks to learning. The psychiatrist interviews the child and studies his attitudes and reactions to the problem as well as his contribution to the disturbed parent-child relationship. Thus the psychiatrist is able to make a diagnosis of the basic psychodynamics involved as well as an estimate of the child's probable response to therapy. Physical factors are studied either by the family physician or pediatrician or by a pediatric clinic. Usually these various studies are pooled at a conference at which a dynamic picture of the genesis and development of the problem can be synthesized and an appropriate plan of treatment evolved.

Teamwork is important not only for diagnosis but for treatment; results are best when someone interviews a parent every time the therapist sees the child. The purpose of these interviews with the parent is to get him to observe himself and to discover a connection between how he feels and acts and how the child behaves. Almost routinely, children improve as soon as the parent gains some insight into himself.

TREATMENT OF THE CHILD

Special methods are used in examining and treating children. Ordinarily an adult wants and asks for help and is able to verbalize his problems. In the case of children verbalization is difficult, and it is an adult who wants the child treated—a parent, teacher, social worker, judge. Children are usually so confused by the fuss stirred up, and so frightened by the idea that there may be something wrong with them, that they initially feel opposed to being examined and treated. Such negative attitudes are often fostered at home. One boy eventually recounted that his father had told him that the psychiatrist was going to cut his head open to find out why he stole. Such negative attitudes have to be overcome by special techniques, e.g., by play therapy. In the psychiatrist's office the child finds a variety of play materials—crayons, paints, clay, dolls, soldiers, trucks, toy pistols, rubber daggers—and is invited to choose something to play with and make up a story about. Through play children freely express their feelings without being aware that they are doing so. One boy had a mother doll punish a boy doll and then made the boy doll attack and beat the mother doll furiously. In this play he was hiding behind the anonymity of the doll, thinking that he was not revealing his own feelings.

The ultimate aim of psychotherapy is that both therapist and patient have a true understanding of the meaning and motivation of the patient's symptoms and behavior. Direct treatment with the child can be divided into three phases. At first an attempt is made to gain rapport by the means I have already described. In this early, getting-acquainted phase, the therapist tries to encourage the child to express himself spontaneously, either verbally or in play. The therapist intrudes his own ideas very little. He is learning how the child thinks and feels. When the child expresses some feeling, this is commented on just to let him know that we are paying attention and trying to understand. As much as possible we try to avoid "why" questions. When a child does something, he becomes upset and disturbed if we ask him why he did it. In the first place, he doesn't know; in the second place, he feels the question as a test and wonders what we expect or what we think is the right answer.

This first phase merges imperceptibly into a middle phase, where most of the treatment is accomplished. In this phase we are able to discern certain patterns of behavior that we can talk about more freely if rapport is good. During this period the child is busy testing us out. Most disturbed children have suffered from inconsistent handling. They crave to find someone who is consistent and whom they can count on. In our office we set definite limits to what the child can and cannot do. This makes him feel safe and less anxious, but at the same time he keeps trying to see if we are really consistent. We discover in this phase other repeated tendencies. Thus he often tries to stimulate us to act just like one of his parents. At this stage in his treatment the child expresses his pent-up emotions. We help him do this without feeling too guilty or anxious. We reassure him about the naturalness of his feelings, and we sometimes dilute the dosage by not encouraging too much release at one time. We also discuss the meaning to him of his feelings.

This middle period merges imperceptibly into the terminal phase, which is characterized by freer verbalization. This phase is more educational. The child, by this time, has expressed his confusions and is practically asking for enlightenment and insight. Many of these children suffer from ungrounded fears, unreal notions, and distorted ideas which can now be profitably discussed. It might seem logical and simpler to bypass most of the therapy as I have described it and, at the outset, tell the child the facts about himself and his life. Unfortunately, we have learned that such early discussions have no effect on the child's problems. Both the doctor and the child must discover the problem and its meaning before such a discussion is fruitful.

Our diagnosis usually reveals some variation of this theme: the emotional growth of the child has been blocked by a variety of circumstances, often involving a parent-child tangle that has developed into a vicious circle. In treatment we attempt to clarify and untangle the situation so that the spontaneous tendencies toward growth, inherent in every child, may proceed relatively freely. In other words, we attempt to free the child from the internal, as well as the external, conflicts that have interfered with his emotional development.

THE CASE OF ONE FOUR-YEAR-OLD

At the time he was referred, the patient was four years, ten months old and had just been dismissed from an excellent nursery school because of his destructive behavior. He was noisy, demanding, dominating, and intensely hyperactive. He was cruel to a cat, which he loved. At home he lied constantly and took money. He cut up sheets and towels with razor blades and, when left in his room, threw things out of the window. This child fought off sleep, and there were always scenes at bedtime that lasted several hours. His parents were unable to control him, and he was destructive in the neighborhood. He shot a BB gun through windowpanes and destroyed flowers in a neighbor's garden.

The boy had been seen in another psychiatric clinic at the age of three years, and the mother had been told that he was subnormal and would probably become a criminal. She had been unable to accept the diagnosis of subnormality and had developed some hostility to psychiatry. She came to our clinic at the suggestion of another mother, whose child had been treated successfully.

The father, aged forty-three, was well educated and came from a home of good middle-class standards. He was described by the mother as a quiet, stable sort of man. The mother, throughout the contact, denied any serious marital maladjustment. She was thirty-three, a high-school graduate, had a rather explosive temperament, and was quite desperate about the patient's increasing behavior difficulties, with which she could not cope. One other child, a girl seven years older than the patient, was a withdrawn, submissive child, who created no problem at home or at school. The mother frequently expressed extreme hostility toward the patient, with marked guilt, admitting that she often wished she had never seen this child. The patient was constantly punished by both parents. Once, early in the treatment period, the mother tied him hand and foot to his bed with a rope. She wanted, and investigated the possibility of, military-school placement for him at the age of five years.

The patient was tested in the clinic, and at the age of four years, ten months, he was exactly one year accelerated intellectually, with an IQ of 121. He showed very superior ability also with tests of the puzzle type. In the test situation he co-operated perfectly and displayed none of the problems described. All subsequent contacts confirmed his superior intellectual ability. His vocabulary and range of interests were well beyond his actual age. He was not above average in manual co-ordination. His hands were small, and he was awkward and careless with them, frequently breaking and spilling things.

The mother was seen by the psychiatric social worker each time the patient was seen for treatment interviews. The mother resisted her part in the treatment process. Although she knew that the patient was bright, she clung to the idea that he was abnormal and for a long time could not see any possible relationship between her attitudes and the patient's problems. Her treatment was interrupted by a change of social workers, and there was a period during which no one saw her. She was, however, quite regular about bringing the patient, although at first she was greatly discouraged, since no improvement occurred. In each interview she would recount the patient's outrageous behavior of the current week, showing great hostility to the child and resisting any effort to come to grips with any part she might have in his problems, although she quoted the patient as saying to her frequently that she did not love him.

Both parents wanted the child placed away from home for treatment and observation, and the mother kept coming back to the question of boarding school. She also referred constantly to her own nervous condition, which she felt was greatly aggravated by the patient's behavior. Attempts were made to get her relaxed and working on the problem of her relationship with the child. During the period when she was seeing no one herself, she was impatient and bored and would buttonhole the child's therapist and express her hostility and discouragement in a kind of temper outburst, often in the child's presence. With the second social worker, she was brought back again and again to the problem of her own attitudes and what they were doing to the patient, and, concurrently, visible improvement occurred in the child. Toward the end of the treatment the mother's attitude was much more relaxed. She had really seen the connection between her own attitudes and the patient's behavior. She began to show some pride in the child and to appreciate some of his boyish qualities.

The patient knew from the start that his woman therapist liked him and felt that he was all right. This made him anxious to hold this regard, and his behavior at first was quite controlled. He always remained anxious to have the therapist think well of him and always became disturbed if the therapist so much as spoke of his mother.

As he was quite young, it was not too practicable to talk to him directly about his problems, and most of the hours were spent in spontaneous play. Early in the contact there were two or three interviews in which he treated dolls representing a family with great hostility. He put them all in bed and said that they had broken their legs. He "scalded" the doll representing the mother in the toy bathtub and threw her in a puddle on the floor. He shot the dolls representing father and mother. He announced that his sister liked to play with matches and had "burned herself to a cinder"; on another occasion he fabricated the idea that his sister had pneumonia. He had reason to be jealous of his sister, who was obviously acceptable to both parents. He was not questioned at all about how his parents treated him, and all this hostility was directed toward the dolls anonymously. They were never identified as his own parents.

As the patient became more secure, he went into a second phase. He became very aggressive and destructive in the office. He spilled water, broke toys, scattered toys all over the place, was noisy and hyperactive. This was permitted within certain limits, for it seemed necessary for a child as disturbed as this to learn that someone could still like him even if he was bad.

Usually he became anxious when he was really destructive and made some bids for reassurance. He would quiet down, come close, and would ask to be read to. As the contact continued, he made more and more bids for direct expression of affection. He sat in the same chair, stood close beside the therapist, and was quiet for twenty or thirty minutes at a time.

About the third month he did several things to suggest that he feared that little girls were better and more loved than boys. Each time this question was brought up in some indirect way, he was given reassurance that the therapist liked boys. Treatment was interrupted for a month by the summer-vacation schedule. He had shown some improvement in the third and fourth months of treatment, but he regressed during the summer.

In the fall he was glad to resume contact, and interviews were much as before. About this time he began to talk about fears and phantasies, and it became clear that he was afraid to go to sleep at night. He talked of a ghost with an electric knife and said, "Cross your heart and promise, or you'll die before morning"—a phrase that must have been said to him. There ensued several interviews full of phantasies about comic-strip characters. At one point he interrupted and said to the therapist, "You love me, don't you!" When asked what he thought, he said confidently, "I know you love me." He brought out a phantasy about marrying the therapist. He brought flowers. He also played being a baby, drinking water from a small nursing bottle.

Treatment now focused on setting up some limits as to what the patient could do in the office. He was told at one point that it is possible to like someone and yet not like everything that that person does. The sessions became more quiet, and the patient showed more and more affection. He began to get over his anxiety about being a boy and showed a lot of playful domination of his therapist. His relationship with his mother improved, and toward the end he told the therapist that he liked his mother best. On that same date the patient suddenly said very seriously, "I think I always liked everybody except myself," and, on being questioned, admitted he was beginning to like himself.

At the next interview he was still preoccupied with that question: "I'm not so sure I like myself. Is it right to like yourself?" He was again reassured and at that point seemed to accept himself. His relationships and behavior outside improved rapidly. The kindergarten reported a great change in him. He gained weight, took on color, and began to sleep normally. The treatment was terminated with plans to send him to a small summer camp, and he was ready and eager to go. The mother and child were told that they might return if things went badly, but they have not been heard from.

This case illustrates several features commonly encountered in the psychiatric treatment of children. First, we observe the vicious circle mentioned above. The mother's rejecting, hostile attitude not only contributed to the child's disturbance, but her attitude, in turn, was aggravated by the child's destructive and defiant behavior. In this case, as in many other child guidance cases, treatment is successful only when changes in attitudes can be effected simultaneously in mother and child. At the same time that the mother becomes more tolerant, the child feels accepted by the therapist, even though he expresses hostile feelings. This acceptance is finally turned back on to the parent. With this break in the vicious circle and the removal of the major obstacles, the child's emotional growth can proceed more normally.

Disrespect For Law Growing

FBI Chief Sees U.S. Becoming Morally Weaker

LOS ANGELES (NC)—The moral fibre of the nation is growing weaker, not stronger, at this most crucial period in world history, J. Edgar [...]

"Crime costs $1.11 each year for every $1 spent on education," he said. "For every dollar we contribute to churches, crime costs us $12."

POLICE DATA

Mr. Hoover, discussing increasing national disregard [...]

2 Dope Suspects Will Face Jury

Two men accused of narcotics peddling were held for the grand jury yesterday after a hearing before City Judge Casimir T. Partyka.

They are Salvatore Falzone, 31, of 208 W. Tupper St., and Joseph Abbinante, 36, of 69 Cottage St. They were charged with possessing narcotics and intent to sell narcotics.

They were arrested May 22 when local, state and federal authorities raided Falzone's apartment in W. Tupper St.

Hot and filthy—
Naked prisoners kept in sweat box 26 straight days

TAMPA, Fla., Sept. 6—(UP)—The Tampa Tribune reported Saturday night it has learned that two prisoners, one a teen-ager, were confined for 26 continuous days and nights in hot, filthy "sweat boxes" at the state road prison camp near Moore Haven.

Woman, 42, Found Shot And Burned

Sarah J. Mead, 42, of 3939 Newdale rd., Chevy Chase, was in critical condition in Suburban Hospital yesterday with third degree burns and a bullet wound in the head.

Montgomery County Police said Mrs. Mead was found by a janitor in her apartment house Friday night. She was lying on a burned mattress which, police said, probably caught fire from a cigarette when she fell on the bed after returning from the bullet wound. Police said she had been shot with a .38-caliber revolver.

Mrs. Mead's husband, Paul, 47, a construction worker, the couple's son and his family had not contacted them since last February, and Mrs. Mead had been depressed. Mead told police he and his son went on a trip to Florida last January with their son, Kenneth, his wife and their [...]

GRAND JURORS BEGIN GAMING PROBE MONDAY

Indianapolis, Aug. 9 — More than 160 bookmakers and bettors from throughout the nation will start testifying as a grand jury Monday when they begin about a defunct multi-million dollar gambling syndicate indicated at Terre Haute, Ind.

The list of witnesses includes wealthy and prominent men believed to have placed bets with the syndicate.

United States District Attorney Don A. Tabbert said about 170 subpenas were [...]

State Closes Penacook Bank; Criminal Action Studied As Valley Trust Books Audited

---

order, we are forced to concede an ever growing national disregard for it," he declared.

Gaming Dens Wide Open in the Suburbs

BY GEORGE BLISS

Gambling continues to flourish in the suburbs, a survey disclosed Wednesday. A tour of notorious handbooks and gambling casinos indicated that Sheriff Joseph D. Lohman's recently avowed war on gambling has had little effect.

Visits were made to the gaming and betting rooms exposed in a recent TRIBUNE series by a reporter who entered the places and participated in the gambling. Altho locations had [...]

FINDS PINBALL GAMING BOOM OUTSIDE CITY

Harmless looking pinball machines, which syndicate gangsters have converted into lucrative gambling devices to lure money from teen-agers and others, are doing a boom [...]

Bank Commission Acts To Prevent 'Run' On Nine-Year-Old Bank

Phillips Moves In By Order of Dwinell

Investigation of Big Loans Started by Atty.-Gen. Wyman; Rand Resigns

Seeks Review of Conviction
Sex-Slayer in Last Chance Appeal to Escape Chair

NEWARK (UPI) — Convicted sex-slayer Edgar H. Smith has one "last chance" for life today as his attorney planned a final appeal less than 40 hours from the ex-Marine's scheduled execution in the electric chair for the murder of a teen-aged girl.

Smith's attorney, John E. Selser [...]

CHICAGO STILL CAFE RACKET PROBE TARGET

Gus Alex Is Called to Senate Quiz

The Senate rackets committee disclosed Saturday that it will reopen its probe of the racket scarred Chicago restaurant business with Gus Alex, Chicago crime syndicate hoodlum and gambling boss, the leadoff witness. The probe may be resumed on Wednesday.

Federal investigators finally caught up with Alex, 46, last Wednesday night as he drove his expensive sports car into the basement garage of the apartment building at 4300 Marine dr. Alex had successfully eluded a committee subpena for three months.

THUG GRABS $4,203 STORE BANK DEPOSIT

Robs Porter Near Baltimore And Charles, Then Escapes

A goateed thug robbed a woman's apparel store porter of a $4,203 bank deposit yesterday afternoon near Baltimore and Charles streets and escaped in the crowded downtown area.

The robbery victim was Charles W. Curry, 57-year-old Negro employee of the Gaxton Company in the 200 block North Charles street. The robbery occurred about 1:30 P.M.

Central district police said they were told by Jerome S. Alperstein, president of the store, that the porter was grabbed from behind by a Negro bandit who [...]

Armed Slayer Eludes Posse, Bloodhounds In Big Swamp

● **Norfolk Negro Goes in Hiding After Gunning Sister-in-Law**

By Robert C. Ramage

NORFOLK—A murder suspect armed with a 12-gauge shotgun defied 80 lawmen who tried all day to flush him from an eastside Norfolk swamp after he killed his sister-in-law Sunday morning.

Aided by an airplane and tracker dogs, the 80 men from Norfolk, Princess Anne County and State Police units, and Game and Fisheries Department, were searching for Otis Newby, a 39-year-old Church street Negro.

Twelve hours after the killing Newby was still eluding the posse in a swamp on the edge of Broad Creek in residential River Oaks.

Hundreds Watch

Hundreds of spectators, held at a safe distance behind police lines, watched the operations. Terrified residents of the area huddled in their homes. Some demanded police protection.

Jaywalking Drive Pushed

Prosecutor Lawrence A. Whipple yesterday asked each public safety director in the county to pledge full co-operation to the anti-jaywalking campaign his office wants to launch to reduce pedestrian fatalities in Hudson County.

In a letter, Whipple said the success of the campaign, which would be patterned after New York's current drive, depends upon "the full co-operation of all public safety officials in the county."

"The urgency of the situation," he wrote, "requires prompt commencement of such a campaign. Therefore, I should appreciate an [...]

Loan Sharks Probers Plan New Arrests

Sensational twists are expected tomorrow in the investigation of loan sharks which [...]

Atty. James L. O'Dea Jr. revealed last night.

"Surprising developments tomorrow in the investigation the public will find very interesting may turn up," O'Dea hinted.

He said those still under suspicion of playing key roles in the alleged loan rackets include a Greater Boston underworld leader and at least one "innocent victim of the [...]

schemes which State [...] say bilked unsuspecting borrowers of more than a million dollars through exorbitant interest rates.

Arraign 12 Tomorrow

The 10 men indicted for violation of the Small Loans Act and two other men who conspiracy charges were arraigned tomorrow in Middlesex Superior Court. Police say the two raced into a $250,000 racket to pay off through the pair, obtained information to the indictments. O'Dea stressed that all under suspicion beside any person holding public office.

"The investigation shows many ramifications," he said. "We are far from through. You can expect more arrests."

A 'PUFF' IS NO LIE, COURT DECLARES

Terms Extravagant Claims for Stock Plan Harmless

By JOHN S. TOMPKINS

Is the ghost of *caveat emptor* rising again in Wall Street twenty-five years after the New Deal buried it?

CHAPTER 4

Crime

Section I: What Is the Problem?

It was at a national conference on crime that a police chief sounded this bitter note: "We have heard criminals called mad dogs. We have heard them called human vultures . . . ; the time is at hand when we must frankly admit that the menace of these mad dogs and human vultures, preying upon the honest, hard-working, sincere people of the United States is a major problem—an infamous, vicious, cancerous growth, the roots of which must be torn out and completely destroyed." Who are these "mad dogs and human vultures"? Who, exactly, *are* America's criminals?

These are criminals: The men and women who, according to the FBI, during 1957 committed 2,796,400 major crimes: murder, manslaughter, rape, robbery, serious assault, burglary, larceny, and theft. Someone is criminally assaulted or killed every five minutes. A larceny is committed every thirty seconds. In 1957, 479 million dollars' worth of property was stolen in 400 cities.[1]

These are also criminals: The organized criminal gangs which are firmly entrenched in our large cities in the operation of many different gambling

[1] Federal Bureau of Investigation, *Uniform Crime Reports,* Annual Bulletin, 1957, **28**, No. 2 (Washington, D.C.: U.S. Government Printing Office, 1958).

enterprises as well as in other rackets, such as the distribution of narcotics and commercialized prostitution. The thriving nature of these organized gangs on the current scene was fully disclosed by the investigation of the 1951 Senate Committee To Investigate Organized Crime (Kefauver Committee), which pointed out that in some cities law-enforcement officials aided and protected these gangsters and racketeers. It has been estimated that anywhere from $6 billion to $15 billion is spent annually in illegal gambling—the rich harvest on which the corruption-bearing crime syndicates chiefly thrive.

And these are also criminals: Those of the higher economic brackets who commit criminal acts in the course of their business. Some twenty years ago, Edwin H. Sutherland examined 70 large corporations and found 980 court decisions against them on such charges as restraint of trade, misrepresentation, patent infringement, and fraud.[2] Among upper-class criminals, million-dollar embezzlers are "small fry," according to Sutherland, who cited large-scale crimes committed by corporations, investment trusts, and public utility holding companies. Since Sutherland made his study, government supervision of stock transactions has been tightened, the "robber baron" has been virtually eliminated, and big business has developed a greater sense of public responsibility. Nevertheless, the kind of crime investigated by Sutherland and called by him "white-collar" crime continues to occur.

These, then, are all criminals: (*a*) the "predatory" criminal, the something-for-nothing offender of traditional low station who attempts to better his standard of living by directly pre-empting other people's property; (*b*) the "service" criminal, who is in the highly organized business of servicing the gambling and vice impulses of the general public; and (*c*) the "white-collar" criminal, who commits his financial crimes in the course of his legitimate business. To these categories must be added those who commit crimes which have no relation to material gain, e.g., sex offenders. These people can all be branded with the single label, "criminal," because they have all committed an unlawful act which the state has declared to be punishable.

However, the bulk of our statutes are civil rather than criminal in nature. These civil laws establish most of our official rules of conduct with respect to such matters as property rights, business relationships, and compensation for personal damages. Civil laws are enforceable by the court, but violators are not punishable. They are not subject to death, imprisonment, or fine. What distinguishes those laws which *do* carry a penalty and which, therefore, make of the violator a criminal?

[2] Edwin H. Sutherland, "Crime and Business," *Annals of the American Academy of Political and Social Science,* **217** (September, 1941), 112–18.

It has been very broadly said that civil law is designed to establish and protect the rights of any given individual in society, while the direct concern of criminal law is to protect society as a whole and the rules by which it operates. For example: in case of assault, an injured person may sue his assailant for personal damages; but the state is also obliged to take criminal action against the assailant, presumably to protect the *principle* that assault is forbidden. In other words, through the instrument of punishment, criminal law protects social values which are considered essential to the order and morale of a society. However, it is clear that not all violations of important social values are covered by criminal law; breach of contract, for instance, is generally covered by civil law. It might be a little more accurate to say that criminal conduct is what society at any given time considers *sufficiently* dangerous to its order and morale to be deemed punishable.

Criminal laws are one index of a community's social values at any given time. The extent of crime can thus serve as a clue to the conflict that exists between *expressed social values* and *actual social conduct*—between what society *says* and what various of its citizens *do*. This conflict is not necessarily limited to a relatively few individuals who are "out of step." Racketeering and illegal gambling depend upon the broad support of the public. On the other hand, people who commit "white-collar" crimes are rarely regarded as being as much out of step as the safecracker.

Different kinds of people are involved in different kinds of crime. How real are these differences and how illusory? What different kinds of groups are involved? What different kinds of conflicts are involved? If there is no single problem or phenomenon of crime, then can there be a single approach to its solution?

Section II: The Faces of Crime

The following "faces" of crime are examined separately, not for the purpose of setting up rigid categories, but as a temporary and perhaps artificial device which may be helpful in determining how much of our criminal picture is created by the existence of a relatively few individuals who are outrageously in conflict with "the laws and customs that all decent people hold" and, on the other hand, how much of it is created by more pervasive value conflicts in our society at large.

PREDATORY CRIME
Dimensions

The FBI lists seven major crimes: (*a*) robbery—stealing by force or violence; (*b*) burglary—breaking and entering; (*c*) auto theft; (*d*) larceny—

all other direct theft, *not* including the use of fraud; (*e*) criminal homicide; (*f*) aggravated assault—with a weapon or intent to kill; (*g*) rape.

At least 95 per cent of the major crimes reported by the FBI each year fall within the first four categories and are classified as "for the purpose of obtaining property." These acts constitute the traditional image of crime: the predatory violation of property by robbery, burglary, or larceny, with or without attendant violence (assault or homicide). Before World War I, to use a convenient historical marker, this was considered the essence of crime as a major social problem. True, there were occasional serious "crimes of emotion," unrelated to the illegal seizure of property, but these were not considered to be in the mainstream of crime. At least, they did not involve the professional or habitual criminal, the lawless "underworld" by which the community felt threatened.

This "traditional" or "conventional" face of crime is still with us. In 1957 the FBI reported that the major crimes, listed above, were climbing at a rate four times faster than the population.[3] Statistics on the extent of crime are, however, notoriously inexact. The most comprehensive figures are provided by the *Uniform Crime Reports,* published semiannually by the FBI. These are constructed from voluntary reports made by some 3,000 city police departments, 2,000 county police agencies, and 15 state police agencies. Only about half of the population is covered, chiefly in

FIGURE 4:1   TREND IN GROWTH OF THE CIVILIAN POPULATION AND INCREASE IN MAJOR CRIMES, 1940–53

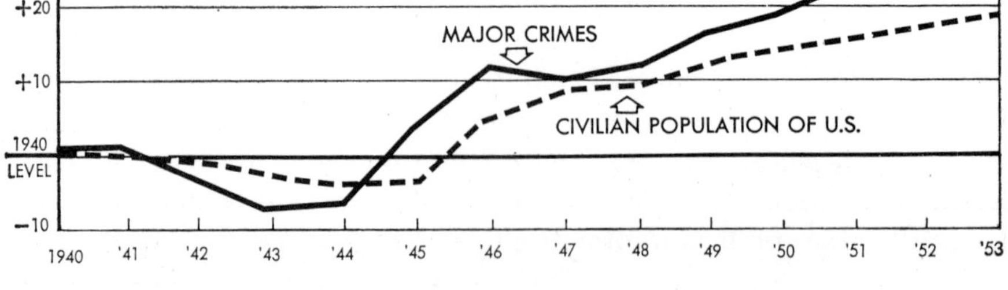

Source: Federal Bureau of Prisons, *Prisoners in State and Federal Institutions, 1950* (Leavenworth, Kansas: U.S. Penitentiary, 1954), p. 8. Civilian population estimates are from the Census Bureau's Series P-25, Nos. 72, 84, and 89; estimates of major crimes are from the Federal Bureau of Investigation's *Uniform Crime Reports.*

[3] *Uniform Crime Reports,* 1957, p. 72.

THE FACES OF CRIME

urban areas, and reporting standards are by no means uniform. Annual court statistics and prison statistics are similarly faulty in both coverage and uniformity of standards. In addition, court statistics and prison statistics have a narrower scope than the law-enforcement-agency statistics gathered by the FBI.

Actually, in any year, major crimes represent only about 3 per cent of all criminal offenses, as reported by the FBI. (About 75 per cent of all criminal offenses come under the heading of traffic violations.) But the overwhelming bulk of these major crimes have to do with predatory theft and make up the traditional face of crime. It is by these criminal activities that men most readily become identified in the public mind as criminals. This is crime at its most visible.

These jungle acts of theft-by-violence, committed by individuals or small bands, are in sharp moral conflict with the overwhelming body of society and its institutions. On the level of actual participation, predatory crime involves a relatively few individuals who are indeed out of step with the rest of the citizenry.

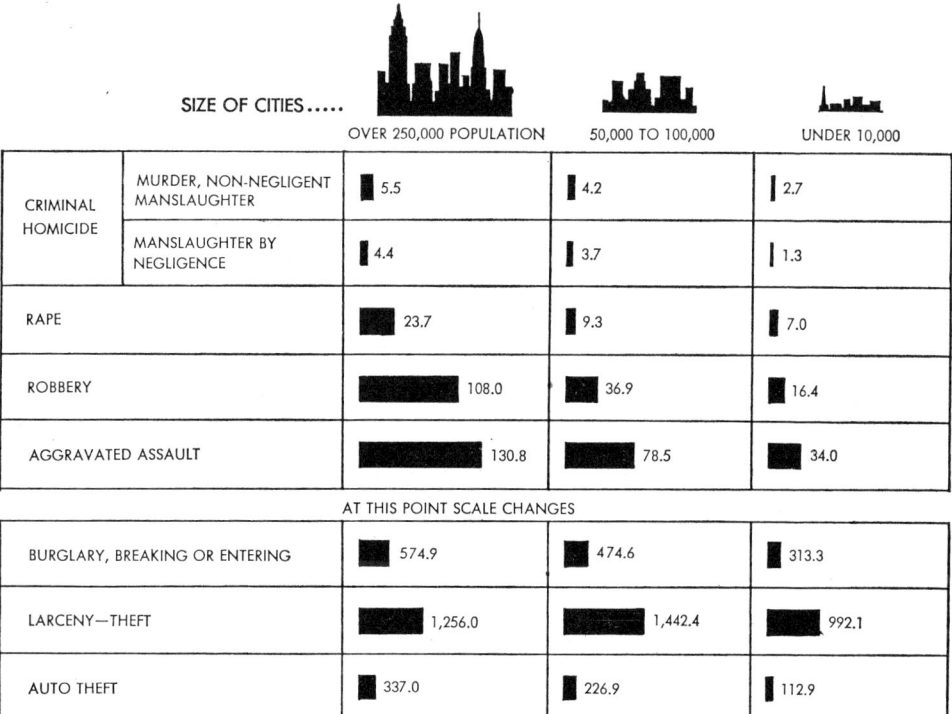

FIGURE 4:2 URBAN CRIME RATES PER 100,000 POPULATION, 1957

		OVER 250,000 POPULATION	50,000 TO 100,000	UNDER 10,000
CRIMINAL HOMICIDE	MURDER, NON-NEGLIGENT MANSLAUGHTER	5.5	4.2	2.7
	MANSLAUGHTER BY NEGLIGENCE	4.4	3.7	1.3
RAPE		23.7	9.3	7.0
ROBBERY		108.0	36.9	16.4
AGGRAVATED ASSAULT		130.8	78.5	34.0
AT THIS POINT SCALE CHANGES				
BURGLARY, BREAKING OR ENTERING		574.9	474.6	313.3
LARCENY—THEFT		1,256.0	1,442.4	992.1
AUTO THEFT		337.0	226.9	112.9

Adapted from Federal Bureau of Investigation, *Uniform Crime Reports,* Annual Bulletin, 1957 (Washington, D.C.: U.S. Government Printing Office, 1958), p. 92.

ORGANIZED "SERVICE" CRIME
Dimensions

A capsule description of the history and operation of organized crime was presented by the U.S. Senate (Kefauver) Committee To Investigate Organized Crime in 1951:

> The structure of organized crime today is far different from what it was many years ago. Its power for evil is infinitely greater. The unit of organized crime used to be an individual gang, consisting of a number of hoodlums whose activities were obviously predatory in character. Individual gangs tended to specialize in specific types of criminal activity such as payroll or bank robbery, loft or safe burglary, pocket picking, etc. . . . New types of criminal gangs have emerged during prohibition. The huge profits earned in that era together with the development of twentieth century transportation and communication made possible larger and much more powerful gangs, covering much greater territory. Organized crime in the last 30 years has taken on new characteristics . . . . Criminal groups today are multipurpose in character engaging in any racket wherever there is money to be made. The modern gang, moreover, does not rely for its primary source of income on frankly predatory forms of crime such as robbery, burglary or larceny. Instead the more dangerous criminal elements draw most of their revenues from various forms of gambling, the sale and distribution of narcotics, prostitution, various forms of business and labor racketeering, black-market practices, bootlegging into dry areas, etc.
>
> The key to successful gang operation is monopoly of illicit enterprises or illegal operations, for monopoly guarantees huge profits. In cities that gangland has organized very well, the syndicate or the combination in control of the rackets decides which mobsters are to have what rackets . . . . They seek to expand their activities in many different fields and in many different geographic areas, wherever profits may be made. We have seen evidence of the operation of the Costello-Adonis-Lansky syndicate, whose headquarters is in New York, in such places as Bergen County, N.J., Saratoga, N.Y., Miami, Fla., New Orleans, Nevada, the West Coast and Havana, Cuba. We have seen evidence of operations of the other major crime syndicate, that of Accardo-Guzik-Fischetti, whose headquarters is in Chicago, in such places as Kansas City, East St. Louis, Miami, Nevada and the West Coast . . . . It is apparent . . . that the leading figures in organized crime do business with each other.[4]

Organized crime, then, takes root wherever there is a widespread market for illegal services. Foremost among these services, and the principal support of organized crime, is gambling. Estimates as to the extent of gambling vary, but they all agree on the great magnitude of the operation. One

---

[4] U.S. Senate, Special Committee To Investigate Organized Crime in Interstate Commerce, *The Kefauver Committee Report on Organized Crime* (New York: Didier Publishers, 1951), pp. 125 ff.

estimate of the amount spent annually on gambling gives the following figures:

Illegal bookmaking	$8 billion
Numbers, policies, and lotteries	6 billion
Slot machines	3 billion
Football and baseball pools	1 billion

These figures do not include the amount spent at race tracks (estimated at $1½ billion) or the amount wagered legally in Nevada (estimated at $1 billion), nor does it include amounts bet at bingo or fairs or at local games. One noncumulative estimate of the number of *people* involved in the different forms of gambling runs as follows:

Horses	8 million
Numbers	8 million
Slot machines	14 million
Punchboards	15 million
Athletic events	19 million
Cards and dice	22 million
Pools, lotteries, and bingo	26 million

Much of this gambling activity is local and decentralized and beyond the monopolistic control of the syndicates. However, the profits from such centrally controlled gambling activities as bookmaking, numbers, and slot machines are the lifeblood of organized crime. These activities could not exist without the eager support of a substantial segment of the "respectable" community and the toleration of the community in general. Prostitution is another "service" provided by organized crime in response to a sizable market in the general community, as were black-market operations and bootlegging.

The criminal syndicates are clearly not addicted to a philosophy of service. They go wherever there seems to be money for an illegal, monopolistic operation. It would be straining the point to ascribe service aspects to business and labor racketeering, although in some cases gangsters made their entry into this field when some businessmen or unions were anxious to hire their violence. The extortion of money from small businessmen on threat of violence, spoilage of goods, or "union trouble" can only be counted predatory crime at its most organized.

The Kefauver Committee reported that it "had before it evidence of hoodlum infiltration in approximately fifty areas of business enterprise." At one time in Chicago it was reported that no less than 168 industries were being preyed upon by racketeers. This infiltration has resulted in unfair trade practices at best and in extortion and violence at normal worst.

GAMBLING—LEGAL AND ILLEGAL

Legal: *Crowd lined up to place bets at a Baltimore race track.*

Illegal: *New York City police raid a "million-dollar" wire service for horse bettors.*

Legal: *Gambling with dice is legal in Nevada. In this "poor man's casino" in Las Vegas the minimum bet is 25 cents.*

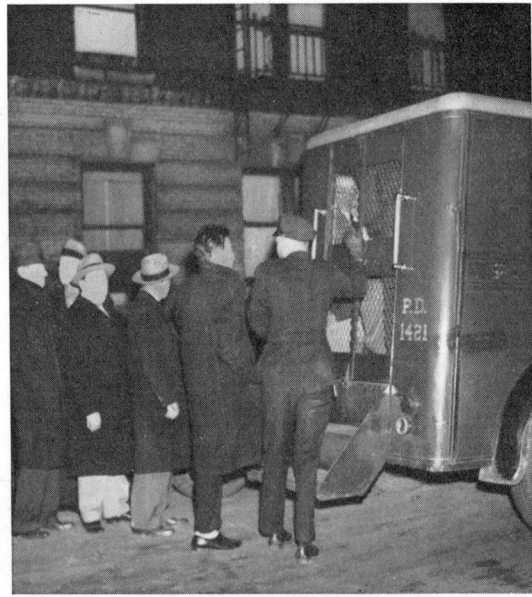

Illegal: *New York City police raid a "floating" dice game and seize 51 men.*

A typical example is provided by the case of one New York racketeer who, after gaining control of a restaurant workers union, exacted tribute from restaurant owners by promising them protection from labor trouble. Restaurant owners who failed to pay tribute were faced with unreasonable labor demands and destruction of their perishable goods.

However, racketeering is not the central operation of the criminal syndicates. Governor Adlai Stevenson of Illinois underscored the point that "the happy hunting ground of organized crime is in the area where too many people are disposed to participate in the breaking of a law."[5] And the Kefauver Committee narrowed it down by stating flatly that "the $2.00 horse bettor and the 5¢ numbers bettors" are providing the money which enables underworld characters to undermine our institutions. In measuring the impact of organized crime on the community, more concern attaches to the undermining of our institutions than to the fact that citizens are engaging in an illegal activity which is bilking them through hopeless odds.

The breakdown of law-enforcement agencies and responsible government in the face of organized crime was described by the Kefauver Committee in this way:

> Despite known arrest records and well-documented criminal reputations, the leading hoodlums in the country remain for the most part immune from prosecution and punishment although underlings of their gangs may occasionally be prosecuted and punished. This quasi-immunity of top-level mobsters can be ascribed to what is popularly known as the fix. The fix is not always the direct payment of money to law-enforcement officials, although the committee has run across considerable evidence of such bribery. The fix may also come about through acquisition of political power by contributions to political organizations or otherwise by creating economic ties with apparently reputable and respectable businessmen and lawyers and by buying public goodwill through charitable contributions.[6]

The point is made that this corruption—the "fixing" of law-enforcement officials and higher-level political entanglements—is not just the product of the peculiar evil genius of the syndicate criminal. This corruption is a natural and inevitable by-product of organized "service" crime as it is created by a willing public and an obliging criminal element.

With regard to gambling and similar "service" crimes which cannot be engaged in as stealthily as conventional predatory crime, Governor Stevenson noted that

---

[5] Adlai E. Stevenson, "Crime and Politics," *Journal of Criminal Law and Criminology,* **41** (1950), 397.
[6] *The Kefauver Committee Report on Organized Crime,* pp. 162 ff.

the law cannot be broken without the connivance of elected officials, and . . . open and long-continued violation inevitably means that there is corruption—a pay-off in some form or another. And corruption is a cancer which cannot be confined—a public official who has gotten in on the take for one purpose has become a captive and his usefulness as a public servant is largely at an end.[7]

The Problem

Service crime, unlike predatory crime, amounts to more than just the existence of service criminals. The syndicate criminal typically has a history of predatory crime before he graduates into his new occupation. In his personal patterns of violence and antisocial behavior he is still in sharp moral conflict with the overwhelming body of society and its institutions. But there is another kind of value conflict involved in service crime, and it is not confined to a relatively few individuals whom we know as "criminals." As Governor Stevenson put it, professional criminals move "in such twilight zones as that of gambling where there are prohibitory laws on the books but no unanimity of moral conviction." In service crime, unlike predatory crime, it is not the criminal alone who participates directly. A substantial portion of the "respectable" public must participate, and the public at large does not consider this participation heinous. This conflict between law and conduct bestrides society itself.

As a result of this "criminal condition" in society, the law-enforcement and political agencies are drawn into participation. This spreading pattern of participation thus becomes institutionalized in society—which is another way of saying that "organized crime" does not just refer to crime that is perpetrated by an organized gang; it refers to a criminal pattern that has been organized and integrated into some of the normal processes of our society. The results are consequently more crippling than the alien and isolated forays of predatory criminals.

Any examination of service crime in isolation is somewhat artificial. It must finally be fitted back into the total picture of criminality. Predatory crime is of course stimulated and protected by the institutionalization of service crime. The Kefauver Committee asserted that the creeping paralysis of law enforcement which results from a failure to enforce the gambling laws spreads to other types of crime and leads to a general breakdown in law enforcement. Even more basic, perhaps, is the fact that widespread participation in, or condoning of, service crime probably contributes to the creation of individual criminals of every stripe. It has been observed, for example, that sometimes the only affluent and respected individuals in a slum area are those associated with racketeering and

---

[7] *Ibid.*, p. 405.

vice—numbers men, gamblers, "hoods," and the like. These are often the only examples of success and status that the young boy has to emulate.

But the fact that society is morally schizoid and in major conflict with its own rules is more than a background factor insofar as service crime is concerned. It is the very substance of organized service crime. If this kind of crime involves something more than the existence of individual criminals, then its control involves more than the control of individual criminals. Crime takes on another dimension, which lies, at least partly, outside the reach of individual punishment.

WHITE-COLLAR CRIME
Dimensions

"White-collar crime" is a term that is used by some criminologists to describe crimes committed by members of the upper socio-economic classes in the course of their business. These include such crimes as embezzlement, fraud, and the violation of laws regulating business practices.

The leading exponent of the theory of white-collar criminality, the late Edwin H. Sutherland, stated that the very nature of this behavior makes its accurate measurement impossible. "The financial cost of white-collar crime," he wrote

> is probably several times as great as the financial cost of all the crimes which are customarily regarded as the "crime problem." An officer of a chain grocery store in one year embezzled $600,000, which was six times as much as the annual losses from five hundred burglaries and robberies of the stores in that chain. Public enemies numbered one to six secured $130,000 by burglary and robbery in 1938, while the sum stolen by [financier] Krueger is estimated at $250,000,000, or nearly two thousand times as much. The *New York Times* in 1931 reported four cases of embezzlement in the United States with a loss of more than a million dollars each and a combined loss of nine million dollars. Although a million-dollar burglar or robber is practically unheard of, these million-dollar embezzlers are small fry among white-collar criminals. The estimated loss to investors in one investment trust from 1929 to 1935 was $580,000,000 [through fraudulent manipulation].[8]

Further evidence of the kind of crime to which Sutherland had reference is the record of illegal business practices by seventy of the country's largest corporations over a period of forty years. These corporations had been found guilty of violating laws against restraint of trade 307 times; of violating laws against infringement of patents 222 times; of violating the National Labor Relations law 158 times; of violating laws against misrepresentation in advertising 97 times; and of violating other business

---

[8] Edwin H. Sutherland, *White-Collar Crime* (New York: Dryden Press, 1949), p. 4.

laws 196 times. Every one of the corporations had violated one or more of the laws. The average was 13 violations per corporation.[9]

There are several reasons why white-collar crimes do not arouse the same outrage as predatory crimes. In the first place, they do not involve physical danger to their victims, and, as a rule, they are not directed against specific individuals. Second, in the case of business-law violations, the nature of the violation is often obscure to the general public. Finally, the laws are implemented differently because of the high social position of the criminals involved. "The crimes of the upper class," writes Sutherland,

> either result in no official action at all, or result in suits for damages in civil courts, and are handled by inspectors and by administrative boards or commissions with penal sanctions in the form of warnings, orders to cease and desist, occasionally the loss of a license and only in extreme cases by fines or prison sentences. Thus, the white-collar criminals are segregated administratively from other criminals, and largely as a consequence of this are not regarded as real criminals by themselves, the general public or the criminologists.[10]

Many criminologists have emphasized the danger of broadening the concept of white-collar crime to include all unethical conduct, even if it breaks no law, or merely any mode of business behavior of which some individual may disapprove. As Paul Tappan points out, it is dangerous to promulgate a system of justice in which the individual may be held criminal without having committed a crime defined with some precision by statute and case law.[11]

However, it is not an indictment of business manners but a criminological point that Sutherland strives to make: Criminality is not so closely associated with poverty—and the correlates of poverty—as is often believed. The prevalence of white-collar crime makes it necessary to find some prime source of criminality that is common to both the lower and the upper social and economic classes. Sutherland invokes, therefore, the prime importance of social learning in the development of criminals. The criminal, upper or lower class, learns his behavior through his associations with people who already have a criminal behavior pattern. The "traditional" criminal learns his behavior, according to Sutherland, through association with delinquents and criminals; the white-collar criminal learns his behavior when he gets into particular business situations in which criminality is "practically a folkway."

[9] *Ibid.*
[10] Edwin H. Sutherland, "White-Collar Criminality," *American Sociological Review,* 5 (1940), 8.
[11] Paul W. Tappan, "Who Is the Criminal?" *American Sociological Review,* 12 (1947), 96–102.

The Problem

When Sutherland refers to white-collar criminality as "practically a folkway," he is pointing to another dimension of crime in which more is involved than a relatively few individuals who are outrageously in conflict with the laws and customs that all decent people hold.

The unofficial sanctions of social disapproval levied against the predatory criminal are notably light in the case of the white-collar criminal. This reflects a feeling that the white-collar criminal has mainly erred in being caught. He has done nothing, in other words, which other respectable citizens have not done with more caution or perhaps better legal advice.

Thus, white-collar crime manifests a pervasive conflict between our economic practices and our moral beliefs. This creates a climate of criminality which is likely to produce criminal behavior not only on the white-collar level but on all levels. In this sense, we are doing little more than restating the causative impact of the delinquent society on criminality in general. However, the complex of white-collar crime uniquely serves to illustrate again, although less specifically than in the case of service crime, that there are value conflicts endemic in society which must be part of any total consideration of crime and which extend, at least in part, beyond the reach of individual punishment and penology.

SPECIAL CRIME PROBLEMS

The bulk of nonprofit crime, and indeed of all crime, is committed in violation of *regulatory* laws, such as traffic laws. These are laws based on administrative necessity rather than moral principle, and their violation is not generally considered by the public as part of the "crime problem," although their contribution to the climate of criminality might well be weighed.

The slim remainder of nonprofit crimes falls mainly within the area of vice.

Sex Offenses

1. *Rape.* Rape is listed by the FBI as one of the seven major crimes. Actually it constitutes only about one-half of 1 per cent of major crimes. Most of these are cases of statutory rape, which automatically calls for charges when females below the age of sixteen to eighteen are involved. For a recent ten-year period, only 18 per cent of rape convictions in New York State were forcible rape. The "Jack the Ripper" image frequently invoked by the newspapers has probably exaggerated the over-all menace of this crime.

2. *Sex deviation.* Such deviations from normal sexual expression as sodomy, incest, indecent exposure, and acts of homosexuality are criminal violations. No connection between this kind of deviant sexual behavior and violence or rape can be assumed. New Jersey's Commission on the Habitual Sex Offender reported that very few minor sex offenders progressed to major sex crimes and that only an estimated 5 per cent of all sex offenders have ever committed crimes of violence.[12] The Commission also pointed out that there are fewer "repeaters" among sex offenders than among other types of offenders, with the understandable exception of murderers.

The problem of sex crime, then, would seem to be a matter more often of protecting the moral values and sensibilities of society than of protecting the citizenry from assault. Also, sex crimes are distinct from the mainstream of crime in being typically psychopathic in origin. New Jersey passed a law in 1949 which called for automatic mental examination of all sex offenders to see, in each case, whether psychiatric treatment or imprisonment was indicated.

Narcotics

The chief relation of narcotics-use to the mainstream of crime would seem to be the market that it provides for organized "service" crime. It is estimated that there are some 50,000–60,000 drug addicts in the United States, although there are many more drug-users. There is no indication that much crime is attributable to the direct physiological stimulation of drugs, although narcotic addicts are frequently driven to petty crimes in order to pay for their habit. Not more than a quarter of those committed to prison for use of narcotics have been convicted of violating other criminal laws, and almost all of these are minor offenders.

Section III: Meeting the Problem
PREVENTION

An old and tempting formula for crime prevention suggests that, since crime is committed by criminals, we have only to eliminate the criminals in order to eliminate crime. This formula begs the question; it is not altogether different from the suggestion that divorce can be eliminated by eliminating divorced people. A society has about as much crime, and as much divorce, as the social process produces. For the most part, criminals are not alien objects that have intruded themselves on society. The criminal population in America is as much a natural fruit of this society as is the number of its philosophers or artists or businessmen.

---

[12] *The Habitual Sex Offender,* Report and Recommendations of the Commission on the Habitual Sex Offender, State of New Jersey, 1950.

Museum of the City of New York; The Jacob A. Riis Collection

Bandits' Roost: A historic spawning ground for criminals in old New York.

Part of society's role in the production of crime-bent or crime-prone individuals has been analyzed in the chapter on delinquency. Delinquency is a broader problem than crime; most delinquents are not "youthful criminals" nor destined for careers of crime. But susceptibility to adult criminal activity is most frequently shaped during youth and is part of the delinquency picture. Two kinds of *habitual* delinquents have been delineated. First, there are those who have absorbed criminal values from the explicitly criminal environments which surround them. They live on subcultural islands of criminality which exist here and there within society. The values of a subculture have been successfully transmitted to them. It can be expected that a professional class of criminals, in some number, will inevitably emerge from these environments.

However, a large number of habitual delinquents emerge from environments that are not explicitly criminal. Their noncriminal environments, espousing positive social values, have failed to imbue them with these values. The subsequent loss of control by the traditional institutions of society is the aspect of modern delinquency that is most disturbing. It is epitomized in the growing recognition that delinquency is not restricted to the "other side of the tracks," where islands of criminality may be expected to exist, but is produced on every level of society. Individual susceptibility to criminal activity is one by-product of this failure of social control, this failure to impart positive social values. In this sense, delinquency prevention is a first step in crime prevention.

However, the thriving existence of institutionalized crime is itself one of the characteristics of the delinquent society that tends to produce delinquents. It is institutionalized crime that provides extensive channels for criminal activity. The "crime problem," insofar as it concerns most people, threatens society, lends a delinquent tone to society, and produces large numbers of professional criminals, is largely a problem of organized, institutionalized, service crime rather than of isolated predatory acts of crime.

Gambling

Illegal gambling remains one of the firm bases of organized crime. There are generally two serious kinds of proposals for the prevention of illegal gambling:

1. Law enforcement should be more effective. The thesis of this approach is that illegal gambling thrives where law enforcement is lax; and this laxity is more often the result of corruption than of sheer inefficiency. A typical proposal is that law-enforcement officers should be paid more so that they will be less vulnerable to corruption. However, there is no indication that law-enforcement officers who are dishonest will be dissuaded

from crime by a relatively small increase in salary. The municipal government will never be able to compete financially with the wealthy illegal gambling industry. Systems of corruption have been rooted out of law-enforcement agencies by diligent reform administrations. In the wake of heightened public concern, special-prosecutor activity has even reached into high places and tumbled some of the "executives" of organized crime. But service crime has always demonstrated regenerative powers and will continue to do so as long as a public demand for the illicit commodities of vice and gambling persists.

2. Gambling should be made legal. The premise of this recurrent suggestion is that "to gamble is human," and the practice might as well be harnessed to the accepted social system. This would make inevitable the collapse of the criminal industry which is based primarily on the illegality of gambling. Instead, gambling could bring needed revenues to the various governments.

Supporters of this proposal point out that a double standard already exists in official society. Gambling at race tracks, which brings substantial revenue to many state treasuries is legal, but "off-track" betting is illegal. Lotteries to raise funds for churches and other philanthropic activities are commonly permitted, while lotteries for profit are prohibited. If gambling is immoral, it is immoral even where the profits go only to government or philanthropy.

It has been the organized church groups who have most often led the vocal opposition to legalized gambling. They customarily point out that as a practical matter it is the average wage-earner who must be prevented from dissipating his earnings. Relatively few can become habitués of a race track. But a legal bookmaker on every corner would be another matter.

In the post-Revolutionary years, legalized lotteries were common in this country. State governments conducted these lotteries for schools and other government funds. However, as the opponents of legalized gambling like to point out, such state supervision did not prevent crime and corruption. Legislators were bribed, unscrupulous promoters reaped large profits, and it was largely as a result of the gross political corruption attending legalized gambling that it was eventually abolished in the various states before the Civil War.

Recurrent modern proposals for legalized gambling claim to take this experience into consideration. It is suggested that certain safeguards can be erected against corruption. The state, rather than license private groups, should maintain complete supervision and reap all the profits. The state agency set up to maintain this supervision should be completely independent and divorced from politics.

Narcotics

There are three remedial paths generally suggested for the reduction of the problem of illegal narcotics.

1. Punishment for narcotic dealers should be more severe. It has even been suggested that the death sentence should apply to habitual narcotic dealers. However, there is no evidence that more severe sentences would deter the illegal sale of narcotics. It has been suggested that such sentences would only serve to drive the market price of illegal narcotics higher than it is. This would make the addict more desperate and even more dependent on petty crime to pay for his habit.

2. There should be compulsory hospitalization and better treatment facilities for addicts. To date, the record of cure for narcotic addicts is dismal, even with relatively good treatment facilities. At best, not more than one out of four patients at the federal hospitals for addicts is "cured" for any length of time, and many consider this an optimistic figure. Former addicts who have "kicked" the habit usually return to the same environments and problems and are often drawn back into the habit by "pushers," who have a business stake in making and maintaining addicts.

Certainly, addicts who desire treatment should be able to find adequate psychiatric and guidance as well as medical facilities. Some communities have established adult guidance centers to help narcotic addicts as well as alcoholics. But there is no reason to believe that the establishment of these facilities, so important from a humanitarian point of view, will seriously disturb the criminal empire and industry that are built on addiction. It is even possible that laws providing for compulsory hospitalization, with its uncertain prospects for medical success, would only drive addicts further underground.

3. Narcotics should be sold legally to addicts. This proposal envisions the establishment of narcotic clinics which would sell drugs to addicts at cost. These clinics, under medical supervision, would not only dispense narcotics but provide some expert guidance. Each applicant would be carefully examined to establish the fact of addiction. All doses would be minimal, sufficient only to prevent the highly painful withdrawal symptoms which all addicts dread. Some therapeutic measures might be taken, but the primary purpose of these clinics would not be the cure of those who are already addicted. One purpose would be to make the life of addicts more tolerable and even useful and to reduce the petty theft associated with addiction. An even more significant purpose would be to destroy the organized crime associated with narcotic sales and prevent a significant amount of new addiction. An amount of heroin worth ten dollars on the legal market can be sold for eighty thousand dollars illicitly. The

underworld therefore could not compete with the clinics in the sale of narcotics. More important, it is customary for the underworld to deliberately "hook" new addicts by offering several free doses or otherwise promoting the use of narcotics, often among teen-agers. This practice would, of course, cease if there were no profit attached to it.

TREATMENT

Punishment for crime has historically been justified on two grounds: retribution and deterrence. Retribution is no longer considered morally defensible in Western society. Nor is it tenable in a political system based on the equal application of the law; there is no slide rule for determining the precise degree of retribution appropriate for every given criminal offense. The concept that a criminal must "pay his debt to society" also implies that when his debt has been paid he is free to run up a new one.

The deterrent value of punishment is clearly limited. It is perhaps reasonable to assume that a number of people are turned from criminal acts, or even from a criminal career, because of the fear of imprisonment. However, there is no evidence to indicate that the bulk of committed and habitual criminals which our society does produce are seriously deterred from further criminal activity by such a fear. Criminals are simply not deterred by the thought of punishment, because they do not expect to be caught as they embark on a criminal venture. Indeed, a majority of offenders are not even apprehended for any given crime. There may be as many as twenty offenses committed for every conviction that is finally obtained.

An extension of the theory of deterrence calls for drastically increasing the penalties. Extreme punishment might serve as a deterrent in some cases, but it must be balanced against other values. A ban against extreme and unusual punishment is part of the basic creed of every democratic political order. It is a safeguard against the cheapening of human life. To impose an inordinate degree of punishment would be to foster a general sense of brutality which might well contribute toward a delinquent society and thus increase the flow of crime. Against these hazards must be laid the fact that most habitual criminals, and those who commit crimes of passion, will not be deterred in any case. Historical evidence is clear on this point. In eighteenth-century England over two hundred offenses were punishable by death, but crime was not eradicated.

On the other hand, it has been suggested that the role of punishment cannot be eliminated. To eliminate punishment, it is argued, would be to hold that no one is accountable for his actions. And indeed some modern approaches to delinquency and crime appear to deny the concept of individual responsibility. Every criminal is regarded as a helpless victim of his environment, his personal history, and his constitutional makeup. Therefore, the criminal, being without free will, cannot be held accountable for his crime; therefore, he cannot be punished. This, of course, is the root concept of delinquency, originally applied to the very small child but now extended to the adult. But even if free will did not exist, society would have to act as though it did. Otherwise, it would be impossible to establish the individual responsibility without which society cannot exist. Rules and values have no meaning or effect if adult individuals are not held to be able to comply with them and accountable for not complying with them.

From this point of view, some penalties must still be applied to those who knowingly violate society's rules. However, the nature and content of these penalties may differ. They may be designed to be retributive and deterrent only. Or they may be aimed at the humanitarian and practicable goal of rehabilitation, the prevention of repeated criminal activity.

In other words, society need not feel guilty about reasonably penalizing its criminals. However, it should do so within the framework of its primary task of rehabilitating them wherever possible.

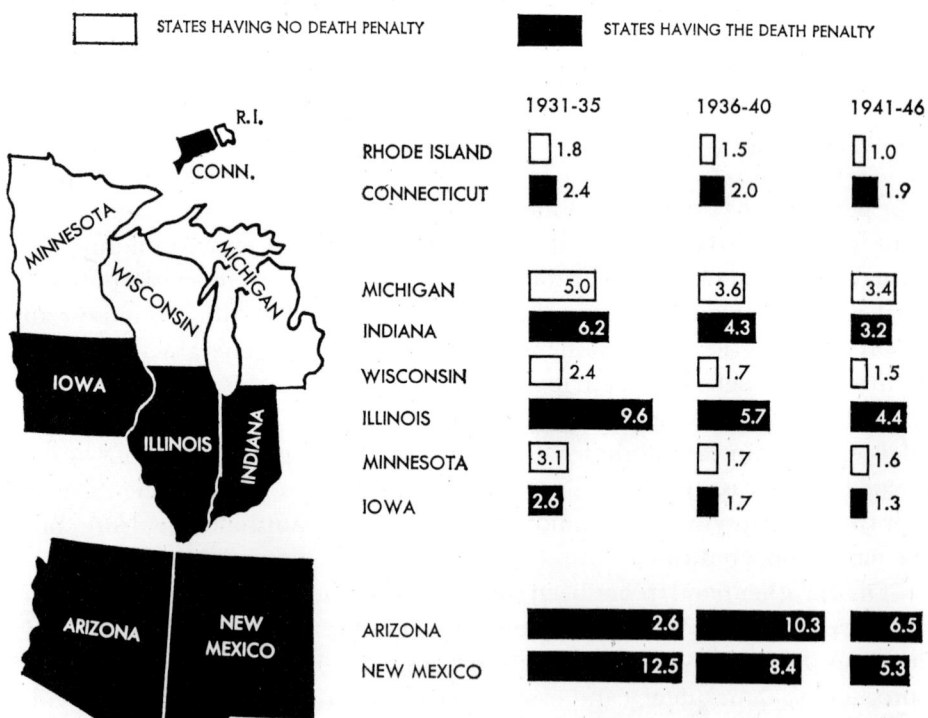

FIGURE 4:3 ANNUAL AVERAGE HOMICIDE RATES IN TEN STATES SELECTED ACCORDING TO CONTIGUITY

Adapted from Karl F. Schuessler, "The Deterrent Influence of the Death Penalty," *Annals of the American Academy of Political and Social Science*, 284 (November, 1952), 54–62.

Bob Benyas; Black Star

Shut Out: The modern prison provides recreational facilities—but remains a prison.

Imprisonment

The same fundamental weaknesses of correctional institutions for delinquents apply to prisons for adults. Prison life is isolated from society and normal social activity; it is stigmatizing; it is "criminal" in environment and even serves as a training course in crime; by its very nature, prison life tends to be brutalizing and to run counter to the requirements of rehabilitation.

Prison life is thus handicapped even where it offers the best in medical, educational, vocational, and psychiatric facilities. But, typically, it does not. Prisons are overcrowded. Classification systems, which ideally should separate the psychopath from the psychologically normal, the younger from the older, the habitual criminal from the one-time violator, break down under institutional pressures. There is not enough work to go around, so idleness is a serious problem. Guidance services and psychiatric treatment are token. In the absence of these facilities, criminals are returned to society in no better condition for leading a noncriminal life than when they entered. In 1956, 63.5 per cent of all federal prisoners were recidivists, that is, had records of previous commitment. Almost half of these had three or more previous commitments.[13]

Ideally, a "rehabilitated" criminal is one who has absorbed positive social values. The mere imposition of external controls such as bars and walls does not establish internal controls and, in fact, often tends to weaken them. The most effective prison experiences, from the viewpoint of rehabilitation, are minimum-security situations, where the men may work outside the prison during the day, live in cottages or cell blocks without locks, and generally develop an internal discipline out of a developed sense of social responsibility. But these minimum-security conditions are most applicable to the least habitual criminals, and perhaps probation or early parole would serve the same purpose more effectively in many of these cases. One summary viewpoint is that prisons should be regarded primarily as an evil necessity. They protect society by keeping certain habitual criminals in custody for a period of time and perhaps establish the social principle of penalty for crime. But it may be doubted that they could ever serve as agencies of rehabilitation.

Parole and Probation

Probation is, in effect, a suspended sentence with two conditions imposed: good behavior for the duration of the "sentence" and the constant supervision by, and co-operation with, a probation officer. Parole is, in effect, the suspension of the remainder of a sentence under the same conditions after part of the sentence has already been served in prison. Parole is usually granted upon advice of a parole board, while probation is usually established by the court. These practices vary widely in the states, but about one out of three major offenders across the country is placed on probation today, and about three out of four releases from state prisons are by parole.

The increasing use of parole has been accompanied by the increasing use of the "indeterminate sentence," or the sentence which indicates both minimum and maximum limits, e.g., "five to ten years." The philosophy of the indeterminate sentence is that an offender may be released, under supervision, at whatever time he seems to have developed into a good risk. Some criminologists recommend parole as a regular practice, thus providing some measure of control over the convicted criminal after he is released. If he has a fixed sentence and serves it, there can be no supervision over him when he returns to society.

Probation and parole, where they can be used, are generally considered more conducive to rehabilitation than imprisonment. The "permanent" success of probation was found to be about 75 per cent in a 1954 United Nations Survey of Britain, Denmark, Norway, Sweden, the Netherlands, and

---

[13] Department of Justice, Bureau of Prisons, *Federal Prisons: 1956* (Leavenworth, Kans.: United States Penitentiary, 1957).

the United States. This finding is supported by statistical data limited to this country. This apparently high degree of success, however, needs to be closely scrutinized.

Most of these offenders might just as assiduously have avoided further crime if they had been imprisoned instead of being placed on probation or parole. Moreover, the hard core of criminal offenders tends not to be placed on probation but sent to prison and, when there, to be denied parole. On this score alone, prisons can be expected to have an inferior record in preventing recidivism. The relative success of parole and probation indicates that courts and parole boards are fairly successful in selecting the good risks and incarcerating the bad risks.

This leaves, in brief, a number of habitual offenders for whom there is no high hope of rehabilitation by known remedial measures. The substantial number of offenders who do *not* repeat their offenses indicates that a new crop of offenders is continuously appearing on the criminal scene. Both observations point up the conclusion that society can perhaps solve the problem of individual criminals, either by custody or by treatment, without solving the problem of crime.

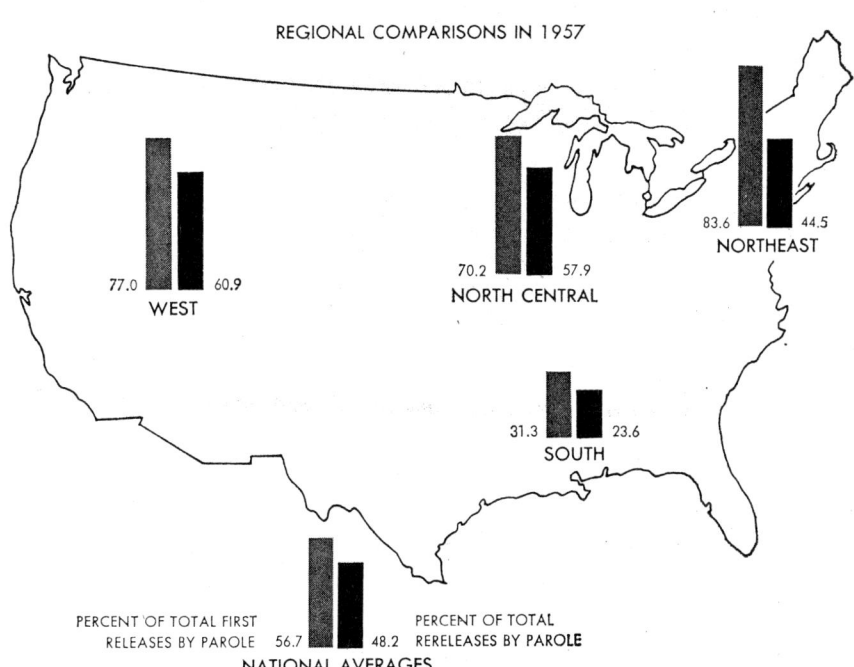

FIGURE 4:4 RELEASES FROM STATE INSTITUTIONS BY PAROLE
REGIONAL COMPARISONS IN 1957

WEST 77.0 60.9
NORTH CENTRAL 70.2 57.9
NORTHEAST 83.6 44.5
SOUTH 31.3 23.6

NATIONAL AVERAGES
PERCENT OF TOTAL FIRST RELEASES BY PAROLE 56.7
PERCENT OF TOTAL RERELEASES BY PAROLE 48.2

Adapted from Federal Bureau of Prisons, "Prisoners in State and Federal Institutions, 1957," *National Prisoner Statistics*, No. 19 (July, 1958).

adaptation 6   PREDICTING PAROLE SUCCESS
AND FAILURE

Abridged and adapted from Lloyd E. Ohlin, Selection for Parole *(New York: Russell Sage Foundation, 1951). Published in this form by permission of the author and the publisher.*

[Because it is impossible in practice to predict with absolute certainty whether any given prisoner will or will not abstain from criminal activity during his parole, parole is necessarily a system of calculated risks. Even with the best intentions, some parolees fail and even commit major crimes. Realistically speaking, every parolee is a risk. The question is: How great a risk?

It has been recognized for some time that it is feasible to calculate with reasonable accuracy and for each case the probability that parole will be a success or, in other words, to determine the degree of risk to society incurred with each release. This calculation does not introduce an entirely new element into parole decision; it is an attempt to arrive at a more accurate assessment of risk than is otherwise attained by common sense, intuition, or prejudice. Nor does it automatically solve the problems of a parole board. Though it tells the parole board what the risks are, it cannot determine its decisions.

Calculations of parole risk tell the board that if it releases 100 prisoners of a designated type, it can expect, let us say, 5 to commit new crimes. It cannot tell the board whether the applicant before it, who happens to fall into the designated category, will be one of the 5 or one of the 95. Nor can it tell the board whether a 95 to 5 risk is one which ought to be incurred. It is the delicate task of the conscientious parole board to balance justice to the individual with justice to the community, to weigh the cost of the continued imprisonment of all 100 against the cost of the 5 crimes that will in all probability occur. Ought the 95 "suffer" for the sake of the 5, or should society "suffer" the 5 for the sake of the 95?

The following is a report by Lloyd E. Ohlin, written when he was research sociologist of the Illinois Division of Correction, on the method devised in Illinois to predict what kinds of parolees are most likely and what kinds are least likely to violate parole or to commit new crimes.]

THE BASIC TASK

To evaluate the probability that prisoner A will no longer be a danger to the community, we ask whether there are factors in the prisoner's situation which experience with past parolees has shown to be statistically related to rehabilitation. Is A the kind of prisoner who in the past has tended not to continue his criminal activity? To take a frivolous example, if A is over six feet tall and if, in the past, 80 per cent of all parolees over six feet tall have been rehabilitated, then, all other things being equal, the probability is 8 to 2 that A is a good parole risk. A prisoner's height is, of course, not significantly relevant to his success as a parolee. The basic task in parole prediction is to discover the factors that in the past have actually been related to parole success.

MEASURING SUCCESS AND FAILURE

It is necessary, first, to decide what constitutes parole success and failure. Unfortunately it is not practicable to secure reliable knowledge concerning the best and most stringent measures of success and failure. The ideal measure of parole success would be the prisoner's achievement of a satisfactory *total* adjustment, a concept which implies not only cessation from criminal activity but firm reintegration into respectable society as well. Here reliable knowledge, though possible to obtain, would be extremely costly. The next best measure would be the prisoner's abstention from all criminal activity, whether or not it had come to official notice. In this case, not only would the cost be prohibitive, but much criminality would still remain unrevealed.

In constructing the Illinois prediction system, it was decided to take issuance and nonissuance of a parole violation warrant as the test of parole success and failure. Parole violation warrants are issued under two circumstances: (1) if the parolee violates parole rules—for example, by associating with criminals or failing to report to his parole officer—and (2) if the parolee commits a new crime. In the former case, the parolee is considered a minor violator; in the latter, a major violator. In either case, if a warrant was issued, parole was adjudged a failure.

This measure has the advantage of being a clear, objective index of success and failure and one easily obtained from the records at minimum expense. Its disadvantages are several.

In the first place, the nonissuance of a warrant is apt to overemphasize the success of parole. (*a*) Many men manage to comply with parole regulations without making any real social adjustment. (*b*) Parole agents are reluctant to issue warrants for minor infractions so long as the hope of rehabilitation remains. (*c*) Where parole supervision is poor, the nonissuance of a warrant often reflects nothing more than lack of knowledge of the parolee's activities.

In the second place, the number of major violators tends to be underestimated by the records. (*a*) Many criminal acts go undetected. (*b*) Because violation of parole rules is often associated with a drift toward criminal association and behavior, parolees suspected of such a drift are often returned for technical infractions of parole regulations which might otherwise be overlooked. As a result, the preponderance in the records of minor over major violators (see Table 4:2, p. 163) inadequately reflects the seriousness of some parole failures. Some minor violators are in fact actual or incipient major violators.

PREDICTION FACTORS

In order to arrive at factors actually related to parole success, the records of past parolees were examined to find violation rates for a variety of proposed prediction factors. These factors were chosen in the light of sociological and psychological knowledge of the conditions associated with criminal behavior.

For example, "social type" was chosen as a factor possibly bearing on parole success. Parolees were classified as belonging to various subclasses under "social type" according to the following definitions:

1. *Erring citizen:* An older man who has apparently been entrusted with responsibility; a substantial and reliable citizen, but one who erred on this occasion.

2. *Marginally delinquent:* A borderline classification between an erring citizen and a socially inadequate person.

3. *"Farmer":* A rural-type person who generally leads a normal social life but becomes easily involved in situations that lead to trouble.

4. *Socially inadequate:* An offender who has failed to establish a place for himself in conventional society, by virtue of mental deficiency, irresponsibility, or an unstable personality. He does not exhibit steadiness in his work history or responsibility in his family relationships.

5. *Ne'er-do-well:* An irresponsible person who seldom seeks work, lives by the easiest way possible, and is considered to have a bad reputation in the community as a thief, gambler, drunkard, etc.

6. *Floater:* A man who drifts about the country, rides freights, lives in jungles, gets tagged for vagrancy, and frequently commits minor crimes en route.

7. *Socially maladjusted:* A person who cannot adjust himself to conventional society by virtue of strong criminal orientation or serious personality disturbances.

8. *Drunkard:* An offender who continually loses his job because of drinking, frequents saloons constantly, and works only to keep drinking. Generally he has a reputation for being an alcoholic, and his crime is related to his drinking.

9. *Drug addict:* A person who has acquired the habit of using narcotics and whose crimes are generally related to this habit.

10. *Sex deviant:* A man who engages in recognized deviant sex behavior as a common practice.

Next, the percentage of parole failures for each social type was calculated and was found to be as follows:

	Per cent
Erring citizen	0
Marginally delinquent	3
"Farmer"	13
Socially inadequate	18
Ne'er-do-well	34
Floater	39
Socially maladjusted	41
Drunkard	44
Drug addict	48

The subclass "Sex deviant" contained too few cases to permit a reliable violation rate to be calculated.

Statistical tests were applied to insure the significance and reliability of the various violation rates. Where the figure for a given subclass, such as "Ne'er-do-well" or "Sex deviant," was deemed statistically unreliable, it was regarded as neutral for parole prediction. Categories with low percentages were held to be favorable to parole success, those with high percentages unfavorable.

Twenty-seven factors were proposed and tried, but only twelve were finally retained as good prediction items. Table 4:1 lists these factors and their subclasses and shows whether the latter turned out to be favorable, neutral, or unfavorable for parole success.

The highest violation rate occurred for the item *inadequate* under the factor "Parole job." Parolees were classified as having inadequate job prospects when they had only very vague notions of job possibilities or if they had arranged for a job inconsistent with their previous work experience, ability, or social type. For such parolees the violation rate was 65 per cent.

SCORING THE PAROLEES

A method had to be devised for scoring each man on all twelve factors. It was discovered that complicated procedures for giving different weights to different items added little predictive force to the final scores. On the face of it, an inadequate job prospect was more unfavorable than drug addiction, yet attempts to take this difference into account did not materially affect the results. The simple device was finally used of subtracting unfavorable from favorable items and counting the neutral items as zero. For example, a parolee had a final score of -4 if he fell into a favorable subclass on two factors, an unfavorable subclass on six, and a neutral subclass on the remaining four.

TABLE 4:1 RATING OF PREDICTION ITEMS, JOLIET-STATEVILLE AND MENARD DIVISION, ILLINOIS STATE PENITENTIARY SYSTEM

Prediction Factors and Items	Rating of Items Favorable	Rating of Items Neutral	Rating of Items Unfavorable	Prediction Factors and Items	Rating of Items Favorable	Rating of Items Neutral	Rating of Items Unfavorable
1. *Type of offense:*				6. *Social type* (continued):			
Homicide and assault	1			Socially maladjusted			x
Robbery		0		Drunkard			x
Burglary			x	Drug addict			x
Larceny and stolen				Sex deviant		0	
property		0		7. *Work record:*			
Forgery and fraud		0		Regular	1		
Sex offenses	1			Irregular		0	
Miscellaneous		0		Casual		0	
2. *Sentence:*				Student		0	
All definite sentences	1			None		0	
All other sentences		0		8. *Community:*			
3. *Type of offender:*				Urban		0	
First	1			Rural		0	
Technical first		0		Transient			x
Occasional		0		9. *Parole job:*			
Juvenile recidivist		0		Adequate		0	
Recidivist			x	Inadequate			x
Habitual			x	None		0	
4. *Home status:*				10. *Number of associates:*			
Superior	1			None		0	
Average		0		One or two		0	
Inferior		0		Three or over	1		
Broken		0		11. *Personality:*			
Institution		0		Normal (no gross			
Left home		0		defects)	1		
5. *Family interest:*				Inadequate		0	
Very active	1			Unstable		0	
Active		0		Egocentric		0	
Sustained		0		Gross personality			
Passive		0		defects		0	
None			x	No record		0	
6. *Social type:*				12. *Psychiatric prognosis:*			
Erring citizen	1			Favorable	1		
Marginally				Problematic		0	
delinquent	1			Doubtful		0	
"Farmer"	1			Guarded		0	
Socially inadequate	1			Unfavorable		0	
Ne'er-do-well		0		No record		0	
Floater			x				

ADAPTATION 6

TABLE 4:2 ILLINOIS EXPERIENCE TABLE—VIOLATION RATES

Score Group	Violators per 100 Cases in Each Score Group		
	Total Violators	Minor Violators	Major Violators
5–10	3	2	1
4	7	5	2
3	10	7	3
2	18	10	8
1	19	10	9
0	29	16	13
−1	40	25	15
−2	46	27	19
−3 and −4	56	34	22
−5 and −6	75	62	13

THE EXPERIENCE TABLE

As a final step, almost 5,000 prisoners were studied to determine violation rates, not for isolated factors, but for score groups. It was found that among those with scores of 5–10 only 3 per cent had violated parole; while among those with scores of −5 and −6, as many as 75 per cent had violated parole. The complete results appear in Table 4:2. This table is called an "experience table" because it sums up past experience with parolees with regard to parole success and failure. Provided it is kept up to date, the experience table can be used to predict violation rates for new parolees; adjusted experience tables have been found to predict accurately with an average error of only 1–2 per cent. In the case of the highest-scoring prisoners, the chances are as high as 97 to 3 that parole will be successful; in the case of the lowest-scoring prisoners, the chances are that 3 out of 4 will violate parole.

The Illinois experience table requires annual adjustment because of the decline over the years of the average parole violation rate in that state. During the period 1925–35 the average violation rate was 44 per cent; during the period 1936–44 it fell to 29 per cent. However, since the drop was spread rather uniformly over the various score groups, their comparative standings remained unchanged. In 1937 a detailed study supported the conclusion that, although better prison treatment and parole supervision undoubtedly had a part, the experience table itself played a significant role in the decline of violation rates by facilitating selection of the better parole risks.

USING THE EXPERIENCE TABLE

1. The experience table is one important factor, though not the only one, in decisions to grant or deny parole. The table acts very much like a traffic

signal. A high positive score signals "go." It tells the board that, unless persuasive negative evidence exists to offset the prospective parolee's high score, he is a good risk. A medium score signals "caution." In these borderline cases, the parolee's score may be given less weight in the decision than other information, such as the nature of the crime, the offender's attitude toward parole, and his response to treatment in prison. A low score, on the other hand, signals a definite "stop" unless there is persuasive evidence that the prisoner can overcome the obstacles to rehabilitation revealed by his score. In short, the experience table indicates to the board whether to concentrate on positive evidence pointing to parole or on negative evidence pointing away from it. It also indicates to the board how much offsetting evidence to look for. Conceivably, all other things being equal, a good attitude toward parole might be decisive for a medium-score applicant but far from sufficient in the case of a low-score applicant.

2. The experience table is sometimes used to decide on the order of parole. Although associates in the same offense are frequently considered for parole at the same time, parole boards are reluctant to release them simultaneously lest continued association occur and result in a drift toward crime. On the basis of the experience table a board may release the higher-scoring individual first on the ground that he is more likely to establish constructive associations before the release of his erstwhile partner.

3. The experience table can also be used to control the average parole violation rate. Let us say a parole board has in one month released 100 prisoners. The board can then calculate, on the basis of the experience table and the scores of the 100 prisoners actually released, what the average violation rate for that month's parolees is likely to be. If the preponderance of these 100 parolees had high scores, the average violation rate will in all probability be low. The parole board may then decide to incur a higher average violation rate and grant more paroles to those with lower scores. On the other hand, if the average violation rate for a given month is predicted to be high, the parole board may be more stringent in the future.

OBJECTIONS TO THE EXPERIENCE TABLE

The chief objection to the experience table is that it will be used mechanically. Although 75 per cent of parolees with a score of -5 or -6 have in the past violated parole, it seems unfair, simply on this ground, to deny parole to every applicant with such a score; perhaps *this* applicant is the one out of four who will not violate parole. Here possible injustice to the prisoner is being invoked. Similarly, though only one out of every hundred parolees with high scores will commit a new crime, this does not absolve the parole board from trying to discover which parolee is that *one*. This argument invokes possible injustice to the community.

In reply it can be said that use of the experience table does not in any way imply its mechanical application. For those with scores of —5 and —6, either evidence offsetting their scores exists or it does not. If it does not, the board has no objective grounds other than the prisoner's low score for granting parole. The prisoner's low score does, after all, indicate that more obstacles than aids to rehabilitation are present in his situation. If offsetting evidence does exist, it can be used, though it may have to be of considerable moment for parole to be indicated.

It must be remembered, moreover, that secure knowledge is not presently available concerning the factors that make for nonviolation in 25 per cent of the low-scoring cases. Consequently, in the absence of such knowledge the board is hardly likely to be able infallibly to select out for parole those low-scorers who will turn out to be successful, and some released low-scorers will eventually violate parole despite the evidence assessed as being in their favor. In fact, as more low-scorers are paroled, the closer their violation rate is apt to approach that of the experience table. In the interests of the community and, therefore, of the continued existence of the parole system itself, caution and stringency must necessarily increase as scores decrease; and the parole board cannot safely ignore the probabilities formulated in the experience table if the average violation rate is not to exceed tolerable limits.

A parole board is in an analogous position in the case of the one parolee in a hundred who commits a new crime despite a high score. So long as it is denied absolute certainty, a parole board can avoid paroling that individual only by denying parole to every applicant, even to those with the highest scores. This is not only a manifest injustice to the overwhelming number of high-scorers who will in fact be successful; it is also a denial of the very rationale of the parole system. But, so long as it cannot infallibly select out the future culprit, as the board releases more and more high-scoring parolees, the greater is the likelihood that it will release that one individual who will commit a new crime.

In the future, more accurate selection may well be possible, largely through the discovery of better prediction factors. There is little likelihood, however, that any one factor or combination of factors will ever be found unequivocally separating out nonviolators from violators. The best that can reasonably be hoped for is a better experience table with a more accurate calculation of parole risks.

In the absence of an experience table, other ways of assessing parole risks must be used. Recent studies show that, in the long run, though the experience table can neither choose all nonviolators nor reject all violators, more of the former and fewer of the latter can be selected with its aid than without it.

Without the knowledge embodied in an experience table, parole decisions are likely to be based either on factors irrelevant to parole success and failure or on criteria other than parole success and failure, for example, the moral offensiveness of the original crime.

Homicide and sex offenses have been found to be relatively favorable to parole success, burglary not. Yet, because the former are almost universally regarded as more serious crimes, there is an understandable temptation to take the heinousness of a crime as a deciding factor in granting or denying parole. If it does this, not only does a parole board lose its unique function and become another punitive authority; it also tends by its decisions to drive the violation rate upward.

Weight should doubtless be given, especially in borderline cases, to the fact that, however seldom parolees originally convicted of homicide repeat their crime, such repetition is a more serious matter than continued burglary. Nevertheless, if the parole system is to exist at all, its aim cannot be to parole those whose continued criminality will only mildly threaten society but those who, on the evidence, appear most likely not to commit further crimes of any sort. The parole system is founded on the belief that, whatever the nature of the original crime, rehabilitation is possible. Its basic task is to assess, not the degree of threat to society of various kinds of crime, but the probability that, whatever the original crime, rehabilitation has occurred and, with adequate parole supervision, will continue.

Finally, the experience table avoids the danger that parole boards will take into account too few factors in judging prospective parolees. The tendency to drift back into criminality is the result not of one factor but of several. Strong family interest in the prisoner and an adequate job can do much to counteract negative factors. Prisoners' scores are an attempt to combine in manageable and succinct form the multiple factors that, according to past experience and theory alike, are important in determining parole success and failure.

---

adaptation 7   *FALLACIES CONCERNING THE*
                  SEX OFFENDER

Abridged and adapted from The Habitual Sex Offender, *Report and Recommendations of the Commission on the Habitual Sex Offender, as formulated by Paul W. Tappan, Technical Consultant to the Commission (State of New Jersey, 1950), pp. 13–16.*

[Few social problems are susceptible of easy and effortless solution. Obstacles of all sorts stand in the way: vested interests, lack of financial and human resources, apathy, human frailty of one kind or another. Not the least of these obstacles is the human emotion of fear and its tendency to distort the facts and provoke hasty action.

In the following report to the New Jersey State Legislature are listed ten fallacies concerning sex offenders. The report makes two main points. One is that, though recent laws concerning sex offenses were presumably designed to safeguard the community from the "sex fiend," their practical result is undue punishment of the minor deviate. The second is that under these laws the sex deviate is deprived of due process (a similar problem arises in the handling of juveniles). Under these laws an alleged sex offender is not charged with a crime and convicted, and imprisoned according to standard legal procedure. Instead he is brought before a civil tribunal and, if adjudicated a sex offender, can be confined to a mental hospital for an indeterminate period of time although he is not insane and has not been declared to be insane.]

It may be useful to consider a number of the propositions upon which public fears have been fed in relation to the sex offender. These assumptions have been a basis for much ineffective legislation enacted in a number of states in recent years. The futility of these laws has proceeded from the inaccuracy of views that have been held widely but without scientific or critical investigation. Their popularity must be attributed in the main not to any foundation in fact but to exploitation of the peculiarly intense anxieties about sex crime that most people feel. Single instances of the crimes of "sex fiends" are given widest currency along with demands for heroic remedies, while more objective studies of the prevalence of such behavior and its possible prevention and treatment are relegated to specialized technical journals, scholarly monographs, and legislative reports such as this one.

Every conceivable variety of approach has been recommended from some quarter in recent months to "meet the sex problem." Most of these have been put into operation somewhere, either legally or extralegally: increased publicity, the death penalty, doubling the prison sentence, life terms, prohibition of parole, castration, sterilization, the administration of sex hormones or goat-gland extracts, psychoanalysis, shock treatment, state hospital custody for life or for indeterminate periods, brain surgery, group therapy, and many others. Some "authorities" recommend in one overheated breath the greatest possible severity of punishment for all sex deviates and in their next impetuous exhalation declare that the problem is medical and must be turned over at once and in its entirety to psychiatrists.

Some of the more significant and prevalent fallacies are presented below very briefly. The immediate purpose is merely to point toward certain crucial areas where error serves only to complicate our difficulties. These are some of the commonly cherished but quite erroneous views that are vitally related to policy considerations:

1. *There are tens of thousands of homicidal sex fiends abroad in the land.* In fact, the vast majority of sex deviates are minor offenders, most of whom never come to official attention. It has been estimated by Dr. Kinsey that not more than 5 per cent of our convicted sex offenders are of a dangerous variety, exercising force or injury upon a victim. Crime reports support this finding. Homicide associated with sex crimes is unusual. A study by the criminologist, E. H. Sutherland, shows that the "danger of murder by a relative or other intimate associate is very much greater than the danger of murder by an unknown sex fiend." Nearly 90 per cent of the murders of females he studied were committed by relatives or suitors, and 25 per cent of those who murdered females committed suicide.

2. *Sex offenders are usually recidivists.* In fact, sex offenders have one of the lowest rates as "repeaters" of all types of crime. Among serious crimes, homicide alone has a lower rate of recidivism. Careful studies of large samples of sex criminals show that most of them get into trouble only once. Of those who do repeat, a majority commit some crime other than sex. Only 7 per cent of those convicted of serious sex crimes are arrested again for a sex crime. Those who recidivate are characteristically minor offenders, such as peepers, exhibitionists, and homosexuals, rather than criminals of serious menace.

3. *The sex offender progresses to more serious types of sex crime.* It is the consensus among psychiatrists—and their views are confirmed by crime statistics—that sex deviates persist in the type of behavior in which they have discovered satisfaction. Any thoroughly frustrated, rigidly repressed personality may conceivably explode into violence, but there is no evidence that this occurs more frequently among sex offenders than among others. Progression from minor to major sex crimes is exceptional.

4. *It is possible to predict the danger of serious crimes being committed by sex deviates.* Reports from 75 prominent psychiatrists reveal a consensus that it is impossible to predict the occurrence of serious crime with any accuracy. This inability to predict is of special importance in relation to recent laws that are designed to constrain individuals who have committed no law violations or are minor sex deviates or even juveniles.

5. *"Sex psychopathy," or sex deviation, is a clinical entity.* Two-thirds of the psychiatric authorities consulted by the writer pointed to wide disagreement among psychiatrists as to the meaning of the term, "sex psychopath." More than half of them maintained that this condition is not a sufficiently clear diagnostic entity to justify legislation concerning the type. Hospital authorities handling cases of "sex psychopaths" committed by the courts find, in fact, a wide variety of psychological types: neurotics, psychotics,

schizoids, feeble-minded persons, epileptics, constitutional homosexuals, alcoholics, and many who are normal. In different states the authorities look for different symptoms as evidence of dangerous sexual psychopathy; the cases they adjudicate as sex deviation display varied forms of behavior and assorted types of personality organization.

6. *These individuals are oversexed.* From the point of view of their treatment and their dangerousness, it is important to realize that most of the sex deviates treated under the laws are undersexed rather than hypergonadal types. A majority are passive or nonaggressive. The problem is very rarely one of drives too strong to control, as commonly recommended programs of castration, sterilization, and close correctional custody would imply.

7. *Effective treatment methods to cure sex offenders are already known and employed.* In fact, as compared with other types of psychological and constitutional abnormality, we are peculiarly at a loss in the handling of abnormal sex offenders. Methods of effective treatment have not yet been worked out. The states that have passed special laws on the sex deviate do not even attempt treatment! The "patients" are kept in bare custodial confinement. This point is central to the atrocious policy of those jurisdictions that commit noncriminals and minor deviates for indefinite periods to mental hospitals where no therapy is offered. Most psychiatrists agree that psychotherapy of some sort should be given to sex offenders, but they also agree that professional staffing is not available to perform this work and that an unknown but undoubtedly very high percentage of deviates would not respond to such treatment. In private practice the treatment applied to the sex deviate by many psychiatrists is designed to help him to accept his peculiarity without guilt feelings and to be more discreet in its expression. The point should be stressed that commitment of a sex deviate to a state mental hospital does not imply clinical treatment. These institutions lack the space, the personnel, the treatment methods, or even the desire to handle deviated sex offenders who are nonpsychotic.

8. *The laws passed recently in one-fourth of the states are getting at the brutal and vicious sex criminal.* Data secured from the several jurisdictions reveal that, although the laws were passed in response to public fears about dangerous and aggressive offenders, in fact these are the types least frequently brought under the statutes in actual administration. Most of the persons adjudicated are minor deviates and rarely if ever "sex fiends."

9. *Indeterminate commitment to a mental hospital of the sex deviate is similar to our handling of the insane and, therefore, human liberties and due process are not involved.* This type of thinking has been used in several states to support long-term custody of minor deviates. Laws have been passed which permit indeterminate confinement of an alleged sex deviate to a mental hospital although he has neither been declared in-

sane nor convicted on a criminal charge. Yet no sound reason has ever been advanced for committing a "peeper" to a mental hospital for an indeterminate period (or any period) of time where he will be segregated from his community and family in an unproductive existence at state expense. Nevertheless, this has become common practice today under recent legislation throughout the country. Moreover, such confinement constitutes in effect not only a kind of punishment but an infringement of individual liberty without due process of law.

10. *The sex problem can be solved merely by passing a new law.* Common sense must indicate the contrary. Certainly experience with these laws reveals the futility of ineffectual legislation. In general the statutes appear to have served the purpose only of temporarily satisfying the public that "something is being done." In fact, and fortunately, very little is being done under the sex-psychopath laws, but that little is worse in effect than leaving the offender to the operation of the traditional criminal law. Thus far no problems have been resolved by the new sex laws. On the contrary, some dangerous precedents have been established: (1) for judging and confining individuals without ordinary due process—in five states, without even a criminal charge; (2) for indeterminate commitments to mental hospitals of individuals who are not insane and who deviate little or not at all from the normal; and (3) for providing hospital custody to a growing body of minor sex deviates who are to be held until "cured"—though without treatment—at great cost to the taxpayer and with serious diminution of the facilities available for those mental patients who *are* seriously disturbed.

SUGGESTIONS FOR FURTHER READING

Herbert A. Bloch, *Disorganization* (New York: Alfred A. Knopf, 1952), Chapters XIII, XIV, XV, and XVI on sexual pathologies.

Estes Kefauver, *Crime in America* (Garden City, N.Y.: Doubleday & Co., Inc., 1951).

John Bartlow Martin, *Break Down the Walls* (New York: Ballantine Books, 1954).

Walter C. Reckless, *The Crime Problem* (New York: Appleton-Century-Crofts, Inc., 1955).

Edwin H. Sutherland and Donald R. Cressey, *Principles of Criminology* (5th ed.; Philadelphia: J. B. Lippincott Co., 1955).

Frank Tannenbaum, *Crime and the Community* (New York: Columbia University Press, 1951).

Clyde B. Vedder, Samuel Koenig, and Robert E. Clark (eds.), *Criminology* (New York: Dryden Press, 1953).

Owen; Black Star

CHAPTER 5

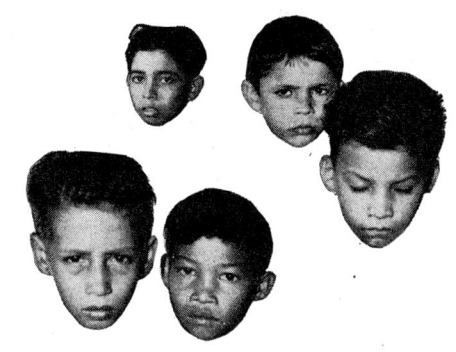

Group Prejudice:

Analyzing the Problem

Section I: What Is the Problem?

Lord Bryce once said that there is a solution to every social problem but one: group prejudice. If this is true in America, it is certainly not because of blanket indifference. Our national leaders have unequivocally laid down America's official attitude toward group prejudice:

President Eisenhower: "We must wipe out every inequality of opportunity." [1]

Bishop Oxnam, as president of the country's largest federation of Protestant churches: "Bigotry breeds sin . . . selfishness . . . Godlessness." [2]

Cardinal Cushing, when he was Archbishop of Boston: "Religious and racial bigotry is a godless disease of the ignorant mind." [3]

George Meany, as president of the nation's largest amalgam of labor unions: "Group hatred breeds itself and smothers the democratic way of life." [4]

---

[1] Los Angeles speech, October 9, 1952, as reported in the New York *Herald Tribune,* October 10, 1952.
[2] Bishop G. Bromley Oxnam, "The Nazis Aren't Licked Yet," *American Magazine,* **140** (October, 1945).
[3] Archbishop Richard J. Cushing, "Parents Are To Blame If Children Display Bigotry to Neighbors," *Boston Sunday Advertiser,* April 22, 1951.
[4] George Meany, *The AF of L Fights Bigotry* (New York: Jewish Labor Committee, 1946).

Eric Johnston, as president of the United States Chamber of Commerce: "Bigotry is expensive foolishness any way you look at it—from the economic or social angle."[5]

Yet during the same period that these uniformly disapproving statements were being made (and generally accepted as noncontroversial), the following facts were noted: A survey of 1,229 business firms conducted by the state of Pennsylvania in 1952 found that 90 per cent of these firms discriminated against minority groups for office, engineering, and sales jobs.[6] A President's Committee on Civil Rights reported an estimate that 80 per cent of the land in one metropolitan city was covered by restrictions designed to exclude certain racial, religious, or nationality groups from residence.[7] The psychologist, Gordon Allport, after a survey of available public opinion poll data concluded that 5 or 10 per cent of Americans are violently anti-Semitic, while perhaps 45 per cent more are mildly bigoted in the same direction. At least 40 per cent express prejudice against the Negro. The number that are anti-Catholic or anti-Protestant varies, but in all cases the proportion is fairly high.[8]

There would seem to be no other area in American life in which the discrepancy between official belief and overt behavior is greater. There are fifteen million Negroes in the United States, nearly a million people of other non-Caucasian racial descent, including orientals and Indians, perhaps five million Jews, and at least two million people of Mexican descent. Despite official doctrine, members of these sizable minorities are objects of group prejudice.

"Group prejudice," when used to describe a social problem in America, has a special meaning. "Group" refers almost exclusively to racial, religious, or nationality groups, and the word "prejudice" takes on more than its usual dictionary burden. The dictionary meaning of "prejudice" signifies a prejudgment which can be either favorable or unfavorable. In speaking of prejudice as a social problem, however, we always have in mind an *unfavorable prejudgment;* prejudice means "prejudice against."

But group prejudice is more than an unfavorable prejudgment. Some unfavorable prejudgments are accurate and reasonable. Having been burned by fire once, we accurately and reasonably prejudge all fires as dangerous. Group prejudice, on the other hand, is not only a prejudgment but a *misjudgment* of the facts. Whole groups are assigned grossly anti-

---

[5] Eric Johnston, *The High Cost of Bigotry* (New York: National Conference of Christians and Jews, 1951).

[6] *Civil Rights in the United States, 1953* (New York: American Jewish Congress and the National Association for the Advancement of Colored People, 1954), p. 51.

[7] *To Secure These Rights,* Report of the President's Committee on Civil Rights (New York: Simon & Schuster, 1947), p. 68.

[8] Gordon W. Allport, *The Nature of Prejudice* (Cambridge: Addison-Wesley Publishing Co., Inc., 1954).

social traits—such as avarice, stupidity, craftiness, vulgarity—and it is believed that these traits are biologically inherent in the racial, religious, or nationality group in question.

It is not, however, simple inaccuracy which is at the heart of group prejudice but rather the quality of *unreason* which sustains that inaccuracy. Reasonable men constantly revise inaccurate judgments to conform to new facts. But group prejudice has a built-in resistance to facts that do not conform to its prejudgment. It ignores or misinterprets facts to suit itself. The prejudiced person seems to have a special attachment to his prejudice.

The example of highly cultured Negroes does not disturb the conviction of the prejudiced person that all Negroes are essentially "primitive"; and Robert K. Merton has summed up vividly the way prejudice interprets facts to please itself:

> Did Lincoln work far into the night? This testifies that he was industrious, resolute, perseverant and eager to realize his capacities to the full. Do the outgroup Jews or Japanese keep the same hours? This bears witness to their sweatshop mentality, their ruthless undercutting of the American standard, their unfair competitive prices. Is the ingroup here frugal, thrifty and sparing? Then the outgroup villain (while doing the same things) is stingy, miserly and penny pinching.[9]

Group prejudice, then, might be initially described as hostility toward certain racial, religious, or nationality groups, based on unreasonable and mistaken prejudgments. Not only does it damage human beings; it also denies those human values which democracy was designed to realize and to protect.

The central focus of American tradition is the individual. The central focus of prejudice is group membership and negation of the individual. Here is the philosophic heart of the problem of group prejudice. Official American belief has it that each man is to be judged and treated in the light of what he is and can do as a unique individual. But group prejudice would have it that at least some men are to be judged and treated according to the racial, religious, or nationality group to which they belong or are assigned. "I won't hire that man *because* he is a Filipino"; "I dislike [all individuals who are] Negroes." Even if we determined that a particular racial, religious, or nationality group *is* statistically more lazy than others, this still would not tell us about the laziness of any given *individual* within that group.

Prejudice is a process of deindividualization. Some people are not eval-

---

[9] Robert K. Merton, *Social Theory and Social Structure* (Glencoe, Ill.: The Free Press, 1949), pp. 186–87.

uated as individuals, and their importance and worth as human beings are depreciated. This depreciation is, in a democracy, not only a moral issue but a severe social problem.

Not all patterns of subordination are products of prejudice. It is almost inevitable that new immigrants congregate together, occupy the lowest rungs on the economic ladder, and have relatively little share in government. But democracy, because of its moral assumptions, is a continuous process of sharing power with new and emergent groups. This ideal is seldom achieved without a struggle on the part of those subordinated, but it is nevertheless the program to which democracy is dedicated and on which it depends for its continued vitality. For democracy stakes its life, its strength, and its prosperity not on an aristocracy of the blood but on the creative energies of all its people. Government and industry must be staffed with talent discovered in the citizenry and developed by mass education. When significant numbers of citizens are prevented from developing or using their full potentialities, democracy is cut off from major sources of talent.

In a democracy, moreover, official values run counter to a policy of frozen subordination, and subordinated groups eventually take on democratic values. They learn the moral principles of official democratic doctrine and acquire the desire to participate fully and as equals in the life of society. Where prejudice stands in the way, frustration and hostility result. The tensions and mutual antipathies thus created must necessarily be a disruptive force in the community. Since World War II, the aspirations of America's largest subordinate group, the Negroes, have sharpened dramatically in conjunction with some almost revolutionary advances in status. It is this condition, rather than any new rise in prejudiced behavior, that has caused the "race question" to become such an active and even explosive problem in this country during the past decade.

Finally, prejudice, in contributing to mass conditions of underprivilege and frustration, contributes to many other social problems. For some groups it means more disease, more crime, more juvenile delinquency. In heterogeneous America, prejudice is nothing less than a root social problem.

Section II: Manifestations of Prejudice

The word "prejudice" is customarily used to describe both a kind of attitude and a kind of behavior. It is necessary, however, to distinguish between prejudiced behavior and prejudiced attitudes, which do not always go hand in hand. For example, two different employers may refuse to hire a qualified man because he is a Negro. The first may do so because he is opposed to any hint of social equality for the Negro. The second may reject the Negro applicant solely out of apprehension about customer reaction. Conceivably he may not have a prejudiced attitude at all, despite the fact that he engages in the same discriminatory behavior as the other employer.

KINDS OF PREJUDICED BEHAVIOR

There are different degrees and levels on which prejudiced behavior can occur. *Discrimination* is the differential treatment of a minority group in ways that directly impose restrictions on its members politically, economically, or socially. Not all prejudiced behavior is discrimination. Social avoidance of minority groups does not qualify as discrimination, because the prejudiced person imposes limitations on his own actions rather than on those of the minority group. For example, he quietly refuses to eat in a restaurant where a Negro is eating, whereas in the case of discrimination the Negro himself is prohibited from eating in that restaurant. Manifestations of prejudice short of discrimination are often called *personal prejudice*. By the same token, acts of *physical violence* must be distinguished from "mere" discrimination.

Personal prejudice may be limited to the area of interpersonal relations without necessarily being translated into an all-pervasive system of political and economic disadvantage for minority group members. Similarly, discrimination may exist without acts of physical violence.

Physical attack, where it exists, is usually the most immediate concern of minority groups, followed by discrimination, followed by personal prejudice. The organized Negro community, for example, was for a time most concerned with protection against outright violence and lynching. Now that lynching has become relatively outmoded, its attention has shifted more urgently to political and economic discrimination. Social equality on an interpersonal level is at present not a major working goal.

A CHART OF PREJUDICED BEHAVIOR

Physical Attack

Genocide: An attempt to exterminate an entire group, e.g., the murder of six million Jews by Hitler's government. This is necessarily an official, governmental policy and is, of course, *not* an American phenomenon.

Violence: "Unofficial" physical attack on individual members of a minority group. Although illegal, it may be abetted by the discriminatory laxity of law-enforcement agencies. Lynching and race riots are the two most spectacular forms of intergroup violence, but they are quite

Dixie Segregation Plan Offered by Judge Ward

By ASSOCIATED PRESS

Arkansas gubernatorial candidate Lee Ward said that if he wins the race he will enlist all Southern governors in a drive to make school segregation legal under federal statutes.

The Paragould Chancellor reiterated campaign statements that he believes in segregation and practices it.

"And I believe in the right of local self-government in matters concerning segregation or integration," he added.

In a televised speech made in Memphis (over WHBQ-TV last night), Ward said ... important question ...kansas and the Sou... to restore our an... local self-governme...

He said recent U... Court decisions or... had taken away th... Ward said one... official acts as go... be to call a confere... ern chief executive... specific change in...

...tion of our federal law, as it is now interpreted by our Supreme Court."

He said Southern governors could get their states' congressional delegations to support the proposed change.

School Closings Loom in Charlottesville As U.S. Judge Signs Integration Order

RICHMOND, Va., Sept. 13 (AP) — Charlottesville, Va., came to the brink of school closings today. A United States District Judge signed an order directing the city to admit twelve Negro pupils to the white schools.

The judge, John Paul, denied the request of city school officials for a stay of his order pending an appeal. He holds that the two schools affected—Lane High School and Venable Elementary School—would not open until Sept. 22, he said there would be ample time for attorneys to try for a stay.

As a result, the state closed the school under its "massive resistance" anti-integration laws. The order Judge Paul signed today is effective immediately. Attorneys for the Charlottesville school board agreed to the...

Negro Political Group to List Candidates
Wednesday Night Mass Meeting

Vote-O-Rama, a group dedicated to getting out the negro vote, will announce tomorrow night the candidates it will support in the coming elections.

J. F. Estes, Vote-O-Rama chairman and a negro attorney, said today there will be a mass meeting at 8 p.m. tomorrow at Temple AME Church, Wellington and Pontotoc, with song and band music.

"Know what and whom to vote," said.

Wilburn, negro candidate to Tennessee Legislature, will advocate areas as state and for negroes, use of county school buildings.

SCHOOL UNIT DEFIES COURT ON NEGROES

Virginia Group Denies Admission To 30 on Race

By The Associated Press

The Charlottesville, Va., School Board, under virtual order to admit some Negroes to white schools this fall, has rejected the applications of all 30 Negroes to those schools.

The action was made known by an attorney for the National Assn. for the Advancement of Colored People a few hours after Gov. Almond met secretly on the school ...

ALABAMA CASE DECRIED

Canadian Judges Say Negro's Execution Would Stir World

Special to The New York Times

TORONTO, Sept. 12—If Alabama electrocutes Jimmy Wilson it will shock the conscience of the world, a group of Canadian judges warned today.

Yesterday the Alabama Supreme Court refused to hear a plea from Wilson, a 55-year-old Negro handyman who is scheduled to die Oct. 24 for robbing an elderly white woman of $1.95.

At a meeting here today, the Canadian Section of the International Commission of Jurists authorized Justice J. T. Thorson, president of the Federal Exchequer Court, to convey to Gov. James Folsom of Alabama a resolution expressing deep concern over the case and asking the Governor to intervene.

The jurists were highly disturbed that the sentence of death should be associated with the crime of night-time robbery with violence, for which the maximum penalty in Canada is life imprisonment with lashes.

NEGRO YOUTH FAILS IN MOVE TO ENTER ALL-WHITE SCHOOL

By JAY JENKINS
Charlotte Observer and Atlanta Journal-Constitution

...C., Sept. 6—A Raleigh Negro failed in his effort to crack ... in the public schools of ...

...ict ...or-...ool ...it ...felt ...iam ...ligh

...ley ...ime ...urt ...be-...ex-...nis-...dies der the state's Pupil Assign[ment]... meant that North Carolina ...

Judge Stanley pointed out the assignment law says that "reassignment of the child to such school will be for the best interest of the child and will not interfere with the proper administration of the school, with the proper instruction of the pupils there enrolled, and will not endanger the health or safety of the children."

The judge added that ... be based on some type ... tainly the board is ... the applicants for rea... to those and other rev...

He added that in cases "mutual good fa... state and its citizens is ...

The Week in ...
Ground was broken ... Bishop Paul N. Garbe... Methodist College, ... Commission and Pie... Railroad Co. reached ... relief to a ... in Charlotte ...

... The Advisory Budget Commission allocated $1.5 million for capital improvements at community colleges in Asheville, Wilmington and Charlotte... The Commission on Reorganization of State Government announced it will recommend a multi-million dollar bond issue to the 1959 legislature for the purpose of erecting a state office building... Judge Basil M. Boyd of Charlotte's Recorder Court stepped down ...

Little Rock Wins Stay; Integration Again Delayed

From AP and UPI

LITTLE ROCK, Ark., Aug. 21 — The Little Rock School Board was granted a court stay today, which means it can avoid integration until the U. S. Supreme Court rules on the issue.

Central High School, torn by rioting and surrounded by troops during the integration crisis last fall, ...

NORTH CAROLINA

Maine: A Glass House

Racial Prejudice Still Rampant At Summer Resorts

By STEVE RILEY (Staff Writer)

The State of Maine is like a big glass house when it comes to discrimination. Its citizens might be well advised not to cast stones at the South until their own house is in order.

For there's plenty of evidence that racial prejudice still exists on a wide scale at Maine summer resorts.

Right now a Jew, with an obviously Jewish name, will find he is not wanted in many resorts and even in some motels.

And there are indications that in the future when Negroes begin to come to Maine in greater numbers they will run into even more trouble finding accommodations.

"If you think the Jewish problem is big," says a man close to the state's vacation-travel industry, "just wait until the Negroes start coming. I just don't know where they'll stay."

That's only one man's opinion, to be sure, but it comes from a person who is close enough to the picture to know what's going on.

Jews Suffering

But because large numbers of Negroes aren't vacationing in Maine, the principal group to suffer from racial prejudice here are the Jews, not only out-of-state visitors, but highly respected Maine residents as well.

Take the routine case of some prominent Portland Jews who were hosts to guests from Canada and, wanting to entertain them well, called to make dinner reservations at a well-known Kennebunkport hotel.

The call was put through and reservations made for the party. Then — but here's the way the Portlander who did the calling puts it:

New Hollywood Movie Has Sensitive Racial Plot

BY ROI OTTLEY

Prominent south side leaders recently witnessed a preview showing of a new Hollywood film, "The Defiant Ones," which proved to be a sternly eloquent handling of the strained relations between white and Negro.

What mostly impressed the assembled Negroes about this movie, starring Tony Curtis and Sidney Poitier, was the forthright handling of one of ...

Sheriff Is Honest

But the film's sweep and honesty to social facts permits it to generalize about white and Negro beyond these two symbolic but hapless fugitives.

For example, the sheriff hunting them is portrayed as a person concerned with the basic concepts of the law. As a consequence, he prevents the chase by a posse from de...

Negro Housing Project Bids Are Opened

$3,737,033 Is Low On 320 Apartments

Memphis Housing Authority got a low bid of $3,737,033 by G. E. Bass Construction Co. of Jackson, Miss., today for building a 320-apartment negro housing project on the south side of Crump Blvd.

Walter Simmons, executive di...

Negroes Win Strike, Store Serves Them

OKLAHOMA CITY, Aug. 21 (UPI)—Store officials at Katz Drug Co., today gave in to Negro youths who went on a "sit-down" strike for fountain service. They began to serve the Negroes.

The youths had occupied all seats of the store soda counter for several hours today, protesting the store's policy of serving Negroes only when they want food to be taken away for consumption elsewhere.

The store's manager, J. B. Masoner, had no comment on the change this afternoon. Earlier today he said the Negroes could sit at the lunch counter "as long as they wish, but they won't be served."

Integration of Families in Eastwick Is Biggest Problem, Report Says

By JOSEPH M. GUESS
Of The Bulletin Staff

Housing must be provided for both whites and Negroes in Eastwick if the $100 million urban renewal project is to succeed.

The problem is: How much Negro housing is feasible in proportion to white housing?

If this can be solved, there's enough demand now and in the future to put Eastwick over the top in a maximum of 13 years.

These are the conclusions reached by the University of Pennsylvania's Institute for Urban Studies after a two-year, top-level survey made for the Philadelphia Redevelopment Authority.

High Cost of Housing

40 minutes of travel time from center city Philadelphia, Eastwick can expect a demand for some 26,400 sales homes and 4,900 rental units by 1970, the ...

...17,860 units—still more than the 8,500 to 10,500 units which will be available under present plans.

The rental picture is quite dif...

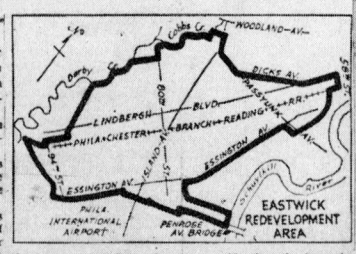

different matters. Lynching, the extralegal execution of a person by a mob, is one-way violence. A race riot is more often two-way violence and indicates a higher level of resistance among minority groups.

Discrimination

In citizenship: Interference with equal participation in government or with equal protection under the law. Prohibited by the United States Constitution, this interference has usually been accomplished extralegally.

In employment: Economic discrimination at its most direct. It may take the form of total exclusion by an employer or union or of selective exclusion, i.e., exclusion of minority members from certain preferred categories of employment. A minority member is often said to be "underemployed" when he is frozen in a job category below his skills or capacities. Employment discrimination may manifest itself in preferential hiring, whereby members of minority groups are hired last and fired first. Or it may take the form of differential wages. Employment discrimination in the professions is more subtle. Negroes are often excluded from local medical societies and thereby from hospitals.

In education: In the South educational discrimination has taken the form of rigid segregation (separate schools). In nonsegregated schools, especially at the vocational and college level, discrimination appears in the quota system (a ceiling on the number who may be admitted from a minority group). Segregated schools have, in practice, meant inferior education for minority members (inferior facilities, less capable teachers, lower expenditures). In the case of trade schools and schools of higher learning, minority members often find themselves without even a segregated school to which they might be admitted, so that they are totally excluded from learning certain types of higher skills, particularly professional skills. Consequently, educational discrimination has not only interfered with self-realization but has been an integral part of economic discrimination. In addition, segregation by public agencies, such as the school, institutionalizes prejudice and makes it an authoritative part of the cultural scene.

In housing: Housing discrimination is essentially a matter of segregation. As in education, this has often meant inferior housing for the segregated, regardless of economic status, because of a persistent shortage of new housing. Housing discrimination results in overcrowding in Negro areas and higher rentals relative to white areas. It also often entails violence when Negroes try to move into white neighborhoods.

In places of public accommodation: Exclusion and segregation also occur in areas of public accommodation where citizens ordinarily mingle: restaurants, transportation facilities, theaters, parks, and other places of amusement. Some feel that exclusion from semipublic community organizations is discrimination rather than personal prejudice. These are the facilities which, even when privately owned, carry a tradition of public responsibility; for example, when a privately run recreation center for the youth of a community excludes Negroes, this is discrimination rather than "mere" personal prejudice because Negro youth are thereby excluded from a community experience.

Personal Prejudice

Avoidance: Avoidance, as a form of prejudiced behavior, does not directly impose any restriction on the object of prejudice. Instead, the prejudiced person imposes restrictions on himself. He does not insist that the minority group avoid him; he takes it upon himself to avoid the minority group and arranges his own social and public life accordingly.

Some forms of social avoidance are forms of discrimination. A group of businessmen who set up a "service" club for the purpose not only of accomplishing some civic purpose but of meeting socially presumably have the privilege of determining their own admission standards. Nevertheless, members of minority groups are thereby excluded not only from personal contacts which might be helpful to them economically but also from an important channel of community leadership, status, and respect. This argument has been extended, less strenuously, to admission standards of private social clubs as well.

Defamation: The prejudiced person may merely "speak" his prejudice. "They are lazy," "They are dirty," or simply "They are different," or "I don't like them." It has been pointed out that avoidance and defamation, especially when practiced by parents and other opinion-molders, transmit and support those attitudes which in others may become discriminatory behavior and even violent behavior. Even latent prejudice is a force which can potentially be "fired" at certain moments of stress.

KINDS OF PREJUDICED ATTITUDES

"Prejudice" is often used in a more limited sense to refer to *attitudes* of prejudice as distinct from *acts* of prejudice. These attitudes may or may not be acted out, and may or may not directly determine prejudiced behavior. These attitudes may vary widely in intensity and quality, partly because any given manifestation of prejudice is usually a *complex of attitudes* which is likely to include some combination of the following elements:

> In July, 1951, Harvey E. Clark, a Negro bus-driver, and his family tried to move into an apartment he had rented in Cicero, a suburb of Chicago. This was a previously all-white residential area. A three-day riot ensued. Thousands of white persons armed with bricks, stones, iron pipes, and other weapons engaged in wholesale attacks upon Negroes, police, and National Guardsmen. At one point there were estimated to be some 4,000 rioters. Firebrands were thrown onto the roof and into the windows of the apartment house. Mobs broke through the police lines and did extensive property damage. Nineteen persons were injured.
>
> In July, 1951, a group of scientists arranged to hold a luncheon at a well-known club maintained by some of Chicago's most respectable citizens. The scientists invited Dr. Percy Julian, eminent Negro scientist, to attend the luncheon. The club refused to admit him. This incident immediately became public knowledge.
>
> The difference in prejudiced behavior between the violent rioters of Cicero and the gentle avoiders of the Chicago club reflected nothing more, perhaps, than a difference in class status. The policy-makers of the Chicago club were undoubtedly shocked by the lawless violence employed at Cicero, as were all the leadership circles in Chicago. But their own policy of exclusion demonstrated that they really had no disagreement with the Cicero rioters about the social undesirability of Negroes.

Overidealization of One's Own Group

Uncritical rejection of other groups is often paired with an equally uncritical acceptance of one's own group, its values, and its ways of behaving. This tendency of an individual to identify strongly with his own group and to devalue whatever is foreign to it has been called "ethnocentrism." The ethnocentric individual is likely to feel at home only with what is familiar, to be uneasy and suspicious in the presence of the new and strange, and to interpret what is merely different as dangerous and threatening.

Stereotypes

Like prejudgments, stereotypes are part of the economy of experience. We cannot always respond to every clerk, every banker, every child, in terms of his unique characteristics. Thus we often develop *stereotyped* ways of responding to whole classes of people, that is, we follow standardized and preformed patterns of behavior in their presence. We may treat clerks arrogantly, bankers respectfully, children condescendingly.

Stereotyped images often accompany stereotyped behavior. We are apt to carry in our heads an image of "the banker"—symbolizing all bankers—as a dignified, gray-haired, distinguished-looking gentleman. It is an image which evokes and sustains "appropriate" attitudes of trust and respect. Like prejudgments, stereotypes may be favorable or unfavorable, but prejudicial stereotypes invariably carry negative overtones. They constitute symbolic images that prompt and foster feelings of disapproval, condescension, and sometimes fear and suspicion. The hook-nosed Jew, the dozing Mexican, the Negro mammy, the sly-looking oriental, are familiar stereotypes in the dreary gallery of prejudice.

Stereotypes, whether favorable or unfavorable, tend to be self-confirming. They are prefabricated images of the world, and the tendency is to shape reality to fit these images rather than to revise the images. For instance, stereotypes can so distort perception that to the highly prejudiced person all orientals may actually seem to have a sly expression in the same way that, to overly sentimental people, all children look innocent. And, even more insidiously, when the deviation of a minority group member from the stereotype is too obvious to be ignored, he is merely made the "exception that proves the rule." When an individual who is Jewish does not conform to the physical stereotype, the stereotype is not rejected as inadequate, but it is said of him that "He doesn't look Jewish."

Sometimes, if strongly enough established, the stereotype can actually bend reality to its image. This is most likely to occur if the individual is given a measure of approval and security when he conforms to the stereotype and meets with hostility when he violates it. The positive stereotype of the honest banker undoubtedly encourages bankers to be honest, but the negative stereotype of the Negro places a burden upon the intelligent and ambitious Negro, who must often resign himself to encountering constant tension and even overt aggression in his relations with whites. By placing a day-to-day liability upon efforts to break through its confines, the negative stereotype has the effect of encouraging Negroes either to be, or to pretend to be, lazy and unintelligent—a tendency that is further strengthened by severe limitation of opportunities for education and achievement.

Scapegoating

Prejudice sometimes carries with it the temptation to blame the minority group against which it is directed for all manner of social ills and problems. At the time of the Roman emperors, the Church Father Tertullian wrote: "If the Tiber overflows, if there is famine or pestilence, at once they cry: 'To the lions with the Christians.'" Frustration in the face of seemingly insoluble problems or of personal incapability and guilt is often the forerunner of scapegoating. There is the need for an identifiable object against which aggression can be directed. Natural catastrophes such as floods, or economic catastrophes such as depressions, do not provide such a simple enemy. Scapegoating is not only a device for evading reality; it is also a means of projecting guilt feelings upon others. The term itself is derived from a Biblical practice of symbolically laying the sins of a community upon the head of a goat and driving the goat into the wilderness; the community then felt purged of its iniquities.

Political demagogues have often deliberately stimulated scapegoating tendencies in order to solidify popular support, to arouse "moral indignation," and to divert public attention from the real sources of prevailing problems. The temptation to look for a scapegoat in situations of social stress and disorganization is a common occurrence, and minority groups, because they are seen as intrinsically antisocial, are particularly vulnerable in this respect. But different minority groups, because of their peculiar histories and because of the peculiar stereotyped images which have been created around them, may serve different scapegoating purposes. Some extreme opponents of school desegregation in the South have attacked the movement for integration as a conspiracy and have settled upon Jews rather than Negroes as its hidden leaders. The stereotype of the Jew commonly includes the myth of political power and conspiracy; the relatively powerless Negro could not so well fit the role.

Some prejudice seems to be little more than a product of ethnocentrism and stereotyped imagery, hardly distinguishable from provincialism and narrow-mindedness, on the one hand, or from snobbery and contempt for the "lower classes," on the other. Prejudice against southern and central European immigrants seems as a rule to be of this order. Anti-Catholic, anti-Negro, and anti-Semitic prejudices, on the other hand, are deeper; they involve the strong emotions of "moral indignation" and fear; often they are bolstered by elaborate ideologies. By an "ideology" is often meant any broad system of ideas, but in the context of prejudice the word is also used to signify a system of thought whose main function is to rationalize some unreasonable belief.

Ideologies differ. Anti-Negro feeling includes allegations of biological inferiority, sexual immorality, and laziness. Anti-Semitism, on the other hand, is rationalized by the somewhat opposite assertions of shrewdness, clannishness, and business acumen. Where the Negro is typically accused of inferiority and shunned, the Jew is typically accused of economic and political chicanery and blamed. The peculiar constellation of emotions and ideology applied to each is in part a reflection of the different positions occupied by Negroes and Jews in American life: Negroes are an economically and educationally depressed group; Jews, as a group, are not. The history and status of the target groups themselves become, then, a factor in shaping manifestations of prejudice.

Section III: Effects of Prejudice

The rock-bottom criticism of group prejudice is that it is morally wrong and conflicts with the value assumptions of our dominant religions and our American political philosophy. But while morality may be its own reward, certain "practical" damages have variously been charged to group prejudice.

SOCIAL AND POLITICAL EFFECTS

On democratic morality. The President's Committee on Civil Rights reported: "The pervasive gap between our aims and what we actually do is creating a kind of moral dry rot which eats away at the emotional and rational bases of democratic beliefs." [10] If a cornerstone principle is flagrantly breached in one circumstance, it is that much less secure in all circumstances and breeds a general cynicism.

On democratic vitality. Subordination of certain groups and mutual antipathies between groups are apparently natural phenomena that have marked every society. But democracy is a society "in constant change," where subordinate groups continuously emerge to share power and provide fresh human resources. This is the essential working process of democracy which can be threatened by the countermovement of prejudice.

On domestic politics. The issue of "white supremacy" has often been used, especially in the South, to becloud the rational discussion of other issues. This "diverting" potential of prejudice is everywhere a danger, especially in times of economic or political stress.

On international politics. The majority of the world's population is dark-skinned, and it is among these people that the current tide of nationalism, with its attendant pride and sensitivities, is strongest. Throughout Asia, Africa, and Latin America, American democracy has been measured by its treatment of racial minorities. Patterns of American discrimination have been exploited and distorted by those who are in ideological competition with America and democracy.

On social problems. The tensions and disabilities that attend group prejudice are obvious factors in many major social problems. Crime and delinquency are the most dramatic examples. In 1945, for instance, about 74 per cent of the adult offenders arrested and 73 per cent of the juvenile offenders arrested in the District of Columbia were Negroes, although

[10] *To Secure These Rights*, p. 139.

Negroes constituted only about 33 per cent of the population. Of course, comparative arrest rate is not a true index of comparative crime rate, particularly with a severely disadvantaged group. The apparent disparity in criminality is further reduced if the proportion of Negroes (or Americans of Mexican or Puerto Rican descent) arrested and convicted is compared with the arrest and conviction rate of native whites in the same socio-economic class. Artificial depression of a group by economic discrimination is always a risk factor in criminality. A point of much profounder implication is made by Gunnar Myrdal, when he states that discrimination often prevents the Negro from identifying himself with society and the law.

ECONOMIC EFFECTS

Lowered productivity and purchasing power. Because of discrimination, many skilled workers cannot secure jobs at which they would be most productive, nor can potentially productive individuals get training to realize their potential. This economically inefficient use of human resources reduces national productivity. In addition, the depressed wages and income of some minority groups reduces the consuming market potential, because very often Negroes are paid less than whites for the same job.

The duplicated costs of segregation. Estimates of the cost of unnecessary duplication in housing and educational facilities because of segregation have gone as high as $3 billion.

Increased public welfare costs. Discrimination keeps many workers unemployed although there are jobs they are qualified to perform. The customarily higher rates of disease and known crime among economically depressed groups are also reflected in the general tax rate.

PSYCHOLOGICAL EFFECTS:
ON THE TARGETS OF PREJUDICE

Ultimately prejudice exacts its greatest cost in the damage done to the psychological well-being of its targets. One of the most important results of prejudice is to incapacitate many minority group members for effective and satisfying participation not merely in the life of society but even within the minority community itself. This manifests itself first of all in higher crime and juvenile delinquency rates for some minority groups. But it manifests itself in other and more subtle ways as well.

Self-degradation. "Protective clowning," or playing the fool, has been a historic technique of the American Negro, particularly where his subordinate role is most fixed. This technique has often enabled him to slip out of trouble and, at the same time, to poke covert fun at his white "master."

Withdrawal. Group isolation is a common (and self-defeating) way of "keeping out of trouble." This has often been accompanied by psychological withdrawal. Sometimes psychological withdrawal takes the form of what appears to the dominant group as secretiveness or slyness. Other times it manifests itself more damagingly as apathy and the atrophy of all goals and ambitions.

Overcompensation. The trappings of status have often had to replace its substance. Ostentation is often a result. One Negro leader in San Francisco described the flashy cars often preferred by Negroes as "aspirin on wheels." They also reflected the fact that many Negroes cannot spend their money on something they might have preferred: better housing.

Self-hate. The target of prejudice is subject to the same cultural influences as everyone else and may finally accept the unflattering stereotype which the dominant group has of him. He may come to hate those characteristics which serve to mark him off from the majority. Thus the light-skinned Negro may shy away from the dark-skinned; the second-generation American may be embarrassed by his parents' accent and old-country customs.

PSYCHOLOGICAL EFFECTS: ON THE PREJUDICED

Psychologists point to two kinds of damage that may occur to the personality of the prejudiced individual:

Loss of contact with reality. Insofar as the prejudiced person builds his prejudices into his mind's picture of the world, he has a distorted view of the world and is less capable of coping with it. Especially when his prejudice provides him with an "explanation" for his and the world's problems, he is detoured from coming to grips with their real causes.

Strain of split values. It is part of the moral tradition of Western civilization that group prejudice is both undemocratic and irreligious. Insofar as he is touched by this tradition, the prejudiced person may feel guilty. Such a feeling of guilt may lead in vicious circles to even greater hostility toward the target of his prejudice. This conflict is, of course, minimized where local or intimate group values strongly support his prejudice.

Section IV: The Objects of Prejudice

Group differences of many kinds exist. But in the main the group differences used to justify prejudice are alleged to be *antisocial* in nature: deficiencies in values, morals, manners, character, and intelligence. Any broad-scale pattern of prejudice rests upon allegations that "they" are not merely different but are different in destructive and harmful ways.

There are certainly biological differences among groups, but scientific evidence points to the conclusion that there is no determining relation between biological traits and the antisocial traits invoked by prejudice. The overwhelming determinants of values, morals, manners, character, and intelligence are social and cultural rather than biological. Swedes behave like Swedes not because they are tall, blond, and robust but because they live in Sweden and have been brought up in a Swedish culture. A person who is short, brunet, and frail, if he is raised in Sweden, will be just as Swedish as anyone else.

By the same token, people raised in a Swedish culture *are* different from people raised in a Chinese culture. All people differ from one another to the extent that (*a*) they are members of distinct social and cultural groups or (*b*) they are accorded distinctive social treatment.

This principle does not apply to racial, religious, or nationality groups only. Sharply different economic classes of similar racial and ethnic background can differ from each other not merely in the matter of income but also in appearance, in manners, in beliefs, in values. Such differences arise inevitably. Different economic groups live in different neighborhoods, undergo different life-experiences, receive more or less education, have only limited communication and interaction with each other. "Being a worker" and "being a banker" are therefore more than occupational categories; they are social categories as well.

In the same way, "being a Negro" is not so much a biological as a social category. Negroes have been assigned a distinctive social role, have been treated in distinctive ways, and have been directed into distinctive areas of achievement. This holds for their "superiorities" as well as for their "inferiorities." Jazz has flourished among Negro musicians partly because the white stereotype has permitted and even encouraged the Negro to develop his musical talent, provided it took a "primitive" and "folksy" direction and required little or no musical training.

The following conclusions would seem to put group differences in their proper framework:

1. The social and cultural traits which characterize human groups are shaped by social and cultural influences and can be *changed* by social and cultural influences. They are not inherent or immutable.

2. They nevertheless *do* exist. When white southern parents *today* complain that the Negro children in their community are, as a group, educationally inferior to and culturally different from white children, they are undoubtedly correct.

3. Most of these social and cultural differences, however, are morally neutral, i.e., they do not involve grossly antisocial traits. Even where some group does exhibit a somewhat higher percentage of antisocial behavior

as a result of environmental circumstances (e.g., delinquency among Negroes), still only a proportionately small number of the group is involved.

4. There is a wide range of individual variation within each group. Group characterizations on the basis of percentage differences cannot be automatically applied to any one individual. This comes back to the heart of prejudice: it is finally directed, not against some abstract group, but against *individuals*.

The specific manifestations of prejudice, related as they are to group differences, are partly rooted in the peculiar history of each target group.

The American Negro

The problem of prejudice in this country is most often identified with the American Negro. Negroes comprise about 10 per cent of the national population and are the largest single target group of prejudice. This is the group that in this country has suffered most severely from prejudice and against which every form of prejudice has been directed. The problem of prejudice against Negroes has been dramatized in recent years by the sharp growth of vehement demands for equality on the part of the Negro community and, further, by the explosive postwar renaissance among the colored peoples of Asia and Africa.

BACKGROUND HISTORY

The pattern of prejudice against the American Negro is an integral part of our national history. This is one pathological condition that was not imported from the Old World. The complex nature of the phenomenon of prejudice against Negroes, and indeed of many aspects of the Negro community itself, becomes comprehensible only against the detailed background of the American past.

The South—Before the Civil War

In 1619 twenty Negroes were sold to Virginia settlers by a Dutch man-of-war. This was the beginning of American slavery, but it was not yet the beginning of racial prejudice as we understand it today.

In 1790 there were over 750,000 Negroes in the country (about 60,000 of them free), nine-tenths of them in the plantation economy of the South. At this time the slave system seemed to be losing ground; the economic need for slave labor was diminishing, and the abolitionist movement in the South was at least as strong as it was in the North. At the turn of the eighteenth century, however, the cotton-textile industry in England boomed, and with it the demand for raw cotton. The value of slaves doubled. Between 1790 and 1808, when the importation of slaves became illegal, over 100,000 slaves were brought into the country, and at least 250,000 were smuggled in subsequently. The fresh need for slavery was accompanied by the fresh need to *justify* slavery; and an extensive literature began to appear, proposing the inferiority and nonhuman status of the Negroes.

However, there was still no race-relations problem. Although there were slave revolts, relations between Negroes and whites were in general so rigidly fixed that they were not at issue.

The South—After the Civil War

The birth of our modern race-relations problem dates from the emancipation of almost four million slaves after the Civil War. During the Reconstruction period (1865–79), an attempt was made to impose equality on the South. The Thirteenth Amendment to the Constitution abolished slavery, the Fourteenth granted citizenship to the Negroes, and the Fifteenth affirmed their right to vote. Other federal civil rights measures were passed, even to the extent of prohibiting discrimination in public places. But they were enforced only when northern troops were present. Secret white societies, such as the Ku Klux Klan, sprang up against the attempt to reverse the social system of the South by force of law. When the military occupation ended, it left the South in economic and political chaos. The South was impoverished, its land cotton-exhausted, and its economic system in a shambles. The unrest of the "poor whites" was turned on the Negro, and political power was consolidated on the basis of antagonism to the Negro. The civil rights emphasis of the Reconstruction was savagely reversed. "White Supremacy" became the rallying-cry of the South, and with it came a deliberate and vocal emphasis on the concept of race prejudice to an extent unknown before Emancipation.

Northward

Following the Civil War most of the Negro population found a place within the marginal agricultural life of the South. They remained as farm laborers, as tenant farmers, or as small farm-owners, sharing to an accentuated degree the poverty of the South. More than half were concentrated in the so-called "Black Belt," which stretched through eastern Virginia, the Carolinas, Georgia, Alabama, and the lower Mississippi Valley. By 1890 there had been some movement to cities, but mainly to southern cities, and four out of five Negroes still lived in rural areas.

During World War I, over a half-million Negroes surged to the burgeoning industrial centers of the North. This movement kept pace with the growth of the industrial North and the continuing poverty of the South. Over two million Negroes left the rural areas of the South between 1900 and 1930. During these decades the Negro population in New York City rose from 97,000 to 343,000; in Chicago from 46,000 to 258,000; in Philadelphia from 85,000 to 222,000; and in Detroit from 5,000 to 128,000. These mass migrations, coupled with housing shortages, recurrent employment problems, and other growing-city stresses, were accompanied by rising levels of race prejudice in the North.

The labor needs of World War II brought an even more dramatic migration of Negroes to the industrial cities of the North and West. Between 1940 and 1950 the nonwhite population of New York City increased from 477,000 to 775,000; in Chicago from 282,000 to 509,000; in Philadelphia from 252,000 to 378,000; in Detroit from 150,000 to 303,000; and in Los Angeles from 97,000 to 211,000. About half the Negro population in the United States is now urbanized, and almost two out of five Negroes live outside the South.[11]

FIGURE 5:1 THE CHANGING PROPORTION OF THE NEGRO POPULATION IN THE UNITED STATES, 1900–1950

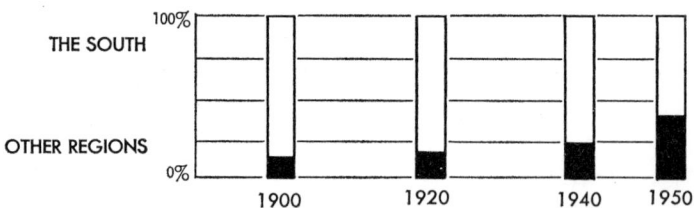

THE CHANGING LOCATION OF THE NEGRO POPULATION, 1900–1950

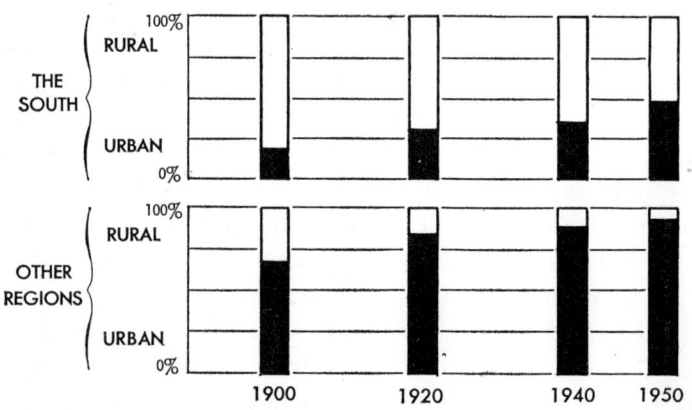

Adapted from Eli Ginzberg, *The Negro Potential* (New York: Columbia University Press, 1956), p. 15.

[11] U.S. Department of Labor, Bureau of Labor Statistics, *Negroes in the United States*, Bulletin 1119 (Washington, D.C.: U.S. Government Printing Office, 1952), p. 34.

PATTERNS OF PREJUDICE

Physical Attack

Lynching has been predominantly a southern phenomenon. According to the National Association for the Advancement of Colored People there have been over 5,000 lynchings since 1882, although more than 1,000 of those lynched have been white people. In the face of growing attention, lynchings have gradually diminished, and no mob lynching has been recorded since 1951. There is no measure of the extent to which less publicity-catching violence exists. The President's Committee on Civil Rights stated in 1947: "We are convinced . . . that the incidence of police brutality against Negroes is disturbingly high."[12] Nevertheless, the end of flagrant lynch law marks a significant turn in the road for the South.

Race riots have been largely a northern or border-state phenomenon; they have occurred mainly as a result of the tensions and migrations accompanying both world wars. Riots were reported in 26 cities in 1919. Major race riots occurred during the second World War in Chicago and Detroit, but more common has been violence on the gang and "small-mob" level. This has often occurred as a secondary expression of delinquency or where some pattern of discrimination has been threatened (e.g., where Negroes were moving into an all-white neighborhood). Violence is, perversely, often a by-product of *weakening* discriminatory patterns.

Discrimination—In Citizenship

A major disability of the Negro in the South has been his disfranchisement. Following Reconstruction, a number of ingenious devices were employed by southern states to prevent the Negro from voting. (1) The so-called "Grandfather Clause" withheld the vote from those who had not been entitled to vote in 1867 or whose ancestors had not been so entitled. This device was held unconstitutional by the United States Supreme Court in 1915. (2) Payment of a poll tax as a prerequisite for voting successfully disfranchised a million whites as well as the mass of Negroes. Originally enacted by ten southern states, it remains in five. (3) The "white primary" was also effective. State political parties held that the primary was a private affair and could legitimately exclude Negroes. In this way Negroes were in effect disfranchised, since nomination in the Democratic primary has in the past been tantamount to election in the South. In 1944 the United States Supreme Court ruled that the primary was an integral part of the election process and could not exclude Negroes. (4) Literacy and educational tests, applied arbitrarily, are tedious but foolproof bars to the Negro vote. Negroes have even been asked to recite the entire Constitution by

[12] *To Secure These Rights*, p. 27.

memory in order to qualify. (5) Sheer intimidation has always remained a final dike against the Negro vote, especially in rural areas. Theodore G. Bilbo, campaigning for re-election to the United States Senate in 1946, told audiences that the best time to tell Negroes about not voting is "the night before the election."

The gradual removal of obstacles to voting and the diminution of solid southern opposition to the Negro vote have apparently marked another clear turn in southern race relations. The number of registered Negro voters in the South rose from about 300 thousand in 1938 to about 600 thousand in 1948 to over 1 million in 1954. In the "hard-core" southern states, however, where the school-desegregation issue is still almost completely unresolved, Negro registration remains low. In Alabama, where Negroes represent 30 per cent of the voting-age population, they constitute but 6 per cent of the registered voters.

Unequal justice in the courts has been a severe hazard for the Negro in many parts of the South, often manifesting itself directly in the outspoken bias of judge or jurors. It has been accentuated in many sections by the systematic exclusion of Negroes from juries. In 1947 the United States Supreme Court ruled that in any case affecting a Negro the patterned, deliberate exclusion of Negroes from juries was ground for a mistrial.

Discrimination—In Employment

Employment discrimination is a major problem for the Negro in all sections of the nation. While some employers will hire no Negroes, the most common pattern has been to bar them from certain types of employment, restricting them to the least visible and least skilled jobs. In 1940 only about 4 per cent of nonwhite male workers were in skilled trades as against about 15 per cent of white male workers. About 2 per cent of nonwhite male workers were in sales or clerical jobs as against almost 14 per cent of white male workers.[13]

This inferior employment status was only partly a function of educational discrimination. According to the 1940 census, the median annual income of the Negro high-school graduate was only $775 as compared with $1,454 for the white high-school graduate. The median annual income of the Negro college graduate was $1,074, as compared with $2,046 for the white college graduate.[14]

This pattern changed sharply during the industrial frenzy of World

[13] U.S. Department of Labor, Bureau of Labor Statistics, *Notes on the Economic Situation of Negroes in the United States* (May, 1958), p. 6.
[14] U.S. Bureau of the Census, "Educational Attainment by Wage or Salary: 1940," *Population —Special Reports*, Series P-46, No. 5 (Washington, D.C.: U.S. Government Printing Office, June 18, 1946).

Violence: A Negro is dragged from a streetcar during the Detroit race riot of June 21, 1943.

War II. At the beginning of 1942 it was estimated that only 3 per cent of those in war industries were Negro as compared with about 8 per cent in the fall of 1944. Between 1940 and 1947 Negro males in the skilled trades increased by 25 per cent. The percentage of Negro women in sales and clerical jobs nearly tripled.[15]

A government study showed that, in 1936, 22 national unions excluded, segregated, or otherwise discriminated against Negroes.[16] In 1953 the Jewish Labor Committee informally estimated that 75 per cent of those unions that had discriminated against Negroes ten years before no longer did so.

The postwar picture continues to show increases in nonwhite employment on the higher levels. The proportion of nonwhite males employed as skilled craftsmen more than doubled between 1940 and 1957, while the

FIGURE 5:2 DISTRIBUTION OF WORKERS BY OCCUPATION, SEX, AND COLOR IN APRIL 1940 AND APRIL 1957

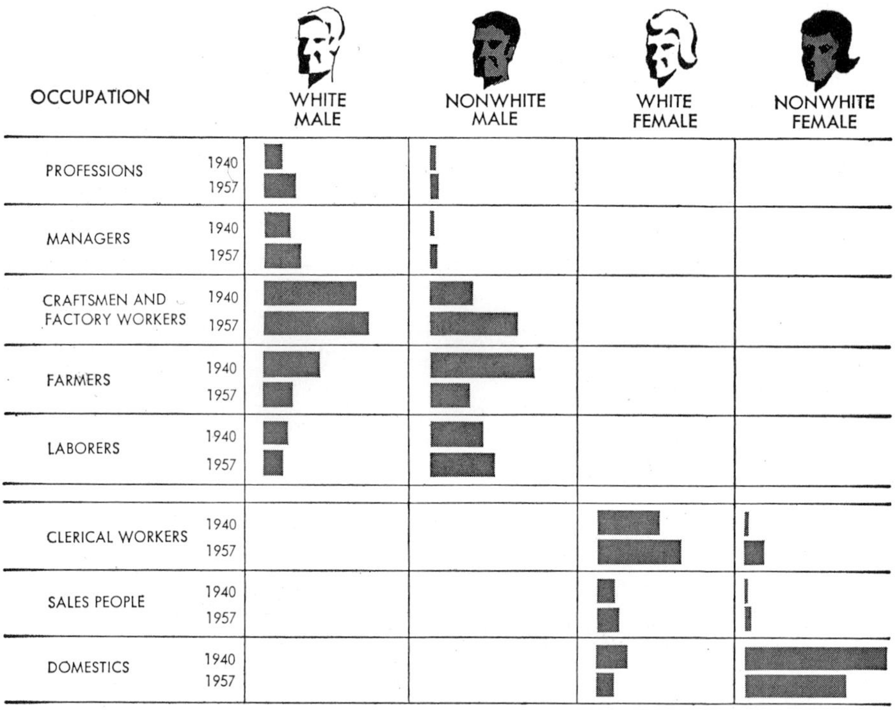

OCCUPATION		WHITE MALE	NONWHITE MALE	WHITE FEMALE	NONWHITE FEMALE
PROFESSIONS	1940				
	1957				
MANAGERS	1940				
	1957				
CRAFTSMEN AND FACTORY WORKERS	1940				
	1957				
FARMERS	1940				
	1957				
LABORERS	1940				
	1957				
CLERICAL WORKERS	1940				
	1957				
SALES PEOPLE	1940				
	1957				
DOMESTICS	1940				
	1957				

Adapted from U.S. Bureau of Labor Statistics, *Notes on the Economic Situation of Negroes in the United States* (Washington, D.C.: U.S. Department of Labor, 1958), p. 6.

---

[15] Robert C. Weaver, *Negro Labor: A National Problem* (New York: Harcourt, Brace & Co., 1946), pp. 15–17.

[16] U.S. Department of Labor, Bureau of Labor Statistics, *Handbook of American Trade Unions,* Bulletin 618 (Washington, D.C.: U.S. Government Printing Office, 1936), pp. 40–48.

proportion of white male workers in that category was rising by about 25 per cent. The proportion of nonwhite males in clerical and sales work more than tripled, while the proportion of white male workers remained about the same.

At the same time, the proportion of nonwhite laborers during this period was also increasing, from 20 to 25 per cent, while the proportion of white male laborers was decreasing from 7 to 6 per cent. Removal of the color bar starts at the bottom of the occupational ladder. The major movement of nonwhite workers from 1940 to 1957 was actually from farm work to lower-grade industrial work. There were still fewer than 15 per cent of nonwhite male workers in the relatively favorable occupations of skilled, clerical, and sales work as against over 34 per cent of white male workers.

A survey of a hundred firms with almost a million workers was made by a governor's commission in Pennsylvania in 1952. The survey showed that almost four out of ten firms discriminated against Negroes in hiring for unskilled jobs; over half discriminated in semiskilled jobs; two-thirds discriminated in skilled jobs; and nine out of ten discriminated in office and engineering jobs. During a ten-week period in 1952, the Cincinnati office of the Ohio State Employment Service reported that 76 per cent of the hiring orders from employers specified "white only." [17]

The median wage of the nonwhite worker was less than 40 per cent of the median wage of the white worker in 1940, and in 1956 it was still little more than half the median wage of the white worker.[18] Moreover, as long as a widespread pattern of discrimination persists, there is no guarantee that in

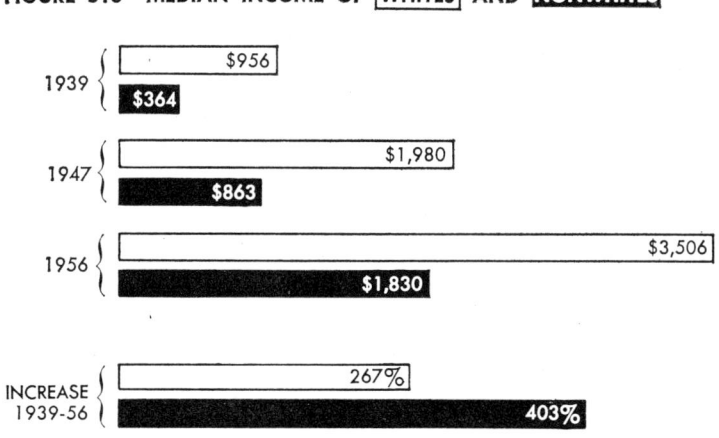

FIGURE 5:3 MEDIAN INCOME OF WHITES AND NONWHITES

1939: $956 / $364
1947: $1,980 / $863
1956: $3,506 / $1,830
INCREASE 1939-56: 267% / 403%

Adapted from U.S. Bureau of Labor Statistics, *Notes on the Economic Situation of Negroes in the United States* (Washington, D.C.: U.S. Department of Labor, 1958), p. 11.

[17] *Civil Rights in the United States, 1953*, p. 51 (see n. 6, above).
[18] *Notes on the Economic Situation of Negroes in the United States*, p. 11 (see n. 13, above).

a period of relatively slack employment recent progress will not be chipped away. Almost half of the skilled Negroes in the nation were displaced from their usual types of employment during the depression period of 1930–36, and their rate of unemployment was high. In 1957, about 3.6 per cent of the white workers in the country were unemployed as against about 7.2 per cent of nonwhite workers. A year later, after a period of economic recession, about 6.7 per cent of the white workers in the country were unemployed as against about 14 per cent of nonwhite workers. Though both percentages doubled, the proportion of unemployed white workers had increased by about 3 per cent, while the proportion of unemployed nonwhite workers had increased by about 7 per cent.[19]

Discrimination—In Education

Segregation in the public schools was legally institutionalized in the South after Reconstruction. In 1896 the Supreme Court decision in *Plessy v. Ferguson* established the principle that segregation was not a violation of constitutional rights so long as "equal" facilities were provided. The specific case at issue had to do with transportation facilities, but the "separate-but-equal" doctrine became the cornerstone of all forms of segregation.

In fact, segregated school systems have in the past never had equal facilities. In 1940, average educational expenditure in nine southern states was $50.00 for each white child, $21.00 for each Negro child. In 1940, capital outlay for school facilities in eight southern states was over $4.00 for each white student, $0.99 for each Negro student. In 1940, white teachers in twelve southern states received an average salary of $894.00 as compared with $487.00 for Negro teachers.[20]

Again, an important change has taken place in this pattern since World War II. Partly to stave off the gathering attack on segregation, the South has been moving toward making its separate educational facilities more nearly equal. In 1952, average educational expenditure for Negro students in nine southern states was 70 per cent of that for white students; it had been 43 per cent in 1940. In 1952, capital outlay in eight southern states for Negro schools was 82 per cent of the outlay for white schools; it had been 23 per cent in 1940. In 1952, Negro teachers in twelve southern states received salaries that were 87 per cent as great as the white teachers'; they had been 54 per cent as great in 1940.[21]

However, opponents of segregation have always argued that separate educational facilities can never be equal because (a) there are always unequal

---

[19] *Ibid.*, p. 8.
[20] Harry S. Ashmore, *The Negro and the Schools* (Chapel Hill: University of North Carolina Press, 1954), pp. 153, 156, 159.
[21] *Ibid.*

factors, such as distance to school; (b) the rigid social isolation is a handicap to the Negro; (c) segregation is meant to imply inferiority. In 1954, the Supreme Court ruled that separate educational facilities were unconstitutional, no matter how equal they seemed to be, and ordered the eventual abandonment of segregation in the schools. According to the Supreme Court decision, "To separate [Negro children] from others of similar age and qualifications solely because of their race may affect their hearts and minds in a way unlikely ever to be undone." In some places, especially in the border states, compliance was immediately undertaken. In the heart of the South, however, long-range campaigns of evasion and resistance were promised and undertaken by state and local governments.

Formal desegregation, even when totally implemented, will not necessarily mean desegregation *in fact*. This is indicated by the situation in the

FIGURE 5:4 CURRENT EDUCATIONAL EXPENDITURES PER PUPIL FOR WHITE AND NEGRO CHILDREN IN THE SOUTH

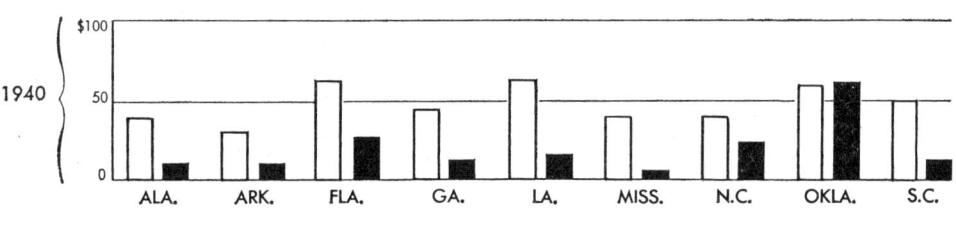

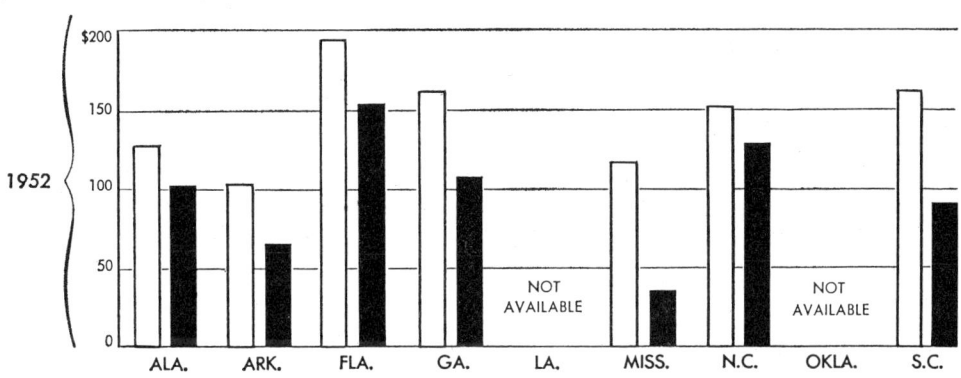

NEGRO AS A PERCENTAGE OF WHITE

Adapted from Harry S. Ashmore, *The Negro and the Schools* (Chapel Hill: University of North Carolina Press, 1954), p. 153. Figures are based on records and reports of state departments of education.

North and West, where it is probable that most Negro children are *somehow* separated in schools from whites. In some areas there is illegal segregation, but more often school segregation is a result of housing segregation and, on occasion, the gerrymandering of school districts. It has been roughly estimated that about one-fourth of Negro school children outside the South go to schools that are thoroughly mixed, one-fourth to schools that are distinctly separate, and about half to schools where there is token mixing. This pattern would largely disappear as a natural consequence of a breakdown in housing segregation.

The segregation system of higher education in the South began to crack before World War II because separate facilities, equal or unequal, often did not exist, particularly in professional and graduate schools. In 1938, the U.S. Supreme Court held that the University of Missouri had to admit Negroes to its law school because there was no similar state law school for Negroes. By 1956 about 2,500 Negro students were attending "white" colleges in the South, private and public, from which they had formerly been barred. More than 25 public and 25 private colleges in the South have admitted Negro students to one extent or another. In professional schools particularly, a quota system often operates against the Negro in all parts of the country.

Discrimination—In Housing

The pattern of geographical segregation is, by and large, more obvious in the North than in the South. In the older cities in the South, following slave and servant traditions, Negroes live on less desirable streets and alleys in all parts of the city. In the North, as in some large cities of the South, the mass migration of the Negro resulted in the formation of distinct Negro areas. Between 1940 and 1950, the urban nonwhite population increased by about

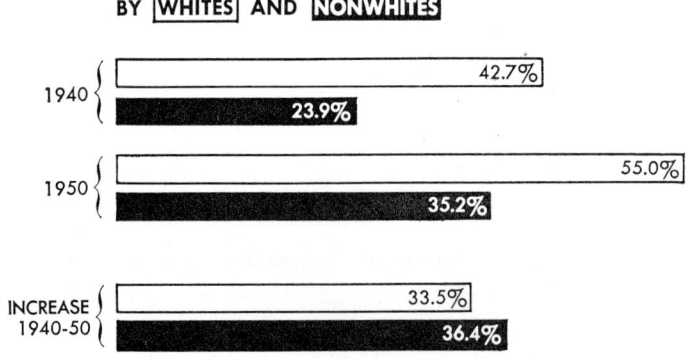

FIGURE 5:5 PROPORTION OF OWNER OCCUPANCY OF HOUSES BY WHITES AND NONWHITES

1940: 42.7% / 23.9%
1950: 55.0% / 35.2%
INCREASE 1940-50: 33.5% / 36.4%

Adapted from U.S. Bureau of Labor Statistics, *Notes on the Economic Situation of Negroes in the United States* (Washington, D.C.: U.S. Department of Labor, 1958), p. 45.

3 million, more than half of it in cities outside the South.[22] Negroes have moved chiefly into the vacuum of slums abandoned by white families. The historic "rhythm of the slums" has called for migrant populations to move out when their socio-economic status rises, to be replaced by a more recent migrant population. But unlike disadvantaged white migrant groups, the Negro has been less able to break out of slum areas.

As a result, the proportion of overcrowding for nonwhites in 1952 was four times as great as for whites. The proportion of substandard housing they occupied was six times as great by U.S. Census standards.[23] This is partly attributable to their economically disadvantaged position. Consequently, the issue of low-rent housing is intertwined with the total problem of discrimination against Negroes. Over 40 per cent of the families in low-rent public housing are nonwhite; well over half of this public housing is segregated, although the trend is running toward increasing integration.

Public housing and urban redevelopment, even if integrated, would be only part of the answer to the slum-locked condition of the Negro community. With the increasing income of the Negro family, private housing discrimination looms as an ever larger factor. From 1935 to 1950 the average income of nonwhite families tripled, but of the 9 million new homes built during that period, less than 1 per cent were open to Negroes.[24]

There is indication that housing developers and financiers are beginning to recognize the untapped market that is represented by the Negro community. Some unrestricted private housing developments are being established in the middle-income range. Most of these become all-Negro developments. The issue then becomes not so much one of poor housing as of socially segregated housing.

Discrimination—In Places of Public Accommodation

Segregation in facilities of public accommodation and public transportation was institutionalized by law in the post-Reconstruction South. Outside the South, discrimination has been a common practice in those facilities which have an element of sociability: restaurants, hotels, and particularly resort hotels. Exclusion from privately owned facilities in the North and West as well as in the South has been a factor in the hyperdevelopment of Negro clubs and fraternal organizations.

Defamation

Defamation against the Negro has two prime characteristics: (*a*) it usually has to do with a supposed inferiority of mentality, morality, or personal

---

[22] *The High Cost of Bad Housing* (New York: Anti-Defamation League, 1952), p. 1.
[23] *Ibid.*
[24] *Ibid.*

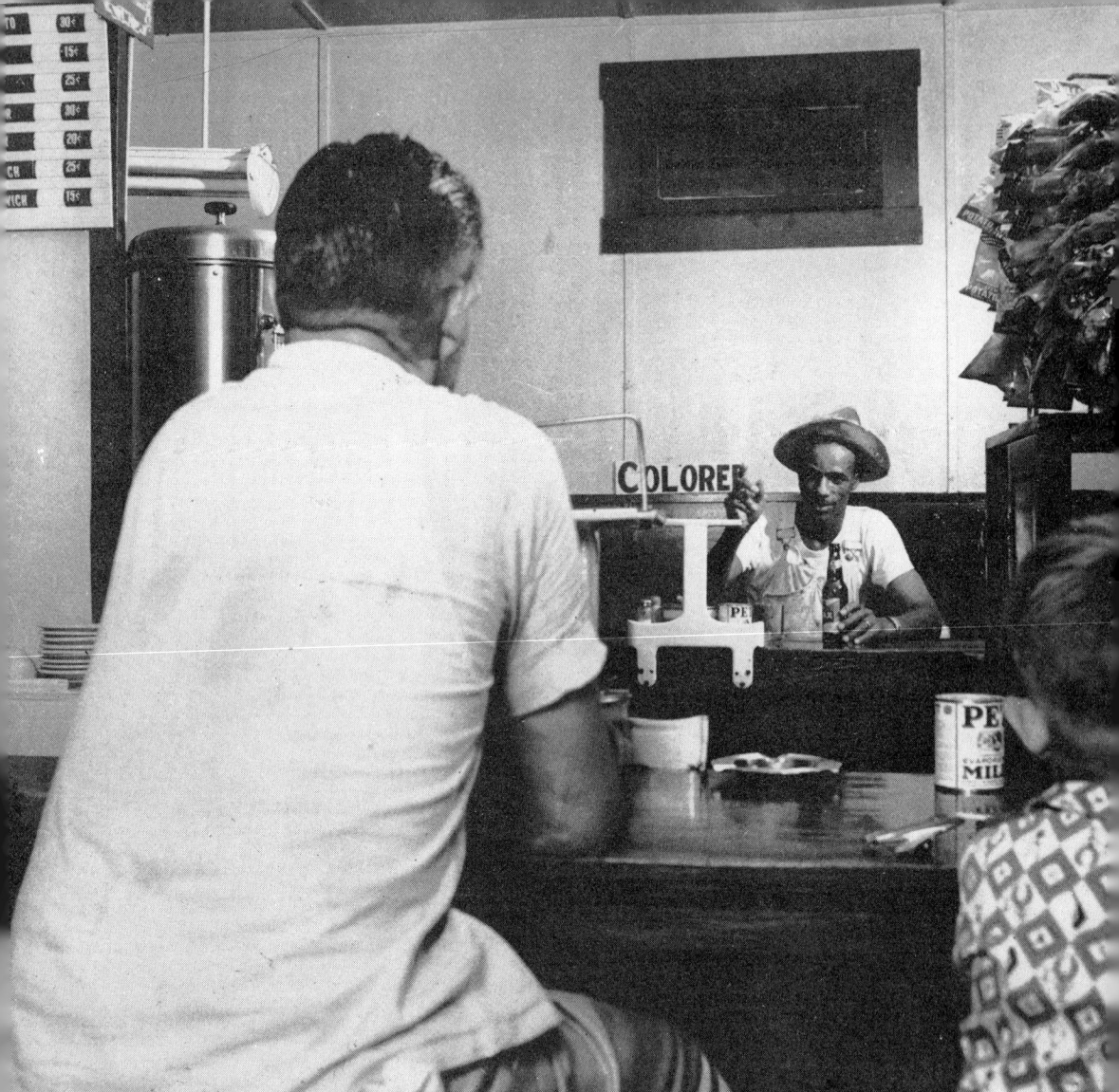

Bern Keating; Black Star

The Imaginary Line: At this Mississippi lunch counter, a Negro and a white man cannot sit together—but they chat freely across the space that divides them.

habits; (*b*) this defamation is usually invoked in direct support of some discriminatory pattern.

The American Jew

BACKGROUND HISTORY

In the sixth century B.C. the first dispersal of the Biblical people known as the Jews was effected by the Babylonian conquest of Jerusalem. During the Hellenic period and following the Roman conquest, the Jews further dispersed into Italy, Spain, France, and Germany. At the beginning of this period the conflicts in which the Jews were enmeshed were not substantially distinguishable from other national conflicts that existed. But as the dispersed Jews began to lose their "single nationality," their religion became the focus for antipathy, and their refusal to abandon their religion became the stimulus for recurrent attacks during the early Christian era. Refusing conversion, the Jews were massacred by the thousands during the centuries following the Crusades. The entire Jewish community of Vienna was exterminated in 1420. The medieval mind created fantastic legends about the Jews: they had horns, they had tails, they engaged in ritual murders.

The social and economic patterns created in the wake of mass persecution abroad have a direct bearing on the status of the Jew in the modern world. A papal decree of 1555, for instance, decreed that Jews were to be segregated strictly in their own quarter, which was to be surrounded by a high wall and closed off at night. The tight ghetto was the living-place for Jewish communities throughout Europe for centuries. Jews were also excluded from most occupations and were thus forced into marginal trades, such as peddling, in which the non-Jew had no interest, and into moneylending, which at that time was prohibited to the Christian.

Cut off from the rest of the world by wall and legend, the Jew became the classical scapegoat for all misfortune. When the Black Plague struck Europe during the middle of the fourteenth century, the rumor became current that it was caused by Jews poisoning the wells. Within two years nearly three hundred and fifty Jewish communities were exterminated.

Meanwhile, many Jews had been pushed eastward by these excesses. Russia refused them entrance, and the refugees piled up in Poland, which eventually had the largest Jewish population in the world. There the persecutions continued. About 100,000 Jews were killed in Poland between 1648 and 1658. And it was in eastern Europe that the medieval oppression of Jews lingered most stubbornly.

The Modern World

The position of the Jews considerably improved with the ascendancy of political liberalism in the late eighteenth and nineteenth centuries. Full citizenship was granted to them by the French Assembly in 1791, and by 1870 political, economic, and religious equality had been officially granted in all of western Europe. But, though the ghetto gates had been opened, the folkways of centuries were not so easily erased. Social exclusion and occupational restrictions persisted. In addition, the medieval role of the Jews as scapegoats for general misfortune was given new impetus in the modern political world. The term "anti-Semitism" was first used by a German journalist in 1873 to describe anti-Jewish hostility having nothing to do with religion. Formerly it had been possible for a Jew to escape persecution by undergoing conversion, but this was no longer possible when "being a Jew" was determined by ancestry. In order to sustain anti-Semitism as a political weapon, it became necessary to establish the myth of the Jew as some kind of distinct biological "race" or as a member of a mysterious international cabal. This image of the mysterious Jew could then be shaped to need.

In the Germany of the 1870's there was deep economic distress and political tension. Many political groups found that it was possible to divert popular unrest into antipathy for the Jews by making the Jews represent different threatening symbols to different segments of the nation (urbanism for the peasants, competition for the middle class, social change for the aristocracy). As late as 1952 an anti-Semitic pamphlet published in Germany announced: "The Jew as a dictator of democracy, Bolshevism and the Vatican, rules over all of you."

The culmination of political anti-Semitism was the murder of 6 million Jews in Europe by the German Nazis. About 4 million Jews died in concentration camps, and about 2 million were killed by extermination squads.[25]

In America

There were about 2,000 Jews in the United States in 1790, most of them of Mediterranean origin. By 1880 the swell of Jewish immigrants from Germany had raised the total to about 250,000. Between 1880 and 1910 about 1.5 million Jews arrived. Most came from Russian Poland, where bloody pogroms were still widely practiced.

Today there are about 5 million Jews in this country, the largest single Jewish population in the world total of 11–12 million Jews. The Jews settled largely in the urban areas and into those occupational roles in which they had been cast by history. Over 2 million Jews live in New York City. A total of another 1.5 million live in Chicago, Boston, Philadelphia, or Los Angeles. About three out of four American Jews live in the ten most populated cities. The others are largely concentrated in the other urban centers around the country. The socio-economic status of the American Jew is overwhelmingly middle class. Recent census studies in six cities (Passaic, Port Chester, Los Angeles, Trenton, Nashville, and Gary) revealed that one-third to one-half of the male Jewish labor force were occupied as proprietors and managers and that 11–19 per cent were professionals or semiprofessionals. In the managerial field the American Jew has been identified with trade and independent retail business rather than with large industry, chain-store operations, finance, or manufacturing. In the census-study cities mentioned above, at

---

[25] The most specific collection of figures is found in Leon Poliakov, *Harvest of Hate* (Syracuse: Syracuse University Press, 1954), which draws directly on the archives of the Nuremberg Tribunal and the testimony at that trial of former Nazi officials.

least 75 per cent of the Jewish labor force were listed in the trade and independent-retail categories or in clerical and sales jobs. Less than 2 per cent were listed as laborers; and less than 2 per cent of the American Jewish working force is in farming pursuits.[26] In New York City in 1935 almost half the Jewish working force were skilled or semiskilled workers, primarily in the garment industry, but this proportion has since declined steadily in a middle-class direction.

Although many of the states in the Colonial period imposed religious disabilities, religious equality was one of the firmest tenets of the young American republic. In a roomy and fast-expanding America there were no significant manifestations of anti-Semitism until the turn of the twentieth century. With the closing of the frontier, the growing congestion of the city, increasing economic competition, and the mass migrations from eastern Europe, the picture began to change.

With the development of a more settled community life, social status became a more important factor, and social discrimination followed in its wake. When a Jewish family was denied admission to a resort hotel in New York in 1877, the incident was novel enough to occasion many condemnatory editorials and pulpit speeches. But twenty years later such an incident was considered commonplace. Widespread economic discrimination followed, and the rise of political anti-Semitism in Europe began to be reflected in the 1920's with the organization of anti-Semitic groups and the mass dissemination of anti-Semitic literature in America. Against this background, the pattern of prejudice against Jews in America took shape.

THE PATTERN OF PREJUDICE

Physical Attack

Violence has been an infrequent expression of anti-Semitism in this country. However, any manifestation of anti-Semitism is haunted by the specter of its blood-letting European past. The extent of concern with discriminatory or latent forms of anti-Jewish feeling can only be understood in that context.

Discrimination—In Employment

Employment discrimination against Jews is fairly uniform in the urban centers of the country. The Chicago Bureau of Jewish Employment Problems surveyed 7,200 job orders received by commercial employment agencies during 1953 and found that 22 per cent expressly excluded Jews.[27] A

---

[26] *American Jewish Yearbook, 1951* (Philadelphia: Jewish Publication Society of America, 1952), pp. 11–12.
[27] *Civil Rights in the United States, 1953*, p. 52 (see n. 6, above).

similar survey of 2,009 job orders by the same agency in 1957 found that 20 per cent excluded Jews. A survey of 5,535 job orders placed with the Los Angeles office of the California State Employment Service in 1951 revealed that 17 per cent of the job openings were barred to Jews; about 27 per cent of the white-collar job openings were closed to Jews.[28]

Employment discrimination against Jews is expressed chiefly in white-collar jobs and is more marked in the higher executive positions. It is least marked in new and service industries. A survey by *Fortune* magazine in 1936 found that there were only 33 Jews among the 420 directors of banks which were members of the New York Clearing House, and the role of Jews in finance was even smaller outside New York. The survey noted the absence of Jews in the country's insurance business and their virtual nonexistence in heavy industry.[29]

As a result of past and present discriminatory patterns, Jews have been disproportionately stimulated to find job security in small businesses and the professions. Approximately 10–12 per cent of the Jewish population are in professions as compared to about 7 per cent of the general population.[30]

Employment discrimination has not made an economically depressed group of the Jews for at least two reasons: the high rate of self-employment and the fact that there are still ample nondiscriminatory job openings for the relatively small number of Jews in the general population. If it is not often a direct economic handicap, employment discrimination nevertheless retards the full integration of the Jew into American society and is a disturbing reflection of continuing anti-Semitic sentiment.

Discrimination—In Education

Discrimination against Jews in education is largely confined to colleges and especially to graduate and professional schools. About 90 per cent of all the colleges and universities in the country require a statement of religion or religious preference before admission. The President's Commission on Higher Education remarked that this is strong evidence that "such information is likely to be used for discriminatory purposes."[31] Medical schools have been particularly subject to criticism on this score. While "quotas" often operate on the undergraduate level, nevertheless the proportion of Jewish students in the colleges is somewhat greater than the proportion of Jews in the population. The average Jewish student, however, has to make more applications than the average non-Jewish student before

---

[28] Report of the Los Angeles office of the California State Employment Service to the Area Minorities Advisory Committee, February 16, 1951.

[29] "Jews in America," *Fortune*, 13 (February, 1936), 79 ff.

[30] Oscar J. Janowsky, *The American Jew* (New York: Harper & Bros., 1942), p. 165.

[31] President's Commission on Higher Education, *Higher Education for American Democracy* (Washington, D.C.: U.S. Government Printing Office, 1947), Vol. I, p. 38.

he finds an acceptance. For example, a survey conducted by the Elmo Roper organization following World War II found that 77 per cent of all Protestant applications were accepted for college admission, 67 per cent of the Catholic applications, and 56 per cent of the Jewish applications.[32] And because of the quotas in certain professional schools, many Jews are effectively prevented from entering a desired profession.

Discrimination—In Housing and Places of Public Accommodation

In most urban areas there can be found neighborhoods or residential buildings which are restricted with respect to Jews. A survey in the Detroit suburbs in 1958 found that one-third of the real estate agents clearly indicated that they did not wish to see or rent to Jews.[33] In all areas of the country there can also be found restaurants, clubs, and resort hotels which are restrictive against Jews. A recent survey of 3,014 resort establishments by the Anti-Defamation League found that over 22 per cent of them clearly discriminated against Jews.[34]

Under the auspices of the "Cornell Studies," conducted under the direction of Robin Williams, Jr., and John P. Dean, a survey was made of social discrimination in 248 cities ranging in population from 10,000 to 500,000. Three tests of social acceptability were used: admission to the Junior League, admission to clubs, and admission to exclusive residential areas. In

FIGURE 5:6 DISCRIMINATION IN COLLEGE APPLICATIONS

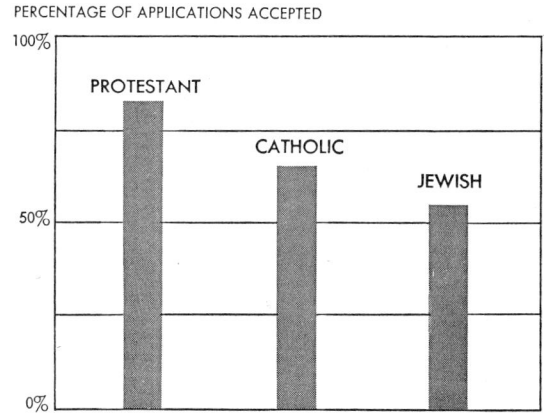

Source: Elmo Roper, *Factors Affecting the Admission of High School Seniors to College* (Washington, D.C.: American Council on Education, 1949), p. 37.

---

[32] Elmo Roper, *Factors Affecting the Admission of High School Seniors to College* (Washington, D.C.: American Council on Education, 1949).
[33] *Housing: The Role of the Real Estate Agent* (New York: Anti-Defamation League, 1958).
[34] *Barriers* (New York: Anti-Defamation League, 1958), p. 36.

one-third of these cities Jews are denied admission to all three. In only 20 out of the 248 cities are some Jews accepted in all of these groups, and most of these 20 cities are the smaller ones.[35]

In 1955, it was estimated that discrimination was still being practiced by at least half of the national college fraternities despite, in many places, vociferous campus opposition.[36]

Defamation

Defamation against Jews often has to do with supposed social traits and is sometimes used in support of a discriminatory pattern. But the major emphasis of anti-Semitic defamation is not on discrimination. Where the Negro is typically accused of inferiority and *shunned*, the Jew is typically accused of political and economic chicanery and *blamed*. The stimulation of such group "blame" is often useful to those who are inclined, or find it advantageous, to inject into some political or social issue the spurious and emotion-rousing image of a "conspiratorial enemy."

In the 1920's the dissemination of scapegoating diatribes against the Jew reached mass proportions. A typical item of distribution was the mythical *Protocols of the Elders of Zion,* which purported to document an international Jewish conspiracy. (This document, which originated in Czarist Russia, was discovered to have been copied word for word from an early French novel; the only change was that the fictional conspiracy concocted by the novel's author was now called a "Jewish conspiracy.") The American industrialist, Henry Ford, alone distributed hundreds of thousands of these pamphlets, a deed for which he publicly apologized in 1927. In the 1930's, under the impact of the depression and Hitler's deliberate propaganda, organized anti-Semitic defamation reached its peak. By midsummer of 1939 as many as sixty anti-Semitic meetings were being held each week in the streets of New York. In 1938 the radio pulpiteer, Father Coughlin, announced that henceforth his organization, the Christian Front, "would not fear to be called anti-Semitic." He had a radio audience of 3.5 million people. It has been estimated that 121 organizations were primarily engaged in spreading anti-Semitic propaganda between 1933 and 1940.

Such public and rabble-rousing defamation of the Jews declined in fashion when the United States entered the war, and the several dozen remaining "professional anti-Semitic" organizations are in general disrepute. But wherever extremists have felt the need to personify the enemy, the myth of the conspiratorial and manipulative Jew has at some point crept in. This mythical Jew has been accused of controlling Presidents Roosevelt,

[35] John Slawson, *Social Discrimination* (New York: American Jewish Committee, 1955), pp. 10 ff.
[36] Alfred McClung Lee, *Fraternities without Brotherhood* (Boston: Beacon Press, 1955).

Wide World Photos

Anti-Semitism in Boston, 1955. An anti-Semitic group protests the opening of a Catholic chapel on the campus of Brandeis University, a nonsectarian institution founded by American Jews. The leader of this group, a former priest, had been excommunicated by the Catholic Church because of heretic activities.

Truman, and Eisenhower. He has been accused of engineering desegregation in the schools. He has been accused of promoting progressive education in order to destroy our school system and the fluoridation of water in order to dull the senses of our populace. He has been accused of starting our wars and of masterminding Communist subversion. When the active anti-Semitic policy of Communist Russia and the Communist satellites was revealed in the 1950's, the mythical Jew was then accused of the ultimate deception: self-destruction in order to throw the world "off the track."

These extremist sentiments have little active currency in America today. But the anti-Semitic myth on which they are based may in some cases be only dormant.

Other Targets of Prejudice

Americans of Chinese, Japanese, Mexican, Filipino, and Puerto Rican extraction have met discriminatory barriers in various regions somewhat similar to those raised against Negroes. On the West Coast "Anti-Coolie" associations were formed against the Chinese in the 1860's and were attended by violence and lynching activities. The mass evacuation of Japanese and Japanese-Americans from the West Coast during World War II was later called by the President's Committee on Civil Rights "the most striking mass interference since slavery with the right to physical freedom."[37] Serious tensions have been reported in New York City, where a sudden influx since World War II has brought the Puerto Rican population in that crowded city to the half-million mark. (These tensions have often found Negro and white united against Puerto Rican.) For the most part, prejudice against these groups has expressed itself in employment policies and in housing and social discrimination. As in the case of the Negro, employment and,

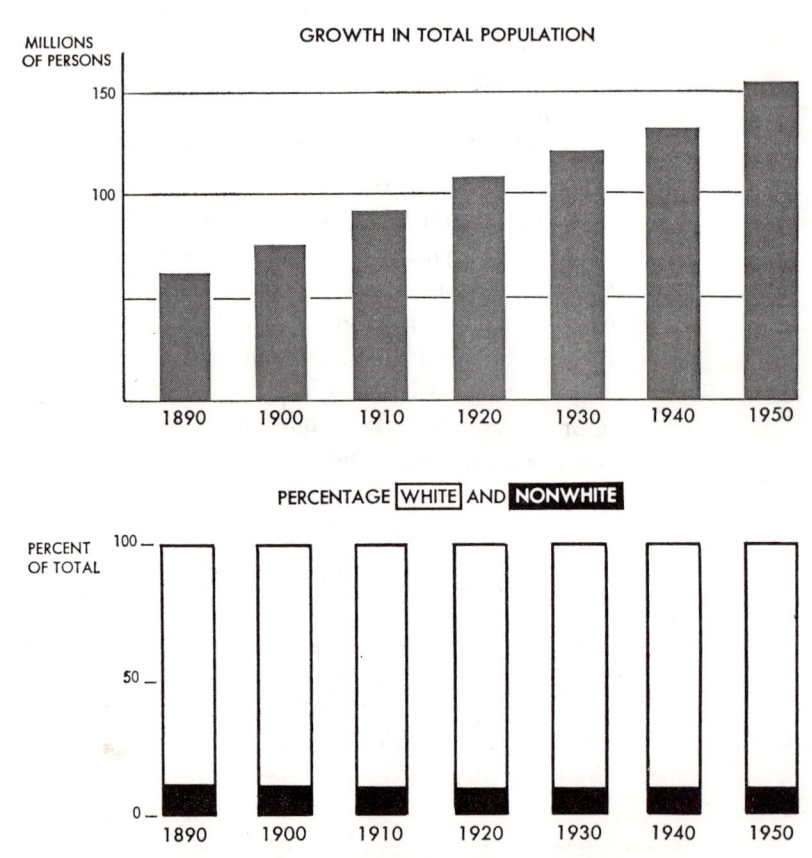

FIGURE 5:7 U.S. POPULATION GROWTH AND RACIAL DISTRIBUTION

Adapted from U.S. Bureau of the Census, *Statistical Abstract of the United States, 1957* (Washington, D.C.: U.S. Government Printing Office, 1957), Table 29, p. 36.

---

[37] *To Secure These Rights*, p. 68 (see n. 7, above).

to some extent, housing discrimination has tapered off since World War II.

Anti-Catholic prejudice more often follows the pattern of anti-Semitic prejudice but is appreciably milder in degree. There are still evidences of employment discrimination and of some discrimination in higher education. But the extent of these behavior patterns is greatly outstripped by the amount of latent prejudice against Catholics revealed in attitude polls.

Section V: Why? The Causes of Prejudice

"What makes prejudice a social problem?" and "What causes prejudice as an attitude and mode of behavior?" are two somewhat different questions. In the first case, the reference is to a mass conflict of aspirations. The Negroes, for example, have aspirations for equal status which are being frustrated by the behavior of large numbers of the white population, many of whom desire to maintain their superior status.

Prejudice and the subordination of groups in a society become active social problems only when significant resistance to them develops within a society. As the aspirations of the Negro community grew, as dissatisfaction with a racial caste system grew among both Negroes and whites, so did the social problem. When a substantial number of Negroes did not aspire to voting privileges, to equal employment opportunity, to equal housing opportunity, these questions were not centers of conflict.

If the inferior status and stigmatization of certain racial, religious, or ethnic groups is successfully transmitted as a "social value" to members of both the dominant and the subordinate group, a conflict in values will theoretically not develop. There have been many factors that have accelerated this conflict in American society. The explicit egalitarian philosophy of this country was sharpened in the public mind by certain historical, patriotic, and political events. During the world wars, for example, our democracy was widely proclaimed; in addition, the more active participation of subordinate groups in our society was needed and promoted. The mass migration of Negroes to the industrial cities of the North and West, and the influx of immigrants in general, increased the political potential of minority groups. The ideal of equal opportunity became a political by-word.

New generations in the subordinate groups, and many in the dominant group, broke sharply from traditional attitudes on this aspect of the social order. Universal education sharpened aspirations. Mobility, and the breakdown of stable patterns of community and family life, fanned these aspirations and freed them from traditional molds. In other words, the *social problem* of prejudice as we know it has been created largely by the changing nature of American society.

However, the remedial key to this aspiration conflict, which constitutes the social problem of prejudice, lies not in modifying the rising aspirations of subordinate groups, for these appear to be not only irreversible but, according to the official values of our American society, legitimate and reasonable as well. The remedial key, rather, lies in modifying the element of this conflict which gives it its name: prejudice; because prejudice, both as attitude and behavior, offers unreasonable resistance to certain aspirations of subordinate groups.

Therefore, the causal theories that are commonly advanced to explain this social problem are those theories which try to explain the source of prejudiced attitudes and behavior.

Basic Causal Theories

Two kinds of causative factors are customarily invoked in attempts to explain prejudice. One approach to prejudice emphasizes *personality factors;* it centers around the idea that special emotional needs and tensions underlie individual susceptibility to prejudice. The other approach attempts to isolate and describe those *social circumstances* which give rise to widespread patterns of prejudice irrespective of special emotional needs.

PERSONALITY FACTORS

Frustration-Aggression Theories

The argument: The frustration-aggression theory can be stated in the following schematic form: (a) A person failing to achieve some important goal tends to respond to his frustration with feelings of aggression and hostility. This aggression is ordinarily vented on the source of the frustration. (b) Often, however, the sources of an individual's frustration are unknown to him or reside in people he fears or cannot control or for whom he also has feelings of affection and identification. In this case, he often deflects his aggression and chooses other people and groups as substitute targets. (c) Substitute targets are usually those who are different from his own group, with whom he feels little or no identification, and who are weak and in no position to retaliate. In other words, frustration and its consequent feelings of hostility may take the form of prejudice. (d) Finally, unable or unwilling to face the real source of his frustration, the prejudiced person soon finds a rationalization for his aggression toward the objects of his prejudice; he accepts beliefs and ideas which seem to him to justify his hostility.

The frustration-aggression hypothesis does not hold that frustration leads necessarily and inevitably to outward aggression. It is usually recognized that extreme frustration may also produce hopeless resignation and apathy.

The evidence supports the view, however, that some fairly direct relation between frustration and aggression exists.

For example, thirty young men at a summer camp first expressed their attitudes toward Japanese-Americans; they were then deliberately frustrated by being prevented from attending a local theater and being forced instead to take a series of complicated tests. When retested at that point, they tended to express more unfavorable attitudes toward Japanese-Americans.[38] Among tested veterans who claimed to have had a bad break in the Army, almost five times as many were prejudiced as not; the majority of those claiming to have had a good break were relatively unprejudiced.[39]

Sometimes the frustration-aggression theory is couched in terms not of "frustration" but of "anxiety" or "insecurity" as the source of displaced aggression and prejudice. Another important variation invokes the concept of "projection": (*a*) A person feels impulses which are in conflict with his conscience (e.g., sexual impulses). (*b*) He expunges awareness of these impulses from his conscious mind, that is, he represses those impulses which make him feel guilty. (*c*) He nevertheless finds an outlet for his impulses through "projection," i.e., he attributes his impulses to others. John Dollard, in his study of a typical southern town, points out that, though most sexual violations are initiated by white males against Negro women, there is widespread belief in Negro male hypersexuality.[40]

Evaluation: 1. The frustration-aggression theory does not explain enough about the specific social conditions which transform "free-floating" hostility into hostility against certain outgroups and not others. Nor does it explain why prejudice becomes the channel for aggression in some societies, individuals, and areas and not in others.

2. However, this theory does explain a function that prejudice may serve for some individuals. It may explain why epidemic conditions of frustration, such as economic depression, may tend to spawn prejudice in a society. And, from a remedial point of view, it may be helpful in explaining some of the resistances to purely "reasoned" attacks on prejudice.

The Authoritarian Personality

The argument: According to some researchers there is a personality type which is particularly susceptible to prejudice. This is the authoritarian personality.[41]

The so-called "authoritarian personality" has the following tendencies:

[38] Neal E. Miller and Richard Bugelski, "Minor Studies of Aggression," *Journal of Psychology*, 25 (1948), 437–42.
[39] Bruno Bettelheim and Morris Janowitz, *Dynamics of Prejudice* (New York: Harper & Bros., 1950), p. 64.
[40] John Dollard, *Caste and Class in a Southern Town* (New Haven: Yale University Press, 1937).
[41] T. W. Adorno *et al.*, *The Authoritarian Personality* (New York: Harper & Bros., 1950).

(*a*) He is a rigid conformist. He cannot tolerate customs or people who differ from what he considers to be the social norm. He is often a puritanical moralist. (*b*) He is ethnocentric. He divides the world sharply into ingroups and outgroups and rejects the outgroups. (*c*) He is a worshipper of authority and strength. He needs an authority to turn to because of his own weakness and lack of confidence. He is attracted to the "man on the white horse" and conversely despises the "weak." (*d*) He is "single-valued." He cannot accept the belief that two conflicting values may both have merit. He cannot stand ambiguity. Part of his need for a clearly defined authority results from an inability to tolerate shadings of black and white, right and wrong. Often correlated with these characteristics are a high degree of prejudice, ultraconservatism, and a lack of sympathy for the democratic process.

The attitude patterns which form the authoritarian personality are conceived to be primarily the result of warped emotional development. As a child the typical authoritarian was subjected to harsh discipline and given little affection. His emotional needs and sense of self-reliance were curbed by heavy parental emphasis on conformity and obedience to authority.

Psychologist Else Frenkel-Brunswik found that highly prejudiced children tend to endorse the following beliefs: [42]

> There is only one right way to do anything.
> If a person does not watch out, somebody will make a sucker out of him.
> It would be better if teachers would be more strict.
> Only people who are like myself have a right to be happy.
> Girls should learn only things that are useful around the house.
> There will always be war. It is part of human nature.
> The position of the stars at the time of your birth tells your character and personality.

Elmo Roper reported that individuals high in anti-Semitism gave a lower proportion of "don't-know" responses in surveys.[43]

A number of people were asked to copy a drawing of a pyramid which had some lopsided dimensions. Sixty-two per cent of the highly prejudiced, as compared with 34 per cent of the little prejudiced, equalized the dimensions, being unable to tolerate the inexactitude.[44]

When asked to list people "most admired," the highly prejudiced usually gave names of "strong men," like Napoleon and Bismarck. The others more typically gave names of authors or scientists, like Einstein.[45]

---

[42] Else Frenkel-Brunswik, "A Study of Prejudice in Children," *Human Relations*, 1 (1948), 295–306.

[43] *Fortune*, 33 (February, 1946), 257 ff.

[44] Jerome Fisher, "The Memory Process and Certain Psychosocial Attitudes, with Special Reference to the Law of Prägnanz," *Journal of Personality*, 19 (1951), 406–20.

[45] Else Frenkel-Brunswik and R. Nevitt Sanford, "Some Personality Factors in Anti-Semitism," *Journal of Psychology*, 20 (1945), 271–91.

In one experiment with middle-class people in a suburban American community, it was found that the most important single factor accompanying a high degree of prejudice was extreme nationalistic feeling.[46]

Evaluation: 1. Critics of the concept which links prejudice to authoritarian personality traits have complained that many of the traits ascribed to basic personality are perhaps more correctly attributable to social and educational factors. It has been pointed out that, though "being superstitious" and "being prejudiced" tend to go hand in hand, this correlation may be a result not of basic psychological propensities but of a lack of education and sophistication.

2. Any effort to delineate personality types has the weakness of all typologies. There are few "ideal" types, and most people fall somewhere "in between."

3. However, the research has had accepted value in pointing out the extent to which prejudice or its absence is built into the individual's total outlook on life and people and in reminding us that democracy must be sustained by people to whom tolerance is psychologically congenial.

SOCIAL FACTORS

Learning: The Normal Transmission of Social Values

The argument: Prejudice may be learned as a matter of custom, just as habits of clothing or diet or etiquette are learned. This approach asserts that there does not necessarily have to be any special personality need in order for prejudice to exist.

In general, an individual learns his social attitudes and behavior by conforming to the attitudes and behavior he finds around him. Indeed, in his earlier years he has little choice. This learning is by indirection as well as by indoctrination. Jokes about minority groups help to build stereotypes. Obvious social avoidance of minority groups by parents leads children to infer their inferiority and undesirability. Advertisements in the classified section of the newspapers reading "restricted" or "gentiles only" also become part of the indirect learning process. In turn, learned prejudices seem to be "proved" by certain unevaluated observations, such as that many Negroes live in slums and that there is a disproportion of Jews in small business. In this way do the effects of prejudice tend to perpetuate prejudice itself.

One investigator found that by the age of five most white boys began to demonstrate a preference for their own race, discovered through their reactions to pictures of white and Negro boys. There was a gradual increase

[46] Nancy C. Morse and Floyd H. Allport, "The Causation of Anti-Semitism: An Investigation of Seven Hypotheses," *Journal of Psychology,* 34 (1952), 197–233.

of preference to the age of fourteen without any corresponding increase in personal contact with Negroes. The conclusion: attitudes toward Negroes are chiefly determined not by contact with Negroes but by contact with the prevailing attitude toward Negroes.[47]

One pair of investigators studying white children found that by the age of ten they had learned to reject Negroes totally, i.e., no favorable quality was ascribed to Negroes more often than to whites. However, at this age their personal conduct was not so deeply affected. They still played with Negro children. At the age of twelve, on the other hand, they were able to ascribe some favorable qualities to Negroes on paper but rejected Negro children more completely in their behavior.[48] In other words, by adolescence, the children had learned the complete adult pattern: they *expressed belief* in the American creed of equality but *acted* on the basis of prejudice.

Evaluation: 1. This approach, by itself, leaves unexplained the different degrees of susceptibility to prejudice and the special resistance to relearning which seems to characterize so much prejudice.

2. However, the approach does serve to point up the widespread existence of a quiet, unemotional kind of prejudice, which stems more from a desire to conform to prevailing patterns than from strong feelings of hostility. Special emotional factors do not have to be present in order for prejudiced behavior to exist.

3. Most significantly, perhaps, this approach points to the fact that prejudices may be rooted in past history rather than in contemporary circumstances. It certainly seems to be the case that, once prejudice is generated by particular historical circumstances, it has a strong tendency to continue as an independent culture pattern. If this is the case, it means that the problem of eliminating prejudice is substantially a matter of re-education rather than wholesale psychological transformation.

Ingroup Emphasis

The argument: A strong cultural emphasis on ingroup idealization and loyalty breeds hostility toward outgroups.

An "ingroup" has been defined by Gordon W. Allport as "any cluster of people who can use the term 'we' with any significance." But where there is a "we," there is also a "they" of some kind. A person actually belongs to many ingroups, but with lessening degrees of intensity as the ingroups become less exclusive.

An extreme form of the ingroup-outgroup theory of prejudice would hold that hostility toward outgroups is a "natural" concomitant of ingroup feel-

[47] Eugene Horowitz, "The Development of Attitudes toward the Negro," *Archives of Psychology*, 28 (January, 1936).

[48] Robert Blake and Wayne Dennis, "The Development of Stereotypes Concerning the Negro," *Journal of Abnormal and Social Psychology*, 38 (1943), 525, 531.

ing and social solidarity. Where ethnic and racial minorities are highly visible outgroups, differing either in physical appearance or in ways of behaving, they are highly susceptible to being defined as "they" and to becoming targets of hostility.

A less extreme approach would deny that ingrouping automatically creates hostility toward outgroups. There is nevertheless the implication that the normal ingrouping process tends to create a divisiveness which extreme ingroup attitudes or ingroup insecurity can seriously aggravate.

In one research study, some seven-year-old children were asked: "Which are better, the children in this town or in [the neighboring town]?" Almost all replied: "The children in this town." Asked why, they usually said: "I don't know the kids in [the neighboring town]."[49]

College students were given a list of nationalities and asked to rate them in order of personal preference. Included on the list were three fictitious nationalities: "Daniereans," "Pirenians," and "Wallonians." It developed that those students who evinced prejudice against actual nationalities also tended to reject automatically the fictitious nationalities because of their "outgroup sound."

Evaluation: 1. Ingroup-outgroup feelings become severe enough to lead to prejudice only under special psychological and social conditions. An insecure person, for example, may depend so heavily upon ingroup support and approval that he develops a complementary hostility toward outgroups.

2. There seems to be great divergence among groups in the degree to which they use hostility toward outgroups as a means of achieving ingroup loyalty and cohesiveness. Becoming a member of a group may require at some point a vivid sense of who is not a member of the group, but there seems to be ample evidence that uncritical distinctions between "we" and "they" are often only temporary and certainly need not lead to strong feelings of hostility. An insecure group may, however, manipulate hostility toward outgroups to increase member loyalty.

3. In attacking the problem of prejudice by relearning, it is undoubtedly more effective to deal with hostility toward specific outgroups than to rely on creating abstract attitudes of tolerance toward outgroups in general.

Risk Conditions

From a remedial point of view, it is worth while to isolate certain aspects of social life in order to see how these various causative factors actually operate. What follows is a cross-sectional application of the causal theories, discussed above, to specific aspects of community life, namely, the prejudiced community, the family, and economic and political tensions.

[49] Gordon W. Allport, *op. cit.,* p. 42.

THE PREJUDICED COMMUNITY

The argument: The individual learns prejudice chiefly by conforming to the models of prejudiced behavior that are prevalent in the community in which he lives and with which he most closely identifies.

1. *Official society.* The attitudes of prejudice explicitly stated by official society tend to be accepted by its members. Such attitudes are expressed by official spokesmen or by law.

There is more than one official society; government exists at the national, state, and local levels. In the case of delinquency, these official societies merge into one official society against lawbreaking; criminal subcultures are not official. In the case of prejudice, however, there are sharp conflicts among various official societies. The national society is today officially on record against prejudice, through its laws, its judicial decisions, and the statements of its executives. This is true also of most of the official societies of the northern and western parts of the country. Most markedly, of course, it is not the case in most of the official societies of the South. There, the laws and the official spokesmen are, to varying degrees, explicitly in favor of unequal racial status, although they are opposed to religious prejudice.

2. *The mass media.* On the national scale, unofficial fashion in prejudice is reflected chiefly in and through the mass media.

In 1944 the Bureau of Applied Research of Columbia University studied contemporary fictional characterizations. In the 195 short stories in widely circulated magazines that were studied, the Anglo-Saxons were predominantly the "good people." The report concluded: "The behavior of these fictional characters could easily be used to 'prove' that Negroes were lazy, the Jews wily, the Irish superstitious and the Italians criminal." Of 100 movies studied, 75 per cent of the Negro characters were stereotyped or disparaging, 13 per cent were neutral, and 12 per cent were favorable. This ratio roughly applied to radio practices as well.[50]

3. *Common customs: the local community.* The individual learns his prejudiced attitudes and behavior most directly from the daily living conditions with which he comes into contact.

Segregation in schools, in housing, in public places, by overtly demonstrating the acceptability of prejudice, fixes the status of the disadvantaged group. This is true whether that segregation is "official" and proclaimed by law, or not. In other words, a segregation law is doubly effective: it expresses an official attitude favoring segregation and also creates an actual condition of segregation. However, segregation and discrimination are no less perceptible community patterns when they exist without benefit of law or even contrary to law.

[50] *How Writers Perpetuate Stereotypes* (New York: Writers' War Board, 1945).

PERSONALIZED SERVICE

Confidential Information to Travel Agents.

HOTEL AND GUEST HOUSE RESERVATIONS.

All reservations are made in YOUR name and all commissions are payable to YOU. Some hotels are restricted. We suggest, therefore, the use of the following code words, particularly in cables, to denote racial origin.

Gentile	Oleander
Jewish	Hibiscus
Negro	Geranium
Asiatic	Poinciana

Our fee for this service is $5.00 per room (plus cable charges, if any), irrespective of whether the accommodation is for one or more persons. Such fees will be billed on confirmation of reservation.

RESTRICTIONS

Anyone suffering from a communicable disease will not be accepted. We cater to Gentiles only. We reserve the right to refuse or cancel stay of anyone at our own discretion.

Type of clientele preferred __Christians__ Restrictions __No Hebrews__

RESTRICTIONS

The Clientele is rigidly restricted to gentiles. Reservations at Paradise Inn are made only for those people who, in the opinion of the manager, will be happy and congenial guests. Guests are selected just as is the membership of the most exclusive club. Paradise Inn reserves the right to refuse accommodations or to terminate reservations without other reason than the judgment of the manager. The homelike and conser-

---

Unofficial patterns of community behavior may be prejudice-bearing whether they are deliberate or not. Though discrimination in employment may be discernible as a deliberate pattern, e.g., through discriminatory advertisement, the prevalent employment of minority groups in low-grade jobs can exist without being the direct and immediate result of discrimination. The low educational level and lack of high-grade skills of a subordinate group resulting from a past history of discrimination may be the immediate factor. The image is nevertheless projected of the Negro as commonly employed in a menial capacity. The image of the Negro as a slum-dweller, for another example, is a result not only of overt housing discrimination but also of his condition of economic disadvantage and his past history of cultural deprivation. In this sense, prejudice is self-fulfilling: many of its objects take on the social characteristics that prejudice would ascribe to them as "natural." The young and the unthinking, however, are apt to "learn" this image and accept it as a natural and inevitable phenomenon.

4. *The "prejudice-prone" community.* Certain characteristics of a community might not be described as "prejudiced" within our established context but may be called "prejudice-prone," in the sense that they foster those social values which are strongly related to prejudice.

A cultural emphasis on extreme nationalism might be an example. The excessive stress on ingrouping might foster a general xenophobia (fear of strangers). An insistence on conformity could contribute toward a generally authoritarian atmosphere. These are background social conditions which make it easier, or at least possible, for the widespread phenomenon of prejudice to flourish.

5. *Group influences.* The individual tends especially to adopt the prejudiced attitudes and behavior patterns of community groups to which he belongs and with which he identifies. Allport cites the recollection by a college student of his first day at prep school:

> One of the older boys remarked about a schoolmate, "Don't you know that Harry is a Jew?" I had never met a Jewish boy before, and personally didn't care whether or not Harry—who seemed a likeable fellow—was a Jew. But the older boy's tone of voice was enough to convince me that I had better not make Harry my friend. Thereafter, I avoided Harry, and, although I could not understand why we should dislike Jews, I gradually accepted the prejudice. It seems strange that a feeling of antagonism toward Harry should grow up in me. But it did. Personally I had no unpleasant experience with him or with any other Jew I ever met.[51]

Evaluation: A community is not necessarily homogeneous with respect to its influences for or against prejudice. Within each community there may be major conflicts and, at the very least, islands of dissent. The least conflict and the fewest islands of dissent probably exist in the South. Where the influences of the general community are overwhelmingly for or against prejudice, the islands of dissent have the most difficulty in maintaining them-

---

[51] Gordon W. Allport, *op. cit.*, p. 287.

selves and exerting their own influence. Where the influences of the general community are in sharp conflict or are not positive in either direction, each group is able to exert its greatest influence.

In addition, the individual's attitudes and behavior are often likely to shift depending on the different group situations in which he finds himself. Prejudice is not a neatly tied bundle that a person carries with him from place to place. An individual may manifest more prejudice in a prejudiced group than he would the next day as part of an unprejudiced group.

Nevertheless, while the role of the prejudiced community is not mechanical and cannot be considered to have a rubber-stamp effect, this does not diminish its central importance in the transmission of prejudiced attitudes.

THE FAMILY

The argument: The family is the center of attitude-learning for the growing child. It is also the place where the frustrated and prejudice-prone personality is initially shaped.

The most direct transmission of prejudice is from parent to child. Transmission of prejudice may be explicit, but it may also be inferred from observing parents' behavior, as witness the following account:

Walking across the playground, a settlement worker found a little Italian boy crying bitterly. She asked him what was the matter. "Hit by a Polish boy," the little boy repeated several times. Inquiry among the bystanders showed that the offender was not Polish at all. Turning again to her little friend, she said, "You mean, hit by a big naughty boy." But he would not have it thus and went on repeating that he had been hit by a Polish boy. The worker made inquiries. She learned that he had lived in the same house with a Polish family and that the Italian mother by constantly quarreling with her Polish neighbor had put into the heads of her children the notion that "Polish" and "bad" were synonymous terms.[52]

General emotional problems which may play a part in any given instance of prejudice are, of course, strongly rooted in family relations. But, more specifically, the genesis of the authoritarian personality has been firmly laid at the family door. A stern, authoritarian parent, together with relative absence of affection, has been found to be the most common background for the development of authoritarian tendencies. In such cases there is a power relationship between parent and child. There is an insistence on conformity; pleasure is de-emphasized; stress is laid on the grim nature of life; the expression of emotion is discouraged. And throughout all this is a strict and inflexible interpretation of right and wrong. The result is often, and logically enough, the individual who was, in a preceding section, typologically described as the "prejudice-prone authoritarian personality."

[52] Bruno Lasker, *Race Attitudes in Children* (New York: Henry Holt & Co., 1929), p. 98.

Other research, without attempting to build the total construct of an authoritarian personality, has indicated a relationship between family disorder and prejudice. During World War II, for example, it was reported that certain seriously maladjusted children, whose maladjustment could be laid to insecure home life, tended to turn against minority groups in America and especially against the Jews.

Evaluation: Perhaps this kind of general evidence is put into proper perspective with the simple statement that the family is the most immediate source of both personality development and social learning for the child. Psychologists have stressed the extent to which the individual's personality is forged on the anvil of early child-parent relationships. In addition, the family is the natural bridge by which cultural attitudes are transmitted from society to the growing individual. Of course, the family is itself normally a product of the community in which it exists. However, the strongest counterinfluence to prejudice is probably the prejudice-free family, even where it exists as an island in a prejudiced community.

ECONOMIC AND POLITICAL TENSIONS

The argument: 1. Economic hardship stimulates prejudice. Economic deprivation is chronic frustration. Where people are unable to understand the real sources of their poverty, either in themselves or in others, they may vent their hostilities upon some scapegoat.

2. It has been argued, however, that economic hardship by itself does not generate prejudice. One study of the attitudes of veterans toward Jews found rabid anti-Semitism most prominent among those who suffered a downward shift in socio-economic status upon their return to civilian life.[53] Economic depression, it is argued, is related to prejudice because it brings with it *relative deprivation;* as people move downward on the socio-economic ladder, they feel deprived relative to their former life. Goals and satisfactions once attainable no longer are. In addition, the drop in status brings to such people the feeling that they have "lost face." Their self-esteem is threatened; they are torn between feelings of having personally failed and of being overwhelmed by outside forces. A scapegoat is someone else to blame, someone who will also embody their conviction that they have been cheated by social forces outside their control.

3. Depressions are periods of competition for scarce jobs and scarce goods, and prejudice easily arises as a generalized effort to exclude whole classes of people from access to the scarcities of life. Such competition may exist even in periods of relative prosperity; for example, as Negroes have migrated in large numbers to northern cities, open hostility has sometimes resulted because of the resulting scarcity of housing.

[53] Bettelheim and Janowitz, *op. cit.*

Evaluation: It is sometimes maintained that prejudice would not be generated even in the above situations without being deliberately suggested and fomented by those who wish to use intergroup dissension as a means of achieving political or economic power or of escaping blame. That there is some justice in this argument is illustrated in the following examples, which have been more fully treated in the previous discussion of the target groups concerned:

The rise of anti-Chinese feeling among union people during the economic depressions in nineteenth-century California, although the Chinese had been welcomed earlier, was deliberately fomented by some union leaders.

Propaganda concerning Negro racial inferiority burgeoned when the Negro slave suddenly became freshly important to the southern economy at the turn of the eighteenth century.

Those seeking political power in the post-bellum South fomented bad feeling between the "poor whites" and the newly freed Negroes.

It has also been suggested that other epidemic tensions, besides economic hardship, can create risk conditions for prejudice. The fear of war, invasion, or subversion arising from international tensions has been offered as an example. During the period immediately preceding World War II, political anti-Semitism found fertile soil in the organized isolationist movement in America and rose to a new peak. A few isolationist leaders found that they struck a responsive chord in some of their constituents when they included an anti-Semitic rationale as part of their argument against involvement in war. It was easier to sustain moral outrage and self-righteousness when a mythical sinister plot for involvement could be invoked.

However, the determinist theory that group prejudice is always the result of deliberate fomentation by some power group is much overdrawn. This possibility certainly represents a risk factor, although power groups, as in the post-bellum South, more often avail themselves of already prevailing prejudice. Furthermore, prejudice has sustained itself handily through periods of economic prosperity and political harmony. As in the case of other social problems, the removal of economic and political frustration is a worthy end in itself, but as an answer it begs the immediate question.

Section VI: Summary

Prejudice serves an emotional function for many people. It permits them more easily to shift blame from themselves to others, to rationalize their aggressions, or otherwise to find an outlet for their special emotional needs. Psychological theories attempt to explain the relationship between emotional needs and prejudice. They thus explain the special susceptibility that *some* people have to prejudice. More than that, these psychological theories explain the special attractiveness that prejudice seems to have for human beings in general. In other words, they help to explain the particular virulence with which some individuals display prejudice; more generally, they also help to explain the particular emotional attachment which prejudiced individuals have for their prejudice.

These theories are thus a significant part of the total causal picture. However, they do not explain the *differential prevalence* of prejudice. They do not explain why prejudiced attitudes and behavior thrive in some places and not in others or why they take different forms in different places. Nor do they explain the phenomenon of *widespread* prejudice.

Political and economic tensions, especially when they are exploited by political demagogues, may explain some of the historical origins of, or the recrudescence of, particular patterns of prejudice. But, more often than not, these tensions merely arouse already existing prejudice.

It is in the transmission of prejudiced attitudes and behavior patterns through the normal processes of cultural learning that the widespread existence of prejudice as a social phenomenon can best be explained. It is indeed toward the redirection of these normal processes of cultural learning that most of the remedial proposals are, in one way or another, directed.

---

adaptation 8   THE SEMANTICS OF PREJUDICE

Abridged and adapted from Felix S. Cohen, "The Reconstruction of Hidden Value Judgments: Word Choices as Value Indicators," in Lyman Bryson, Louis Finkelstein, R. M. MacIver, and Richard McKeon (eds.), Symbols and Values: An Initial Study, Conference on Science, Religion, and Philosophy (New York: Harper & Bros., 1954), pp. 545–61. Published in this form by permission of the publisher.

[The late Dr. Felix S. Cohen, son of the eminent American philosopher, Morris R. Cohen, and himself an outstanding lawyer and scholar, was for many years an official of the Bureau of Indian Affairs in the United States Department of the Interior. From 1939 to 1940 he was Chief of the Indian Law Survey conducted by the United States Department of Justice. He was particularly interested in the ethical, judicial, and administrative implications of prejudice, especially as they affected American policy toward its native Indian population.

In the following analysis Dr. Cohen analyzes the "language of prejudice."

He shows that by choosing one word rather than another we often structure the world into ingroups and outgroups and create unfavorable attitudes toward those we designate as "they."**]**

Bertrand Russell has called attention to the possibility of conjugating value-weighted adjectives in the following way: "I am firm; You are obstinate; He is a pig-headed fool."

Almost any human characteristic may be described either in honorific (favorable and approving) or in pejorative (unfavorable and disapproving) terms. If we examine the words used to describe particular human traits, we see that some are noncommittal and neutral, some favorable and "upgrading," and others unfavorable or "downgrading." For example, if we take a fairly neutral attitude toward a young man, we call him simply "young." If we have an unfavorable attitude toward him and wish to "downgrade" him in the eyes of others, we say that he is "immature." On the other hand, if we want to emphasize his vigor and freshness, we call the same person "youthful." What word we use often depends upon some implicit value judgment we have made of a person and upon our desire to arouse the same attitude in others. The following list of some of the adjectives used to describe human traits shows how easy it is to create favorable or unfavorable attitudes toward the same behavior simply by a judicious use of language:

Favorable, Upgrading	In Between, Neutral	Unfavorable, Downgrading
Discreet	Cautious	Cowardly
Loyal	Obedient	Slavish
Careful	Meticulous	Fussy
Devoted	Self-subordinating	Fanatical
Kind	Soft	Mawkish
Warmhearted	Sentimental	Mushy
Tolerant	Nondiscriminating	Nigger-lover, Indian-lover, etc.
Generous	Liberal	Spendthrift
Courageous	Bold	Reckless, foolhardy
Mature	Old	Decayed
Youthful	Young	Immature
Sound	Conservative	Reactionary
Open-minded	Liberal	Unsound
Practical	Aware of material factors	Mercenary
Realistic	Suspicious	Cynical
Humanitarian	Idealist	Do-gooder

In the eyes of the satisfied employer, the servant is "loyal" and therefore possessed of an important virtue. In the eyes of the social critic, the same servant may be "slavish," implying that his relationship to his employer is to be condemned. The same person may be called "generous" by those who approve of him and a "spendthrift" by those who do not.

Not only adjectives but nouns as well are used to express attitudes of approval and disapproval and to create them in others. Consider, for example, the varying connotations of respect or disrespect involved in choosing among the following ways of describing the position of a given individual:

Favorable, Upgrading	In Between, Neutral	Unfavorable, Downgrading
Official	Office-holder	Bureaucrat
Statesman	Policy-maker	Politician
Officer	Policeman	Cop
Investigator	Detective	Flatfoot
Governess	Nursemaid	Servant
Business executive	Employer	Boss
Financial leader	Banker	Moneylender
Pilgrim	Migrant, refugee, immigrant	Alien
Orator	Influential speaker	Rabble-rouser

In her own language the nursemaid may be a "governess," but to her employer she may be a "servant." Early Puritan refugees are praised as "pilgrims," but later refugees are "aliens." "Statesmen" are always "orators," while "politicians" are usually "rabble-rousers."

Verbs, too, fall on a value scale. The following list covers only a few of the key word-choices that, when applied to any controversial issue, may help us to identify the moral or political standpoint of the word-user and the direction in which he wishes to influence opinion, attitude, and policy:

Favorable, Upgrading	In Between, Neutral	Unfavorable, Downgrading
Discern	Think	Theorize
Demonstrate	Assert	Allege
Co-operate	Act in concert	Conspire
Assist	Aid	Abet
Clarify	Retract	Admit error
Advice	Urging	Behest
Serve	Control	Interfere
Administer	Manage	Manipulate

Favorable, Upgrading	In Between, Neutral	Unfavorable, Downgrading
Enlighten	Report	Propagandize
Inspire	Motivate	Inflame
Catalyze	Stir to action	Instigate
Counsel	Recommend	Incite

So we find that as a rule majorities are "inspired" but minorities are "inflamed"; and where the former "co-operate" with each other, the latter "conspire."

Generally speaking, words of the first column in the three lists may be classed as "we" words. They are words we customarily apply to ourselves and our ingroups. Words of the third column, on the other hand, are "they" words, used to describe the actions of those outgroups from whom we are inclined to separate ourselves. Sometimes the relation between "we" words and "they" words involves no more than the addition of the three-letter pejorative suffix, "ism." We and our friends are for peace, or psychology, or social progress, or isolation. But our enemies are for pacifism, psychologism, socialism, progressivism, or isolationism.

The use of downgrading words helps to establish others as "they." At the same time, the use of "they" words often serves to encourage unfavorable, downgrading attitudes. When a white judge refers to a defendant as a Negro, Indian, or savage, he is using an "outgrouping" line of demarcation that separates himself from the defendant. On the other hand, a judge who refers to the same defendant as a citizen, taxpayer, father, husband, or veteran is using an "ingrouping" delineation that includes himself or honored friends. Perhaps the most significant effort of attorneys on opposite sides of a case is to persuade the judge or jury or both to think of the defendant in "we" terms or "they" terms. Many American newspapers refer to arrested or suspected criminals as "Negro" or "alien," if they are either; on the other hand, they do not use words like "white" or "seventh-generation American" or "Protestant" or "freckled." This technique helps to build popular impressions as to the criminality of Negroes or aliens which are often very far removed from the facts. What may be called "the technique of the irrelevant adjective" is a smear technique that is difficult to answer. When a New York congressman objected to being referred to as a "Jewish congressman from New York," the answer was, in effect: "Well, you are Jewish, aren't you? Why be ashamed of it?"

The real issue here is not whether a racial or religious adjective is accurately descriptive of an individual but whether the adjective is properly relevant to the context in which it is used. The adjective "Negro" may be entirely relevant to a discussion of the medical effects of sunburn, and the adjective "Jewish" may be entirely relevant to a discussion of religious ritual. These adjectives are irrelevant to a court trial or a report of a crime wave except upon the unstated premise that Negroes or Jews, Indians or immigrants, are especially disposed to criminal activity. Such unstated premises make the difference between sympathetic or unsympathetic accounts of the same event and bear upon the possibility of reaching a just judgment, based on the merits of the individual case.

---

adaptation 9   THE "MINORITY" CULTURE OF THE
AMERICAN NEGRO

Abridged and adapted from Gunnar Myrdal, An American Dilemma *(New York: Harper & Bros., 1944), primarily Chapters 33 and 44. Published in this form by permission of the author and the publisher.*

[*An American Dilemma* is an intensive study of the American Negro, conducted in the United States under the leadership of a Swedish social scientist. In this study, American society is seen from the point of view of a scholar not himself a product of American culture.

In the following adaptation of portions of *An American Dilemma,* the author addresses himself to the question of whether there exists an American Negro culture distinct from the dominant white culture. He notes that, even when they do not mean to be unfriendly to Negroes, whites often feel that certain aspects of Negro life are different or peculiar. To the extent that they exist, are the differences or peculiarities of Negroes attributable to their African origins?

The author concludes that the American Negro community is in most respects merely a pathological and distorted form of the American community. Apparent *differences* of behavior are often in reality only *excesses* of behavior; they are exaggerations or intensifications of traits and tendencies which characterize American society as a whole. Family instability, religious emotionalism, high crime rates—these are phenomena which in general differentiate America from many other countries (such as England or the Scandinavian nations). They find intensified expression within the Negro community. This intensification is the product not of a distinctive Negro culture but of the social isolation, disorganization, and degradation that, especially in a democracy, accompany segregation and discrimination.

The author makes it clear that his observations hold largely for southern Negroes or for new migrants from the South, i.e., for those on the lowest socio-economic levels. They do *not* hold *at all* for middle-class Negroes, nor do they apply to many Negroes on lower occupational levels. Most of Myrdal's conclusions are based on the Negro community in the deep South; they are valid only insofar as old patterns linger and continue to exert their influence.]

THE PATHOLOGICAL NEGRO COMMUNITY

Negro institutions are similar to those of the white man. They show little similarity to African institutions. In his cultural traits the Negro is akin to other Americans, and his allegiances are characteristically American. He believes in the American creed and in other ideals held by most Americans, such as getting ahead in the world, individualism, the importance of education and wealth. He imitates the dominant culture as he sees it, insofar as he can adopt it under his conditions of life. For the most part he is not proud of those things in which he differs from the white American.

In practically all its divergences, American Negro culture is not generally independent of general American culture. It is a distorted development or pathological condition of the general American culture. The instability of the Negro family, the inadequacy of Negro educational institutions, the emotionalism in the Negro church, the insufficiency and unwholesomeness of Negro recreational activity, the plethora of Negro sociable organizations, the narrowness of interest of the average Negro, the provincialism of his political speculation, the high Negro crime rate, the cultivation of the arts to the neglect of other fields, superstition, personality difficulties, and other characteristic traits are mainly forms of social pathology which for the most part are created by the pressures of prejudice.

The Family

The uniqueness of the Negro family is the product of slavery. Most slaveowners either did not care about the marital status of slaves or for economic reasons were interested in seeing that they did not form strong marital bonds. In addition, the internal slave trade broke up many slave families. Certain cultural practices grew up in slavery which retain their influence to the present day in rural southern areas; marriages sometimes occur by simple public declaration or in a ceremony conducted by a minister but without a marriage license.

At the close of the Civil War the slave states legalized all existing common-law marriages, and, with the disappearance of slavery, there was a great increase in family stability. Nevertheless, an easygoing attitude toward marital relations still remains a part of rural and lower-class Negro culture insofar as it differs from the official white pattern. (That this attitude is by no means universal is pointed up by the existence of a large class of Negro families among whom there is such strict adherence to the ideal of the monogamous, partriarchal Christian family that Frazier has called them "Black Puritans.")

Perhaps the best index of family stability available is that of illegitimacy. For the United States as a whole the figures indicate that the Negroes have about eight times as much illegitimacy as native whites. There seem to be fewer cases of illegitimacy in the North than in the South (there is no regional difference among whites), and fewer in rural areas than in urban areas. Despite the greater concentration of Negroes in rural farm areas, where broken families are least frequent, 30 per cent of all Negro families in 1930 were broken as compared with 20 per cent of native white families.

The Negro masses undoubtedly have many more of those characteristics which define family disorganization in the traditional American sense. At the same time, they also have certain other cultural traits which tend to reduce the disorganizing effect of these characteristics. Considering common-law marriage and temporary marriage, there are probably significantly fewer unattached Negro adults than unattached white adults. Neither common-law marriage nor illegitimacy are seriously condemned in the Negro community, except among the upper classes, and they therefore have fewer disorganizing effects on the individual. The Negro community also has the healthy custom of attaching no stigma to the illegitimate child, freely adopting illegitimate children and orphans into established homes. There are few unwanted children.

The existence of these practices does not mean that the Negro community has no moral standards. "Fast women," philandering men, and "fly-by-night affairs" are condemned. In the rural South the rule is that a person may cohabit with only one other person for a given period, and there is little promiscuity. The important point is that the Negro lower classes, especially in the rural South, have built up a type of family organization conducive to social health even though their practices are outside the American tradition. When these practices are brought into closer contact with white norms, as occurs when Negroes go to cities, they tend to break down and to cause the demoralization of some individuals.

The Negro Church

The Negro church differs from the white in three respects: the greater importance of religion and church life in the Negro community, the proliferation of sects and extradenominational "storefront" churches, and the greater emotionalism of the church service.

At least 44 per cent of American Negroes were officially claimed as members of Negro churches in 1936 as compared with 42.4 per cent of the white population in white churches. Actually the discrepancy between white and Negro church participation is much greater. The census figure neglects the significant number of Negroes who are members of white churches; it leaves out many of the small sects to which Negroes adhere more often than whites; it ignores the fact that fewer Negroes than whites belong to churches which, like the Catholic, count membership from birth.

To an outsider the main observation about Negro churches and Negro religious life is that they adhere so closely to the common American pattern. There are differences, and they are important; but more important are the similarities. In this case as in many others, the caste system forces the Negro to become an "exaggerated" American.

Americans generally are a religious people, southerners are more religious than the rest of the nation, and Negroes are probably a little more religious than white southerners. America as a whole is still predominantly Protestant in spite of the "new" Catholic and Jewish immigration; southern whites and Negroes are even more Protestant. In America, and especially in the South, low-church denominations with less formalized rituals have always been predominant; the great majority of Negroes belong to the Baptist and Methodist churches or to small sects which have branched out from them. Compared with other countries, American Protestantism has always been marked by relatively more emotionalism; revival meetings and evangelists have played a greater role, and the regular church services have exhibited more emotional traits. The South is somewhat extreme in this respect, too, and Negroes still more so. American religious emotionalism dates back to the Great Revival of 1800, a time of mass Negro conversion to Christianity. But this was a white movement, and its practices are still retained, even in extreme form, by many lower-class whites in isolated rural communities in the South.

As in the white population, there is a class as well as a geographical differential in regard to degree of emotionalism in religious services. Emotionalism in religion tends in general to be associated with poverty and social isolation; to the degree that there is exaggerated emotionalism in the Negro church, it testifies to the greater frustration and deprivation of its members. As in the white American population, the small upper class among Negroes tends, more than the lower classes, to belong to the Episcopalian, Congregational, and Presbyterian churches and to frown upon practices which still prevail in the lower classes. Even among the latter, however, emotionalism is fast disappearing in the large, well-established urban churches.

In the face of adversity and social isolation, the Negro church has given hope and a sense of community. In a society callous to their needs and aspirations, Negroes have had to place their hopes for a better life in religion. In addition, the Negro church was from the beginning the only place where Negroes could congregate freely and publicly. The Negro church became a community center par excellence. In the South there are few public buildings for the recreation of Negroes. Negro homes are almost always too small to have more than two or three guests at a time. Only the church is left, and in many ways it is well fitted to serve as a community center. For one thing, it is owned by the Negroes themselves. They feel free to do what they please in it, the white man's respect for religion giving it an unusual freedom from intrusion. The Negro church is so important that it might almost be said that anyone who does not belong to a church in the rural South does not belong to the community.

The ministry was once the chief outlet for Negro ambition. For a long time, taking up preaching provided practically the only opportunity for advancement for the individual; under slavery, and after, the preacher stood out as the leader and spokesman for his group. Even today, new Negro churches and sects seldom begin because of theological differences but because more people are "called" to preach than there are legitimate positions available. As opportunities expand, the desire and capacity for initiative and leadership are being expressed not as a "call" to the ministry but in business and the professions. "It is not too much to say that if the Negro had experienced a wider range of freedom in social and economic spheres, there would have been fewer Negroes 'called' to preach and fewer Negro churches."

For Negroes the church has in the past been the major center of community life and the preacher the major leader of the community. But this is changing rapidly as the Negro community becomes diversified, as other professionals are becoming more numerous, as an upper and middle class have developed among Negroes, as a minister does not advance as rapidly in education and sophistication as do the youth of his community. The Negro church has declined in relative importance since 1880, and the prospects are for a continued decline. Nevertheless, the Negro church means more to the Negro community than the white church means to the white community—in its function as a giver of hope, as an emotional cathartic, as a center of community activity, as a source of leadership, and as a provider of respectability.

Voluntary Associations

As many foreign observers have pointed out, America has an unusual proliferation of social clubs, recreational organizations, lodges, fraternities, sororities, civic-improvement societies, self-improvement societies, occupational associations, and other organizations which may be grouped under the rubric of "voluntary associations." While this is true of Americans generally, Negroes seem to have an even larger relative number of associations. In Chicago in 1937, when the total Negro population of the city was less than 275,000, there were over 4,000 formal associations the membership of which was wholly or largely Negro. In this respect, again, Negroes are "exaggerated" Americans.

There are a number of reasons for regarding this situation as pathological. In the first place, Negroes are highly active in voluntary associations because they are not allowed to participate in most of the other organized activity of American society. Second, Negro voluntary associations tend to follow a pattern which is about a generation behind the general American pattern. Lodges with secret rites and elaborate rituals became unpopular at least thirty years ago and now seem to the white American as ludicrous as they once seemed fashionable. More important is the fact that most of these organizations are "sociable" clubs, which do little to improve the position of the Negro in American life and have failed to provide the Negro community with a united and effective leadership.

Crime

Statistics on Negro crime have special weaknesses due to certain characteristics of the Negro population. One of the basic weaknesses is that people who come in contact with the law are generally only a sample of those who commit crime. Negroes by and large are more likely to come into contact with the law when they commit a crime than is the white population. This is reflected in the comparative statistics.

Negroes are seldom in a position to commit white-collar crimes. They commit the crimes which much more frequently result in apprehension and punishment. In the South, inequality of justice seems to be the most important factor in making the statistics on Negro crime and white crime not comparable. Negroes are more likely to be arrested than are whites, more likely to be indicted after arrest, more likely to be convicted in court and punished. The popular belief that all Negroes are inherently criminal operates to increase arrest, while the Negroes' lack of political power prevents a white policeman from worrying about how many arrests he makes. In a southern court a Negro's testimony will often be ignored, if he is permitted to express it at all. When sentenced he is usually given a heavier punishment, and in many southern communities there are no special institutions for Negro juvenile delinquents or for the Negro criminally insane as there are for whites.

In the North it is not so much discrimination that distorts the Negro's criminal record as it is certain characteristics of the Negro population. For example, unorganized crime is much more prevalent in the South than in the North among both whites and Negroes; and when the Negro goes North, he brings his high crime rate along with him. Another cause of distortion of the Negro's crime record is his poverty: he cannot bribe the policeman to let him off for a petty offense; he cannot have a competent lawyer to defend him in court; and, when faced with the alternatives of fine or prison by way of punishment, he is forced to choose prison. The Negro's ignorance acts in a similar fashion: he does not know his legal rights; he does not know how to present his case; and he also lacks, of course, influential connections. In general, our attitude toward crime statistics must be that they do not provide a fair index of Negro crime. Even if they did, a higher crime rate would not mean that the Negro is addicted to crime either in his heredity or his culture, for the Negro population has certain external characteristics (such as concentration in the South and in the young adult ages) which give it a spuriously high crime rate. With this attitude in mind, we may examine some of the statistics.

According to Bureau of Census figures in 1940 there were about three times as many Negro males in prisons and reformatories as there were native white males in proportion to the sizes of their respective populations, and the rate for Negro women was more than four times as great as that for native white women. The difference between Negroes and whites in this respect is much larger in the North than in the South. In the South the number of Negro male felony prisoners is only two to two and one-half times as great in proportion to population as the number of white male felony prisoners. In the North, however, the Negro rate is almost five times as large as the white rate. This would seem to be due mainly to the fact that northern Negroes are concentrated in cities, where social disorganization is greatest and law enforcement most efficient.

Fundamental is the Negro's hatred of the whites. A not insignificant number of crimes by Negroes against whites is motivated by revenge for discriminatory or insulting treatment. The revenge motive may also lead to a cold and calculating crime. It is said by many Negro social scientists that mugging—the robbing and beating of a victim by a group—was originally practiced in Negro neighborhoods on white men who were thought to be searching for Negro prostitutes. But the reaction to prejudice is much more general. It prevents the Negro from identifying himself with society and the law. Because the white man regards him as apart from society, it is natural for a Negro to regard himself as apart. He does not participate in making the laws in the South, nor is he given a role in their enforcement.

The slavery tradition and its aftermath are also reflected in the low regard for human life that characterizes lower-class southerners generally, and especially Negroes. The slave's life had only a money price, not a legal or ethical value. After emancipation the use of violence to support the caste system maintained this low regard for human life. Negroes have taken over the white man's attitude and have even exaggerated it. Assault and murder are relatively more common among Negroes. Such crimes are rarely premeditated, and they are the result of a moment's anger when it is not inhibited by a developed respect for life and law.

Certain traits present everywhere, but more developed in the Negro as a consequence of his slavery background and patterns of prejudice, have also been conducive to a high Negro crime rate. Sexual looseness, weak family bonds, and poverty have made prostitution more common among Negro women than white women. Social organization is generally at a low level among southern Negroes, but disorganization reaches its extremes only when Negroes migrate to the cities and to the North. The controls of the rural community are removed, and the ignorant Negro does not know how to adjust to a radically new type of life. Negroes are especially prone to take over the criminal patterns of the urban slums, since they have such difficulty in getting regular and decent jobs. More Negro mothers have to work for a living and therefore do not have the time to take care of their children properly. Negro children more than white children engage in street trades. The overcrowdedness of the home and the consequent lack of privacy prevent the development of ideals of chastity and are one element in encouraging girls to become prostitutes. The friction that is bound to develop in a poverty-stricken household, especially where there are no strong family traditions, weakens family control over children still further.

We know that Negroes are not biologically more criminal than whites. The great bulk of crime among Negroes has the same causes as that among whites. There are the same variations in the crime rate between social classes among Negroes as among whites. The upper and middle classes among Negroes are at least as law-abiding as the corresponding classes among whites, and much of the differential in gross crime rate lies in the fact that the proportion of lower-class Negroes is so much greater.

Negro Leadership

One of the striking characteristics of recent trends within the Negro community has been the growing development of a relatively strong and independent Negro leadership. This is partly the result of the rapidly rising educational level of Negroes. It is also the result of the fact that Negro leadership is becoming more and more indispensable to *both* Negroes and whites as a means of communication between them. Even in the South, master-servant relations are no longer apt to lead to feelings of subservience to white opinion; Negroes are no longer so willing uncritically to accept white patronage. Whites are therefore more and more compelled to attempt to reach and influence the Negro community through a strong and effective Negro leadership with whom it can deal.

Direct contact between Negroes and whites is becoming more and more limited to direct contact between their leaders, each acting on behalf of his own bloc. Like two foreign nations, Negroes and whites in America deal with each other through the medium of plenipotentiaries. The contact is not, however, between equal powers. On the contrary, power is almost all on the white side; and to this power the Negro leadership is often forced to accommodate.

Where caste restrictions are rigid, as in the South, there is still a strong tendency for leadership to devolve upon the most accommodatively inclined members of the Negro community. In the old South, and in rural sections today, this has usually meant an "Uncle Tom" leadership. From the Negro point of view, this is almost always an inadequate leadership. It tends to project into leadership those Negroes—"good old darkies"—who represent white stereotypes rather than Negro aspirations.

The role of the favored and trusted "darky," never a factor in the North, is fast disappearing even in the South. As wealth and education become more attainable by Negroes, those who have them gain prestige in the Negro community no less than in the white community. In the North and on a national scale, education is a necessary condition for that section of Negro leadership which deals with white society, though in the white South resistance to the educated, "uppity" Negro is still strong.

In recent years, especially in the North and nationally, Negro leadership has increasingly been trying to effect a compromise between accommodation and protest. In the Deep South, where militancy sometimes invites economic reprisals and even death, the compromise is often more formal than real.

The following conversation with the president of a branch of the National Association for the Advancement of Colored People in one of the smaller capitals of the Deep South reveals the extraordinary difficulties which Negro leadership faces. He was asked whether there were any other organizations besides the NAACP in the city:

"Yes, there is the League for Civic Improvement."

"Why do you bother to have two organizations with the same purpose of trying to improve the position of the Negroes?"

"Sir, that is easily explainable. The NAACP stands firm on its principles and demands our rights as American citizens. But it accomplishes little or nothing in this town, and it arouses a good deal of anger in the whites. On the other hand, the League for Civic Improvement is humble and 'pussyfooting.' It begs for many favors from the whites, and succeeds quite often. The NAACP cannot be compromised in all the tricks that Negroes have to perform down here. But we pay our dues to it to keep it up as an organization. The League for Civic Improvement does all the dirty work."

"Would you please tell me who is president of this League for Civic Improvement? I should like to meet him."

"I am. We are all the same people in both organizations."

[The situation in the American Negro community has been shifting rapidly since Myrdal's study. A dramatic example of the transition toward militance in the South was provided by a Negro boycott of municipal buses in Montgomery, Alabama, in 1956. City and state law required segregated seating sections on all public transportation. This often resulted in a situation in which Negroes were unable to find bus seats even though there were empty seats in the "white section." Growing out of one specific incident, an effective boycott was organized by Negro leadership in Montgomery. Negroes formed car pools or walked to work. Since the municipal transit system depended largely on Negro riders, its revenue was very seriously reduced. Further than that, the effective and organized boycott in defiance of segregation law was apparently disturbing and embarrassing to white leadership in the community. Negro leaders, including many ministers, were arrested on charges of organizing a boycott in violation of an old state law. The arrested Negro leaders proclaimed that the boycott would continue, although they warned the Negro community against holding demonstrations or mass meetings. Negroes carefully walked to work singly or in small groups in order to avoid violence or any apparent show of strength.

In the Montgomery bus boycott, we nevertheless find illustrated several of the "peculiarities" noted by Myrdal which at present mark the Negro community:

1. Ministers played a larger and more important role in the boycott than ministers ordinarily play in corresponding "action" situations in the white community.

2. Church meetings apparently provided a substitute for mass meetings. The latter would probably have been regarded by the white community as provocative and would very likely have met with reprisals. The church remains a Negro sanctuary.

3. The boycott represented a striking instance of compromise between accommodation and protest. Passive resistance and nonviolence were the watchwords, yet there was no doubt about the "protest" nature of the citywide boycott or about the active and independent role of Negro leadership in this Deep South city.]

SUGGESTIONS FOR FURTHER READING, CHAPTERS 5 AND 6

Nathan W. Ackerman and Marie Jahoda, *Anti-Semitism and Emotional Disorder* (New York: Harper & Bros., 1950).

T. W. Adorno et al., *The Authoritarian Personality* (New York: Harper & Bros., 1950).

Gordon W. Allport, *The Nature of Prejudice* (Boston: Beacon Press, 1954).

Harry S. Ashmore, *The Negro and the Schools* (Chapel Hill: University of North Carolina Press, 1954).

Morroe Berger, *Equality by Statute* (New York: Columbia University Press, 1952).

Kenneth B. Clark, *Prejudice and Your Child* (Boston: Beacon Press, 1955).

John Dollard, *Caste and Class in a Southern Town* (New Haven: Yale University Press, 1937).

E. Franklin Frazier, *The Negro in the United States* (New York: The Macmillan Co., 1957).

E. Franklin Frazier, *The Negro Family in the United States* (Chicago: University of Chicago Press, 1939).

Eli Ginzberg, *The Negro Potential* (New York: Columbia University Press, 1956).

Alfred McClung Lee, *Fraternities without Prejudice* (Boston: Beacon Press, 1955).

Leo Lowenthal and Norbert Guterman, *Prophets of Deceit* (New York: Harper & Bros., 1949).

C. Wright Mills, Clarence Senior, and Rose Kohn Goldsen, *The Puerto Rican Journey* (New York: Harper & Bros., 1950).

Arnold N. Rose (ed.), *Race, Prejudice and Discrimination* (New York: Alfred A. Knopf, 1951).

George E. Simpson and J. Milton Yinger, *Racial and Cultural Minorities* (New York: Harper & Bros., 1953).

Marshall Sklare, *The Jews: Social Patterns of an American Group* (Glencoe, Ill.: The Free Press, 1958).

Jacobus ten Broek, Edward C. Barnhart, and Floyd W. Matson, *Prejudice, War and the Constitution* (Berkeley: University of California Press, 1954).

Helen G. Trager and Marian Radke Yarrow, *They Learn What They Live* (New York: Harper & Bros., 1952).

C. Vann Woodward, *The Strange Career of Jim Crow* (New York: Oxford University Press, 1955).

Ben Kertin; Black Star

CHAPTER 6

Group Prejudice: Meeting the Problem

There are in existence hundreds of national and local agencies and organizations which have as a primary objective the reduction of prejudiced patterns and attitudes. In a way the nation has become a huge laboratory for the testing of deliberate attitude-changing techniques. These techniques fall within four general categories of approach:

A. *Law*
   The attempt officially to prohibit certain forms of prejudiced behavior.
B. *Direct Action*
   The attempt to deal with specific cases of prejudiced behavior where there is no effective recourse to the law.
C. *Education*
   The attempt to alter prejudiced attitudes through formal education and the mass media.
D. *Community Organization*
   The attempt to shape the organized community in ways that will weaken patterns of prejudice.

The *National Association for the Advancement of Colored People (NAACP)* and the *American Jewish Congress* are two national organizations with prime programmatic emphasis on the law. The NAACP, with a reported membership of 100,000, preponderantly Negro, has spearheaded the postwar court battles against segregation. Its branches have been active in the development of local legislative programs. The American Jewish Congress, its membership largely concentrated in the metropolitan areas, has often worked with the NAACP in promoting new legislation.

The *National Urban League,* on the other hand, is essentially a social work agency designed to enlarge economic opportunities for the Negro through direct action. Conferences and negotiations are conducted with industry and labor. Consultative assistance is provided for the harmonious integration of Negroes into any given work force. Branches of the Urban League are scattered through about thirty states in the nation, some of them affiliated with the local Community Chest. The *Anti-Defamation League,* an arm of B'nai B'rith fraternal lodges throughout the country, is traditionally concerned with the direct handling of anti-Semitic "incidents" by negotiating with the offenders or in some cases by bringing the incidents to the attention of the public. Many local groups of an interdenominational and interracial composition have been set up to deal primarily with incidents of racial discrimination on such a case-handling basis. In some cities, official commissions or "Mayor's Committees" have been established for this purpose. The *Congress of Racial Equality* is a less typical interracial organization, with branches in about a dozen cities, which tries to bring dramatic public attention to discriminatory establishments by picketing, sit-down strikes, leaflet distribution, and similar techniques.

Most of the organizations in the field consider education to be their prime function. The *National Conference of Christians and Jews* has over fifty branches throughout the country for the promotion of educational material, intercultural workshops for teachers, and National Brotherhood Week, celebrated during February of each year. More than any other national organization of size, the National Conference of Christians and Jews steers clear of specific issues and addresses itself to general attitudes of prejudice and to intercultural education in the schools. It also supports a continuing research program oriented toward improving teaching techniques in intergroup education. The Anti-Defamation League, in addition to handling anti-Semitic incidents, emphasizes mass-media education, and produces films, display material, and large quantities of pamphlet material for distribution to church groups, other adult groups, and the schools. The *American Jewish Committee* mounts a similar educational program and, more than either the American Jewish Congress or the Anti-Defamation League, has sponsored leading academic research in the field of prejudice. Both the Anti-

Defamation League and the American Jewish Committee have a programmatic interest in publicly exposing organized bigotry, and both are more likely than the National Conference of Christians and Jews to carry their educational activity into specific "action" areas of concern, such as seeking fair employment practices legislation. The interracial *Southern Regional Council* carries on research and such educational activities as news publications and interracial conferences.

The variance in the programs of these and similar organizations is to some extent grounded in the different nature of their constituencies; for this same reason the organizations often differ, also, in their perception of goals and urgencies. Even within a minority group, different organizations may characteristically have constituencies of different socio-economic status. These status differences are often accompanied by characteristically different attitudes about social-action techniques such as picketing or governmental intervention. But whatever the motivational background, the validity of these various programmatic philosophies can be measured—insofar as they can be measured at all—only by their effectiveness.

Section I: Law

"There ought to be a law" is a perennial cry of the aggrieved. And civil rights law has been a major occupation of American politics since the end of World War II. "Civil rights," in its current usage, is equivalent to "minority rights," and has often been distinguished from "civil liberties." The right to vote is a civil liberty applying to all Americans, but an anti-poll-tax law is usually referred to as "civil rights" legislation because it is primarily concerned with a minority group's privilege to vote. "Civil rights" has also been extended to mean not only the protection of constitutional political liberties for minorities but also the prohibition of "private" economic and social discrimination in community life.

Despite the furor, there has been no substantial federal civil rights legislation since Reconstruction. At the present time it is virtually impossible to pass federal civil rights legislation because of the use of the filibuster by southern senators. Rule 22 of the Senate, the cloture rule, allows a senator or group of senators to speak indefinitely, and thereby "kill" a pending bill, unless two-thirds of the senators present vote for cloture. Perennial attempts have been made to change this rule so that a simple majority of senators, or even a majority of those present, can effect cloture. Without the co-operation of southern senators, this change is impossible to obtain.

However, "the law" includes not only the making of new laws by the legislature but the interpretation of existing laws by the judicial and administrative branches of government. Since the beginning of World War II there has been a ferment of activity, not only in state legislatures but in federal and local courts and administrative agencies. This has been the result of a number of factors: the requirements of war; new global pressures on the United States; a rising "fashion of opinion" against prejudice; the increasing political weight of minority groups; and, against this background, a long-range campaign of litigation in the courts.

CONSTITUTIONAL QUESTIONS

Attempts to mitigate prejudice by law have raised some constitutional questions. It is frequently argued that the legal campaign against prejudice is itself a violation of rights granted by the Constitution. It is claimed, for example, that federal civil rights legislation would be a violation of state sovereignty as defined by the Constitution. It has also been suggested that the constitutional rights of private citizens are violated by laws regulating the hiring policies of employers or the practices of restaurant proprietors, property-owners, or labor unions. Finally, much debate has centered around proper interpretation of the Fourteenth Amendment to the Constitution and its guarantee of "equal protection of the laws" to all.

Federal Action: Are States' Rights Violated?

Some of the opponents of federal civil rights law—whether it be legislation or judicial or administrative interpretation—have invoked the danger of too much federal control. They have contended that civil rights matters rightfully belong within the jurisdiction of the states themselves.

Some "hard-core" southern states have threatened to resurrect the doctrine of nullification, now called "interposition," as an extreme expression of states'-rights philosophy. According to this doctrine, the states are the original source of sovereign power. If any federal law or decision of a federal court is thought by the states to exceed the limited powers granted by the states to the federal government, then the state may "interpose" itself between the federal government and the people of that state. It is contended that this act of interposition automatically nullifies the federal ruling with respect to the state that takes such action. This nullification can be legally overcome only by a constitutional amendment specifically granting the disputed powers to the federal government. Such an amendment requires the ratification of 36 states and therefore—like restriction of the filibuster—the assent of at least some southern states.

Other supporters of states' rights do not invoke the legalistic doctrine of interposition. They acknowledge that the national government has the legal right to ban segregation, if the Supreme Court so interprets the Constitution. But, they argue, is this not a dangerous abuse of federal prerogative when local desire and custom are so flagrantly ignored? Is it not the road to an undemocratically centralized and too-powerful government? In his first inaugural address, Abraham Lincoln reaffirmed a fundamental point in his platform:

> . . . the maintenance inviolate of the rights of the States, and especially the right of each state to order and control its own domestic institutions according to its own judgement exclusively, is essential to that balance of power on which the perfection and endurance of our political fabric depend.[1]

This belief in states' rights, like the belief in the rights of the individual, is ultimately based on the same desire to protect the citizen from governmental abuse of power. In theory there is no conflict between states' rights and individual rights; both are safeguards against absolute power.

Now, however, many feel that the "domestic institution" of segregation conflicts with our basic constitutional order, just as the "domestic institution" of slavery, which Lincoln had in mind, later seemed in his judgment to conflict with preservation of the Union. The right claimed by state governments to segregate their citizens appears to contradict the constitutional right granted to all United States citizens to equal treatment from *all* governments, whether federal or state.

Official Acts of Prejudice: What Is Equal Treatment?

The basic law of the land, as expressed in the Thirteenth, Fourteenth, and Fifteenth amendments to the Constitution, states in effect that neither the federal nor any state government may treat one citizen in a manner different from the way it treats another.

This law regulates the official acts of government as they relate to people in their role as *citizens*. It clearly applies to such matters as citizenship rights and due process of law; it would also seem to apply in any area in which the government is a party, such as public housing, publicly owned facilities, public education, and public employment.

This principle of "equal treatment" is already law and is subject only to interpretation by the judicial, and enforcement by the executive, agencies of government. The most spectacular executive enforcement of "equal treatment" since World War II, and indeed since Reconstruction, has been the desegregation of the armed forces by the national administration. The most far-reaching judicial interpretation has been the desegregation of the public schools throughout the nation ordered by the Supreme Court.

Very little debate has centered around desegregation in the armed forces, for there is no question of the right of the federal government to make and enforce its own regulations within its own domain. To school

---
[1] Abraham Lincoln, First Inaugural Address, March 4, 1861.

CIVIL RIGHTS AMENDMENTS TO THE UNITED STATES CONSTITUTION

Article 13. [1865]

1. Neither slavery nor involuntary servitude, except as a punishment for crime whereof the party shall have been duly convicted, shall exist within the United States, or any place subject to their jurisdiction.

2. Congress shall have power to enforce this article by appropriate legislation.

Article 14. [1868]

1. All persons born or naturalized in the United States, and subject to the jurisdiction thereof, are citizens of the United States and of the State wherein they reside. No State shall make or enforce any law which shall abridge the privileges or immunities of citizens of the United States, nor shall any State deprive any person of life, liberty, or property without due process of law, nor deny to any person within its jurisdiction the equal protection of the laws.

2. Representatives shall be apportioned among the several States according to their respective numbers, counting the whole number of persons in each State excluding Indians not taxed. But when the right to Vote at any election for the choice of Electors for President and Vice-President of the United States, Representatives in Congress, the executive and judicial officers of a State, or the members of the Legislature thereof, is denied to any of the male inhabitants of such State, being twenty-one years of age, and citizens of the United States, or in any way abridged, except for participation in rebellion, or other crime, the basis of representation therein shall be reduced in the proportion which the number of such male citizens shall bear to the whole number of male citizens twenty-one years of age in such State.

[Sections 3 and 4 do not have current Civil Rights application.]

5. The Congress shall have power to enforce by appropriate legislation the provisions of this article.

Article 15. [1870]

1. The right of the citizens of the United States to vote shall not be denied or abridged by the United States or by any State on account of race, color, or previous condition of servitude.

2. The Congress shall have power to enforce the provisions of this article by appropriate legislation.

desegregation there has been strong resistance. Two different kinds of questions are involved. One is the legal contention of a number of southern states that "equal but separate" school facilities do not violate the doctrine of "equal treatment." The other is the practical question of whether the federal government can effectively force its constitutional interpretations on unwilling local governments.

"Private" Acts of Prejudice: Can the Citizen Be Controlled?

Constitutional provisions do not apply to the treatment of one private citizen by another. This area is, then, chiefly a matter of new legislation; here the most comprehensive efforts have been made in state and local fair-employment laws. However, in a few areas, where the private affairs of a citizen are somehow government-connected—where, for example, a businessman sells his products to the government or a transportation system comes under the jurisdiction of the Interstate Commerce Commission—courts and administrative agencies have sometimes stepped in on the basis of constitutional law.

In any case, the outstanding question is the extent to which the attitudes and actions of private citizens can be shaped by law. Most of the current efforts to mitigate either official or private acts of prejudice date from World War II, and there has been little time for definitive research and evaluation. However, there is a slowly increasing body of evidence for interpretation.

LAW AND PRIVATE DISCRIMINATION

Private Employment

At the end of the 1958 legislative season, fifteen states and about three dozen cities had some kind of Fair Employment Practices (FEP) law. More than one-third of the American population fell within the jurisdiction of these laws. An FEP law typically has these characteristics: (*a*) it declares discrimination in employment, public or private, to be against public policy; (*b*) it may or may not set up a commission to carry on an educational campaign against discrimination; (*c*) it may or may not empower a commission to hold public hearings, with full subpoena powers, for each individual complaint of discrimination; (*d*) it may or may not provide, where negotiations fail, for fines and/or imprisonment for continued violation of the law. Some proponents of FEP legislation feel that the law is ineffective unless it contains all four provisions, especially the last. Others believe that public hearings are in the long run the most effective lever. Others feel that the main purpose is accomplished by declaration of public policy.

In 1952 the U.S. Senate Labor Subcommittee surveyed FEP operations in seven states and two cities that had fully enforceable laws. In about half of the 5,900 complaints handled, discrimination was verified after investigation.[2] All but six of these cases were settled by informal conciliation without formal hearings. In addition, the state commissions claim a wide effect on patterns of employment over and beyond individual cases handled. Massachusetts reported that "literally thousands of jobs, for the first time, have been opened to representatives of minority groups." The New York Commission made a special study of the 334 cases it reviewed in 1951 and reported that in 85 per cent of the cases there was an improvement in the employment pattern over and beyond the original case in question. But there are nowhere reliable statistics on the actual number of jobs that have been opened up.

FEP laws also make the practice of discrimination somewhat more difficult. They typically prohibit discriminatory advertising. They prohibit the use of discriminatory questions in employment application blanks, although a recent survey indicated that a large number of private employment agencies in New York were still doing discriminatory screening of some kind for their clients.

There has been reported no instance of discord in any union or business operation which has complied with an FEP order.

Government-Connected Private Employment

In 1941, following pressure from Negro groups and a threatened "March on Washington," President Roosevelt issued an executive order which prohibited discrimination by any firm doing business with the government. During the war this FEP order affected most of the large industries and unions. A commission was set up to investigate and hold public hearings on any grievance connected with this order. During its five-year tenure this commission handled over 10,000 complaints and reported that almost 5,000 were successfully negotiated.[3]

In 1946, this wartime FEP Commission went out of existence largely as a result of southern opposition to it in Congress, but executive orders have continued to make nondiscrimination a qualifying clause in all government contracts. About 85 per cent of American industry does some work under government contract. There is, however, only a small staff assigned to ensure compliance, there are no enforcement procedures, and few complaints are filed. The chief effort has been educational, e.g., the issuance of pamphlets and posters to contracting industries.

[2] John A. Davis, "Negro Employment: A Progress Report," *Fortune*, **46** (July, 1952), 102 ff.
[3] Fair Employment Practice Committee, *Final Report* (Washington, D.C.: U.S. Government Printing Office, 1947).

Higher Education

Following the example of New York State's Fair Educational Practices Act of 1948, other northeastern states have taken steps to outlaw discrimination in private colleges and in trade and vocational schools. There is no conclusive evidence on the effects of these laws. Relatively few complaints have been submitted. During 1952, for instance, only two complaints were made under the New York law (both dismissed) and one under the New Jersey law. In 1953 the two major organizational proponents of fair-education laws, the American Jewish Congress and the NAACP, reported:

> There appeared to be little abatement of discrimination against Jews and Italian-Americans at the large private colleges and medical schools of the Northeast. The fair education laws in effect in New York, New Jersey, and Massachusetts were not being effectively invoked either by their administrators or by rejected applicants.[4]

The main efforts of the administrators of these laws have been educational and mediatory. More recently there has been evidence that the use of the quota system in northeastern states has been diminishing. An official survey in 1955 indicated that perhaps twice as many Jewish applicants were being accepted in the medical schools of that state than had been accepted in 1940.[5] There have been no studies to indicate how much of this advance has been, directly or indirectly, the result of legislation.

Discrimination in Public Places

At least nineteen northern and western states have laws (often called "civil rights laws") outlawing discrimination in public places, most of them dating back to the Civil War situation. Unlike the modern fair-employment and fair-education laws, they did not originally have provisions for commissions or investigatory procedures, and it was generally agreed that they were largely ineffective. Regular law-enforcement officers did not take them seriously, and not many people felt it was worth the trouble to prosecute. When cases were prosecuted, fines were small ($10–$100) and were often merely charged by the offending management to public-relations expense. Since World War II, at least five northeastern states have broadened the powers of already existing antidiscrimination commissions to include the investigation of discrimination in public places.

---

[4] *Civil Rights in the United States, 1952* (New York: American Jewish Congress and the National Association for the Advancement of Colored People, 1953), p. 66.

[5] Harold Braverman, "Medical School Quotas," in N. C. Belth (ed.), *Barriers* (New York: Anti-Defamation League, 1958).

In 1953, for example, the Connecticut Commission reported 23 complaints; Massachussetts, 16; New Jersey, 44; New York, 31; and Rhode Island,11.[6] Investigation found about half of these to be justified, and in almost all cases the offending policy was reported corrected. The modified laws have generally included prohibition against the use of discriminatory signs or advertisements by places of public accommodation.

Government-Connected Accommodations

Since World War II a number of decisions by federal courts and the Interstate Commerce Commission have held that segregation in interstate carriers (and their station facilities) is illegal. In 1950, for example, the U.S. Supreme Court ruled that segregation in interstate dining cars, specifically that practiced by the Southern Railway, was illegal. The Southern Railway promptly established a rule of seating "same with same" that was ostensibly much wider than racial in principle. Not only were Negroes to be seated with Negroes, whites with whites, but also young people with young people, old people with old people, and so forth. The Interstate Commerce Commission ruled, by a majority of seven to four, that this rule did not violate the injunction against racial discrimination. In 1953, the American Jewish Congress and the NAACP summed up the situation in these words: "Though the principle was far from being established in practice, there was a noticeable decrease in segregation in many of the Southern carriers."[7] In November, 1955, the Interstate Commerce Commission laid down a more comprehensive ruling, banning any segregation of interstate passengers in rail and bus transportation.

Presumably, discrimination by *intrastate* transportation facilities is also illegal in those states which have general civil rights laws. Relative to the Montgomery, Alabama, bus situation, a federal district court ruled in 1956 that state or local laws ordering segregation in intrastate transportation facilities were unconstitutional.

Housing

The U.S. Supreme Court has ruled that restrictive covenants in real estate deeds and documents cannot be enforced by the courts. This ruling did not serve to make housing discrimination illegal. It did, however, establish the principle that any agreement made by the buyer of a piece of property that he would not resell to a nonwhite was not legally binding. It therefore removed a control device for those who wished to discriminate. Recent New York, Pennsylvania, and Connecticut laws provide that

---

[6] *Civil Rights in the United States, 1953* (New York: American Jewish Congress and the National Association for the Advancement of Colored People, 1954), p. 121.

[7] *Civil Rights in the United States, 1952*, p. 100.

private housing developments which are publicly assisted (e.g., by tax exemption) are prohibited from discriminating. In 1955 New York pioneered a law prohibiting discrimination in any housing which is financed through the Federal Housing Administration or the Veterans' Administration; the implementation of this law falls to the state's Commission against Discrimination. In 1957 New York City passed the first law in the country which prohibits discrimination in the sale or rental of private housing even where no government funds or agencies are involved in any way; this law applies to "multiple dwellings," which includes tracts and apartment houses with ten or more units. In 1958 a California court ruled that any discrimination in the sale of housing which involved Federal Housing or Veterans' Administration funds was unconstitutional. If this finding is confirmed by other courts, the need for special legislation would seem to be diminished.

LAW AND PUBLIC DISCRIMINATION

Public Employment

The Federal Civil Service Commission operates on a policy of nondiscrimination. Most states in the North and West, either by law or administrative order, also prohibit discrimination in public employment.

In 1948 President Truman, by executive order, forbade discrimination in the armed forces and set up a committee to administer its enforcement.

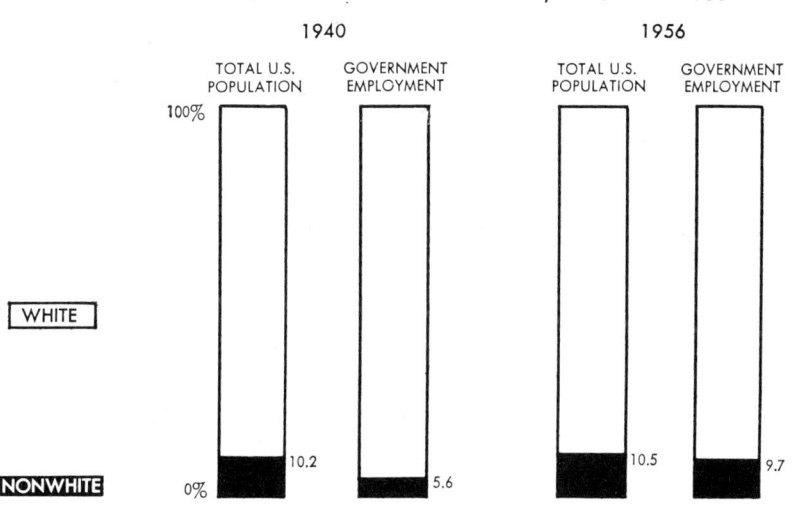

FIGURE 6:1 RESULTS OF FAIR EMPLOYMENT PRACTICES IN GOVERNMENT EMPLOYMENT, 1940 AND 1956

Adapted from U.S. Bureau of Labor Statistics, *Notes on the Economic Situation of Negroes in the United States* (Washington, D.C.: U.S. Department of Labor, 1958), p. 18.

Private civil rights organizations have continued to check on its progress and to maintain pressures on the government. Desegregation was the immediate goal, and in the directive atmosphere of the armed services it was quickly accomplished. By 1954 it was reported that there were no longer any segregation policies in the Army, Air Force, or Navy. Neither sleeping, eating, entertainment, nor any other official facilities are segregated.

During the war a research branch of the Army found that contact experience with Negro soldiers shaped the attitudes of white soldiers favorably toward further associations with Negroes. In divisions where there were no colored platoons, 62 per cent of the white soldiers said they would "very much" dislike association with Negroes. Where there were colored troops in the same division but not in the same regiment, 24 per cent of the white soldiers gave the same answer. Only 7 per cent of the white soldiers in companies that had a Negro platoon gave this response.[8]

After the accomplishment of complete desegregation, an Army survey concluded that "it works."[9] Desegregation rarely led to friction. Some base commanders reported less racial friction than had been the case under circumstances of segregation. Overnight, it seemed, the white and Negro soldier had learned to work, live, and even play together. A white Army sergeant from Virginia made this comment after his experience with desegregation: "Many guys didn't like it. I was one of them. They didn't like the idea of going to the same mess hall with them. There was a lot of talk about what would happen. Nothing actually happened. In about two weeks it wore in. I slept with one right beside me. I resented it at first. It's all in your mind. Once you get it out, you're okay. If you can live with whites you can live with most colored."

The permanence of new attitudes was not so clearly established. What happens when the white soldier returns to his community and to old patterns? At least some white soldiers were able to adjust harmoniously to the temporary situation without any major revisions of attitude. One white soldier, expressing satisfaction with his own desegregation experience, nevertheless hedged: "I wouldn't be surprised if they all [the Negroes] got rated by a psychologist as to who's fit to go into a white outfit."

In addition, veterans returning to the South are, for the most part, younger men who are not in a position of strength to oppose patterns of segregation in the community. However, it can be assumed that Army policy now contributes to reduction of rigidly prejudiced attitudes instead

---

[8] Samuel A. Stauffer *et al.*, *The American Soldier* (Princeton: Princeton University Press, 1949), Vol. I, p. 594.

[9] Department of Defense, *A Progress Report on Integration in the Armed Services, 1954* (Washington, D.C.: U.S. Government Printing Office, 1955).

of strengthening them by the maintenance of segregated patterns. Nor can it be overlooked that an important effect of armed forces integration is to raise the level of aspiration of southern Negroes who return to their communities from the desegregated services.

Public Education

In May, 1954, the Supreme Court ruled that separate public school facilities, even if equal, were discriminatory and therefore unconstitutional. The Supreme Court in 1896, in *Plessy* v. *Ferguson,* had come to an opposite conclusion. Referring to this reversal, the Supreme Court decision of 1954 remarked: "Whatever may have been the extent of psychological knowledge at the time of *Plessy* v. *Ferguson,* this [desegregation] finding is amply supported by modern authority."[10] Presumably out of "sociological" considerations, the Supreme Court also ruled that the lower federal courts could decide what the pace or method of desegregation should be in any given region.

The reactions of the seventeen southern states were scarcely uniform. By the beginning of 1958, five border states (Kentucky, Maryland, Mis-

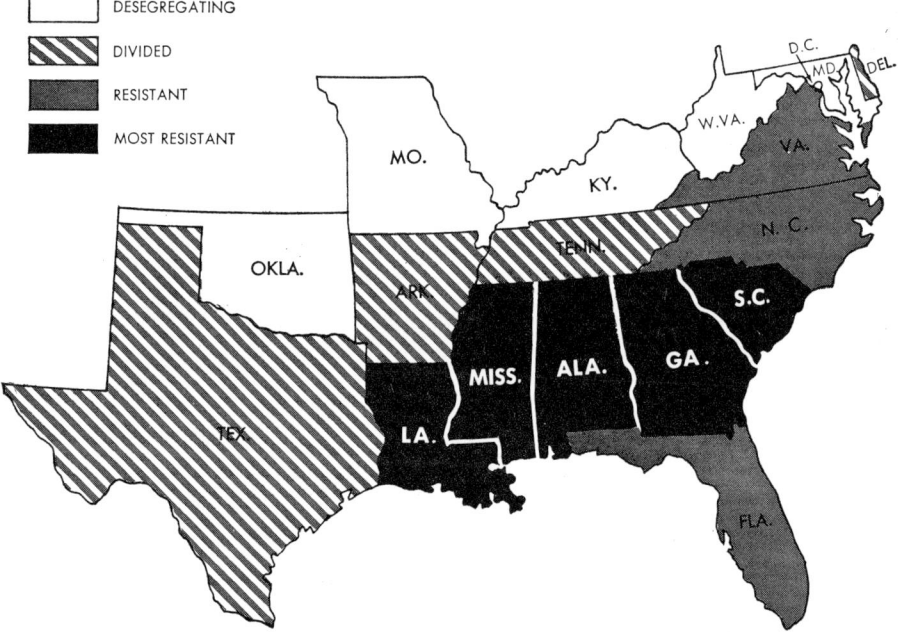

FIGURE 6:2 ATTITUDES OF SOUTHERN STATES TOWARD SCHOOL SEGREGATION

---

[10] *Oliver Brown* et al. v. *Board of Education of Topeka, Shawnee County, Kansas,* et al. (1954), 347 U.S. 483, 74 S Ct 686.

souri, Oklahoma, and West Virginia) and the District of Columbia had begun to desegregate schools in many localities within their borders. Major, if not total, compliance in these states seemed destined within a relatively short time. These states have a white population of about 12.5 million and a Negro population of about 1.5 million.

In addition, six other states had either initiated some desegregation or had given indication that they would. Some counties of Arkansas, Delaware, Tennessee, and Texas had desegregated; other sections had resisted. Some sections of North Carolina had indicated readiness to desegregate. Florida was reportedly making some plans for desegregation. These were states in which compliance would be uneven and delayed but in which the pattern of change had already begun, or showed some promise of beginning, as a result of the Supreme Court decision. These states comprise a white population of about 16 million and a Negro population of about 3.5 million.

Integration, where it occurred, was not always unattended by "incidents." In Baltimore, for instance, three weeks after 52 schools were integrated in September, 1954, picketing and public demonstrations by students took place. These activities made headlines; but actually no more than six schools were ever involved, and the hard facts were that 97 per cent of Baltimore's public schoolboys and girls were not withdrawn from school but, instead, attended classes without interruption. At the opening of the school year in the fall of 1956, the nation's newspapers were filled with headlines about violence in a half-dozen communities of Tennessee, Kentucky, and Texas as crowds gathered to try to prevent the desegregation of public schools. In Kentucky and Tennessee the governors called out the state militia to protect the Negro children who were attending the schools.

The most publicized and significant "incident" took place in Little Rock, Arkansas, in 1957. There were already a number of desegregated school facilities in the state, and plans had been made for the desegregation of Central High School in Little Rock. As a matter of fact, the Board of Education in Little Rock announced its intention to comply with the Supreme Court decision three days after the decision was issued, and in May, 1955, it published a concrete plan for desegregating the schools. It was a gradual plan, to be accomplished over a period of not less than eight years. It was to begin in September, 1957, with the admission of 10 Negro students into the Little Rock Central High School, which had a student body of about 2,000 students. The plan was widely publicized and was explained to about two hundred local groups and organizations. Major opposition to it came from those who considered the plan "too slow." A suit was filed by members of the Negro community, asking that the plan be accelerated, but the United States district court ruled that it constituted compliance and was consistent with the Supreme Court decision.

However, in September, 1957, just before the opening of the school semester which was to see the first Negro students in Central High School, Governor Orval Faubus of Arkansas surrounded the high school with units of the National Guard. He stated that this action was taken not to prevent integration but to preserve civil peace and order. However, he added that he did not think civil peace and order could be preserved at that time if the Negro students were to enter the school. He told the nation he had evidence that there would be violence. In any case, the National Guard units refused to permit the Negro students to enter.

After the school board had brought this situation to the official attention of the United States district court, envisioning the possibility of suspending its plan, the court issued an injunction against the state government to prevent it from further obstructing the entry of the Negro students into the high school. Governor Faubus said that he would reluctantly comply with this order and withdrew the state troops.

By this time the emotions of the community had been brought to a boil, and there had been deliberate attempts to inflame opposition to integration. On the school day following the withdrawal of state troops, scenes of interracial violence were common in Little Rock, and the mob outside the school itself attacked all Negroes in sight. The Negro students managed to get into the school, but the mob uproar led the authorities to request these students to stay away until adequate protection was made available. The police were incapable of handling the mobs, and requests to Governor Faubus for troops to protect the Negro children went unheeded. The situation was clearly out of hand. It was headlined in newspapers around the world.

The same day, President Eisenhower issued a proclamation requesting the mob to cease its illegal activity. When the situation continued to deteriorate on the next day, the President ordered federal troops into Little Rock to enforce the court orders for the removal of obstructions to lawful integration. The federal troops were immediately flown in, they established order without bloodshed, and the Negro students returned to school. The principle had been established that the federal government would not tolerate the physical obstruction of federal law as duly interpreted by the courts. However, the problem of integration in Little Rock was not thereby laid. The school board requested permission to delay integration because of the local situation, and the court battles continued to rage.

In six states there still seemed, in 1958, to be almost total resistance to any desegregation move. These states—Alabama, Georgia, Louisiana, Mississippi, South Carolina, and Virginia—have a white population of about 12 million, a Negro population of about 5.5 million. All had enacted some

SCHOOL INTEGRATION BEGINS IN THE SOUTH

An *eleven-year-old student enters school on the first day of integration in Greensboro, North Carolina.*

Jack Moebes; *Greensboro Record*, Greensboro, N.C.

George Harris; Black Star

A teacher with her kindergarten class in St. Louis, Missouri—one of the first cities to lay plans for compliance with the Supreme Court decision.

The end of the day at a recently integrated high school in San Antonio, Texas.

Ivan Massar; Black Star

kind of legislation designed to evade the Supreme Court ruling, e.g., by providing for a "private" school system to be subsidized by the state. The evasions were not generally expected to withstand judicial scrutiny, and a major break in this wall of total resistance appeared early in 1959, when the schools of Norfolk, Virginia, began to desegregate. On January 19, 1959, the Supreme Court of Appeals of Virginia declared that Virginia's "massive-resistance" legislation was unconstitutional under the *state* constitution, which requires a system of free public schools. This legislation had provided for the closing of any Virginia public school in the event that a federal court ordered its immediate integration.

Bitterness has run high in these states and in recalcitrant sections of some of the "divided" states. "Citizens' Councils" were formed, disavowing violence but employing drastic economic pressures against Negro and white protagonists of desegregation. State legislators and ex-governors were counted in the ranks of some of these Citizens' Councils, which also included some prominent local businessmen and labor leaders. Although these Councils for the most part attempted to disassociate themselves from the tactics of the discredited Ku Klux Klan, some of their local leaders were invariably at the forefront of the occasional violent action against desegregation. In several cases these leaders were arrested for assault or inciting to violence.

On the surface, at least, a resolution of the school-desegregation issue does not yet appear to be in sight in these "hard-core" areas. On the other hand, there is a continuing court battle, county by county, by such organizations as the NAACP. There is recognition on the part of some industrial and political leaders in the South that stability is needed to attract northern industry and insure industrial growth. There is at least an audible murmur of protest from groups of parents and students in some of the southern cities which have closed their schools rather than submit to a court order for integration. During 1958 dissatisfaction with a policy of total resistance was being expressed by groups of citizens who were not identified with, and indeed were in principle opposed to, the goal of desegregation. But the closing of the schools placed the education and the future of their children in jeopardy. Even where private schools have been established, the effectiveness and accreditation of these schools are in serious question. As court actions multiply, and if in the wake of these court actions more and more public schools are closed, it is expected that the situation will become intolerable for southern parents, especially in urban areas. It is in these slowly developing factors that the protagonists of desegregation in the South have placed their hopes. In addition, the southern population has demonstrated a rather extensive unwillingness to resort to violence when legal resources to block integration are finally exhausted. The dynamiting, in 1958, of schools and other buildings in Tennessee and Georgia by fanatical segregationists brought swift condemnation from both the officials and the community at large in the cities involved.

Public Housing

At least a half-dozen states and over a hundred communities have statutes prohibiting segregation in new public housing. As a result, at least 15 per cent of the nation's public housing projects have an integration policy. There have been no serious "incidents" reported as a result of the introduction of Negroes into formerly segregated projects, although there have been instances of white families moving when Negroes were admitted. On the other hand, integrated projects report long waiting lists of both white and nonwhite applicants. A series of studies by New York University in four public housing projects concludes that "from the point of view of reducing prejudice and of creating harmonious democratic intergroup relationships, the net gain resulting from the interracial projects is considerable." In the two genuinely integrated projects studied, 59 per cent and 62 per cent of the white housewives indicated that their attitudes toward the Negro people had changed in a favorable direction. Only 3 per cent and 7 per cent indicated that their attitudes had changed in an unfavorable direction. (For a more detailed analysis of this study see Adaptation 10, pp. 279 ff.)

Summary evaluation: 1. *The enactment and enforcement of law depend partly on the state of public opinion.* In a democratic society most laws cannot come into being without some prior process of community education. Fair employment practices laws have passed in those states in which opinion is already most unfavorable to employment discrimination. It has been possible for laws against the Ku Klux Klan to be passed in southern states in recent years because public opinion with regard to racist violence has changed.

The desegregation decision has been implemented most readily in those southern states which have the most favorable climate of public opinion. There are still widespread patterns of employment discrimination in states covered by fair employment practices laws. Many employment agencies, for example, have found devious ways of serving employers who wish to hire on a discriminatory basis.

2. *However, law can shape public opinion by altering the social conditions under which opinions are formed.*

a) Laws can create conditions of intergroup living. The scientific evidence indicates that interpersonal contact can reduce prejudice, provided minority and majority group members are of roughly the same socio-economic status. Such contact has been created most spectacularly by integration in the armed forces, in public housing, and potentially in public education. Even the partial reduction of educational and employment barriers helps to destroy stereotypes, raise socio-economic status, and make intergroup contact more constructive.

b) Laws can directly alter the visible signs of prejudice. Fair employment practices and enforceable civil rights laws can effectively eliminate discriminatory advertising from the community scene. Laws can drive prejudice at least partly underground, thereby modifying the cultural environment, especially for the younger generation.

3. *Laws can also exert a direct "conformity pressure" on behavior and attitudes.* For those who have mixed feelings about prejudice, or for those whose behavior and attitudes are strongly shaped by a desire to conform, established law can tip the scales. This principle obviously does not apply where there is overwhelming rejection of the law by the community and in-group.

Hadley Cantril has suggested this law of public opinion: "When an opinion is held by a slight majority, or when an opinion is not solidly structured, an accomplished fact tends to shift opinion in the direction of acceptance." [11] He points out that, prior to American entry into World War II, public opinion polls showed a 10-per-cent increase in responses favorable to repeal of neutrality legislation and enactment of a conscription law immediately after these actions had in fact been taken by Congress.

Conversely, law also serves to break up the conformity pressures *for* prejudice. Employers have often been motivated to "hold the color line" because of a reluctance to break ranks with fellow-employers in the community or neighborhood. A fair employment practices law helps release these employers from such ties. It also helps to support those employers who say they have not instituted an open hiring policy because of the resistance of their present employees. In those states which are divided on implementation of the desegregation ruling—and indeed in the southern states as a whole—the solid front of conformity pressure has obviously been cracked.

Section II: Direct Action

Direct action, in this context, is the handling of specific cases of discrimination by persuasive methods where there is no effective recourse to the law. Direct-action techniques fall mainly into the following categories.

[11] Hadley Cantril *et al., Gauging Public Opinion* (Princeton: Princeton University Press, 1944), pp. 226–30.

> The National Association of Attorneys General had scheduled its annual meeting in December, 1954, at a famous resort near Phoenix, Arizona. It was discovered that this resort had an avowed "rigid policy of 100 per cent Gentile clientele." This fact was brought to the attention of the attorneys general by the Anti-Defamation League. In answer to a disturbed query from the attorney general of Arizona, the resort's management wrote on September 30:
>
> "The embarrassing position this places you in has hastened us to make a change in our policy.... Henceforth from this date we will refrain from using the objectionable 'restricted clientele' terminology in our advertising and in our correspondence."
>
> On October 18 the Anti-Defamation League wrote directly to the resort manager, asking whether this letter meant only that the hotel would refrain from discriminatory *advertising* or whether the "changed policy" would in fact mean that "no guest will be rejected on the grounds of religious faith."
>
> The resort replied, on October 20, that "our policy in guest selection will remain the same as it has been in the past." The manager indicated that the advertising material in the future would refer to "selected clientele" rather than "restricted clientele," but affirmed the continuing practice of discrimination in fact.
>
> This was brought to public attention by the Anti-Defamation League in newspaper stories around the country. Several attorneys general indicated that they would not stay at the resort in the light of its policy. The Association canceled its reservation and moved its convention site to West Virginia.

NEGOTIATION

Negotiation consists of private conferences with the parties responsible in an attempt to point out the moral and practical disadvantages of discrimination. Often this is a matter of negotiating specific complaints, usually in regard to employment or housing discrimination. In some cases, critical areas of discrimination are sought out by organizations and acted upon without waiting for a complaint. The Urban League, for example, has traditionally sought to break down patterns of discrimination in an industry by negotiating with key members of that industry. It has had success, for example, in persuading department stores in certain communities to employ Negroes as salesgirls for the first time; in such cases, they help the department store to find especially well-qualified Negro employees. In other cases, attempts have been made to overcome the biased behavior of one homeowner in the hope that the total neighborhood pattern might change.

PUBLIC EXPOSURE

When private negotiation fails, generally the leverage of public exposure can be applied successfully only insofar as the climate of opinion is sympathetic and only when the offending party is responsive to the pressure of unfavorable public opinion.

BOYCOTT

Implicit in public exposure is the danger of resultant economic boycott. Organizations such as the Anti-Defamation League and the Urban League frown on organized boycott, feeling it is morally improper for a private agency to attempt to be punitive. Because of the moral impropriety, there is always the practical danger of a public-opinion boomerang.

Where explicit boycotts have been successful, they have usually been based on the special economic leverage of the minority group itself, e.g., picketing of stores in Harlem which depended almost exclusively on Negro trade but did not hire Negro personnel.

Evaluation: 1. *Relatively few individual complaints are handled by private agencies.* These cases probably number in the hundreds—a "drop in the bucket" compared with the known extent of discrimination.

2. *The case-by-case approach does not reach hidden patterns of discrimination.* Many minority members, for instance, do not bother to apply for jobs in areas where discriminatory patterns are notorious.

3. *A private agency is not as effective as a legally established agency.* It can neither make a proper public investigation nor implement the results of investigation.

4. *Nevertheless, casework may be effective in making prejudice less "respectable."* Sometimes prejudice is only forced underground, as when an apartment-house management persists in a quiet discriminatory policy but eliminates advertisements, signs, or public statements to that effect. Still, even in such a case, the moral point has been made and accepted that, at the very least, public expression of prejudice is offensive.

5. *Casework can establish models of nondiscrimination.* Where one department store satisfactorily eliminates discrimination in its employment policy, other department stores in the community become more hospitable to change. The experience has been that, in general, hiring minority employees has met with acceptance by both customers and other employees.

6. *Casework can give relief to individual victims of prejudice.* Even where full satisfaction is not obtained, members of a minority group have the security of knowing that there is some organization that will take up their cause. They do not feel entirely helpless or isolated.

Section III: Education

It has been demonstrated that direct action and law are potent weapons of "education," by any reasonable use of the word. The difference between these techniques and any formal category of education must be initially spelled out in terms not of effect but of approach. Law and direct action are approaches to behavior (and through behavior to attitudes). Education is an approach to attitudes (and through attitudes to behavior). Education, broadly defined as "an approach to attitudes," would include what is commonly called "propaganda." In other words, it includes both the educative approach, whose goal is to develop the resources of an individual so that he can rationally construct his own attitudes, and the manipulative approach, whose goal is to implant a given attitude by any means.

THE SCHOOLS

In the belief that the most comprehensive *preventive* program must lie with the schools, a number of organizations have been created to deal exclusively with the development of such a program. The Bureau of Intercultural Education, formed in 1934, comprises a wide range of laymen who conduct a research, literature, and consultative program. The New York University Center for Human Relations Studies is concerned with research and training in the field. The National Conference of Christians and Jews has intercultural education in the schools as a major concern of its program; to a less exclusive extent, so do the American Jewish Committee and the Anti-Defamation League. Many school departments in the North and West have themselves developed special programs in this area.

The research evidence is limited. Most of the evaluative studies are preliminary, and few are scientifically convincing. However, the evidence that does exist, buttressed by what we know in general of educational techniques, suggests certain tentative generalizations.

Direct vs. Indirect Content

What is taught may have a relatively direct or indirect bearing on prejudice. An analysis of anti-Semitism and its logical flaws would be "direct." A study of the Jewish religion, in the hope of breaking down barriers of suspicion as a by-product, would be "indirect."

Henry Kagan conducted an experiment with two groups of Christian students with these different approaches.[12] The "indirect group method" dealt with the Jewish origins of and contributions to Christianity and the values of the Bible shared by Christian and Jew alike. The "direct group

---

[12] Henry E. Kagan, *Changing the Attitudes of Christian toward Jew* (New York: Columbia University Press, 1952).

method" concerned itself specifically with the problem of prejudice against Jews and the correction of prejudicial misinformation about Jews. He concluded that the indirect approach did *not* decrease the degree of prejudice toward Jews, but a significant decrease of prejudice did follow the use of the direct approach.

The students involved in the Kagan study were willing participants and hospitable to the direct approach. If deeper resistances had been involved, the direct approach might not have been so successful. It has become almost axiomatic among educators, however, that, unless the concrete implications are spelled out, indirect learning is apt not to carry over. An understanding of the principles of brotherhood does not automatically create an understanding of the need for integrated housing. During World War II it was found that a rejection of Nazism did not necessarily entail a rejection of Nazi anti-Semitism. The indirect approach often serves only as a useful entree to the main subject.

Intellectual vs. Participating Techniques

Obviously, no rigid dichotomy can be set up between intellectual and participant learning, but they do represent two separable approaches. Classroom presentation of factual material about other ethnic groups would be an intellectual approach; even a lively discussion of intergroup problems, involving the students, would be considered essentially an intellectual approach—and probably a more effective one. Setting up and working with other ethnic groups in an actual intergroup situation would be a participating approach. In a sense, it is the difference between "being told" and "learning for oneself" through experience.

Schoolroom evidence indicates that participating programs are more successful than the merely intellectual and factual. Increases in favorable attitudes toward minorities do not keep pace with increases in information about minorities or about prejudice. However, participating approaches will be most disappointing when they have only the appearance of participation. Intergroup contact which involves nothing more than physical propinquity would be a case in point. Participation in a common project is more likely to involve the participants, stimulate genuine interaction, and induce positive attitudes.

Again, the carry-over from school-connected experience to concrete attitudes about minority groups is not automatic. The implications of the experience must often be spelled out directly and specifically.

Possibility of Changing Attitudes

Comprehensive school programs in intergroup relations, applying the best knowledge in the field, have regularly shown a statistical decrease of prejudiced attitudes. However, these decreases have either been slight or of dubious import.

A comparative study was made of graduates of the "Springfield Plan," a long-range and omnibus approach to intercultural education in Springfield, Massachusetts.[13] Students were tested with the Bogardus Social Distance Scale, which asks which groups the subjects would not admit to their country, to their neighborhood, to close kinship, and so forth. The higher the score, the higher the degree of prejudice. Those educated in Springfield had a mean score of 64.76. The control group had a mean score of 67.60. This difference was small and of bare statistical significance; i.e., had the difference been a little less, it would have had to be attributed to chance.

Summary evaluation: 1. *Formal education is but one segment of a child's life.* Its influence may be limited because it is competing with potent educational forces in the home and community.

2. *The "educative" approach is too slow.* Disadvantaged minority groups, concerned with current patterns of discrimination, do not like to feel that they have to depend upon attitude changes that will not bear fruit for a generation.

3. *Schools cannot greatly outstrip the sentiments of their communities.* In many of the communities that need it most, intergroup education is not likely to exist at all.

4. *However, schools have the opportunity of providing life-experiences.* While school is only a segment of a child's life, it is nevertheless an important segment. If there is the possibility of intergroup contact, the schools have the means of making that contact meaningful rather than perfunctory.

5. *The hidden effects of direct education are not revealed by research evidence.* Research evidence does not indicate what delayed effect education may have upon individual attitudes and public opinion. One person's prejudice may not be immediately altered by accurate knowledge about racial differences, but it is nevertheless important that there is no longer any "respectable" race theory.

6. *The schools can build leadership.* A base of intellectually sound and emotionally convinced citizens is essential to other community efforts against prejudice, including efforts by law. The schools can provide the motivation, and certainly the needed resources, for such future leadership.

THE MASS MEDIA

One of the advantages of the school situation is that it can reach the entire juvenile population. The most nearly analogous situation in the adult

---

[13] Dorothy T. Spoerl, "Some Aspects of Prejudice as Affected by Religion and Education," *Journal of Social Psychology,* **33** (1951), 69–76.

community is the existence of mass media: television, radio, moving pictures, newspapers, periodicals, streetcar cards, and so forth. By its very nature, the mass-media approach has several distinctive characteristics:

1. It is divorced from any of the "participating" techniques of education.

2. To the extent that its audience is adult, it must be concerned with re-forming rather than forming attitudes.

3. Its methods tend to be (although they are not necessarily) manipulative. Because it is so difficult to alter prejudiced attitudes with facts or logic alone, and because participating techniques are not possible with mass media, there is heavy emphasis on propagandistic approaches. The key to the propagandistic approach is its attempt to induce acceptance of a new attitude by attaching it to an already present and potent emotion.

Agencies which operate primarily in the mass-media field typically circulate dramatic radio transcriptions, films for television use, car cards, and the like. They help to plan magazine and newspaper articles. They attempt to "salt" their message into the regular radio and television programs. They arrange newsworthy events, such as meetings and conferences which are reported by the press.

It is even more difficult than in the case of school or legislative programs to assess the effect of a mass-media program. Cartoons created to combat prejudice were found by two sets of observers to be successful for some of the audience, to have no effect on others, and frequently to boomerang. Bernard Berelson has suggested this ironic formula: "Some kinds of communication on some kinds of issues, brought to the attention of some kinds of people under some kinds of conditions, have some kind of effect." [14]

These studies remind us that individuals are not wholly manipulable. What are some of the conditions under which propaganda is successful or unsuccessful? How far can and should propaganda go in inducing new attitudes? Research evidence tentatively supports the following generalizations with regard to changing individual attitudes:

1. *As a rule, propaganda is successful only when a proposed attitude fits in with an individual's basic value structure;* that is, when it does not conflict with, or when it strengthens or reinforces, other attitudes which seem fundamental and important to him. A strong prejudice against foreigners may help to encourage opposition to the United Nations. A firm belief in democracy may help to make acceptable and convincing an appeal that racial prejudice be abandoned.

For this reason, mass-media technicians try to attach their "message" to widely accepted and highly respectable values. A program motivated by a desire to improve intergroup relations may be presented within the frame-

---

[14] Bernard Berelson, "Communication and Public Opinion," in Wilbur Schramm (ed.), *Process and Effects of Mass Communication* (Urbana: University of Illinois Press, 1954), p. 345.

Propaganda: This widely distributed poster attempts to make bigotry disreputable by association.

work of a generally patriotic theme. A crude example is the poster shown above, which attempts to link prejudice with the general distaste of the American public for communism.

2. *The more deeply an attitude is held, the more difficult it is to modify.* A mass-media campaign designed to turn an audience to a new brand of face soap can be swiftly successful. It would not be easy, on the other hand, to persuade an American audience not to use soap at all.

3. *People tend to protect their important attitudes by rationalization,*

evasion, and distortion. The prejudiced person with strong negative stereotypes about Negroes, for example, will typically evade the example of a Negro who does not fit the stereotype by dismissing him as "different." Already cited was the example of the southern white soldier who got along fine with the Negro soldiers in his Army unit but suggested that they had been specially chosen.

4. *Attitudes may be strengthened or weakened but rarely reversed.* One experiment subjected an audience opposed to the Tennessee Valley Authority to propaganda supporting it. Intensity of opposition was frequently reduced, but few actual conversions were made. One observer remarked: "Opinions have this in common with entrenchments, that they offer obstinate resistance to a frontal attack but not to a turning movement." [15]

5. *People tend to expose themselves only to what they want to hear.* Lazarsfeld, Berelson, and Gaudet studied the voters of Erie County, Ohio, in the presidential election of 1940.[16] They reported that about two-thirds of the constant partisans managed to see and hear more of their side's propaganda than the opposition's. About one-fifth happened to be exposed more frequently to the other side, and the rest were neutral in their exposure. But the more strongly partisan the person, the more likely he was to insulate himself from contrary points of view.

According to the measurements of these three investigators, the effects of the campaign were as follows:

Reinforcement or activation of predispositions	67%
Conversion	5
Partial conversion	12
No effect	16

However, though it is easy to avoid an obvious political address on radio and television, it is not so easy to avoid a dramatic program which, it develops, has an intergroup theme.

6. *An attitude is more readily adopted if it is held by people whom the individual respects or with whom he identifies.* In some people the need to conform to "respectable" opinion is highly developed; but in any case, it is always difficult for an individual to "buck" the opinions of people he likes or has to be with.

7. *An attitude is often more acceptable if it represents majority opinion.* In one experiment, student opinion on campus issues was changed merely by making the majority view known. The group involved need not be the general community but merely the people with whom the individual comes

---

[15] Joseph T. Klapper, "Mass Media and Persuasion," *ibid.,* p. 306.
[16] Paul F. Lazarsfeld, Bernard Berelson, and Hazel Gaudet, *The People's Choice* (New York: Columbia University Press, 1944).

into contact or with whom he feels an affinity. A prejudiced person who moves in unprejudiced circles is apt to keep silent about his feelings if their expression would threaten his social relations, while a person who moves in highly prejudiced circles is apt to acquire prejudices he never had before.

8. *An attitude is difficult to change if it is one of the sources of group solidarity.* By the same token, if an attitude is irrelevant to the basis for association and to a feeling of "we-ness," it is more susceptible of modification. Southern attitudes toward the Negro are difficult to change because they are often part of what it means to a southerner to be a southerner. For a person living in the North, attitudes toward the Negro are usually not part of his identification of himself as a northerner. Many unions readily adopt resolutions and policies opposing discrimination and segregation and institute programs of education to combat prejudice despite the fact that, as individuals, their members are often prejudiced. This can happen in part because the prejudice of the members is not a dynamic element in their self-identification as union members and in their loyalty and commitment to the union.

9. *Propaganda that does not specifically touch on the attitude involved may have little immediate effect.* For this reason, moralizing propaganda is likely to have little specific result. A Protestant may accept the belief that all religions seek truth without modifying his strong anti-Catholic prejudice; if this prejudice is to be modified, anti-Catholicism must be specifically dealt with.

10. *Propaganda on specific attitudes may not influence general moral beliefs.* In an intensive study of the effect of propaganda films on Army audiences, Hovland, Lumsdaine, and Sheffield concluded that the films shown had "only a very few effects" on general opinion items not specifically covered by the material shown.[17]

Summary evaluation: 1. *Mass-media efforts have little immediate effect on individual attitudes of prejudice.* Prejudice characteristically protects itself with a hard and complex shell of rationalization. It therefore resists and evades rhetorical attack and is least directly amenable to the nonparticipating approach.

2. *Manipulation of public opinion is immoral.* Insofar as mass-media techniques tend to be propagandistic and manipulative in nature, they help to breed and strengthen nonrational approaches to human problems. Minds have not been helped to think their way maturely out of a problem; their immaturity has merely been "properly channeled." But such a mind is always dangerous. If it cannot be "trapped back" into prejudice by some

---

[17] Carl Hovland, Arthur A. Lumsdaine, and Fred D. Sheffield, *Experiments on Mass Communication* (Princeton: Princeton University Press, 1949), p. 64.

superior manipulative trick, then it is always vulnerable to some other irrational and perhaps antisocial trap.

3. *Nevertheless, the mass media are an important part of the cultural environment.* Mass media are themselves one of the social conditions under which private opinions are normally shaped. Like the law, they are a mirror of society and are therefore a potent educational influence. The role of the mass media in sustaining negative stereotypes of minority groups has long been recognized.

4. *The mass media can exert conformity pressure.* Like the law, the mass media are a factor for those people who have some need for conformity. This effect of mass media is obviously qualified by the manner of its use and the extent of the monopoly which can be obtained.

5. *The hidden effects of mass-media education are not revealed by research evidence.* The delayed effect of mass-media education is difficult to measure. Hovland, Lumsdaine, and Sheffield, when they rechecked attitudes nine weeks after the initial presentation instead of after the usual one week, found that factual information suffered about a 50 per cent loss of retention; there was some regression of attitude changes; however, there were also some increases of opinion change over and above the earlier tests, and in some cases increases were eleven times the size of the short-term effect.[18] It is the deeper value beliefs which seem to be more subject to delayed-reaction changes. Even where mass-media education is not a prime mover of attitude changes, it may eventually be the *sine qua non* of such changes. The mass media, like the schools, have helped to destroy the respectability of unscientific race theories.

6. *The mass media are relatively accessible.* A sizable proportion of the mass-media outlets are national in scope. They are not bound by local or regional prejudices and are hence more open to the approaches of intergroup-relations agencies. They are often more easy to negotiate with than, say, thousands of schools or adult forum groups around the country. Motion pictures, radio, television, periodicals, reach millions with each impact. The percentage of success with each impact does not have to be great to make the effort worth while. With their limitations, the mass media are often the only practical and significant means of adult education available to intergroup agencies.

Section IV: Community Organization

"Community organization" describes the attempt to modify public opinion and behavior through the use of existing patterns of influence in the community. This effort entails many different kinds of activities and ap-

[18] *Ibid.,* p. 184.

proaches: the organizing of individuals into an effective association; the organizing of existing associations into a unified force; the enlisting of support from influential individuals. In the context of social action, the concept of community organization encompasses the attempt to place the various elements of the community into effective relationship to one another with respect to some goal. Community organization is increasingly considered basic to all efforts to combat prejudice, whether by law, direct action, education, or the mass media.

PATTERNS OF INFLUENCE

In 1958 in one city of 800,000 population there were at least 2,000 voluntary citizens' associations. People gather together in such associations to share certain common goals and values. Trade associations and labor associations are, for example, based primarily on self-interest; fraternal organizations have sociability as their chief aim; while other associations, such as religious groups, are based not so much on specific goals as on common beliefs.

Because of the nature of its membership, however, a formal association may be stamped with values that extend beyond its ostensible reason for being. A businessmen's service club, for example, may have been organized to perform certain community services while providing a measure of sociability. Nevertheless, the fact that its members are businessmen is usually taken to signify that the association is operating within the framework of certain "businessmen's values." A neighborhood improvement association may be organized for the purpose of protecting property values, but the socioeconomic character of the neighborhood it represents may imply a larger framework of values.

Although not connected with a formal association, individuals may be key forces in a community because they are personally identified with some particular package of goals and values or because, for one reason or another, their opinions are respected.

AIMS OF COMMUNITY ORGANIZATION

The aims of community organization are (1) to reach people through the organizations of which they are members, (2) to influence the attitudes of the community at large through its key leaders, and (3) to bring specific pressures to bear upon legislators and administrators.

Reaching Memberships

People are less likely to offer resistance to new attitudes when these are proposed through an association with which they identify. If a veterans' organization emphasizes an appeal against prejudice or against a discriminatory pattern, the members of that organization are less likely to resist such appeals as unpatriotic and may even be prepared to incorporate that appeal into their system of patriotic values.

Not only is it potentially easier to reach members of organized associations, but it is probably more important to reach them than it is to reach the unorganized members of the community, for they are more likely to be interested and articulate persons who serve as opinion-molders in their circles of the community. By the same token, a minority group can most clearly focus on and learn about its collective aims and techniques for equality when its articulate members are organized in an association.

Influencing the Community

The symbolic weight of an association or individual can effectively influence the community at large on an issue relating to prejudice. All other things being equal, if a prominent businessman serves as chairman of a committee to promote a fair employment practices law, those in the community who identify themselves with business interests are that much more likely to reduce their resistance to such a law, while the community as a whole is that much less likely to feel that the law is "not respectable."

Bringing Pressures to Bear

Public officials and legislative representatives are susceptible to organized forces. These forces represent the articulate elements of their constituencies and are a primary index of public opinion. Not only do they represent organized groups of voters; they are also agencies for general community persuasion. If a labor union important to a legislator's support indicates a real interest in a law against discriminatory housing, he is realistically moved to give that law greater consideration. And where minority group members are gathered into an appropriate association, not only can they more clearly establish such a law as one of their communal goals; they can also present a front of some political importance. A minority association with clearly established goals and leadership carries an economic as well as a political potential. For example, in many northern cities, some vulnerable business firms, such as city-wide grocery chains, have altered their discriminatory patterns in order to avoid stigmatization by Negro organizations. It is common for them to consult immediately with the leadership of these organizations in order to quash unfounded rumors of discrimination that periodically arise.

WHO ARE KEY FORCES?

Prejudiced behavior and attitudes have been found to be highly situational in nature, i.e., the same person will have different attitudes or act in

United Press International

In northern cities the candidate must cultivate all groups in order to win.

a different fashion depending on the situation or frame of reference in which he finds himself. In Panama it is common to find Panamanian Negroes conforming to discriminatory practices on one side of the street, which falls in the United States Zone, and white Americans conforming to nondiscriminatory practices on the other side of the street, which falls in Panamanian territory. An individual may find no objections to working with Negroes in his place of business, where the union has established a strong nondiscriminatory policy, but may object strenuously to having Negroes move into his neighborhood, where the civic improvement club has an exclusionist policy.

In much the same way, individuals and organizations may be key forces in one situation but not in another. Furthermore, not all individuals and organizations are key forces for the same reason.

Relevance to the Issue

The most significant impact is likely to be made by the association most inherently related to the issue at hand. A man may highly value his labor union, his veterans' group, and his civic improvement association, all of which may have conflicting views on certain issues. But he may take his strongest cue on economic issues from the labor union, on politics from the veterans' group, and on segregated housing from his neighborhood improvement association. Sometimes a boomerang effect of resentment results when a leader in one area of affairs offers advice in another and apparently unrelated area.

However, the effectiveness of an individual's or association's support of an issue is often in inverse proportion to the extent that this support seems to be self-serving. Minority group support of a fair-employment ordinance may have some significance to the politician, but it probably does not impress the general community. Conversely, minority group opposition to a specific fair-employment ordinance *would* impress the general community. A minister's support of such an ordinance would not be as impressive as a representative businessman's, for the minister is "supposed to" feel this way in accordance with his moral obligations and has "nothing to lose."

Subject matter, however, is not the only point of relevance between an issue and the effectiveness of an association or leader. A national labor union and its leadership may oppose discrimination within its ranks; but many local unions within such national associations may nevertheless continue to practice discrimination because there are more immediate pressures operating. Many southern AFL and CIO unions publicly attacked and disagreed with the strong national policies of support for school desegregation. There was even talk of disaffiliation, and union organizers reported that it was practically impossible to organize workers during this period in the Deep South because of the desegregation position of the national labor federations. Similarly, the strong position of the national Catholic religious authorities on the question of school desegregation met with open rebellion in some southern Catholic communities, and the emphatic position of other national church bodies was also widely ignored by their local denominations in the South.

Against the background of these general factors must also be laid the fact that prejudice, with its many-sided manifestations, is not a single issue. It is sometimes a housing issue, sometimes an employment issue, sometimes a citizenship issue, sometimes an issue of general social status or general morality. The campaign against prejudice normally raises different specific issues at different times and at different places. The key forces may change accordingly.

Practical Considerations

Some associations and individuals are of key importance in community organization efforts because of certain practical necessities. Especially where the attempt is being made to institute policies in advance of general public opinion, there is usually an urgent need for funds, for an aura of legitimacy and respectability, and for access to government and sources of political power.

1. *Fund-raising.* Significant efforts to launch an educational campaign, initiate a social-action project, promote legislation, or generally influence the community require working funds. Not the least of these needs is often the employment of a community organizer. With the growing need to reach and influence public opinion, it has become more and more necessary to expend funds in order to attract the attention of the public. If the effort is to be a substantial or sustained one, then it is generally impossible to raise the necessary promotional funds from small per capita membership fees or donations. It is often necessary to find some special sources of financial support. The key forces in this case are usually found in the business community or among people or associations with access to the business community.

2. *Conservative respectability.* Organizational fund-raising necessities are only one reason for the special "key" quality of business elements in the community. Their support is often important for people in political life. In addition, businessmen are relatively free agents in the community. They are not subject to the same direct economic sanctions as others. For example, dissident ministers may find it difficult to raise church funds, lawyers may lose clients, schoolteachers often fear that their careers will suffer.

Also, the business element epitomizes "conservative respectability" to most of the general community. The aura of conservative respectability has often been a critical goal for attitude-changers in the field of prejudice. Any deliberate attempt to induce forward changes in social attitudes is likely to meet with problems of inertia and caution on the part of the public. But the issue of prejudice has been particularly complicated by the profusion of fringe groups and groups considered politically radical which have attempted to attach themselves to the issue. Patterns of prejudice in America have been a target of Communist propaganda abroad. The Communist Party in this country has had civil rights high on its public agenda, although its shifting and often contradictory program in this area has convinced minority leadership that the Communist Party's interest is one of destructive expediency rather than genuine principle.

Other elements of the community presumably having a vested interest in the status quo may also have a key value in helping to create respectability—the head of an established and conservative craft union, for example, or a socially prominent individual. With the general limitations indicated above, a minister may serve to add initial respectability to a project, depending on the nature of his congregation and the personal reputation he enjoys in the community.

3. *Political power.* Where legislative reforms are an aim, and political pressures are called for, the support of leaders of large, organized, and pressure-oriented organizations is almost indispensable. Minority leadership would eminently qualify, as would leaders of a labor or veterans' organization. Educators and most ministers would not qualify, since they are not leaders of organized forces. However, individuals of high socio-economic status might, since they tend to travel in circles with access to top public officials.

INVOLVEMENT OF KEY FORCES

Minority Organization

A minority association for equal rights has a unique "key" quality. Especially under conditions of discrimination and segregation, minority members can be reached and influenced only through their own leaders. Conversely, minority leadership develops most responsibility toward the community when it is in turn responsible to a membership and to a substantial association. It is through such an association that a minority group can crystallize and express its aims and most effectively act as a spur to the conscience of the "liberal" nonminority community. Minority organization for equal rights superficially seems to be a contradictory exercise in self-segregation, but it is a necessary step in the struggle for civil rights.

Progressive Involvement of Leaders

Very often it is initially necessary to widen the gap between the key leaders and their associations or the people who fall within their sphere of influence by inducing them to take positions in advance of their followers. It is easier to create this gap in the case of leaders who have been chosen for other than sociability factors. Leaders of unions or professional associations are often relatively free to deviate from membership opinion without fear of losing their position. The cohesiveness of some groups, however, is based upon strong similarities in the total social and personal outlook of their members. Where this is the case, leaders do not "lead" in the sense of being more responsible or more far-sighted than the members; they are chosen as leaders because they typify so strongly the personality and beliefs of the ordinary member. Not only are they less able to deviate from the attitudes of their membership without jeopardizing their leadership, but they are less likely to have attitudes in advance of their membership. This occurs most often in groups where sociability is an important factor in holding members together. These are usually local groups, and it is a common experience that national leadership is often more advanced than local leadership.

However, even those leaders who are not in advance of membership attitudes are relatively vulnerable to attitude-changing influences. They have a public role and are thus drawn into public formalities and activities. They tend to travel in other leadership circles. They are subjected to other leadership attitudes. Through this process, leaders who are otherwise indifferent often become progressively involved in the issue of prejudice, i.e., this involvement typically leads from the general to the specific. An individual may be asked to participate in an innocuous and general "Brotherhood Day" program. He may be given some responsibility for the execution of this program. This may lead to his participation in a research committee to discover the extent of discrimination in the community. By this time he may come to have a genuine personal interest and stake in this issue. Other leaders ideologically sympathetic to begin with have, by the same process, become more actively and emotionally involved.

The Progressive Involvement of Associations

Once the gap between the key leaders and their associations or spheres of influence has been widened, it is necessary to bring the membership up to the level of its leadership. The enlistment of the leader in his symbolic capacity is itself a step in that direction. He may become a member of an *ad hoc* citizens' committee against segregated housing. He may appear in this capacity in radio and television programs or be quoted in the newspapers.

But the association itself may be involved through its leadership. The movement again is often from the more general to the specific. A resolution against prejudice in general may be passed at an organizational convention, although the mass of the membership may be indifferent to the issue. The resolution may appear first on a national scale, then on a regional and local level. This commitment, aside from whatever symbolic weight it may have in the community at large, may open the way for more specific resolutions. Perhaps, with the guidance of the leadership, committees may be formed within the membership to conduct an educational or action campaign. Sub-leadership involvement can in this way be developed within the organization.

A strong note of caution would seem to be in order. The people of a community are not so many helpless robots who can be pushed from attitude to attitude by the mathematically proper application of key forces. This skeletonized description of community organization emphasizes its manipulative aspects, especially when skilled community organizers are involved. But community organization is also an educational effort directed toward both leaders and community and competing in the market place of ideas with other educational efforts. A skilled community organizer cannot, presumably, sell an idea that has no relation to the needs and events of the time. Within these limits, however, community organization can affect the dynamics of a community so that it will be moving as swiftly and strategically as possible in the direction of desired attitudes.

Section V: The Strategy of Approach

The concept of community organization serves to integrate all of the deliberate approaches to the changing of prejudiced patterns and attitudes. All of these approaches—by law, education, direct action, or mass media—buttress each other, and none of them is absolutely better than the others; but each has unique applications, depending on several sets of factors.

DIFFERENCES IN AGENCIES

The agencies which are attempting to change prejudiced patterns have inherently different competencies. Often they must play different roles because they have different constituencies and therefore different philosophies. The following story is told of the procedures of three different agencies in the field when a serious national issue arose relating to discrimination.

Agency A, a mass-membership organization, instructed its units around the country to immediately organize large public meetings in order to arouse the communities and register protest; Agency B, with a markedly middle-class membership, instructed its chapters to quietly enlist and register the protest of leadership elements in the community; Agency C, comprised of a relatively small group in the upper socio-economic range, had its president immediately confer with a high official in the White House. These dissimilar approaches were dictated by the nature of the different constituencies. To put it another way, if any one of these agencies had not existed, many of its members would probably not have belonged to any agency, and their support and energies might well have been completely lost in this field. Some individuals will support only educational efforts; others will support only efforts by law. Ancillary to this is the fact that tax-exempt agencies cannot engage directly in legislative activity. (The fund-raising capacity of many organizations depends upon the fact that contributors can deduct their contributions from taxable income.)

DIFFERENCES IN ISSUES

Some issues inherently limit the approach that may reasonably be made to their solution. An example can be found in the case of the fringe-group professional bigot, the person whose only livelihood is selling bigoted literature, making bigoted speeches, or collecting donations for an organization to do both. His prime need is free publicity, which is hard to come by. He is not afraid of opposition but of indifference. He has only a relatively small market for his wares, and somehow he must reach the people who constitute this market and enlist their support. On the other hand, he is considered potentially dangerous because, the wider he manages to make his circle, the more widely will his baseless rumors and canards circulate in the general community. Should his small meetings be picketed? Should he be widely attacked by name in the general press? Should an attempt be made to pass a law against group libel, and then prosecute? All of these alternatives would seem to provide him with both the publicity and the martyrdom which he needs in order to widen his circle of influence. The consensus among the agencies is that such an individual, unless he has already gained some prominence, must be publicly ignored if his purposes are to be defeated. The only specific remedy perhaps lies in education directed generally against the kind of message he would purvey.

The possible boomerang effect of law is another example. Most agencies in the field have rejected the idea of a group-libel law because of the inherent danger to civil liberties which seems to lie within such a law, which would be directed against the expression of certain beliefs rather than against specific behavior. Opponents of proposed group-libel laws believe that a person has a legal right to be prejudiced and to be protected against laws interfering with his private opinions. On the other hand, many also feel that there is no legal or moral objection to laws which regulate a person's *public behavior* and thus *indirectly* influence his personal attitudes.

Section VI: Summary

The deliberate efforts to change prejudiced patterns in the last two decades can be described as the progressive involvement of the community and nation. It has been an involvement from the more general to the more specific; at different stages of development in different regions different approaches have been significant in deepening this involvement.

Fair-employment laws, or integration in the Army, or a school-desegregation decision by the Supreme Court would have been improbable twenty years ago. The community was not prepared for them. The minority groups within the community were themselves not prepared for them. It was in the mass media and at the level of public opinion that the modern revolution in race relations was first spurred. In the beginning it was expressed at the generalized level of "brotherhood" as an American principle. Buttressed by increasing scientific knowledge concerning ethnic and racial differences, a rhetorical stress on the official values regarding equal status became an increasing part of the daily experience of the American public. The historical

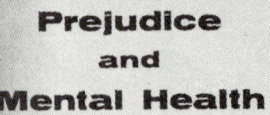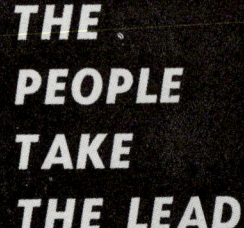

circumstances were ripe, to be sure; internal wartime needs, a racist enemy, the renaissance of Africa and Asia, the involvement of America in a global ideological war, the political significance of Negro populations newly massed in the industrial centers of the North, all made prejudice impractical. But the propaganda barrage to which the public was constantly subjected was deliberately stimulated on every side. Brotherhood was invoked as never before from the rostra, from the pulpits, from the mass media of the nation. In the North employers began to disguise their discriminatory hiring policies; in the South lynchings became anachronistic. In the North it became possible to pass laws against employment discrimination; in the South it became possible to pass laws against the Ku Klux Klan. And where laws became possible, they usually accelerated shifts in public opinion more swiftly than would have been possible by any other means. More specific targets, e.g., housing, were singled out, and more specific laws were passed. This snowballing progress has not been just the by-product of historical change; its swiftness of movement and its direction have been fashioned by deliberate social action.

INTERRACIAL HOUSING adaptation 10

Abridged and adapted from Morton Deutsch and Mary Evans Collins, "Intergroup Relations in Interracial Public Housing: Occupancy Patterns and Racial Attitudes," Journal of Housing, *7 (April, 1950), 127–29, 134. Published in this form by permission of the authors and the* Journal of Housing. *A detailed description of the study appears in Morton Deutsch and Mary Evans Collins,* Interracial Housing *(Minneapolis: University of Minnesota Press, 1951).*

[One of the arguments against "mixed" housing is that, however desirable and just it may be, it will not work. Close contact between different races will bring conflict and hostility; the only way in which Negroes and whites can live in peace is at a distance.

The following account, which summarizes some of the results of an intensive study of interracial housing, points to quite the opposite conclusion. The authors found that, when Negro and white tenants were *not* segregated, prejudice and hostility were markedly reduced.]

SEGREGATED AND INTEGRATED HOUSING

In segregated housing projects, Negro and white families live in the same project but are assigned to different buildings or parts of the project. In integrated projects, Negro and white families are assigned to apartments without regard to race. "Koaltown" and "Sacktown" are the fictitious names of two integrated projects studied; "Bakerville" and "Frankville," of two segregated projects. The attitudes of white housewives in both types of housing were investigated and compared with regard to: (1) the Negro people in the project, (2) Negro people in general, (3) other minority groups, and (4) living in an interracial project.

All the measures of racial attitudes employed in the study gave the same result: *Housewives in the integrated projects were considerably less prejudiced than those in the segregated projects.* In referring to Negroes, for example, almost three times as many women in segregated projects (36 and 31 per cent as compared with 13 and 10 per cent) spontaneously used words like "aggressive," "dangerous," "trouble-makers."

ATTITUDES TOWARD THE NEGRO PEOPLE IN THE PROJECT

Table 6:1 indicates that in the integrated projects the overwhelming majority of white housewives respect their Negro neighbors. In the segregated projects, on the other hand, housewives regard the Negro people as inferior almost as often as they feel them to be equal to their white neighbors.

Another striking difference in attitude is revealed when the number of housewives who wish to be friendly with their Negro neighbors is compared with the number of housewives who do not. In the integrated projects, approximately two housewives want to be friendly to every one who does not. In the segregated projects, only one wishes to be friendly to every ten who do not.

ATTITUDES TOWARD NEGRO PEOPLE IN GENERAL

It might be objected that the tenants in the integrated projects were, to begin with, favorably disposed toward Negroes and that the above results re-

TABLE 6:1 ATTITUDES TOWARD NEGROES OF WHITE HOUSEWIVES IN BIRACIAL PUBLIC HOUSING PROJECTS

	INTEGRATED PROJECT		SEGREGATED PROJECT	
	Koaltown	Sacktown	Bakerville	Frankville
Views Negro people as equal to white people in project	72%	79%	43%	39%
Not sure	17	8	20	26
Views Negro people as inferior to white people in project	11	13	37	35
Total number of interviews	102	90	100	101

TABLE 6:2 WHITE HOUSEWIVES' ATTITUDES TOWARD NEGROES PRIOR TO RESIDENCE IN BIRACIAL PUBLIC HOUSING PROJECTS

	INTEGRATED PROJECT		SEGREGATED PROJECT	
	Koaltown	Sacktown	Bakerville	Frankville
Originally favorable	15%	36%	13%	17%
Originally neutral	26	29	48	47
Originally unfavorable	59	35	39	36
Total number of interviews	99	89	99	100

flect initial differences rather than differences arising out of participation in their respective housing arrangements. Table 6:2 summarizes the reports of housewives regarding their attitudes toward Negroes prior to moving into the projects. It is apparent that, though housewives in Sacktown were initially less prejudiced, housewives in Koaltown were initially more prejudiced than those in the segregated projects. The relatively more positive attitude toward Negroes finally expressed by housewives in the two integrated projects seems to be attributable, therefore, to their experience in their housing project rather than to any greater original friendliness toward Negroes.

In addition, as Table 6:3 shows, a far greater change in the direction of acquiring favorable attitudes occurred in both integrated projects than in the segregated projects. Detailed results which cannot be presented here indicate that housewives who were highly prejudiced at the outset tended to lose their prejudice more often in the integrated than in the segregated community. More striking is the fact that, though unprejudiced housewives continued on the whole to remain unprejudiced, there was in one of the

TABLE 6:3 CHANGES IN WHITE HOUSEWIVES' ATTITUDES TOWARD NEGROES FOLLOWING RESIDENCE IN BIRACIAL PUBLIC HOUSING PROJECTS

	INTEGRATED PROJECT		SEGREGATED PROJECT	
	Koaltown	Sacktown	Bakerville	Frankville
Changed in favorable direction	59%	62%	27%	18%
Remained the same	38	31	66	69
Changed in unfavorable direction	3	7	7	13
Total number of interviews	99	89	99	100

segregated projects some tendency for the unprejudiced to become prejudiced.

Interviews provided dramatic illustrations of the attitude changes that occurred among many of the housewives in the integrated projects. Thus, one woman when asked how she felt about living in the project, said:

> I started to cry when my husband told me we were coming to live here. I cried for three weeks. . . . I didn't want to come and live here where there were so many colored people. I didn't want to bring my children up with colored children, but we had to come; there was no place else to go. . . . Well, all that's changed. I've really come to like it. I see they're just as human as we are. They have nice apartments, they keep their children clean, and they're very friendly. I've come to like them a great deal. I'm no longer scared of them. . . . I'd just as soon live near a colored person as a white, it makes no difference to me.

In contrast, the following remarks express typical findings in the segregated projects:

> I don't have anything to do with the colored people . . . they don't bother me . . . I don't mingle with them. I guess I don't like them because they're colored . . . the Bible says "God created them equal," so I guess they're equal, but I don't like them. I don't like living so close to them. I think they ought to be in separate projects. Let them live their lives and let us live ours. . . . My ideas haven't changed any since I've lived here. . . . They're colored and I'm white. They don't like us and we don't like them.

Approximately 70 per cent of the women in the integrated projects, in contrast to 50 per cent in the segregated projects, *disagreed* with the following statement: "Generally speaking, colored people are lazy and ignorant." One woman in an integrated project made the following remarks: "I thought I was moving into the heart of Africa. . . . I had always heard about how they were . . . they were dirty, drink a lot . . . were like savages. Living with them, my ideas have changed altogether. They're just people . . . they're not any different." Another one said: "I was prejudiced when I moved in here but not any more. . . . I know the people, I've been in their homes. . . . I know they're not dirty. My doctor is colored . . . my dentist is colored. He's a surgeon and he's wonderful."

In other words, many of the women in the integrated projects have not only come to respect and like the Negro people with whom they have associated but they have also changed their notions about Negroes in general. Their experiences in the project have become partially generalized, so that they now have more favorable attitudes toward Negroes as a group. It should be pointed out, however, that not all women who became more favorable to Negroes in the project become more favorable to Negro people in general. The fact that the projects were all located in deteriorated, delinquent Negro neighborhoods may be one of the main factors limiting the generalization of their project experience. Unpleasant experiences in the neighborhood, and the association of "deterioration" and "delinquency" with "Negro," may to some extent have offset their pleasant experiences in the project.

ATTITUDES TOWARD OTHER MINORITY GROUPS

Questions were asked about Chinese and Puerto Ricans to see whether changes in attitudes toward Negroes would be accompanied by changes in attitudes toward minority groups with whom the women had little or no contact (less than 1 per cent of the project residents were Puerto Rican or Chinese). Some change did apparently occur. There was more change in attitude toward Chinese than toward Puerto Ricans, the former being considered, in all projects, to be of lower social status than the latter. As might be expected, the most significant change occurred in feelings about having Chinese as neighbors in the same building, the integrated projects being considerably less prejudiced in this respect than the segregated projects.

ATTITUDES TOWARD LIVING IN AN INTERRACIAL PROJECT

Table 6:4 summarizes responses to the following question: "On the basis of your experience of living in a project where there are colored and white families, what plan do you think that the city should follow in new projects? Do you think that colored and white families should be given apartments anywhere in the project, no matter what their race is *or* do you think colored and white families should only be allowed to live in separate buildings in the project *or* do you think projects should be all white or all colored?" The opinions of the housewives in the integrated projects are in sharp contrast to those in the segregated projects. The majority of respondents in the

TABLE 6:4 RECOMMENDATIONS OF WHITE HOUSEWIVES REGARDING SEGREGATION OR INTEGRATION IN FUTURE PUBLIC HOUSING

	INTEGRATED PROJECT		SEGREGATED PROJECT	
	Koaltown	Sacktown	Bakerville	Frankville
Any place	53%	53%	4%	6%
Separate buildings	9	7	23	25
Separate projects	38	40	73	69
Total number of interviews	96	88	100	96

former favor the integrated pattern, while housewives in the latter would overwhelmingly prefer to have completely separate projects for Negro and white families. A number of housewives who, though they felt satisfied with living in an integrated interracial project, nevertheless did not recommend it as public policy. People who are positive in their attitudes toward living in an integrated interracial project may still find it difficult to buck the prejudices of the larger community. Others, who would just as soon have Negroes as neighbors, may feel that many white people are prejudiced and might cause trouble.

RELATIONS WITH NEGRO PEOPLE IN PROJECT

The segregated projects did not lead to bad personal relations between Negroes and whites. Instead they were characterized by the absence of relations, whether friendly or otherwise. In the integrated projects, as Table 6:5 shows, Negro-white relations were preponderantly friendly. Many women in the integrated projects made statements of this nature: "We get along beautifully . . . . When I was sick, Mrs. Jones across the hall noticed it and she came in and helped. She used to bring food in and go shopping for me. A lot of white people wouldn't do that for you." Others did not achieve friendliness but nevertheless maintained a neutral attitude unmarked by hostility. This *accommodative relationship* is characterized by such remarks as "I've had no trouble. They mind their own business, or they smile and say 'Good morning.' But with me it's 'Hello and goodbye,' I don't bother much with the people here." The *mixed reaction* is evidenced by phrases like "Some are nice, but some are nasty." None of the instances of *bad relations* were characterized by physical violence; they took the form of an intense discomfort or dislike. Thus, one housewife in an integrated project, who was rated as having bad relations with the Negro tenants, said: "I've never liked them. I guess they know it and have told their kids. They

TABLE 6:5 NATURE OF HOUSEWIVES' RELATIONS WITH NEGRO PEOPLE IN PROJECT

	INTEGRATED PROJECT		SEGREGATED PROJECT	
	Koaltown	Sacktown	Bakerville	Frankville
Friendly relations	60%	69%	6%	4%
Accommodative relations	24	14	5	1
Mixed relations	7	11	2	3
No relations	5	0	87	88
Bad relations	4	6	0	4
Total number of interviews	102	90	100	101

call me 'white trash' whenever they see me. I have to keep careful watch on my kids or else the colored kids will gang up on them." The incidence of bad relations was nonetheless no greater than had previously been found to exist between different nationality groups in an all-white project.

In the integrated projects, closer contacts with Negro neighbors brought not only an increase in personal friendliness but also a decrease in racial prejudice. Knowledge of how their Negro neighbors lived did not confirm their prejudices but, on the contrary, tended to create a sense of identification and fellow-feeling. Since the segregated projects were characterized by a striking absence of all relations between Negro and white, it is not surprising that marked changes in attitudes did not occur.

CONCLUSIONS

1. Integrated housing projects have the effect of reducing racial prejudice, while segregated projects show only a slight gain in this direction.

2. In integrated projects, relations between Negroes and whites are preponderantly friendly; in segregated projects, they are practically nonexistent. The segregated community, by not providing opportunities for close contact between the races, also does not provide the conditions for friendly relations, knowledge of the other group, and the mitigation of prejudice.

3. Neither the segregated nor the integrated interracial projects studied were characterized by interracial strife. Moreover, instances of bad relations among Negro and white tenants were no more frequent than those found to exist between members of different nationality groups in an all-white project.

4. Favorable attitudes toward Negro neighbors in the project were often but not always accompanied by favorable attitudes toward Negroes in general. The location of interracial projects as islands in deteriorated Negro neighborhoods probably works against the reduction of prejudice even in integrated projects.

5. Living in an integrated project helped to create attitudes favorable toward integrated housing as public policy (53 per cent in both cases). However, living in a segregated project did not create corresponding attitudes favorable to segregated housing as public policy (23 and 25 per cent).

6. Many who found integrated housing a satisfactory personal arrangement still did not favor it as public policy. Of these, however, very few advocated segregated housing, but rather complete separation. It is probable that many satisfied residents of integrated housing took the prejudices of the larger community into account when asked to formulate public policy.

[*Comment:* The authors point out that intimate contact does not always mitigate prejudice. Certain conditions have to be fulfilled before increased knowledge and interaction promote tolerance. Among these conditions are the following:

1. The minority group must not be of markedly lower socio-economic status than the majority. This means, among other things, that the minority must not have standards of conduct which appear to the majority to be of a lower order than their own. The minority must also have approximately as much education and income as the majority, though both may have relatively little of either.

2. The contact must take place within a structured situation, that is, in a situation where people have some goals in common, where they feel part of some common community, and where at least at the outset there are certain formal rules and social amenities which guide their behavior toward each other. A housing project is such a structured situation; we call it "structured" partly because we all know how to behave toward neighbors even when we do not approve of them and wish to demonstrate a feeling of aloofness and social distance. We also call it "structured" because, when we feel we have been imposed upon by a fellow-tenant, we can apply for redress through a formal authority, that is, the project manager or superintendent. Hostility need not be expressed in personal outbursts; it can instead be "channeled."

In contrast, intimate contacts in nonstructured situations (for example, on the streets or in places of public recreation) sometimes foster outbursts of personal hostility. People do not feel constrained by a sense of shared goals or the public opinion of a common community, nor do official channels exist through which anger can be rerouted. It is apt, therefore, to be expressed directly, personally, and on the spot.

3. Contact must take place within a context which encourages and supports tolerance. A housing project, even though it is a structured situation, would perhaps not lead to the mitigation of prejudice if it were managed by an official unwilling to throw his weight on the side of tolerance and fair play.]

---

adaptation 11   PHILADELPHIA RACE RIOT

Abridged and adapted from Hannah Lees, "How Philadelphia Stopped a Race Riot," The Reporter, 12 (June 2, 1955), 26–28. Published in this form by permission of the author and The Reporter.

[The following report describes what happened in Philadelphia when a Negro family moved into an all-white neighborhood. It shows the crucial importance of community organization in preventing violence and mediating group conflict. There existed in Philadelphia a Commission on Human Relations whose job it was to deal with interracial tensions; behind it lay the prestige and authority of the city government. However, it was the policy of the Commission, from its position of prestige, to take advantage of the power structure of the community as it already existed. It worked with those people in both the white and the Negro communities who, by virtue of their leadership, were most apt to have a strong sense of community responsibility.]

A young Negro car-washer named Wiley Clark borrowed $300 from a loan company and made a token payment on a house in an Irish-Italian section of Philadelphia. Clark and his wife simply wanted a real house with a yard where their four children could play; they were tired of living, all six of them, in a room and a half in a crowded Negro neighborhood. Clark was making about $40 a week. His wife made another $25 doing housework. A relative took care of the children during the day.

The house, a former gift shop, at the corner of Judson and Cambria, had been bought at a sheriff's sale by another Negro named Williams, who makes his living picking up houses at forced sale and reselling them fast at a small profit. During the eight months it had been vacant, neighborhood gangs had smashed in the store front and ripped out most of the plumbing. There was hardly a housing ordinance it didn't violate, but Clark bought it with a promise to put it in livable condition before moving in. The terms were $200 down and $50 a month until a $1,500 payment had been made, after which, if he had managed to keep up the payments, he would get a deed and mortgage. It was a bad buy, and Clark was in no position to make the renovations, but he went ahead nevertheless.

The first the neighbors knew of all this was when they saw Clark working around the house evenings and weekends. When they asked what was happening, he got scared and said he was getting it ready for the owner.

The neighborhood is one in which most of the families own their own homes. Most of the men work at skilled trades, and most of the women stay home and take care of their houses. Many of them grew up in the neighborhood. They watched Clark night after night clumsily filling in the store front with cinder block. They saw he sometimes had a bottle of whiskey with his bag of lunch. They eyed the growing pile of rubbish in the back yard. The nearest Negroes at that time lived four or five blocks away, and the whites didn't want them any nearer. Especially, they decided, not Clark.

THE CLARKS MOVE IN

Late on the night of August 18, Wiley and Bertha Clark moved in, having left the children with a relative (later they were sent to Clark's mother in Virginia) so they could be free to work on the house. Almost their only furniture was a bed and a large television set Clark had bought on time. When the community woke up the next day to find they did in fact have the Clarks for neighbors, the whites started a riot.

The Clarks had gone off to work early and uneventfully that Thursday morning, but by the time Wiley Clark got home he found some windows broken and a crowd of boys milling around and looking for trouble. He tried to find out who had done the damage. Somebody laid hands on somebody. A bigger, angrier crowd began to gather, and Clark went for the police. The first station house he went to was out of his district, so they sent him to another. It was a couple of hours before he could get anyone to take him seriously enough to phone headquarters that a disturbance was under way at Judson and Cambria. Meanwhile, Bertha Clark had returned from work but was afraid to go into the house when she saw the crowd. When the police arrived, they found her standing on the sidewalk waiting for her husband, with the mob shouting at her. Officer Max Weiss, a police expert in interracial relations, persuaded her and Clark, who came back about then, to go into the house and stay there. The police would get the mob under control, he told them, and the Commission on Human Relations would be along any moment to straighten everything out.

THE COMMISSION ON HUMAN RELATIONS

In 1951 Philadelphia, contemplating its fast-growing Negro population —one Philadelphian in five now is a Negro—had written into its new city charter a department called the Commission on Human Relations, with a staff trained to handle interracial tensions and paid from the city budget just like the police and health departments. Most big cities today have something of the sort, but the Philadelphia Commission has the widest powers and the biggest budget of any in the country.

George Schermer, executive director of the Commission, got word of the trouble from police headquarters about ten-thirty. Schermer, a relaxed but completely uncompromising man who got his training in Detroit, where things are considerably tougher interracially than in Philadelphia, lives in Germantown in a racially mixed upper-income neighborhood with his wife and four children. By eleven o'clock Schermer and community-relations expert Mike Jefferson, one of whose assets to the Commission is that he is a Negro, were inside the house with the Clarks. Mrs. Anna McGarry, top trouble shooter for the Commission, and John McDermott, both Catholics, were mingling with the predominantly Catholic crowd outside. By three in the morning, when the police had got most of them to go home for the rest of the night, the experts added up what they knew and began to make plans.

CLARK MUST STAY

The mob seriously believed that Clark had been planted either by Father Divine (leader of a Negro religious sect) or by the Communists in order to open up the neighborhood to Negroes. They didn't want and they weren't going to have Clark. He was just no good: Look at all the trash, the sloppy way he dressed, the whiskey, and the way he had lied about having bought the house. Besides, he was breaking the law living in a house with no plumbing. And nobody had started anything until Clark got rough with some of the boys. This was the story from outside.

Clark's story was that he had bought the house in good faith and had worked like a dog to fix it up; the local boys had thrown his stuff around and broken the windows from the start, but he had tried to manage without calling the cops. Even when the mob turned up, he hadn't done a thing but try to find out who had broken his windows. Sure he had been afraid to say he was going to live there, they had been so unfriendly. Sure he had had a drink while he was working. Why not? He didn't know about the housing ordinances, and Williams had said he was getting him a building permit. He had been planning to clean up the yard. But now all he wanted was out.

This would have been an easy solution, since the neighborhood didn't want Clark and Clark no longer wanted to stay. But it would have given a green light to every potential rioter in town. As Schermer later told some of the leaders of the Judson-Cambria neighborhood, if they felt Clark was a bad neighbor, they could have gotten him out by peaceful means because he was violating the law; if they had left him alone, he would almost certainly have defaulted on his payments in a few months and moved away. But the minute they rioted, they forced the Commission to find some way to help the Clarks stay where they were and make the neighbors accept his right to stay there. No city today could afford to let a race riot succeed.

ORGANIZING CITIZEN ACTION: STRUCTURING THE SITUATION

It wasn't a job a mere dozen or so trained staff workers could cope with. It was going to take citizen action, and marshaling citizen action is the Commission's specialty. For the next three days, some hundred plainclothes, traffic, and motorcycle cops patrolled the area, keeping an angry mob, numbering at times as many as five or six hundred, from doing any damage to the house or from attacking any Negroes who came by, and also stifling any attempts at retaliation. Meanwhile, Schermer and his staff worked in three different directions at once. They answered angry phone calls from leading Negro citizens with an invitation to come and discuss the problem and invited a good many who didn't phone. They got to work on an open letter that would tell exactly how and why Clark had bought the house and help counteract the wild rumors flying around. Mrs. McGarry and McDermott and some of the other workers wandered in and out of churches and clubs and saloons near the trouble spot, picking up the names of local men who carried weight whom they could also invite to a meeting. On Sunday, local churches distributed four thousand of the open-letter fact sheets on official City of Philadelphia letterheads.

COMMUNITY ORGANIZATION

On Monday, by special invitation, a group of angry leading Negro citizens—ministers, doctors, architects, editors—met in the Commission quarters. One of the nine unpaid Commissioners of Human Relations, a woman lawyer who is herself a Negro, chaired the meeting. Schermer let their anger boil around him. He felt it was partly justified; with better pipelines he might have known Williams was selling the house to Clark and could have started working soon enough to prevent trouble. Then he told them all he knew, the bad with the good. Clark might not be a very desirable symbol of interracial living, but symbol by now he definitely was. It would be rough on interracial relations if he were driven away. But to stay, he needed help and a lot of it—help the Commission had no power to give. At the end of the meeting a grimly determined delegation from the meeting went to call on Wiley Clark. Then, under police protection, they went to the corner of Judson and Cambria to look the house over and see what had to be done to put it in habitable condition.

A Citizens' Committee for Wiley Clark was formed, with subcommittees to raise money to buy materials and organize crews to work on the house and a very special select committee to work on Wiley Clark himself and help him become a better interracial ambassador.

Two days later, twenty-three Irish and Italian home-owners from around the corner of Judson and Cambria met at Commission quarters. This meeting was chaired by another of the nine unpaid Commissioners, an Irish Catholic lawyer. It was an even angrier meeting than the one with the Negro delegation. In spite of the fact sheet, they were still sure it was all a plot. They resisted both fact and logic. But after a couple of hours of bitter argument a local real estate dealer named Di Gregorio, a forceful personality his neighbors are used to listening to, began talking sense. Already a dozen houses near the Clarks had FOR SALE signs. Enterprising realtors reading of the riot had rushed soliciting letters to every home-owner in the neighborhood. If a panic set in and everybody tried to sell, they would all lose money. Take it easy, Di Gregorio counseled.

A few days later, under Di Gregorio's leadership, the Judson-Cambria citizens held a mass meeting in a funeral parlor and formed the North Penn Civic Improvement Association. They appointed two men to each block in the vicinity of the Clark home to talk to neighbors and calm them down. Another purpose may well have been to find a legal way of getting Clark out, but if so they reckoned without Philadelphia's Negro citizens.

On September 14 the Citizens' Committee for Wiley Clark and the North Penn Civic Improvement Association met together at Commission offices. The Citizens for Wiley Clark said they were sorry Clark had not been a better neighbor and they aimed to help him become one. They expressed bitter disapproval of the riot. Di Gregorio and his group in return expressed regret that the riot had happened. They blamed it all on some reckless teen-agers. They said frankly, however, that they still didn't want Clark for a neighbor. The Committee said equally frankly that if they could swing it, Clark was there to stay. No lasting friendships were formed, but there was no violence.

AFTERMATH

In the next two months the Citizens' Committee for Wiley Clark, with the aid of Fellowship House—a Philadelphia volunteer center for interracial and interfaith good will—and of two or three dozen other church and citizen groups, raised two thousand dollars in cash, and gave another two thousand dollars' worth of work and materials to get Clark's house in a state he could be proud of and neighbors could not criticize. Clark temporarily quit his regular job and worked day and night with a series of volunteer crews.

On November 8 the Clarks brought their children up from Virginia and moved back into their completely renovated house. The Citizens' Committee had taken over the mortgage from Williams and got him to reduce the price, which had been too high all along. They had helped Clark get a better job at somewhat higher pay. They had taught him some things about budgeting and filled him with a sense of his responsibility to his race and to the community. A gala housewarming was held, which the president of the North Penn Civic Improvement Association attended, perhaps more to inspect than to offer friendship, but there he was. The house looked good to him, even though the Clarks still did not. People began taking down their FOR SALE signs, and fewer and fewer police were needed in the district.

From November to January everyone marked time, watching and waiting. Not a single family sold its house and moved away, Di Gregorio says, but not a single family moved in either. From January to June, however, Di Gregorio's office sold twenty-six houses, all of them to relatives or friends of the old-time settlers. Values hadn't dropped, and the community has settled down to its old tranquillity.

The neighbors still only tolerate Clark. They have not really accepted him, and it may be a long time before they do. But Wiley Clark and his wife and children are living at peace in the house Clark chose and bought and moved into. The Commission has protected his right to do so and shown all other Philadelphians what they are apt to be up against if they take a notion to start a race riot.

adaptation 12   PROMISING PRACTICES IN
INTERGROUP EDUCATION

Abridged and adapted from Marion Edman and Laurentine Collins, Promising Practices in Intergroup Education (Detroit: Board of Education of the City of Detroit, 1947). Published in this form by permission of the authors.

[The authors have attempted to evaluate current classroom practices in intergroup education in this outline, which was originally prepared for the Detroit public schools. They take particular pains to point out the potential boomerangs that may exist in some of the more time-honored and usually simple techniques of intercultural education, such as the stereotype potential in emphasizing "folk contributions." The total impact of this evaluation is to stress the need for a total school orientation toward intergroup education as against reliance on any single curricular approach.]

THE "CONTRIBUTIONS" APPROACH

In the "great-man" approach, children are told about the achievements of outstanding individuals in various groups. A unit on "Famous Americans Who Were Foreign" or on scientists or artists or the biography of George Washington Carver gives children information on men and women of note who are explicitly identified as members of the minority group.

The "folk-contribution" approach describes the way of life of some group in America either here or in its home country: its art, music, handicraft, dance, folklore, food, festivals, or religion. This material is frequently supplemented by an activity program of firsthand experiences. Children sang the songs, danced the dances, ate the food, wore the costumes, handled the exhibit materials.

Estimate

The merit of the approach lies in the extent to which it achieves its goal, namely, mutual respect among members of different groups. The facts and observations can be used to develop the understanding that cultural pluralism is one of the glories of the composite known as "the American way of life." When properly handled, this approach may also help overcome feelings of inferiority in members of minority groups. A subsidiary merit of the approach lies in its interest for children, the wealth of material, and the ease of its integration into the curriculum.

Effective as this approach can be, it conceals a number of pitfalls for the unwary. The most obvious danger is that of making generalizations from one or a few facts. In the school a child is somehow led to adduce that all Negroes are good people because of Carver. Outside of school he may conclude that Italians are bad people because of Capone. Approach to the individual rather than the group must continually be emphasized.

In addition, it is necessary to screen the factual materials to distinguish between culture items that are historical and those that are current. It is extremely hard, it seems, to give up a false notion that Dutch children generally wear wooden shoes, that all Negro children sing beautifully, that all Eskimos live in igloos. The tendency toward the romantic, the sentimental, and the "cute" derives, at least in part, from a deliberate avoidance of basic issues in intergroup living.

THE "PEOPLE-ARE-ALIKE" APPROACH

In certain aspects this approach overlaps the contributions approach. There, however, the orientation is to differences between people, while here the attempt is made to convey the basic characteristics common to all men. The whole emphasis is to show that historically and scientifically mankind is essentially one in both physical and social aspects. When viewed in the light of ways in which all men are alike, differences are dwarfed into inconsequential proportions.

A unit on early man, for instance, emphasized the common origin of man, the development of physical differences, the growth of languages and customs. (In an elementary school!) That difference does not constitute inferiority was brought out again and again. Cartoons were drawn to show that in so-called "racial types" a great deal of overlapping is evident in many physical characteristics. Even at the kindergarten level the essential likeness of all people is stressed. One of the schools used pictures of "five little babies," which showed that mothers of varied racial strains share strong maternal affection. In one first grade it was pointed out that all little girls and boys of like age lose their front teeth no matter where they live or what their skin color or way of life. In another first grade a collection of pictures was made, showing that many kinds of people make up America. For religious groups careful explanation was made of the likenesses as well as the differences; Judaism as the foundation of Christianity was a case in point.

Estimate

This approach supplies the basic data for all learning and thinking about human relations. If nothing else, the information supplied is a counteragent to the erroneous notions that many children bring to school. Also, the scientific method implicit in the approach may help guide children into the proper procedure for gathering facts and verifying assertions. In addition, the approach has been found feasible at all age levels and develops naturally out of most existing subject matter.

The fundamental practical drawback to this approach is that textbooks do not give generally fair and adequate treatment to minority groups, and many teachers do not have the training or time to fill those gaps with information. Finally, since it is realized that facts alone do not change attitudes, it would appear that this approach would be effective only as part of a wider activity program.

THE STUDY-OF-PREJUDICE APPROACH

This approach attempts to make clear the reasons for stereotyped and bigoted thinking by analyzing the psychological, economic, historical, and social causes of group frictions. Such techniques of prejudiced thinking as name-calling, segregation, scapegoating, and spreading rumors are pointed out and analyzed.

In one intermediate school all 9A classes studied the causes of rumors and their effects on perpetuating false ideas about minority groups. One class listed common erroneous beliefs about Negroes, analyzing and discussing each. The results of hate and the effects of discrimination and prejudice, both on personality and on the social structure, were approaches used frequently. Ignorance as a basic factor in perpetuating ignorance was an approach used as early as the third grade. The economic factors causing prejudice were studied, particularly at the high-school level.

Estimate

One great advantage of the study of prejudice is that it is a realistic grappling with things as they are. It gives children insight into psychological and economic processes and attempts to discover causes that suggest remedies. A psychological drawback to this approach is that, unless it is carefully handled, members of the minority groups discussed may become self-conscious and resentful. The practical hindrance is that most printed materials are intended for use in intermediate and high schools; not many materials are available for lower grade levels, where this approach is needed even more. In schools organized about usual subject matter, it is also necessary to develop special units.

THE PRECEPT APPROACH

This approach aims to give children an understanding of what "the American way of life" really means by explanation of basic American documents, such as the Declaration of Independence, the Bill of Rights, the Four Freedoms, and others. In addition, schools reported such activities as a detailed discussion of the sentence, "All men are created equal"; a joint essay contest on "One World" by the pupils of two schools, one predominantly Negro, one predominantly white; special assemblies to stress the American ideal; conference periods devoted to discussing "respect for other persons' feelings, rights, and beliefs"; a detailed study of the meanings of the Golden Rule and the meaning of the pledge of allegiance to the flag.

Estimate

This approach can make more meaningful the bases of the program in intercultural education, namely, the moral and ethical principles underlying democracy as a way of life. On the other hand, children may end up with nothing but meaningless abstractions. Reciting creeds, devising codes, memorizing pledges, by themselves lead to no improvement in everyday contact with people. In addition, there is a danger of relying on prestige appeal. To urge children to be understanding merely because General Eisenhower or someone else of his status says it is good Americanism to do so is to foster bad habits of reasoning.

THE DEMOCRATIC-PROCEDURES APPROACH

The democratic-procedures approach can add content and meaning to the verbal study of democratic precepts. Stress must be laid on the development of democratic procedures in the classroom. Teachers, children, and administrators should plan and work co-operatively.

In the elementary schools most of the reports indicated that democratic living was achieved primarily by building good group morale between teacher and children rather than through formal organization. (Only a few schools at this level reported any form of student government.) It was emphasized that every child in school received exactly the same consideration as every other child, the same punishment, the same condemnation.

Intermediate schools and high schools reported a considerable number of student-teacher committees to plan and carry out programs for intercultural education. An example might be the pattern of a principal inviting the faculty to advise him on school policies. A committee elected by the teachers might consider grievances, present them to the principal, and offer suggestions about decisions. Similarly, representatives to the student council should be elected in each home room.

At daily meetings problems and projects are explored with the guidance of faculty advisers. The council decides what matters should be carried to the administration. As one example, the students were dissatisfied with the varied bases used by teachers for citizenship marks, so they worked out a new method that was adopted by the faculty. In a large number of schools students are encouraged to exercise a large amount of self-direction in some departments, particularly home economics and shop classes.

Estimate

This approach is basic. Democracy must be lived as well as talked about in schools. Obviously a great deal remains to be done before American schools become truly democratic institutions. But, like the other approaches, this one cannot be used in isolation. It is necessary to communicate to children the principles out of which democratic procedure arises, so that what they do is meaningful as well as enjoyable.

THE IDEALS-VS.-PRACTICE APPROACH

In this approach the "American dilemma" is presented. The contrast is pointed up between what America stands for and what some Americans actually practice in dealing with minority groups. (This is a study of prejudice in the *concrete*.) The schools report such activities as the study of restrictive covenants as they operate in Detroit; discussions of organizations formed to restrict property sales within the community; a study of "Problems of Negroes Today"; surveys of local newspapers to show types of discrimination contained in news and advertising sections; discussion of the Ku Klux Klan; and the study of zoning and housing restrictions in the community.

Estimate

One great merit of this approach is that it is honest and realistic. It motivates children's thinking by leading them to see what should be done to make America what its ideals proclaim it. In realizing that their own neighborhoods and communities have unsolved problems in group relations, children may become less smug and chauvinistic. Such realization is best obtained when children can see at first hand the results of discrimination, but care must be taken in such trips that the children understand that they are witnessing the results of discrimination and not the derelict behavior of individuals. On the other hand, the approach is disillusioning and puzzling to immature children. They find it harder to reconcile the discrepancy between profession and practice in a country which has always been highly idealized for them. The hope is that realization of the dilemma will eventually lead to intelligent efforts to resolve it rather than to rationalize its acceptance.

THE VICARIOUS-EXPERIENCES APPROACH

Fortunately there is an adequate and growing body of books for all age levels dealing with intergroup living and with the daily life of minority groups. These books portray normal, healthy characters among all kinds of people who share the activities and feelings of mankind everywhere. Such portrayals help break down stereotyped thinking. The use of skits, plays, and movies and the comparatively new technique of psychodrama or role-playing (in which children are presented with a situation involving human relations and are then assigned roles and asked to act out some solution on the spot) was reported with frequency.

Estimate

This approach gives children an opportunity to identify emotionally with people of minority groups. Again, as in the other learning materials and approaches, the teacher must guard against books and other media containing false or sentimentalized treatments of minority group members. Too many of the books, also, are deliberately remote, showing Latin-American children, for instance, living in Mexico rather than in Michigan. Even most of the books that are realistic treat their subjects, such as a Negro family, as an isolated entity rather than as a part of a larger society. A fundamental limitation of this approach is that, in spite of the emotional appeal, it probably has little effect upon the many children who have difficulty in learning from words unrelated to their activities.

THE SCHOOL-ACTIVITIES APPROACH

This approach stresses a program of inculcating co-operation and mutual respect in *all* aspects of school life for *all* the children. It is particularly important in schools with mixed populations. Steps were taken to insure good integration in all types of activity. These included integrated clubs and groups. Taking pictures of mixed groups and displaying them on the bulletin board or printing them in school newspapers was a frequent occurrence. The election of pupils from minorities as group and class leaders was common. In the assignment of roles in dramatics and games, no attention was paid to color. Special care was taken to insure the integration of pupils in making locker assignments, and showers in swimming classes were always mixed.

Estimate

This approach was based on a principle that many consider the only really effective one for achieving democratic human relations: living and working together for mutually desired goals. Children learn that the only sensible criterion for co-operative work is the effective contribution of each individual and that his religious or ethnic background is irrelevant to this contribution. The function of the teacher in this approach is to multiply opportunities for co-operative activity to assure absolute impartiality to all individuals and groups. Special attention may have to be given to children who still display evidence of feelings of prejudice.

THE GUIDANCE APPROACH

The conscientious teacher may find that, before her students can enter wholeheartedly into co-operative activities, she has to undertake some preliminary but important efforts in personal guidance and reorientation. While not much is known about the factors that produce healthy, integrated personalities and those that cause bigoted personalities, there is good reason to believe that psychological insecurity is a breeder of prejudice and scapegoating. Therefore, various attempts were made to help children feel secure, particularly in their school relationships. A number of schools used conference periods during which individual and group problems were ironed out. Deviating children of all types were given special assistance and guidance. A visiting teacher conferred with parents.

Much of the work took place in the classroom itself—that little world composed of tightly organized cliques, shifting friendly circles, and partly or completely rejected children. Some teachers were alert to spot the gangs and cliques both within and outside the schools and to discover who the rejected individuals in the class were. Attempts were made to integrate into class activities children who were left out. Attempts at self-segregation by any group were carefully guarded against.

Estimate

This approach can be of the highest effectiveness when properly used in conjunction with democratic procedures of multiplying opportunities for group work. In addition to increased feelings of security, children are spurred to their best individual and co-operative efforts when they know someone is taking a personal interest in their individual success.

The approach is made difficult by the amount of time and individual attention it demands of the teacher. What is undoubtedly needed is a reappraisal of what should be taught, with fresh decisions as to what uses of the teacher's time should receive higher priority.

THE PERSONAL-CONTACT APPROACH

In addition to the wider contacts within each classroom that grow out of the preceding approaches, it is considered desirable to make deliberate efforts to multiply pleasant experiences with members of other groups in other ways. This approach can be fully effective only when a policy is maintained of making appointments to the administrative teaching and service staffs strictly on the basis of merit. In some schools benefits were reported in the use of Negro substitutes. However, schools with comparatively homogeneous populations must usually make special arrangements for outside contacts. One important technique is interschool visits. These were always planned with some specific goal—to present a program or an exhibit or to engage in discussions and sings. Very often, opportunity was planned for mingling of the pupils through teas, tours of buildings, and other social contacts as a supplement to the more formal part of the visit. Joint visits to community centers or joint attendance at meetings were other techniques used. The girls from one high school having no Negro pupils attended a state meeting with a mixed group from another high school, all participating and living as a unit.

Estimate

While pleasant contacts between groups are fairly easy to arrange, there is a valid theoretical objection to their indiscriminate use. We have all heard of the anti-Semite, some of whose best friends are Jews, and of the patronizing southerner who knows and likes individual Negroes but still insists on segregation. Obviously, contacts must be meaningful as well as pleasant; that is, they must be on a basis of equality as part of a pattern involving democratic procedures concerned with shared activities. The teacher will have to prepare participants before the contact and evaluate the experience afterwards. The impression must also be avoided that contacts are "staged." In order to avoid generalizations, members of minority groups must be approached as individuals who have some interest and skill and knowledge and not as "representatives" of that group.

THE COMMUNITY-PARTICIPATION APPROACH

No matter what heights of intergroup education a school might otherwise attain, its fullest potentialities have not been exploited unless the children become aware of the fact that the school is part of the community and that the community has resources relevant to their own interests. Other aspects of this approach are participation by teachers in community activities and education of parents in reference to what the schools are doing.

As a preliminary to this approach, it is helpful to make a survey of some aspects of the community, i.e., a study of how people work together and play together in their community, a map showing where the chief minorities live, a survey of recreational facilities in the neighborhood. The most frequently reported method of school-community co-operation was the preparation of programs dealing with intercultural education for parents' groups.

Second in frequency was the use of community resources: speakers, public libraries, community centers.

Estimate

One merit of this approach is that it helps erase the artificial barrier often erected between school and "real life." This cushions the shock of disillusionment that may attend the discovery of standards and values vastly different from those preached in school. In addition, there is the positive enrichment of the school program derived from the use of community resources.

---

adaptation 13   A SOUTHERNER'S VIEW OF DESEGREGATION

>Abridged and adapted from Thomas R. Waring, "The Southern Case against Desegregation," Harper's Magazine, *212* (January, 1956), 39–45. Copyright, 1955, by Harper & Brothers. Reprinted from Harper's Magazine. *Published in this form by special permission of the author.*

[Some southern white spokesmen stand by segregation on principle. Others oppose the Supreme Court decision ordering public school integration on the ground that, though integration is morally just and desirable, the time for it has not yet come. They hold that the historical pattern of segregation, and the deep cultural differences resulting from it, cannot be reversed overnight; they are also of the opinion that other sections of the country do not quite appreciate the social dislocations which would ensue were the Supreme Court decision to be enforced now. In the following summary, Thomas R. Waring elucidates the "clash of cultures" between Negroes and whites as many southern whites view it. He does not hold that these cultural differences are permanent and inevitable, but he states that they currently exist and must be understood in order to appreciate much southern resistance to immediate desegregation by law.]

The differences between Negro and white children in the South may eventually be removed, but these differences are too great *at present* to encourage white parents to permit their children to mingle freely in school. This has nothing to do with the frequent practice of children of both races playing together when young, or with cordial relationships in many other contacts of ordinary life.

Volumes could be written on racial differences from many angles, including anthropology and sociology. I shall merely try to summarize five of the differences that most immediately come to the minds of white parents in the South. These are health; home environment; marital standards; crime; and a wide disparity in average intellectual development.

HEALTH

Negro parents as a whole—for reasons that white people may sympathetically deplore but which nevertheless exist—are not so careful on the average as their white neighbors in looking after the health and cleanliness of their children. The incidence of venereal disease, for instance, is much greater among Negroes than among whites.

Statistics to document this statement are difficult to come by, though the statement itself would be generally accepted in the South. The U.S. Public Health Service some years ago quietly stopped identifying statistics by race. South Carolina figures, available for 1952–53, give a clue to the situation in that state; it probably is much the same elsewhere in the South. Out of a population 60 per cent white and 40 per cent Negro, 6,315 cases of syphilis were reported, of which 89 per cent were among Negroes. Infection with gonorrhea was found in six Negroes to one white person, but some physicians report that many cases of gonorrhea among Negroes go unrecorded.

During the same period—1952–53—a campaign against venereal disease was carried on, county by county. A spot check of four representative counties in different parts of South Carolina showed that cases of syphilis were found among 1.3 per cent of the white persons examined. This was a fairly constant percentage. The percentage of infection among Negroes ranged in the same counties from 8.5 to 10.8 per cent, averaging more than 9 per cent.

Fastidious parents do not favor joint use of school washrooms when they would not permit it at home, and there's no use to tell them that it is unlikely that anyone will catch venereal disease from a toilet seat. They just don't want to take risks of any kind with their children.

HOME ENVIRONMENT

For most colored children in the South, the cultural background is different in many ways from that of their white neighbors, and while these differences may have various explanations, they add up in the public's mind as racial. Slavery is so long in the past that nobody thinks about it any more, but the master and servant, or boss and laborer, relationship between whites and Negroes is still the rule rather than the exception. The emergence of a middle class among the Negroes has been extremely slow; again, the reasons count for less in the minds of white parents than the fact itself. Indeed, the professional and commercial class among Negroes is so small that its members are in perhaps the most unenviable position of all. They have progressed beyond the cultural level of the vast bulk of their own people, but are not accepted among the whites, who fear to let down any dikes lest they be engulfed in a black flood.

Someone may suggest that there is an opening wedge for integration in the schools by admitting a few well-scrubbed and polished colored children of cultivated parents. In reply, let me say that this would be no more acceptable to the colored people than to the whites. The solution, perhaps—as it is among upper-bracket white people who do not send their children to public schools—might be private schools for prosperous Negroes as for prosperous whites. In any case, white people feel that cultural gaps on other levels should be filled in before discussing integrated schools.

MARITAL HABITS

Many southern Negroes' marital habits are, to state it mildly, casual—even more so, in fact, than among the often-divorced personalities of northern café society. Many Negro couples—the statistics are not readily available, for obvious reasons—do not bother with divorce because there was no actual marriage in the first place. Statistics on the results of such casual unions, however, are available. On the average, one southern Negro child in five is illegitimate. It is possible that the figure may be even higher, since illegitimate births are more likely to go unrecorded. Even among Negroes who observe marriage conventions, illegitimacy has little if any stigma.

Many white persons believe that morals among their own race are lax enough as it is without exposing their children to an even more primitive view of sex habits. Moreover, while these parents do not believe there is any surge of desire among their offspring to mate with colored people, they abhor any steps that might encourage intermarriage. They believe that lifting the racial school barriers would be such a step. Miscegenation has been on the wane in recent years. Whatever mixing of blood may have occurred—and admittedly that was due largely to lustful white men seeking out acquiescent Negro women—has been without benefit of either law or custom. On some levels of society, breaking the racial barriers might lead to mixed marriages. The mixture of races which white southerners have observed in Latin-American countries gives them a dim view of legalizing cohabitation with Negroes.

CRIME

For many years, crime in the South has been more prevalent among Negroes than among white people. Though the northern press no longer identifies criminals by race, white southerners have reason to believe that much of the outbreak of crime and juvenile delinquency in northern cities is due to the influx of Negro population. They believe the North now is getting a taste of the same race troubles that the South fears would grow out of mixed schooling, on a much bigger scale. They want no "blackboard jungles" in the South.

Maintaining order is a first concern of southerners. What they have heard about the fruits of integration in the North does not encourage them to adopt the northern race pattern. In Chicago, three hundred policemen have been assigned for a year or more to guard a nonsegregated housing project with no bigger population than a southern village where a single constable keeps the peace. In the County of Charleston, South Carolina—with 190,000 population, nearly half Negro—the total law-enforcement manpower of combined city and county forces is 175.

While the homicide rate in the South is high, it is due in large measure to knifings and shootings among colored people. Interracial homicide is relatively rare. (One of the reasons why the ghastly killing of Emmett Till in Mississippi made hot news—and some of that news was superheated and garnished with prejudice for the northern press—was the very fact that it *was* unusual. No lynching, as even most northerners now realize, has occurred in years.)

With racial bars down and rowdies of both races daring one another to make something of the vast increase in their daily contacts, opportunities for interracial strife are frightening. Conservative, law-abiding people—and believe it or not, they constitute the bulk of southern whites—are deeply fearful that hatred and bloodshed would increase without separation of the races.

And they know that, in the long run, if there is riotous bloodshed it will be for the most part Negroes' blood. The thin tolerance of the ruffian and lower elements of the white people could erupt into animosity and brutality if race pressure becomes unbearable. Schools would be a focal point for such disturbances, first among pupils themselves and later by enraged parents. Instead of learning out of books, the younger generation would be schooled in survival—as several northern sources have told me is already happening in some areas of New York, Philadelphia, and Washington, D.C.

INTELLECTUAL DEVELOPMENT

Again for whatever the reasons may be, southern Negroes usually are below the intellectual level of their white counterparts. The *U.S. News and World Report*—the fairest nationally circulated publication I am acquainted with, in its treatment of the race issue—has reported that in Washington colored children are about two grades behind the whites in attainment. This discrepancy, I believe, is about par for other communities. In Washington it was found that there were even language difficulties to surmount. The children used different terms for some things.

Some advocates of integration say the way to cure these differences is to let the children mingle so that the Negroes will learn from the whites. The trouble with this theory is that, even if it works, a single generation of white children will bear the brunt of the load. While they are rubbing off white civilization onto the colored children, Negro culture will also rub off onto the whites.

Few southern parents are willing to sacrifice their own offspring in order to level off intellectual differences in this fashion. They reason that their children will get along better in later life if they have, as youngsters, the best available cultural contacts. Such an attitude is not, I understand, altogether unknown in the North. Many parents in New York City, for example, make considerable financial sacrifices to send their children to private schools to spare them the undesirable associations and the low-geared teaching standards of most public schools.

If this sounds snobbish to a northern reader, let me ask you to examine your own conscience. Can you honestly say that you are eager to send your own child to a classroom where the majority of other pupils will be considerably more backward in their studies and extremely different in social background and cultural attainment? Which would you *really* put first—your theory of racial justice, or justice to your own child?

---

adaptation 14 THE SUPREME COURT ON SCHOOL SEGREGATION

[The following is the decision of the Supreme Court in *Oliver Brown* et al. v. *Board of Education of Topeka, Shawnee County, Kansas,* et al., 347 U.S. 483 (1954); only footnote and bibliographical references of the Court are omitted. In this decision, usually referred to as *Brown* v. *Board of Education,* the Supreme Court ruled that segregation in public schools violates the guarantee of equal protection of the laws to all persons contained in the Fourteenth Amendment to the Constitution. The decision actually encompassed four different appeals to the Supreme Court for reversal of rulings by lower courts denying Negro children admittance to public schools on an equal basis with white children.]

Mr. Chief Justice Warren delivered the opinion of the Court.

These cases come to us from the States of Kansas, South Carolina, Virginia, and Delaware. They are premised on different facts and different local conditions, but a common legal question justifies their consideration together in this consolidated opinion.

In each of the cases, minors of the Negro race, through their legal representatives, seek the aid of the courts in obtaining admission to the public schools of their community on a nonsegregated basis. In each instance, they had been denied admission to schools attended by white children under laws requiring or permitting segregation according to race. This segregation was alleged to deprive the plaintiffs of the equal protection of the laws under the Fourteenth Amendment. In each of the cases other than the Delaware case, a three-judge federal district court denied relief to the plaintiffs on the so-called "separate but equal" doctrine announced by this Court in *Plessy* v. *Ferguson*. Under that doctrine, equality of treatment is accorded when the races are provided substantially equal facilities, even though these facilities be separate. In the Delaware case, the Supreme Court of Delaware adhered to that doctrine, but ordered that the plaintiffs be admitted to the white schools because of their superiority to the Negro schools.

The plaintiffs contend that segregated public schools are not "equal" and cannot be made "equal," and that hence they are deprived of the equal protection of the laws. Because of the obvious importance of the question presented, the Court took jurisdiction. Argument was heard in the 1952 Term, and reargument was heard this Term on certain questions propounded by the Court.

Reargument was largely devoted to the circumstances surrounding the adoption of the Fourteenth Amendment in 1868. It covered exhaustive consideration of the Amendment in Congress, ratification by the states, then-existing practices in racial segregation, and the views of proponents and opponents of the Amendment. This discussion and our own investigation convince us that, although these sources cast some light, it is not enough to resolve the problem with which we are faced. At best, they are inconclusive. The most avid proponents of the post-War Amendments undoubtedly intended them to remove all legal distinctions among "all persons born or naturalized in the United States." Their opponents, just as certainly, were antagonistic to both the letter and the spirit of the Amendments and wished them to have the most limited effect. What others in Congress and the state legislatures had in mind cannot be determined with any degree of certainty.

An additional reason for the inconclusive nature of the Amendment's history, with respect to segregated schools, is the status of public education at that time. In the South, the movement toward free common schools, supported by general taxation, had not yet taken hold. Education of white children was largely in the hands of private groups. Education of Negroes was almost nonexistent, and practically all of the race were illiterate. In fact, any education of Negroes was forbidden by law in some states. Today, in contrast, many Negroes have achieved outstanding success in the arts and sciences as well as in the business and professional world. It is true that public education had already advanced further in the North, but the effect of the Amendment on Northern States was generally ignored in the congressional debates. Even in the North, the conditions of public education did not approximate those existing today. The curriculum was usually rudimentary: ungraded schools were common in rural areas; the school term was but three months a year in many states; and compulsory school attendance was virtually unknown. As a consequence, it is not surprising that there should be so little in the history of the Fourteenth Amendment relating to its intended effect on public education.

In the first cases in this Court construing the Fourteenth Amendment, decided shortly after its adoption, the Court interpreted it as proscribing all state-imposed discriminations against the Negro race. The doctrine of "separate but equal" did not make its appearance in this Court until 1896 in the case of *Plessy* v. *Ferguson,* involving not education but transportation. American courts have since labored with the doctrine for over half a century. In this Court, there have been six cases involving the "separate but equal" doctrine in the field of public education. In *Cumming* v. *County Board of Education* and *Gong Lum* v. *Rice* the validity of the doctrine itself was not challenged. In more recent cases, all on the graduate school level, inequality was found in that specific benefits enjoyed by white students were denied to Negro students of the same educational qualifications: *Missouri* ex rel. *Gaines* v. *Canada; Sipuel* v. *University of Oklahoma; Sweatt* v. *Painter; McLaurin* v. *Oklahoma State Regents.* In none of these cases was it necessary to re-examine the doctrine to grant relief to the Negro plaintiff. And in *Sweatt* v. *Painter* the Court expressly reserved decision on the question whether *Plessy* v. *Ferguson* should be held inapplicable to public education.

In the instant cases, that question is directly presented. Here, unlike *Sweatt* v. *Painter,* there are findings below that the Negro and white schools involved have been equalized, or are being equalized, with respect to buildings, curricula, qualifications and salaries of teachers, and other "tangible" factors. Our decision, therefore, cannot turn on merely a comparison of these tangible factors in the Negro and white schools involved in each of the cases. We must look instead to the effect of segregation itself on public education.

In approaching this problem, we cannot turn the clock back to 1868 when the Amendment was adopted, or even to 1896 when *Plessy* v. *Ferguson* was written. We must consider public education in the light of its full development and its present place in American life throughout the Nation. Only in this way can it be determined if segregation in public schools deprives these plaintiffs of the equal protection of the laws.

Today, education is perhaps the most important function of state and local governments. Compulsory school attendance laws and the great expenditures for education both demonstrate our recognition of the importance of education to our democratic society. It is required in the performance of our most basic public responsibilities, even service in the armed forces. It is the very foundation of good citizenship. Today it is a principal instrument in awakening the child to cultural values, in preparing him for later professional training, and in helping him to adjust normally to his environment. In these days, it is doubtful that any child may reasonably be expected to succeed in life if he is denied the opportunity of an education. Such an opportunity, where the state has undertaken to provide it, is a right which must be made available to all on equal terms.

We come then to the question presented: Does segregation of children in public schools solely on the basis of race, even though the physical facilities and other "tangible" factors may be equal, deprive the children of the minority group of equal educational opportunities? We believe that it does.

In *Sweatt* v. *Painter,* in finding that a segregated law school for Negroes could not provide them equal educational opportunities, this Court relied in large part on "those qualities which are incapable of objective measurement but which make for greatness in a law school." In *McLaurin* v. *Oklahoma State Regents* the Court, in requiring that a Negro admitted to a white graduate school be treated like all other students, again resorted to intangible considerations: ". . . his ability to study, to engage in discussions and exchange views with other students, and, in general, to learn his profession." Such considerations apply with added force to children in grade and high schools. To separate them from others of similar age and qualifications solely because of their race generates a feeling of inferiority as to their status in the community that may affect their hearts and minds in a way unlikely ever to be undone. The effect of this separation on their educational opportunities was well stated by a finding in the Kansas case by a court which nevertheless felt compelled to rule against the Negro plaintiffs:

"Segregation of white and colored children in public schools has a detrimental effect upon the colored children. The impact is greater when it has the sanction of the law; for the policy of separating the races is usually interpreted as denoting the inferiority of the Negro group. A sense of inferiority affects the motivation of a child to learn. Segregation with the sanction of law, therefore, has a tendency to retard the educational and mental development of Negro children and to deprive them of some of the benefits they would receive in a racially integrated school system."

Whatever may have been the extent of psychological knowledge at the time of *Plessy* v. *Ferguson,* this finding is amply supported by modern authority. Any language in *Plessy* v. *Ferguson* contrary to this finding is rejected.

We conclude that in the field of public education the doctrine of "separate but equal" has no place. Separate educational facilities are inherently unequal. Therefore we hold that the plaintiffs and others similarly situated for whom the actions have been brought are, by reason of the segregation complained of, deprived of the equal protection of the laws guaranteed by the Fourteenth Amendment. This disposition makes unnecessary any discussion whether such segregation also violates the Due Process Clause of the Fourteenth Amendment.

Because these are class actions, because of the wide applicability of this decision, and because of the great variety of local conditions, the formulation of decrees in these cases presents problems of considerable complexity. On reargument, the consideration of appropriate relief was necessarily subordinated to the primary question—the constitutionality of segregation in public education. We have now announced that such segregation is a denial of the equal protection of the laws. In order that we may have the full assistance of the parties in formulating decrees, the cases will be restored to the docket, and the parties are requested to present further argument on Questions 4 and 5 previously propounded by the Court for the reargument this Term. The Attorney General of the United States is again invited to participate. The Attorneys General of the states requiring or permitting segregation in public education will also be permitted to appear as amici curiae upon request to do so by September 15, 1954, and submission of briefs by October 1, 1954.

It is so ordered.

United Press Photo

CHAPTER 7

Immigration

Section I: What Is the Problem?

"Rarely in American history," commented the *Christian Science Monitor,* "has there been a piece of Federal Legislation as bitterly attacked or as extravagantly praised."[1] This comment marked one stage in the controversy that has boiled up around the "immigration issue" since the end of World War II. The heat of debate has laid bare the several deeply drawn and dramatic issues which underlie the usual charts of cold immigration statistics. Reflected is a conflict not only about *how many* but also about *what kinds* of people the United States can best absorb; and this conflict, in turn, reflects even deeper feelings about one of the most unique characteristics of the American community: the heterogeneity of its people.

"With the idea of quotas in general there is no quarrel," said President Harry Truman, and he continued:

Some numerical limitation must be set so that immigration will be in our capacity to absorb. But the over-all limitation of numbers imposed by the national origins quota system is too small for our needs today, and the country-by-country limitations create a pattern that is insulting to large numbers of our finest citizens, irritating to our allies abroad and foreign to our purposes and ideals.

To put it baldly, [the idea behind the national origins quota system was that]

[1] Quoted in *Platform,* April, 1953 (Weekly Publications, Inc., New York), p. 2.

Americans with English or Irish names were better people and better citizens than Americans with Italian or Greek or Polish names .... Such a concept is utterly unworthy of our traditions and our ideals.[2]

Epitomizing an opposing view, a columnist for a Negro newspaper wrote:

Culturally this is a Western European—specifically an Anglo-Saxon—nation regardless of its racial composition, and in the past many of our social difficulties have stemmed from indigestible elements in the population. Contrary to the ideal this nation is not actually a melting pot, but a polyglot stew with the morsels staying pretty much separate. We may not like it but that's a fact.... People of divergent cultures simply do not mix well when living together.[3]

The issue, then, revolves around the acceptability of foreigners in general and of certain foreigners in particular.

Our present population is the fruit of the migration of more than 40 million people to the United States in search of space, opportunity, and freedom. There is no American except the native Indian who is more than a dozen generations removed from a foreign country. Immigrants have swept in from every part of the world, at varying times and in varying numbers depending upon homeland pressures and American barriers. From 1820 to 1954 more than 33 million emigrated from Europe. More than 5 million have come from countries of the Western Hemisphere, and almost 1 million from Asia.

Americans have come in substantial numbers from at least fifty nations, bringing with them many distinctive cultures and many different patterns of social, political, and religious thought. Even after four decades of restricted immigration, America is still an immigrant nation. One out of five Americans has at least one parent who is foreign-born. There are some forty language groups in the country sizable enough to support over a thousand foreign-language newspapers and periodicals. These are indicative of the many national subcultures which have run through the American fiber.

Despite this background, restrictionist sentiment in this country has proved strong enough to win handily every legislative test. There has been in recent years no major proposal to radically raise the over-all immigration ceiling. Current debate substantially concerns the question of "whom" rather than "how many" we shall let in. Under these circumstances, current restrictionist sentiment would seem to be based on qualitative rather than quantitative concerns. The premise is that America is essentially an offspring of Anglo-Saxon and western European culture. This may not be a

---

[2] "Immigration and Nationality Act—Message from the President of the United States" (House Doc. No. 52), *Congressional Record*, Vol. 98, Part 6 (June 25, 1952), pp. 8082–85.

[3] George S. Schuyler in the *Pittsburgh Courier*, January 10, 1953.

"better" culture, but it is at least a distinctive culture. The indiscriminate removal of restrictions would result in the failure of immigrants to be integrated into American society. It would also result generally in a basic modification of the national character.

To determine how much of this concern is grounded in fact and how much can be laid to prejudice, we can examine the adjustment record of our immigrants, especially in the past seventy-five years. In this way we can perhaps discover how disruptive are the culture clashes inherent in a heterogeneous and immigrant-receiving nation such as we have been. Against the background of this information and in order to evaluate it, these questions must be posed: What is the value of heterogeneity? What is its price? What is the value of homogeneity, and what is *its* price? What adjustments to America can and should be expected of immigrants and their near descendants? These are of one piece with a final generic question: What is America . . . and what is an American?

Section II: The Growth of the Problem

Immigration to America, virtually uncontrolled before World War I, was largely shaped by world history and the changing pressures upon populations abroad. Different people have come to America at different times, for different reasons, and in varying numbers. Similarly, each period of immigration has had different consequences, has raised different problems, and has evoked different reactions from those already settled in America.

STAGE I: EARLY IMMIGRATION (1607–1830)

Who and How Many

About three-quarters of a million immigrants came voluntarily to America from the time of its Colonial beginnings in 1607 to the eve of the Revolution in 1770. Their national origins can be roughly estimated by examining family names at the time of the first United States census in 1790, at which time the total non-Indian population was about 4 million. It is believed that about 60 per cent were of English or Scotch-Irish descent and that about 20 per cent were Negro. The rest were largely German, Dutch, Scandinavian, French, Spanish, and Portuguese.

Immigration Policies

During this period there were no general restrictions on immigration either as to numbers or origins. Immigration policy in the early colonies was liberal. Religious and political tolerance was advertised as an inducement, and the ground rules were deliberately shaped for an immigrant nation: for office-holding, no religious test was required, and only the President had to be native-born. However, naturalization was restricted to those who were free and white.

Adjustment Problems

Immigrant difficulties in Colonial days had mainly to do with religious differences. At one time or another all the colonies except Rhode Island had some kind of discriminatory legislation against Catholics and Jews. Some fears were expressed during the post-Revolutionary period about the assimilability of some of the foreign-language groups. Benjamin Franklin once voiced concern about the fact that the German population in Pennsylvania

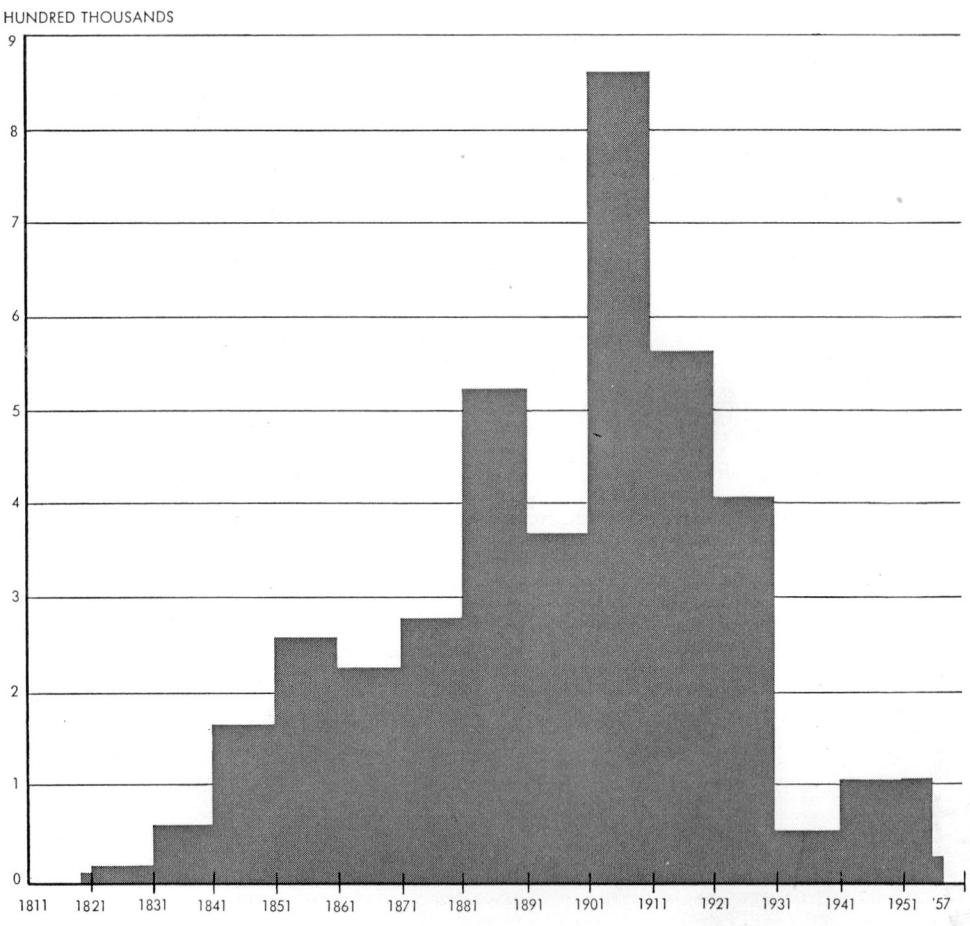

FIGURE 7:1 IMMIGRATION TO THE UNITED STATES, 1820–1957

Source: U.S. Department of Justice, Immigration and Naturalization Service.

clung so persistently to its own language. But there were no major group-adjustment problems until the first big wave of immigration in the 1830's.

STAGE II: THE "OLD" IMMIGRANTS (1830–80)

Who and How Many

In the three decades between 1830 and 1860, almost 5 million immigrants came to America. This sudden acceleration was spurred by a liberal land policy in the United States, political upheaval in Europe, and improved transportation. Of these 5 million immigrants, only 30,000 were from southern and eastern Europe. The rest were from northern and western Europe, the majority being from Germany and Ireland. These German and Irish immigrants represented the first large-scale ethnic differentiation in America.

The Irish immigrants (almost 2 million in three decades) fled absentee landlords, an alien church, and stark poverty aggravated by famine. The German immigrants (about 1.5 million) came mainly for economic reasons, although a number of them were political refugees from the unsuccessful revolutions in Germany. The rural elements in these migrant groups played a large role in developing frontier society. The city settlers provided the manpower to build the spawning cities and the railroads and canals reaching into the West.

Toward the end of this period, the "national-origin" base of immigration began to broaden, but immigrants from northern and western Europe still outnumbered southern and eastern European immigrants by about sixteen to one.

Immigration Policies

No restrictive laws were enacted during this period. Government emphasis, particularly in frontier states, was still on the positive encouragement of immigration.

Adjustment Problems

During the 1830–60 period, America had its first attacks of "immigrant indigestion," centering around the unprecedented size and nature of the Irish and German migrations.

The Irish immigrants, who arrived penniless in the big cities of the East and tended to remain there, became the principal objects of nativist displeasure. They offended by being conspicuously poor and devoutly Catholic. They crowded together into squalid "shanty-towns." Political corruption followed in the wake of their poverty as they were gathered in by the big-city party machines. Fraudulent voting, the ward heeler, and political favor flourished. In addition, preachers and pamphleteers attacked them as "popish idolaters" whose primary allegiance was to a "foreign potentate."

The German immigrants of this period offended American opinion by importing strong ideas about social reform and by adhering to continental living habits, which did not include Puritanical observance of the Sabbath. Though most German immigrants came in search of land, a leavening of political refugees stayed in the cities to exercise their passion for social reform. When they also insisted on their traditional Sunday entertainment and beer, they were accused of being not only radical but immoral.

A mutual bitterness built up around these various religious, political, and cultural divergences, and some uneasiness began to be expressed by native workmen about "lowering of living standards." Anti-immigration pamphlets reached flood peak. Protestants and Irish Catholics fought in the streets. A convent was burned in New England. There were "beer riots," involving Germans. This feeling climaxed in the Know-Nothing Party of the 1850's, directed mainly against Irish Catholics and radical German organizations and demanding severe restrictions on immigration. Although this party achieved enough influence to control the governments of at least a half-dozen states, none of the demanded restrictions was effected at that time, and the storm passed with the Civil War period. During the war, immigration was encouraged anew; and the war served both to demonstrate the loyalty of the immigrant groups who fought in the Union forces and to diminish some of the cultural differences.

STAGE III: THE "NEW" IMMIGRANTS (1880–1920)

Who and How Many

Immigration to America took its second spectacular jump in the 1880's, when it more than doubled that of the previous decade. In the forty years between 1880 and 1920, more than 23 million people coursed through the "Golden Door," representing more than half our total immigration from 1600 to the present. More important, the extra bulge in immigration was made up largely of people from southern, central, and eastern Europe, who were, in addition, predominantly Catholic or Jewish. In these forty years over 4 million from Italy, almost 4 million from Austria-Hungary, and over 3 million from Russia migrated to this country, whereas up to 1880 total immigration from each of these countries had been less than 100 thousand. During this forty-year period, almost twice as many "new" immigrants (from southern and eastern Europe) came in as did "old" immigrants (from northern and western Europe), and toward the end about five times as many "new" as "old" immigrants were being admitted.

The "new" immigrants came as escapees from poverty and, particularly in the case of Russian Jews, from religious oppression. Too late to take a large role in America's territorial expansion, they settled in the cities and provided the manpower for America's prodigious industrial expansion.

Immigration Policies

The first federal legislation to control immigration was passed in 1882. This was designed to exclude paupers, criminals, and diseased persons, formerly a function of port-of-debarkation states. Also in 1882, America's first restrictive *group* law was passed. This was the Chinese Exclusion Act, later extended to include most orientals and reputed by some to have played an important part in the deterioration of Japanese-American relations.

In 1917 a first attempt was made to slow down immigration, particularly the influx of "new" immigrants, by the device of a literacy test. This failed as a restrictive measure and made no apparent dent in the flow of immigration, "old" or "new." Until 1921 there were no direct quantitative restrictions on non-Asiatic immigration, which seemed to be limited only by the amount of available shipping.

Adjustment Problems

Their greater numbers, their deeper-going cultural divergencies, and the changed nature of America itself made the adjustment problems of the "new" immigrants considerably more complicated than those of the "old" immigrants. Their mass concentrations in the cities became conspicuous communities-in-themselves, whose very size encouraged cultural self-sufficiency and served to insulate the new immigrants against rapid assimilation. This tendency was further strengthened by the fact that the "new" immigrants were predominantly Catholic and, less so, Jewish. In the last quarter of the nineteenth century the Catholic population practically doubled. Large eastern cities elected Catholic mayors for the first time, while the growth of parochial schools stimulated national debate.

Aggravating these cultural conflicts was the fact that the census of 1890 officially declared that the frontier was now "closed." There was no longer extensive opportunity for "horizontal" expansion, there was less sense of unlimited living space, and huge concentrations of people began to build up in the industrial cities.

Two notorious "hate" groups thrived and waned during this period: the American Protective Association, which was essentially anti-Catholic, and the reborn Ku Klux Klan, which was anti-everything but white Protestant. But more respectable American institutions joined the cry against unlimited immigration. Fearing cheap labor and strikebreaking, the Knights of Labor, and then the American Federation of Labor, called for restrictions. Many labor leaders blamed immigration for the depression of 1893.

The apparent growth of socialist thought abroad, and particularly the Bolshevik Revolution of 1917, brought new fears. For the first time, big business began to lend its weight to the restriction of immigration, along with such groups as the American Legion and the National Grange. The country was ripe for the period of controlled immigration, which began in 1921.

STAGE IV: CONTROLLED IMMIGRATION (1921–52)

Restrictive Policies

Until 1921, all immigrants except Asiatics were admitted on the basis of *individual* qualifications. In that year America's immigration policy took on the national-origin emphasis it has retained to this day when Congress passed the "Three per Cent Law." This law restricted the annual immigration of each nationality outside the Western Hemisphere to 3 per cent of the total number of foreign-born of that country who had been in the United States in 1910.

This did not satisfy the restrictionist sentiment, and in 1924 Congress passed the Reed-Johnson Act, which established a temporary two-per-cent formula (based on the number of foreign-born in the United States in 1890) and set up a permanent National Origins Quota System, which went into effect in 1929.

The National Origins Quota System

This National Origins Quota System, under which we are still operating, specified that the total number of immigrants to be allowed to enter the country under the quota system would be restricted to one-sixth of 1 per cent of the white population of the United States in 1920. This total immigration "pie," about 154,000, was cut up into different-sized slices for each nation according to the proportion of people of that national descent who had been in this country in 1920. It was estimated that 40 per cent of the white people recorded in the 1920 census were of English origin; therefore, 40 per cent of the total annual "quota pie" was allotted to Great Britain. It was estimated that about 4 per cent of the white people recorded in the 1920 census were of Italian origin; therefore, 4 per cent was allotted annually to Italy. Thus, less than 6,000 Italian immigrants could enter the United States each year as compared with 55,000 permissible British immigrants.

The National Origins Quota System laid a heavy premium on immigration from "old-immigration" countries of northern and western Europe (82 per cent of the total). Since the quota supply for these countries was generally larger than the demand, the only immigration that was actually

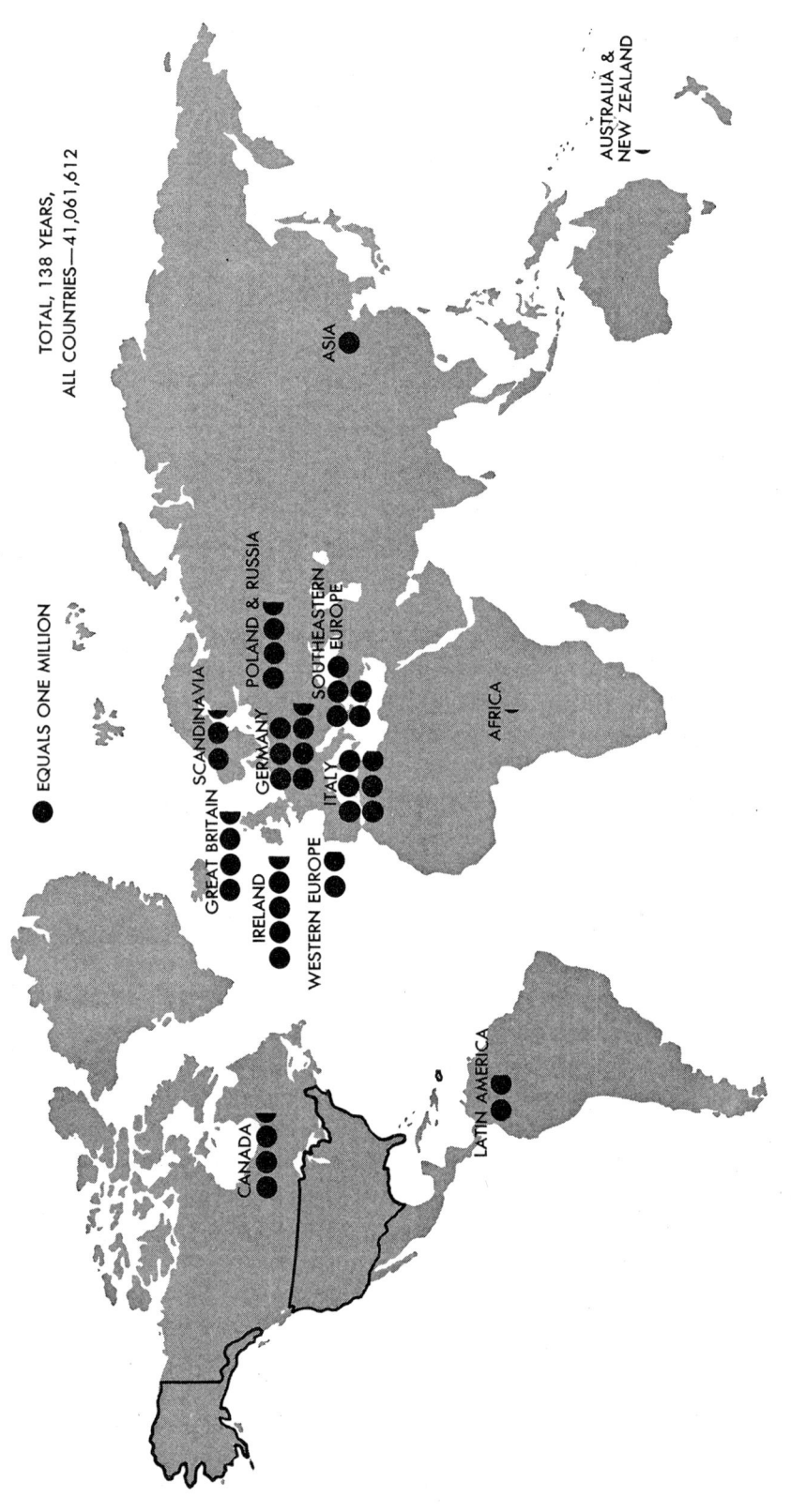

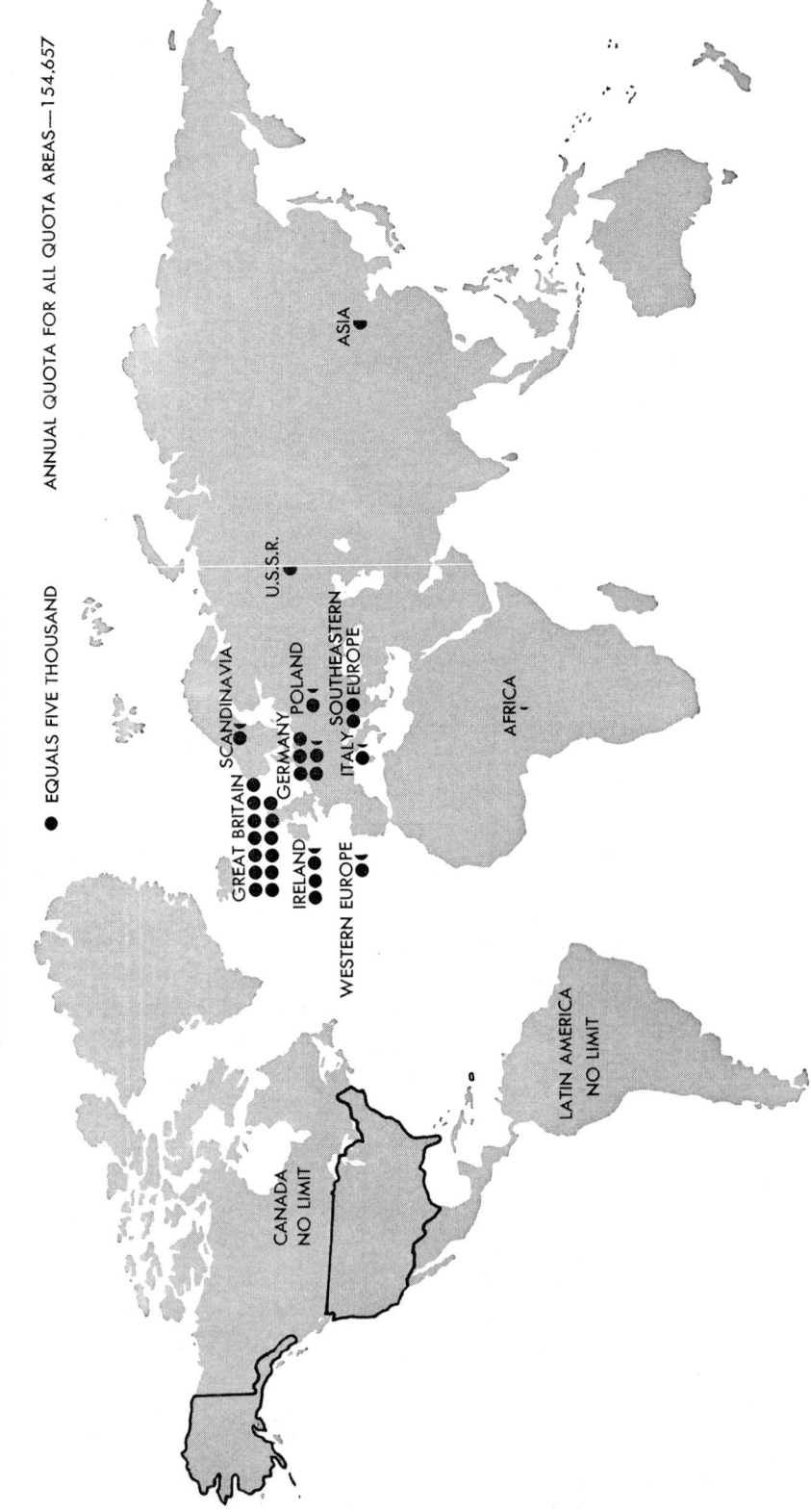

FIGURE 7:3 CURRENT ANNUAL IMMIGRATION QUOTAS

Source: U.S. Bureau of the Census, *Statistical Abstract of the United States, 1957* (Washington, D.C.: U.S. Government Printing Office, 1957), p. 93.

restricted by this Act was from the "new-immigration" countries of southern and eastern Europe, which normally have had long waiting lists in excess of their quota allotments. Orientals, excluded from naturalization, were automatically excluded from immigration. This situation lasted until World War II, when restrictions on Chinese Nationals were loosened in the light of their participation in the war. The Chinese Exclusion Act was repealed in 1943, when the Chinese were granted naturalization rights and a token annual immigration quota of 105 persons.

Who and How Many

1. *Quota immigration.* The theoretical immigration figures set up by the National Origins Quota System have not resembled actual immigration figures for several reasons. (*a*) The large quotas set for countries of northern and western Europe exceed immigration applications from those countries and are largely unfilled; Great Britain, for example, has filled only a little more than 10 per cent of its allotted quota. (*b*) Immigration from southern and eastern European countries, which normally have waiting lists in excess of quotas, was artificially stemmed by the war and by Nazi and Communist captivity. (*c*) Unused quota visas cannot be carried over to following years or be shifted from one country to another. For example, Greece has an annual quota of 310; if only 210 immigrants of Greek origin enter the United States in one year, the unused quota of 100 cannot be filled the following year or be transferred to some other country.

Theoretically, about 25,000 immigrants from southern and eastern Europe are permitted annually, but from 1930 to 1948, because of depression and war, only about half that number have entered on the average each year under the quota system. Table 7:1 shows the quotas allotted by the Reed-Johnson Act of 1924 and compares them with the actual number of quota visas used for a nineteen-year period (1930–48).

2. *Nonquota immigration.* Nearly half of the actual immigration since the law of 1924 has been nonquota immigration, which falls into these categories: (*a*) special classes of people exempt from quota provisions; (*b*) immigration from the Western Hemisphere; and (*c*) emergency "refugee" immigration, provided for by special legislation.

a) Exempt classes: The wives, the minor children, and in some cases the husbands of American citizens, as well as ministers and professors, were exempted from the quota restrictions of the 1924 Act. Such exemptees, coming in outside the quota system, have comprised about one-sixth of the total immigration from Europe. This includes the large number of "GI" brides and children admitted after World War II.

b) Western Hemisphere: Countries of the Western Hemisphere were exempted from the National Origins Quota System. Some had no nationals

TABLE 7:1 UNUSED QUOTA VISAS, EUROPEAN COUNTRIES, 1930–48*

NORTHERN AND WESTERN EUROPE

Country	Quota for 19 Years	Quota Visas Used in 19 Years	Percentage of Quotas Unused
Belgium	24,776	8,540	66%
Denmark	22,439	6,717	70
France	58,634	20,554	67
Germany	493,183	199,193	60
Great Britain and No. Ireland	1,248,699	161,464	87
Iceland	1,900	417	78
Ireland (Eire)	239,207	43,171	82
Luxemburg	1,900	628	67
Netherlands	59,907	16,019	73
Norway	45,163	12,046	73
Sweden	62,966	10,782	83
Switzerland	32,433	8,784	73
Total	2,391,207	488,315	80% av.

SOUTHERN AND EASTERN EUROPE

Country	Quota for 19 Years	Quota Visas Used in 19 Years	Percentage of Quotas Unused
Albania	1,900	1,854	3%
Austria	15,433	7,537	52
Bulgaria	1,900	983	48
Czechoslovakia	54,606	25,427	53
Danzig	1,900	728	62
Estonia	2,204	1,080	51
Finland	10,811	4,606	57
Greece	5,890	5,112	14
Hungary	16,511	11,026	33
Italy	109,937	46,593	58
Latvia	4,484	2,428	46
Lithuania	7,344	4,468	39
Poland	123,956	59,989	52
Portugal	8,360	5,984	29
Spain	4,788	4,274	11
Turkey	4,294	3,579	16
U.S.S.R.	53,162	20,069	62
Yugoslavia	16,241	8,088	50
Other countries	8,200	744	91
Total	457,440	220,761	52% av.

* This table, illustrating disparity in unused quotas between northern and western Europe and southern and eastern Europe, has been drawn to 1948, because of the passage in that year of the Displaced Persons Act. The admission figures were distorted for the next few years; the increased admissions were illusory because they represented the "mortgaging" of future quotas.

SOURCE: William S. Bernard, *American Immigration Policy* (New York: Harper & Bros., 1950), p. 306, and U.S. Immigration and Naturalization Service, *Annual Report* for the years 1947 and 1948 (Washington, D.C.: U.S. Government Printing Office).

in the United States on whom to base a quota, and restriction would presumably have hampered the "Good Neighbor" policy. About a third of all immigration to this country since 1924 has been nonquota immigration from the Western Hemisphere. This is the breakdown of *nonquota* immigration to the United States for the years 1925–47:

>   From Europe (exempt individuals)...................... 319,919
>   From Mexico and Latin America.......................... 396,041
>   From Canada and Newfoundland........................ 575,774
>   From Asia, Africa, and the Pacific (exempt individuals).... 34,137

This total of 1,325,871 *nonquota* immigrants for the years 1925–47 compares with a *quota* immigration during this period of 1,392,135.

Because of the absolute visa-issuing powers of consular officers, immigration from the Western Hemisphere has by no means been totally unrestricted. Especially in the case of Mexico, whose poverty and proximity have stimulated prospective immigration, our consular officials have carefully held down immigration through widespread use of the clause which denies visas to those who "might become public charges."

In the wake of this policy, a special problem of illegal immigration from Mexico has been created. In 1952 an immigration official estimated that Mexicans were illegally entering the country at the rate of one a minute. Termed "wetbacks," because so many of them literally swim the Rio Grande, more than half a million illegal Mexican entrants were apprehended and deported in 1950. The actual traffic is estimated to be at least twice that figure, although there are undoubtedly a large number of repeaters. The chief goals for these wetbacks are the seasonal-crop areas of the Southwest. It was estimated that in 1949 at least 400 thousand of the 1 million migratory farm laborers were illegal Mexican immigrants. Among the consequences of the "wetback invasion" listed in 1951 by the President's Commission on Migratory Labor was serious depression of wage and health standards.[4] The border patrol numbered about five hundred men at that time, and it was questioned whether anything short of a standing army would be able to patrol the extensive Mexican-American border.

A complicating problem, according to the President's Commission, is the enforcement of national immigration law in an area which is unsympathetic to that law. The lack of sympathy for immigration-law enforcement on the part of some farm employers, according to the President's Commission, is partly the result of labor needs in seasonal-crop areas and partly the result of the fact that the wetback traffic has severely depressed farm wages. The Commission suggested that if the profit were removed from wetback

[4] President's Commission on Migratory Labor, *Migratory Labor in American Agriculture* (Washington, D.C.: U.S. Government Printing Office, 1951).

employment (by requiring adherence to minimum-wage standards) and the risk of such employment were increased (by making the employment of a wetback a crime), this illegal traffic would soon diminish.

In 1948 Congress passed the first Displaced Persons Act for admission of some of the millions of Europeans who had been uprooted by the war and who for political or economic reasons could not or would not be resettled in their native lands. Additional emergency legislation of this character was passed in 1950. As a result of these bills, some 394 thousand refugees were admitted to this country.

STAGE V: THE PRESENT—RENEWED CONTROL

Public Law 414, the Immigration and Nationality Act of 1952, reaffirmed the immigration policy of the preceding three decades without major alteration. The over-all tendency of the Act was toward greater rather than less restriction. Public Law 414 is a comprehensive codification of all immigration regulations, with these controversial highlights:

Over-All Quota

The formula of the 1921 Act based on the 1920 white population was retained. Adjustments raised the total annual quota figure from 153,714 to 154,657.

National Origins Quota System

The national-origins formula of the 1921 Act was maintained without change for European countries. (Provisions had always existed for making adjustments for shifting national boundary lines in Europe.)

Racial Barriers

1. *Naturalization.* All barriers to the naturalization of Asiatics were lifted. Most notably, this gave many foreign-born Japanese a chance to become citizens for the first time.

2. *Asia-Pacific Triangle.* For the first time an annual quota of about one hundred was established for certain Asian countries and areas, including Japan. However, the Act provides that any person attributable by as much as one-half of his ancestry to races native to the Asian-Pacific zones shall be chargeable to the quota of his ancestry, *no matter where he was born.* All other immigrants are charged to the land of their birth, no matter what their ancestry. For example, immigrants born in China of French parents or born in France of even one Chinese parent are charged not to the French but to the Chinese quota.

3. *Colonial immigration.* Especially in the case of Jamaica and other British colonies in the West Indies, Negro immigrants had formerly entered

Loomis Dean—courtesy of LIFE Magazine

Nonquota Immigration: Having crossed the border illegally, Mexicans follow the power lines north across the desert.

freely under the ample British quota. Public Law 414 abolished that right and instead established for each of these areas a maximum annual quota of 100.

Nonquota Immigration

All husbands of U.S. citizens are now included in the nonquota category, along with wives and children; but professors lost their nonquota status. Immigration from the Western Hemisphere continued unrestricted by quota (except for those of Asiatic ancestry).

Meanwhile, an "emergency act" passed by Congress in 1953 provided for the possible admission of about 200,000 nonquota refugees, mostly escapees from Communist countries.

Visa Preferences

Previously at least half of each national quota was reserved for applicants on a first-come, first-served basis. The only two preference groups were close relatives of citizens and skilled agricultural workers. Under Public Law 414, half of each quota is available to "immigrants whose services are determined by the Attorney General to be needed urgently in the United States" because of education, training, or experience. The remaining half is available to close relatives of citizens. Whatever is unused may be assigned on a first-come, first-served basis. This is a symptomatic move in the direction of more selective immigration.

Security Emphasis

1. *Admission.* The law continues the double-headed administration of immigration: through consular officials, who have absolute visa-issuing powers abroad, and through the Immigration and Naturalization Service, under the Department of Justice, at United States ports of debarkation. Consular officials have been authorized to refuse visas if they "have reason to believe" that the entry of an immigrant would be prejudicial to the security of the United States. Unless he has redeemed himself, no one can enter who has been a member of a party that has advocated totalitarianism for the United States. This applies uniformly to Communists, but it has not been clear whether it applies to all former German Nazis.

2. *Deportation of aliens.* The law multiplies the number of reasons for which an alien may be deported (e.g., present or former membership in the Communist party; any serious criminal offense; failure to file a notice with the Attorney General within ten days of a change of address).

3. *Denaturalization.* The law also broadens the grounds for revoking the citizenship of naturalized citizens (e.g., the concealment at time of naturalization of a material fact with or without proof of fraud; conviction of contempt for refusing to testify before a congressional committee concerning subversive activities; affiliation with a subversive group).

Section III: Immigrant Adjustment

The U.S. Senate Committee on the Judiciary made the following report in 1950, preliminary to the introduction of the Immigration and Nationality Act of 1952:

The adoption of the national origins formula was a rational and logical method of numerically restricting immigration in such a manner as to best preserve the sociological and cultural balance in the population of the United States. There is no doubt that it favored the peoples of the countries of northern and western Europe over those of southern and eastern Europe, but the subcommittee holds that the peoples who had made the greatest contribution to the development of this country were fully justified in determining that the country was no longer a field for further colonization, and, henceforth, further immigration would not only be restricted but directed to admit immigrants considered to be more readily assimilable because of the similarity of their cultural background to those of the principal components of our population.[5]

The immigrant obviously brings with him the customs and traditions in which he has been steeped all his life—living habits and attitudes which were attuned to the social and legal as well as the political and economic institutions of his former country. But just how disruptive of American community life *is* the resultant culture-clash?

STAGES OF ADJUSTMENT

Accommodation

The first necessity for the immigrant is to earn a living. His first adjustment, therefore, is on the job. Standardization in dress and the learning of the English language typically follow. The immigrant deliberately learns to conform to basic American manners and rules in order to avoid conflict with the general community. But, except for the necessary contact he must have with the general community, he tends to confine himself to his own national-origin group. There he speaks his native tongue, reads foreign-language newspapers, and joins nationality associations for cultural, social, and fraternal purposes. The concept of "mutual accommodation" requires merely that the general community tolerate the immigrant and his differences.

This initial stage of adjustment serves as an important bridge for the immigrant. He has the security of a familiar environment while he is adjusting to new ways. Not uncommonly, he displays more interest in the culture and affairs of his old country than he did before he emigrated, partly because he has a freedom of expression in America that he never had in the "old country." This, too, is part of the growing adjustment to America, even where it is initially done in a foreign language.

This first stage of accommodation is shorter at present than it once was, partly because of restricted immigration but also because of modern pressures toward standardization and conformity. Radio, television, and films

---

[5] U.S. Senate Committee on the Judiciary, *The Immigration and Naturalization Systems of the United States,* Senate Report 1515, 81st Cong., 2nd Sess. (1950), p. 455.

become almost immediately a part of the immigrant's new environment. He is not likely to seek out a nationality "ghetto." He quickly acquires an automobile; in this and other ways he becomes acquainted with the many facets of American community life far sooner than did his early-century predecessor. Through union membership, for example, he has more initial points of contact with the community.

Integration

In the stage of accommodation, community standards are still alien to the immigrant, though he conforms to them in order to get along. He becomes integrated, however, as these basic standards are absorbed and become second nature to him. An integrated immigrant may very well retain certain nationality habits of diet, recreation, humor, etiquette, belief and ritual, but these habits will not interfere with his ability to move in the general community and share in general community interests and activities. Mutual adjustment on this level requires that the general community accept his participation in public and semipublic affairs despite his continuing differences. But, at the very least, he has come by second nature to conform to the major rules and institutions which govern social behavior in his new society.

Assimilation

To assimilate means "to become like," and its use as an immigration term is varied. When an immigrant has become integrated in the manner described above, he has "become like" native Americans in his *basic* pattern of community conduct. In one sense, then, he has become assimilated. However, many people demand of the immigrant and his descendants that they not only fit into American life but that they be utterly indistinguishable from anybody else in order to be counted as "assimilated." To satisfy this definition, the immigrant must lose virtually all of his nationally distinctive customs and characteristics. He must be free of all national-origin contacts and interests. He must become culturally indistinguishable from the native population.

THEORIES OF SATISFACTORY ADJUSTMENT

The satisfactory adjustment of an immigrant group depends not only upon the desires and abilities of the immigrant group but also upon the demands of the native population. Different views as to the nature of a satisfactory adjustment have been current at various times. Early in our history a laissez-faire attitude prevailed. Frontier society badly needed immigrant labor, services, and initiative; it tended not to demand conformity even in language.

The Melting-Pot Theory

In the decades immediately preceding World War I there emerged, as a response to the great wave of new immigration, the theory of the melting pot. This held that the foreign-born would fuse with the native stock with great rapidity and that a new type of composite American would result.

To some extent the melting-pot theory was justified, especially as it denied widespread fears that the immigrant would remain forever a foreigner and an "enemy" of the "true" American. In time, the descendants of immigrants do indeed become integrated into American life and often wholly assimilated, while the Anglo-Protestant character of American society has undoubtedly been modified by values derived from other national strains and religions.

In other respects the melting-pot theory seems from our present vantage point to have been mistaken. For example, though American Protestantism, Catholicism, and Judaism undoubtedly differ in many important respects from their European counterparts, three separate religions and groups of religious organizations nevertheless remain. There is no new, composite American who belongs to a new, composite American church. The melting-pot theory also underemphasized the regional variations in American society. A parish in Louisiana and a county in Montana, a ranch in Texas and a farm in Iowa, exhibit differences in speech, diet, recreation, humor, and etiquette; living together in a national community does not require a composite American. Moreover, democracy does not require the obliteration of all group differences but prides itself upon its willingness and ability to mediate among them and to employ them in fruitful, enriching ways.

Sometimes the melting-pot theory was couched not as a factual belief but as a demand: the immigrant *ought* to fuse rapidly with the native stock. In this guise, its influence was less than beneficent. For one thing, it failed to appreciate the importance of group-belonging for personal security and fulfillment. The family group, immigrant or not, is the primary source of the individual's values, attitudes, and sense of security; it is only at considerable psychological cost that a person can renounce to any great degree what was inculcated in him as a child. Moreover, everyone feels most at home with those who share with him customs and ways of behaving, however superficial, to which he has become accustomed. In addition, phrased as a demand, the melting-pot theory seemed to suggest that neither immigrant values nor native values were ever worth defending for their own sake and intrinsic worth. It also seemed to suggest that the best ideals were always a mixture and a blending. In practice, given the inferior status of immigrants, this meant that immigrants often depreciated and forsook their own values even when these were worth preserving.

The Americanization Theory

The third conception, an outgrowth of the nationalism and drive for unity inspired by the first World War, was the Americanization theory. Its aim was not a blending of cultures but standardization and the obliteration of European attitudes and customs. Actually, however, its goal was to Anglicize rather than to Americanize; it tried to make the foreign-born conform to an Anglo-Protestant culture. It overlooked the fact that our American culture has always contained numerous other groups besides the English. It also created serious personality problems for the foreign-born and their children by carrying the implication that foreign languages and cultures were inferior.

The Theory of Cultural Pluralism

A fourth theory is called "cultural pluralism." This concept supports the right of groups to maintain their cultural life and traditions without interference or censure. In its most common usage, it is not a laissez-faire theory. It emphasizes the responsibility of individuals and ethnic groups not to permit their differences to conflict with the welfare of the larger American society. Cultural pluralism, however, does imply the existence of cultural islands in the midst of political and economic unity.

Supporters of this approach point out that cultural pluralism in this country has not in fact led to the existence of a series of cultural islands within our society. When an immigrant or any descendant of his absorbs the major rules, institutions, and mores of America, then he has become part of the American culture. He may retain a taste for some of the cultural trappings of his country of origin, such as a distinctive kind of cooking, but this is not an essential part of any national culture. He may still be interested in the literature or destiny of his country of origin, but there is an important difference between being "interested in" and being "of" a culture. Given successful integration, our normal democratic principle of personal freedom can be applied without danger, and no constraint can or need be laid on citizens who have a special interest in other cultures or nations.

AIDS TO ADJUSTMENT

A framework for comprehensive aid to immigrant adjustment already exists in this country under the auspices of private organizations. The United Service for New Americans, the Church World Service, and the National Catholic Resettlement Council have local affiliates throughout the country designed to bridge the way for the immigrant. Emergency financial aid is available through these sources, as well as vocational training and employment services. In addition, these agencies provide a broad program of

American Family: An Italian immigrant couple with their American-born children and grandchildren.

social services, including individual and family counseling. Adult education in the English language and in citizenship subjects is provided by these as well as many other organizations, such as the YMCA and YWCA, and by Boards of Education in metropolitan areas. The American Association of International Institutes, with many local affiliates, offers a variety of counseling services and special group activities leading to social and cultural adjustment. In addition to these specialized agencies, there are available today in all cities a wide range of social services which were not available to the immigrant thirty years ago, e.g., employment service, welfare service, and rehabilitation service for individuals and families.

THE RECORD OF ADJUSTMENT

The effect of immigration on American society has generally been assessed from three different angles: the American economy; American political life and philosophy; and American social standards.

Economic Adjustment

While America was physically expanding, there was no question about the economic value of immigrants in quantity. They were needed to extend the frontier, build the railroads, dig the mines, and man the mushrooming factories. Their earnings were plowed back into the agricultural and industrial expansion of the country. In 1909, in the United States Bureau of the Census, *A Century of Population Growth*, it was estimated that during the nineteenth century our population swelled by thirty million people and our wealth by $40 billion as a result of immigration.

In the first decade of the twentieth century the frontier seemed to be closing, the runaway industrial boom slowing down, the cities filling to capacity. Yet immigrants were pouring off the boats in unprecedented numbers. This situation was investigated by the United States Immigration Commission of 1907–11.[6] The forty-two-volume report of this Commission provided the background for forthcoming restrictive laws by making these charges:

1. Immigration lowered the American standard of living. First, by creating an oversupply of unskilled labor, immigrants depressed wages. Second, immigrants brought with them such a low standard of living that they were content to live in slums and work for low wages under sweatshop conditions.

2. Immigration created unemployment. Immigrants displaced native workers, especially by being willing to work for lower wages.

3. Immigration increased the number of public charges. Many immigrants arrived without funds and became public charges or made public charges of others by depriving them of jobs.

[6] U.S. Immigration Commission, *Abstracts of Reports* (Washington, D.C.: U.S. Government Printing Office, 1911).

The target of these charges was not merely the "how many" but also the "who" of immigration. It was supposedly the southern and eastern Europeans who brought with them the low living standards of their poverty-stricken countries, who were willing to work in sweatshops for low wages, who were unskilled, who were impoverished on arrival. These charges have colored the popular discussion of immigration ever since. They have been subject to the following criticisms:

1. *Standards of living.* The report of the 1907–11 Immigration Commission concluded that the economic status of the immigrant was directly related to the length of his residence in this country. It was only a matter of time before an immigrant, of whatever national origin, accepted the American standard of living. This time lapse has been almost entirely eliminated since 1911 by such developments as broad-scale unionization, laws covering minimum wages and working conditions, and the universal impact of the mass media.

The standard of living aspired to is also related to their occupations—in the case of immigrants, to their occupations prior to immigration. Since the first decade of the century, the occupational pattern of immigrants has changed radically, partly because political oppression has become an important reason for immigration, partly because occupational patterns have been changing in other countries. This changing pattern is dramatized in Table 7:2, which shows the percentages of incoming immigrants in various occupational categories in several periods between 1908 and 1954. From 1908 to 1923, for example, approximately a quarter of all immigrants were unskilled or common laborers; from 1951 to 1954 only about 8 per cent were unskilled workers.

TABLE 7:2   OCCUPATIONS OF IMMIGRANTS *

OCCUPATION	YEAR OF ARRIVAL			
	1908–23	1930–34	1940–44	1951–54
Professional	3%	10%	26%	13%
Skilled	22	32	26	35
Farm laborers	25	9	1	3
Common laborers	26	12	6	8
Commercial		5	25	22
Servants	24	20	8	8
Farmers		6	2	7
Miscellaneous		7	7	5

* Column 1 (1908–23) is taken from Harry V. Jerome, *Migration and Business Cycles* (New York: National Bureau of Economic Research, 1926). The sources for the other columns are the Bureau of the Census' *Statistical Abstracts of the United States, 1946* and *1955*. The high percentage of professional immigrants in 1940–44 reflects the high proportion of political refugees during that period.

2. *Unemployment.* In underdeveloped areas, where farm land is limited and poor and farming methods remain primitive, populations can indeed increase beyond the available food supply and famines result. In an industrialized society with rich natural resources, such as the United States, a relatively small portion of the population can produce food and raw materials for a total population many times its numbers. Hence the capacity for population expansion is correspondingly increased. Beginning in the nineteenth century, the United States was able to divert much of its manpower to building its transportation and industrial plant; in recent years it has been able to turn its energies to an unprecedented expansion of consumer goods and services.

The historical fact is that, because of industrialization, population increases have been outstripped by job increases. During the fifty-year period of greatest immigration, 1870–1930, American population increased about threefold while the number of gainfully employed increased about fourfold.[7] Louis Bean, economist for the Department of Agriculture, testified in 1953:

> The immigration restrictions for the past 25 years have retarded the economic growth of this country. We would have today 16 to 17 million more people in this country, producing at least $35 billion more of the national output, nearly $30 billion more of national income, $15 billion more in wages and $3 billion more in farm cash income.[8]

At a time of depression and high unemployment, large-scale immigration would undoubtedly worsen the situation. The historical fact, however, is that during the five-year heart of the depression, from 1932 to 1936, 136,000 more people emigrated *from* than *to* America.

But whatever the economic considerations, the question is one of maximum population size, *whether native or immigrant.* There is no reason to suppose that a surplus of immigrants creates unemployment while a surplus of native-born employables does not. Nor is there any reason to suppose that a surplus of immigrants from one part of the world creates unemployment while a surplus of immigrants from another part of the world does not. And this is the context of the current immigration controversy, into which the question of unlimited immigration does not enter.

3. *Dependency.* Statistics indicate that immigrants have been substantially as self-supporting as the native-born. In 1940, a time of relatively high unemployment, the U.S. Census Bureau reported that about 9 per cent of

---

[7] William S. Bernard, *American Immigration Policy* (New York: Harper & Bros., 1950), p. 70.
[8] Jewish War Veterans of America, *Measuring Up* (Boston: Department of Massachusetts, Jewish War Veterans of America, 1953), p. 33.

the native-born white males and about 10 per cent of the foreign-born white males were unemployed. Further, the stipulation that every immigrant must be individually screened as to the possibility of his becoming a public charge is *not* at issue in the current immigration debate.

Political Adjustment

The political aspects of immigration are perhaps closer than the economic to the heart of the current immigration issue. These two related questions have been asked about the political effects of immigration: (1) How well are immigrants from the various nations able to understand and participate in our democratic system of self-government? (2) How strained is the political allegiance of immigrants to America?

1. *The immigrant and the democratic process.* According to Senator George of Georgia, who was in the Senate when the original 1924 law was passed and again when its principles were reaffirmed in 1951, one of the real purposes of the law is "to preserve . . . something of the character of the men who loved self government, who understood it and who had some concept of it."[9] Such men, the law implies, are to be found mainly in western Europe, where the principles of American self-government originated. It is generally agreed that during the periods of mass immigration, at the end of the nineteenth and the beginning of the twentieth century, the preponderance of immigrants were: (*a*) unfamiliar with the practice of voting and other democratic procedures; (*b*) unfamiliar with and uninterested in the basic issues of American politics; and (*c*) preoccupied with personal problems of job and adjustment rather than with politics.

Under these circumstances was born the "immigrant boss," who served as a link to the bewildering new world for his compatriots. He was able to "fix" things for them, to interpret the new rules, and often to find jobs for them; in return, they were quite willing to follow his political lead. The immigrant boss was a cornerstone of the big-city political machine. These machines were bolted together by personal favors rather than by political philosophy. As a result, they fostered political corruption and political illiteracy.

With respect to the current immigration issue of national-origin selection and limited immigration increases, the following points have been made:

a) The immigrant boss and the political machine were as prevalent in areas populated by Irish and German immigrants as in areas populated by southern and eastern Europeans. National origin, then, was not an essential factor.

b) Immigrants are no longer as cut off from the mainstream of American

[9] "Revision of Laws Relating to Immigration, Naturalization, and Nationality," *Congressional Record*, Vol. 98, Part 5 (May 22, 1952), pp. 5756–77.

life as they were at the turn of the century. All of the standardization pressures are operative. In addition, there are now numerous nonpolitical agencies to help meet the adjustment needs of new immigrants.

c) Immigrants tend to be more politically conscious today than they were at the turn of the century. Indeed, political motivation has become a major factor in immigration.

2. *Immigrant loyalty.* Immigrants have been accused not only of failing to understand democratic processes of government but of maintaining a loyalty to their homeland which interferes with their loyalty to the United States. They have been called "hyphenated Americans."

By a "hyphenated American" is meant someone who retains a major interest in the welfare of his former country, or country of descent, and shapes his political opinions accordingly. Thus, in 1914 a number of German-Americans urged our government to take a sympathetic view toward Germany. After the war, Italian-Americans pressed President Wilson to support their motherland in demanding the Brenner Pass. In 1946, a number of Irish-Americans went on record as opposing the huge loan to Great Britain. During the years preceding World War II, numbers of Americans of German origin joined an American version of the Nazi Bund. These are clearly "special interest" national-origin groups within our political community.

The special interest of American citizens in some aspects of foreign policy has not always been based on national origin. When Israel was established by the United Nations as a homeland for the Jewish refugees of Europe and Asia, the Jews of America manifestly took a special interest in the welfare of that nation. When regular diplomatic representation at the Vatican was proposed by President Truman, the Catholics of America manifestly took a special interest in supporting and promoting that proposal; conversely, much of the opposition which resulted in the ultimate failure of the proposal came from organized Protestant church sources. "Special interest" in foreign affairs may spring from many sources in heterogeneous America. However, these qualifying points have been made:

a) "Dual loyalty" cannot be meaningfully applied to every citizen who has a special interest in a foreign country. Such special interest is common, whether for reasons of ancestry or for reasons of sentiment or economic interest having nothing to do with national origin. Such interest may, of course, help to shape the citizen's judgment as to the foreign-relations program of the United States, but it does not necessarily involve a conscious conflict between his concern for the welfare of this country and the "other" country. "Dual loyalty" can be properly used only where such a conflict exists—where devotion to another country would actually interfere with allegiance to America.

b) These special interests in a native land have more often resulted in na-

Werner Wolff; Black Star

Screening the Immigrant: Two prospective Polish immigrants are questioned through an interpreter by a Board of Special Inquiry at Ellis Island.

tionality relief funds and cultural societies than in effective attempts to alter the main course of American foreign policy.

c) In the case of war, the records show no hazard to this country as the result of defective loyalties, even on the part of those born in countries with which we have been at war. In 1917, out of 24 million draft registrants, some 4 million were aliens. Two and a half million of these had as yet declared no intention to seek citizenship and therefore would have been exempted, had they requested exemption. In the second World War, official government statistics show that aliens contributed their proportionate share to the armed forces. Although there were many tales, even on the floor of Congress, about espionage activities on the part of Japanese living in America during the early days of World War II, J. Edgar Hoover, chief of the FBI, later reported that there had not actually been a single case of treason or espionage.

d) With respect to the *current* immigration issue, special interest in land of descent is certainly as notable in the case of northern and western European nationalities as in the case of southern and eastern European nationalities.

In modern times, however, the most disturbing questions of loyalty have involved dual national loyalty coupled with *ideological* defections from the democratic way of life. "Party" Communism is an international political ideology with built-in Russian patriotism. The Senate Committee on the Judiciary which prepared the McCarran-Walter Act stated in its report that "the Attorney General of the United States presented before the subcommittee an analysis conclusively establishing that the Communist organization, the Communist apparatus in the United States is overwhelmingly under the control of aliens and foreign-born persons."

The Attorney General had studied 4,984 of the more militant members of the Communist party as of 1947. The analysis showed that 2,202, or 44 per cent, of these were born in Russia, or had at least one parent who was born in Russia, or were married to persons of Russian stock. Another 614, or 12.5 per cent, of the militants were "either of stock from the countries adjacent to Russia (Poland, Finland, Rumania, Lithuania, Turkey, Latvia and Estonia) or were married to persons of such stock." An additional 1,739 persons, or 34.9 per cent of the Communist militants, were "either of stock from other foreign countries or were married to stock from other foreign countries." Altogether, 4,555, or 91.4 per cent, of the 4,984 militant Communists studied were either of foreign stock or were married to persons of foreign stock (one parent or both parents born abroad).[10]

In the light of the current policy issue, however, the following comments have been made:

a) At the time that the Attorney General's study was made, there were in the United States about 35 million persons of "foreign stock." The additional number of people who were "married to foreign stock" was unmeasured. Can we conscionably make national policy on the basis of the records of 4,555 (less than one ten-thousandth) of these people?

b) There are no statistics available as to the disproportionately large number of foreign-born who, because of their experience, are militantly and passionately anti-Communist and anti-Nazi. A good number of those who sought or are seeking immigration to this country are specifically fleeing Communism. *Individual* screening of immigrants for possible subversive tendencies is the only screening method consonant with good sense and democratic principles.

Social Adjustment

Perhaps the most objective method of evaluating the record of social integration is by examining immigrant conformity to the formal rules of society. This record was made by immigrants of preponderantly southern and eastern European origin.

All studies of criminal statistics show that the foreign-born have consistently contributed less than their due proportion to the total criminal population, even where age and sex factors have been taken into account.[11]

---

[10] U.S. Senate Committee on the Judiciary, *Subversive and Illegal Aliens in the United States*, Progress Report, 82nd Cong., 1st Sess. (1951).

[11] C. C. Van Vechten, "The Criminality of the Foreign-Born," *Journal of Criminal Law and Criminology*, **32** (1941), 139–47.

On the other hand, there has been statistical evidence pointing in the direction of higher crime and delinquency rates for the children of foreign-born parents than for the children of native-born parents. The meaning of these statistics is not clear. More significant would be a comparison of delinquency rates between children of foreign-born and native-born parents *of the same socio-economic class*. Many of the same risk factors of delinquency would then apply, e.g., residence in delinquency areas, greater susceptibility to police action, a greater degree of family disorganization and individual frustration. There is, however, one risk factor which would seem to apply particularly to children of immigrants and which has a national-origin dimension: marginality.

The phrase "marginal man" was coined by Robert E. Park to describe a person who, like the second-generation member of an immigrant group, lives on the margin of two ways of life, knowing both but participating fully in neither. Brought up from childhood in a home with one set of values, traditions, and habits, he has to make his way in a society based on another set. His parents' ways, he soon finds, are unacceptable in America; this experience undermines his confidence in parental rightness and authority. On the other hand, because American ways are not inculcated in him in earliest childhood, he often has an inadequate understanding of the new society and a diminished loyalty to its code. Under these circumstances, there is some risk that the individual will not feel constrained by the morality of either his parents or the outside world.

This condition of marginality applies not only to the children of immigrants. Negro families are often marked by the same conflict. Many Negro parents are still ruled by a code found in a rural South; their morality is based on submissiveness, noncompetitiveness, frugality, and strong religious belief. Their children are taught—in northern schools, for example—quite another code, which stresses go-getting competitiveness and the value of nonreligious goals.

For child or adult, the "lack of belonging" characteristic of marginality can certainly bring with it problems of insecurity and the hazard of personal and social maladjustment. On the other hand, "being on the outside," however painful, may enable the marginal man to be a particularly objective and creative critic of both cultures in which he is partially involved.

Section IV: Meeting the Problem

The immigration problem must be met largely on the level of national policy rather than by direct community action. With regard to immigration quotas, there have been two kinds of legislative proposals regularly offered since 1952 toward revision of current policy. One calls for the complete abandonment of the national-origins quota system, substituting for it an allocation system based on American and immigrant needs without regard to national origin. The other calls only for the pooling of unused quotas and their allocation without regard to national origin. The latter approach would modify the restrictive intent of the current law, since the high-quota countries of western and northern Europe regularly use only a small part of their allotted quotas. However, the initial philosophy of national-origin preferences would remain intact.

Both approaches have generally been coupled with the proposal that the latest census, rather than the 1920 census, be used as the basis for determining the over-all immigration ceiling. According to the 1950 census, this would call for a ceiling of about 251,000 immigrants as against the current maximum of about 154,000. Either the abandonment of the national-origins quota system or the policy of "using unused quotas" would tend to make this ceiling an *actual* figure and not a hypothetical maximum which is never reached.

It has been an almost unanimous opinion among political observers that, while many other changes may be made, the philosophy of the national-origins quota system will remain untouched in the foreseeable future. On the face of it, this determined resistance is an anomalous situation which bears exploring. At least at the national leadership level the weight of opinion expressed against the national-origins philosophy has been substantial. National leaders of all of the major religious denominations have uniformly expressed opposition to the national-origins philosophy as discriminatory. The National Council of the Churches of Christ in the U.S.A. has officially stated that Congress should remove "all discriminatory statutes based upon consideration of color, race, or nationality."[12] Similar criticism has been forthcoming from such sources as Cardinal Mooney of Detroit, Cardinal McIntyre of Los Angeles, the National Catholic Welfare Council, the National Lutheran Council, and the National Episcopal Council. The national policy-making bodies of the American Federation of Labor and the Congress of Industrial Organizations have expressed opposition to the national-origins philosophy. So did Republican President Eisenhower and, before him, Democratic President Truman.

Yet the legislative representatives of the American people have overwhelmingly resisted any effort to revise the national-origins philosophy. When President Truman vetoed the McCarran-Walter Immigration bill in 1952, he made its allegedly discriminatory provisions one of the prime bases of his objection. The House of Representatives promptly passed it over his

---

[12] Quoted in *U.S. Immigration Policy: Statements of Position* (New York: Committee To Improve U.S. Immigration Law, n.d.).

MEETING THE PROBLEM

veto by a vote of 278 to 113, and the Senate by a vote of 57 to 26. This vote engendered no public repercussions. It seemed clear that there was no ground swell of public opinion contradicting the tenor of this congressional vote.

There is no way to make a clear analysis of the national inclination to retain the national-origins philosophy. Many factors are involved in the passage of immigration legislation, and no definitive effort has been made to separate out the various elements of the public attitude toward the law.

It is perhaps significant, however, that there is a direct correlation between the congressional vote to override President Truman's veto and the proportion of foreign stock (foreign-born and children of foreign-born) in the various states. The representatives from the ten states with the lowest proportion of foreign stock to general population (about 1 to 24) registered a total vote of 3 to sustain the veto and 69 to override (a proportion of 1 to 23). The representatives from the ten states with the highest proportion of foreign stock to general population (about 1 to $1\frac{1}{2}$) registered a total vote of 81 to sustain the veto and 95 to override (a proportion of somewhat less than 1 to $1\frac{1}{2}$).

These figures might serve suggestively to support the opinion that the mainspring of restrictionist sentiment at this point in history is an attitude

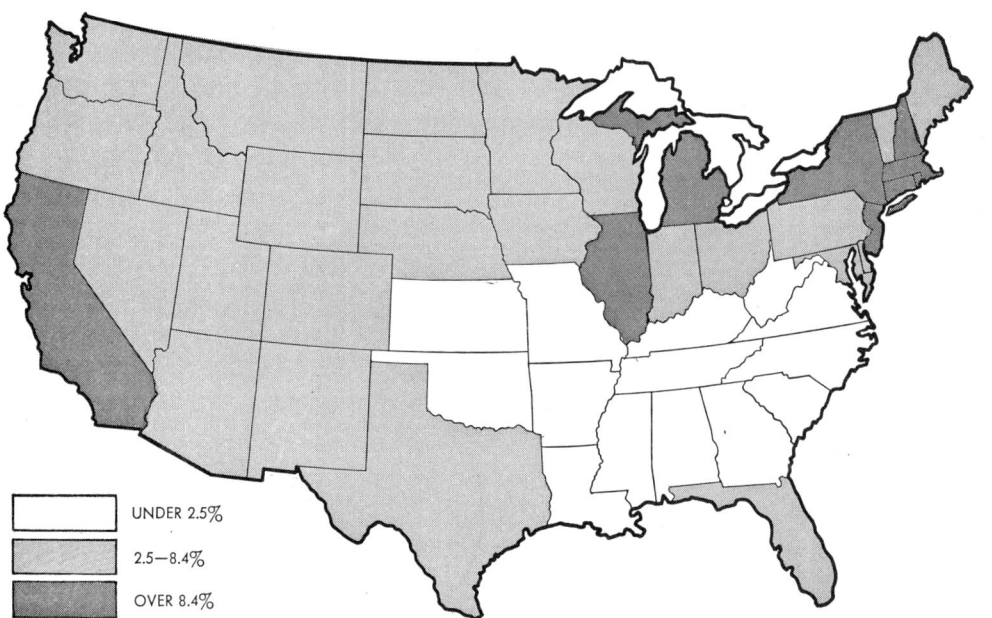

FIGURE 7:4 PROPORTION OF FOREIGN BORN WHITES BY STATES, 1950

UNDER 2.5%
2.5–8.4%
OVER 8.4%

Source: U.S. Bureau of the Census, *Nativity and Parentage*, 1950 Population Census Report P-E, 3A (Washington, D.C.: U.S. Government Printing Office, 1954), p. 71.

of "nativism" and a converse suspicion of the "alien." At the least, some of the elements of prejudice, such as ethnocentrism and stereotyping, would seem to be strongly operative. The current immigration issue, after all, does not involve the prospect of wholesale lowering of the immigration bars. The resistance to any tampering with the national-origins system would be at least partly explained by the widespread existence of prejudicial attitudes toward foreigners in general and toward non-Anglo-Saxons in particular. Partly explained also would be the resistance of the general public to the rhetorical demands of their national leaders, religious and otherwise.

This is not to say that all protagonists of restricted immigration are prejudiced or that there are not legitimate and rational concerns in the restriction of immigration. But it is important to recognize that there is an element of group prejudice affecting both the formulation of national policy on immigration and the adjustment of those immigrants whom we do receive.

Apart from prejudice per se, however, and against a background of what we know about the realities of immigrant adjustment, we are faced finally with the necessity of choosing a viewpoint in answering the question: What shall our immigration policy be?

---

adaptation 15 — WHOM WE SHALL WELCOME

Abridged and adapted from the President's Commission on Immigration and Naturalization, Whom We Shall Welcome *(Washington, D.C.: U.S. Government Printing Office, 1953).*

[In September, 1952, a special commission was appointed by President Truman "to study and evaluate the immigration and naturalization policies of the United States." After holding public hearings throughout the country, this commission issued its report in January, 1953, sharply criticizing the current immigration law and epitomizing the argument for a liberal immigration policy.]

An immigration law is a key to whether Americans today believe in the essential worth and dignity of the individual. It is a clue to whether we really believe that all men are entitled to those "inalienable rights" for which our nation was created. It indicates the degree of American humanitarianism.

An immigration law is an index of the extent of our acceptance of the principle that tyranny is forever abhorrent and that its victims should always find asylum in the land of the free. It indicates our outlook on the future of America. Those who have faith in a dynamic, expanding, and strong American economy see immigration not only as a part of our heritage but also as essential to our future. On the other hand, those who regard the future of America in terms of a static economy and a maximum population view immigration with alarm.

An immigration law is an image in which other nations see us. It is also an expression of the sincerity of our confidence in ourselves and our institutions. An immigration law which reflects fear and insecurity makes a hollow mockery of confident world leadership.

Immigrants have supplied a continuous flow of creative ability and ideas that have enriched our nation. The American story proves that great cultural diversities do not mean the existence of superior and inferior classes. American national unity has been achieved without sacrificing diversity of opinion and individuality.

For the following major reasons the current immigration and nationality law embodies policies and principles that are unwise and injurious to the nation:

1. It reflects an attitude of hostility and distrust toward all aliens.
2. It discriminates against human beings on account of national origin, creed, and color.
3. It ignores the needs of the United States at home and abroad.
4. It provides unnecessary and unreasonable restrictions and penalties against individuals.

The Commission believes that we cannot be true to the democratic faith of our own Declaration of Independence in the equality of all men and at the same time pass immigration laws which discriminate against people because of national origin, race, color, or creed. The Commission recommends the complete abolition of the National Origins System and institution of a Unified Quota System. Allocation of visas should be made under five categories:

1. Right of asylum: to provide haven for the oppressed of other lands.
2. Reunion of families.
3. Needs in the United States: persons whose skills, aptitudes, and knowledge are necessary or desirable for our economy, culture, or security.
4. Special needs in a free world: economic, political, and social conditions of other nations directly affect our capacity to preserve peace and freedom, develop international trade, and promote friendship abroad.
5. General immigration: desirable individuals who do not fit into other categories. This plan would eliminate not only the national-origins bases of our law but also such racist provisions as the "Asiatic-Pacific Triangle" and the restriction of colonial Negroes.

Other recommendations made by the Commission are these:

1. The maximum annual quota immigration should be one-sixth of 1 per cent of the population of the United States as determined by the *most recent* census. Under the 1950 census, quota immigration would be open to 251,162 immigrants annually instead of the 154,657 now authorized.

2. All immigration and naturalization functions now in the Department of State and the Department of Justice should be consolidated into a new and single agency.

3. There should be a Board of Immigration and Visa Appeals so that aliens can have full hearing in exclusion and deportation cases.

4. The grounds for deportation of aliens should bear a reasonable relationship to the national welfare and security; they should not be technical or excessive nor be retroactive, penalizing aliens for acts which were not prohibited when committed. A primary function of the restrictions in our immigration law is to protect the United States against aliens who are actually or potentially undesirable. But it is difficult to reconcile this sound and important aim with the excessive punishments contained in our immigration laws or with the attitudes of suspicion and distrust which seem to motivate them.

5. Aliens who have been members or affiliates of any totalitarian party, including Communists, Nazis, and Fascists, should be denied admission into the United States except where their membership was involuntary or unwitting, or if they have repudiated and now oppose such totalitarianism.

6. There should be a ten-year statute of limitations on both deportation and denaturalization.

7. The law should not discriminate against naturalized citizens but should place them in the same status as native-born citizens except where citizenship was procured by fraud or illegality.

It is necessary to revise our immigration law, along these lines, from beginning to end. The present law is unwise, injurious to the nation, displays distrust of all foreigners, and applies racial and other discriminations. It is rooted in the period of America's blindest isolation.

---

adaptation 16   IN DEFENSE OF NATIONALITY

Abridged and adapted from Henry Pratt Fairchild, Race and Nationality *(New York: Ronald Press, 1947). Published in this form by permission of the Ronald Press.*

[The late Professor Henry Pratt Fairchild was, from the early days of immigration-policy controversy, an outstanding and influential philosopher of restriction. The following is an adaptation of one of his many statements on the subject of immigration.]

The essence of nationality is *feeling*. A nationality is a group of people who feel alike and together about a considerable number of major interests and values of life. They have the same or similar ideas, ideals, standards, aspirations, and life-objectives. They recognize a spiritual, emotional, and intellectual kinship, and on the basis of these bonds they wish to be united into a sympathetic, harmonious, and homogeneous unit.

There are feeble nationalities, and there are strong nationalities. There are stable nationalities and there are shaky nationalities. How much community of feeling and identity of interests, how much uniformity of institutions, how much sharing of basic activities must be present in order to constitute a true nationality cannot be definitely stated. It is certain, however, that there must be a well-established community with reference to several of the basic interests, values, and institutions of organized social life. Foremost among these requisites are language, religion, and family.

One's native tongue is such a dear and precious thing to him that he is positively hurt by its abuse or mishandling. One of the penalties that an American of the older stock has to pay for residence in New York City is the constant bombardment of his ears by multitudinous varieties of tortured and mutilated English.

Scarcely inferior to any of the foregoing in its hold upon the emotions of individuals is the matter of food. Hardly anything arouses more acute disgust, even to the extent of physical nausea, than the spectacle of someone indulging in foods that by the observer are regarded as improper, dirty, or unnatural. While food habits, dress, decoration, and recreation have no immediate connection with the persistence or welfare of a group, yet they have their own acute sense of rightness and propriety.

The central principle emerges that every single one of these things is the occasion of feelings of sympathy among the members of the ingroup and of antipathy toward those in the outgroup. Taken in the aggregate, they constitute an absolutely overpowering and irresistible stimulus to feelings of togetherness or apartness. And these feelings are the very essence of nationality.

Just how much uniformity there must be, and with respect to what major interests, in order to constitute a true nationality is a question that cannot be categorically answered. One thing is certain, however; there must be enough fellow-feeling with respect to a few of the major concerns of life to create the indispensable feeling of spiritual community. Ordinarily these must include language, religion, and family system, the economic structure, and the basic moral code. A lack of identity in any one of these areas is a serious threat to nationality and a detraction from its completeness. However, history has shown that if there is a substantial identity in two or three of the major fields, uniformity may be dispensed with in one of the others. The United States is an outstanding example of the conviction that if the nation has uniformity in sufficient other fields, it may be strong enough so that it can safely dispense with identity in the matter of religion.

The true nation, thus constructed, is the most stable and humanly significant large-scale group yet produced by the process of social evolution. It has more of the elements of solidarity, personal comfort, and satisfaction, promise of continuity, and resistance to internal and external attack than any other known group—almost than any other imaginable group.

The problem of blending nationalities would be near enough to impossibility if the ingredients were limited to only two nationalities, but, with respect to the United States, there are dozens of nationalities involved. The foreigner has to be "denationalized" and "renationalized" at the same time. And let no one imagine for a moment that this is a bland and placid experience! It involves an upheaval of the very depths of emotional experience. Indeed, so difficult and deep-reaching are the changes involved that it is doubtful whether any immigrant who makes the transfer after early childhood can ever be completely assimilated in a new land. (This means, incidentally, that the foreigner is not to be blamed for his foreignness or subjected to any persecution on account of it. If there are any objections on that score, they ought to be imposed at the port of entry or, much better, at the original point of departure.)

The problem involved in the great immigration current to the United States was that of maintaining national homogeneity and solidarity in the face of large and increasing contingents of members of foreign nationalities. It was to a considerable extent a quantitative problem, which remained within the bounds of practical solution as long as the annual accessions from any one foreign group, or all together, did not exceed the possibilities of establishing normal contacts with the basic American population within two or three generations at worst. But when the numbers of any particular outside group became so great and the conditions of their life in their adopted country so unfavorable that, instead of developing varied and close relations with the true American nationality, they tended to form isolated communities of their own, then the menace to national integrity became acute.

There is excellent reason to believe that the United States has gone just about as far as it can safely go in permitting, in the name of humanitarianism and liberalism, the dilution of its own nationality. If there be not tranquillity, order, discipline, and harmony within, how can there be effective leadership toward peace without? The problems of international participation are going to be sufficiently acute and insistent to test all the stability and vitality that the American nation can possess at best, without having it weakened and undermined by dissensions, conflict, and disharmonies among more or less irreconcilable elements within its own body politic.

THE ASSIMILATION OF MINORITY GROUPS adaptation 17

Abridged and adapted from Louis Wirth, "The Problem of Minority Groups," in Ralph Linton (ed.), The Science of Man in the World Crisis (New York: Columbia University Press, 1945), pp. 347–72. Published in this form by permission of Columbia University Press.

[An important question for minority groups is the extent to which assimilation is both desirable and possible. By "assimilation" is here meant the merging of the minority group with society at large and the loss of its own unique identity. Assimilation has two aspects. One is the willingness of the minority to be absorbed; the other is the willingness of the majority to accept members of the minority into the life of society.

In the following treatment the author delineates the social conditions which encourage or discourage assimilation. One of his conclusions is that a resistance to assimilation is apt to characterize the initial stages of a minority's struggle against domination and discrimination. Cultural differences are apt to be emphasized rather than underplayed in the effort of the minority to fortify itself with self-respect and self-confidence. We may expect, therefore, in this period that minority groups will make efforts to strengthen the individual's loyalty to his ethnic ingroup and will not encourage his efforts to participate in the institutions of the dominant majority.

According to the author, if the dominant majority can tolerate this initial stage of the accentuation of differences, there is a strong tendency for assimilationist attitudes to develop on the part of both minority and majority groups. Although the author's discussion treats specifically of ethnic minorities, much of it applies to racial minorities as well.]

WHAT IS A MINORITY?

A minority is a group of people who, because of physical or cultural characteristics, are singled out for differential and unequal treatment and who regard themselves as objects of collective discrimination. The existence of a minority implies the existence of a corresponding dominant group enjoying higher social status and greater privileges. Minorities objectively occupy a disadvantageous position in society. They are debarred from certain opportunities, economic, social, and political, and these deprivations circumscribe the individual's freedom of choice and self-development. Members of minority groups are held in lower esteem and may even be objects of contempt, hatred, ridicule, and violence. They are generally socially isolated and frequently spatially segregated. For all these reasons they suffer from more than the ordinary amount of social and economic insecurity.

Minorities tend to develop attitudes, forms of behaving, and other subjective traits which tend further to set them apart. One cannot long discriminate against people without generating in them a sense of isolation and persecution and without giving them a conception of themselves as more different from others than in fact they are. Whether a minority comes to suffer from a sense of its own inferiority or develops attitudes of rebellion and protest depends in large part upon the total social setting in which it finds itself. Where a caste system has existed over many generations and is sanctioned by religious and other sentiments (as in India), the attitude of resignation is likely to be dominant over the spirit of rebellion. But in a secular society, minorities are not likely to accept their inferior status and deprivation without some effort to improve their lot. However, it is not conflict with the dominant groups but nonparticipation in the life of the larger society, or in its important aspects, that more particularly marks off a minority people and perpetuates their status as such.

CLASSIFYING MINORITIES

There are various ways to classify and catalogue minorities. One is to classify them according to the criterion on which discrimination is based, such as race, national origin, language, or religion. Such a classification is, however, apt to be superficial; for it is not their ethnic or racial traits that mark a people as a minority but the attitude of some other group in the society toward those traits. Characteristics which once served as marks of dominant status may at another time and under other circumstances symbolize identification with a minority. In prewar Poland under the czarist regime, the Poles were a distinct ethnic minority. When they gained their independence at the end of the first World War, they lost their minority status but reduced their Jewish fellow-Poles to the status of a minority. As immigrants to the United States, the Poles again became themselves a minority.

A less conventional way to distinguish among minorities is on the basis of the attitudes which a minority bears toward the dominant majority. There are differences among minorities in the way they conceive their relation to the dominant group, in their self-conceptions, in the aspirations they project for themselves. We shall distinguish among four types of minorities: the pluralistic, the assimilationist, the militant, and the secessionist.

The Pluralistic Minority

A pluralistic minority is one which seeks toleration for its differences on the part of the dominant group. Implicit in the quest for toleration (as opposed to a more complete assimilation) is the conception that variant cultures can flourish peacefully, side by side, in the same society. Indeed, cultural pluralism has been held out as one of the necessary preconditions of a rich and dynamic civilization.

Toleration requires that the dominant group feel sufficiently secure in its position to allow dissenters a certain leeway. Those in control must either be convinced that the issues at stake are not too vital, or else they must be so thoroughly imbued with the ideal of freedom that they do not wish to deny to others the liberties which they themselves enjoy. If there is a great gulf between their own status and that of the minority group, if there is a wide difference between the two groups in race or origin, the toleration of minorities may go so far as virtually to perpetuate several subsocieties within the larger society.

The range of toleration which a pluralistic minority seeks may at first be quite narrow. As in the case of the Jews in medieval Europe or the Protestants in dominantly Catholic countries, it may be confined to freedom to practice a dissenting religion. Or, as in the case of the ethnic minorities of czarist Russia and the Austro-Hungarian Empire of the Hapsburgs, it may take the form of a demand for the recognition of a language as the official medium of expression for the minority and the right to have it taught in their schools. While on the one hand the pluralistic minority craves the toleration of one or more of its cultural idiosyncrasies, on the other hand it resents and seeks protection against coerced absorption by the dominant group. Above all, it wishes to maintain its cultural identity.

Coupled with the demand for cultural autonomy is usually the struggle for economic and political equality or at least equalization of opportunity. Although the pluralistic minority does not wish to merge its total life with the larger society, it does demand for its members a greater measure of economic and political freedom if not outright civic equality.

The wish to maintain cultural identity characterizes ethnic minorities in the period of their awakening. During this period, minority movements undergo cultural renaissances. The primary emphasis in this stage of development is upon accentuating the religious, linguistic, and cultural heritage of the group and striving to obtain recognition and toleration for these differences.

A homely folk tongue, an alien religion, an obscure lore, and eccentric costume are transformed into objects of pride, in which the intellectuals among the minority take an especially avid interest and the promotion of which becomes the road to their leadership and power. The aim of the pluralistic minority is achieved when it has succeeded in wresting from the dominant group the fullest measure of equality in all things economic and political and the right to be left alone in all things cultural.

The Assimilationist Minority

Unlike the pluralistic minority, which is content with toleration and the upper limit of whose aspiration is cultural autonomy, the assimilationist minority craves the fullest opportunity for participation in the life of the larger society with a view to uncoerced incorporation in that society. It seeks to lose itself in the larger whole by opening up to its members the greatest possibilities for their individual self-development. Rather than toleration and autonomy, which is the goal of the pluralistic minority, the assimilationist minority works toward complete acceptance by the dominant group and merger with the larger society.

Whereas a pluralistic minority, in order to maintain its group integrity, will generally discourage intermarriage and intimate social intercourse with the dominant group, the assimilationist minority puts no such obstacles in the path of its members but looks upon the crossing of stocks as well as the blending of cultures as wholesome end products. Since assimilation is a two-way process, however, the emergence of an assimilationist minority rests upon a willingness of the dominant group to absorb and of the minority group to be absorbed.

The success of such a "melting-pot" experiment depends in part upon the relative numbers involved and the period of time over which the process extends. Assimilation is apt to proceed apace when the influx of immigrants is gradual. In the early years in the United States the vast spaces and resources of the new continent also facilitated settlement and absorption of newcomers.

For later immigrants the path of assimilation has not been without serious obstacles. Each immigrant group not only has its own language, which serves as a barrier to intergroup communication, but also its own religious, social, and even political institutions, which tend to perpetuate group solidarity and to inhibit social intercourse with members of the "out" group. Moreover, each ethnic group in the United States, especially in the early period after its arrival, tends to occupy a characteristic niche in the economy which generates certain definite similarities among its members in occupation, standard of living, place of residence, and mode of life. On the basis of such likenesses within the group and differences without, stereotypes are built up and fixed attitudes arise which inhibit contact and develop social distances and prejudices. Overanxiety about being accepted sometimes results in a pattern of conduct among minorities that provokes a defense reaction on the part of the dominant group; these defense reactions may take the form of rebuffs which are likely to accentuate minority consciousness and thus retard assimilation.

No ethnic group is ever unanimous in all its attitudes and actions, and minority groups are no exception. They, too, have their internal differentiations, their factions and ideological currents and movements. The Jews furnish an excellent illustration of a minority which especially in modern times has vacillated between pluralism and assimilationism. When the "out" group was favorably disposed toward the Jews, assimilation proceeded apace, even in the face of occasional rebuffs and persistent discrimination. When the dominant group made entry of the Jews difficult, when intolerance movements became powerful and widespread, and when persecution came to be the order of the day, the Jews as a minority group generally withdrew into themselves. The most conspicuous example of this transformation is to be found in the shift in the attitude of the German Jews. Before the Hitler epoch they could have been correctly characterized as an assimilationist minority. Upon the advent of Hitler their optimum longing was for a modicum of toleration. Among Jews in this country a similar differentiation is found. The older settlers and those who have climbed the economic and social scale seek on the whole full incorporation into the larger society and may truly be regarded as an assimilationist minority. The later-comers and those whose hopes have been frustrated by prejudice, those who through generations of persecution in the Old World retain a more orthodox ritual and a more isolated and self-sufficient community life, generally do not seek full cultural identification with American society at large. They aspire to full social and economic equality with the rest of the population, but they seek to retain a degree of cultural autonomy.

The Secessionist Minority

The secessionist minority represents a third distinct type. It repudiates assimilation, on the one hand, and is not content with mere toleration or cultural autonomy, on the other. The principal and ultimate objective of such a minority is to achieve political as well as cultural independence from the dominant group. If such a group has had statehood at an earlier period in its career, the demand for recognition of its national sovereignty may be based on the cultivation among its members of the romantic sentiments associated, even if only in the imagination, with its former freedom, power, and glory. In such a case, the minority's cultural monuments and survivals, its language, lore, literature, and ceremonial institutions, no matter how archaic, are revivified and built up into moving symbols of national grandeur.

In this task the intellectuals among the minority group play a crucial role.

They can find expression for their talents by recovering, disseminating, and inspiring pride in the group's history and civilization and by pleading its case before world public opinion. Having been rejected by the dominant group for higher positions of leadership, and often having been denied equal opportunity and full participation in the life of the larger society, the intellectuals of such minorities tend to be particularly susceptible to a psychic malady bordering on an oppression psychosis.

The Irish, Czech, Polish, Lithuanian, Estonian, Latvian, and Finnish nationalistic movements, which culminated in the achievement of independent statehood at the end of the first World War, were examples of secessionist minority groups.

The Militant Minority

The goal of the militant minority reaches far beyond toleration, assimilation, and even cultural and political autonomy. The militant minority has set domination over others as its goal. Far from suffering from feelings of inferiority, it is convinced of its own superiority and inspired by the lust for conquest.

Thus, for instance, the Sudeten Germans, aided and abetted by the Nazi propaganda, diplomatic, and military machine, made claims on the Czechoslovak republic which, if granted, would have reduced the Czechs to a minority in their own country. The problem of finding a suitable formula for self-government in India would probably have been more readily solved if the Hindu "majority," which considered itself a minority in relation to British imperial rule, could have been satisfied with an arrangement which stopped short of Hindu domination over Moslems.

CONCLUSIONS

The initial goal of an emerging minority group, as it becomes aware of its ethnic identity, is to seek toleration for its cultural differences. By virtue of this striving it constitutes a *pluralistic* minority. If sufficient toleration and autonomy are attained, the pluralistic minority advances to the *assimilationist* stage, characterized by the desire for acceptance by and incorporation into the dominant group. Frustration of this desire for acceptance and full participation is likely to produce *secessionist* tendencies, which may take the form of the establishment of sovereign nationhood. Secessionist tendencies, finally, may lead to the goal of domination over others and the resort to *militant* methods of achieving that objective. If this goal is actually reached, the group sheds the distinctive characteristics of a minority.

[It should be emphasized that this typology of minorities is a theoretical construct rather than a description of actually existing groups. We should not expect to find any one of these types occurring in pure form either in the past or in the present. All minorities contain within themselves tendencies and movements in which we can discern the characteristic features of one or more of these types, although the history of American minorities has been notably free of secessionist or militant tendencies.]

SUGGESTIONS FOR FURTHER READING

William S. Bernard (ed.), *American Immigration Policy* (New York: Harper & Bros., 1950).

Maurice Rae Davie, *Refugees in America* (New York: Harper & Bros., 1947).

Henry Pratt Fairchild, *Race and Nationality* (New York: Ronald Press Co., 1947).

Oscar Handlin, *Race and Nationality in American Life* (Boston: Little, Brown, & Co., 1957).

John Higham, *Strangers in the Land* (New. Brunswick. N.J.: Rutgers University Press, 1955).

Milton R. Konvitz, *Civil Rights in Immigration* (Ithaca, N.Y.: Cornell University Press, 1953).

R. A. Schermerhorn, *These Our People* (Boston: D. C. Heath & Co., 1949).

Lyman Cromwell White, *300,000 New Americans* (New York: Harper & Bros., 1957).

Leon Levinstein

CHAPTER 8

The Family

Section I: What Is the Problem?

A sober warning that "the family of the last few decades has grown ever more unstable, until it has reached the point of actual disintegration," has been issued by Pitirim A. Sorokin.[1] Carle C. Zimmerman expresses his alarm in this way: "The western world has entered a period of demoralization comparable to the periods when both Greece and Rome turned from growth to decay. Divorce, premarital sex experience, promiscuity, homosexuality, versatility in sex, birth control carried to excess, spread of birth control to every segment of the population, positive antagonism to parenthood, clandestine marriage, migratory divorce, marriage for sex alone, contempt for familism . . . all are increasing rapidly."[2] And, he goes on to argue, they bespeak a deepening family crisis which in turn portends the decay of Western civilization.

But other observers, such as Burgess and Locke, are not displeased with what they see: "The black picture of the family . . . painted by Sorokin arises from his failure to perceive that present trends represent not only disorganization but reorganization."[3] The old family system is decaying but

---
[1] Pitirim A. Sorokin, *The Crisis of Our Age* (New York: E. P. Dutton & Co., 1941), p. 188.
[2] Carle C. Zimmerman, *Family and Civilization* (New York: Harper & Bros., 1947), p. 632.
[3] Ernest W. Burgess and Harvey J. Locke, *The Family* (New York: American Book Co., 1953), p. 650.

a new family unity is being forged, "based neither upon compulsion nor upon contract but upon the binding affections and loyalties growing out of intimate associations in the companionship family."[4]

In similar vein, Joseph Kirk Folsom argues that "if we build *merely* a narrow program to 'conserve *The Family* as a sacred institution' . . . we shall not be saved."[5] What is required is instead a policy of supporting and realizing even more fully the positive values of the new family system.

These sharply divergent judgments flow from a common agreement that in less than two generations the American family has been transformed from a relatively close-knit group with considerable authority over its members to a rather loose, atomistic arrangement in which divorce is relatively frequent and early emancipation of the young not only occurs but is actively encouraged. The hold of the family over its individual members has greatly diminished, while the freedom of the individual to strike out for himself has increased.

Where the individual is irrevocably bound into the family orbit, the individual, whether youth, husband, or wife, pays prime loyalty and grants ultimate authority to the family. His own behavior is circumscribed accordingly. If necessary, he sacrifices his own felt desires and fulfillment rather than disrupt the family and undermine its stability, unity, and authority. In short, the family is more sacred than he is.

At the other end of the scale, the family receives loyalty and is granted authority only insofar as it effectively serves the individual and his goal of self-fulfillment. If it serves that purpose, he clings to it and participates in it. When it fails to serve that purpose, he feels free to leave it if it is feasible for him to do so. As an individual he is more sacred than the family as such. Presumably it is in this latter direction that we are moving.

The family has indeed changed. But disagreement exists as to the meaning of this change. Those who deplore the current trend believe that contemporary emphasis upon individual fulfillment is leading to the destruction of the family as an effective social unit and, since the family is the basic building block of society, to the eventual deterioration of the social order itself. They see in diminishing family loyalty an open invitation to individual irresponsibility and rootlessness. They argue that only the tightly knit, all-embracing family can exercise the kind of control over individuals which society requires in order to survive. Those who take this pessimistic view of modern developments are not, as it may appear, insensitive to the question of individual happiness. On the contrary, they maintain that the individual needs to be firmly bound into the family group for a sense of

---

[4] *Ibid.*, p. 651.

[5] Joseph Kirk Folsom, *The Family and Democratic Society* (New York: John Wiley & Sons, Inc., 1943), p. 680.

personal security and "belonging." Because it inevitably threatens family fealty, the modern demand for personal happiness and individual self-fulfillment is regarded not as merely frivolous but as dangerously and tragically self-deceptive. The lonely individual without ties of love and obligation to family simply cannot find the happiness and self-fulfillment he so ardently seeks. Where they do not despair, proponents of this position typically call for a return to the traditional family, the reinstatement of male authority, and a renewed regard for marriage as a hallowed institution, in which divorce, if not absolutely forbidden, is at least extremely difficult to obtain.

On the other hand, those who look with optimism upon recent developments usually interpret the modern "permissive" family system as the extension of freedom and democracy into family life. They hold that the family is not disintegrating but is merely evolving into a different kind of unity in response to modern conditions—and, what is more, into one better equipped to meet the challenges of contemporary society. Because old patterns persist and new patterns have not yet been stabilized, it is inevitable that dislocations and conflicts should occur, but the present disorganization of family life is only temporary. The American family, being in a state of transition, is simply experiencing the growing pains that always accompany important social change.

This position argues that the family is in the process of adapting itself to changes that have taken place in society at large and over which it has little or no control. The traditional family, it is pointed out, was a rural family; the new family is an urban family. It lives in an industrialized, cosmopolitan, "open" society which has made the monolithic family obsolete and rendered the subjugation of women and children not only socially anachronistic but morally offensive. To proponents of this position, subordination of the individual to family authority is a form of slavery we are well rid of; whatever the difficulties and shortcomings of modern family life, there is no going back. Mutual affection, not submission, ought to be and is indeed becoming, they argue, the "tie that binds."

What is the modern family like? And how does it differ from the American family of the past?

The rural family which once predominated in American society was, incomparably more than the present urban family, an all-embracing form of group life. It was society's basic economic unit; a family not only lived together but worked together. Women were, as a rule, totally dependent economically; but neither could a man operate a farm successfully without a wife. The economic partnership of husband and wife, which in time encompassed the children as well, was reflected in day-to-day dependence upon each other, not for mere money income but for essential skills and services.

The rural family's geographical isolation further increased the mutual interdependence of its members; the family was thrown upon its own resources for entertainment and sociability. Because the rural family seldom came into prolonged contact with outsiders, it tended to develop unity of beliefs and attitudes. It was, moreover, part of a community of people who shared familiar experiences and had a similar outlook on life. The individual's contacts with the larger world outside the family tended not to compete with but to strengthen and reinforce family ways.

The American family has been steadily moving from the farm to the city, from rural areas to metropolitan areas. The typical American family now lives in the city or, as is becoming more likely, in the suburbs. The husband is away from home most of the day, working in an office or a factory. The newly wed wife probably continues in a job until the couple "decides" to have children. The wife is then likely to devote herself to being a housewife, but this may be experienced by her as a period of withdrawal and social isolation. While the children are still young, the mother is likely to remain at home, though it is becoming increasingly the case that, especially as the children reach school age, the wife may, like her husband, work outside the home. In 1954 a little more than a quarter of all married women were working; of those in the 35–44 age group, about one-third worked outside the home.[6]

If the family is upper middle class or professional, the child is almost certain to be deposited in nursery school sometime before the age of four or five; at the tender age of three he may already be spending a significant part of his time outside the home with adults and peers who are not part of his family. By adolescence, most children are spending most of their time outside the home, either in school or in the company of their peers.

Our mass-production society, commercialized entertainment, and the possibility of easy contact with others in an urban environment make for a radical separation between home and family on the one hand, and work and play on the other, which was almost unknown in a predominantly rural economy. The net result is that, in many American families, father, mother, child, husband, wife, each goes more or less his separate way. Each has his own goals and activities, and there is little common experience out of which genuine interest in and understanding of the other can naturally grow.

Can this kind of individualistic, atomized family do the job it is supposed to do? Our relatively high divorce rate seems to indicate that much disharmony and tension characterize modern marriage. Our relatively high delinquency rate has been attributed to the inability of contemporary family life to win the affection of its youth and to inculcate those positive values and

---

[6] Metropolitan Life Insurance Company, "The American Wife," *Statistical Bulletin*, **36** (October, 1955), p. 3.

Joe Covello; Black Star

Dinner Time: It has occasionally been suggested that television will reunite the fragmented family.

self-discipline that are required for rewarding participation in society. Many also see in teen-age revolt a sign that even the best-situated families are finding it difficult to control their children.

Many psychologists believe, moreover, that neurotic incapacities and difficulties are on the increase and are attributable to the failure of the modern family to provide individuals with basic and indispensable emotional satisfactions. Although inherited traits are undoubtedly the raw material, the family is apt to be the most important single influence upon the growing child's personality and character. Playmates, school, job, a hundred other experiences, will also leave their mark, but always upon a foundation laid in earliest life. If childhood experiences are severely distorted, this is apt to be reflected in distortions of adult personality and character, in eventual unhappiness, malaise, and failure. For adults, the lack of common goals which strongly unite husband and wife may lead to emotional alienation and a mutual sense of abandonment and deprivation.

Thus, three major sources of current concern—divorce, delinquency, and problems of mental health—are all laid at the door of the modern family system. They are seen as consequences of its individualism and atomization. But the modern family can too easily be made into a scapegoat. Family unity, authority, and interdependence are being impinged upon and threatened, not by individual perversity of will or failure of nerve, but by the larger society in which the family now lives. Areas of life once contained in or intimately related to day-to-day family experience are now being taken over by other institutions: the factory, the corporation, the school, the peer group, the mass media of communication and entertainment. This shift places a burden upon the community. As impersonal institutions take over functions which formerly belonged to the traditional family, they are by the same token invested with correlative responsibility. If by usurping family functions they weaken the family, presumably they have the duty to take up the slack. But here the question arises: Are other groups and institutions capable of doing the family's job? If they are not, can we find ways of supporting and reinforcing the authority and unity of the modern family?

Section II: Divorce

Divorce has been portrayed in two lights. At one extreme it has been interpreted as an infallible sign of the intrinsic shortcomings of the modern family system. This point of view tends not only to analyze divorce as a sign of social disorganization but to condemn divorced individuals for irresponsibly furthering the disintegration of society. It is inclined to see a close and causal relation between juvenile delinquency and our relatively high divorce rate, to stress the devastating effects of divorce upon the children of a marriage, and to be impatient with adult demands for "happiness."

At the other extreme, divorce has been viewed positively as the belated extension of freedom to marital relations. This point of view is inclined to stress the unhappiness of adults trapped in an unfortunate marriage and to argue that children can be even more seriously damaged in the conflict-ridden though still formally intact home. It tends to assert that our relatively high divorce rate, though probably signifying some increase in marital disharmony in contemporary marriage, also reflects present freedom to escape from marital disharmony when it exists. It is also apt to argue that former marital unity was often more apparent than real, resulting from the submission of women and children to male authority and often purchased at the cost of their self-fulfillment.

We shall consider three principal questions: (1) How prevalent is divorce, and among what groups is it most prevalent? (2) What are the causes of divorce? Do they really lie in the intrinsic shortcomings of modern family life? (3) How serious are the consequences of divorce for the social order?

THE DIVORCE RATE

The United States divorce rate has risen steadily for over a half-century until it is now more than three times what it was in 1900. Table 8:1 lists the crude divorce rate from 1920, when it was already significantly above nineteenth-century levels, to recent years. The crude divorce rate states the number of divorces per 1,000 population. In 1900 there were 0.7 divorces per 1,000 population, or one divorce for every 1,450 inhabitants; in 1955 there were 2.3 divorces per 1,000 population, or one divorce for every 435 inhabitants.

The crude divorce rate, measured against total population, would give us an unreliable picture of the divorce trend if the proportion of married people in the total population had changed radically during the past fifty years. Table 8:1 also lists the crude marriage rate from 1920 to 1956. Despite considerable fluctuation from year to year, our marriage rate has re-

TABLE 8:1 CRUDE MARRIAGE AND DIVORCE RATES, UNITED STATES, 1920–56 * (Rates per 1,000 Population)

Year	Marriage Rate	Divorce Rate	Year	Marriage Rate	Divorce Rate
1956	9.5	2.3	1937	11.3	1.9
1955	9.3	2.3	1936	10.7	1.8
1954	9.2	2.4			
1953	9.8	2.5	1935	10.4	1.7
1952	9.9	2.5	1934	10.3	1.6
1951	10.4	2.5	1933	8.7	1.3
			1932	7.9	1.3
1950	11.1	2.6	1931	8.6	1.5
1949	10.6	2.7			
1948	12.4	2.8	1930	9.2	1.6
1947	13.9	3.4	1929	10.1	1.7
1946	16.4	4.3	1928	9.8	1.7
			1927	10.1	1.6
1945	12.2	3.5	1926	10.2	1.6
1944	10.9	2.9			
1943	11.7	2.6	1925	10.3	1.5
1942	13.2	2.4	1924	10.4	1.5
1941	12.7	2.2	1923	11.0	1.5
			1922	10.3	1.4
1940	12.1	2.0	1921	10.7	1.5
1939	10.7	1.9	1920	12.0	1.6
1938	10.3	1.9			

* Adapted from U.S. Department of Health, Education, and Welfare, Public Health Service, National Office of Vital Statistics, "Marriages and Divorces . . . 1956," *Vital Statistics—Special Reports,* 48 (April, 1958), p. 58.

mained fairly stable; the proportion of the population which married in 1955, for example, was exactly the same as that at the turn of the century. The crude divorce rate thus gives us a fairly reliable picture of the long-term upward trend of divorce. Roughly the same proportion of our population continues to marry, but a larger proportion now gets divorced.

The crude divorce rate does not tell us what percentage of marriages ends in divorce or, expressed another way, the probability that a marriage will end in divorce. Because of the relative constancy of our marriage rate, however, the crude divorce rate does provide a rough guide to the percentage of marriages dissolved by divorce. In 1900 about 7 of every 100 marriages were terminated by divorce, while at present we can expect about 25 of every 100, or one in four, marriages to end in divorce.

The long-term upward trend in the divorce rate is not confined to the United States but has occurred throughout the Western world. Table 8:2 lists the divorce rate for a number of countries from 1915 to 1947. Though the divorce rate has always been higher in the United States than abroad, it has recently increased far more rapidly in other nations.

Two interrelated factors have contributed to the increase in divorce in Western society, thus making comparison of divorce rates difficult: (1) a probable increase in the sheer number of marriages experienced as unsuccessful and (2) the removal of social, legal, moral, and financial obstacles to divorce.

Two general considerations encourage the conclusion that the increase in the divorce rate in Western society points to a heightening of marital difficulties in recent years. In the first place, the very conception of what constitutes a satisfactory marriage has changed within the past half-century. Expectations have altered, and a marriage regarded as successful in an earlier era may today be regarded as unsuccessful.

In the second place, marriage is now subject to strains not experienced in earlier and more stable periods, strains that are part and parcel of modern industrial, urban society. The fact that women are acquiring individual aims which make them less single-minded in their devotion to family goals is enough to make marriage less stable than it once was. Any group—even if it consists of only a married couple—is weakened when its members have important individual aims that compete with shared goals. Indeed, this emergence of individual aspirations accounts in large part for the extraordinary contemporary emphasis upon the emotional and sheerly personal relations between husband and wife and, later, between parents and children. Because family goals have decreased in importance, the principal bond must necessarily be the emotional attachment of the individual members of the family to one another. Romantic love between the sexes has thus come to have a historically new and unprecedented value for modern man; but unless it is supplemented by considerable sharing of common goals and activities, it is unlikely to provide an adequate foundation for family life.

The long-term rising divorce rate reflects therefore both a basic change in the Western conception of marriage and new strains placed upon marriage by the urbanization of Western society. It also reflects the increasing availability of divorce through the removal of legal, moral, social, and economic obstacles. This obvious fact becomes important when we wish to compare the divorce rate of one country, area, or group with that of another.

According to Table 8:2, the United States divorce rate in 1915 was about 50 times that of England and Wales. From this we cannot conclude that marriage was that many more times more unsuccessful in the United States or that the United States was that much more urbanized and industrialized. Legal, religious, and social strictures against divorce existed in Britain which did not exist here. In 1938 British divorce law was liberalized; Table 8:2 shows that the British divorce rate was about 7 times as great in 1947 as it was in 1938.

Ireland provides another illustration of the difficulty of making inferences from divorce statistics. Wholehearted acceptance of Catholic restrictions virtually rules out divorce in Ireland. Yet from this we cannot infer the extraordinary success of Irish marriage. In 1941, only about 35 per cent of Irish males in the 30–34 age group had ever married as compared with about 80 per cent of American males in the same age group. In the 60–64 age group, about 30 per cent of Irish males had never married as compared with about 10 per cent of American males.[7] The tendency in Ireland is either to marry very late or to avoid marriage altogether. Where moral or religious strictures against divorce exist, the difficulties that attend marriage may be expressed in a low marriage rate rather than in a high divorce rate. The same strictures may also manifest themselves in a high desertion rate after marriage has been entered into. In this country there is some evidence that more white Catholics than white Protestants resort to desertion, and an increasing Catholic divorce rate might signify fewer desertions rather than more unhappy marriages.[8]

Differences in legal availability of divorce may also account for differences in divorce rate; this is strikingly illustrated by the divorce statistics of Nevada and New York. In 1950, Nevada had a divorce rate of 55.7 per 1,000 population, New York about 0.08.[9] Most Nevada divorces were, of course, "migratory" divorces granted to out-of-state citizens who had satisfied both the six-week Nevada residence requirement and Nevada's liberal divorce

---

[7] Metropolitan Life Insurance Company, "Increase in Early Marriage," *Statistical Bulletin*, 34 (May, 1953), p. 8.

[8] William M. Kephart and Thomas P. Monahan, "Desertion and Divorce in Philadelphia," *American Sociological Review*, 17 (1952), 710–27.

[9] U.S. Bureau of the Census, *Statistical Abstract of the United States, 1957* (Washington, D.C.: U.S. Government Printing Office, 1957), p. 73.

TABLE 8:2 TREND OF DIVORCE IN SPECIFIED COUNTRIES, 1915–47*
(Ratio per 1,000 of Divorces in Each Year to Average
Annual Number of Marriages in Preceding Decade)

Year	United States	Canada	England and Wales	Australia	Denmark	France	Netherlands	Sweden	Switzerland
1947	292.9	74.0	138.5	†	193.3	†	121.4	115.2	124.7
1946	399.7	72.9	81.0	†	212.1	207.2	147.5	116.0	128.6
1945	323.9	49.6	42.3	105.6	166.3	101.2	68.2	109.9	113.3
1944	269.8	38.1	33.0	85.9	153.8	70.9	68.0	94.9	96.1
1943	250.2	34.4	26.6	73.0	142.7	68.7	66.9	86.0	99.4
1942	236.8	35.0	20.7	59.9	132.3	55.6	58.7	79.4	100.3
1941	226.8	29.8	17.7	59.1	113.4	57.0	51.6	68.5	97.6
1940	212.0	30.6	22.4	60.5	106.7	46.1	46.3	69.8	98.5
1939	204.4	27.6	23.9	61.6	114.9	71.5	52.8	74.3	95.5
1938	201.1	30.3	19.1	62.1	109.1	87.0	53.4	75.4	108.4
1937	209.6	25.6	15.2	56.9	110.3	81.8	57.0	70.2	108.7
1936	201.4	22.4	12.9	52.4	109.1	80.5	54.1	66.1	104.1
1935	188.3	20.7	13.1	50.6	104.8	72.5	50.8	65.2	98.2
1934	178.0	16.4	14.1	49.8	109.3	71.5	50.6	67.4	100.2
1933	142.4	13.6	13.4	42.7	101.5	69.7	50.4	63.9	99.6
1932	139.9	14.7	12.9	36.7	93.0	68.4	49.9	60.2	101.8
1931	158.7	10.1	12.4	41.7	92.2	68.3	51.1	59.7	95.6
1930	163.4	12.5	11.5	37.7	86.4	60.4	48.2	56.7	90.2

TABLE 8:2—continued

Year	United States	Canada	England and Wales	Australia	Denmark	France	Netherlands	Sweden	Switzerland
1929	172.8	11.5	10.8	43.6	85.9	63.8	46.6	56.1	90.7
1928	170.7	11.6	12.8	40.6	89.0	64.2	46.8	55.2	85.6
1927	168.2	11.0	10.4	43.6	84.2	56.7	45.0	51.3	85.6
1926	160.0	9.1	8.5	38.1	76.4	62.5	42.1	46.7	77.3
1925	154.0	8.2	8.3	43.2	67.4	66.8	39.9	46.3	80.1
1924	152.6	8.1	7.3	36.0	72.6	69.9	39.2	43.8	78.1
1923	150.1	7.4	8.5	34.7	81.7	74.1	38.4	41.6	74.6
1922	137.1	8.1	8.3	31.7	58.5	82.8	38.1	40.4	79.1
1921	150.1	8.4	11.5	36.0	64.2	105.5	40.4	40.4	75.6
1920	165.5	7.2	10.4	29.1	57.1	132.1	41.8	38.1	88.2
1919	140.9	†	5.8	22.6	63.1	83.5	33.7	35.4	78.9
1918	116.7	†	3.9	18.6	54.5	40.2	31.5	32.8	67.4
1917	125.4	†	2.5	17.5	50.4	34.5	30.8	31.4	63.9
1916	119.9	†	3.5	17.0	46.1	17.8	29.9	23.4	59.7
1915	111.8	†	2.5	18.5	44.2	6.6	26.9	25.9	54.8

* Adapted from Metropolitan Life Insurance Company, "World-Wide Increase in Divorce," *Statistical Bulletin*, 30 (April, 1949), 2.
† Not available.

law. New York, on the other hand, permits divorce only on the ground of adultery, and some Nevada divorces are in fact granted to citizens of New York.

Finally, a rising divorce rate may signify that certain groups in society to whom divorce was formerly inaccessible are now availing themselves of it. For those lower on the economic ladder it may portend an increase not in marital disharmony but in economic prosperity. Our own early and continuing high divorce rate as compared with other Western nations may also be a reflection of the fact that the status of workers and of women has always been relatively higher and less tradition-bound in this country. Furthermore, people who are only loosely integrated into society may not feel it necessary to formalize their marriages and therefore have no need to seek formal divorce. A rising divorce rate among American Negroes, for example, might point to an increase in the number of formal marriages and growing acceptance of the officially approved moral order.

WHO GETS DIVORCED?

In democratic United States all kinds of people get divorced: farmers and city dwellers, rich and poor, white and nonwhite, Protestants, Catholics, and Jews. But in order to arrive at some understanding of the causes of divorce, we need to know among what groups divorce is most prevalent. For example, divorce has been attributed to the intrinsic shortcomings of the new, democratic, permissive family. If this is true, we might expect to find divorce most prevalent among those groups in which the new conception of family life has taken firmest hold, that is, among the middle class or those with relatively high incomes and educational level. Or, if religious sanctions are an important factor, we should expect to find a low or nonexistent divorce rate among Catholics.

In point of fact, analysis of group divorce statistics results in some mixed and unexpected findings. Not unexpectedly, farmers have a relatively low divorce rate. But how do income, education, religion, and race affect divorce?

Income

Popular opinion has it that divorce is most prevalent in the higher income brackets. Available evidence does not support this belief. In 1950 the median income of men still married was $2,959, of divorced men $2,242, and of men separated from their wives $1,750.[10]

Aside from farmers, occupation level appears, on the whole, to be inversely related to divorce: the higher the occupational level, the lower the

---

[10] U.S. Bureau of the Census, "Marital Status and Household Characteristics: April, 1951," *Current Population Reports,* Series P-20, No. 38 (April 29, 1952), p. 13.

divorce rate. Kirkpatrick devised an occupational "divorce quota" from census figures for 1948.[11] He found that divorce rates among professionals, proprietors, managers, and officials were considerably below "normal," while those of laborers, service workers, and clerical employees were above "normal." The divorce rate among laborers was by far the highest.

Another such calculation was made by Goode for 1949.[12] If we take the figure 100 as an arbitrary base, the following tabulation shows the deviations upward and downward in extent of divorce among men in various occupations:

Professional, semiprofessional	67.7
Proprietors, managers, officials	68.6
Clerical, sales	71.8
Craftsmen, foremen	86.6
Operatives (semiskilled)	94.5
Service workers	254.7
Laborers (except farm and mine)	180.3

Goode also calculated a similar scale for income brackets.[13] Again taking 100 as a base, the following tabulation indicates that for men of low incomes the divorce rate is considerably above the base and that for men of higher incomes, considerably below:

$ 1–$ 999	188.6
1,000– 1,999	134.8
2,000– 2,999	92.9
3,000– 3,999	89.2
4,000 and over	66.7

A study of Peoria, Illinois, related the 1930–34 divorce rates for different neighborhoods to their socio-economic characteristics. It was found that, the more relief cases in a neighborhood, the more divorce; the higher the average rent, average annual income, and percentage of home-ownership, the less divorce.[14]

From our previous analysis of the relation of juvenile delinquency to poverty, we can guess that divorce is a consequence not of poverty per se but of the social disorganization with which poverty is so closely linked in urban life. Low-income families are highly vulnerable, moreover, not only to divorce but to other factors which effectively dissolve the family: desertion, separation, death of a spouse. In his study of one American community, Hollingshead found that about 85 per cent of both upper-middle- and lower-middle-class families were intact after fifteen or more years, but a third of

---

[11] Clifford Kirkpatrick, *The Family* (New York: Ronald Press Co., 1955), p. 529.
[12] William J. Goode, *After Divorce* (Glencoe, Ill.: The Free Press, 1956), p. 46.
[13] *Ibid.*, p. 54.
[14] Clarence W. Schroeder, *Divorce in a City of 100,000 Population* (Peoria: Bradley Polytechnic Institute Library, 1939), pp. 50–51.

the working-class families and half of the lower-class families were broken by divorce, desertion, or the death of a spouse while the children were still dependent.[15] In addition, it is likely that the incidence of psychological alienation in low-income families is even greater than their high divorce and desertion rates indicate. For many, divorce may never be a serious and realistic alternative either because of resigned acceptance to unhappiness and conflict as essential ingredients of life or because financial obstacles to divorce are still insurmountable.

The chapters on juvenile delinquency discussed the fact that in urban society there is a close, though by no means necessary, relation between poverty and social and family disorganization. The loss of shared family goals, the lack of integration of the family and its members into community life and the social order, the conflict and attenuation of values that are apt to characterize urban life—though these are not exclusively the burden of the urban poor, nevertheless they bear down most heavily upon them. The statistics on divorce support the conclusion that lower-income groups suffer more than the middle class does from atomization and family disorganization. The same factors which make for loss of control over their children also make for alienation and conflict between husband and wife.

Hollingshead has tried to account for the fact that popular opinion sees divorce as an upper-class phenomenon. He distinguishes between established families, which have been in the upper class for at least two generations and have the security of inherited wealth and social standing, and those "new" families whose money is only currently being earned and who lack both solid financial security and unquestioned social status. It is among the latter, he conjectures, that divorce is relatively frequent and highly conspicuous; without ties to a past and lacking social acceptance and the firm assurance of inherited wealth, newly rich families may turn to the gross and purchasable symbols of their recently acquired status. The result is often conspicuous expenditure and fast living, and "we find divorces, broken homes, alcoholism, and other symptoms of disorganization in a large number of new families."[16] Because these new families are conspicuous both in their consumption and in their behavior, they stand out and become representative of upper-income groups in general. Hollywood, though hardly representative of the newly rich, is nevertheless a case in point.

Education

In general there is a direct relation between education and income in our society; the more education, the higher the income. Therefore we should

---

[15] August B. Hollingshead, "Class Differences in Family Stability," *Annals of the American Academy of Political and Social Science*, **272** (November, 1950), 39–46.
[16] *Ibid.*, p. 42.

expect to find divorce less prevalent among the college-educated than among those with less education. While this does obtain for white males, it does not appear to hold either for women or for Negro males. College women appear to have a higher divorce rate than both college men and women of only grade-school education.[17] Similarly, in contrast to white males, the college-educated Negro male seems more likely to be divorced than the Negro male with only a grade-school education.[18]

A number of circumstances probably combine to make at least some of the well educated in our society especially vulnerable to divorce.

1. It may be the case that, among those with only a grade-school education, women and Negro males are less likely than white males to avail themselves of legal procedure.[19] There may be fewer unhappily married college women than women with only grade-school education; but if a college-educated woman is unhappily married, she is probably more likely to initiate a divorce. However, of all women, the college-educated woman appears least likely to be separated from her husband or to be deserted by him.[20]

The higher divorce rate of the college-educated Negro male may be attributable to the fact that among Negroes with only minimal education many marriages are not formalized and are therefore never legally dissolved. There are probably fewer broken marriages among college-educated Negroes than among Negroes with only grade-school education, but for the college-educated the marriages that are terminated are far more likely to be terminated by formal divorce.

2. For women and nonwhite males a college education may be the source of considerable frustration. Education serves to raise aspiration levels. In the case of white males who are college-educated, opportunity to achieve tends to keep pace with aspiration. In the case of college-educated women and nonwhites, this is not so. Both find it difficult to find satisfying and socially accepted expression of their capabilities; in any case they are faced with highly ambiguous attitudes on the part of society. What society thinks they ought to want to achieve, what they do want to achieve, and what they actually can achieve may be three different things. The level of frustration and dissatisfaction is therefore likely to be higher among college-educated women and Negro males than among college-educated white males and may be expressed in a higher rate of marital discontent.

3. Present ambiguities in the role of women tend to exacerbate marital conflict, and these are probably heightened when the woman is college-educated. Desire for a career may be thwarted by the responsibilities of

---

[17] Kirkpatrick, *op. cit.*, p. 530.
[18] Goode, *op. cit.*, p. 54.
[19] *Ibid.*
[20] Kirkpatrick, *op. cit.*, p. 530.

motherhood. Moreover, as a wife she is likely to resent the fact that old patterns of male dominance continue to be sustained not only by built-in habits and training but also by the husband's undiminished economic responsibility and actual importance in the world of affairs. Conversely, the husband is apt to resent the fact that his wife, though anxious to assume the prerogatives of traditional male status, is often unwilling or unable to assume its responsibilities. The husband finds that his wife merely talks equality. Thwarted in his expectations of a submissive wife, willing to subordinate herself to his comfort and happiness, the husband is further burdened with a permanently dissatisfied partner, apt to be alternately, and confusingly, aggressive and dependent.

Religion

Most of our information on divorce comes from analyses of official United States Census Bureau data. Since in the past these have not included religion, what we know of the relation between divorce and religion is based on spot studies made by different investigators in different areas. Despite differences in detail, they nevertheless tend to agree in their major conclusions.

At the present time, marriages in which both partners are Catholic appear to be marked by less divorce than are marriages in which both partners are either Protestant or Jewish. The differences in divorce rates for same-religion marriages are, however, not striking.[21] When divorce, desertion, and separation are combined, there seems to be little difference in the percentage of Catholic and Protestant homes that are broken. The relatively high desertion rate among Catholics, especially on the lower income levels, tends to offset their lower divorce rate. The Jewish home appears to be the most stable.

Mixed-religion marriages and those in which both partners profess no religion are much more vulnerable to divorce and dissolution than same-religion marriages. Landis found the percentage of broken Catholic, Jewish, and Protestant homes in his study to be 4.4, 5.2, and 6.0, respectively, but about 14 per cent of mixed marriages and about 18 per cent of no-religion marriages were broken.[22] These figures are roughly typical of other studies.

Similarity of outlook in the partners to a marriage is conducive to a good relation. For this reason, if for no other, we should expect rural marriages, which usually occur between people of highly similar backgrounds, to be more stable than urban marriages, which are more apt to occur between people of diverse origins. Dissimilarity, including that of religion, puts a

---

[21] Judson T. Landis, "Marriages of Mixed and Non-Mixed Religious Faith," *American Sociological Review,* 14 (1949), 401–7.
[22] *Ibid.,* p. 403.

strain on any relation, and we should normally expect mixed marriages to exhibit more instability than same-religion marriages. The fact that differences in religion are often accompanied by differences in national and cultural origins only adds to the difficulties.

However, we should not take it for granted that religious differences are actually the important factor in the poor adjustment rate of mixed marriages. In the first place, it is highly likely that in most mixed marriages neither partner adheres strongly to his or her religion. In our secular society, furthermore, religion tends to be a once-a-week ritual rather than an integral part of individual and family life; differences in religion do not make for marked differences in day-to-day style of life except for a small minority of the pious and devout. Finally, there does not appear to be a great difference in the adjustment record of mixed and no-religion marriages.

Marriages tend to be weak wherever individuals are poorly integrated into society and the family has, as a unit, few ties to community life. The mixed marriage is eloquent testimony to the fact that the young adult's ties to the family, group, and church of his origin have already been sufficiently weakened to make the choice of an "outside" marriage partner possible. One study indicates that the rate of mixed marriages between Catholics and non-Catholics varies from area to area depending upon the extent to which Catholics retain an ethnic identity. Where Catholics of Irish or Mexican parentage still maintain their ethnic solidarity, mixed marriages are rare; as the ethnic community breaks down, mixed marriages increase.[23]

In no-religion marriages, there is no church membership; thus the absence of religion cuts off the individual and the family from an important form of institutionalized participation in community life. Furthermore, though religious affiliation is not the only source of idealism and morality, breaking the religious tie often goes hand in hand with the attenuation of moral discipline. For many sectors of our society, nonreligious sources of discipline such as education, achievement through work, or even status-striving are simply not present or accessible, and the loss of religion often bespeaks a loss of morality and that degree of disciplined responsibility which any social relation, including marriage, requires.

The Negro Family

In every respect Negro families suffer great instability. Not only divorce, separation, and desertion but death as well make normal family life among Negroes extremely precarious. Figure 8:1 is based upon a study of Maryland youth made in the late 1930's. It shows that for the better-situated

---

[23] John L. Thomas, "The Factor of Religion in the Selection of Marriage Mates," *American Sociological Review*, **16** (August, 1951), 487–91.

Negro families not on relief the percentage of homes broken by marital discord was less than that of white families on relief. This bears out the hypothesis that marital discord and economic status are in general inversely related and that this holds for Negroes as well as for whites. However, the figures also show that death struck the Negro family considerably more often than the white family, whatever the economic plight of either. Undoubtedly some nonwhite women with children report themselves as widows when they have been deserted by common-law husbands, but being widowed (or deserted) at an early age and left with still-dependent children is a considerable risk run by the Negro wife. In 1951, 20 per cent of all nonwhite widows but only 7 per cent of white widows were less than 45 years old. Of all nonwhite women between the ages of 45 and 54, 23 per cent were already widowed as compared with only 10 per cent of white women in the same age group.[24]

Because of segregation and discrimination, every strain which bears upon the low-income white family bears all the harder upon the low-income urban Negro family. In addition, the Negro family is burdened with a history of marital instability which expresses itself not only in a high divorce rate but in a high desertion rate. Slavery and the attitude of masters toward female slaves prevented the formation of strong ties between Negro men and

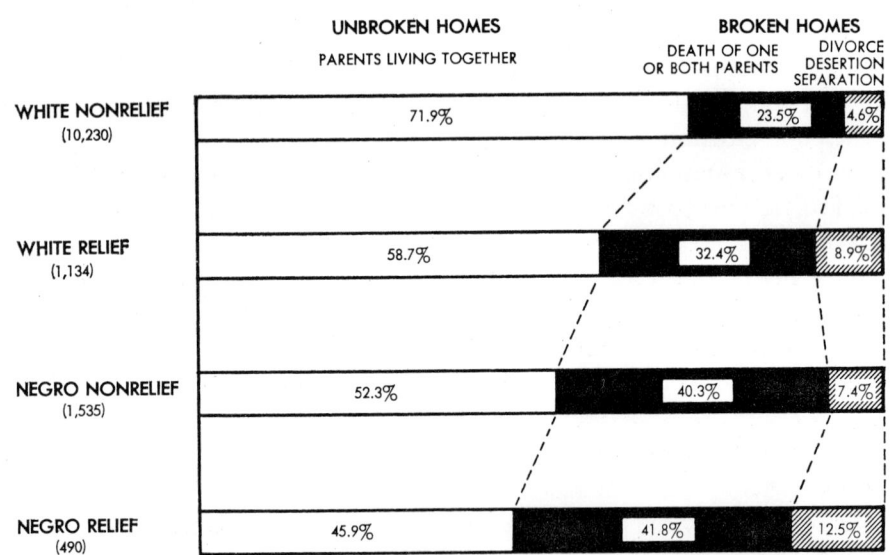

FIGURE 8:1 STABILITY OF THE HOME IN RELATION TO RACE AND RELIEF

Source: Howard M. Bell, *Youth Tell Their Story* (Washington, D.C.: American Council on Education, 1938), p. 20.

[24] Metropolitan Life Insurance Company, "Widows Increasing in Number," *Statistical Bulletin,* **36** (January, 1955), 6.

women. Unions between them were often broken at will by white masters, while unions between white men and Negro women had no official status. The central and often the only enduring family relation was that between the mother and her children. This was perforce the case when the children were the offspring of a white master, but it tended also to hold where the father was a slave. The mother, or grandmother, was as a rule the head of the household into which the adult Negro male was often only superficially integrated.

The employment difficulties of the Negro male in urban areas and the continued opportunity for domestic work for Negro women have tended to preserve the old rural slave patterns despite migration to the cities. Marital ties and male responsibility tend to be weak, while the relation of the mother to her children tends to be protective and strong. Desertion and separation occur frequently, with the mother often assuming sole responsibility for the children. Where the husband has employment security and the family has middle-class status, old patterns disappear rapidly.

DIVORCE AS A SOCIAL PROBLEM

Doubtless, for the individuals involved, divorce is usually an extremely painful personal experience. But how serious is divorce as a *social* problem? Dire conclusions are often drawn concerning the consequences of divorce for the very fabric of our social order. Divorce, it is sometimes charged, is an important causal factor in juvenile delinquency; divorce signifies the destruction of marriage and the family as the basic unit of our society and eats away at the foundations of our social order; divorce encourages marital and parental irresponsibility and portends the gradual weakening of our moral fiber.

The long-term upward trend of our divorce rate is incontrovertible. So is the fact that, by almost any standard, it is high. There are, however, a number of considerations which somewhat soften the picture and which support the view that not divorce itself but the causes of divorce constitute the basic social problem.

1. The sharp increase in the divorce rate during World War II was sometimes interpreted as a sign of the suddenly accelerated breakdown of contemporary marriage as such. But it appears to have been transitory and to have been a response to the especially unsettling circumstances of the period.

During the World War II period the incidence of divorce among those married five years or less rose sharply from 1942 on, that is, the divorce rate was abnormally high for those people who married during the war period.[25]

---

[25] Metropolitan Life Insurance Company, "Divorce and Wartime Marriage," *Statistical Bulletin,* **29** (March, 1948), 1.

The sharp increase in divorce during World War II can in large measure be attributed to the fact that wartime encourages the kind of marriage which even in peacetime has little chance of success. During wartime, many individuals are separated for a long period from the familiar social controls and personal satisfactions of family and community life. This was especially the case during World War II and held true for both men and women, the latter entering the labor force in unprecedented numbers. Such uprootedness encouraged the formation of hasty and superficial alliances between lonely people who under less extreme circumstances would have been more inclined to consider their mutual suitability. Prolonged separation of husband and wife put an abnormal strain upon already existing marriages which might otherwise have survived. Moreover, since unmarried men were as a rule the first to be conscripted, desire to postpone service in the armed forces further swelled the number of premature and highly vulnerable marriages entered into for the wrong reasons. Young men 18–20 years of age were required to register for Selective Service in June of 1942; a study of New York State marriages (exclusive of New York City) showed that almost three times as many young men under 20 were married in 1942 as in 1939.[26]

The postwar divorce rate has returned to, and continued at, a level close to that of 1942. Many students of the family now believe that, though our divorce rate will in all probability remain high, it will not follow an inexorable path upward. According to this view, our divorce rate has now begun roughly to approximate the actual proportion of unsuccessful marriages; with the reduction of social, moral, and financial obstacles to divorce, most people who seriously want divorces now appear to be getting them.[27]

2. Our high divorce rate has sometimes been said to signify the breakdown of marriage as an institution. Yet, despite our high divorce rate, getting married has remained a stable element in our conception of what constitutes a normal and presumably desirable way of life. In Figure 8:2, which presents in graphic form the crude marriage and divorce rates of Table 8:1, the marriage rate fluctuates rather widely, but the fluctuations tend to iron themselves out. Especially during economic depressions, people tend to postpone getting married, and the marriage rate drops; but they do not renounce marriage forever, and troughs in the marriage curve are soon followed by peaks. Despite the roughly 25 per cent probability that a marriage will end in a divorce, Americans continue to enter marriage at an unabated rate.

3. The remarriage rate of divorced persons appears to be high. One survey revealed that about 75 per cent of those divorced during the period

---

[26] Metropolitan Life Insurance Company, "Wartime Changes in Age at Marriage," *Statistical Bulletin*, 25 (May, 1944), 5.

[27] Kingsley Davis, "Statistical Perspective on Marriage and Divorce," *Annals of the American Academy of Political and Social Science*, 272 (November, 1950), 18.

1943–48 had remarried by 1948; of those divorced between 1934 and 1943, about 86 per cent had remarried by 1948.[28] Of women aged 25–29 who married in 1950, one quarter were divorcees; of those aged 35–44, nearly one half were divorcees.[29] Of 110 women, Goode found that, twenty-six months after divorce, eight of the ten who were 20–24 years old and half of those who were older had remarried.[30] This occurred despite the fact that "another man" was rarely the reason for the divorce.

If relaxed moral attitudes help to facilitate divorce, they also help to facilitate remarriage. A generation ago the word "divorcee" had connotations of unrespectability, but today the divorced woman is virtually without moral stigma. However, there is some evidence that remarriages of divorced persons are on the whole not as stable as first marriages, indicating that some people are "divorce prone." It is against such persons that the strictures of the conservative critics of easy divorce would seem to have most weight. For those already so disposed, easy divorce is an open invitation to marital irresponsibility. It might be agreed that strict divorce laws would at least act

FIGURE 8:2 CRUDE MARRIAGE AND DIVORCE RATES; 1900–1956

RATES PER 1,000 POPULATION

Source: U.S. Bureau of the Census, *Statistical Abstract of the United States, 1957* (Washington, D.C.: U.S. Government Printing Office, 1957), p. 56.

[28] Paul C. Glick, "First Marriages and Remarriages," *American Sociological Review*, 14 (1949), 729 ff.

[29] Metropolitan Life Insurance Company, "Current Pattern of Marriage and Remarriage," *Statistical Bulletin*, 34 (June, 1953), 6.

[30] Goode, *op. cit.*, p. 279.

as a constraint even if they could not transform the personalities of those unable to fulfill the responsibilities of marriage.

4. An increase in the divorce rate does not necessarily signify an increase in the incidence of broken homes. Desertion, separation, and death also result in broken families and often raise more serious problems of dependency and community responsibility than does divorce. As a matter of fact, taking death and divorce together, the proportion of broken families appears to be somewhat lower today than it was in 1890.[31] Figure 8:3 presents a picture of the relative importance of death and divorce in the dissolution of marriage from 1890 to 1948. Though divorce has greatly increased as a factor, it has tended to be offset by the rise in life-expectancy.

Figure 8:4 estimates the present relative importance in the dissolution of marriage of death and divorce on the basis of 1947 figures. Though divorce is by far the principal hazard in the first five years, sometime before the fifteenth year it becomes increasingly likely that a marriage will be dissolved not by divorce but by the death of one spouse, more probably the husband. Because it tends to occur later in a marriage and to leave the wife behind,

FIGURE 8:3 MARITAL DISSOLUTIONS BY DEATH AND DIVORCE, 1890–1948

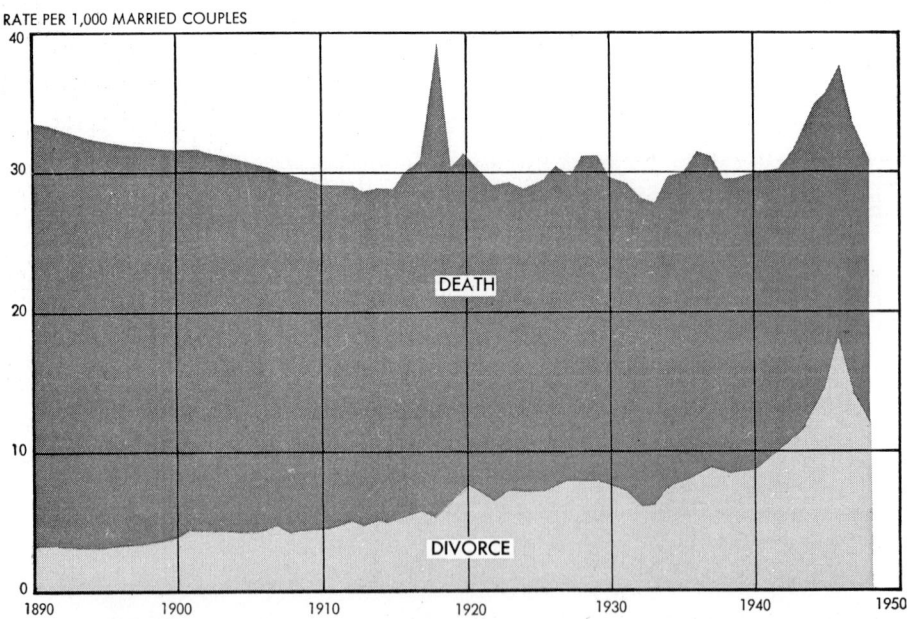

Source: Metropolitan Life Insurance Company, "Have Broken Families Increased?" *Statistical Bulletin*, Vol. 30, No. 11 (November, 1949), p. 2.

[31] Metropolitan Life Insurance Company, "Have Broken Families Increased?" *Statistical Bulletin*, **30** (November, 1949), 1.

death can in many cases raise graver problems of dependency than divorce, which is apt to occur early and to affect younger rather than older adults.

In 1953, in about two-thirds of marriages terminated by death, it was the husband who had died;[32] in 1940, in two-thirds of the cases where the widow was under 45, she had dependent children under 18.[33] Though the proportion of widowed in our population has been declining, the number of widows has been increasing rapidly. Both men and women live longer at present, but the wife is still apt to outlive her husband. Between 1920 and 1953 the number of widows rose by almost 90 per cent, while the adult female population increased by only 63 per cent; in 1920 there were less than four million widows, while in 1953 there were over seven million.[34]

In 1956, about 66 per cent of American females over fourteen were married, and about 12 per cent were widowed. Of those not married, 2.4 per cent were divorced; but of the women still married, the husband was absent

FIGURE 8:4 MARITAL DISSOLUTIONS IN THE FIRST 40 YEARS OF MARRIAGE, 1947

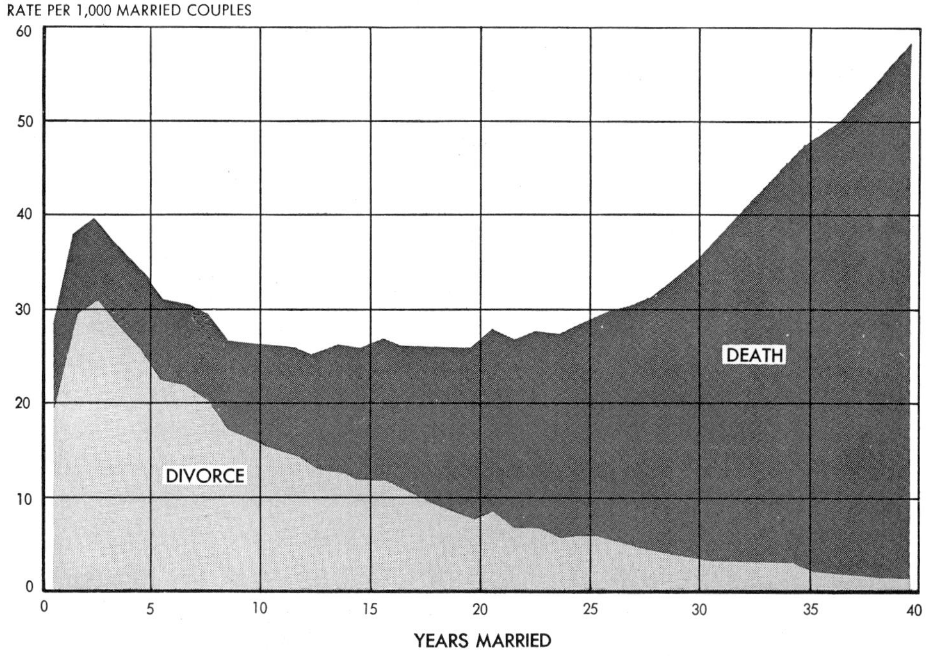

Source: Metropolitan Life Insurance Company, "Have Broken Families Increased?" *Statistical Bulletin*, Vol. 30, No. 11 (November, 1949), p. 3.

[32] Metropolitan Life Insurance Company, "Widowhood and Its Duration," *Statistical Bulletin*, **34** (September, 1953), 1.

[33] Metropolitan Life Insurance Company, "The American Family Stands Firm," *Statistical Bulletin*, **25** (July, 1944), 10.

[34] Metropolitan Life Insurance Company, "Widows Increasing in Number," *Statistical Bulletin*, **36** (January, 1955), 6.

in 3.8 per cent of the cases for some reason or other, including separation.[35] Separation includes, for example, imprisonment of a spouse; it also includes desertion. To some extent our rising divorce rate probably reflects a decreasing desertion rate, especially on the lower socio-economic levels. Desertion has been called the "poor man's divorce," but there is reason to believe that formal divorce is replacing desertion as an escape from marriage. In addition, it must be remembered that a rising divorce rate may signify a decrease in the number of informal alliances that do not require legal dissolution.

Where divorce is a substitute for desertion, it is in most cases the healthier and more socially responsible alternative. Desertion typically implies abandonment of all relation to the children of a marriage and flight from financial responsibility. Divorce, on the other hand, usually involves the legal fixing of rights and duties, especially with regard to the children of a marriage.

In general, divorce rates are inadequate measures of family stability unless they are supplemented by separation and death rates and are evaluated in the light of the ease with which divorce may be obtained. Where divorce is not accepted as a legitimate recourse, we cannot infer from the absence of divorce the absence of family disorganization or inversely the presence of marital harmony. This reminder is especially important as we interpret the meaning of the long-term historic rise in our divorce rate. The same factors which make for family disorganization and a high divorce rate among the urban poor today undoubtedly made for family disorganization among the urban poor a century ago, even though legal divorce was then a rarity. Today, though Catholic religious doctrine on the sanctity of marriage and the family appears in some measure to hold down the Catholic divorce rate, it does not seem able to forestall family disorganization when the social conditions which make for it are overwhelmingly present. Caught between family disorganization and official Catholic doctrine, many Catholics apparently have recourse to the compromise of separation or desertion.

Similarly, the fact that the urban Negro divorce rate appears to be higher than the white is but a partial reflection of the actual greater incidence of broken families among Negroes. Not only a high desertion rate but a shorter life-expectancy makes the Negro family a far more fragile unit than is revealed by official divorce statistics.

Children and Divorce

The effect upon the children of a dissolved marriage is one of the most forceful arguments against easy divorce. Though we have no genuine knowledge concerning the lasting effects of divorce upon the children involved,

---

[35] *Statistical Abstract of the United States, 1957*, p. 46 (see n. 9, above).

DIVORCE

we know that for children as well as for adults divorce can be a bewildering and emotionally painful experience.

Data for 1948 indicate that the divorce rate is considerably higher for childless couples than for couples with children.[36] Figure 8:5 shows that in the third, fourth, and fifth years of marriage it is about three times as high; after fifteen years it is still about twice as great. Since divorce rate tends to decline with duration of marriage, it is not surprising that divorce rate varies inversely with size of family. In 1948 the divorce rate per 1,000 couples with one child was 11.6, with two children 7.6, with three 6.5, and with four 4.6, while the corresponding rate for childless couples was 15.3.[37]

It is sometimes argued by traditionalists that having children is an important factor in holding a marriage together. Nevertheless, in any year we can expect about two of every five divorces to be granted to couples with chil-

FIGURE 8:5 DIVORCE RATE FOR COUPLES WITH AND WITHOUT CHILDREN UNDER 18, ACCORDING TO DURATION OF MARRIAGE, 1948

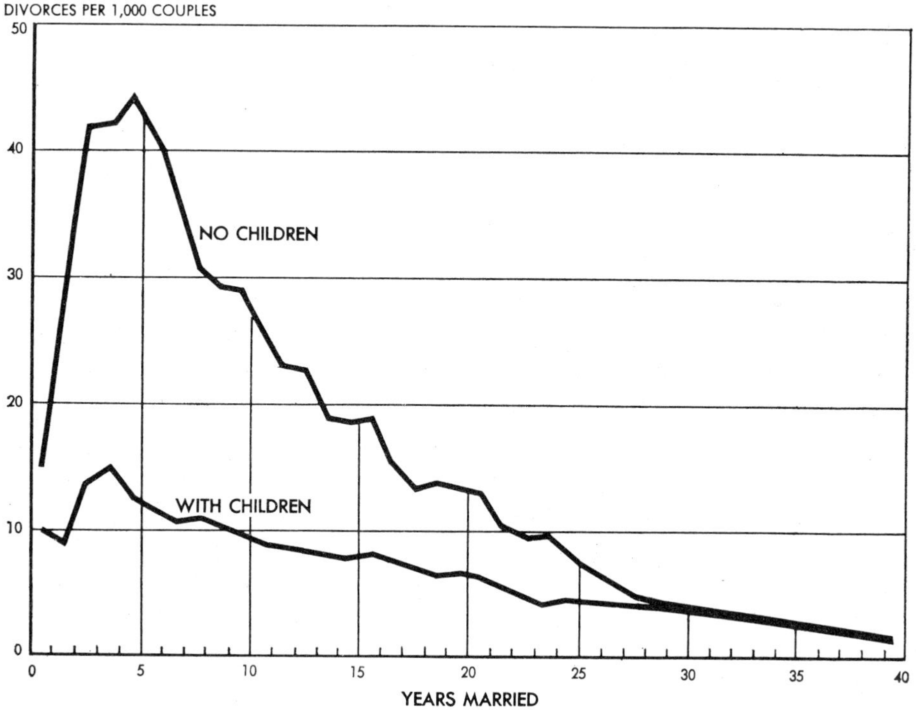

Source: Metropolitan Life Insurance Company, "Divorce and Size of Family," *Statistical Bulletin*, Vol. 31, No. 2 (February, 1950), p. 3.

---

[36] Metropolitan Life Insurance Company, "Divorce and Size of Family," *Statistical Bulletin*, **31** (February, 1950), 3.
[37] *Ibid.*, p. 2.

dren.[38] In many cases, moreover, the presence of children keeps the marriage formally but not emotionally intact.

The absence of children in the majority of divorces and the higher rate of divorce among the childless are probably the combined result of a number of factors which have little to do with the alleged contribution of children to marital happiness.

1. At present many couples, whether happily or unhappily married, put off having children for a few years. Since divorce tends to occur in the early years of marriage, it is not surprising that many are childless.

2. The unhappy couple without children is more likely than the unhappy couple with children to decide upon divorce. For one thing, the presence of children often raises insurmountable financial obstacles; for another, the woman with children may resist divorce because she believes her chances of remarriage are decreased.

3. Couples who want children early in a marriage are often the kind of people who strongly value marriage and family life and are ready to make whatever adjustments are necessary to stay married. Conversely, the divorce-prone personality is apt to shun the responsibility of parenthood.

Divorce and Delinquency

It is occasionally contended that divorce is an important causal factor in juvenile delinquency. Studies of delinquents usually find that the percentage who have divorced parents is high; figures ranging between 20 and 50 per cent have been reported. On the correct assumption that the percentage of nondelinquent children in the United States who have divorced parents is considerably less, it is sometimes concluded that divorce contributes significantly to delinquency.

However, delinquents, or at least those officially designated as such, tend overwhelmingly to come from the urban poor, and the urban poor are in general characterized by a high divorce rate. So, even if divorce had nothing at all to do with delinquency, we should expect delinquents to be far more likely than children in general to come from homes in which divorce or separation had occurred.

We need, therefore, to compare delinquents not with all nondelinquents of all socio-economic classes but with nondelinquents of similar economic and social background. In the Gluecks' study (see Adaptation 2, p. 78) boys from similar slum neighborhoods were compared. It was found that about 22 per cent of the delinquents and about 13 per cent of the nondelinquents had parents who were divorced or separated. Though delinquents were indeed more apt than nondelinquents to come from homes marked by divorce

---

[38] *Ibid.,* p. 1.

or separation, the difference is not striking; there is a fairly high probability that *any* child in a low socio-economic neighborhood will come from a home broken in some way. In any case, the majority of delinquents in this study came from homes in which no divorce had occurred.

There is little reason to suppose that divorce by itself is of causal importance in delinquency. The most significant element in delinquency appears to be a home characterized by neglect, irresponsibility, the incapacity to give and receive affection, and the personal disorientation and demoralization of the parents. It is such homes, of course, that are likely also to be broken by divorce, separation, or desertion; adults who are inadequate to fulfill the parental role are apt to fail also in their marital roles. But such homes may still be formally intact. Moreover, the broken home appears to be an adequate home if the remaining parent is able to maintain a responsible and concerned attitude toward the child.

Divorce and delinquency are both primarily urban phenomena highly correlated with low economic status, because it is among the urban poor that social disorganization is most severe. Both are symptomatic of the fact that family relations, both marital and parental, tend to deteriorate among those whose integration into society is marginal. People without a secure place in the life of society are likely to be both emotionally impoverished and lacking in the self-discipline required to fulfill social and personal responsibilities.

Not all delinquents, of course, come from homes marked by adult demoralization. Discrimination and segregation are sometimes enough to alienate Negro or Mexican-American youth from even the best of homes. Nor is all divorce the product of gross adult inadequacy. Although we have no real knowledge, the evidence suggests that divorce has little or no consequence for delinquency when the parents are genuinely concerned about their children, are in fact bound to them by ties of affection, and continue to fulfill as best they can their parental roles. However painful to the child partial or total loss of one parent may be, he need not lose the conviction of being loved and cared for. In any case, the emotional difficulties of the protected child of middle-class parents, divorced or not, are more likely to be expressed in self-punishing personality disturbances than in aggressive juvenile delinquency.

WHY DIVORCE?

It is important to recognize that to speak of the causes of divorce is not necessarily to speak of the causes of marital disharmony. In periods and countries where the divorce rate was once nonexistent or negligible, there was, presumably, some marital disharmony. Yet divorce was not regarded as an acceptable escape from an unsatisfactory marriage. Part of the answer to the question of the causes of divorce concerns the growing acceptability of divorce in Western society.

We can best understand the acceptability of divorce by asking what has happened to transform marriage from an institution to which commitment was once in effect absolute to a "personal" relation to be judged and weighed in the light of individual satisfaction. No doubt the secularization of Western thought has, over the centuries, diminished the claim not only of marriage but of all institutions to be sacred and inviolable. For the civilized, rational man in modern society, no loyalty can be absolute; he concedes to no commitment or relation the right to be immune to test, judgment, and, if need be, rejection.

The secularization of Western thought has its roots in a fundamental social change in Western society: the growing independence of the individual from *specific* group membership. The individual, if he is to participate in society, can never isolate himself totally from group life; people participate in society not as individuals but through institutions and groups of which they are members. Nevertheless, modern man tends not to regard any *particular* group or institution as having an absolute claim on his loyalty and devotion. He feels more free to break his bonds to others when he becomes convinced, whether rightly or wrongly, that his own self-fulfillment is being thwarted. It is evident that, in present-day Western society, people are as committed as they have always been to marriage as a desirable institution, but there is a weakened commitment to any particular marriage, and there is a willingness to "cut loose" and try again.

Thus, in analyzing the causes of divorce, we have two things to consider. First, what makes for harmony or disharmony in marriage? Second, what makes for the acceptability or unacceptability of divorce when marital conflict *is* present?

1. When the family shares basic goals, self-fulfillment is seen as identical with group achievement. Here conflict is minimized because strong individual aims do not emerge to conflict with group aims. The old farm family is the best example of the family as a common enterprise because it was a production unit with great mutual interdependence. Because so much of contemporary urban life can be pursued outside the family, the group character of the urban family is less fundamental and more precarious. Not only do individual aspirations emerge that often conflict with family goals, but disharmony, where it exists, is not so readily tolerated.

2. When the individual is economically dependent upon the family, disharmony is apt to be suppressed or tolerated. The urban wage-earning husband is no longer economically dependent upon his wife, as was the farmer or small shopkeeper, nor is the wife so dependent upon her husband. The increasing work opportunities for women have in all probability done much

to increase the divorce rate. The woman's new economic independence has made not only the wife but the husband as well more willing to entertain the idea of divorce even where children are present. It has also opened up the prospect of easy remarriage; if the second wife works, it is not economically impossible to support two households.

3. Where the family is an important avenue to participation in the basic life of society, individual loyalty to marriage is apt to be enhanced. When the family farm was the basic economic unit, being married was almost essential for participating in the important economic and political life of the community. Participation in the life of the community depended far more than it does now on being a member of a household.

In modern urban society, much participation is on an individual basis. Though most wage-earners are in fact married, their economic role and function have little to do with their being married. The husband works outside the home with people who may never meet his wife nor she them. Who she is or what she is is largely irrelevant for a significant segment of his life. Much the same situation obtains for the growing proportion of American wives who work outside the home.

The family still plays, of course, an important sociability function. The woman, especially the older woman, is still greatly dependent upon her marriage in this respect. Nevertheless, getting married and having children is apt to be sensed as a curtailment rather than an enrichment of her social experience and importance. Many women now work before they become married, and they are likely to regard marriage and motherhood not as a road to becoming solidly integrated into the significant life of society but as a status which isolates and cuts them off from it.

The decreasing importance of the family as a vehicle for social participation has facilitated divorce by making divorce far less disruptive of the individual's life. Divorce has few repercussions when home is just a place to hang one's hat.

Section III: The Family, Society, and the Child

The human being, though born with the potentiality for social life, must nevertheless undergo a long and often arduous process of socialization. He must first learn how to live with others and then to participate in his society in satisfying and rewarding ways. This by no means requires the slavish acquisition of conventional values; it does require, however, that some ethic of self-discipline and self-respect be transmitted, not merely for the sake of the social order but for the sake of individual happiness.

In our society many institutions beside the family participate in the moral education and training of the young, e.g., the school and the church. Nevertheless, the family is still regarded as the single most important agency for the inculcation of those basic social values and character traits which make for the child's eventual responsible participation in the life of society. The recent history of the family represents a gradual but inexorable loss of function and importance in the larger community, but the job of child-rearing still belongs to it. The family is of course responsible for the physical care of the young, but to it is also entrusted the moral education of the young. When things go wrong, as in juvenile delinquency, common sense tends to place the onus squarely upon the family and on shortcomings in the home.

Common sense is supported in its judgment by much modern psychological thinking. The ultimate origin of personality and character is traced to the dynamics of the parent-child relation, and early childhood experience within the home is seen as the most important single factor in the formation of basic adult attitudes and behavior. Family responsibility is inescapable, of course, because the family tends to have sole physical access to the very young child. But far more important is the fact that the intimacy of family life gives the family a psychological access to the young available to no other institution in society. Because family life revolves around basic needs and satisfactions, both physical and emotional, parents are in a position to inflict painful deprivations and thereby to exercise considerable influence in molding and shaping their children. Indeed, as community life has diminished and the effective family no longer includes a host of kinfolk, responsibility for training the young has come to rest more and more exclusively with the parents; if they fail, there are rarely others present in the environment to take up the slack. In this sense the importance of the parents for the psychological well-being of their children has increased rather than diminished.

There are at least two important and related factors which are making it difficult, however, for the modern family to accomplish the core socialization job which is still required of it. One is the loss of family function and importance; the other is the fact that so much of the socialization process now occurs outside the home.

LOSS OF FUNCTION

1. Sharing in group activity, especially if it is centered around a job of work or a common goal, is one of the contexts in which the individual learns to discipline his behavior and takes on standards and ideals of achievement. One of the ways the child learns to be good is through discovering that disruptive behavior incurs group disapproval and frustrates the achievement of goals in which he himself has a vital stake. In order for co-operation to occur, certain minimum standards of behavior must be observed.

As the family has been shorn of common goals, it has also lost opportuni-

John B. Titcomb; Black Star

Love and performance.

ties to inculcate discipline and ideals in the normal course of everyday life. For example, to the extent that the family is no longer a production unit, it has few opportunities to transmit the disciplines and values that center around work. Because it does not arise out of the necessities of common family enterprise, discipline now often appears arbitrary and irksome, not only to children but to their parents as well. Parents feel uneasy and anxious in exercising their authority; the old-fashioned farm mother who insisted that her daughter do the evening dishes had no reason to suspect herself a tyrant; her fatigue was sufficient to validate the discipline. But the modern mother, viewing her mechanical dishwasher, may doubt the justice of any such claims upon her daughter.

Because authority and discipline do not flow as naturally as they once did out of the concrete realities of experience, parents now tend to look to child-rearing theories for guidance in their parental role. Reliance is more often placed on abstract rules.

2. Where shared activities and goals are at a minimum, less time is spent together and there is decreased interaction. The capacity of the parents to influence and mold the child in desired ways is thus reduced.

3. The development of technology and mass production has relieved the

family of the task of transmitting specific occupational skills to its children. Before the advent of the mass-production society, manual skills were far more important than they are now, and formal education far less so. In a rural society, children are still apt to grow up to be farmers and wives of farmers, and their chores as children are not arbitrarily imposed tasks but a genuine preparation for their adult roles. In urban life there is no telling what the future occupation of the children will be. Even though the children of workers tend also to be workers, the father may work in an automobile factory, the son in a refrigerator plant. The same obtains for the middle class. Father and son may be corporation executives but in entirely different fields. There is very little concrete training which the parents feel is worth transmitting to the child.

4. Finally, because the family has lost much of its importance as a unit in the life of society, the young person is less dependent upon it. The family has thereby lost an important source of control and discipline. The child is no longer dependent upon the family for learning skills essential to his future livelihood and adult role, nor does the young person have to remain an integral part of the family in order to sustain himself. Except for certain old-line wealthy families, the family does not determine as it once did the status and respectability the individual has within the larger community. And finally, the family is no longer the unit of participation in community life. The individual can relate to society apart from family participation.

The loss of function on the part of the family has the inevitable consequence that the child must learn occupational skills and much of his social skill outside the home. In short, the family now shares the socialization job with many other institutions and groups in society, many of which are hostile to rather than supportive of parental values.

SHARING SOCIALIZATION

The School

One of the salient characteristics of modern technological society is the growth in importance of formal education. As a matter of fact, education has come in common parlance to be synonymous with "formal education," that is, education by the separate and largely impersonal institution of the school. Modern education is also becoming more formal in another sense as well. It imparts abstract skills rather than concrete arts. Adequate participation in modern society requires even of unskilled workers a fairly high level of literacy and general knowledge, but even more important is the sheer intellectual competence required to manage our complex technological apparatus. People in our society on whatever level need to acquire intellectual skills which have very little to do with immediate goals.

Although formal education has existed in Western society for some time, more and more young people are now spending most of their youth in school, and more and more are going beyond high school to spend their young adulthood in college and professional training. Beginning, indeed, with nursery school, the family now relinquishes the child to other people and other more impersonal institutions for a good part of the day and for almost the entire period of youthful dependence. The relinquishing of the family's educative role to the school is most important during adolescence and early adulthood, when the problem of relating to society and to people outside the family becomes acute.

Once it was primarily through participation in family life and work that the adolescent learned about group life and took on social values. Prior to the wholesale extension of education beyond the fundamentals of grade school, adolescence was the period which the individual spent with his family learning the skills which would prepare him for adult life. This part of his education was informal. The young person learned skills in the execution of daily tasks, learned about the realities of social life by participation in adult society, and took on an image of his or her future role as husband or wife, father or mother, through intimate observation of family life.

The formal nature of present-day education is most sharply revealed by the school's invasion of areas once regarded as highly private and personal, that is, by the presentation of formal courses in marriage, social poise, sex, and the rearing of children. These were once matters of informal education passed on from parents to children in day-to-day interaction and learned primarily through participation in family and community life. In present urban society, where the "nuclear" family is small and the young person does not come into frequent contact with aunts and uncles and cousins, the young woman may be totally unskilled even in the physical care of infants, never having observed younger children within the context of family life.

The present-day formal nature of most education, even that once reserved to the family, has deprived the family of a great part of its training function and gives parents only limited opportunities to pass on their ideals and traditions. In many cases, moreover, the ideals of the school are at variance with those of the family. For example, in the school we find an emphasis upon new knowledge rather than the reverence for tradition and old ways, and this has the tendency to undermine parental authority in general.

The Peer Group

The extension of formal education beyond childhood into late adolescence and early adulthood also encourages the relatedness of the young to each other rather than to their parents, their family, and the larger community. The young spend most of their time with one another, and out of this fact arises the natural tendency for them to value the approval of their peers at least as much as that of their family. When family ideals are in sharp conflict with peer-group ideals, this creates tension between parents and youth and tends to reduce the effectiveness of parental control.

The interrelatedness of age-mates in peer groups has come to have a new significance in modern society. Where the family is the important unit of social participation, relatedness cuts across the generations, and children very early observe and take part in adult society. As a matter of fact, the shrinking of the family to parents and their offspring has resulted in the growth in importance of peer groups for parents as well as for children. Married couples tend to associate with their age-mates, and grandparents are supposed to find satisfaction in groups of their age-mates. The old are isolated from the family life of their children, and there is an ever-increasing tendency for the problem of the aged to be interpreted as one of finding a way to create a society of the aged.

As the family has diminished in function and no longer works together, play has become an increasingly important activity of the young. The young are regarded as having their significant experiences in the peer play group. Indeed, parents themselves regard peer interaction as one of the primary devices for socializing their offspring. The nursery school, for example, is a place where mothers hope their children will learn how to get along with others. But the consequence of intensive peer interaction is that the child must perforce give great weight to the values and attitudes of his peer group, and the capacity of parents to pass on their values is diminished.

Teen-Age Revolt

The failure of the family to maintain control and authority over its members is particularly important in the case of the adolescent. There is very little known in a scientific way about the problem of the teen-ager; many would even deny that such a problem exists. Many observers are agreed, however, that conflict between adolescents and their parents has increased, that adolescent behavior tends to be more undisciplined than it once was, and that the teen-ager has become a new social category.[39]

Certainly a significant portion of the mass media now caters to the teen-agers as a separate social group. That the adolescent should have values and modes of behavior peculiar to his age group is not a new phenomenon. What does seem unprecedented is the extensive elaboration of these values and modes of behavior, many of which are in sharp and almost brazen conflict with parental and traditional values, and the emotional intensity with which the teen-ager identifies with the symbols—the fads and fashions—of

[39] Kingsley Davis, "The Sociology of Parent-Youth Conflict," *American Sociological Review,* 5 (1940), 523–35.

Leadership: The peer group helps the child to find out who he is.

his peers. Moreover, what appears to be occurring is not merely the sharp differentiation of adolescents into a social category but their independence from adult control.

Some observers tend to identify teen-age revolt with juvenile delinquency, interpreting the latter as merely a more intensive expression of the former. This seems to be an extreme interpretation of the present plight of the adolescent, especially in view of the fact that the behavior problems of juvenile delinquents tend to start very early, long before the onset of adolescence and its special tensions. Nevertheless, there does seem to be some truth in the belief that in present-day society the family is apt to lose control or to find it exceedingly difficult to maintain authority over their children during adolescence and early adulthood, even when in a few years it turns out that their children have acquired a surprising respectability and morality.

There are a number of factors which make it difficult not only for the present-day adolescent to accept any other authority than that of his peer group but for the peer group itself to develop an adequate degree of responsibility and self-control. Probably most important is the fact that the family is in a position to do little to define and structure the adolescent's present and future participation in the life of society at large. The family is itself isolated from the major workings of society. Not being as integral and functioning a unit in society as it once was, it can do correspondingly little to integrate the adolescent into the social order.

Adolescence marks, of course, an important biological development; the capacity to engage in adult sexuality is as a rule accompanied by new and often upsetting responses to the other sex. Adolescence is therefore typically conceived of as a period of intense emotional upheaval. But this aspect of adolescence can easily be overemphasized. The adolescent is also becoming an adult in a social as well as a biological sense. The teen-ager has to learn how to deal with others not as a dependent child but as a preadult. He has to find a place, a position, a niche for himself, not within the family but outside it. He has to learn the realities of the social order outside the protective circle of his family, e.g., how to treat any member of the other sex, how to respond to nonparental authority, what the going rules are not only within his own family but in the community at large. Adolescence is the period, then, in which *social* self-definition becomes an acute problem.

Outside the family, the only important institutional relation the adolescent has is to the school. But the school as an institution is scarcely better equipped than the family is to relate the adolescent to the concrete and living reality of his society. Since so much of education is perforce formal, it is divorced both from specific future adult roles and from the day-to-day life of the community.

The adolescent, as a result, exists in a kind of social limbo, securely anchored to social reality neither by his school nor by his family, and therefore forced back upon his own kind for an introduction into social experience. The peer group becomes the source of his knowledge of what is proper and not proper; it also becomes the only social group in which he can test his social "know-how" and find his place within some structure of social relations. Here he discovers whether he is a leader or a follower, a good mixer or a fringe participant. The peer group is almost the only social group which can readily provide the young person with an image of what he is as a social being.

But the peer group in our society is, as a rule, almost entirely a sociability or play group, operating largely outside the framework of adult life and institutions. Therefore, it is easy for it to develop its own independent and irresponsible norms. With the growth of mass communication, moreover, the adolescent is very early exposed to knowledge about adult prerogatives, but he is not simultaneously checked by responsible participation in adult society. Except for school, the adolescent is usually taskless and does not participate with his family or other adults in important social institutions. For those young people whose future goals are clearly related to formal education, the school may serve as a major source of task-oriented discipline. But for those to whom school is a mere legal requirement, formal education may have little effect as either a discipline or a source of ideals. As a consequence, the adolescent is apt to have little opportunity to internalize attitudes of responsibility. His primary source of social control easily becomes conformity to the standards of his peer group. But because the peer group is cut off from adult society, these standards are apt to be inadequate and uncontrolled.

Section IV: Meeting the Problem

The problem of the family is its diminishing capacity to maintain unity and cohesion among its members. Because of this incapacity, there is a deterioration of the family's ability to act as society's basic mechanism of social control, as the transmitter of social values and aspirations. This would seem to be the most serious hazard the atomistic family presents to organized society. However, because of the same incapacity, there also tends to be a loss in the family's ability to act as a satisfactory and effective emotional matrix for the growing child and in its ability to provide stable and gratifying social roles for its adult members. These tendencies contribute further to the fragmentation of family life. This downward spiral of family ineffectiveness is at the root of many of the specific social problems which exist in our society. At the same time, of course, the ineffectiveness of the family is a direct product of our society. It is a result not of the ignorance or willful waywardness of family members but of the impact of modern history on the institution of the family itself. Many claim that some of the changes in familial institutions are in keeping with the times and are ultimately for the best, e.g., the democratization of family relations and increased emphasis on the importance of the individual. They also claim that the problem of apparent disunity which attends this timely change is a transitional problem of adjustment to new circumstances.

Transitional or not, this "problem of the family" is important background to much current social pathology. Because of its multiple and pervasive sources, because it is inseparable from the entire historical fabric of our times, this problem is not easily subject to any direct and deliberate community remedy.

The deep-rooted nature of the family problem emphasizes the necessarily limited and partial effectiveness of programs designed to remedy those specific social problems, such as juvenile delinquency, that are, in part, only manifestations of this more fundamental problem. This does not negate the ability of limited programs, when soundly conceived, to ameliorate some of the symptoms of family inadequacy. The human values involved demand ameliorative efforts even when the root difficulty is left untouched. But even more, direct attacks on the symptoms of family disorganization can serve to develop those values, concerns, and insights which are needed for successful attack upon the basic sickness itself. The intelligent involvement of citizens in the problem of delinquency can lead to a greater awareness of fragmented family life as a central disability and can add impetus to certain current developments toward greater family unity.

INFLUENCES TOWARD FAMILY UNITY

A number of recent developments appear to be spontaneous efforts on the part of the modern family to achieve greater unity and to counteract the tendency to treat the home as merely a place to hang one's hat.

Consumption Goals

Consumption goals appear to be becoming increasingly important as goals to be shared by all the family, the allocation of money resources for family purchases replacing the former allocation of human resources for family work. From a unit of production, the family seems to be turning into a more and more important unit of consumption.

The middle-class family with an adequate and rising income is apt to achieve a considerable degree of unity centered around consumption goals; in this way it probably does not differ significantly from economically comfortable families in the past. Acquisition, moreover, is one way the family has of relating itself to the community, for it validates and enhances status and prestige. For working-class families, acquisition can provide a major sense of participation in our predominantly middle-class society.

In poverty-stricken families, however, the goal of acquisition can hardly serve as a source of family unity; indeed, the inability to acquire may serve to disrupt family life partly because it so easily stamps the parents as failures in the eyes of youth. In any case, however, consumption goals can hardly serve as a profound and ultimately satisfying basis for family unity; the significant relation of family members is not to one another but to the goods that can be bought and the status they bring in the eyes of others.

Do-It-Yourself

There is some evidence that the modern family senses the inadequacy of consumption goals and is striving to incorporate work goals into family life.

There has grown up in recent years a do-it-yourself movement; in his spare time the husband may turn his hand to carpentry, the wife to sewing. Advertisements for home woodworking equipment and dress patterns are now directed not to the farmer or to those with a low cash income but primarily to the urban and suburban middle-class family.

In an economy based on mass production, the do-it-yourself trend appears to be something of an anomaly. No doubt part of it signifies the almost unlimited desire of Americans for material possessions and middle-class status. But it probably also signifies a desire on the part of both husband and wife to be related to the home in more personal, direct, and work-oriented ways than the roles of money-earner and purchaser provide.

The Child-Centered Home

The modern husband and wife are physically and socially separated from each other for most of the day. The husband works outside the home in a place which is usually totally unfamiliar to his wife and which relates to people she has never met. It is part of the wife's accepted role that she listen sympathetically to her husband's work and career problems; but except for their implications for her social and financial status, her interest is almost bound to be more polite than genuine. The world in which her husband is deeply involved is not one in which she participates or of which she has much firsthand knowledge.

Correlatively, the wife has now come to have exclusive concern with the children during the day. Whereas the farm father came into daily intimate contact with his sons, at least, the contemporary father sees his children only in the evening. Though fathers are still often expected to wield ultimate parental authority and no doubt are as interested as mothers in their children's well-being, responsibility for the children, both male and female, is now relegated largely to the wife. But just as wives can be only superficially interested in their husbands' work problems, so husbands are apt to be impatient with the problems of child-rearing.

The fact that the main preoccupations of husband and wife are so unrelated and separate them for most of the daylight hours makes the problem of finding some area of shared activity crucial. Since the wife cannot participate in her husband's domain, the only alternative is that he share in hers. This has resulted, especially in middle-class families, in a greater sharing by husbands in household duties and child care, and it has also encouraged the extremely child-centered character of the American middle-class family. Husband and wife can at least share the common goal of "giving their children the best." Moreover, the children also provide a rationale for much shared family sociability; weekends are often devoted to amusing the children. In fact, sociability in American middle-class life is pretty exhaustively divided between seeing other married couples of one's own age group and doing things to keep the children happy.

Community Participation

There appears also to be some tendency for the middle-class couple to find a set of common goals in shared community participation. This community participation, though a surrogate, perhaps, for the community involvement of the "old" family, nevertheless differs from it. The new participation is essentially formal and organizational. Husband and wife join committees devoted to causes, participate in organizations devoted to civic affairs, or devote their time to youth groups, such as the Boy Scouts. Many times, of course, it is the wife who is most active in community life, largely because this is practically the only avenue open to her for a kind of participation in society which is not family or sociability centered. Husband and wife may join different community organizations. Nevertheless, a shared interest in community affairs and local political events seems to be replacing, in some cases, the more informal participation in community life which tended to characterize the family in the past.

Home-Ownership

Finally, the new migration out of the city into the suburbs and the large increase in home-ownership in recent years are also working to provide the family with common goals. Owning a home provides a family with some common focus of concern and interest and perhaps with a heightened sense of itself as a unit. It also gives the modern family some stake in community life and therefore some sense of relatedness to the immediate community. Taxes, schools, roads, even the state of the neighbor's lawn, become not only matters of vital concern but, because the suburb is usually a smaller political unit, matters on which the family feels it can exert some influence.

In addition, suburbs are far more homogeneous, socially and economically, than urban areas. Sharp and valid criticism has been made of suburban conformity and provincialism, but in point of fact most parents find in the suburb an atmosphere which is supportive rather than destructive of their own values and those which they wish to transmit to their children.

It must be noted, however, that recent evidence points to rising delinquency rates in suburban areas. Since World War II the suburbs are no longer so exclusively middle class. Low-cost housing has not only created the working-class suburb but has probably reduced the degree to which home-ownership and stability of family life are related. We do not yet know whether the rising suburban delinquency rate is attributable to the fact that more delinquency-prone families are moving into the suburbs or whether the suburban family is in general becoming more delinquency-

United Press Photo

The role of women in politics has been expanding from simply voting (above) to the staffing of polling places (above), political organization activity (lower left), and candidacy for elective office (lower right).

UPI Telephoto United Press International

prone. Nor do we know whether the rising delinquency rate is nevertheless lower than it would be for the same socio-economic groups in cities and without home-ownership. In addition, the rise is undoubtedly also due to the fact that people often move into the suburbs when their children are very young. Sufficient time has now elapsed since the postwar housing and baby booms for these children to have reached the age of delinquency.

SOCIAL SERVICES

Specific community programs directed toward the generic problem of family disharmony and disunity have not been seriously designed to solve that problem in itself but rather to mitigate its harmful effects on given individuals.

Family Casework

Family casework agencies are typically independent organizations supported by the community chest or by religious or other charitable funds and staffed by trained social workers. Cases come to them directly or through referral by schools, churches, courts, or hospitals. There is usually a sliding-fee arrangement, adjusted according to income. Though family counseling and guidance in general are provided, the objective of social workers, with the aid of consulting psychiatrists, is frequently psychiatric in nature: to diagnose and develop insights into the nature of severe problems of family relationship either between parent and child or between husband and wife. If the emotional problem seems beyond the technical capabilities of the agency staff, referral is made to a psychiatric agency. The ability of these agencies to give helpful guidance, counseling, and support to families in dramatic trouble has been limited by the interrelated unavailability of adequate funds and trained social workers.

Family-Life Education

There has been an increasing emphasis on high-school, college, and adult-education courses on family life. The chief goal of these programs has been to provide some anticipatory awareness of the demands and responsibilities of married life. Romantic love is typically depreciated, and some of the psychological hazards of modern family life are expounded. Frequently some kind of anticipatory sex education is included in the curriculum, and even more frequently, especially in adult-education programs, there is some generalized guidance for actual or prospective parents in child-rearing.

Family Courts

Family courts, or courts of domestic relations, have developed rapidly as specialized jurisdictions in many cities. These courts sometimes deal with parent-child relationships, as in cases involving adoption or custody, and with marital relationships—most specifically, with divorce. These courts typically serve as a kind of social as well as judicial agency. Ideally, they have the services of social workers for investigation prior to the court hearing, and they have access to medical and psychiatric services. In matters of divorce, the effort of these courts is presumably to effect a reconciliation if this is at all possible. It has been argued that these efforts are ill conceived and that it is socially harmful to impose an artificial bond upon a marriage that is not successful. On the other hand, it has been argued that more marriages would become successful if husbands and wives were somehow compelled to "work at it" a little. This is, of course, the nub of the debate as to whether divorce laws should be more or less liberal. There is no clear record of the success of these courts or the permanence of the reconciliations they effect.

MARRIAGE—A CULTURAL PERSPECTIVE   adaptation 18

Abridged and adapted from M. F. Ashley Montagu, "Marriage—A Cultural Perspective," in Victor W. Eisenstein, M.D. (ed.), Neurotic Interaction in Marriage *(New York: Basic Books, Inc., 1956), pp. 3–9. Published in this form by permission of the author and the publisher.*

[Marriage is viewed by some as a changing social institution to which different values accrue at different times; by others, as a basic and immutable religious value around which the social institution must be built. These interpretations of marriage do not conflict at every point and indeed may have substantial areas of working agreement.

In heterogeneous America both views are strongly represented. The following adaptation presents the secular approach of the anthropologist, M. F. Ashley Montagu.]

In our twentieth-century, technologically advanced Western culture, no less than in the primitive cultures of peasant China or the Pacific Islands, marriage is a cultural product. In primitive and more stable societies the cultural influences are readily apparent. In our highly complex and rapidly changing society, they may be more difficult to perceive but they are fully as significant.

Perhaps one of the most striking characteristics of marriage in our culture is the fact that it is based upon the concept of romantic love. The concept of love, developed in the twelfth and thirteenth centuries among the nobility of France, was characterized by complete abdication of all selfish motives, complete fealty, and a complete idealization of the beloved. Love was held to be a matter of free exchange, and that which was freely given was conceived to be vastly superior to the dutiful relationship supposed to exist between husband and wife in marriages that were arranged by parents or overlords.

This concept of romantic love, appealing as it did to women, has been handed down through the centuries and is now held by most women in our culture, but not by most men. Romantic love does, of course, govern the male's courtship behavior. During this period he behaves much like the adoring lover described by the twelfth-century troubadours. But after marriage, the male—because he has never been culturally conditioned to it—cannot maintain the role of romantic lover, and the wife's disillusionment at the change in him is one of the causes of marital dissatisfaction. Such disillusionment does not occur of course in other cultures, in which romantic love plays no part.

Closely related to the romantic ideal is the notion that a principal function of marriage is to increase one's personal happiness. This view, too, is peculiar to Western culture and does not exist in those cultures in which marriage is arranged by parents or has essentially an economic basis. Since happiness is not likely to be achieved by purposeful pursuit, this hedonistic view leads almost inevitably to some degree of disappointment and disillusionment in marriage.

In almost every society the division of labor between husband and wife is an important determinant of the stability and happiness of marriage. In nonliterate societies this division of labor is clear cut: the wife is usually the domestic worker, taking care of the feeding and clothing of the household and gathering the agricultural products, whereas the man is the hunter and maker of implements. In our culture today, however, males and females are educated in virtually the same skills. As a result, the woman acquires aspirations which are necessarily truncated after marriage; and her resulting frustrations are by no means lessened when she sees her husband able to pursue freely both the aspirations and the skills which he developed in the course of the same kind of education. The additional fact that the husband usually earns a living in a place remote from the household and often by means of a skill so highly complex as to be unsharable by the wife produces a barrier to communication between husband and wife and reduces sharply their area of common interests. If, on the other hand, the wife pursues her skills in an active career, the culture tends to make her feel guilty about forsaking her duties as housewife and mother.

The social mobility that is characteristic of our own culture is another source of tension in marriage. In our culture, more than in any other, individuals marry outside their social class and find adjustment to the customs and values of the spouse's class difficult, repugnant, or even impossible. Horizontal social mobility—the movement of individuals geographically and occupationally without change in socio-economic level—tends to produce marriages with partners outside one's own ethnic or racial group, a practice virtually unheard of and socially proscribed in nonliterate societies That differences between partners of such exogamous marriages contribute to marital instability is corroborated by considerable empirical data. Perhaps one reason for the instability of exogamous marriages is that they lack the stabilizing influences of the tribe or kinship group. Marriage in nonliterate societies involves not only the two spouses but also the extended family groups of each of them. The multiplicity of interrelationships of each spouse with the other's kinship group promotes a stability that is often entirely lacking in the marriage of two essentially family-less individuals.

The relative ease of separation or divorce which is characteristic of our culture may be due in part to the lack of influence of the kinship group, but in its own right it can promote marriage instability by permitting a tentative approach to marriage. Such an attitude toward marriage may of course be favorable for the mental health of the individual who is involved, even though it produces statistics that bode ill for the stability of marriages.

The premium placed upon youthfulness and physical beauty is another peculiarity in our culture that can make for difficulties in marriage. The value of beauty is so strongly and so pervasively stressed that many men seem to make a marriage choice largely on the basis of being able to display their wives. Marriage on the basis of physical attractiveness has had such disastrous consequences that society has been forced to permit the dissolution of such unions by making divorce more easily possible.

The sheer complexity of our society makes our marital roles much more complex than those in any other society. The wife must be competent not only as housewife and mother but also as companion and helpmeet even when neither her personality nor her learned skills are suited to such a diversity of roles. Her husband must be competent not only as a breadwinner but also as the head of the family even though most of his waking hours are spent far away from the home on matters not even remotely connected with home or family, and even though he could not as a child learn his future roles by observing the activities of adult males.

Virtually everything we have noted thus far would seem to indicate that marriage in our own culture is complex, difficult, and precarious, and, by implication, that marriage in nonliterate societies involves infinitely fewer complexities, tensions, difficulties, and handicaps. In actual fact, very few studies have been made of marriage in nonliterate societies; but the systematic studies available and the incidental observations of anthropologists, studying other institutions, make it quite clear that in every society there are tensions, insecurities, and difficulties. For us, marriage is beset by a number of difficulties that are unknown in simpler societies; but it also offers more opportunity for the full development of personality and self-expression. In a stable society, marriage is likely to be stable; but it is also likely to be devoid of challenge and devoid of the satisfactions arising from the successful meeting of challenge. Moreover, the very complexity of our society permits deviations that are not possible in simpler societies, and as a result, the deviant personality not only can make a better adjustment but can contribute to the enrichment of the society itself.

---

adaptation 19 DIVORCE—A CATHOLIC VIEW

Abridged and adapted from Clement S. Mihanovich (ed.), Marriage and the Family *(Milwaukee: Bruce Publishing Co., 1952), Chapter I, by John L. Thomas, S.J., and Chapter XII, by Clement S. Mihanovich. Published in this form by permission of the authors and the publisher.*

[The preceding adaptation presented an anthropologist's approach to marriage as a secular institution. The following summarizes the position of two sociologists formally identified with the Catholic Church.]

Those who reject the Christian teaching on marriage and the family, or who deny that there are any fixed ends and laws regulating these institutions, look upon modern trends in regard to the family as inevitable. For them the present disorganization of the family represents the more or less necessary family maladjustment which accompanies the transition from one type of family organization to another. They see in the present disorganization of the traditional family form elements of reorganization. They believe they can discover a new form arising, the "democratic" family. This new form will serve primarily as a vehicle for the personality development of the mates; its only bonds will be the emotional attachment and affection of the parties involved.

Those who look upon marriage in this way can be divided into two general groups. There are those who look upon the change as inevitable but are content to let things take their proper course. Opposed to this passivist group are the radicals. They are not content to wait for inevitable changes but would hasten the day of "liberation" by launching violent attacks against the old traditional forms. Among the first of these were some of the early "feminists" who looked upon marriage as the instrument of the slavery or servitude of women. The early Marxists used somewhat the same argument but for different reasons. The Marxist attack on private property necessarily entailed an attack on the traditional form of the family as the basis of social privilege and inheritance. All those who advocate greater sexual freedom and loosening of the monogamous bond are also attacking the family. Many of them base their contentions on the theory that all repression of sexual desire is unhealthy and will lead to psychic and nervous disorders. Some go so far as to look upon the family as a breeding ground for every kind of neurosis.

The less radical but more subtle attack on the family comes from those who look upon the family as primarily a vehicle for the development and satisfaction of sexual wants. Marital happiness is equated with perfect sexual harmony. If this is not achieved in marriage, then the family should be broken up and a new mate sought out. They believe that mismatches would result less often if there were greater sexual freedom before marriage, and some advocate a kind of trial marriage which would enable them each to find out if they were compatible. This way of thinking receives strong support from motion pictures and the popular magazines. Here love is portrayed as a mysterious visitation, to be recognized by the sudden glow of passion aroused at the first sight of the new lover. This some-enchanted-evening-you-will-see-a-stranger philosophy of love, more commonly called the "romantic cult," falsifies the marital expectations of the unmarried by identifying physical attraction with love.

One of the most serious attacks on the family comes from those who contend that the traditional family is not able to prepare and educate the youth of the country for life in the modern world. The mothers overprotect, the fathers are too authoritarian, the brothers and sisters arouse jealousy. In general, in one way or another, the poor child is thought to be ill prepared to mix with the larger society and to take his place as a balanced citizen. Either parents must be re-educated by the child psychologists, or the training of the children should be turned over to "specialists."

ROOTS OF THE FAMILY CRISIS

The family is in crisis today, however, not only because the structure of the family and the functions which it performs have changed so greatly. Historically man has ever been adapting his institutions to changing external conditions. However, adaptation requires that individuals be convinced that the ends and values embodied in the old are really worth preserving. If the participants in a particular institution are confused or in doubt about the ends and values traditionally embodied in it, they are not likely to make many sacrifices to preserve these confused and doubtful ends. It is such confusion and doubt which have precipitated the crisis of the family today.

The roots of this change are found in the Renaissance. Humanists such as Erasmus sought to free the family from much of the traditionalist family control. The Reformation insisted that marriage was not a sacrament and reduced it to a pure contractual basis. This setting-aside of the supernatural sanction which had surrounded marriage had far-reaching consequences. Once the divine sanctions were removed from the family, it was a short step to bypass all social control and consider marriage as a private affair concerning only the individuals involved. Thus the institution of the family was established on the unstable basis of personal satisfaction. The consequences of this shift from the sacramental to the contractual basis of marriage became apparent only with the increasing secularization of Western society. Emancipation from religious restraint and the substitution of the "scientific" approach to all problems were considered the absolute prerequisite of progress. The splendid advances achieved in the natural sciences induced men to believe that they could as easily uncover "laws" of human action. This belief was helped immeasurably by the discoveries of Freud and the psychologists of other schools. Granting the very real contributions they made to our knowledge of human motivation and action, their ready generalizations as conveyed to the general public resulted in the belief that restraint and self-discipline were either unwise or illusionary.

The consequences for marriage and the family in all these trends are apparent today in the two major motifs controlling man's thinking on marriage. These are the romantic cult and individualism. On the negative side one can look at the romantic cult as a reaction against the "Puritanism" exemplified in the American tradition. Positively it is based on modern psychological theory as seen through the eyes of a novelist in Hollywood. If the mysterious glow of love dies down after the honeymoon, then you have made a mistake and there is little to do but break up the union and start to search all over again! The second motif running through thinking on modern marriage is that of individualism, which is really complementary to the romantic cult. Marriage and family are looked upon as vehicles for the personality development of the persons involved. They are good only if they contribute fully and freely to his personality development as conceived by the individual. They are intolerable if they hinder this. However, the exigencies of family life are such that considerable limitation and restraint on individual desires and impulses are imperative, so that individuals must either change their philosophy of life or seek escape from intolerable situations through divorce.

THE EVILS OF DIVORCE

As a result of these developments, the American home in the twentieth century has been ravaged by a cancerous phenomenon, divorce, which has all but threatened to destroy this basic cell of human existence in civil society. As old as the human race, and second only in importance to man himself, is the channel of life whereby the family has been perpetuated and preserved through the ages. When the sacredness of family life is undermined, civilization itself is endangered. No nation is stronger than the homes of which it is composed. As the family goes, so goes the nation. Indeed, divorce may be considered from several different aspects besides its usual legal definition as a legal dissolution of marriage bonds. It may be viewed as a pathological condition in society. It may in turn be viewed as a painful personal tragedy. But divorce may also be viewed as a violation of divine precept.

During the Christian era marriage was elevated to the dignity of a sacrament, and the Saviour taught with the greatest explicitness: "Wherefore now they are no longer two, but one flesh. What therefore God has joined together, let no man put asunder" (Matthew 19:6). He stated further: "Whoever puts away his wife and marries another, commits adultery against her: if the wife puts away her husband, and marries another she commits adultery" (Mark 10:11; Luke 16:18).

By the tenth century the Catholic teaching on the dissolubility of marriage had been incorporated into the civil laws of every Catholic country. The Protestant Reformation, however, rejected Catholic teaching, and the pre-Christian concept of marriage was reassumed. This pre-Christian concept held that marriage was merely a natural contract and therefore could be terminated by a civil divorce.

In the United States, canon law and the ecclesiastical court system have never been integrated with either the state or the federal legislative departments. Marriage was never recognized legally as a sacrament and is, of course, not now recognized legally as a sacrament. Divorce is considered a privilege granted by the state.

Because of divorce, the marriage contract becomes subject to whim and caprice; easy opportunity is afforded for the disruption of homes; conjugal instability is encouraged; the care and education of children are undermined; and the seeds of discord find fertile soil in the encouragement furnished by easy divorce legislation and administration.

Since it is true that, for the disintegration of the family and the decadence of the state, nothing is so powerful as the corruption of morals, it is apparent that divorce is one of the greatest dangers to the welfare of families and nations.

adaptation 20

THE ADOLESCENT

Abridged and adapted from Nathan W. Ackerman, M.D., "The Adaptive Problems of the Adolescent Personality," in The Family in the Democratic Society, Anniversary Papers of the Community Service Society *(New York: Columbia University Press, 1949), pp. 85–120. Published in this form by permission of the author and Columbia University Press.*

[The following analysis of the adolescent personality and the tensions characteristic of adolescence in contemporary society represents a fusion of psychoanalytic and sociological insights. Biologically, adolescence is the period of sexual maturation. Fundamental to the author's analysis of adolescence is, however, an emphasis on the interdependence of the processes of sexual, psychic, and social maturation.]

THE ADOLESCENT PERSONALITY

For psychiatrists the vicissitudes of adolescent behavior have fundamental significance. Out of the fiery crucible of adolescent change is precipitated not only the permanent structure of the adolescent personality but also the major forms of mental disease. Adolescence is a normal crisis in the growth process. It is also the deepest crisis in the growth process. The personality undergoes a basic shift in equilibrium. It is during this transitional period that the culture exercises a profound shaping influence on personality; it selectively reinforces or weakens specific character tendencies. Hence, during adolescence, conflict emerges at all levels of the emotional life.

The typical manifestations of adolescent change are familiar to all of us: the pervasive insecurity; the instability of mood and action; the egocentricity; the prominence of the sexual drive; the exhibitionism; the loyalty to the same sex and mistrust of the opposite sex; the shifting concepts of self; the confusion; the self-consciousness; the lack of ease with one's own body; the preoccupation with physique and health; the vulnerability of self-esteem; the exaggerated feelings of difference; the conflict concerning authority, social forces, religion, and philosophy; the rebelliousness; the craving for independence; the obstinacy; the hero-worship and the susceptibility to outside influence; the fear of inadequacy and inferiority; the tendency to depression and social withdrawal; and, finally, the aspiration to be outstanding in some field of human achievement.

Underlying these rapid, radical shifts of behavior are the fundamental biological processes of pubescence. Changes in glandular function produce changes in physique, in physiological balance; with these changes, the sex drives emerge. Throughout, the elements of physical change are accompanied by a shift in emotional, social, sexual, and intellectual behavior. Inequalities of development in these various spheres tend to intensify the usual instability. Not only are there tremendous variations from one individual to the next, but, perhaps even more important, every conceivable type of imbalance may occur within one individual—a factor which sharply stimulates anxiety, self-consciousness, feelings of difference, and inferiority.

Adolescence may be characterized as the critical stage of development in which the anatomic unity of personality is temporarily dismembered and reformed. It is a transitional adaptation between childhood and adulthood. Adolescence, therefore, is an in-between phenomenon reflecting features of both the child and adult. It is characterized, however, by one dramatically positive feature of its own, namely, sexual maturation. This series of changes in personality, impelled by sexual differentiation and maturation, is in turn conditioned by the surrounding cultural pattern. The complex of adolescent behavior is a product, on the one hand, of the impact of growth changes, with particular emphasis on sexual development, and, on the other hand, of the pressure of cultural forces.

The adolescent does not mature in a consistent, forward movement; instead, anxiety induces an irregular movement, alternately forward and backward. The adolescent loses the protection of childhood but does not yet have the strength and privileges of the adult. The realities of adult living still represent an unknown and undefined menace. Fear of being a child pushes the adolescent forward. Fear of being an adult pushes him backward.

THE ADOLESCENT AND THE GROUP

The closeness of the adolescent to his group life is of central significance. Often the interchange between the adolescent and his group is so fluid and rich that the respective identities of the adolescent and his group can hardly be separated. The distinction, therefore, between what is properly inside and outside the adolescent's self cannot always be clear. Within the family circle the adolescent rebels. Outside the family the need of the adolescent to conform to dominant group standards is often extreme.

Culture at all times has played a large role in dictating the adolescent's place in the social scheme and in shaping adolescent personality. Culture, for the adolescent, comprises a far wider group of cultural influences than those which surround the child. The adolescent moves out to make contact with an expanding variety of groups bound by common religious, recreational, intellectual, and economic interests. In so doing, adolescents achieve new privileges but also must assume new responsibilities. They must evolve into approved versions of men and women.

Each individual society imposes a distinct set of standards. Discrepancies between one society and another are often striking. Earlier societies were often less complex in pattern, but more rigid; cultural influences tended to be more definite, more static, more consistent. The established patterns of social and sexual conduct were sharply delineated. The price of achieving adulthood was impressed on adolescents in a manner not to be denied. The adolescent's task of assimilating the cultural standards was then presumably easier. The role of present-day culture is more difficult to assay. The standards of modern society are extremely unstable and contradictory. Social aims and values are in themselves in a state of transition. This is an inevitable expression of the vast social crisis which is the outstanding feature of our time. Group standards are inconsistent, confused, and at times frankly chaotic or occasionally simply nonexistent. At such times, safe standards are difficult to find.

For example, the moral code with which children are indoctrinated is not the same as that which dominates the scene in adult society. Children who were taught to share, to co-operate, to be truly considerate of the rights of other persons, are ill prepared for the ruthless, competitive aggression which prevails in the adult world. In addition, members of our society have little opportunity for experiencing a positive sense of security in their group affiliations, since such groups are no longer as stable and hallowed as before. Thus, in contrast with earlier forms of society, the relations between the adolescent and contemporary culture are extraordinarily complex. The adolescent has little security in surrounding groups; the interrelationship is vague and menacing in its uncertainty. There are not the familiar guideposts that adolescents of older generations got from their parents. The adolescent today never knows exactly what to expect or where he stands. This is complicated by the highly developed technology and the trend toward specialization. The necessity for long apprenticeship, in preparation for the special tasks of adult life, imposes on the adolescent the status of prolonged dependence.

Inevitably disillusioned in the standards of his parents, the adolescent searches for new and more satisfying standards. To replace the shattered ideal of his parents, he seeks a new ideal. The unusual features of modern society render the adolescent's problem of choice more difficult. Feeling constricted and threatened in the larger culture, the adolescent strives to create his own culture, to mold social realities to his own liking. Adolescents try hard to create within their own group a small world of their own, with unique standards and values, carefully suited to their needs. They make a place for themselves if the world outside fails them. To whatever extent they do not feel accepted, they will withdraw and create their own separate community within the larger community. This trend is akin to the attitude of eccentrics, oedepians, artists, and writers, who, uncomfortable under the pressure of ordinary social realities which they feel are hostile and unsympathetic, withdraw and create their own community. Here is the effort to block off a smaller world within a larger one. The adolescent's defense is to build an "island culture." This is never really successful. In the end, interpenetration between the "island culture" and the parent culture inevitably occurs. But the defensive group behavior of adolescents must be regarded as a reflection of the failure of the parent culture to provide an adequate place for the expression of adolescent need.

SELF-ASSERTION AND SELF-ESTEEM

Against this background we may turn to the inner factors, the intrapsychic vicissitudes of adolescence. The fluidity of the concepts of self, the changing aims and aspirations, the instability of repression, the effort to rebuild a conscience suited to maturity, the imperious quality of the sex drives, bring into sharp focus every conflict, past and present, which has failed to achieve solution. All this adds up to one central feature, the understanding of which is indispensable for correct interpretation of all and any manifestations of adolescence, namely, the instability and vulnerability of the adolescent personality. At no period in life do human beings feel as exposed and defenseless as in adolescence. This is conspicuously expressed in the presence of diffuse, pervasive anxiety, the sense of exposure, the embarrassment and self-consciousness. This is the matrix in which is nourished the adolescent's belligerent defense of his privacy.

Of first importance is the adolescent's effort to achieve a feeling of adequacy. Every single aspect of the adolescent's effort to adapt to reality is influenced by his sense of worth and confidence or the lack of it. The actual experience of success in achievement and the feeling of strength and mastery in coping with the issues of life are essential for good emotional balance. Lack of confidence releases a host of defensive attitudes, among which we must group humility, submissiveness, gullibility, or the other extreme, excessive rebellion, belligerence, and the urge to intimidate others. These emotional vicissitudes are easily recognized as the adolescent's identity conflict—his struggle to resolve his identification with his parents and from this to build an individual identity uniquely his own. The uncertainty and confusion which characterize these transitional shifts in sense of self radiate outward to affect all of the adolescent's attitudes toward life. His fear and anxious searching for identity and orientation are paralleled by an expanding interest in social and economic conflicts and in religion and philosophy. The adolescent, in a time of rejection of parental images and temporary disillusionment in self, seeks to identify with something larger than himself. His urge is to ally himself with a cause greater than his own. Economic and religious groups often offer such opportunities. The allegiance to a group characterized by a special economic philosophy, especially one which seeks social reform or even revolution, serves to conceal the disappointment in parents and to reinforce the unstable repression of hostility to parental authority. It also buttresses the unstable repression of adolescent sexual drives. The excessive religiosity of adolescents or, on the other hand, their radical turn from it to atheism, is alleged often to be motivated by the need to reinforce the repression of unconscious passive, dependent strivings.

Some of the more conspicuous adolescent conflicts center in real or fancied injury to self-esteem. Adolescents show extraordinary sensitiveness concerning their concept of self. Since the image of self is in a state of flux, they are especially vulnerable to other persons' judgments. Adolescents often disclose with astounding vividness memories of deep early injuries to their pride. They painfully relive these childhood hurts. They dread renewed assaults on these old but exposed wounds. Against this background the compensatory drives can be readily understood—the urge to be big, powerful, to be "top dog," completely to obliterate all possible rivals, and to rely for such purposes on fantasies of omnipotence. Of special significance are the highly developed narcissism, the sensitive vanity, and the exhibitionist drives of adolescence. The misplaced assertion of these compensatory drives often impels a neurotic adolescent to commit acts of delinquency.

THE SEARCH FOR STANDARDS

Still another level of conflict has to do with the reformation of the conscience during adolescence. During adolescence, the guilt reactions are peculiarly labile. At first they are rather rigid and are clearly based on the standards laid down in childhood, influenced by the earlier trends of parental approval or disapproval. The temptation to transgress is accompanied by fear of punishment and loss of love of the parents. As the adolescent detaches himself from his parents, he shifts his dependence to persons and groups outside the family—occasionally to other adults but more conspicuously to peers and older adolescents. New patterns of aspiration emerge, based on these new affiliations. For a time the standards laid down by the peers may completely dominate the adolescent's conduct and bring about a severe clash with the parents' ideals. This struggle over standards is often bitter because of the adolescent's fear of losing control over his sexual and aggressive urges. The temptation to release these drives is intense, but the adolescent, dreading the loss of control, clings tenaciously to his childhood conscience and the parents from whom it was derived.

In this period of unstable transformation there are lightning shifts of behavior, characterized alternately by restraint and self-indulgence. Strivings which represent elements of unconscious conflict are released impulsively. Inevitably, such "acting-out" is followed by a resurgence of guilt and anxiety; and this, in turn, impels the reimposition—temporarily, at least—of childhood patterns of restraint. Of some relevance here is the adolescent's addiction to excitement and danger, the thrill of deliberately daring the powers of authority to catch and punish him for his excesses. In this behavior he seeks to measure his power against that of authority. He craves the satisfaction of outwitting and triumphing over symbols of authority, but behind this façade always lurks the apprehension of the day of judgment. This type of motivation sometimes finds expression in irrational and delinquent acts, such as walking over a roof ledge, stealing automobiles, etc.

The guilt related to sex drives and the corresponding aggression are often intense, but in this connection one important point must be made: adolescents are not guilty regarding the sex urge per se but only as the release of the sexual urge is conceived as an act injurious to some other person. In oedipal conflict, the guilt is not derived from the wish to possess the mother's love but rather from the urge to inflict injury on the rival figure. Because of the excessive nature of the guilt, a variety of defensive devices is brought into play in an effort to allay it. One means for evading conscious guilt is provided in the mechanism of externalizing the functions of conscience. This is a device for displacing responsibility to the person who personifies conscience—"let so and so do the worrying for me." Still another device for dealing with guilt is the assumption of a defensively passive attitude. This is an effort to avoid responsibility for the initiative—"let the other person do it first." Another defense closely related is the avoidance of completion of an act which will incite guilt; the act may be begun, and it may be carried through to near-completion, but, by magical thinking, so long as the act fails of actual completion, there need be no conscious guilt. When the quantity of guilt is large, there is a strong trend toward masochistic motivation. The pleasure element may be mostly or entirely concealed, and in its place we see more the experience of suffering, which reflects the need for self-punishment. Sometimes the suffering clearly outweighs the pleasure; sometimes the pleasure is highly significant but is covered up by the more obvious suffering.

Of course, the sexual evolution of the adolescent and the resolution of identity conflict are tremendously influenced by the individual vicissitudes of past personality development. During the crucial changes of adolescence, character traits established by past experience, the fixation points and the regressive weaknesses of the individual, clearly reveal themselves; they condition both the form and content of adolescent conflict. During adolescence, anxiety, emotional confusion, erratic social behavior, shifting concepts of self and the outer world, weaknesses of reality perception, vaccillating moral standards, instability and irregularity of impulse control, fickle, ambivalent interpersonal relations, may all be part of a normal transitional development.

SUGGESTIONS FOR FURTHER READING

Nathan W. Ackerman, *The Psychodynamics of Family Life* (New York: Basic Books, Inc., 1958).

Ruth Nanda Anshen (ed.), *The Family: Its Function and Destiny* (New York: Harper & Bros., 1949).

Ernest W. Burgess and Harvey J. Locke, *The Family* (New York: American Book Co., 1953).

Ernest W. Burgess and Paul Wallin, *Engagement and Marriage* (Philadelphia: J. B. Lippincott Company, 1953).

Joseph Kirk Folsom, *The Family and Democratic Society* (New York: John Wiley & Sons, Inc., 1943).

Clifford Kirkpatrick, *The Family* (New York: Ronald Press Co., 1955).

Judson T. Landis and Mary G. Landis, *Readings in Marriage and the Family* (New York: Prentice-Hall, Inc., 1952).

Paul H. Landis, *Adolescence and Youth* (New York: McGraw-Hill Book Co., Inc., 1952).

Jerome M. Seidman, *The Adolescent* (New York: Dryden Press, 1953).

Robert F. Winch and Robert McGinnis, *Marriage and the Family* (New York: Henry Holt & Co., 1953).

Carle C. Zimmerman, *Family and Civilization* (New York: Harper & Bros., 1947).

By Gertrude Samuels, The *New York Times*

CHAPTER 9

The Schools

Section I: What Is the Problem?

"The public sees no point in much of what is done in the name of education and has developed a justifiable skepticism toward education itself," complains a professor at the University of Illinois.[1] "The fundamental base of the 'activity program' [in our public schools] is the same base upon which communism rests, a materialistic, anti-religious base," warns a Chicago employers' association.[2]

No other formal institution in our society is under such constant and severe attack as our school system; these two complaints illustrate the widely varied sources of this attack. The varied nature of the charges can be read in the following bill of particulars: Item: The school does not teach the "3 R's" properly; there are too many "fads and frills" in the schools. Item: The schools fail to teach moral and spiritual values; they are "godless" and leave their students morally rudderless. Item: The schools are attempting to usurp the rightful functions of the home; they should concern themselves less with the "personality" of the child and concentrate on teaching subject

---

[1] Arthur E. Bestor, *Educational Wastelands* (Urbana: University of Illinois Press, 1953), p. 1.
[2] Cited in Robert A. Skaife, "They Sow Distrust," *The Nation's Schools,* 47 (January, 1951), 27–30.

matter. Item: The schools are teaching "welfare-state collectivism"; they serve as a shield for subversive influences.

The schools seem variously to be held responsible for delinquency, lack of religion, general moral laxity, and the marginal state of cultural literacy which marks so many of our high-school and college graduates. These accusations have become more than charges of technical incompetence; they relate to the basic values and goals of the public school system.

Such charges are apparently made in the face of the rather simple axiom that the school system is at least as much a product as a producer of society. The educational system largely reflects the morals, values, aspirations, and confusions of the society of which it is an instrument. The school, by itself, cannot maintain values which are crumbling in the community around it. The school is subject to the same forces which are constantly reshaping society. It is directly affected by many of the specific pathologies of that society—such as intergroup prejudice and juvenile delinquency—whose remedy must range far beyond the scope of the school.

However, the school system does provide an ideal public arena in which many of the basic value issues of society can be openly debated. The institution of the family is at least as often used as whipping boy for a wide range of social problems and deficiencies, but the family is not publicly supported, nor is it under formal public control. The schools are. Furthermore, with the virtual achievement of universal education, the school is the only controlled public institution through which all members of society must pass. It is the "youth movement" of America. It is society's official training ground. It is at this point, therefore, that organized society must have a clear conception of what it is about, where it is going, what values it cherishes.

RECENT SOCIAL ISSUES AND THE SCHOOLS

Where major value conflicts or tensions exist, they are very likely to come to specific contention in the restricted arena of public school issues. In recent years a number of major social issues have come to public debate in the guise of "school issues."

Equality of Opportunity

A democracy depends upon the practical ability of submerged groups to rise to the surface of society. Otherwise, the legal and political institutions of democracy would mean little and would have lost their purpose. A democracy cannot afford to depend on the talents of those who have been chosen by arbitrary standards to be its leaders and subleaders, its professionals and technicians. Education is obviously the key to a working democracy, not only by providing needed skills but by providing equal opportunity to develop those skills. The extended battle for free and universal schooling was, at base, a struggle for this concept of democracy. Today, it is not surprising that the most crucial struggle against racial subjugation is being fought on the school front. In many southern states the battle is being fought frankly within its larger context, for a "way of life." But in many other communities throughout the nation the same battle is being made more covertly, as part of a "school issue." Throughout the past decade, training and materials in intergroup relations have frequently been the targets of attack in public discussions about so-called "progressive education" and "subversive influences in our schools." In one bitter and celebrated community controversy "about the schools" in California, a thinly hidden issue was the proposal to bring Negro students into formerly all-white schools. (See Adaptation 21, pp. 450 ff., below.)

Religious Diversity

Interreligious conflict and tensions in the United States cannot always be subsumed under the heading of intergroup prejudice. Prejudice has often colored interreligious conflict, and interreligious conflict has often served as a base for prejudice; but the two are not the same. Prejudice is based largely on mistaken judgment, distorted stereotyping; interreligious conflict is based largely on *genuine* ideological and creedal differences. There are two major and evangelical religious groups living side by side in America: Protestantism and Catholicism. Their relationships to each other, to other religious sects in the country, and to the making of public policy are a potentially serious point of friction in our democratic society. That this friction is often kept beneath the surface emphasizes the delicate nature of these relationships and the importance to our society that such friction be kept within bounds. Certain creedal differences cannot be reconciled, and their application to organized society is often expressed at the level of discussion about the schools. The place of religion in our public schools is one focus of such discussion; the relationship of private parochial schools to organized society is another.

Social Change

Is there a fixed image of the political, social, and economic nature of America and of American communities? Or does the image of America include the element of constant and unlimited change? These questions underlie much discussion "about the schools." Are the schools to serve as a stamp of authority on "what is"; are they to open up unlimited horizons of "what might be"; do they have the responsibility to try to delimit the directions of future change? Much of the controversy about curriculum content, teaching methods, alleged subversion in the schools, and academic freedom relate to decisions which society must make in wider areas than the schools.

The Ultimate Values of Our Society

In some quarters there has grown the concept that the schools should be geared primarily to the training of future citizens to fill an active and useful role *in a democratic society*. Others believe that the schools should attempt primarily to bring every student to his fullest intellectual capacity. Is our first object in teaching English, for example, to provide communications skills for democratic living or to open the door to truth and beauty for every individual? One objective may well lead to the other, as is usually claimed; but this possibility does not alter the nature of the debate. Why, indeed, are we dedicated to the democratic form of government? Are our basic values identical with the concept of democracy, or is democracy only a tool for the realization of our basic values? Is democracy primarily an end, or is it primarily a means? These are questions that come to specific issue in discussions of school curriculums and of the role of the school in our society.

There are many purely technical and practical matters which draw the attention of the citizenry, e.g., what pedagogical methods will most effectively teach a child to spell, how communities are to meet rising school costs, etc. But even the debate about these issues more often than not comes to involve the deeper controversies for which the public school system provides a handy arena.

Section II: Educational Purposes—For Whom and For What?

BACKGROUND

Colonial America inherited the European social-class approach to education. General education was considered to be appropriate only for the upper class and as a preparation for leadership in church and state. Only vocational, or at best the most elementary, education was required for the lower classes. The broadening of the concept of education during this period turned chiefly on two motivations; one was the strong Protestant drive for Bible-reading literacy, and the second was the birth of a substantial middle class in a developing mercantile system. Both motivations were strongest in New England and weakest in the South. The Massachusetts School Law of 1647, which first established community-supported education, was known as the "Old Deluder" law. This law justified the need for universal literacy by proclaiming that it was "one chief project of that old deluder, Satan, to keep men from the knowledge of the Scriptures as in former times, by keeping them in an unknown tongue." But as the new middle class emerged, it created new educational demands beyond that of Bible-reading—demands dictated primarily by new vocational requirements.

During the pre-Civil War period, a booming business life and the expanding frontier intensified the goal and possibility of economic success for any man, regardless of his background. There was consequently less satisfaction with limited vocational education. When an educator suggested expanded facilities for craftsmanship education in 1930, his proposals were met with resistance in workingmen's circles.

In addition, as school attendance became more nearly universal, it became apparent that the schools would bear a vital relationship to the growing political institutions, national consciousness, and citizenship requirements of the new nation. The concept was established of secondary education as a kind of "people's college," providing more than vocational skills but less than a college education.

The social-class approach to education began to break down after the Civil War. Around the turn of this century especially, with an increasingly complex urban, industrial, and political life and with the large influx of immigrants, it became clear that our democracy would have to draw needed economic, political, and technical leadership from "the ranks." Advanced training in vocational skills was no longer enough. Nor was a terminal "people's college" sufficient. What was needed was an opportunity for anyone to prepare for higher education.

THE CURRENT ISSUES

The educational system in America is now charged with satisfying the students' aspirations, whether they are vocational, professional, or intellectual. Graduation from high school may be terminal, or it may not. The high-school graduate may become a worker in a factory or a teller in a bank; a doctor, a lawyer, or a chemist; an executive in business, a government administrator, or a professor. For some, school is primarily a preparation for a career; for others, school is primarily a source of general knowledge and intellectual training; for still others, school is merely a legal requirement.

As a result, educational needs that are *common* to *all* students, whatever their vocational horizons, have come to be featured. This is partly the result of the growing universality of secondary and even higher education. Also, educational opportunity in America has already reached the point where every person theoretically has the opportunity to obtain the educational background he needs in order to satisfy his economic aspirations; most of these aspirations do not require specialized training in depth. In addition, as we approach universality of education, it becomes clear that the schools provide society with opportunities that go beyond the vocational preparation of its youth.

Under these conditions, the "citizenship" theme in education has come to the fore. The schools are considered the prime instrument of democracy and democratic training. The rise of psychiatric and social-welfare concepts has also added another motivation: the creation of a "well-adjusted" population. Special vocational purposes still exist within the present-day school system, but they are no longer the larger part of it. In a sense, the schools have come full circle and have returned to their earliest philosophy: general, universal education for the moral and ethical training of every child. But while this common education was to be provided three centuries ago by a few years of Bible-reading and training in religious precepts, today it is to be compounded of psychology and democratic philosophy.

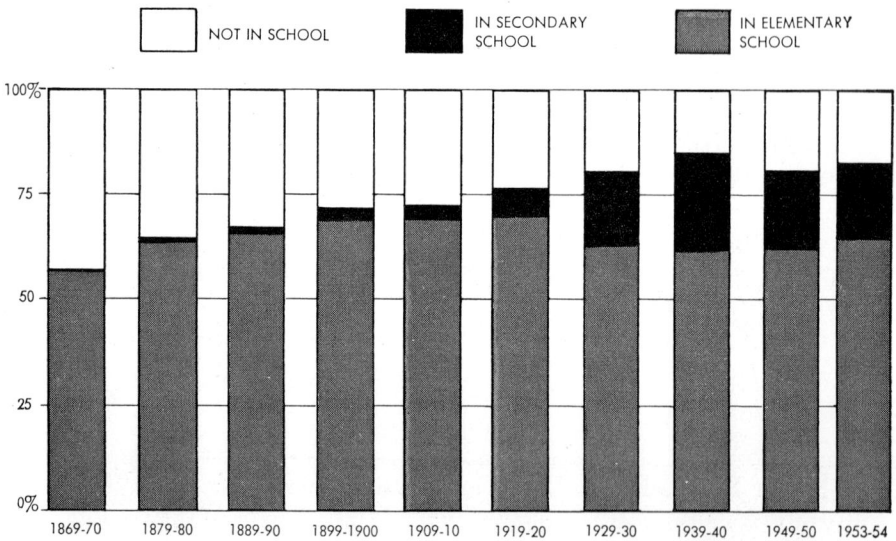

FIGURE 9:1   PERCENTAGE OF SCHOOL-AGE POPULATION ENROLLED IN THE PUBLIC SCHOOLS, 1869–1954

Source: U.S. Office of Education, *Biennial Survey of Education in the United States, 1952–54*, Chapter 1, "Statistical Summary of Education, 1953–54" (Washington, D.C.: U.S. Government Printing Office, 1957), p. 20.

Section III: The Educational Instrument—Public or Private?

BACKGROUND

Technical authority over education was from the beginning formally vested in the various Colonial governments by England. However, the primacy of religious authorities in matters of education was generally accepted by these governments. In the South, particularly, church authorities were delegated the right to supervise and control schools. In New England the civil authorities themselves took the initiative, although in fact there was

Chicago Sun-Times Photo

First School Day: A Chicagoan begins his formal education.

little separation between church and state during this period. The Massachusetts School Law of 1647 ordered that every township of fifty householders or more should appoint someone to teach all children to read and write. The New England schools were dominantly religious in purpose; but control by governmental authority created no special problem, since there was relative uniformity of religion. This was not the case in the middle colonies, whose population was more diverse in religious faith. Consequently, there grew in these colonies a demand on the part of religious groups to initiate and control their own schools. As the religious diversity of the Colonial population became more pronounced, the pattern of privately controlled church schools grew.

The Colonial trend of delegating school authority to private sources was reversed in the early days of the republic. Universal public support of elementary schools was firmly established. This grew partly out of what was felt to be a political need of the country—the achievement of national cohesion—and partly out of what was felt to be a democratic need—the equalization of educational opportunity.

The bitter and prolonged public debate about the elementary schools centered around the question of taxation. Each stage was typically reached only after a battle: first, taxation by local communities, with state permission, to support free education for all; then, state laws *requiring* certain minimum rates of school taxation. By the time of the Civil War, the principle of compulsory taxation for universal elementary education had been firmly established.

The most tentative beginnings were also made during this period to bring into being a publicly supported secondary school system. Some attempts were made to integrate existing private secondary schools into the public school system. The first public high school, English High School of Boston, was established in 1821. By 1860 there were about forty public high schools in the country.

Higher education also began to receive public funds. In their zeal, some state legislatures attempted to take over private colleges but were rebuffed by the Supreme Court; so they set about to establish their own colleges. The new states were aided by the federal grant of public lands for this purpose, and by 1860 there were twenty-one such state colleges in twenty states.

The great struggle during the post-Civil War period was the establishment of public support for free high schools. In 1862 the Supreme Court of Michigan ruled that it was legal for communities to impose taxes for the support of free high schools. Pointing to the existence of a state university, the court concluded that the state had intended everyone to have an equal opportunity to proceed on to higher education.

However, in 1901, the United States Commissioner of Education said: "It is doubtful that the Constitution permits the education of the people in free high schools. District schools are all right but our forefathers never intended to furnish a liberal education to all children at the expense of the taxpayer."[3] Taxpayers associations supported this point of view, as did the owners of private academies. But the pressure for free, tax-supported high schools was inexorable, much of it generated by the fact that large numbers of children, now being graduated from the tax-supported elementary schools, would not be able to continue their education except in free high schools. In 1860 there were about 40 free high schools in the country, in 1890 there were about 2,500, and in 1918 there were about 25,000.

Meanwhile, the private parochial school system, primarily Roman Catholic, was growing side by side with the public school system. In 1910, over a million children were enrolled in private Catholic parochial schools, representing well over 5 per cent of the total elementary-school population. Parochial high schools grew along with public high schools.

THE CURRENT ISSUES

The principle of public support for education has now been fully established on all levels. Since the achievement of universally free secondary education, the only possible area of advance is in higher education, where the *principle* of public support has already been established. Today, about half of the students enrolled in institutions of higher learning are enrolled in publicly supported and controlled institutions, and the proportion is increasing.

But the private parochial school system existing side by side with the public school system continues to grow. About 13 per cent of all elementary- and secondary-school students are enrolled in parochial schools. It is estimated that there are about 200,000 Protestant children attending some 3,000 Protestant parochial schools; a major proportion of these are supported by the Lutherans.[4] At least 9,000 children are enrolled in Jewish parochial schools. About three and a half million children—over 98 per cent of parochial school enrollments—are in Roman Catholic schools; these represent about 60 per cent of Catholic children of school age. Monsignor Frederick E. Hochwald, director of the Education Department of the National Catholic Welfare Conference, has said: "Every effort will be made to achieve the ideal of a place in the Catholic school for every Catholic child."[5]

---

[3] W. T. Harris, "Recent Growth of Public High Schools in the United States as Affecting the Attendance of Colleges," *Journal of Proceedings and Addresses,* National Education Association, 1901, p. 174.

[4] National Council of the Churches of Christ in the United States of America, *Information Service,* May 3, 1952, p. 1.

[5] A speech at a 1952 convention of the National Catholic Educational Association as reported in the *New York Times,* April 20, 1952.

The constitutional question of the right to maintain private schools has been established by the Supreme Court on at least two separate occasions. Between 1917 and 1921, in a postwar fever of nationalism, over thirty states passed laws requiring all instruction in schools to be given in English. In 1923 the Supreme Court ruled these laws unconstitutional on the ground that they interfered with the private rights of parents to seek for their children the kind of education they saw fit, within the framework of any reasonable regulations the state might lay down. In 1925, the "Oregon decision" of the Supreme Court prevented the closing-down of certain Catholic schools. It argued that though the state had the right to regulate both private and public schools and to compel attendance at some school, it had no right to compel attendance at a public school.

However, the existence of the parochial school system has continued to be a subject of criticism in some quarters. In 1952, James B. Conant, president of Harvard University, triggered a nation-wide debate by making the public statement that our national unity and principle of equal opportunity depended on all children attending the same school system. Professor John L. Childs, of Teacher's College, Columbia University, has suggested that, for

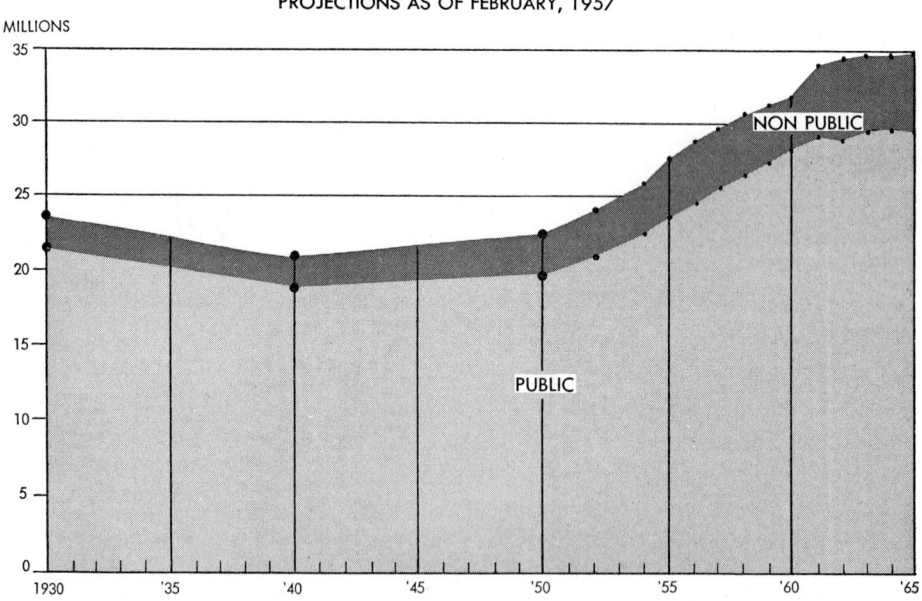

FIGURE 9:2 ELEMENTARY SCHOOL ENROLLMENTS, 1930 TO 1965

PROJECTIONS AS OF FEBRUARY, 1957

Source: U.S. Office of Education, Research and Statistical Services Branch, "Enrollments in Kindergarten and Grades 1–8 in Public and Nonpublic Day Schools: Continental United States, 1930, 1940, 1950, 1952, and 1954 (Actual); and 1955–1965 (Estimated)" (mimeographed report; Washington, D.C.: U.S. Department of Health, Education, and Welfare, May 26, 1958).

purposes of national unity, all children be required to spend at least half of their school lives in a public school.[6]

The chief argument of the supporters of the parochial school system is that religious and moral training is too important to be a casual part of a child's education. Religion, they say, must be a constant thread throughout education. They answer the charge of "divisiveness and cultural ghettoism" by stating that, to the contrary, the parochial school system reinforces the democratic concept of educational freedom and cultural diversity. Large elements of the population believe that their children can be educated properly only in schools of their own religion and that a separate private school system relieves the evils potential in a state monopoly of education.

Many critics depreciate the need for parochial schools by suggesting that effective religious training belongs in the church and home, and they add that the public schools produce no greater proportion of delinquents or smaller proportion of useful citizens than do the religious schools. This argument, of course, does not touch on the primary religious motivation be-

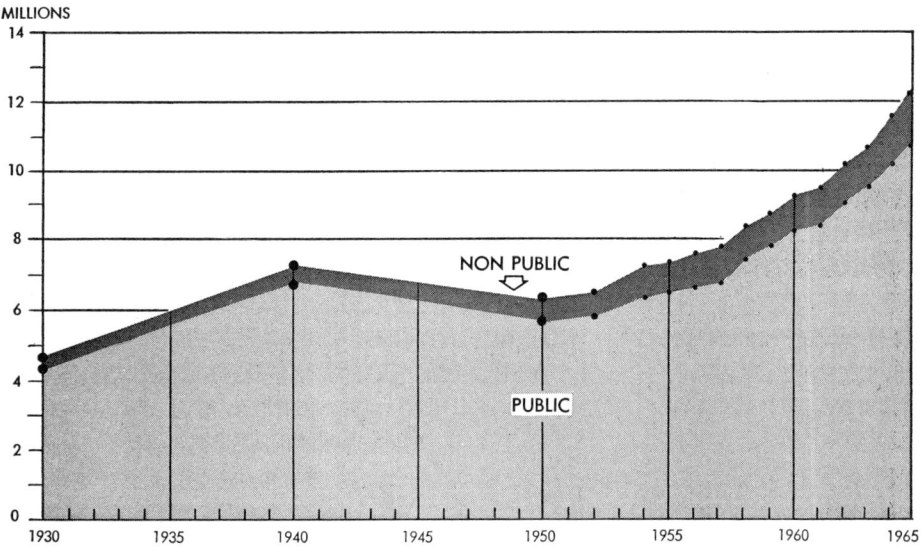

FIGURE 9:3 SECONDARY SCHOOL ENROLLMENTS, 1930 TO 1965

PROJECTIONS AS OF FEBRUARY, 1957

Source: U.S. Office of Education, Research and Statistical Services Branch, "Enrollments in Grades 9–12, Including Postgraduates in Public and Nonpublic Day Schools: Continental United States, 1930, 1940, 1950, 1952 and 1954 (Actual); and 1955–1965 (Estimated)" (mimeographed report; Washington, D.C.: U.S. Department of Health, Education, and Welfare, May 26, 1958).

---

[6] John L. Childs, "American Democracy and the Common School System," *Jewish Education*, **21** (1949), 32–37.

hind the parochial schools, which is not expressed in terms of general social but rather of specific religious values.

While three-fourths of the states provide by law that education in private schools shall be equivalent to that of public schools, some educational critics have complained that in most states inspection and regulation of parochial schools by state authorities is perfunctory and that the teaching personnel, equipment, and educational standards of some parochial schools compare unfavorably with those of the public schools.

It cannot be ignored that much of the criticism of the parochial schools stems from some historically rooted feelings about the Catholic Church itself. This often finds expression in the charge that education under authoritarian influence is not suitable training for democratic life.

However, the constitutional right of the parochial school system to exist is not currently in serious question. Current arguments supporting and criticizing the parochial schools revolve around another issue: How far, if at all, should public funds be used for the support of the parochial schools? The debate on this question runs constantly and sometimes feverishly through community life in America. The intensity of feeling is perhaps underestimated because, like the proverbial iceberg, most of it lies beneath the surface. The mass media and most civic leaders tend to treat the issue gingerly, airing publicly only its most dispassionate legal aspects.

The parochial school issue is a symptom as well as a cause of the still sharp Catholic-Protestant ideological conflict. No precise comparison is possible between membership figures offered by Protestant and Catholic sources. Most Protestant churches count as members only persons who have attained full membership, usually at the age of thirteen. Catholics regard all baptized persons, including children, as members. According to these measures, about 35 per cent of the American population belong to Protestant churches, while about 20 per cent is Catholic. About 3 per cent of the population is Jewish. Of course, most of the population who are not church members are ancestrally and culturally Protestant. However, Catholics, like Jews, are "visible" beyond their numbers, partly because of their heavy concentration in metropolitan centers.

The still-simmering historical conflict typically boils up when Catholic religious requirements touch on public matters. For example, the Catholic Church has been most prominent in its opposition to less stringent divorce laws; in its support of adoption procedures which require that children of Catholic parentage be placed only in Catholic homes; in its opposition to the practice of "planned parenthood" or its promotion by public institutions; in its attempt to remove "indecent" literature from the newsstands of the nation—an attempt which has sometimes been charged with being censorship. These are all continuing centers of controversy, which can presumably be argued on their own merits but often become invested with an emotionalism rooted in an earlier era of Protestant-Catholic conflict.

Public Aid to Private Schools

The parochial school issue engenders the most serious and consistent expression of Catholic-Protestant conflict. The parochial school is a bulwark of the Catholic Church. The Catholic community is sensitive to this fact, as are those who, for whatever motivation, have some fears of or antagonisms toward the Catholic Church in America.

Interreligious tensions seem to have had a rebirth in recent years, as witness the formation in 1948 of the organization called "Protestants and Other Americans United for Separation of Church and State" (POAU). This organization was launched with a manifesto signed by, among others, the president of the Princeton Theological Seminary, a Methodist bishop, and the president of the Southern Baptist Convention. This organization has grown rapidly, has set up local chapters, and has involved many prominent local Protestant clergymen throughout the country. POAU was vehement in its opposition to President Truman's proposal to appoint an ambassador to the Vatican, and it has been extremely active in opposing public aid to parochial schools on every level. In stating its opposition to such aid in its original manifesto, this organization declared: "We are determined to pursue a course that cannot be justly characterized as anti-Catholic, or as motivated by anti-Catholic animus."[7] The press and spokesmen of the Catholic Church, however, have maintained that this organization is mainly motivated by anti-Catholic prejudices, akin to those of the Ku Klux Klan.

In this interreligious issue are bound up, sometimes indistinguishably, genuine intellectual conviction and historical prejudice. It touches vitally on the basic problem of two major and proselytizing religions existing side by side in a democratic society. The question of public aid to parochial schools is in many ways a more delicate, probably a more enduring, and perhaps a more critical question than the more sensational matter of desegregation of schools.

The increasing financial burden on the parochial school system, as a result of the broadening of education in general, has sharpened this public debate. The annual cost of the Catholic school system is over a billion dollars. The necessity for capital expenditures to expand the system for a growing school population is proportionately at least as great as for the public schools. In the Catholic schools some 90 per cent of the teachers are nonsalaried members of religious orders, but there may soon develop the need to expand the lay teaching personnel.

[7] Joseph M. Dawson, *Separate Church and State Now* (New York: Richard R. Smith, 1948), p. 210.

On the surface, most of the debate about public aid to parochial schools has centered around two questions: whether this aid is constitutional, and whether the parents of parochial school children deserve some relief from "double taxation." The First Amendment to the Constitution reads: "Congress shall make no law respecting an establishment of religion or prohibiting the free exercise thereof." The Supreme Court interpreted this in 1946 as follows:

> Neither the state nor the federal government can set up a church nor pass laws which would aid one religion, aid all religions or prefer one religion over another.... No tax in any amount can be levied to support any religious activity or institution, whatever they may be called.[8]

In conformity with this interpretation, state constitutions and codes have established the principle that state funds cannot be used for parochial school purposes. But questions of further interpretation have arisen. Are there not ways, within this constitutional law, that the state can provide financial relief to the parochial school system? If there are such ways, should they not be implemented in light of the fact that the parochial school system has substantially relieved the financial burden of the state? Thirteen per cent of America's school children are being educated without expense to the state, although Catholic parents of parochial school children pay their tax share toward the support of public education. Critics of this argument reply that this is a wasteful and unwanted "saving" and that, in any case, public school education is of benefit to all members of society, not just to the parents of school children.

There are various patterns by which the parochial schools do or could conceivably obtain public support:

1. *Tax exemption.* The exemption of religious groups from taxation of property is generally accepted and is essential to the maintenance of parochial school systems. A full-fledged assault against tax exemption for parochial schools in the state of California was launched in 1952 by a taxpayers' association, which claimed that such exemption violated the constitutional provisions of the First Amendment. The California Supreme Court rejected the argument by a four-to-three vote in 1955; a year later the U.S. Supreme Court refused to review that decision, thereby indicating that the constitutionality of tax exemption for parochial schools was not at issue. In 1958 a referendum proposing abolition of tax exemption for parochial schools was defeated by California voters.

2. *Direct support.* It has already been noted that the direct grant of funds to parochial schools is prohibited by almost every state in the nation.

---

[8] *Everson v. Board of Education* (1946), 330 U.S. 1, 67 S Ct 504.

3. *Child-welfare grants.* It is possible for grants to be made by the state directly to parochial school children rather than to their schools. Such grants can be made for "auxiliary" welfare services available to all children in the state. The provision of milk and hot lunches for parochial school children is an example of a service to which no segment of the community takes exception. However, the providing of secular textbooks to parochial schools out of public funds is not so universally accepted as falling within the definition of welfare services to children.

The most controversial question of possible public support concerns transportation to parochial schools. With the increasing consolidation of schools, free transportation has become a significant item of educational expense. Over seven million public school pupils are transported each year at a cost of about a quarter of a billion dollars. About eighteen states provide free transportation for parochial schools on the grounds that this is aid and support to the pupils rather than to the schools. The New York Court of Appeals rejected as illegal the use of public funds for transportation to parochial schools on the basis that

the purpose of free transportation is to promote the interest of the private [religious] schools . . . . Without pupils there could be no schools. It is illogical to say that the furnishing of transportation is not an aid to the institution while the employment of teachers and furnishing of books, accommodations and other facilities are an aid.[9]

The dissenting opinion, however, declared that

The statute in question does not have the effect of giving public money, property or credit as an aid or maintenance of a religious school . . . . There is no benefit to the schools, except perhaps if one may conceive an accidental benefit in the sense that some parents might place their children in a religious school when they anticipate transportation provisions though they may hesitate to do so if the children were compelled to make their own way.[10]

The U.S. Supreme Court in the Everson case of 1947 specifically ruled that the transportation of parochial school students at public expense did not violate the federal Constitution, since such transportation was essentially a welfare service to the children. (See Adaptation 23, pp. 464–68.) In effect, the Court acknowledged in this decision that the parochial schools themselves might be aided by free transportation, but it held that where there is a clash between the provisions of the First Amendment and the welfare of children, the latter interest is supreme.

4. *Federal aid.* Federal aid to parochial schools could take the form of

---

[9] *Judd* v. *Board of Education* (1938), 278 New York 200, 15 N.E. 2d 576.
[10] *Ibid.*

URGE MEMBERS TO OPPOSE U. S. AID TO SCHOOLS

The Illinois State Chamber of Commerce urged its members...

'Emergency' in Schools to Continue? Decision Due

By William F. Smiley
Tribune Education Writer

Whether Utah will enter a... The other was a proposal for a continuing state aid program.

...mand another 454 for a total of 1,639 new classrooms needed by the end of the biennium.

...current taxes and reserves will provide all but $6,638,500. Only five districts of the state's 40...

School Merger Plan Faces Fight

By FRED TAYLOR
Staff Writer, The Birmingham News
Special to The Atlanta Journal-Constitution

MONTGOMERY, Ala., Sept. 6 — Twin proposals for consolidation of state-supported colleges in Alabama under a single board and merger of county and municipal schools into one system in each of the 67 counties held the attention of education leaders throughout the state.

And these movements, spearheaded by State Sen. A. C. Shelton of Calhoun, a veteran school leader, were certain to bring heated battling when the Legislature meets next spring...

Fred Taylor

Parents to Seek Arrest of Teacher

The parents of a suspended sixth grade student at School 37, Carlton and Orange, said last night they would seek a warrant for the arrest of a teacher who, they alleged, struck their 13-year-old daughter during an altercation at the school Monday.

The student, Patricia King, daughter of Mr. and Mrs. Wilbur Dobbs of 173 Maple St., was arrested and suspended from school following the incident. She is free pending a hearing...

113,000 Enrolled In Hudson

Increase Noted In 10 of 12 Communities

By DICK LISS

Hudson County is expected to follow the national trend of increasing elementary and high...

Education Of Public School Teachers Sets Off Big Row

This is the first of a series of six articles on teacher education and certification in New Hampshire. This first article surveys the problem. The second will discuss teacher certification requirements and the teachers college curricula. The third will present the defense of the teachers' colleges. The fourth will discuss what teachers' college students think of their program of studies. The fifth article is the considered view of a member of the Department of Education, and the last will be a summary of the situation...

...could improve. Critics of the present system reply "poorly" and demand sweeping changes.

What is Mr. Average Citizen supposed to believe 'midst the tumult and the shouting?...

CATHOLICS ADD 40 MILLION TO SCHOOL PLANS

5 Year Program to Meet Rush

BY WILLIAM O'SHEA
(Quigley Seminary, Senior)
(Picture on page 2)

Msgr. William E. McManus, superintendent of Catholic schools in Chicago, on the... with the... superior... "We... better sch... he satisfi... doing, Sa... o stagna... work."

Msgr. ... n 1939, s... postgradu... University Washingto... o 1957 h... ector of...

HOUSE VOTES 900 MILLIONS IN SCHOOL AID

Scholarships Stricken from Bill

Washington, Aug. 8 — The House passed a 900 million dollar aid-to-education... after stripping... scholarship pr...

ESTE AÑO?

Soon 4th Graders To 'Parlez Vous'

By SUE CONNALLY

Dallas school officials are considering a plan to introduce foreign language courses in elementary schools here, possibly this year, The News learned Thursday.

"I don't think the program will be delayed," declared R. L. Dillard Jr., member of the Dallas Board of Education.

"We will undoubtedly have a class in the experimental language arts section before midterm."

A survey to find out how many teachers are competent to teach such courses will be made "right after the beginning of school," he added.

Dillard said there is a possibility of starting with Spanish,... headed by E. O. Cartwright.

Although the teaching of foreign languages in elementary schools in the United States is scattered, educators have been giving it wider study in the last several years.

Dillard said he has been in correspondence with officials in upper state New York where such programs are in operation, and also noted that Washington, D.C. schools have foreign language taught in their elementary schools.

School Supt. W. T. White pointed out that there are "many practical aspects to be considered" in having the program. He named teacher supply, pupil and parental interest and time allotment...

RESULTS SOMETIMES INCREDIBLE

Educators Hail Teaching on TV

By RICHARD ASHWORTH

The Fulton County school system's first year of experience in educational television has shown vast new fields in which TV teaching can be employed.

New Grade School Reading Plan Demonstrated to Justice PTA

A crowd of approximately 150 people jammed the gymnasium of Justice Addition Grade School last night to learn of... plan for teaching... will be instituted... County Elementary... Grade School near Sha... Ernest B. C... superintendent... County Element... Chris Holt,... Grade School... gram for th... school's final P... meeting. Craddock and...

Schools. According to Craddock, every state in the union with the exception...

The Joplin plan for reading is carried on in grades four, five and six, with from three to eight dif...

High Point Man Heads Effort

Education of Retarded Child Is Growing in North Carolina

By Robert Marks
High Point Enterprise

TAYLOR KENNERLY
... Helping hand ...

...by Mrs. L. B. Bryant of Charlotte, President of the association last year. Mrs. Bryant is now its executive secretary and handles most of the correspondence and other paper work.

Other presidents have been Robin Hood of Marion and Dr. Courtland Davis of Winston-Salem. Dr. Davis is a member of the board of directors of the national association. Mrs. Paul Stoker of Lexington will become president this fall.

Major Problems

Kennerly says the association faces several major problems. One of the biggest, he says, is finding the local ch... would als... of state-in... for retar... years of... or over... ted to cit... or Goldsb...

The ass... first gene... fall. The... to the G... ceptional... lem.

Every Moment

Elected president of the new association, Kennerly spent every moment of his spare time for the next year working for the organization. Writing letters, making telephone calls, traveling extensively, he saw the association gradually acquire a solid foundation and begin to grow.

Kennerly, who two weeks ago resigned his position with the Federal Housing Administration in Greensboro to head the Taylor Kennerly Construction Co., devotes most of his spare time to the association. But the duties the president have been lighte...

Teacher Aides Suggested as Method Of Relieving Nation's School Problem

By G. K. Hodenfield
Associated Press

What the country needs — besides a good 10-cent cigar — is a miracle solution to the most critical problem facing American education today: the twin shortage of classrooms and good teachers.

There is no miracle to one suggested remedy. And yet it seems to promise better teaching, happier teachers. And maybe even an eventual end to the teacher shortage.

It's a simple remedy: Just hire untrained assistants to do the regular teachers' clerical and "housekeeping" chores, thus freeing the teachers for fulltime work with the pupils.

The idea has been suggested time and again, but hasn't seemed to catch on in the vast majority of school systems.

Tried in Area

It has been tried, and found workable. It's not expensive. Research indicates school costs would increase little, if any. Teachers find themselves with more time to devote to each type of learner, the slow, the average, the fast. This, in turn, challenges and inspires each student to do his best work.

[Montgomery County tried teacher aides in a few schools several years ago to assist teachers with extra-large classes. The plan was "not too favorably received," according to a school official, and was discontinued after a two-year trial. There are no plans now to try the system again.

In Fairfax County, two fully-qualified teachers are assigned to those classes which are on half-day sessions, in order to permit maximum use of teaching time.

[Other area school systems have not attempted the teacher aide method.]

With one important qualification, most of the teachers, superintendents, parents and even the pupils themselves who have participated in the plan are enthusiastic about it.

either direct aid or indirect child-welfare aid. Bitter debate has marked the introduction of various congressional bills to provide assistance to all schools. The dominant controversy and perhaps the chief deterrent to passage of any of these bills has been the parochial school issue.

Symptomatic of the emotion-wrought character of the issue was the series of public controversies over the introduction of a federal-aid bill into Congress in 1949 by Representative Barden of North Carolina. The bill proposed to limit aid to public schools; furthermore, it specifically excluded federal assistance for transportation or welfare services. Barden and his bill were attacked by Catholic spokesmen around the country as "bigoted," "un-American," and "anti-Catholic." Eleanor Roosevelt, in commenting on the controversy, said that the parochial school system was legitimate and worth while but that it should not be supported by public funds. She was thereupon charged with being prejudiced and anti-Catholic by Cardinal Spellman of New York. Tempers burned high, and congressmen reported that only on rare occasions had they received such a volume of mail on a single issue. Politically sensitive legislators took note of this deep and bitter division, which has been a block to passage of *any* federal-aid legislation.

Section IV: The Educational Method—Curriculum

BACKGROUND

A dual system of education characterized the Colonial period. For members of the upper class there was college, and there were Latin schools to prepare them for college. There were elementary schools and apprenticeship schools for the lower classes. This has become known as a "double-track" system, because there was no normal procedure for moving from one system to the other, and there was normally no place for the graduate of the elementary school to continue his education. The rise of the middle class, however, occasioned the rise of the so-called "English school," a private secondary school. This was not a college-preparatory school but a terminal school in primarily utilitarian subjects.

The "three R's" of the elementary schools in the Colonial period were reading, writing, and religious orthodoxy. There was little else. The curriculum of the Latin schools was heavily classical, revolving around Latin and Greek. The English school featured a much broader curriculum. The vocational skills of the new merchant class were taught: mathematics, bookkeeping, penmanship, surveying, and sometimes chemistry. The commercial languages of Portuguese, Spanish, and Italian were taught. However, the aspirations of the middle class were not strictly vocational. With new wealth, freedoms, and cultural horizons opening for them, they were anxious to acquire the more polite skills. So the private English schools included in their curriculums such subjects as French, music, dancing, arts and crafts, and advanced English grammar. Of religious content there was little or none.

The dual system of education began to break down with the phenomenal rise of the so-called "academies." The academies, which were privately supported, combined the content and objectives of the Latin school and the English school. For the first time under the same roof students could obtain either a utilitarian and terminal or a college-preparatory education. By 1860 there were well over six thousand such academies.

The "single-track" system of education became firmly established with the development of the free and comprehensive high school after the Civil War. In addition, the tendency became clear to extend the "single track" of public education in both directions. The kindergarten was instituted as the first rung in the educational ladder, and the concept of the junior college was introduced. Institutions of higher learning grew apace, both state and private; and graduate professional study on the university level began to come into its own.

By and large there was still a dominance of college-preparatory subjects in the high schools, but as they became more of a universal "people's college," the business and industrial subjects grew in proportion. By 1918 there were some subjects common to both terminal and college-preparatory students, although the split curriculum was still the order of the day.

THE CURRENT ISSUES

The American "single track" of publicly supported education now extends from kindergarten to higher education. Kindergartens are integrated into about 60 per cent of our school systems, and about 10 per cent of our cities operate preschool nurseries, while graduate professional training in many fields is an increasing part of the task of tax-supported state universities. Although about two-thirds of all institutions of higher learning are under private control, about half of all college and university students are in the publicly supported institutions.

Curriculum

The primary debate about curriculum still centers around the high schools, although its implications necessarily spread both downward and upward. The modern high-school curriculum is charged with the fulfillment of four major purposes: preparation for college; training in vocational and prevocational skills; training in citizenship skills; and personality development, or the development of those personal skills which relate to everyday living. The last two objectives presumably apply to *all* students.

The Whole Child: Mothers take notes on their children's behavior. The question: Is my child shy?

Consequently, the curriculum has tended to lose its compartmentalized character and to become more uniform for all students. There is provision, of course, for some specialization in certain commercial skills or toward certain college interests. There is increasing provision of specific craft skills for students with special needs. But the primary curricular emphasis is on the area of educational purpose common to all students. Perhaps the pioneer statement of modern curricular objectives was made by a committee of the National Education Association in 1918:

The purpose of democracy is so to organize a society that each member may develop his personality primarily through activities designed for the well-being of his fellow members and of society itself. Consequently education in a democracy both within and without the schools should develop within and without the individual the knowledge, interests, ideals, patterns and powers whereby he will find his place and use that place to shape both himself and society towards nobler ends.[11]

This "common" approach has developed not only out of the concept that education must train students to be members of a democratic society but also out of the belief that the high-school curriculum was not meeting the specific needs and interests of most young people. As a result of this belief, the so-called "life-adjustment" movement among educators appeared with new vitality after World War II. Educators pointed out that, while as many as 90 per cent of our youth could afford to remain through high school, only 80 per cent entered high school and only 50 per cent graduated.

The following explanation was offered of the mass "dropouts." Not more than 20 per cent of Americans are employed in skilled occupations which require extensive and specialized vocational training; about 20 per cent are in professional and technical occupations which require college and university training; the prime needs of the other 60 per cent, therefore, are neither vocational nor college-preparatory in nature. For this 60 per cent the purpose of high school was conceived to be that of training in "life-adjustment." But life-adjustment education is regarded as applying not only to this "forgotten" 60 per cent but to all students. "Life-adjustment education," concluded one national educators' work conference in 1948, "is designed to equip all American youth to live democratically with satisfaction to themselves and profit to society." [12]

This "common" approach led to a direct emphasis on practical problems of everyday life: diet, marriage, rearing of children, courtship, budgeting, investing, computing taxes, leisure-time skills, the art of conversation, talking to groups, engaging in politics. In some cases "how-to-do-it" subjects found their way into the curriculum. This has been one of the points of complaint made by many of the critics of modern education. Courses in folk-dancing, driver-education, and first aid are attacked as "frills and fads." What does it avail a citizenry, ask some critics, to learn how to apply first aid if it is not equipped to make decisions that may prevent an atomic war? Businessmen, parents, and others—sometimes college professors—who complain about the spelling and reading abilities of high-school graduates suggest that the time might be better spent on fundamentals. Organized taxpayers' groups often seize upon such "frill-and-fad" courses as dramatic reasons for opposing increased budgets for the schools.

While "how-to-do-it" courses have appeared, in widely varying degrees, in

[11] U.S. Bureau of Education, *Cardinal Principles of Secondary Education*, Bulletin 35 (2d ed.; Washington, D.C.: U.S. Government Printing Office, 1928), p. 9.
[12] U.S. Office of Education, *Life Adjustment Education for Every Youth* (Washington, D.C.: Federal Security Agency, 1948).

curriculums around the nation, they do not genuinely reflect the mainstream of life-adjustment education. As expressed by its chief advocates and practitioners, life-adjustment education does not have the object of de-emphasizing reading, writing, mathematics, science, or the social studies. On the contrary, it is claimed that its object is to make these basic studies more effective and meaningful. Unlike past eras, the schools are no longer peopled by those who have some special vocational or cultural motivation for learning traditional subjects in traditional ways. Rather, the bulk of students today must have their interest kindled and their learning related to their own present and future living situations. Mathematics is to be approached directly through a consideration of such daily problems as budgeting, buying insurance, investing, and computing taxes. Arithmetic is to be learned not for its own sake but as a tool for meeting life-problems. This does not mean, according to the advocates of life-adjustment education, *less* mathematics, but mathematics presented in a more purposeful way. English is to be approached by way of daily needs in communication and leisure habits. The social and natural sciences are no longer to be split up traditionally and artificially into isolated subjects. They are to be unified around specific and visible modern-day problems in the community, the nation, and the world.

Supporters of this educational movement point to comparative studies of the spelling ability of modern students and those of twenty-five and fifty years ago. The modern students are invariably superior as a group. This evidence is used to support the belief that many complaining members of the older generations are trapped by nostalgia for an excellence of "old-time" schooling that has no basis in fact. It is held that this new curriculum approach is required to meet the needs and interests of a majority of our expanding school population, so many of whom are actually dropping out of school or are at least receiving little benefit from it because their needs and interests are not now being met.

Those who support the traditional curriculum insist that the life-adjustment approach is an abdication of educational responsibility. It is not for the teachers to succumb to the trivial interests of their students, but rather it is their mission to build an intellectual interest even where none exists. The prime purpose of education is to help create a thinking individual. It is argued that this is indeed the most effective "common" approach for meeting all four of modern education's major objectives. The student must be given "an education, not a head full of helpful hints." If he is to get this education, this basic equipment for living, he cannot avoid the orderly and often grinding study of facts, theories, and methods of analysis discovered and developed by the various disciplines.

Of course the traditionalists do not proscribe the relating of this classroom knowledge to the larger problems of current life. The two approaches, in practice, are not totally dissimilar; only at the poles of rigid and doctrinaire theory are their virtues, or evils, mutually exclusive. While conflict may be sharp in the realm of educational philosophy, actual school practices are usually eclectic and tend to conform to neither philosophic extreme. Each school system must be evaluated individually to determine its excesses or deficiencies.

Teaching Methods

Pedagogical methods and curriculum content are indivisible. When educators talk about a school being "child-centered" rather than "subject-centered," they are talking about curriculum content as well as teaching method. The cornerstone of good pedagogy is to arrange subject matter in a way that will interest and motivate the pupils. This is a premise, for example, of life-adjustment education.

The roots of this emphasis on life-adjustment in teaching methods are to be found in the educational philosophy identified with the pragmatist philosopher, John Dewey, and popularly identified as "progressive education." This educational philosophy was concerned not just with sound intellectual training but with sound personality development—in other words, with "the whole child." The same basic teaching methods were claimed to be effective for the development of both the intellect and the personality of the child. Extending the "object-lesson" technique, this educational philosophy holds that the study of a subject ought to be carried on in life-situations which are familiar to the child. For example, a school "store" is set up, complete with cash registers, and the study of arithmetic is carried on in relation to such everyday problems as making change. Under such circumstances, it is said, the children learn more quickly and surely as a result of being more thoroughly and consistently self-motivated to learn. But, in addition, such a situation is an actual life-situation rather than an artificial one. Education, the maxim runs, *is* life, rather than a preparation for life. Thus education in life-situations does more than develop intellectual skills. The child interacts with other children and, under skillful guidance, can also develop skills in human relations and a mature sense of responsibility toward others not possible in a rigid classroom situation.

Many educators claim, however, that the application of these concepts has gone far beyond their proper or intended scope and has been abused, to the disadvantage of education. Some feel that pedagogical methods should not be allowed to deflect education from its ultimate purpose of providing intellectual training. It is easier to educate a child if you can interest him; but interesting him is not in itself education. A good teacher should spend as much effort as possible in advancing the social adjustment of the child, but a well-adjusted child is not, per se, an educated child. Attempts to motivate small children are commendable, but in the higher grades, and especially in the high schools, such methods are misplaced and time-wasting.

In any event, the term "progressive education," applied originally to advanced pedagogical practices in the lower grades and admittedly a major contribution to teaching methods, has virtually lost its meaning. The term is now incrusted with many years of excess and of general public misunderstanding. It is used by different people to describe different practices. Consequently, the use of the term more often confuses than clarifies public discussion.

Controversial Subjects and Academic Freedom

The conception of the school as a place where universal citizenship training can take place has brought into sharp focus the question of how the school should deal with controversial public issues.

A traditionalist view is that the school should concentrate on the analytical study of history and other subjects to enable the future citizen to deal with these problems on his own. Another point of view, not largely held within educational circles, is that the schools should uncritically indoctrinate the prevailing values of the American society of which it is merely an arm.

The modern educational approach to the social sciences would, on the other hand, typically *start* with current issues as they actually appear in communities and encourage pro-and-con discussion of controversial subjects.

Against the background of cold-war tensions, this has been one of the most disruptive areas of debate about the public schools. Often the issue is posed in terms of whether Communists should be allowed to teach, but in actuality this has been one of the least controversial questions. The National Education Association has declared that membership in the Communist party and "the accompanying surrender of intellectual integrity render an individual unfit to discharge the duties of a teacher in this country." [13] The American Federation of Teachers has also upheld the doctrine that membership in the Communist party disqualifies a teacher and is grounds for his dismissal. There is a minority opinion in both organizations, shared by the Association of University Professors, that a teacher should not be automatically disqualified by membership in a subversive organization but should rather be judged by his conduct in a classroom. To dismiss a chemistry teacher who is a member of the Communist party but who does not bring his politics into the classroom is not an act of educational protection,

---

[13] Educational Policies Commission, *American Education and International Tensions* (Washington, D.C.: National Education Association, 1949), pp. 39–40.

it is argued, but of economic sanction. Critics of this position point out that any teacher is potentially able to influence youth, and his exercise of that influence cannot be constantly monitored. Given the discipline and ideology of the Communist party, the state has the right and the duty to protect itself by refusing to hire teachers who are members of the party. This sentiment has prevailed.

Since World War II the proscription of Communists has often been extended to those considered "suspect." The Feinberg law, passed by the New York State Legislature in 1949, ordered the dismissal of all teachers who belonged to any organization which the state Board of Regents deemed subversive, presumably including the many "front" organizations which had been set up by the Communist party. The U.S. Supreme Court ruled in 1952 that the law was constitutional. As the majority decision of the Court explained,

> the school authorities have the right and the duty to screen the officials, teachers and employees as to their fitness to maintain the integrity of the schools . . . . One's associates, past and present, as well as one's conduct may properly be considered in determining fitness and loyalty. From time immemorial one's reputation has been determined in part by the company he keeps . . . ; we know no rule, constitutional or otherwise, which prevents the state, when determining the fitness or loyalty of such persons from considering the organizations and persons with whom they associate . . . in the exercise of its police power to protect the schools from pollution and thereby to defend its own existence.[14]

The minority Supreme Court position objected that

> the present law proceeds on a principle repugnant to our society—guilt by association . . . . Youthful indiscretions, mistaken causes, misguided enthusiasm, all long forgotten, become the ghosts of a harrowing present . . . . Fearing condemnation, [the teacher] will tend to shrink from any association that bestirs controversy. In that manner freedom of expression will be stifled . . . . That is only part of it . . . ; spying and surveillance with accompanying reports cannot go hand and hand with academic freedom.[15]

In addition, a number of states have enacted legislation requiring special loyalty oaths to be signed by schoolteachers. Most of the teachers' organizations, including those which would support the dismissal of Communist teachers, oppose these special oaths. Some of the oaths are vaguely worded and could conceivably lead to dangerous state control over teachers' attitudes. It is argued that they do not actually serve the purpose of revealing subversives, who will of course sign the oaths, but that they do serve to

[14] *Adler* v. *Board of Education* (1952), 342 U.S. 485, 72 S Ct 380.
[15] *Ibid.*

raise to exaggerated proportions in the public mind the problem of subversiveness among teachers.

In many communities the public furor over this emotion-charged issue has resulted in the muting of controversial issues in the classroom. A poll of 250 social-science teachers in the Los Angeles school system in 1954 revealed that 53 per cent felt less free to discuss "all phases of social studies, history, geography, political science and international relations" than they had five years before. Over 20 per cent of these teachers said they felt that it was dangerous for them to discuss the Bill of Rights in the classroom. Over half of them felt that students "are being deprived educationally as a result of the uproar about controversial subjects." [16]

Religion in the Curriculum

The movement toward public support of education meant that the problem of religious education for a religiously diverse population had to be resolved. A Massachusetts law of 1827 stipulated that a town school committee "shall never direct any school books to be purchased to be used in any of the schools . . . which are calculated to favor any particular sects or tenets." As a substitute for sectarian religious teaching, Horace Mann and the educational leaders of the state attempted to introduce a "common-core" religion into the school, i.e., those elements of the prevalent religions that are free from sectarian controversy. By the orthodox religionists, Mann and his followers were accused of creating immoral schools which produced irreligious delinquents. But the major complaint was raised primarily by those who claimed that this "common-core" religion was a Protestant common core, free only of differences among the Protestant sects. As the Roman Catholic population grew, especially in New England and the Middle Atlantic states, this complaint became increasingly cogent. The curriculum of the public schools began to lose its religious emphasis.

After World War I, organized pressures developed to return to the public school curriculum some of the religious content which had been lost during the buildup of tax-supported schools. These pressures were renewed after World War II. Organized Protestant forces, traditionally supporters of separation of church and state, have been the consistent base of this movement toward more religion in the schools. Organized Catholic forces, most outspoken in their belief that religious training belongs in the schools, have generally opposed this movement, with notable and relatively recent exceptions. Organized Jewish forces have been in opposition to all religious manifestations in the schools, with only rare exceptions.

Public arguments for more religious emphasis in the schools have leaned on the premise that religious education is an antidote for delinquency,

[16] *Time,* **63** (April 5, 1954), 46.

crime, and subversive philosophies. Further, if the schools are to reflect American society, they should reflect the religious basis of that society. Finally, to exclude religion from the schools is to give aid to atheism, which was not the intent of the First Amendment. The answer has been made that there is no indication that religious training, of the limited kind possible in the schools, has any effect on delinquency, crime, or subversion. Indeed, delinquency research supports the belief that there is no connection. Rather, one of the prime functions of the schools is to serve as a unifying force in a diverse America. Any emphasis on religion is necessarily a divisive force.

The varying patterns of support and opposition to religion in the schools have developed around different interpretations of the First Amendment and of the term "nonsectarian." There is general agreement that the public school curriculum cannot legally favor any one religious sect as against another. Some insist that the First Amendment meant only this; as long as no sectarian bias was present, it did not mean to set up an impenetrable barrier between religion and the schools. Others insist that an impenetrable barrier between education and religion, whether sectarian or nonsectarian, was indeed the intent of the First Amendment. But, even if "nonsectarian religious aid" is to be permitted to the public schools, how is the standard to be applied in practice? The evaluation has to be made for each of the several types of "religious aid" which have been suggested for the public schools:

1. *Bible-reading.* This is perhaps the most prevalent of the several practices; typically it consists of reading certain passages from the Bible each day at assembly or in the classroom. Over thirty states have *some* form of Bible-reading in some of the schools in the state. The Supreme Court has never specifically ruled on the constitutionality of Bible-reading in the schools, although it has ruled that the exclusion of the Bible does not violate constitutional rights. Decisions of the state courts have differed, but the majority have supported the legality of Bible-reading. Most of these decisions have been based on the argument that the Bible is nonsectarian, especially when the selections are from the Old Testament.

However, the basic argument against Bible-reading remains: that it is a breach in the wall separating church and state and violates the constitutional right of all students to freedom of conscience. Not only should children of Catholic families not be forced to listen to the Protestant version of the Bible, even occasionally, but children of nonbelieving families should not be forced to listen to any version. There are usually provisions for students to be excused from these sessions at parental request, but it is argued that this is a divisive procedure and one that imposes unconstitutional duress on the students involved.

2. *Released time.* The released-time program typically excuses children about an hour and a half before the end of the school day, perhaps once

a week, so that they can attend their respective churches for religious instruction. Only those children who have parental permission are so released. The others remain in school for a study program or some other activity. The school administers the program to the extent of keeping attendance records and making other administrative arrangements.

The released-time plan originated in Gary, Indiana, in 1913, has grown in use since World War II, and is estimated to be in operation in about 1,000 communities around the nation. Only 14 states have specific laws permitting such a plan, but many school districts in other states have adopted the scheme in the absence of specific prohibitions.

However, some communities have reported abandonment of a released-time plan because of insufficient participation. The statistics available reveal that the largest enrollment comes from Catholic students in public schools. In New York, for example, 81 per cent of the children released are Catholic, although only about 25 per cent of the population is Catholic. A survey in Chicago in 1948 showed that only 4,500 of the 18,000 children released were Protestant.[17]

Protestant forces have historically promoted the released-time program in the public schools. At one time this promotion was made in the face of the opposition of Catholic groups. This opposition has faded, and Catholic participation in these programs is characteristically strong. Conversely, some Protestant groups have found the released-time program less effective than they had once envisioned and are concentrating more of their energies on the enactment of Bible-reading programs, which would reach a larger number and wider variety of public school students.

Two recent decisions of the Supreme Court have dealt with released-time programs. In 1948, in the McCollum case, the Supreme Court ruled that the released-time program in the schools of Champaign, Illinois, was unconstitutional. In 1952, in the Zorach case, the Supreme Court ruled that the released-time program of the State of New York was constitutional. The majority opinion in the latter case pointed out that in the Champaign program the instructors came to the schools and used the classrooms for religious instruction, while in the New York plan the released students went out to their own religious centers. In other words, if a program uses tax-supported facilities, it is illegal; if it merely suspends operations to allow students voluntarily to attend their own religious centers, it is legal.

The constitutional question, though officially settled for the time being, still rages in debate. Three sharply dissenting opinions were written by three of the Supreme Court justices in the Zorach case. They felt that the physical use of school property was a trivial difference between the Cham-

[17] "Religious Instruction on Time Released from Public School," *The Humanist,* 7 (Spring, 1948).

paign and New York plans and that the two plans were the same—and both unconstitutional—in one essential: they both used school administrative machinery to promote private religious instruction. The schools were not really "suspending operations"; they were only doing so on the condition that the released students attended religious classes. "The First Amendment," wrote Justice Black, "has lost much if the religious follower and the atheist are no longer to be judicially regarded as entitled to equal justice under the law." [18]

Supreme Court Justice Jackson wrote in his dissent: "The wall which the Court was professing to erect between Church and State has become even more warped and twisted than I expected. Today's judgement will be more interesting to students of psychology and of the judicial processes than to students of constitutional law."

These sharp words perhaps serve to underline the extent to which the religious question in a creedally diverse America is still a living, powerful, and complex historical undercurrent. It also serves to indicate that at present the religious question is often formulated as a public school question.

3. *Core religious instruction.* Some attempts have been made to distinguish between religious exercises as such and instruction in those common moral and spiritual values which rise from religious precepts. For example, a Los Angeles "guiding statement" for the teaching of moral and spiritual values starts off with seven versions of the Golden Rule from seven different religions. Nonsectarian as they may be in intent, these programs appear to many to be "religious" in nature and to raise again some controversial questions. A proposed New York City public schools guiding statement on moral and spiritual values indicated that "the public schools must reinforce the program of the home and church in strengthening belief in God." The Catholic Archdiocese of New York supported this contention; the Protestant Council was deeply divided; the Board of Rabbis was opposed. Supporters of this statement claimed that to ignore God as the source of moral law was, at the very least, to give public aid to atheism, which was not the purpose of the First Amendment. Critics claimed that *any* attempt to "strengthen belief in God" was outside the authority and competence of the schools; furthermore, it would inevitably lead to sectarian emphases. Many educators feel that the development of moral values has always been a responsibility of the good teacher, whether or not he employs explicit religious precepts. The Educational Policies Commission of the National Education Association concluded: "Schools that exemplify moral values are better than lessons that preach them." [19]

[18] *Zorach* v. *Clauson* (1952), 343 U.S. 306, 72 S Ct 679.
[19] Educational Policies Commission, *Moral and Spiritual Values in the Public Schools* (Washington, D.C.: National Education Association, 1951), p. 61.

Section V: Meeting the Problem

MAKING THE DECISIONS

At the heart of the various school issues are value decisions which the citizenry must make on matters which are not uniquely attached to the schools. However, these school issues provide an opportunity for citizens to deliberately consider these values within a specific and practical context. Such deliberate consideration has been typically complicated by a number of factors and attitudes:

1. The oft-held attitude that broad educational principles, as well as methods, are highly technical matters best left to the pedagogues.
2. The prevalent attitude that those laymen who should be most interested in monitoring the educational system are the parents of school children.
3. The desire of many taxpayers and taxpayers' groups to hold down educational costs.
4. The vocal dissatisfaction of some parents, employers, and others with the educational "products" of the schools.
5. In an era of cold war, sharp ideological debate, and political machinations, the real or expressed fear that the schools are engines of misguided social thought.
6. The belief in many circles that there is a rising tide of delinquency, irreligion, and a general loss of moral tone.
7. The deliberate stimulation of "attacks" on the schools by organized propaganda groups. These attacks characteristically attempt to wrap up all possible fears into one package. The average citizen is unable to separate one issue from another or the genuine issues from the spurious.

The only specific antidote which the organized community can apply to this tangle of confusion and avoidance of real issues is the provision of machinery to stimulate public interest, public knowledge, and public participation in school affairs. In the words of the Committee for the 1955 White House Conference on Education:

In the final analysis, it is only the public which can create schools and nurture them . . . . Schools depend upon the public not only for their material support but for a sense of direction . . . . Even the best professional school administrators and teachers cannot take the place of public interest; they can only be the instruments of it; [but] public interest is aroused only by knowledge of problems and intentions, and it can exist only if the public can play an active part in school affairs.[20]

The traditional citizens' organization concerned with the public schools is, of course, the Parent-Teacher Association, founded at the turn of the century, which now has more than 7 million parents as members in about 38,000 units. The PTA, however, does not involve the total community; it is geared primarily for the member as parent rather than as general citizen. Since World War II, over 5,000 local "Citizens' Committees" have been initiated to help meet the need of full public participation, and a national organization now exists to promote such committees.

The local citizens' committees are typically independent but attempt to maintain a co-operative working relationship with the legally established authorities. Involving as wide a cross section of the community as possible, these committees study and make recommendations on problems pertinent to the schools.

A White House Conference on Education was called by the President of the United States in December, 1955. Representatives from state conferences, two-thirds of whom were noneducators, attended the White House Conference and drew up recommendations on several fronts, based on local thought and experience. Among the recommendations for increased citizen knowledge and participation were these: [21]

1. School districts should utilize the services of citizens' committees which are broadly representative of the community to act as advisory bodies to the board of education. Many have been initiated by boards of education, but they can also be initiated by any responsible group or individual. State-wide citizens' committees have been effective in co-ordinating the efforts of community groups.

2. Every school district should have regularly scheduled conferences devoted to the re-examination of school problems and progress. Both laymen and professional educators should take part, but the laymen should be in the majority. These annual or biennial conferences should culminate in state-wide conferences. Periodically the need for a national conference should be considered.

3. In both conferences and standing committees, all community organizations, including businessmen's associations, labor unions, veterans' organizations, women's clubs, and civic, fraternal, and service groups should be involved.

4. With few exceptions, meetings of both local and state boards of educa-

[20] Committee for the White House Conference on Education, *A Report to the President* (Washington, D.C.: U.S. Government Printing Office, 1956), p. 7.
[21] *Ibid.*, pp. 83 ff.

tion should be open, with dates and agenda publicized in advance and results made public.

5. School leaders and those responsible for mass media should work together to present a steady flow of accurate facts about the schools. Other public-relations techniques, such as special "open-house" days, "school-and-business" days, or special programs with business, labor, and other segments in the community, should be emphasized.

6. School buildings should be used as community centers for adult education, social events, and any worthy purpose.

7. Organizations working for a closer relationship between parents and teachers (PTA) should be encouraged to emphasize programs and activities explaining school policies.

8. Schools should teach students more about schools—their history, role, and problems.

STAFFING THE SCHOOLS

It is self-evident that, given sound school policies, facilities, and community participation, the success of an educational system finally rests in the hands of its teachers. There is a critical shortage of teachers. The great rise in the birth rate during and after World War II and the fact that an increasing percentage of children are going to school mean that more teachers will be needed every year. Every year over 125,000 new teachers are needed in the public elementary and high schools. In addition there is a backlog need of at least 80,000 teachers to relieve already overcrowded classrooms and to replace unqualified teachers. But the schools are getting only about 60,000 new teachers a year from all teacher-training institutions. The number of new teachers is declining, while the number of teachers on emergency or substandard certificates is growing.

Major contributing factors to the teacher shortage seem to be low salaries, overwork, and low status.

Low Salaries

Teachers comprise the only major occupational group whose real earnings have fallen since 1940; the real earnings of industrial workers, for example, have gone up about 50 per cent. The average salary in elementary schools ranged in 1956 from about $3,000 in small towns to $4,800 in large towns; the range in high schools was from $4,000 to $5,500. By contrast, workers in the automobile industry in 1956 averaged $4,900 and railroad conductors $6,600. The schools find it difficult to compete with private industry for the services of college graduates. Some 80,000 teachers leave the school system every year. This failure to compete is particularly critical in certain fields, such as science and mathematics.

Overwork

Already 90 per cent of the nation's classes are overcrowded. With an educationally desirable maximum of 25 pupils to a class, 40 or more in one room is not unusual. This creates not only pedagogical but disciplinary problems. In addition, the teacher is called upon to handle extracurricular activities, including lunchroom and study-room supervision.

Low Status

Low salary schedules and the imposition of nonprofessional duties are also interpreted as signs of the relatively low status of the teaching profession at the present time. This is a less tangible but clearly strong factor in

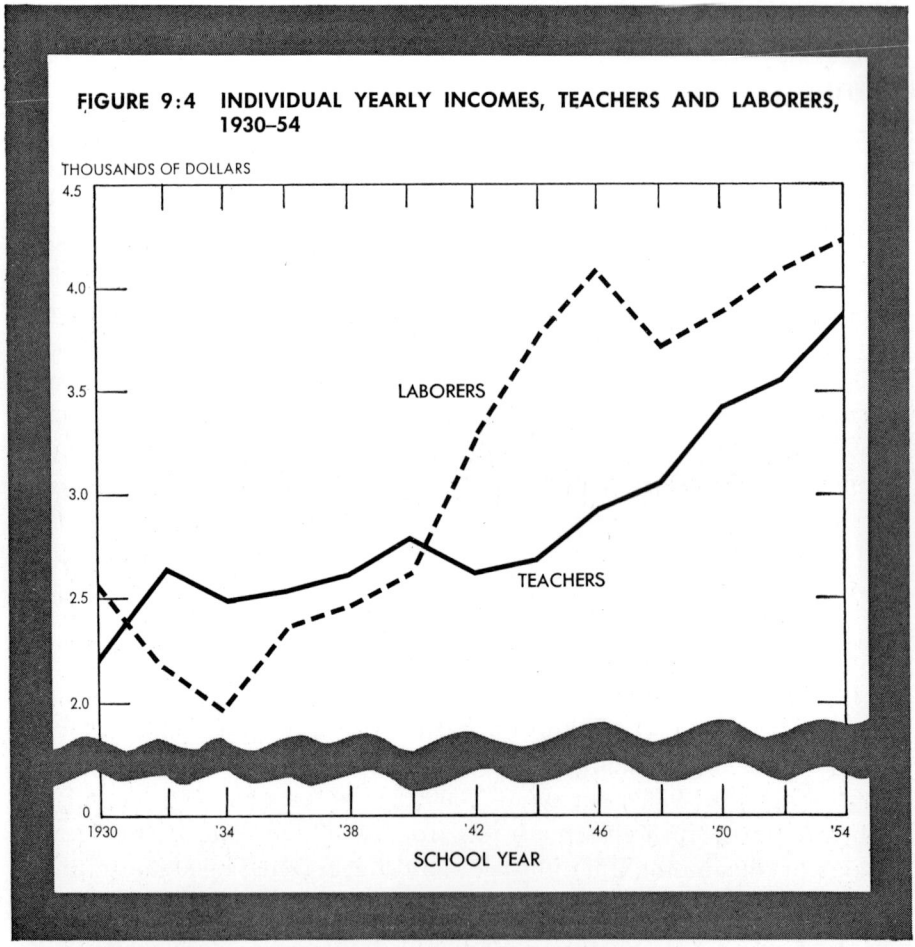

Source: U.S. Office of Education, *Biennial Survey of Education in the United States, 1952–54*, Chapter 1, "Statistical Summary of Education, 1953–54" (Washington, D.C.: U.S. Government Printing Office, 1957), p. 31.

reducing the competitive position and professional character of teaching.

The recommendations of the White House Conference on Education included the following: [22]

1. Teachers' salaries must be competitive with those in private industry.

2. There should be merit-recognition for teachers. However, proposals for merit salary raises have been opposed by many teachers' groups fearful of the arbitrary standards which might result. Salary increases made on the basis of continuing professional training are now a standard part of many salary schedules.

3. Teachers' jobs should be analyzed to see which duties can be safely and economically delegated to nonteaching personnel. Some experiments have already been made with "teachers' assistants" to fill general supervisory and extracurricular roles.

4. College programs for the preparation of teachers should be "made more functional, freed from unnecessary repetition, geared to the abilities

[22] *Ibid.,* pp. 34 ff.

Learning by TV: These young children are listening to a French lesson.

LIFE Photo by Lisa Larsen; © 1956, Time, Inc.

of the better students and should provide greater emphasis on practical classroom experience." In addition, there should be more financial assistance provided to capable students to enable them to complete their professional education.

5. There should be intensive programs for the professional preparation of former teachers who have been out of classroom service for a long time, liberal-arts graduates who have not prepared for teaching, and inadequately prepared teachers now working on emergency certificates. In recent years, for example, the Ford Foundation has made special grants to colleges and students for a program to provide professional training to liberal-arts graduates.

6. Special behavior problems should not be the central responsibility of classroom teachers. The White House Conference suggested that "parents have full responsibility for the deportment of their children during the preschool years, and they must also carry their full share of responsibility for discipline throughout the years of school attendance." The addition of qualified counselors and psychiatric personnel to the school staff would also serve to reduce the total responsibility of the teacher.

7. A stronger program should be undertaken to promote teaching as a profession among high-school and college students.

FINANCING THE SCHOOLS

The teacher-shortage problem is primarily, though not entirely, a matter of adequate community financing. There is also a serious problem of raising funds for additional school construction. For almost two decades, from 1930 to 1948, school construction lagged. During the depression credit was restricted, interest rates were high, and the public refused to support bond issues. With the advent of World War II and again during the Korean campaign, there were restrictions on the use of building materials. The increasing birth rate and rate of school attendance have further aggravated the situation. In the past eighty years, for example, the population has tripled, but high-school attendance has multiplied about seventy-five times. About a quarter of a million additional classrooms were needed in 1956, while the construction rate was only about 60,000 a year. In addition, in the interests of sheer safety, one out of every five schools needs to be remodeled or demolished, and it is estimated that this would cost about $15 billion. A final complication rests in the great shifts of population that have taken place within the country in the past two decades. Almost half the states reported at the White House Conference in 1955 that they were losing rather than gaining ground in the continuing battle for new school construction.

Public school costs—a total of over $12 billion for elementary and secondary schools in 1958 [23]—are still primarily supported by local community revenues, although the proportion of state support has been steadily increasing. In 1890, 76 per cent of public school support came from the local governments and less than 19 per cent from the states; in 1954, 61 per cent came from the local governments, while 37 per cent came from the states. The disparity in support among the states was quite marked, however. Delaware provided about 89 per cent of school support, but some other states furnished 5 per cent or less.

It has been pointed out that school costs are not really outstripping the nation's ability to pay for them. It is estimated that the number of children of school age will have increased by 34 per cent from 1955 to 1965, while the gross national product during the same period will have increased by 44 per cent. The following factors seem to stand in the way of adequate financing.

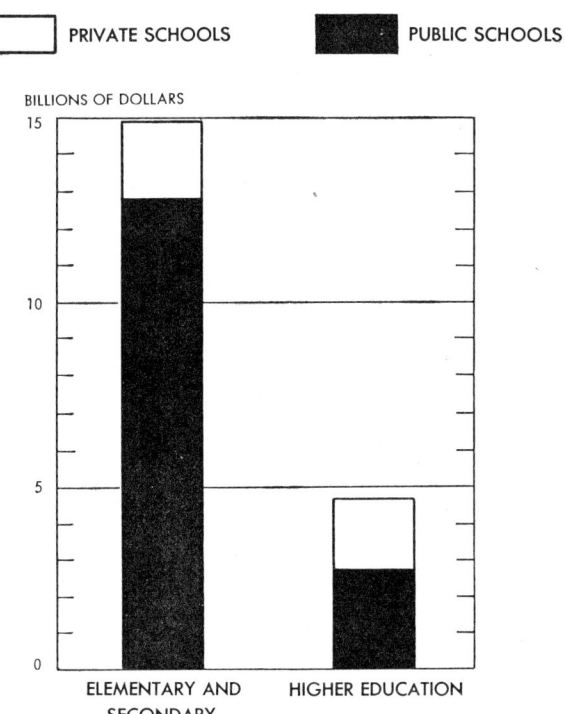

FIGURE 9:5 EXPENDITURES FOR EDUCATION, U.S., 1957–58

Source: U.S. Office of Education, Research and Statistical Services Branch, "Estimated Expenditure, Including Capital Outlay, by Level of Instruction and by Type of Control, Continental United States, 1957–1958" (mimeographed report; Washington, D.C.: U.S. Department of Health, Education, and Welfare, January 8, 1958).

---

[23] U.S. Office of Education, *Estimated Expenditures, 1957–1958* (Washington, D.C.: U.S. Government Printing Office, 1958).

1. The hesitancy of the taxpaying public to support bond issues and tax rates sufficient to fully meet public school needs.

2. The widely differing ability of local school districts to support their schools. Some districts are markedly less wealthy than others. Some have a relatively low legal limit on the tax rate they may impose. In addition, assessment practices in relation to the true value of property vary widely. Since most of the local revenue for public schools comes from property taxes, these practical factors are significant.

3. The wide disparity among states in their ability to support local school systems. The income per child of school age is six times greater in New York, the wealthiest state in the nation, than in Mississippi, the poorest. However, the proportion of total income expended on education is greater in Mississippi than in New York. For example, the school revenue per classroom unit in New York State in 1954 was $9,675; for Mississippi it was $2,404. Yet in Mississippi 2.7 per cent of the total income of the people in the state was spent on education, while only 2.2 per cent of the income of New York State was used for this purpose. Or, to put it another way, the national average of revenue per classroom was $7,025 per state—well over twice that of Mississippi—while the national average of income percentage used for education was 2.7 per cent, the same as that of Mississippi. Eleven states were able to provide less than $5,000 per classroom unit for educational expenditure.

FIGURE 9:6 SOURCES OF INCOME FOR PUBLIC SCHOOLS, 1948–58

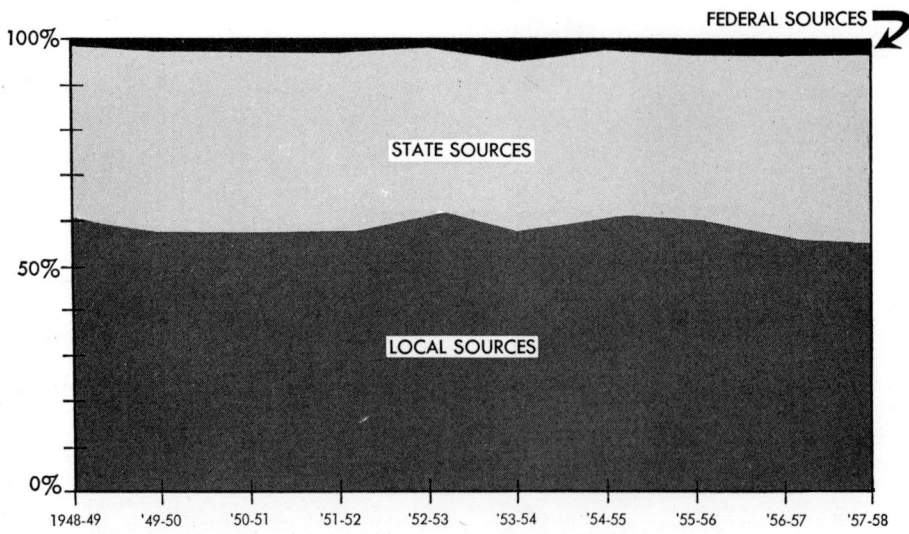

Source: National Education Association, Research Division, *Advance Estimates of Public Elementary and Secondary Schools for the School Year 1957–58* (Washington, D.C.: National Education Association, November, 1957), p. 16.

MEETING THE PROBLEM 449

The White House Conference on Education offered these general recommendations: [24]

1. Each state should reorganize local school districts so that all will have

FIGURE 9:7 NATIONAL INCOME AND EXPENDITURES FOR EDUCATION, 1929–58

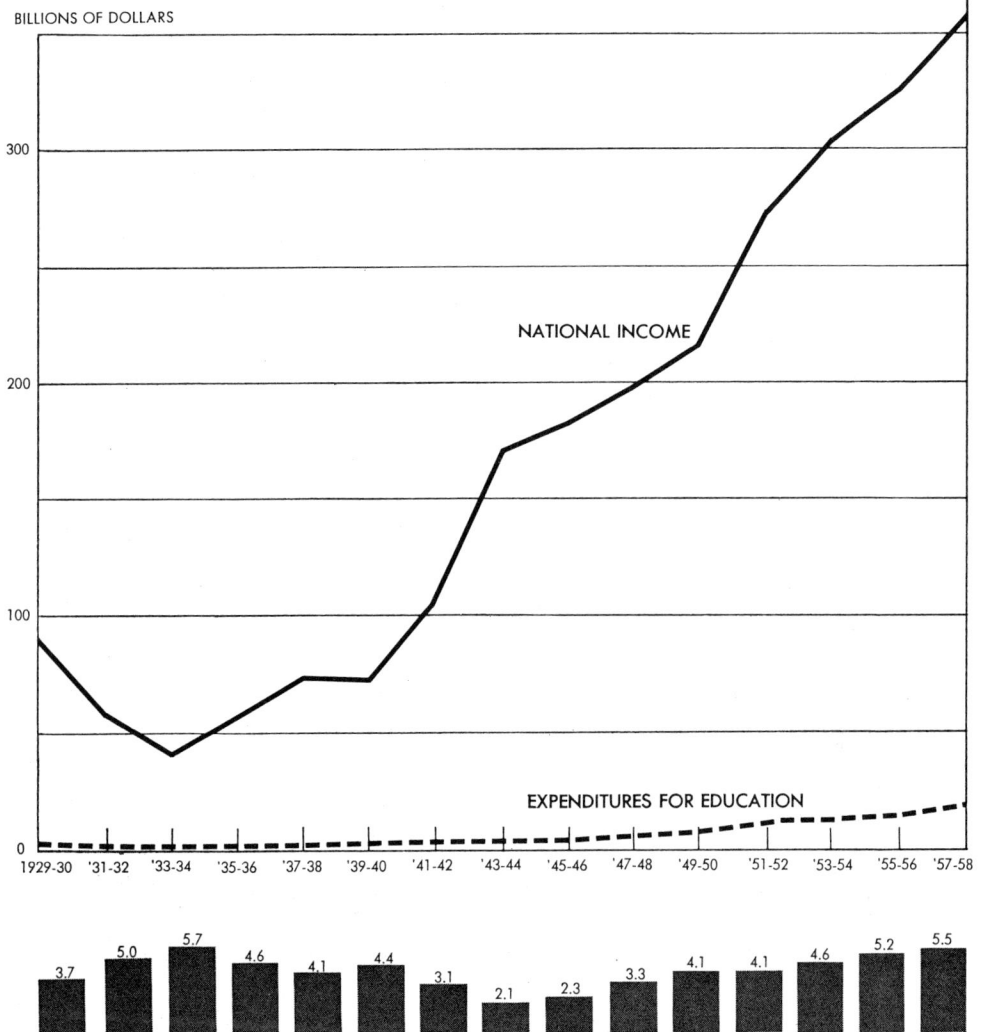

EXPENDITURES FOR EDUCATION AS PERCENTAGES OF NATIONAL INCOME

Source: U.S. Office of Education, Research and Statistical Services Branch, "Total Expenditures for Education (Elementary, Secondary, and Higher, Both Public and Private) as a Percentage of National Income, Biennially from 1929–30 to 1957–58" (mimeographed report; Washington, D.C.: U.S. Department of Health, Education, and Welfare, May 7, 1958).

[24] Committee for the White House Conference on Education, op. cit., pp. 51 ff.

an economic capacity to support an adequate public school system. In many areas there should be fewer and financially stronger school districts.

2. The constitution and statutes of each state should give the people of each school district the power to levy taxes high enough to meet actual needs.

3. States should provide uniform standards and procedures for the assessment of property by the districts.

4. The states should assume primary responsibility for removing inequities in educational opportunity. In some cases this may require increased support from the state. State governments derive their funds for public schools primarily from general-funds appropriations accumulated from many tax sources. These funds increase more rapidly under favorable economic conditions than do the relatively stable taxes on property on which local governments depend. In a period of rising costs, the income of the state is therefore better able to keep step.

5. The federal government should provide aid for building schools to states on a short-term emergency basis. Each state would be required to match federal funds in proportion to its economic ability.

The White House Conference made no recommendations concerning aid for ongoing operational costs of the public schools. The majority of states represented at the conference did not favor such general aid. There was constant insistence that any measure of federal control be avoided, even where federal funds were forthcoming only for construction purposes. At present the federal government provides about 3 per cent of the revenue available for the public schools, but these funds are earmarked for special purposes, such as vocational education and school lunches.

---

adaptation 21   *PUTSCH IN PASADENA*

Abridged and adapted from Milton A. Senn, "Putsch in Pasadena," Frontier, *2 (February, 1951), 5–9. Published in this form by permission of the author and* Frontier.

[Many communities throughout the nation in the past decade have been the scenes of violent public debate about the school system. In such debates, the critics of the schools have not always been ingenuous defenders of an educational philosophy. In some cases the attackers have been motivated primarily by a desire to reduce taxes. In a few other cases, their motivations have apparently been more sinister. One of the attacks on the public schools that attracted attention throughout the nation in 1950 is described in the following account by Milton A. Senn.]

Why was Dr. Willard E. Goslin ousted as superintendent of the Pasadena Public Schools? Up and down the land educators are startled and bewildered. Dr. Goslin, past president of the American Association of School Administrators, is acknowledged to be one of America's foremost educators. The sudden and unorthodox dismissal even jolted most Pasadenans, and consternation and anger still stalk the Crown City.

In Denver, Los Angeles, and Eugene, Oregon, to name but a few of the communities where the public schools are under fire, there is some apprehension that Pasadena has been the testing ground for the techniques of the forces opposed to modern education. That the conflict has national import is underlined by the joint investigation initiated by the National Education Association and the American Association of School Administrators.

TAXES AND THE THREE R's

A quarter of a century ago Upton Sinclair revealed, in *The Goslings,* the potent influence of the economic Bourbons on America's public schools. For them the institution was a burden on the public purse and economy rather than a self-supporting enterprise. Essentially antitaxationists, the Bourbons have opposed since its inception the system of free public education in the nation. Unable to halt its growth, however, they arrogated to themselves— as the large and affluent source of the taxes applied to public purposes—the right to dictate the character of education for young Americans, to interfere in the administration of the educational establishment, and, by other and diverse means, to bend the system of public education to their service.

Though many were shocked by Sinclair's disclosures, the Bourbons, with notable exceptions, continued to resist more taxes for public schools and to intrude their conceptions of the functions of free public education upon school boards, administrators, and teachers wherever they found the opportunity. Frequently they found ready allies in another group, sometimes referred to as the "educational traditionalists." These latter have consistently striven to contain American education within the framework of the three R's, to limit its function to serve the ends of those who employ its products, to resist the modification or enlargement of curriculum in the light of constantly developing social-scientific data, and to oppose numerous other activities designed to develop the whole personality of the child and relate the learning process to the business of living.

The putsch against the Pasadena school system is the latest proof of the power which this coalition still wields.

Dr. Goslin came to Pasadena in the summer of 1948. Pasadena hired him after canvassing the nation's outstanding educators and educational institutions for recommendations. It knew all about his philosophy of education and his previous experience and concluded that he was a "middle-of-the-road" educator. Dr. Goslin attempted to work within the educational philosophy and policies he found in the Pasadena system. While he sought further to refine them, he initiated nothing so startling as to violate the conscience of his colleagues of the Board of Education or to affront the sensitivities of parents and other citizens.

Why, then, was he so unceremoniously booted out?

The answer may be found by examining the character of the campaign waged by the antitaxationists and the educational traditionalists, the relationship of the school board with Goslin and the community, and Dr. Goslin's own public relations. The attack on the school system was made by a coalition of forces representing the Pasadena Realty Board, Property Owners Association, Pro-America, and a group known as the Pasadena School Development Council (hereinafter referred to as SDC). Pro-America has been characterized as the right-wing women's organization of the Republican Party. Pasadena's principal newspapers, the *Independent* and the *Star-News,* supplemented by the Los Angeles *Times* and the Hearst press in Los Angeles, were the opposition's channels of communication to the community.

SDC, the spearhead of the attack, was in reality a synthesis of all of the elements in its allied organization. Its president was Frank Wells, an engineer and father of two children in the city's schools. Among its articulate personalities were Mrs. Morgan Padelford, daughter of ex-Senator Albert Hawkes, and a leader in Pro-America; Mmes. Janet Schwartz, F. P. Bartlett, and R. E. Hallburg, other leading lights in Pro-America; and Dr. W. Ernest Brower, who succeeded Wells as SDC's head. When the Board of Education unanimously approved Dr. Goslin's 1950–51 budget, calling for an increase of almost $400,000, it also ordered a special election which, according to law, was necessary to boost the elementary-school tax rate. For years the tax ceiling had been 90¢ per $100.00 property evaluation. The Board proposed to increase it to $1.35, and pointed out that while no more than 30¢ of the increase would be used in the next year, it was planning for a five-year period. Between 1947 and 1950, twenty-eight elementary-school districts in Los Angeles County had increased their tax on the average by 25¢.

In 1944, children enrolled in Pasadena's elementary schools numbered 7,800; in 1949 there were 10,870. On the basis of tested predictions, the Board had estimated that by 1954 there would be in excess of 16,000 children in the elementary grades. The approved budget provided, among other things, for the opening of three new elementary buildings; eliminated the half-day elementary schedules and double sessions in the kindergartens; allowed for some increase in teachers' salaries; and made possible necessary additional guidance, counseling, and health services.

REZONING

One other Board action ought to be noted as spurring the SDC to mobilize and strip for action. This was Dr. Goslin's proposal to rezone certain school boundaries. He had outlined the plan in February as an effective and desirable answer to the complicated problem of transfers with which the administration was plagued. Also, the community and school population had grown appreciably. By eliminating the "neutral zones," as they were called, he expected to utilize more efficiently the school facilities to serve the children involved, shorten the distances some had to travel, and reduce the traffic hazards to which some were exposed.

But many discerned that the abolition of neutral zones would stop an observable trend toward segregation of Negroes and Mexican and Japanese-American children. This factor was probably uppermost in Dr. Goslin's mind when he warned the Board: "The transfer situation is a 'hot potato.' If you don't think so, just try holding it." For this was Pasadena, where social mobility was rigorously regulated and social stratification strictly policed; where few made bold to change the pattern of residential segregation or abolish the institution of racial restrictive covenants; where talk of equal rights for minorities was usually labeled as "drivel."

Following a public hearing on the question, the Board unanimously adopted Dr. Goslin's plan.

Though the rezoning plan was loathsome to SDC (it called the public hearing "obviously a concerted move"), it chose not to make a strong issue of it. Instead it girded its loins for the all-out offensive against the tax boost. Late in April, SDC had adopted a statement of principles concerning taxation for public school purposes. It proposed that an analysis of the school budget and expenditures be made and that, meanwhile, "educational costs, due to new teaching innovations, should not be entertained except to accomplish demonstrable benefits."

THE ATTACK ON PROGRESSIVE EDUCATION

SDC also asserted, quite correctly, that "the people of each community can and should determine the kind of training which is being given its children." It qualified "people" by stating "the best judges of the success of our educational system are those who employ and work with its products." To parents it tossed the fillip that their evaluation of the educational system "is far superior to the theories of those administering the process, or of abstract written tests of somewhat questionable validity." Proclaiming that the community is "capable of debating educational methods on an even footing with the school administration" and accepting "no inferior status for parents in counseling with school authorities," SDC, the Realty Board, and the Chamber of Commerce hired Louis J. Kroeger and Associates to analyze the proposed school budget.

According to Kroeger's findings, the tax increase was unwarranted. In fact, SDC said, by reshuffling the present budget and eliminating certain expenditures, teachers' salaries could be increased, new elementary schools opened, and half-day sessions ended. Its opposition to the tax levy reinforced by Kroeger's study, SDC now urged a complete review of the schools. The hiring of personnel and supervision of the study, however, it demanded be placed in the hands of groups "independent of, but co-operating with, the School Board and . . . appointed by the Chamber of Commerce, the Realty Board, and SDC." Charging that the report was "so filled with inaccuracies as to be misleading," Dr. Goslin debated with Kroeger before the Chamber of Commerce. Following the discussion, the Chamber's Board of Directors voted unanimously to endorse the tax boost.

Kroeger's analysis passed into limbo as SDC hauled up its really big guns. "If you are in favor of progressive education, you must automatically be in favor of constantly increasing taxes," was the first salvo. "The issue is increased taxes for more progressive education which means less real education . . . . What we want and stand for is more education for less cost." It called upon the Board to "eliminate extravagant 'progressive frills' and close the fiscal year with an actual surplus"; it was confident that "our children can be trained to be literates instead of victims of modern education."

SDC next resorted to the familiar device of equating progressive education with subversive indoctrination. "Progressive education," it warned, "is basically wrong and is dangerous to our children and our American heritage; . . . our children are being taught . . . that other European forms of government are superior." While rallying all patriots with the battle cry "pragmatic progressive education wrecks the individual and promotes socialism and opposes individualism," it alerted parents that such education "produces juvenile delinquency," in proof whereof "today we have our 'Wolf Packs.'" Grateful for ammunition from any quarter, SDC leaned heavily upon A. Allen Zoll's National Council on American Education. Zoll, termed a subversive by Attorneys General Biddle and Clark, had authored the pamphlets *Progressive Education Increases Juvenile Delinquency* and *They Want Your Child*. Both were distributed in quantity at SDC meetings and elsewhere in the community. Mrs. Schwartz, who stated publicly that she was a member of NCAE, credited the organization as the source of most of the information on progressive education and its advocates in America.

Too late the people of Pasadena learned that Zoll was also a strong supporter of G. L. K. Smith, Elizabeth Dilling, and Father Coughlin; that he had opposed the appointment of Justice Felix Frankfurter on the sole basis of his religion; that the American Legion's National Americanism Commission had condemned the literature issued by NCAE; and that General Wainwright, Senator Vandenberg, Gene Tunney, and Father Casassa (of L. A.'s Loyola University), among others, had resigned as sponsors of NCAE when they learned it was a front for Zoll.

On election eve, SDC laid down another intimidating barrage by revealing the stark and sinister implications of the national conspiracy in which Pasadena was involved. "The 'education party' is a growing political force," it charged, on all governmental levels. This new group, with "leaders in the progressive cult at New York and Columbia Universities, directing this latent, national 'education party,' are aware of the importance of 'thought control'; . . . 'controlled' dictums, passed down from such 'headquarters' to local chapters, make the task of local progressive administrators far simpler when they organize machines with local backing."

With such a frightful tocsin ringing in their ears, it is no wonder that more voters bestirred themselves to the polls than had ever before turned out for a special election on school issues. Of the 32,067 ballots cast, representing about 37.25 per cent of the qualified voters in Pasadena and Altadena, 22,067 were against the elementary-school tax increase. Compare 1946, when there was no fight against the tax-limit increase for the high-school district; 6,707 out of 88,000 eligible voters—a scant 7.6 per cent—cast ballots then. Or 1948, when, on the elementary-school bond issue, 17,414— or 20 per cent of the voters—marched to the polls. Or 1949, the year of the regular school election, when 15,016—16.2 per cent of those eligible—voted.

Flushed with victory, the opposition now interpreted the defeat to the community. "The Board of Education and the school superintendent asked for a vote of confidence," crowed a representative for the Property Owners, "and the people have replied." Frank Wells interpreted the vote as virtually supplanting the Board and Goslin with SDC. "We fully realize our responsibility of leadership," he said, "given us by the voters . . . ," and he invited the citizens to "help in making this a successful fight against progressive education and progressive taxation, a crusade for the further safety of our community and nation."

Confident that it had the green light, SDC requested that Dr. Goslin and his immediate staff be removed before the opening of school in the fall.

THE OUTCOME

Pasadena's School Board was once full of admiration and respect for the ability, judgment, and integrity of its superintendent. It stood as one with him on such dynamite-laden issues as rezoning and increased taxes. "We are prepared," President Wopschall told SDC on one occasion, "not only to support this tax measure, but we will also continue to support the kind of educational program which Mr. Goslin and his associates are developing in this community."

On the eve of election, Wopschall assured the community that "this school system is doing a good job" in educating the children to meet the needs of present-day conditions through a program that develops "honesty, dependability, work habits and emotional control." It was a Board of three men and two women—a paint merchant, lawyer, mortician, retired schoolteacher, and a housewife—which adamantly refused to yield one particle of its responsibility to a small coalition of some of the most powerful and influential forces in the community. It lashed out at SDC's proposal for a survey with the statement: "No special-interest group, not elected by the people as a whole, has any business dictating policy to the School Board or school administration."

These five elected officials resisted harassment ("end wanton wastefulness," "who could be more representative . . . than leading business men, taxpayers and parents?") and vilification ("a rubber stamp for the administration," "has ceased to represent the people who elected it"), and charges that the school accounts had not been audited in eighteen years, to the best of their ability. That is, until the defeat of the tax levy.

SDC had dinned into the community that Dr. Goslin was the root of the evil. Its entire campaign was calculated to demonstrate lack of public confidence in the superintendent and, by extension, in the Board which supported him. SDC hammered away at its new theme that the election was a mandate to ride Dr. Goslin out of town.

Dr. Goslin's failure to answer SDC demands for an ideological investigation, particularly after he had requested permission to reply, must have irritated the Board. The Board was roused even more by the superintendent's request for approval of vouchers for a child-study project and for Dr. Dan Prescott, a human-relations expert brought to Pasadena from the University of Chicago for consultation. The Board chided the superintendent for committing the school system to these expenditures without its prior consent. The hiring of George Gerbner, a public-relations man, was just about the last straw. The 3–2 vote for his employment was the first overt split in the Board.

Rumors of dissension among the teaching staff apparently had some basis, the Board reasoned, else why would 200 teachers sign petitions endorsing the administration? Professional jealousies aside, though not unimportant, the antagonisms and animosities which some of Dr. Goslin's colleagues evince toward him may be traced to his retiring and diffident personality.

An engaging and provocative figure on the platform, he seemed to have difficulty establishing rapport in his personal relationships with people. While he addressed an Arrowhead Springs conference of Pasadena school administrators, he remained aloof, for the most part, from the numerous workshops and small deliberative sessions that occurred during the four-day period. Many gained the impression that he preferred the role of "lone wolf."

Other criticism of him seemed to support this impression. He failed to consult with his fellow-administrators on such an important matter as the elimination of neutral zones. Many principals learned of his plans for the first time from parents in their school districts. Moreover, he seldom visited his principals in their own schools and made little effort to know the schools in his system, their personnel, and their problems through field visits.

Complaints from some disgruntled members of the administrative personnel, even threats from some to ask Dr. Goslin to resign, coupled with the connivance by a few others with the opposition, pricked the Board into its final and secret act. It telegraphed its request for his resignation because, as they said, "We know that the opposition will not wait for us as they have plans to meet your plane [Dr. Goslin was in New York] with a demand for your resignation."

Gone was the last shred of confidence in Dr. Goslin. Gone was all pretense of doubt about the significance of the election. At hand, finally, was proof positive that peace could be had and the shrill voices stilled only by lopping off the school system's head. What other alternative? they asked themselves. How else to preserve their own equilibrium and restore harmony to the community?

However, despite the fact that the Board said, in its wire to him, "The main controversy in Pasadena settles around you as an individual," Dr. Goslin was merely the symbolic target for the antitaxationists and educational traditionalists.

With the dismissal of Dr. Goslin, the opposition accomplished its primary mission. Yet they gained but a Pyrrhic victory. For they provoked in Pasadena the most important issue of all—one that yet remains to be solved: What is meant by education, and who determines what kind of education shall be given to the children of this community?

What happened in Pasadena has also happened in other communities as well, though often in less dramatic form. Antitaxationists have on some occasions masked their opposition to increased educational expenditures by mounting an attack on what is carelessly labeled "progressive" education. Together with the educational traditionalists, they have organized a vocal opposition that has usually centered around the person of the superintendent.

adaptation 22   EDUCATIONAL WASTELANDS

Abridged and adapted from Arthur E. Bestor, Educational Wastelands *(Urbana: University of Illinois Press, 1953). Published in this form by permission of the author and the publisher.*

[Attacks on modern educational method and purpose come from several different kinds of sources. One is the so-called "traditionalist," who is genuinely interested in the development of the public schools but has strong disagreements with certain aspects of modern educational theory. It may seem that the entire school system is the target of his barbs, although typically his remarks apply only to the most extreme of his philosophical antagonists. For this reason he has sometimes been accused of setting up straw men for attacks. Others accept his remarks as useful caricatures, not to be taken altogether literally but as saying incisively some valid things about tendencies present in modern educational theory. One of the most provocative traditionalist approaches in recent years is that of Arthur E. Bestor, professor of history at the University of Illinois.]

The men and women who are professionally engaged in education have allowed themselves to become confused about the purposes of education, and they have transmitted their confusion to the public. They have sponsored school and college programs which make no substantial contribution to knowledge or to clear thinking and which could not conceivably make such a contribution. The public sees no point in much of what is done in the name of education and has developed a justifiable skepticism toward education itself.

We talk so much about overcrowding that we are apt to forget the significant fact that the equipment and the resources of the public schools have increased far more rapidly than attendance. Approximately four times as many children as in 1870 are now in school, but we spend more than ninety times as much on their education. A child of today enjoys a school year twice as long. The proportion of teachers to pupils is greater, and teachers are required to spend far more time in training. Compared with 1870 (after adjustments have been made for the changed value of the dollar) we find that nine times as much money is spent per year on the education of each child, and nearly thirteen times as much is invested in buildings and equipment. And yet on almost every count there is general dissatisfaction with the results of the twelve years of education currently provided by most of our public schools, and it is an exceedingly important fact that criticism comes with the greatest intensity from those who believe most strongly in the value and importance of education. Discontent with the training which public schools provide is all but unanimous, I discover, among members of the liberal arts and professional faculties of the universities and colleges. It is almost equally widespread among doctors, engineers, clergymen, lawyers, and other professional men throughout the nation. Businessmen are dismayed at the deficiencies in reading, writing, arithmetic, and general knowledge displayed by the high-school and college graduates they employ. Parents are alarmed. The criticism is not that of "reactionaries." Among college and university faculties the criticism does not come primarily from classicists and the older "traditional" branches of learning; it comes with perhaps greatest intensity from professors in the sciences and mathematics and in the other disciplines directly connected with the problems of the modern technological world.

THE FAILURE OF THE SCHOOLS

No serious critic of modern American education is asserting that the public schools enjoyed a golden age in the past. It is the shortcomings of the school today that concern us. We did not set out to make a fourth-rate educational system into a third-rate one. If we are to have improvement, we must learn to make comparisons, not with the rigidly inadequate public schools of former generations but with the very best schools of which we can obtain knowledge. If the schools are doing their job, we should expect educators to point to a significant and indisputable achievement in raising the intellectual level of the nation—measured, perhaps, by larger per capita circulation of books and serious magazines, by definitely improved taste in movies and radio programs, by higher standards of political debate, by increased respect for freedom of speech and of thought, and by a marked decline of such evidences of mental retardation as the incessant reading of comic books by adults. We should expect superintendents to report that because of improved methods of instruction, longer school years, and better-trained teachers, they have been able to teach successfully in the high schools many of the fundamental disciplines to which students were formerly introduced only in college. We should expect school administrators to produce testimonials from employers, professional men, college professors, and officers of the Armed Services to the effect that young men and women are coming out of high school with sounder intellectual background and greater skill and competence than ever before. No such claims are being advanced and no such comparisons are being made by the men and women to whom we have entrusted the control of our public schools. They do not ask that American public schools be judged by such standards, because, by and large, they no longer accept these as valid standards, with honorable exceptions. The most influential men in the field of elementary and secondary education have for a generation been redefining the purposes of the public schools in a fashion that amounts to repudiation of these objectives. The charge which the public advances is that professional educationists in their policy-making role have lowered the aims of the American public schools. In the last analysis, it is not lack of effort but lack of direction that has resulted in the mediocre showing of our public high schools. The professional educationists are fond of clouding the issue by suggesting that those who believe in discipline and intellectual training deny the importance of good teaching. Nothing could be further from the truth. It is sheer presumption on their part to pose as the only persons in the academic world with a concern for good teaching. The issue in American education today is not drawn between those who believe in scholarship, but are indifferent to good teaching, and those who believe in good teaching, but are indifferent to scholarship. The issue is drawn between those who believe that good teaching should be directed to sound intellectual ends and those who are content to dethrone intellectual values and to cultivate the techniques of teaching for its own sake, in an intellectual and cultural vacuum.

THE NEED FOR INTELLECTUAL TRAINING

Intellectual training may seem a formidable phrase, but it means nothing more than the deliberate cultivation of the ability to think. There is no sharp contrast between the intellectual and the practical. Knowledge does, of course, become more abstract and reasonably more intricate as one proceeds farther into each of the fields of science and learning. But this does not mean that knowledge becomes less practical or less applicable to human affairs as it advances. Quite the contrary. It becomes more practical because it becomes more powerful. A formula is abstract, not because it has lost touch with facts, but because it compresses so many facts into a small compass. And only an abstract statement can sum them up. The modern scientist or scholar knows that the principal value to society of man's cultivating the power of abstract thought is that he is thereby enabled to deal more effectively with the problems of modern life.

The school that sticks to its job of intellectual training is not thereby indifferent to the vocational needs of its students, to their physical development, or to the problem of moral conduct. Such a school merely recognizes that it must deal with these matters in the context provided by its own characteristic activity. By knowing its capabilities and its limitations, the school can make a more effective contribution to vocational training and physical education and to ethics than if it cherishes the delusion that it is a home, a church, a workshop, and a doctor's office rolled into one. To say that the primary purpose of the school is intellectual training is not at all the same thing as saying that intellectual activity is the most important thing in human life. One can say that the primary function of the medical profession is to safeguard the health of the nation without either affirming or denying that good health is the most important thing in human life. The school exists to serve the needs of man, but, like the hospital or the post office, it is not designed to provide all kinds of services indiscriminately. It is designed to provide intellectual training, and the cornerstone of such training must be the fundamental intellectual disciplines.

THE PRIMACY OF THE ACADEMIC DISCIPLINES

What I call the fundamental "disciplines"—history, chemistry, mathematics, philosophy, and the like—have become, in the jargon of secondary-school education, "subject-matter fields"; but a discipline is by no means the same thing as a subject-matter field. The one is a way of thinking; the other is a mere aggregation of facts. The liberal disciplines are not mere chunks of frozen facts; they are not facts at all, but the powerful tools and engines by which a man discovers and handles facts. Without the scientific and scholarly disciplines, he is helpless in the presence of facts.

Consider how the disciplines of science and learning came into being. Before man could deal with the great tangle of confused perceptions, he had to differentiate one experience from another and to discover relationships among them—similarity and diversity, cause and effect, and the like. Gradually he discovered that one kind of relationship can best be investigated in one way (by controlled experiment, it may be) and another relationship in another way, perhaps by the critical study of written records or fossil remains. Thus the separate disciplines were born, not out of arbitrary invention but out of evolving experience. Admittedly a course may bear the respected label of an academic discipline and yet be in reality no more than a "subject-matter field." In my own field of history there are college textbook "survey" courses which would suggest to even an intelligent student that the discipline of history consists of the memorization of facts rather than in the weighing of evidence and the investigation of relationships. Academic courses which teach men to manipulate laboratory apparatus but not to think scientifically, to carry out intricate computations but not to think mathematically, to remember dates but not to think historically, to summarize philosophical arguments but not to think critically, these advance no man toward liberal education. To be perfectly honest, one must admit that higher education has lost repute because so many offerings in the liberal arts and sciences have failed to provide the intellectual discipline which they promise. But the answer is surely not to abandon the ideal of discipline and intelligence in favor of an educational program which offers nothing to liberate and strengthen men's minds. The answer is not to banish the scholarly, scientific disciplines but to hold them rigorously to their task.

EDUCATION FOR DEMOCRACY

Is a good education of the kind described above undemocratic? Democracy implies the right of every citizen to develop his intellectual powers to the fullest extent possible. It also assumes that intellectual ability is independent of the accidents of wealth and social position. Today many public school administrators and professors of education assert that a school which concentrates its efforts upon intellectual training is an aristocratic school. But if a privileged class once monopolized for itself the kind of education we call "liberal," we are not perpetuating an aristocracy but destroying it if we make the same education available to all of the people. We shall never create a genuinely democratic intellectual and cultural life if, as victory comes almost within our grasp, we repudiate the very purposes we set out to achieve. Much is made of the fact that the students in an aristocratic school system were a selected group, while those in the American public schools of today are not. But much of the force of this argument vanishes once we recognize the fact that the aristocratic few were selected for reasons totally unconnected with intellectual capacity. Inherited wealth and social position are no guarantees of mental ability.

OUTLINING A PROGRAM

What kind of training should the schools offer if they are to endow future citizens with the intellectual power that is the end of liberal education?

Effective thinking, I would suggest, involves at least four things. (1) A thorough command of the essential intellectual tools, namely, the ability to read, which means the power to grasp the full meaning of the written word; the ability to write, that is, to put complex thought into intelligible prose; and some command of mathematical thinking. (2) A store of reliable information which the mind can draw upon. It is commonly said that men do not need to carry information in their minds because they can look it up in reference books. Reference books merely explain one thing in terms of another. A man must bring to the reference book a fund of ready knowledge sufficient to make these references intelligible. (3) Practice in the systematic ways of thinking developed within the various basic fields of scholarly and scientific investigation. (4) Finally, but only finally, the culminating act of applying this aggregate of intellectual powers to the solution of a problem. This act presupposes the preceding steps; one cannot teach men to think by training them to perform this final act alone, any more than one can build a house from the roof downward.

Such an education would require not just a restructuring of curriculums but a total training, e.g., a return to the intellectual emphasis of rigid examinations and to essay examinations. But the cornerstone of reorganization must be a new curriculum for the education of teachers, a curriculum based on the liberal arts and sciences rather than upon the mere vocational fields of pedagogy. This will do more to restore the repute of the public schools than any other step that can be taken. Not only will teachers be adequately trained in the disciplines they undertake to teach; they will also be imbued with respect for those disciplines and will be prepared to resist the anti-intellectualism that currently threatens the schools. And when the tide begins to turn, young men and women of genuine intellectual interest and capacity will be attracted in increasing numbers to the profession of public school teaching. They will not be repelled at the outset by being asked to lay aside their intellectual interests and to fritter away their time in the courses of the pedagogues.

All this does not mean that a liberal education cannot properly include preparation for the making of a livelihood. However, education ceases to be liberal if it is directed exclusively to that end, because then it produces not free citizens but men enslaved by their occupations. Some of the offerings, viewed simply as isolated, optional courses, could be defended on utilitarian grounds. The student, alongside of his serious academic work, might profitably pick up some practical training in accounting or pedagogy or public speaking or home economics or library cataloguing. But university administrators permitted the development of departments and even whole colleges devoted to these academic byways, and, naturally, students were allowed to take degrees in them. Popular sneers at "book learning" are not really directed at learning in the liberal sense. It is not the liberally educated man who becomes a laughingstock; it is the journalism major who writes in sentences that no editor would print, the speech major whom no one would hear with patience in a public hall, the home-economics major who is unable to run her own house, the education major who knows less about the subject she teaches than the parents of her own pupils, the commerce major who cannot carry on a business as successfully as the man who never took a business course in his life.

The school makes itself ridiculous whenever it undertakes to deal directly with real-life problems instead of indirectly through the development of generalized intellectual powers. Besides being ineffective, formal instruction in trivial problems of vocational and personal life is dangerously mis-educational in its effect. It generates in the student the belief that he cannot deal with any matter unless he has taken a course in it. Timidity, self-distrust, and conformity are pathetically evident among the graduates of American teacher-training colleges. For many of the poor souls seem to doubt their ability even to open a schoolroom window until they have been told in a textbook or by a professor of education how it should be raised. The citizen of today needs an education, not a head full of helpful hints.

adaptation 23 PAROCHIAL SCHOOLS AND THE
FIRST AMENDMENT

Excerpted from Everson v. Board of Education *(1946) 330 U.S. 1,
67 S Ct 504.*

[In his dissent from the Supreme Court decision in *McCollum* v. *Board of Education* (1948), 333 U.S. 203, a case which involved religious instruction in public schools, Supreme Court Justice Frankfurter wrote: "The mere formulation of a relevant Constitutional principle is the beginning of the solution of a problem, not its answer. This is so because the meaning of a spacious conception like that of the separation of Church from State is unfolded as appeal is made to the principle from case to case."

One of the landmark cases in the current interpretation of the First Amendment as it touches on education was the 1946 majority decision of the Supreme Court in *Everson* v. *Board of Education* that it was constitutional for the state of New Jersey to provide tax funds for parochial school transportation. Following are unedited excerpts from the majority opinion and minority dissent in that case.]

The "establishment of religion" clause of the First Amendment means at least this: Neither a state nor the Federal Government can set up a church. Neither can pass laws which aid one religion, aid all religions, or prefer one religion over another. Neither can force nor influence a person to go to or remain away from church against his will or force him to profess a belief or disbelief in any religion. No person can be punished for entertaining or professing religious beliefs or disbeliefs, for church attendance or nonattendance. No tax in any amount, large or small, can be levied to support any religious activities or institutions, whatever they may be called, or whatever form they may adopt to teach or practice religion. Neither a state nor the Federal Government can, openly or secretly, participate in the affairs of any religious organizations or groups and vice versa. In the words of Jefferson the clause against establishment of religion by law was intended to erect "a wall of separation between Church and State."

We must consider the New Jersey statute in accordance with the foregoing limitations imposed by the First Amendment. But we must not strike that State statute down if it is within the State's constitutional power even though it approaches the verge of the power. New Jersey cannot consistently with the "establishment of religion clause" of the First Amendment contribute tax-raised funds to the support of an institution which teaches the tenets and faith of any church. On the other hand, other language of the amendment commands that New Jersey cannot hamper its citizens in the free exercise of their own religion. Consequently, it cannot exclude individual Catholics, Lutherans, Mohammedans, Baptists, Jews, Methodists, Non-believers, Presbyterians, or the members of any other faith, *because of their faith, or lack of it,* from receiving the benefits of public welfare legislation. While we do not mean to intimate that a state could not provide transportation only to children attending public schools, we must be careful, in protecting the citizens of New Jersey against state-established churches, to be sure that we do not inadvertently prohibit New Jersey from extending its general State law benefits to all its citizens without regard to their religious belief.

Measured by these standards, we cannot say that the First Amendment prohibits New Jersey from spending tax-raised funds to pay the bus fares of parochial school pupils as a part of a general program under which it pays the fares of pupils attending public and other schools. It is undoubtedly true that children are helped to get to church schools. There is even a possibility that some of the children might not be sent to the church schools if the parents were compelled to pay their children's bus fares out of their own pockets when transportation to a public school would have been paid for by the state. The same possibility exists where the state requires a local transit company to provide reduced fares to school children including those attending parochial schools, or where a municipally owned transportation system undertakes to carry all school children free of charge. Moreover, state-paid policemen, detailed to protect children going to and from church schools from the very real hazards of traffic, would serve much the same purpose and accomplish much the same result as state provisions intended to guarantee free transportation of a kind which the state deems to be best for the school children's welfare. And parents might refuse to risk their children to the serious danger of traffic accidents going to and from parochial schools, the approaches to which were not protected by policemen. Similarly, parents might be reluctant to permit their children to attend schools which the state had cut off from such general government services as ordinary police and fire protection, connections for sewage disposal, public highways and sidewalks. Of course, cutting off church schools from these services, so separate and so indisputably marked off from the religious function, would make it far more difficult for the schools to operate. But such is obviously not the purpose of the First Amendment. That Amendment requires the state to be a neutral in its relations with groups of religious believers and non-believers; it does not require the state to be their adversary. State power is no more to be used so as to handicap religions than it is to favor them.

This Court has said that parents may, in the discharge of their duty under state compulsory education laws, send their children to a religious rather than a public school if the school meets the secular educational requirements which the state has power to impose. It appears that these parochial schools meet New Jersey's requirements. The State contributes no money to the schools. It does not support them. Its legislation, as applied, does no more than provide a general program to help parents get their children, regardless of their religion, safely and expeditiously to and from accredited schools.

The First Amendment has erected a wall between church and state. That wall must be kept high and impregnable. We could not approve the slightest breach. New Jersey has not breached it here.

Affirmed.

* * *

Mr. Justice Rutledge, with whom Mr. Justice Frankfurter, Mr. Justice Jackson, and Mr. Justice Burton agree, dissenting.

No one conscious of religious values can be unsympathetic toward the burden which our constitutional separation puts on parents who desire religious instruction mixed with secular for their children. They pay taxes for others' children's education, at the same time the added cost of instruction for their own. Nor can one happily see benefits denied to children which others receive, because in conscience they or their parents for them desire a different kind of training others do not demand.

But if those feelings should prevail, there would be an end to our historic constitutional policy and command. No more unjust or discriminatory in fact is it to deny attendants at religious schools the cost of their transportation than it is to deny them tuitions, sustenance for their teachers, or any other educational expense which others receive at public cost. Hardship in fact there is which none can blink. But, for assuring to those who undergo it the greater, the most comprehensive freedom, it is one written by design and firm intent into our basic law.

Of course discrimination in the legal sense does not exist. The child attending the religious school has the same right as any other to attend the public school. But he foregoes exercising it because the same guaranty which assures this freedom forbids the public school or any agency of the state to give or aid him in securing the religious instruction he seeks.

Were he to accept the common school, he would be the first to protest the teaching there of any creed or faith not his own. And it is precisely for the reason that their atmosphere is wholly secular that children are not sent to public schools under the *Pierce* doctrine. But that is a constitutional necessity, because we have staked the very existence of our country on the faith that complete separation between the state and religion is best for the state and best for religion.

That policy necessarily entails hardship upon persons who forego the right to educational advantages the state can supply in order to secure others it is precluded from giving. Indeed this may hamper the parent and the child forced by conscience to that choice. But it does not make the state unneutral to withhold what the Constitution forbids it to give. On the contrary it is only by observing the prohibition rigidly that the state can maintain its neutrality and avoid partisanship in the dissensions inevitable when sect opposes sect over demands for public moneys to further religious education, teaching or training in any form or degree, directly or indirectly. Like St. Paul's freedom, religious liberty with a great price must be bought. And for those who exercise it most fully, by insisting upon religious education for their children mixed with secular, by the terms of our Constitution the price is greater than for others.

The problem then cannot be cast in terms of legal discrimination or its absence. This would be true, even though the state in giving aid should treat all religious instruction alike. Thus, if the present statute and its application were shown to apply equally to all religious schools of whatever faith, yet in the light of our tradition it could not stand. For then the adherent of one creed still would pay for the support of another, the childless taxpayer with others more fortunate. Then too there would seem to be no bar to making appropriations for transportation and other expenses of children attending public or other secular schools, after hours in separate places and classes for their exclusively religious instruction. The person who embraces no creed also would be forced to pay for teaching what he does not believe. Again, it was the furnishing of "contributions of money for the propagation of opinions which he disbelieves" that the fathers outlawed. That consequence and effect are not removed by multiplying to all-inclusiveness the sects for which support is exacted. The Constitution requires, not comprehensive identification of state with religion, but complete separation.

Whatever might be said of some other application of New Jersey's statute, the one made here has no semblance of bearing as a safety measure, or indeed, for securing expeditious conveyance. The transportation supplied is by public conveyance, subject to all the hazards and delays of the highway and the streets incurred by the public generally in going about its multifarious business.

Nor is the case comparable to one of furnishing fire or police protection, or access to public highways. These things are matters of common right, part of the general need for safety. Certainly the fire department must not stand idly by while the church burns. Nor is this reason why the state should pay the expense of transportation or other items of the cost of religious education.

I have chosen to place my dissent upon the broad ground I think decisive, though strictly speaking the case might be decided on narrower issues. The New Jersey statute might be held invalid on its face for the exclusion of children who attend private, profit-making schools. I cannot assume, as does the majority, that the New Jersey courts would write off this explicit limitation from the statute. Moreover, the resolution by which the statute was applied expressly limits its benefits to students of public and Catholic schools. There is no showing that there are no other private or religious schools in this populous district. I do not think it can be assumed that there were none. But in the view I have taken, it is unnecessary to limit grounding to these matters.

Two great drives are constantly in motion to abridge, in the name of education, the complete division of religion and civil authority which our forefathers made. One is to introduce religious education and observances into the public schools. The other, to obtain public funds for the aid and support of various private religious schools. In my opinion both avenues were closed by the Constitution. Neither should be opened by this Court. The matter is not one of quantity, to be measured by the amount of money expended. Now as in Madison's day it is one of principle, to keep separate the separate spheres as the First Amendment drew them; to prevent the first experiment upon our liberties; and to keep the question from becoming entangled in corrosive precedents. We should not be less strict to keep strong and untarnished the one side of the shield of religious freedom than we have been of the other.

The judgment should be reversed.

SUGGESTIONS FOR FURTHER READING

John Dewey, *Education Today* (New York: G. P. Putnam's Sons, 1940).

Harl Douglass (ed.), *Education for Life Adjustment* (New York: Ronald Press, 1950).

Sidney Hook, *Education for Modern Man* (New York: Dial Press, 1946).

Ernest O. Melby and Morton Puner (eds.), *Freedom and Public Education* (New York: Frederick A. Praeger, 1953).

Leo Pfeffer, *Church, State and Freedom* (Boston: Beacon Press, 1953).

C. Winfield Scott and Clyde M. Hill, *Public Education under Criticism* (New York: Prentice-Hall, Inc., 1954).

W. Lloyd Warner, Robert J. Havighurst, and Martin B. Loeb, *Who Shall Be Educated?* (New York: Harper & Bros., 1944).

Stan Lee; Black Star

CHAPTER 10

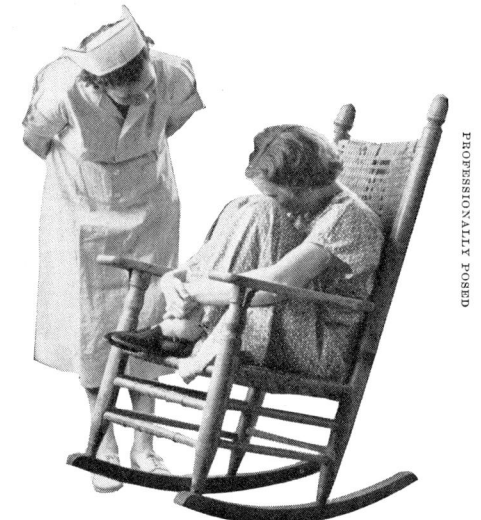

Dependency

Section I: What Is the Problem?

"In a modern industrial society banishment of destitution and cushioning the shock of personal disaster on the individual are proper concerns of all levels of government, including federal government."

With these words did President Eisenhower, in his 1954 message to Congress On the State of the Union, express the modern welfare philosophy of this country. He was expressing more than a pious hope. During 1954 the federal, state, and local governments dispensed over $16 billion for basic welfare purposes. By any fiscal measurement, except for defense requirements on the federal level and public education on the local level, American government is primarily in the welfare business. Although 1954 was a year of relatively high employment and prosperity, about 5 million people were dependent on direct financial assistance through public programs, and many more millions were dependent on public health and welfare services which, by and large, they could not otherwise afford.

Society understands more clearly than ever before, first, the effect of dependency on costly social problems such as delinquency and intergroup conflict and, second, its economic stake in making the dependent once again a productive member of society. Official society's rapidly accelerating acceptance of responsibility for citizen-dependents rests on two developments: the changing nature of the family and the changing concept of dependency.

CHANGES IN FAMILY RESPONSIBILITY

At one time family responsibility was great. The normal dependency of children was, of course, expected to be borne by the parents, as was the normal dependency of the mother and homemaker. It was fully expected that children would assume the responsibility for parents who, because of age, had become dependent. But, further than that, it fell upon family units to accept reasonable responsibility for stray uncles and aunts and cousins who had come to a dependent state.

For a number of reasons this pattern of family responsibility has been changing. The old pattern was generally based on the ability to absorb new dependents into one household, under one roof. This ability diminished as families became part of the urban mass. Household units are now constructed for the small and immediate family. Maintaining dependents in separate households is not economically feasible for most families. The mobility that has come with our industrial economy and urbanization has fragmented large families and has thus made it difficult for people to assume responsibility for others.

Even more significant, perhaps, is the fact that mobility and urbanization have contributed toward the loosening of family ties in general. As a result, there is no longer the *feeling* of responsibility for members of the family beyond the immediate household. The legal and moral responsibility of parents for their children, of course, remains firm. However, the responsibility of grown children for their aged parents has blurred. Generally, before it will accept responsibility for the aged, society requires evidence of the inability of grown children to lend support; but, increasingly, this is a formalistic step, and substantial personal sacrifice is not demanded. The feeling has grown that the fundamental responsibility of young adults is not to take care of their parents but to provide their children with a good home and a good education. The moral pressures have receded with the legal. The family has become a limited welfare unit, and society at large has had to accept the increased responsibility.

CHANGES IN THE CONCEPT OF DEPENDENCY

At one time a "minimal standard of living" meant simply adequate food, emergency medical attention, some shelter, and perhaps adequate clothing. The American people have now become accustomed to a new picture of a basic standard of living. Squalor, even if the stomach is reasonably full, does not fit into that picture. There has been growing recognition that human needs have a cultural and psychological dimension as well as a physical

Post-Dispatch Pictures; Black Star

The TV Set: Reception is poor in this part of the Ozarks, but this elderly couple still feels the need of a television set.

dimension. There has been a growing acceptance of the fact that self-esteem belongs alongside groceries as a basic human necessity.

This means not just a full stomach but the absence of degradation and the provision of human comforts beyond the absolute necessities. The absence of degradation even implies a standard of living which is not radically inferior to the average. A basic standard of living no longer means just warm clothing, but decent-looking clothing; it may even mean the ability to purchase a television set, at a time when there is one in almost every American home.

However, the imperative of self-esteem encompasses more than a growing roster of material needs. There has developed an understanding of the psychological concomitants of dependency. An individual's financial incapacity is generally an index of his inability to fill the kind of productive role for which society in its normal economic process would ordinarily recompense him to the extent of his needs or the needs of his family. It is now recognized, however, that economic dependence requires more than economic assistance; economic dependence often results in loss of self-esteem and demoralization.

Our psychological life partly consists of filling roles in society. It is in this way that the people around us have an image of us, and that we have an image of ourselves. For most people, it is important that they fill the roles that are set by their culture as significant. "Wage-earner" is of major importance among such roles. If a man cannot fill that role, he is likely to be beset by emotional problems that are not directly related to his impoverishment. This may be seen most clearly where impoverishment is not actually a factor. Older men who have been retired from work have often lost their major role in life, as have older women who have lost their family responsibilities. The importance of the emotional factor is now recognized and has affected the philosophy and techniques of working with dependents, whether they be the aged, the disabled, or just men who have lost their jobs. It is no longer considered adequate simply to offer financial assistance, and efforts are increasingly directed toward offsetting the demoralization that easily sets in when the dependent is deprived of a social role and the self-respect which goes with it. The problem of the indigent is no longer regarded as only or even primarily the problem of providing financial assistance.

At the same time, the bare fact of indigence is no longer regarded as the only warrant for an individual's receiving help from society. Child-care

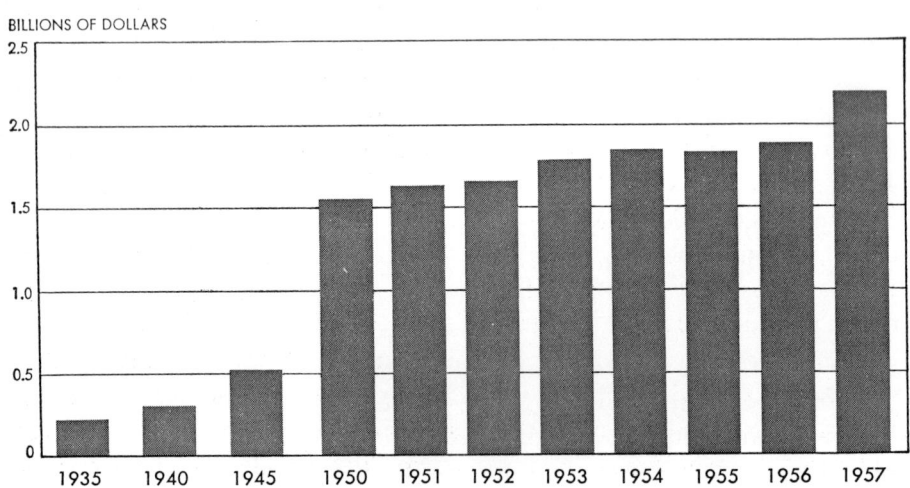

FIGURE 10:1   FEDERAL GRANTS TO STATE AND LOCAL GOVERNMENTS FOR WELFARE PURPOSES, 1935–57

Source: U.S. Bureau of the Census, *Statistical Abstract of the United States, 1958* (Washington, D.C.: U.S. Government Printing Office, 1958), p. 266.

clinics, for example, are not based on the absolute inability of parents to pay for private medical care. They are based instead on the conviction that all children deserve good medical care even though, let us say, parents might have paid for private care with money spent on the family television set.

INSURANCE VS. DOLE

The growing recognition of the psychological man as well as the physical man and the growing acceptance of self-esteem as a major human need have given rise to the concept of "insurance" as against "dole."

There has clearly already taken place a severe de-emphasis of a person's ability to produce or his past history of production as his only legitimate warrant for receiving anything from society. The idea that help in situations of dependency is a natural right of all members of society has become more widespread. But short of that, the factor of self-esteem as a legitimate human aspiration has led to an attack on the idea that financial support should come as a charity or dole from society to its dependent members.

The establishment of social insurance, in the form, for example, of social security or unemployment insurance, was partly motivated by the desire to remove the stigma from dependency. It was ostensibly, of course, an effort to make the widespread support of dependency economically feasible and to establish an automatic procedure by which the individual could provide for his own potential dependency.

However, the use of the term "insurance" in the current social insurance program is, in an actuarial sense, illusory. Social insurance differs in many ways from insurance obtained through private companies. For example, contributions to the system are not made by the individual alone. More significantly, the amount that he pays bears no relation to the potential amount he can receive. A dependent with a family can benefit more than a single dependent, although his total premiums amount to no more. In this respect, since payments are almost universal, the social insurance program is more a general tax-supported program than an insurance program. It more closely resembles, for example, the fire-fighting protection available to citizens who need it but paid for by taxes levied against all. However, in the welfare field, so long dominated by the "dole" concept, the insurance approach has the psychological advantage of involving to some degree the participation of all and, therefore, their sense of "entitlement."

Many fear, however, that the government will become a gigantic welfare machine and point to the dangers inherent in an increase in the sheer bureaucratic size of government. Others see another danger in the continual widening of the definition of dependency. Such a widening of the concept of dependency would destroy the human dignity which modern welfare systems are designed to protect. Citizens might come to think of themselves not as free men but as children of the state, or dependent wards of the state.

These are all issues which must be evaluated, at least to some degree, for each given situation, rather than generally, because of the infinite varieties of dependency and the different factors which each involves.

Section II: Dependency because of Physical Disability

There are two related forms of dependency caused by physical disability: that which renders people fully or partially unemployable, so that they must be supported by others, and that which through catastrophic medical expense imposes an impossible economic burden even where the family wage-earner is not chronically unemployed.

Extent and Nature of the Problem

The precise extent of physical disability is not easy to establish. Many disabilities never become a matter of official record. Though there are local, regional, and national health surveys, most of them are incomplete, swiftly outdated, or difficult to collate because of the use of differing sets of criteria. However, on the basis of these surveys, some estimates are possible.

A survey by the U.S. Public Health Service in 1957 indicated that, on an average, there were about sixteen days of illness disability per person in the country per year. There was an average of over five days per person spent in bed each year because of illness.[1] These figures, of course, include both children and older people, who are not normally wage-earners but whose disabilities represent a burden which the state must assume if the family cannot. In the case of older people, the dependency problem is increased by the fact that their disability is likely to be chronic.

The 1957 survey of the Public Health Service found an annual rate of about eight work-loss days per employed person, or a total of over half a billion workdays lost per year because of illness.[2] The dislocation to the national economy in terms of man-hours lost is obvious. More significant perhaps, from the point of view of dependency, was the finding that about 10 per cent of the population had some type of chronic disability. About 3 per cent of the population were chronically limited in other than their major activities; about 5 per cent were chronically limited in the pursuit of major activities, such as housework or employment; and about 2 per cent

---

[1] U.S. Department of Health, Education, and Welfare, *Preliminary Report on Disability*, Public Health Service Publication No. 584-B4 (Washington, D.C.: U.S. Government Printing Office, 1958), p. 1.
[2] *Ibid.*

of the population were unable to carry on major activity of any kind.[3]

It is estimated that there are over 2½ million people suffering from orthopedic handicaps, of whom about 350,000 are totally incapacitated. More than a quarter of a million Americans are blind, and another half-million have severe sight defects. There are at least 3 million who suffer from serious hearing defects. Perhaps 4 million adults can be considered handicapped by heart trouble.

It is estimated that 15 per cent of American families are in debt to hospitals, physicians, or other providers of medical goods or services to the extent of almost a billion dollars out of a total annual medical bill of over $10 billion. In 1953, about 1 million families incurred indebtedness for personal health services equal to or exceeding one half of their annual income; about half of these million families incurred indebtedness equal to or exceeding their entire annual income.[4]

Meeting the Problem

Society has four different kinds of action concerns in meeting the problem of dependency resulting from physical disability. Its long-range concern is to reduce the incidence of serious disability by preventive measures. More immediately, it attempts to reduce dependency by organized plans to meet medical expenses and by the swift rehabilitation of the disabled. Finally, there is the need to give financial assistance to the disabled where all else has failed.

PREVENTION AND TREATMENT

The prevention of serious physical disability means primarily three things: (a) the prevention of disease and congenital disorders, especially through research; (b) the prevention of accidents; and (c) early and adequate medical treatment.

Research

From the nineteenth century until well into the twentieth century, medical research was preoccupied with the infectious and communicable diseases, such as pneumonia, tuberculosis, and intestinal disorders, which were at that time the leading causes of disability and death. Dramatic research advances, coupled with public sanitation control and better nutrition, have radically reduced the incidence of such diseases.

Tuberculosis, for example, caused a death rate of about 194 per 100,000

---

[3] *Ibid.*
[4] Odin W. Anderson with Jacob J. Feldman, *Family Medical Costs and Voluntary Health Insurance* (New York: McGraw-Hill Book Co., Inc., 1956).

population in 1900; at mid-century it was down to about 26. Influenza and pneumonia had a death rate of about 202 in 1900; at mid-century it was down to about 30. The death rate from typhoid fever has dropped from about 30 to almost zero; diphtheria has almost disappeared as a cause of death, although it had registered a death rate of about 40 per 100,000 at the turn of the century.[5]

As infectious diseases declined and the life-span was extended, the illnesses of an aging population began to attract major research attention. Cancer, for example, increased as a cause of death from about 64 per 100,000 in 1900 to about 138 fifty years later. The death rate from heart disease increased from about 137 to 348 in those years.[6] Medical research began to take new directions and expanded its activities.

Before World War II, medical research expenditures in this country totaled about $20 million a year. In 1951, over $180 million was spent for research. Over 40 per cent of this cost was borne by government, about 30

FIGURE 10:2 AVERAGE LENGTH OF LIFE FROM ANCIENT TO MODERN TIMES

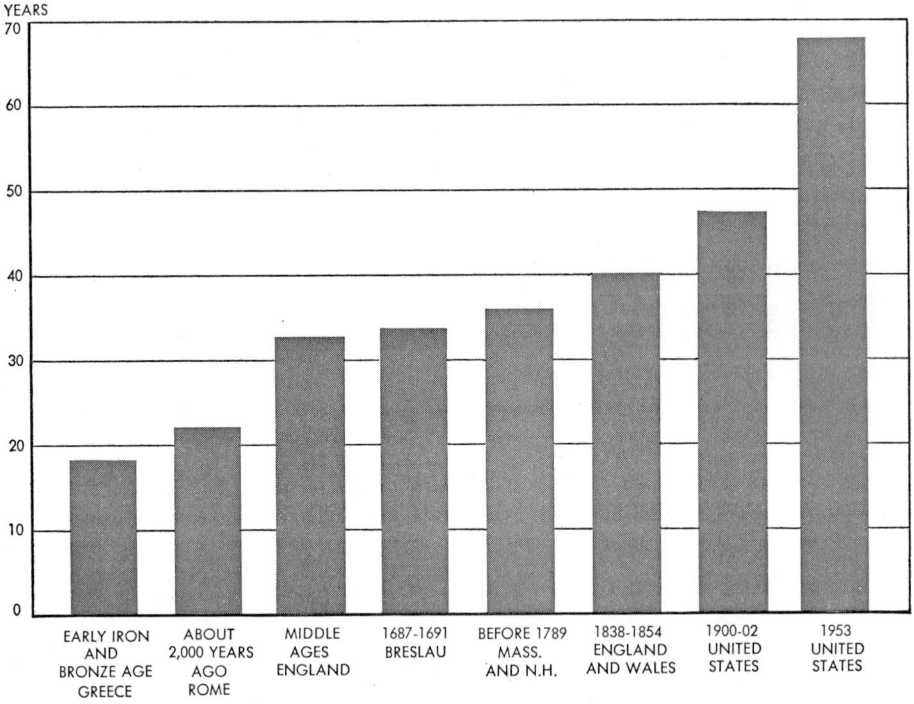

Source: Health Information Foundation, *Progress in Health Services,* 5 (May, 1956), 1.

[5] U.S. Bureau of the Census, *Statistical Abstract of the United States, 1955* (Washington, D.C.: U.S. Government Printing Office, 1956), p. 71.
[6] *Ibid.*

per cent by the pharmaceutical industry, and the rest by medical institutions or other sources of private philanthropy.[7] The federal government has established seven research centers, most of them since World War II: the National Institutes of Cancer, Heart, Allergy and Infectious Diseases, Mental Health, Dental Research, Arthritis and Metabolic Diseases, and Neurological Diseases and Blindness. These institutes carry on research and make grants to hospitals and universities, where most of the research is actually conducted.

The chief complaint against the medical research program in this country is that there is still not enough of it. Because research is expensive and must be highly co-ordinated, the federal government has generally been elected as the only agency able to meet the cost of an adequate program. Critics point out that total expenditure for medical research is only a fraction of 1 per cent of the nation's defense budget. It is claimed that voluntary citizens' health associations, such as the Cancer Society and the Heart Association, are limited both in their fund-raising abilities and in their economic efficiency. In 1954, for example, the Heart Association raised $11 million, but only a little more than one-third of this sum went for research. About 15 per cent of the total collected was actually spent in fund-raising and another 12 per cent in administrative expenses; the rest was spent on

FIGURE 10:3 DEATH RATES BY SELECTED CAUSES, 1900–1957

PER 100,000 POPULATION

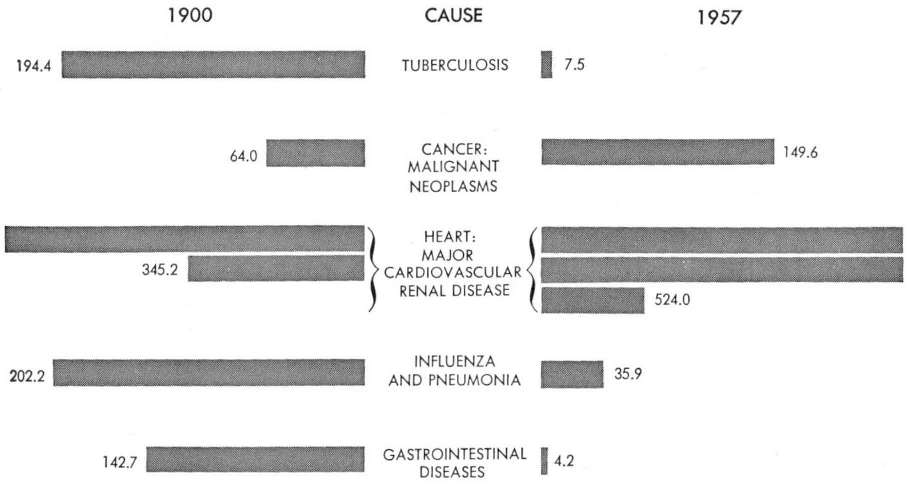

1900	CAUSE	1957
194.4	TUBERCULOSIS	7.5
64.0	CANCER: MALIGNANT NEOPLASMS	149.6
345.2	HEART: MAJOR CARDIOVASCULAR RENAL DISEASE	524.0
202.2	INFLUENZA AND PNEUMONIA	35.9
142.7	GASTROINTESTINAL DISEASES	4.2

Source: U.S. Bureau of the Census, *Statistical Abstract of the United States, 1958* (Washington, D.C.: U.S. Government Printing Office, 1958), p. 68.

---

[7] Justus J. Schifferes, "Who Pays for Medical Research?" *Medical Economics,* 28 (July, 1951), 66.

much-needed public and professional education and community services. The Cancer Society in the same year spent about one-fourth of the $23 million it raised on research and about 16 per cent on fund-raising and administration. How much is collected by these national private agencies tends to depend on the fund-raising ability of the agency rather than on the significance of the disease itself. In 1954, for example, the National Foundation for Infantile Paralysis raised twice as much money as the Heart Association and Cancer Society together, although more than a hundred times as many Americans were victims of heart disease and cancer as were victims of polio. (See Adaptation 24, pp. 511 ff., below.)

Accident-Prevention

It is estimated that about two out of three cases of orthopedic handicap and one out of five cases of blindness result from accidental injury. Fatal accidents have become less common over the years. In 1906 there was an approximate death rate by accident of almost 100 per 100,000 population. In 1956 the death rate by accident was less than 60.[8] This drop occurred despite a 500 per cent increase in deaths by automobile accidents. The dramatic reduction of fatal nonvehicle accidents can perhaps be ascribed to the changing nature of the industrial scene, to stringent industrial and public safety regulations, and to the educational activities of insurance companies and such groups as the National Safety Council.

Strict enforcement of traffic regulations, the building of better roads, widespread use of safety belts, and the new safety consciousness of automobile designers may diminish the rate of serious automobile accidents; but unless there is some radical departure from the present automotive pattern in this country, there is probably an irreducible minimum of accidents that may be expected on the road, as there is in industry and in the home.

Early and Adequate Medical Treatment

Perhaps the most practical approach to the prevention of serious and disabling disease at any given time is the provision of early and adequate medical treatment. This depends in turn on the existence of adequate medical resources and the widespread ability to pay for these resources.

There has actually been a decrease in the proportionate number of doctors in the country since the turn of the century. In 1910 there were about 135,000 doctors, or about 1 doctor for every 680 persons in the United States. In 1955 there were about 218,000 doctors, or 1 doctor for every 750 persons.[9]

---

[8] "Accidents in the United States," in *Progress in Health Services,* bulletin of the Health Information Foundation (New York, October, 1957), p. 1.

[9] U.S. Department of Health, Education, and Welfare, *Health Manpower Chart Book,* Public Health Service Publication No. 511 (Washington, D.C.: U.S. Government Printing Office, 1957), p. 14.

Nor is this a complete picture. Almost 50,000 of these physicians are not in private practice, are retired, are in the armed forces, or are interns. Even more significant is the distribution of those physicians who are in private practice. The Middle Atlantic states have nearly twice as many physicians per capita as do the southeastern states. The great metropolitan centers have nearly four times as many physicians per 100 thousand people as do rural areas.[10] In 1955, Mississippi had about 1 doctor for every 1,300 people, while New York had 1 doctor for every 500 people.[11] These disparities are not being reduced, and it is estimated that 25,000 to 30,000 more physicians are required in order to give reasonably comprehensive care to the whole of the population. There are only about 80 approved medical schools in the country, which admit about 8,000 freshmen and graduate about 7,000 doctors a year. Critics complain that the medical schools have placed an artificial ceiling on the number of medical students who may be trained. There are at least two applicants for each place now available in the medical schools. About a quarter of the approved internships in American hospitals remain unfilled. The average work week of the practicing physician is almost 70 hours.

Again, most suggestions for remedy have turned around the necessity for government, usually the federal government, to step into the breach. Medical training facilities are costly. A recurrent bill in Congress proposes a

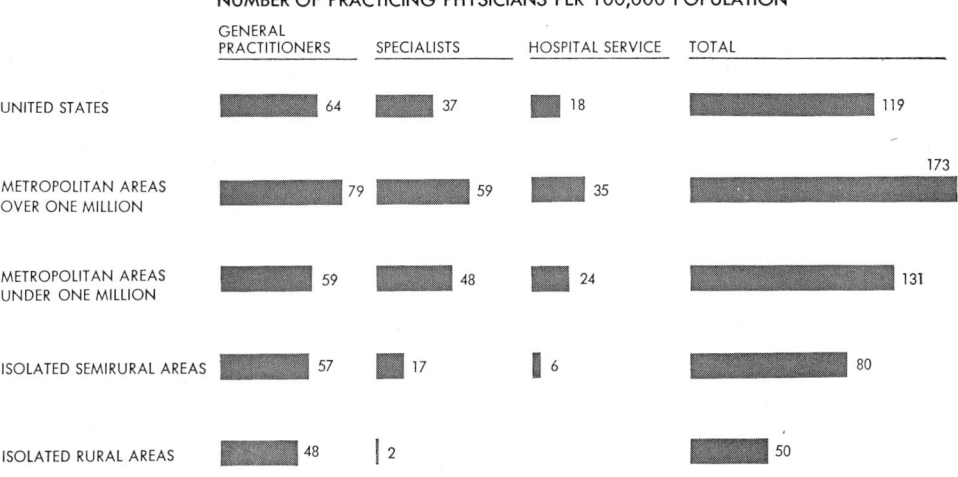

FIGURE 10:4 ACTIVE PHYSICIANS IN URBAN AND RURAL AREAS IN 1949

NUMBER OF PRACTICING PHYSICIANS PER 100,000 POPULATION

	GENERAL PRACTITIONERS	SPECIALISTS	HOSPITAL SERVICE	TOTAL
UNITED STATES	64	37	18	119
METROPOLITAN AREAS OVER ONE MILLION	79	59	35	173
METROPOLITAN AREAS UNDER ONE MILLION	59	48	24	131
ISOLATED SEMIRURAL AREAS	57	17	6	80
ISOLATED RURAL AREAS	48	2		50

Source: U.S. Public Health Service, *Health Manpower Chart Book,* Publication No. 511 (Washington, D.C.: U.S. Government Printing Office, 1957), p. 29.

---

[10] *Ibid.,* p. 28.
[11] *Ibid.,* p. 25.

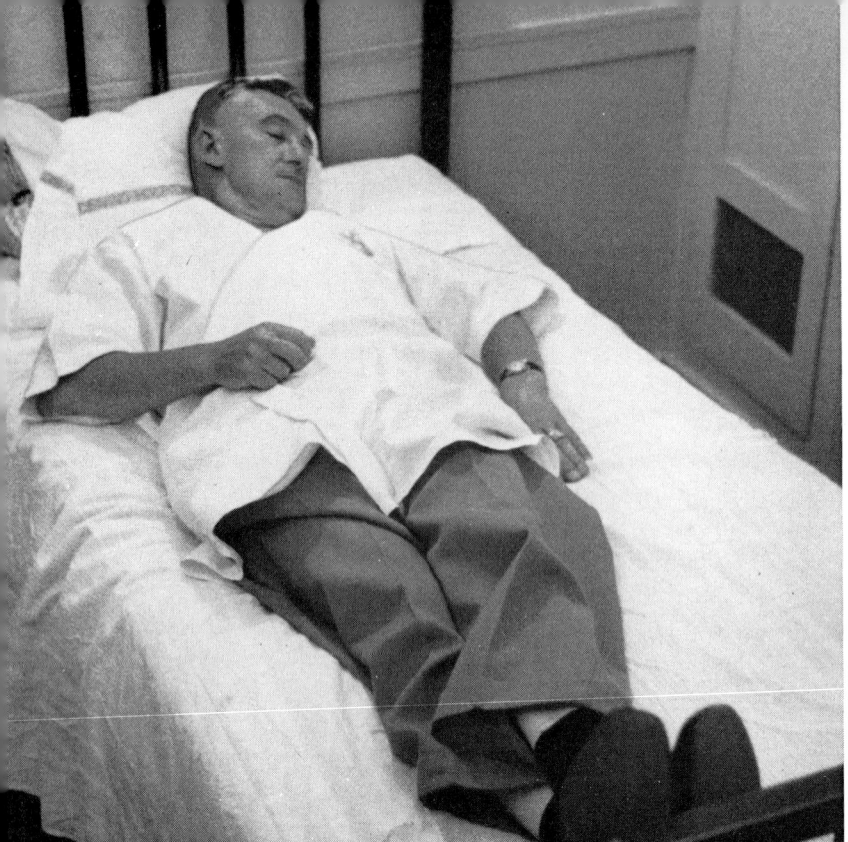

Nolan Patterson; Black Star

Between Emergencies: The American doctor works an average of 70 hours a week.

quarter of a billion dollars of federal aid for the creation of additional medical training facilities, which, it is estimated, would add about 850 places for first-year medical students. It has been further suggested that the maldistribution of physicians will probably not be eased without the establishment of medical treatment centers and hospitals in disadvantaged areas. This, too, would probably require initial government aid and perhaps, in some cases, continuing subsidies.

The 40 per cent of the counties which have a severe shortage of doctors also have in common the absence of an acceptable general hospital. There are about 5,000 general hospitals in the country, providing a little more than 4 beds per 1,000 population. According to the 1953 report of a President's Commission on the nation's health needs, more than half again that number of beds is needed to provide adequate care. This figure is complicated by regional disparities. For example, the Southeast needs more than twice as many hospital beds as it now has.[12]

[12] President's Commission on the Health Needs of the Nation, *Building America's Health* (Washington, D.C.: U.S. Government Printing Office, 1953), Vol. I, p. 23.

MEETING THE FAMILY MEDICAL BILL

Medical economics has two bearings on the question of dependency. Although lack of money is not the only factor, families often do not, for budgetary reasons, seek early treatment of minor ills or get preventive medicine. In addition, extraordinary or catastrophic medical expense often serves in itself to place a family in a position of dependency. About 30 per cent of the population reported in 1946 that they "put off going to a doctor because of costs." [13] Paul de Kruif comments:

> The doctor must be on the watch to avoid sending his sick patients from the frying pan of disease into the fire of subsequent worry about unbearable medical debt.... Where doctors are individual business men dealing with the average sick man, they dare not sell all the science they have to offer. Their regard for the average individual's pocketbook makes it necessary for them to withhold the full power of that science.[14]

A variety of medical prepayment plans have been proposed to deal with both normal and extraordinary medical needs. However, most prepayment plans are designed primarily to meet catastrophic situations. Plans which propose to meet the normal medical expenses of an individual or family have been bitterly opposed by spokesmen of the organized medical profession, on the grounds that such plans usually require aspects of group practice, which the American Medical Association does not feel is in the best interests of the nation, the nation's health, or the medical profession. The American family, it is argued, has not been educated to regard normal medical expenses, including those for preventive diagnosis and treatment, as a standard budget item like food and rent. In fact, the American seems much less reluctant to budget a regular amount for the care and treatment of his automobile than he does for medical care. The organized medical profession agrees that some insurance plan is desirable to help meet large, unexpected medical bills for such contingencies as surgery and hospitalization, and it has helped to sponsor two such plans.

Limited Voluntary Health Plans

Over 100 million Americans are covered by some form of "catastrophic" medical insurance. The largest enrollment is in the Blue Cross Plan, a nonprofit organization controlled by hospital administrators. Blue Cross covers hospital costs primarily, together with certain surgical and medical services in hospitals. The Plan, which differs in different states, typically covers the cost of a ward bed for from 30 to 120 days per illness. The services of the

---

[13] Clarence A. Peters, *Free Medical Care* (New York: H. W. Wilson Co., 1946), p. 94.
[14] Paul de Kruif, *Kaiser Wakes the Doctors* (New York: Harcourt Brace & Co., Inc., 1943), p. 36.

physician are covered only when he performs them in the hospital for the hospitalized patient. The Blue Shield Plan, organized and controlled by the medical profession, is similar in nature, although in some cases it provides for certain services to be performed in the doctor's office. First visits for minor ailments, however, are not covered. Some industries and unions have comparable plans, as do commercial insurance companies. It is estimated that these plans, dealing primarily with hospitalization, surgery, and connected services, cover about 50 per cent of the costs of illnesses that require hospitalization but almost none of the costs of illnesses that do not require hospitalization.

Comprehensive Voluntary Health Plans

About 5 million people in the country belong to comprehensive health plans which cover 80–90 per cent of their total medical costs. These plans typically provide full hospitalization costs, including all surgical and medical costs connected with hospitalization; in addition, they cover any and all physician's and laboratory services, usually with the payment of a nominal fee. The Permanente Plan in California, for example, charges a dollar for each office visit. Under these plans, however, the patient must choose from a closed panel of doctors, though he is free to change doctors if he wishes.

Critics of these plans, including the American Medical Association, charge that (a) the closed-panel arrangement prevents the client from seeking out any doctor he desires in the community; (b) physicians on retainer fee do not tend to give as individual or leisurely treatment as they do on a fee-for-service basis; (c) where a doctor's services are not freely contracted, the proper doctor-patient relationship is damaged.

Supporters of co-operative health plans emphasize that (a) one of their stated purposes is preventive medicine; clients are urged and able to secure early treatment of minor ills and regular diagnostic checkups; (b) the finest medical care is made available, because this is group practice at its most intense; a panel of specialists is provided in every field; (c) physicians like the regular hours, take turns at night duty, have opportunities for advanced study; (d) the plans avoid the usual fee-for-service arrangement because it discourages full medical care; where there is a fee charged for each item of service, it is alleged, the emphasis is upon sickness rather than health, upon quantity rather than quality.

National Health Insurance

England, France, Germany, Norway, and New Zealand have some form of universal tax-supported health insurance. This is essentially a plan for comprehensive medical coverage. The U.S. Congress has entertained several such proposals, which typically would cover about 85 per cent of the population, although others might join voluntarily. According to one proposal considered after World War II, 3 per cent of all income would be taxed for this purpose; the government would contribute about 1 per cent of its general revenue. All necessary medical expenses, including physicians' services, hospitalization, laboratory work, and medicines would be provided. Patients would have free choice of doctors, who, if they entered the system, would have to accept fixed payment for their services from the government.

Supporters invoke all the advantages of a comprehensive medical insurance plan and point out that only under a national health insurance plan of some kind will a substantial portion of the population be able to afford such coverage. Critics, including the American Medical Association, strongly oppose government interference with physicians, which they consider socialistic. Apart from charges that such a plan would be harmful to proper medical practice, general fears of a growing bureaucracy and the centralization of government power are voiced.

REHABILITATION

The return of the disabled to a productive role in society involves these basic factors: (a) special medical attention aimed toward reducing the disability as much as possible, such as the provision of artificial limbs or other special appliances; (b) occupational counseling and training to help fit the disabled individual into as productive a niche as possible; and (c) individual counseling to help the disabled person adjust psychologically to his limitations.

The Office of Vocational Rehabilitation of the U.S. Department of Health, Education, and Welfare estimates that there are about 2 million disabled Americans who could be benefited by vocational rehabilitation and that this number is increased by 250,000 each year. Some private philanthropic organizations, such as the Goodwill Industries and various associations for the blind, have specialized in rehabilitation programs, but the basic, over-all rehabilitation program has been governmental. State agencies have provided the rehabilitation services with guidance and financial grants from the federal government. In 1957 more than 70,000 handicapped men and women were restored to useful occupations through this public program.[15] In 1954 Congress passed special legislation designed to help close the gap between the 60,000 handicapped persons who were being rehabilitated each year and the much larger number who needed rehabilitation. The legislation chiefly provided more financial assistance for state programs.

The economic soundness of rehabilitation expenditures was vividly demonstrated by the Office of Vocational Rehabilitation in 1957. That year over

---

[15] U.S. Department of Health, Education, and Welfare, *Annual Report, 1957* (Washington, D.C.: U.S. Government Printing Office, 1957), p. 215.

70,000 men and women had been rehabilitated through the public program. Their annual rate of earnings had increased from $21 million to $141 million, a net gain of $120 million in the nation's purchasing power. In addition, it was calculated that the increased federal income taxes received from these rehabilitated persons in the course of their working lives would more than return the cost of that year's program.[16]

SUPPORTING THE DISABLED

There are chronically handicapped people who, for many different reasons, cannot be or have not been rehabilitated, and there are those whose short-term disabilities can create a disastrous loss of basic income. For these people, direct financial support is necessary.

The chronically unemployable are now substantially covered by government welfare programs. The Federal Public Assistance Program has authorized financial aid to the blind since 1935 and financial aid to the permanently and totally disabled since 1950. In both cases, the individual states set up and administer their own programs within basic regulations established by the national government, which provides a little more than half of the money needed for these state programs. In April, 1958, 108,000 blind people were assisted with monthly payments averaging about $57. In the same month 305,000 permanently and totally disabled persons received payments averaging about $60 a month.[17]

Temporary disability resulting from on-the-job injury or occupational disease is covered by state Workmen's Compensation laws. These set up insurance programs which provide medical care for job-connected injuries or diseases, but they also disburse cash benefits to a worker who has been disabled on the job. Most states limit the number of weeks for which benefits may be paid, although some continue to pay the worker for as long as he is totally disabled. Three out of four wageworkers are covered by workmen's compensation.

A new development in the 1940's was the establishment of state programs for temporary disability of nonoccupational origin. Rhode Island, California, New Jersey, and New York pioneered these programs, which are being considered in other states. These programs involve insurance plans. In California, payments are financed exclusively by employee contributions of 1 per cent of wages up to $3,000. In other states, employers bear part of the cost. Maximum benefits range from $25 to $30 for 13–26 weeks.

Finally, all states have General Assistance programs for those who need "relief" and do not qualify under any insurance or other public assistance

---

[16] *Ibid.*, p. 218.
[17] U.S. Department of Health, Education, and Welfare, *Social Security Bulletin,* Vol. 21, No. 7 (Washington, D.C.: U.S. Government Printing Office, 1958), pp. 30, 32.

334 NEW CASES OF TB FOUND IN SUBURBS IN '57

32.7 Pct. Discovered in Minimal Stage

Good case finding practices enabled the Suburban Cook

Unwed Mother Relief May Top $10 Million

Smith Gives Estimate Disagreeing With DPA's Figures

By DUKE KAMINSKI
Bulletin Harrisburg Bureau

Harrisburg, Aug. 2 — Auditor

Better Care To Be Sought For Aged Ill

Joint Meeting Set Up Monday to Improve Conditions in Homes

By Eve Edstrom
Staff Reporter
A major effort to

---

7 FAMILIES AID RESEARCH INTO BLOOD DISEASE

Seven families who have lost a relative to blood diseases have set up a joint memorial fund to provide money for scientific research by the American Blood Research society.

nd sponsors in-
e Kaplan Roth
Mrs. Irving L.
Lake Shore dr.;
ovay memorial
Schneiderman,
e dr.; the David
rial by Mrs.
artz, 4934 N.
and the Irene
memorial by
ield, 1737 W.

re the Rosalyn
by Mrs. Sam
Hoyne av.; the
htenstein me-

10,000 See Free Film On Cancer

More than 10,000 Dallas County women turned out Tuesday to see the American Cancer Society's movie which teaches the technique of self-examination for possible breast cancer.

Half of the ten Dallas theaters which showed the film were packed to capacity, including the

Additional details Part 1, Page 2.

big 2,100-seat Palace downtown. "Breast Self-Examination" will be shown again at 10 a.m. Wednesday at 10 Dallas County locations listed in a separate story.

Hundreds of women Tuesday, too late to get seats, stood through the 18-minute movie and 30-minute question-and-answer period at the Palace, Casa Linda, Texas, Inwood and Wilshire Theaters. Many had to be turned away.

Near-capacity crowds were reported at the Grove and Crest

State Medical Fund Low for Aged, Disabled

The Utah Department of Public Welfare is slowly running out of funds to pay medical costs to persons on welfare.

The department is seeking an answer to the problem — but it hasn't found an acceptable one yet.

The trouble, according to James G. Kerr, director of the

department's public assistance bureau, is that medical expenses for persons on old age assistance and for disabled persons receiving aid are depleting the entire medical care fund.

Mr. Kerr said that a cash balance in the "medical pool" allows time for decision-making.

But, meanwhile, the costs of medical care are exceeding

revenues into the pool by $5,000 a month.

Eventually, he said, costs will have to be cut.

The medical pool is financed 50-50 by the state and the federal government. Recipients of aid under the various welfare programs are eligible for financial aid to pay medical costs.

But two categories of aid—

COMBINED FUND GOAL IS RAISED BY 2 MILLIONS

Community, Red Cross Drive Opens Oct. 1

Poor Farm Sale Proposition to Benefit Indigent is Discussed

In addition, the dist
1957 had 3,275 persons
tered in its clinics. A
those are inactive TB
still requiring periodic
ups and treatment, an
charged cases which co
treatment on an out-p
basis.

Psychiatrist Says Jobs Fill Many Needs

The desire to work is a characteristic of the emotionally healthy person, a psychiatrist told a workshop on vocational rehabilitation of hospitalized mental patients at the University of Buffalo yesterday morning.

Dr. Louis Linn of the staff

Ared Persons Active In Retarded Program

Rep. Gertrude F. Koskoff of Plainville is one of several Connecticut citizens who will serve with the Connecticut Assn. for Retarded Children on a financing program. The study follows on the heels of a $15,000 grant to the state organization. It is sponsored in cooperation with the two state institutions for the

HIKE IN SOCIAL SECURITY TAX BRINGS CLASH

BY WILLARD EDWARDS
[Chicago Tribune Press Service]

Washington, Aug. 8 — The

County Board Seeking Out Peoples Feelings on Issue

A proposition to sell the Saunders County Poor Farm north of Wahoo and take the proceeds to build cottages for indigent ne
before the W
weekly meetin
Tony Kriz, Saun
fare Director; Tho
Clerk; and Georg
ounly Attorney w
r reports by Ben
tainment chairm
Members of the
rd of Supervisor
ests at the mee
Mr. Kriz, first t
oposition said.

Where Can Our Old People Go?

Need More Homes for Aged, Better Programs to Aid Them

First in a Series
By JACKIE OWEN
Staff Reporter

"It's her favorite poem," said the superintendent of the home for the aging.

The white-haired old woman smiled agreement from where she sat stiffly in a wheelchair. Her hands, mottled and blue-veined, rested primly in her lap.

She started to recite in a thin but cheerful voice.

They say that I am growing old,
I've heard them tell it times untold . . .
In language plain and bold.
But I'm not growing old.
The frail old shell in which I dwell
Is growing old I know full well—
But I am not the shell . . .

Development of a Medical Plan For Community Is Long Overdue

THE new cooperative venture being discussed by the medical staffs of the community's three hospitals and the Bowman Gray
For 2
been
of th
and n
Ide
joined
ston-S

velop such a plan, then the w
open for the community at lar
late it into bricks and mortar.
w look at the
pment in the

'Too Early To Guess' Effect Of Defeat Of Housing Bill

ways of uti
lities to be
y involve:
f where an
will be pr

House defeats $975,000,000 housing bill by 6 votes .. Page 1

Jobless Pay Claims Rise By 19,500

NEW YORK, June 11 (UPI) — Unemployment insurance claims rose by 19,500 last week, for the first time in seven weeks, the e Department of Labor re-
d today.
laims for the week totalled
000, an increase of 89 per
over a year ago, the Depart-
said.
Outside of N
w claims las
700, mostly
tered layoff
temporary n
umber of ind
tment said.

Alcohol Led Him to Moral Bankruptcy, Then AA's Showed Him the Way Back

By JAMES H. WHITE, *Press-Scimitar Staff Writer*

"I'm an alcoholic," said the little man with the mustache, "but by the grace of God, I'm sober today!"

He spoke to 300 others who knew by their own past experiences what he was talking about. They were all alcoholics, or members of an alcoholic's family.

The occasion was the third anniversary of the Whitehaven Chapter of Alcoholics Anonymous. Other AA chapters from five surrounding states sent representatives to the dinner-meeting at St. Paul's Catholic Church last night.

Now an Executive

The speaker, now a successful Shreveport, La., printing executive, was giving a testimonial speech:

"One never knows when he will cross that invisible line between social drinking and chronic alcoholism," he said.

"I guess I drank socially 35 years. I swelled with pride when my friends commented on how well I could 'hold' my liquor.

"But one day I started drink-

ing earlier in the day. I began the first drink up to 5 p.m., then 3 p.m., 1 p.m. — finally, I couldn't get thru the day without a morning drink.

"After that came the DTs (delirium tremens)—I was more than human being. I was at the end of my rope when I found AA."

'Moral Bankruptcy'

He said what had started as harmless self-indulgence deteriorated into "physical and moral bankruptcy."

"But AA's 12-step program gave me back sobriety—I haven't had a drink now in six years four months and 20 days," he said.

"Alcoholism is the third most serious health problem in the world today," he said. "There are 4,000,000 alcoholics in America alone today. With drinking such an accepted part of American life, we should at least treat it with respect and guard against crossing over that line to alcoholism."

Around the room sat people from all walks of life—doctors,

lawyers, truck drivers, businessmen, old people and young—

Each had a story to tell.

Next to this reporter sat a stockily built Memphis man, about 30. Beside him sat his pretty young wife.
sible to tell which
holic.

Lost $10,000 J

"I didn't have
some do," the m
people have to g
gutter, before th
from the AA. I
self-respect, but I
I couldn't leave t
It cost me a $1
wrecking my lif
had.

"I had thought
for winos and
but I decided to
anyway. Since th
life has changed,
people and can ho
again. I even th
now."

His pretty wife
proved that she
years ago when
husband "for bet
smiled happily.

Rehabilitation Center Urged

State Sen. Mitchell Pledges a Bill

State Sen. Tom Mitchell, running for another term, said he is in favor of a rehabilitation center for the physically handicapped in the Memphis Medical Center.

"I will introduce and support legislation to create a rehabilitation center in the Medical Center to diagnose, treat, train and secure employment for all handicapped persons going there, including the blind."

Slump Erases Merged Welfare Dept. Savings

BY RUDOLPH UNGER

y savings to taxpayers in first six months of operat- e merged city and county re department have been fied by the recession, ond M. Hilliard, director e department, reported sday to Daniel Ryan, y board president.

wever, in his six month t to the board, Hilliard the merged department aved the state treasury ,000 by its ability to er 10,322 cases from state supported general to federally aided spe- lief programs.

ger Permits Transfer

"It would have been impossible to transfer anywhere

economic conditions, save substantial sums of money," the welfare chief said. "They won't come so much in administrative costs where we need a full staff, but in the case load savings such a staff can provide.

"Ho
keep o
belong
on rel
them
help c
thus e
of che
returne

Golden Agers Plan Program for Season

PLAINVILLE — The Golden Age Club will begin its fall program at the Municipal Building, 2 p.m., on Wednesday, it was announced today.

Persons 55 years of age or over are eligible for membership.

Tickets for entrance into two movie theaters will be available at the meeting for persons 60 years old or older.

of the many
e and public
simple but
feeling of

heelchair is
a national.
rly for the

restricts the
ie, but still
ed,
on, superin-
ire 134 resi-
80 per cent
125 per cent

ental ward
65
psy-
ere
said
ake
of-
der

program. General Assistance funds are provided exclusively by state or local governments or both. Qualifications and amounts of assistance vary widely from region to region.

Some groups of people are covered for medical benefits and disability by special plans. The Railroad Retirement Act, an insurance plan, provides both short-term and long-term disability relief for certain qualified railroad workers. Veterans, of course, receive continuing medical care for service-connected disabilities and under certain conditions can qualify for hospitalization for nonservice-connected disabilities. Compensation is received for partial and total service-connected disabilities and for total disabilities which are not service connected. Medical coverage, usually under a limited voluntary health insurance plan, and disability payment plans have also been set up under many private group health and welfare programs established by labor unions and industry in collective bargaining. Such plans received great impetus during World War II, when wages were fixed and employers could bargain in a tight labor market only by offering "fringe benefits."

Section III: Dependency because of Emotional or Mental Disability

There is a certain artificiality about making a distinction between physical and mental disability; overemphasizing the distinction can do a disservice. Both physical and emotional difficulties can incapacitate the individual and prevent him from normal participation in society. Both require treatment and care. One sometimes leads to the other: brain injury may result in mental disability; emotional difficulties are sometimes at the root of such everyday physical disabilities as asthma, headaches, excessive fatigue.

It is probably most valid to distinguish between physical and mental illness in the following way: physical illness may or may not result in dislocations of social and personal behavior, but mental illness in general *consists of* dislocations of social and personal behavior. It is far more difficult to say what constitutes mental illness than to agree on what constitutes physical illness.

1. Characterization of a person as mentally ill has something to do with the severity of the problem. In cases of physical illness, a person who has a mild cold and a person who has pneumonia are both recognized as being physically ill. Where mental illness is concerned, however, the severity of the symptoms is an important factor in deciding whether a person is or is not mentally ill.

2. There is also the difficulty of deciding whether every personality difficulty and every dislocation of social behavior is a case of mental illness. Few

people always behave normally; yet we probably would not want to conclude that everybody is mentally ill to some degree or another. One of the difficulties is that we want to be able to decide when dislocations of social behavior, such as crime or juvenile delinquency, are products of mental illness and when they are not.

Extent and Nature of the Problem

Despite these difficulties, mental incapacities or illnesses are often categorized in the following way, though the distinctions are tenuous and overlapping: (a) mental retardation; (b) clinical emotional disorders, generally classified as psychoses or neuroses; and (c) personality disorders, which do not fall in the clinical category but nevertheless result in disorders of social behavior.

MENTAL RETARDATION

The mentally retarded are those who are born with such low powers of intelligence that they can never make a normal adjustment to life and society. This phenomenon is distinct, for example, from the degeneration of intelligence sometimes found in the aged.

The IQ can serve as a kind of rough standard for mental retardation. According to traditional usage, idiots are those with an IQ below 25, imbeciles those with an IQ from 25 to 50, and morons those with an IQ from 50 to about 70. It is probably more helpful to describe this range of retardation by age-behavior. The lowest grade, corresponding generally to the idiot, has an intelligence of less than the average three-year-old. Consequently he cannot take care of his most simple needs, learn any skills, or utter more than a few words. The middle grade, corresponding to the imbecile, has the intelligence of a child from three to seven or eight years old. He can manage his bodily needs, can speak or even read simple sentences, and can learn certain elementary tasks, none of which, however, are economically useful. Socially, he needs constant supervision. The high-grade mental deficient, corresponding to the moron, has the intelligence of a child from eight to ten or eleven years. It is possible for him to learn certain economically useful manual tasks which can make him self-supporting. However, his social judgment is poor, and he can often be victimized or led into antisocial behavior by others.

This last group comprises about 2 per cent of the American population, or about $3\frac{1}{2}$ million in a population of 180 million. The low-grade mental deficient, a term which is becoming more prevalent and encompasses those who have traditionally been known as idiots and imbeciles, makes up about 1 per cent of the American population.

Causes

At the present stage of knowledge about mental retardation, it is estimated that not more than half, and probably fewer, of the cases are hereditary in nature. Brain damage may take place during pregnancy, through certain illnesses of the mother, or in early years through prolonged fever illnesses, such as encephalitis, or through physical injury. Glandular and other physical defects, such as an excess of fluid surrounding the brain, may cause mental deficiency. Actually, at the present time, there are no clues to either hereditary or nonhereditary causes in about one out of every three cases of mental retardation.

CLINICAL EMOTIONAL DISORDERS

One out of every ten persons in the country, at the present rate, will sometime during his life suffer so severely from a mental illness that he will have to be hospitalized. Over 670,000 persons, or 51 per cent of all patients comprising the average daily hospital census of 1957, were patients in psychiatric hospitals.[18] In 1957, over 350,000 new patients were admitted to mental hospitals and psychiatric units of general hospitals.[19] The total annual cost in 1957 was over $1 billion.[20] It has been further estimated that the patients in mental hospitals would earn and spend about $3–$4 billion a year and would be paying the government about $450 million a year in taxes if they were not ill.[21] This is dependency on a massive scale, and it does not take into account the unnumbered millions who are not hospitalized but are partially and seriously disabled by mental illness. In 1955, some $2\frac{1}{2}$ million people were treated for some form of mental illness in hospitals, clinics, or by private psychiatrists.[22] Many more who needed help never sought or received treatment. A rough index of the general prevalence of the problem may be found in the fact that of the 5,800,000 men rejected by the armed services in World War II, 24 per cent were rejected for neuropsychiatric reasons other than mental deficiency, and for the latter cause about 14 per cent were rejected.[23]

Largely on a symptomatic basis, serious emotional disorders are usually

---

[18] *Hospitals,* Journal of the American Hospital Association, Vol. **32**, Part 2 (August, 1958), p. 378.

[19] *Movement of Population, Summary, for All Mental Institutions, by Type of Hospital or Institution, by Control for the U.S., 1954* (New York: Joint Information Service, American Psychiatric Association–National Association for Mental Health, January 8, 1957).

[20] *Hospitals,* Vol. **32**, Part 2 (August, 1958), p. 378.

[21] *What Are the Facts about Mental Illness?* (Washington, D.C.: National Committee against Mental Illness, 1957), p. 11.

[22] *Ibid.,* p. 3.

[23] Daniel Blaine and John H. Baird, "The Neuropsychiatric Program of the Veterans' Administration," *American Journal of Psychiatry,* **103** (1947), 463.

broken down into two inexactly bounded categories: the psychoses and the neuroses.

The Psychoses

Into the general category of psychoses fall the most severe mental illnesses—those that require the most urgent medical attention and that most completely disable the victim. About 80 per cent of all first admissions to mental hospitals are termed psychotic. By and large, these are the people who were once generally known as "insane." The psychotic is most generally characterized by some sharp break with reality, e.g., through delusions or complete withdrawal or severe moods unrelated to reality. His whole personality tends to be markedly transformed by his illness.

Some cases of mental illness are clearly organic in origin (e.g., those resulting from brain injury). Other cases, more clearly rooted in emotional factors, are called "functional." Since there are probably both organic and functional factors involved in many cases of mental illness, the terms are not usually intended to denote more than a general primacy of factors. About 35 per cent of all new psychotic admissions to hospitals suffer from psychoses that are related to the aging process and are clearly organic in origin. These are the psychoses that accompany cerebral arteriosclerosis, or senile brain disease, and commonly and variously cause delusions, loss of mental capacity, and extreme depression or agitation. As medical science increases the age level of the population, we can expect these psychoses to increase unless new knowledge is obtained. Because of their high death rate, these patients make up only about 13 per cent of the mental hospital population.[24]

About 30 per cent of all new psychotic admissions to the hospitals suffer from schizophrenia. This is typically a disease of the young (those aged 15–44), and it has not been highly susceptible of treatment. As a result, because of their low death rate, schizophrenic patients tend to accumulate from year to year and actually make up more than half of the mental hospital population. Schizophrenia is the classic retirement into private worlds manifesting itself in many forms: delusions, persistent hallucinations, incoherence, extreme stupor, and sometimes attempts at suicide or sudden acts of violence. Other functional psychoses of indistinct origin are mainly characterized by sharp fluctuations of mood and deep depression, such as the manic-depressives, who make up about 5 per cent of first psychotic admissions and whose prognosis is relatively good.

There are psychoses which sometimes accompany primary organic conditions other than those related to old age, such as general paresis or exces-

[24] *What Are the Facts about Mental Illness?*, p. 5.

sive alcoholic intoxication. All in all, more than half of all first psychotic admissions are the result of some discernible organic condition. However, since most of these conditions are associated with old age, perhaps it is the functional psychoses, such as schizophrenia, which represent the greater loss to society and certainly the greater dependency burden.

The Neuroses

The psychoneurotic is generally differentiated from the psychotic in that he still has a grip on basic reality even though he may use devices to avoid that reality.

For illustration: a neurotic, out of fear of not succeeding at a new job, may develop actual pains in his heart or paralysis of a limb, although there is nothing organically wrong with either. With that exception, however, he is fully aware of his situation; he understands that he may lose the job, for example, and worries about it, but he does not see what he can do about it in the light of his "ailment." A corresponding psychotic reaction, however, might be to believe that he is the richest man in the world and therefore does not need a job. A neurotic, out of whatever anxiety, may feel so compelled to keep free of germs that he is unable to enter a restaurant and imposes impossible standards of sanitation on his wife, such as the necessity to wash utensils before as well as after meals. His compulsion is built around bacteria which actually exist. A psychotic reaction might be the compelling belief that there is a conspiracy to kill him by poisoning his utensils.

It is evident that there can often be a murky borderline between the neurotic and the psychotic, and the therapist does not generally worry about how to classify his patient. But it is also evident that there is an equally vague borderline between the neurotic and the nonneurotic. One individual may feel more apprehensive than another about a new job. He may even have palpitations of the heart during the first few days; but, unlike the neurotic, he will not be seriously disabled from doing the job. One individual may be more concerned about bacteria than another. Perhaps, in restaurants, he will carefully wipe off his utensils with a napkin; but, unlike the neurotic, he will not find it impossible to eat in restaurants.

It would be less than helpful to identify every manifestation of emotional disturbance or weakness as mental illness. The man who is too fat, or is not of average muscular strength, or indeed has a slight chronic limp is not considered physically ill, even though some of these characteristics may be warning signs or close him out of certain highly specialized roles. Similarly, it takes more than a neurotic or "neurotic-like" reaction to make a neurosis. A neurotic person is one whose pattern of neurotic reactions pains and disables him in some significant way. He attempts to deal with his psychological problems in unrealistic and misdirected ways that only add to these problems, as in the case of the man who develops "heart trouble" in facing a new job. In this sense, he is often caught in a trap, in a vicious circle that can only become worse unless it receives attention.

In short, the difference between those who are ill and those who are not is often a difference of degree; practically speaking, it is a difference in the degree of disability.

For reasons of definition alone it is impossible to say with authority how many psychoneurotics there are at any given time. Psychoneuroses constitute only about 3 per cent of first admissions to mental hospitals. In the general population, individuals currently in psychotherapy probably are a fraction of those who either need or think they need treatment.

PERSONALITY DISORDERS

The term "personality disorders" has the least medical significance. It is essentially used to describe gross behavior deviations stemming from personality disorders that are psychologically based. It is sometimes limited to deviations where clinical neurotic or psychotic patterns, such as extreme anxiety or delusions, are *not* present. But the serious psychological inability to adjust to society's demands must on the face of it be subsumed under "mental disability," whether or not personal symptoms of clinical neurosis or psychosis are observable. Chronic alcoholism where there are no clinical symptoms is an example. So is the serious inability to hold a job, vagrancy, chronic irresponsibility, and general demoralization. Some would refer to all such conditions as "personality disorders"; others would more technically restrict the term to describe these conditions when they are unaccompanied by clinical symptoms of neurosis or psychosis.

Because the term "personality disorder" is so much a creature of arbitrary definition, a number of cautions seem in order. It is easy to be trapped into common-sense reasoning like the following: all behavior is a function of the personality; therefore, all deviant behavior is a function of a disordered personality; therefore, all deviant behavior denotes mental illness. Such a conclusion, of course, reduces both "personality disorder" and "mental illness" to meaningless absurdities. Personality is a product of constitutional factors, cultural learning, and psychological history. An individual may engage in deviant behavior primarily because his subculture so trained him, as studies in delinquency and crime have demonstrated. He has absorbed criminal values. He did not turn to them because of some special psychological need or emotional disturbance.

Therefore, if the term "personality disorder" is to have precise meaning, and if it is to be considered within the context of mental illness, it must connote the primacy of psychological factors in any given case of social deviation.

Alcoholism

A specific dependency problem which is generally considered to be based on personality disorders of one kind or another is alcoholism. The chronic alcoholic is sometimes defined not by the amount or regularity of his drinking but by his uncontrollable compulsion to drink. It has been estimated that there are as many as a million such serious alcoholic addicts in the country. However, the alcoholic has also been defined as one whose drinking has become enough of a problem to interfere with his major activities and with a successful and happy pattern of life. It has been estimated that there are some 5 million Americans who qualify under this definition and who lose an average of 22 working days each year from alcoholism alone.[25] Expenditures for liquor, time lost from work, and loss of employment because of drinking contribute to a substantial part of the dependencies that come to the attention of the official agencies.

CAUSES OF MENTAL ILLNESS

Research in mental illness is so primitive that it is possible to discuss causation only in the most general terms, except for those illnesses which are specifically related to an organic disorder, such as arteriosclerosis. It is clear, however, that a specific mental illness is almost never inherited in the mathematically predetermined Mendelian sense. A mental deterioration called "Huntington's chorea" is one of the rare exceptions, wherein three out of four children born to a parent who has this illness will themselves suffer from it. However, research suggests that predisposing constitutional factors, whatever they may be, *can* be inherited—as indeed constitutional factors which predispose toward physical illness can be inherited.

In addition, the individual's constitution is subject to change by physical environment that has no relation to genetic factors. The relation of the intra-uterine environment to tissue changes in the brain or glands is a case in point.

However, individual psychological history can also play an important part in the production of mental illness. The specific relationships that develop between a child and his parents seem often to be a major factor in shaping the individual's basic pattern of anxieties and internal conflicts. This approach in psychological depth often provides a basis for individual remedial treatment. But it does *not* explain the genesis of specific and differential phenomena of mental illness, such as the various neuroses and psychoses. The most accurate formula, at this stage of knowledge, would seem to be that *some* people with *some* kinds of psychological history and

---

[25] *Facts and Figures* (New York: National Council on Alcoholism, 1958), pp. 3, 4.

under *some* kinds of psychological stress will develop *some* kinds of emotional illness. The psychiatrist can use this formula in probing an individual patient, but it is not of much assistance in determining broad causal patterns of mental illness in society.

At the present stage of knowledge, it is not safe to generalize about broad risk factors in society. For example, there is always a temptation to suppose that the alleged swift pace, excessively competitive spirit, or heightened international tensions of our time *must* contribute to increasing mental illness. But the evidence for such supposition is weak and needs much more exploration.

In evaluating the sharp rise in hospitalization for mental illness, it is necessary to consider the increase in facilities, the increasing acceptance of these facilities, the rising age of the population, and the large proportion of mental illnesses that are directly related to old age. One research study compared admission rates to mental hospitals in Massachusetts from 1840 to 1885 with the present rate, equating age and class of patients and traditions affecting hospitalization, and found that admission rates are no higher today than they were a hundred years ago for comparable patients under fifty years of age.[26] In short, there is no conclusive evidence that the rate of functional psychosis has increased or that it has any correlation with present-day social conditions. It is impossible, of course, to so compare the rate of neurosis. The general belief is that the rate of neurotic illness has risen and *is* correlated with social conditions, but many questions have to be answered before that belief can be accepted.

There is reason to suspect the significance of superficial correlation between mental illness and specific social conditions. For example, rates of suicide are sometimes loosely invoked as general evidence of the prevalence of mental illness. If we were to apply here the broad generalization that the reprehensible social phenomena of our time are productive of mental illness, we would find little supporting evidence. Suicide rates are highest in peacetime, not in wartime. Suicide rates are relatively high among the highest, not the lowest, income groups. Suicide rates are much lower among Negroes in this country than among whites. And the suicide rate in this country was exactly the same in 1953 (10.2 per 100,000) as it was in 1900.[27]

Such statistics must be interpreted cautiously, but they help to point up the weakness of the theory that mental illness is directly related to social catastrophe. They also point up the complexity of causation in mental illness and the need for basic research in this field, which is now beginning to be widely undertaken.

---

[26] Herbert Goldhamer and Andrew W. Marshall, *The Frequency of Mental Disease* (Santa Monica: The RAND Corporation, 1949).

[27] *Statistical Abstract of the United States, 1955*, p. 71 (see n. 5, above).

Meeting the Problem

Society's agenda for meeting the dependency problems of mental disability are much the same as those required by physical disability: attempts to reduce the initial incidence of disability; improved means of treating illness; the swift rehabilitation of those who have been disabled; and, finally, the support of those who are dependent because of mental disability. Mental retardation and emotional disorders, because of the radical difference in their characteristics, call for different approaches on most remedial levels.

MENTAL RETARDATION

There is no known cure for mentally retarded children. It is possible to fit some of them for useful and self-supporting roles in society by special training. For the others it is only possible to develop their full capacity for personal care and to make their lives as pleasant as possible. Sterilization has often been proposed and sometimes practiced as a means of preventing the occurrence of mental retardation. All other questions aside, the role of heredity in general and in given cases of mental deficiency would have to be much more clearly determined than it is today before society could justifiably launch such a program.

Special School Facilities

Because of mental deficiency, at least 2 per cent of all school children need special classes and courses of study involving simplified lessons in the basic subjects and special training in manual skills. Specially trained teachers are required, and small classes are indicated for the best results. A number of the larger school systems have instituted such classes, against the constant handicap of slim budgets. For children who need more intensive care and supervision than their homes can provide, special all-day nurseries and schools have been recommended.

Institutions

When there is no special program for the mentally retarded child in a community or its schools, when the home is incapable of caring for him, or when a family might be overburdened by his care, institutionalization is called for. There are about 200 private boarding schools for the mentally deficient in the country, but the cost is too high for most families. Public prolonged-care hospitals for this purpose are usually part of the state mental hospital system. These hospitals are typically marked by long waiting lists and overcrowded conditions; and since they lack trained personnel, they also lack adequate training programs. However, less than 3 per cent of our mentally retarded children are institutionalized, and many of these are in institutions only because of the absence of community facilities. It is primarily in the community that the answers must be found.

Employment Assistance

Once they have been trained to the best of their ability, the mentally retarded who can work must still be given constant vocational guidance. They are eligible for assistance under the various state rehabilitation programs. In some instances communities have set up "sheltered workshops," where production is adapted to limited talents. In any case, there should ideally be some continual supervision by a social agency. Personal and financial guidance is often necessary to supplement proper vocational placement.

Home

Guidance for the parents of the mentally retarded is still a largely unmet need. Unwarranted fears, guilt, and shame on the part of parents often prevent the fullest development of their deficient children. The National Association for Retarded Children was formed in 1950 not only to promote the kinds of community facilities indicated above but also to provide help and enlightenment to parents of the mentally retarded.

EMOTIONAL DISORDERS

Research

Research in the various mental illnesses is still at a primitive stage compared with other medical research. It is generally agreed that any major effort to combat mental illness must be based on more knowledge than is presently available. Here again, the larger part of the cost of research is borne by government. In 1957 a total of about $27 million was spent on research by the major state and national agencies interested in mental illness. Over $15 million was in federal funds, dispensed primarily by the National Institute of Mental Health. Approximately another $10 million was spent by the various states. The Ford Foundation expended about $1.5 million for research.

Basic research proceeds along two broad avenues: biological research into the functioning of the brain and central nervous system, and psychological research into the effects of life-experiences on personality development. In addition, there is continuing research toward the practical improvement of treatment methods.

Treatment

There are two broad categories of treatment for mental illness on both the hospital and the out-patient level. *Psychotherapy* is primarily built

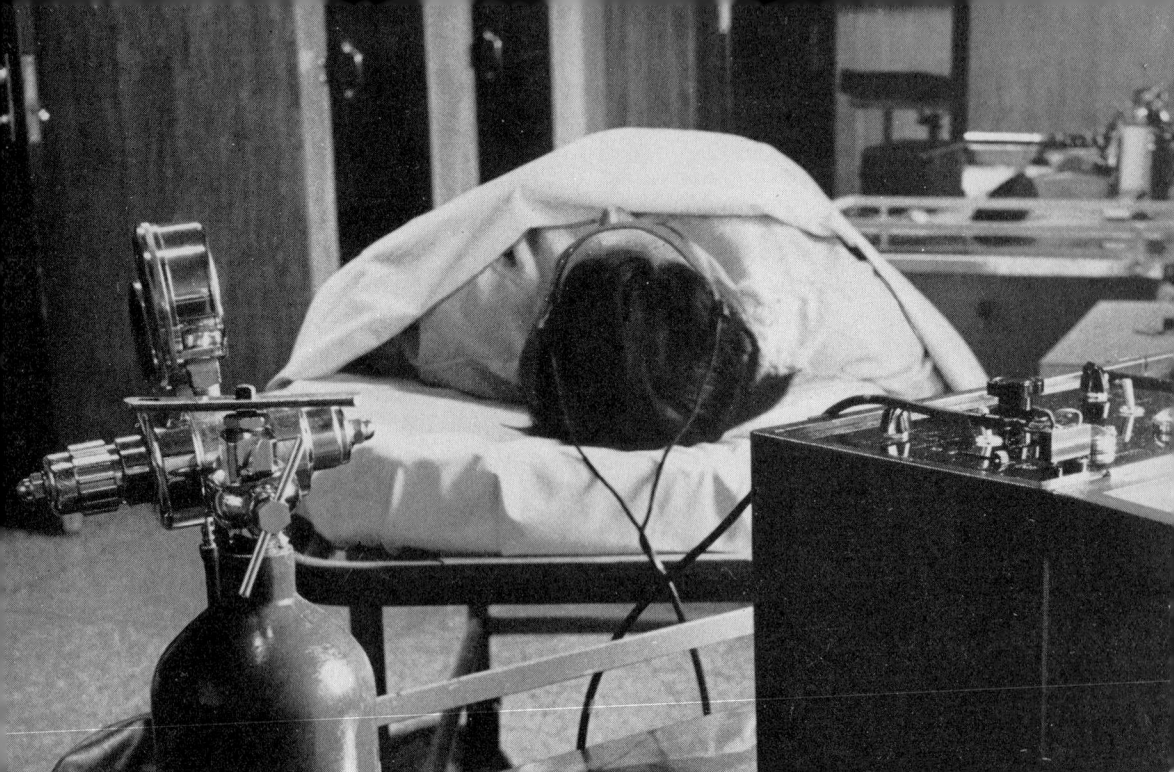

St. Louis Post-Dispatch; Black Star

Electroshock.

around the attempt to develop in the sick individual some insight into the nature of his emotional problems. The psychiatrist, in this process, is not in a magical role but is rather a skilled technician in assisting the individual to meaningfully probe his own personality and experience. *Somatotherapy* refers to those physical techniques which sometimes serve to bring a very sick person back into touch with reality so that he can return to society or at least become accessible to psychotherapy. Insulin shock was the first of such techniques; it has been largely superseded by the use of electric shock. More recently the new tranquilizing drugs have so far proved even more successful than the shock techniques. However, they are considered by psychiatrists to be an aid to psychotherapy rather than a cure.

1. *Hospitals.* The cost of psychiatric treatment is relatively high, and mental illness commonly creates total economic dependency. It is patently impossible for most families to bear the full costs of total and prolonged hospitalization. As a result, about 98 per cent of all hospitalized mental patients are in public hospitals. This requires a total maintenance expenditure of over $1 billion a year out of public funds, not including new construction costs. The bulk of this expense is borne by the states.

However, the magnitude of the problem is such that this expenditure is still far from meeting minimal needs. In 1955 mental hospitals had only about 56 per cent of the beds needed for good care.[28] Almost all were, and still are, overcrowded and short of psychiatric personnel. To meet the minimal standards set up by the American Psychiatric Association, an estimated 3,740 more psychiatrists were needed in these hospitals during 1955.[29] In practice there is little therapeutic help for patients, and nearly all state hospitals play more of a custodial than a treatment role.

It is also clear that the mental hospital situation has been improving since the end of World War II. In 1956, for the first time in history, there were fewer resident patients in state mental hospitals at the end of the year than at the beginning. The fact that a record number of mental patients were admitted to the hospitals in that year underlined the hospitals' new success in returning patients to the community. Part of this success is ascribed to increasing expenditures for state hospitals. In 1945 the average daily expenditure for each mental patient was a little more than a dollar; by 1956 this figure had more than tripled. In 1945 there was one full-time employee

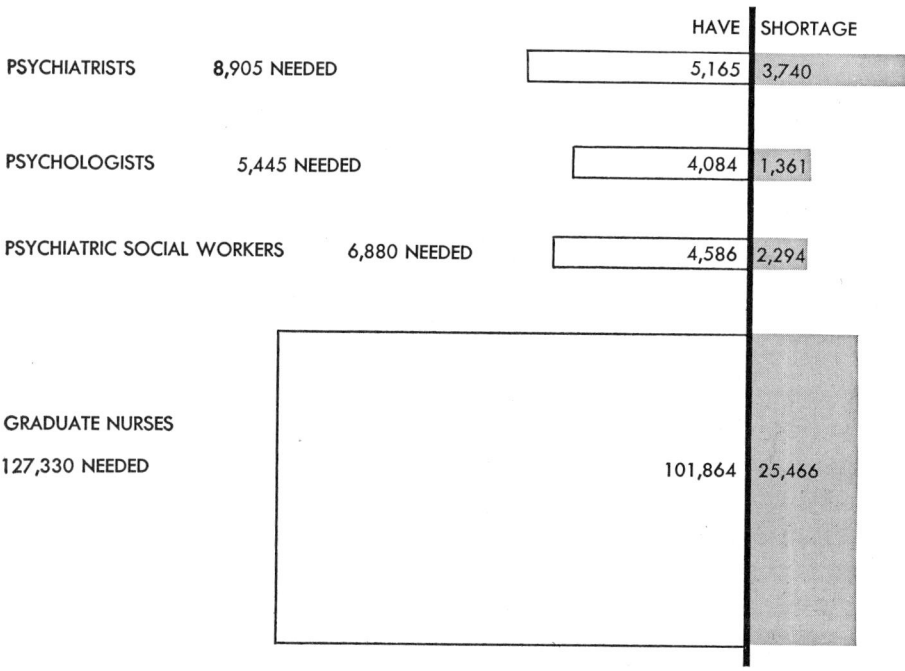

FIGURE 10:5 STAFF PERSONNEL IN STATE MENTAL HOSPITALS, 1955

ACCORDING TO MINIMUM STANDARDS OF THE AMERICAN PSYCHIATRIC ASSOCIATION

Source: National Committee against Mental Illness, *What Are the Facts about Mental Illness?* (Washington, D.C.: National Committee against Mental Illness, 1957), p. 33.

---

[28] *What Are the Facts about Mental Illness?*, p. 13.
[29] *Ibid.*, p. 32.

for every 6.8 patients; in 1956 there was one full-time employee for every 3.6 patients.[30]

The use of tranquilizing drugs has contributed in almost revolutionary fashion to the ability of the hospitals to return patients to the community. In 1956 the New York State hospital system reported a 23 per cent increase in discharges, ascribing it largely to the use of the drugs.[31] Psychiatrists warn that the tranquilizing drugs are not magical potions capable of eliminating the problem of mental illness. Though they are often an important first step, they are useless in many cases. Much of the effect of the drug, where it is successful, is to enable patients to take advantage of psychotherapy. Facilities and personnel for such therapy must be increasingly available.

There is evidence that we could expect dramatic results if maximum treatment were available at all mental hospitals. The Boston Psychopathic Hospital and the Topeka State Hospital have both launched intensive treatment programs, and both have been able to discharge 80 per cent of their patients as improved or recovered within the first year. Our state hospitals have, by comparison, been able to discharge only about 40 per cent of their patients within a five-year period.[32]

2. *Out-patient clinics.* The prevention of serious mental illness in the present stage of knowledge is primarily a matter of early treatment, whereby some illnesses may be brought under control before they result in hospitalization and total dependency. Local out-patient psychiatric facilities are needed, for the hospitals do not provide an answer for the emotional disorders that are partially disabling but do not warrant hospitalization. At present there are only about 1,200 such out-patient clinics in the country, and only half of these operate on a full-time basis. More than half of them are in the Northeast, which contains only one quarter of the population, and almost all of these have waiting lists of from three months to a year. It is estimated that there must be five times as many full-time clinics as now exist in order to meet the minimal need.

A new development which perhaps points to the future is embodied in the community mental health programs of New York and California. Essentially, they provide that the state will reimburse any community for half the cost of establishing and maintaining local psychiatric facilities. A strong emphasis is on the establishment of local out-patient clinics. However, there is also a trend toward the establishment of short-range-treatment hospitals in the community. There is also experimentation with arrangements whereby patients may stay at the hospitals at night, continuing to work during the day; or they may stay at the hospital during the day and return to

[30] *What Are the Facts about Mental Illness?*, p. 35.
[31] *Ibid.*, p. 19.
[32] *Ibid.*, p. 30.

their homes at night. There is also, in these plans, an emphasis on the need for child guidance clinics in the community and child guidance services connected with the schools.

3. *Social agencies.* Part of any community picture of psychiatric facilities are the social agencies which specialize in child and family guidance. The social workers attached to these agencies attempt to provide a certain amount of consultation on emotional problems. They also serve to detect those serious emotional difficulties in need of intensive psychotherapy, if this is available in the community.

Rehabilitation

There have been about 200,000 patients discharged annually in recent years from mental hospitals.[33] They are discharged because they are accounted well enough to return to and live in the community. Many of them are convalescent and need continued help in order to make full recovery. Social-work staffs provided by state governments generally attempt to offer some personal assistance after discharge, but they are typically too understaffed to meet the prolonged needs of many returned patients. Some communities have begun to experiment with so-called "Half-Way Houses," where discharged patients may reside for a temporary period of adjustment while receiving assistance in achieving integration into the community. In some cases these are no more than "Friendship Clubs," where discharged patients may meet for recreational activity and discussions under trained leadership.

However, the most obvious hazard to the returned patient who is trying to find his way back into the community is the matter of employment. Employers have been traditionally reluctant to hire former mental patients. The rehabilitation services of the state and of social-work services are available to former patients for employment assistance, but serious progress on this front can be made only when the stigma is removed from mental illness. This task of public education has been assumed as a major responsibility by a private citizens' movement, the National Association for Mental Health.

Disability Support

The state mental hospital systems automatically assume the support of their patients who are totally disabled and indigent. For those who remain in the community but are disabled because of mental illness, all of the channels of support are available that are available for the physically disabled. Over 10 per cent of those receiving assistance under the total-disability provision of the social security system are mentally ill or mentally defective.

---

[33] *Statistical Abstract of the United States, 1955,* p. 81.

However, there are no medical insurance plans which cover psychiatric treatment, and it is very likely that the need for public hospitals and for more public psychiatric out-patient clinics will continue.

Section IV: The Dependency of Old Age

Some of the problems of old age are aggravated problems of physical and mental disability, which have a sharply rising rate of incidence among older people. These are compounded, however, by certain social disabilities which accompany old age and which are especially marked in modern urban, industrial society.

Extent and Nature of the Problem

The percentage of the population 65 years of age and older is steadily increasing. In 1850 only about 3 per cent of the population fell into this age bracket compared with about 8 per cent a hundred years later. It is estimated that about 14 per cent of the population will be 65 years of age or over by the year 2000. Since the turn of the century, average life-expectancy at birth has risen from about 50 years to about 70 years as a result of advances in medical science and better standards of living.

"Old age" is an arbitrary and relative denomination, marked by these characteristics: (a) diminution of physical powers and health; (b) loss of economic function; (c) loss of family life; and (d) attendant psychological problems, particularly loss of status and social isolation.

DIMINUTION OF PHYSICAL POWERS AND HEALTH

In a strict biological sense, aging begins at conception. As the individual grows older, the capacity of his body for cell growth and tissue repair is retarded. There is a decrease in the metabolic rate, in speed, and in strength. The rate of decline of these functions varies widely among individuals.

This physical degeneration leaves older people relatively more vulnerable to disease and less capable of recovery from it. In addition, as the communicable diseases have been brought under control, the proportion of illness that is strictly degenerative in nature has naturally become higher. Most of the deaths of people over 65 are the result of diseases of the heart, circulatory system, and kidneys. These are often attended by long periods of disability. The over-all result is that perhaps half of the population over 65 have some form of chronic disease. Disability and ill health are a special problem of those who are aging at the same time that they are often the least able to cope with the special medical costs entailed.

OLD AGE

LOSS OF ECONOMIC FUNCTION

Older people in our society are typically faced with compulsory retirement and limited employment opportunity. In 1949, 50 per cent of the jobs available through the employment service in Dallas and 90 per cent of those available through the Birmingham employment service carried some age restrictions. These restrictions become strongly apparent at about 45 years of age and increase rapidly.

There are a number of factors involved. One is the realistic factor that the population 65 and over are somewhat disabled by illness about 44 days per year per person as compared with about 14 days per year per person for the 25-44 age group and with about 21 days per person per year for the 45-64 age group.[34]

The changing nature of our economy has increased the significance of this disability rate. In the farm life of yesterday, the older person could perform useful economic chores even if he had lost the full economic productivity of his youth. As industry has become larger, personnel practices have necessarily become more depersonalized. The statistics of disability are applied uniformly, without regard to individual differences. There is less possibility for the older person to find a niche where he can perform useful functions with his reduced capacities.

Also, pension systems and workmen's compensation have become commonplace. Many employers now argue that it has become impossible to

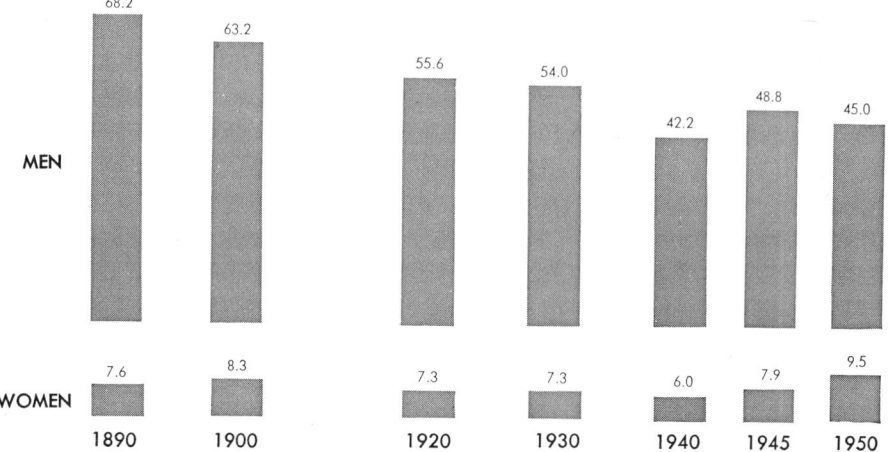

FIGURE 10:6   PERCENTAGE OF MEN AND WOMEN 65 AND OVER WHO WORK

Source: Federal Security Agency, *Fact Book on Aging* (Washington, D.C.: U.S. Government Printing Office, 1952), p. 54.

---

[34] *Preliminary Report on Disability*, p. 11 (see n. 1, above).

hire older persons because they drive insurance rates too high, and it is uneconomical to maintain welfare plans that are not uniformly applied. However, discrimination against older workers exists with or without the existence of pension systems and health insurance plans.

The inability of older people to hold or secure employment creates a typical condition of dependency. In 1955 fewer than three out of every ten persons above the age of 65 secured their income from employment; about five out of every ten in this age bracket received some kind of government assistance. Though the maximum amount that a couple over 65 can receive from social security benefits is $162.80 a month, the average couple receives not much more than $100.00 a month. The typical insufficiency of income for the older person is complicated by the increasing fragmentation of family life.

LOSS OF FAMILY LIFE

The urban and industrial trends in our society have altered the traditional relationship of the older people to their children, grandchildren, and other relatives. Homes in the city are designed to accommodate two-generation and not three-generation families. Children cannot afford to maintain separate households for their aging parents. The mobility of our population has resulted in fewer children remaining in the same locale as their parents. Son-in-law, daughter-in-law, and grandchildren are relative strangers to the older generation. In general, the family is a less cohesive unit than it once was. Along with these developments has grown the explicit philosophy that society in general, rather than the family, is responsible for the support of its aged. Children and relatives, less able to provide support, have been willing to accept this welfare philosophy, as have the dependent aged themselves.

In addition to the economic factor, the fragmentation of family life has made it less possible for the older generations to find companionship, recreation, and social recognition within family circles. This problem of social isolation is aggravated by the fact that while about 80 per cent of people in adulthood are married, only about 70 per cent of the men and 40 per cent of the women over 60 years of age are living with a mate.[35]

LOSS OF STATUS AND SOCIAL ISOLATION

The loss of economic function creates other than economic problems for older people. For many men the role of breadwinner has been their most meaningful role in society, providing not only their chief claim to social status but also the activity that occupied most of their time and energies.

---

[35] Federal Security Agency, Committee on Aging and Geriatrics, *Fact Book on Aging* (Washington, D.C.: U.S. Government Printing Office, 1952), p. 48.

For many women the role of mother and household manager was comparably significant. The loss of these roles leaves great gaps of time, meaning, and status.

Age differences are, in part, cultural differences. Because of the swiftly changing nature of our society, the cultural differences between the older and younger generations are often marked. In a period of relative stability, the older generation can serve as an effective bridge between the traditions of the past and the future; when traditions are not so sacrosanct and are being constantly reshaped to fit new needs, this function loses some of its significance. Attempts to integrate older people into a family home are complicated by these, as well as economic, factors.

In short, the older people in our society tend to feel useless, unimportant, out of place, in the way, discarded, isolated, lonely, and idle. It has been said that this feeling is deepened by the accent on youth in our society. The pleasures of youth, the romance of youth, and the energies of youth have been enshrined in our advertising, our mass media, and our general attitudes.

Meeting the Problem

In most respects, the aged have the same problems as the rest of the population, only "more so." The problem of adequate care for physical and mental health, which the entire population shares, affects the older group most sharply. The changing shape of the traditional family is a problem of adjustment for all of society, but it has special implications for the various age groups. Society's responsibility for the unemployable in general has special quantitative pertinence to the aged as a group. The root problems involved here are general dependency problems. Meanwhile society has only recently begun to consider specific projects for the mitigation of these problems as they specifically affect the aged.

EMPLOYMENT

Among the proposals for relieving the special employment problems of older workers are these: (*a*) laws to prevent discrimination against older workers; (*b*) special counseling and placement services; (*c*) reshaping of community and employer attitudes; and (*d*) sheltered workshops.

Laws To Prevent Employment Discrimination

Massachusetts, New York, Pennsylvania, and Rhode Island now have laws to prevent employment discrimination against older workers, which follow the pattern of fair-employment laws against racial and religious discrimination. There is no evidence that these fair-employment laws have yet been able to open wide avenues of employment for the aged. Such laws are more difficult to administer than those prohibiting discrimination on the basis of race or religion. There are legitimate considerations of physical ability and training capacity which the employer can individually apply to the disadvantage of older workers even under an employment-on-merit system.

Counseling and Placement Services

There are many jobs which are particularly suitable for more mature workers. It is necessary, however, to provide some apparatus whereby the older worker and the job opportunities make contact. Vocational counselors can guide these workers into the more likely channels of employment. A number of state employment services have set up special departments to record job opportunities suitable for older people.

Reshaping Community and Employer Attitudes

Before the special placement of older workers can become a significant reality, employers must be convinced that it is socially necessary and economically feasible. In one sense, this is an educational job directed against the prejudiced stereotyping of older people. The principle of employment on merit, regardless of age, must be accepted. In addition, employers need more knowledge of the kinds of jobs which older people can handle and to which they can, moreover, bring the advantages of maturity. For example, traditional physical requirements for many heavy jobs have been reduced by the use of mechanical handling devices. Automation in general, plus the shorter working day, may serve to bring older workers back into the labor market for alert employers.

Sheltered Workshops

The concept of the sheltered workshop, applied principally to the physically handicapped as such, has on occasion been suggested as a means of filling in the work vacuum of the aged. These workshops are typically supported by private agencies; where the goods they produce are sold competitively and the older workers are paid prevailing wage scales, it is usually necessary to subsidize these workshops to some extent. The psychological adjustment of their clients, rather than production efficiency, is the prime objective of these shops. It is generally agreed that while such operations have some usefulness, they are not a substitute for integration into the normal economy.

ECONOMIC SUPPORT

An alternative concept to the economic integration of the aging is the idea that the older person has *earned* his retirement by the contributions, economic and social, that he has made to society. Of course, this approach does not satisfy the psychological needs of the older person unless he also accepts the concept and is fully prepared to abandon his work career.

This is, however, still an academic debate. Whether it has been justified philosophically and psychologically or not, the hard fact remains that larger and larger numbers of older people are without occupation; and organized society is still wrestling with plans to provide them with income.

Old Age and Survivors Insurance

The Social Security Act of 1935 established a national insurance system to provide a guaranteed income for workers upon their retirement after age 65. Today, more than nine out of ten American workers and self-employed people who earn more than $400 a year are covered by Old Age and Survivors insurance or some other government insurance plan. The only notable exceptions are lawyers, physicians, and dentists, who through their professional associations have opposed such coverage. There are several other exceptions, presumably for reasons of administrative difficulty, e.g., migratory farm workers who work for one farm operator for less than three months; in some cases, e.g., clergymen and employees of charitable organizations, coverage is voluntary.

The ostensible principle of old age insurance is that a worker should be compelled to save against the future and therefore have his retirement income as a right rather than as a government largesse. Employer and employee contribute equally through payroll taxes. A reserve is thereby built up, administered by the government, invested in government securities, and drawn upon when needed. Each worker pays, as a monthly "premium," a percentage (2 per cent through 1958; 2.5 per cent thereafter through 1964) of the first $350 of his income. His employer matches his payments. The worker receives benefits that are based on his average monthly wage, up to $350. These benefits are therefore commensurate with the amount of the "premiums" he has paid into the fund. In these respects, the Old Age and Survivors insurance plan follows the lines of private insurance financing.

However, the deviations from the actuarial principles of private insurance financing are noteworthy. A worker does not pay "premiums" when he is unemployed or not engaged in employment covered by the law. Yet, there are certain ways in which he can permanently qualify for benefits even if there are lapses in his coverage and therefore in his "premium" payment. For example, workers become permanently insured whenever they have had ten years' coverage. They are also insured if they have been covered for roughly half the time between 1950 and the date they become 65, or for roughly half the time between the date they become 21 and the date they become 65.

Even if he permanently qualifies, the worker receives benefits only in accordance with his average monthly wage; but he may omit five years of low earnings or nonexistent earnings in calculating this average. In addition, amounts of benefits have increased regularly to meet rising general costs without reference to past premiums paid. There are other disparities in payments which bear no relation to the amount of "premiums" paid. For example, a retired worker who has a wife will receive higher benefits than one who is unmarried, although he may have contributed no more or perhaps less to the general fund.

In other words, the benefits available under this insurance system bear only the roughest relationship to the premiums paid. In that sense, it has been argued that this is not a true insurance system; rather it amounts to government assistance to the aged, primarily distributed according to certain criteria of need rather than contribution and financed by a special universal payroll tax.

This aspect of the federal insurance plan has occasioned criticism from two sides. On one side, it has been attacked as an illusory insurance system by those who would eliminate any compulsory federal insurance in favor of voluntary private insurance. This is today, however, a relatively small voice in America. On the other side, many have criticized the present system as too *illiberal* because of its illusory insurance aspect. They argue that the system is being financed by a general payroll tax which is not *progressively* assessed beyond $350 a month and which therefore places an undue burden on the lower income brackets of the population. They argue that the old age payments should be made out of a general government fund raised by the income and corporate tax, which *is* progressively graduated according to income. If it is proper and necessary to raise funds for the armed forces by this means, then it is proper and necessary to use this means to raise funds for a system of welfare which is as important to our social structure.

This proposal has certain practical impediments, e.g., the opposition of those who argue that any further significant rise in general, graduated taxation will further hamper the expansion of industry by decreasing venture capital, which is basic to our system of private enterprise. There are, however, other questions raised by the proposal. Will the elimination of the insurance aspect of these benefits mean, on the one hand, that the aged will receive their income not as a right but as a charity? Or, to the contrary, will it mean that the aged will receive their income as a natural human right based only roughly, if at all, on the amount of their past income or the general taxes they have paid on that income?

There are criteria other than its contributory or noncontributory nature which mark the benefits of the present Old Age and Survivors insurance plan as a right rather than a charity. There is, notably, no means test. The qualified recipient is entitled to his benefits no matter how much personal property he may own or how much savings or other resources he may have. He must, indeed, be "retired," i.e., earning less than $1,200 a year, in order to receive his full benefits, but this requirement is considered a retirement test rather than a means test. The state of his personal wealth, as such, is not at issue. Similarly, the receipt of his benefits is not subject to the ability or inability of his children or other relatives to support him.

Old Age Assistance

The Old Age Assistance program, initiated in 1935, provides matching federal grants to the various state programs for the needy aged who are not covered or are inadequately covered by the insurance program. It was designed primarily to fill the gap until the insurance program was fully established. Until the end of 1950 there were more aged on the various assistance rolls than on insurance rolls; at that time 2.6 million people were receiving old age insurance; 2.8 million were receiving old age assistance. Since then the old age insurance program beneficiaries have outnumbered the assistance beneficiaries by a larger number each year.

The assistance program is unequivocally rooted in a charity philosophy. A means test is typically applied. California, relatively liberal in its restrictions, disqualifies applicants with real or personal property assessed in excess of $3,500 and $1,200, respectively. Most states require that the children of an applicant support him if possible. Payment is made according to need, which is evaluated in a different manner in each state. Each applicant is subject to an investigation to determine need and eligibility.

Other Old Age Pension Plans

The broad social security system of the government includes old age insurance systems for certain special groups, such as government employees and railroad workers. In addition, the social security system has been supplemented by the rapid rise of private industrial pension plans. In 1950 there were about 10 million employees covered by private pension plans, more than half of them written into collective bargaining agreements between labor and management.[36]

There are, of course, wide variations in these plans. Some pensions, for example, are payable only after thirty years of service. Eligibility requirements vary, as do time-of-service requirements and policy as to the extent to which a worker has a vested interest in a private pension plan when he leaves a job before retirement date.

---

[36] *Pensions in the United States*, A Study Prepared for the Joint Committee on the Economic Report by the National Planning Association, 82nd Cong., 2nd Sess. (Washington, D.C.: U.S. Government Printing Office, 1952), p. 11.

Medical Care

Perhaps the most dramatic economic characteristic of the aged as a group is their medical indigence. As a group, the aged are those most in need of medical services, yet they are the least capable of paying for even normal medical services. As a final but economically logical irony, they are the least eligible for medical insurance plans. Industrial group-insurance plans typically terminate upon retirement. Private medical insurance plans typically reject older applicants or charge higher premiums which most cannot afford. Only about one out of four people over 65 has some hospitalization insurance, and this does not necessarily cover the needs of chronic illness. Provision for the medical care of the aged falls generally within the charity field. The Social Security Act now provides matching funds to the various states to help pay for the medical care of the needy aged. This is part of the Old Age Assistance program, subject to all its charity restrictions; it is also generally acknowledged that, in low-income states especially, funds are insufficient to meet the cost of adequate medical services. Proponents of a national health insurance plan suggest that only through such a comprehensive insurance plan will the medical needs of the aging population be satisfactorily met.

LEISURE-TIME ACTIVITIES

Communities around the nation have begun to establish recreational and social projects designed specifically for the elderly. "Senior Citizen" and "Golden Age" clubs have sprung up to serve, first of all, as places where the older people of a community can make social contacts. These clubs usually provide facilities for arts and crafts activities, discussion groups, and recreational programs. Attempts are sometimes made to help older citizens feel socially useful in the course of these activities, e.g., toy-repairing projects for hospitalized children. Such activities are carried on by private agencies created for this purpose or as part of the program of existing group-work agencies such as the YWCA, and they are sometimes partly supported by public adult-education programs.

It is generally agreed that such "idle-hands" activities, while filling an important gap in community service, do not answer the retirement question. They do not prevent large numbers of older people from feeling cut off from and discarded by society. The central problem, according to many observers, is not confined to the aged; it is a general leisure-time problem; too many people do not know how to live meaningfully. Too often during the younger and middle years recreational activity consists of a filling-in of time between working hours, of escape instead of self-fulfillment, of anesthetic rather than creative pursuits.

This picture is, perhaps, overpessimistic. The trend in America, despite TV-saturation, is toward participation in more active and more rewarding leisure pursuits. In 1952, for example, hobbyists spent about $60 million on woodworking tools as compared with about $6 million only five years earlier.[37] Attendance at serious musical concerts increased about 90 per cent between 1941 and 1951, and the number of local symphony orchestras almost doubled.[38] In a national survey in 1947, more than two-fifths of all adults questioned indicated that they were interested in securing further education; and in 1950 at least $2\frac{1}{2}$ million people were formally enrolled in some adult-education activity.[39]

Such figures would suggest the potential that exists for full-time, participant, and personally satisfying leisure-time activities. For this potential to be realized, it is necessary for society to equip its members *from an early age* for creative leisure-time activities; creativity is not a spigot that can suddenly be turned on at age 65 and retirement. Such training would be a responsibility of the schools at least as much as vocational training or training for democratic living; it would entail the fullest development of total individual capacities *for their own sake*. According to this point of view, the central psychological problem of old age would approach solution in the realization that there are activities that are of social and human value outside the realm of economic productivity and homemaking. In this sense, the problem of the aged merely dramatizes a problem that exists in less aggravated form for the entire adult population.

THE FIGHT FOR FUNDS adaptation 24

Abridged and adapted from Marguerite Shepard, "The Battle for Health . . . and Dollars," St. Louis Globe-Democrat, *February 12–20, 1956. Published in this form by permission of the author and the* St. Louis Globe-Democrat.

[The traditional pattern of charity work and donations has changed drastically in the past several decades. Basic responsibility for the indigent and the disabled has shifted from private community charity to public responsibility. There are still many private welfare agencies in the communities of the nation, supported by "voluntarily" donated funds. These funds

---

[37] *Wall Street Journal*, October 14, 1952.
[38] Fenton B. Turck, "Science on the March: The American Explosion," *Scientific Monthly*, **75** (September, 1952), 188.
[39] The Gallup Poll, March 17, 1950.

support or partly support recreation centers, hospitals, medical clinics, social-work agencies, homes for dependent children and the aged, and a galaxy of other activities designed for community betterment and augmenting the fundamental responsibility for the dependent which government has come to accept. Frequently, in the larger cities, these local welfare agencies have banded together in Community Chests for the purpose of central fund-raising and central social planning. The multiplicity of these agencies and their fund appeals seemed to make such a device finally necessary.

However, more recently, a new and often disturbing element has been added to this private welfare picture, namely, the large national health agencies, with local affiliates, which were created to combat the major diseases of the nation, notably the National Foundation for Infantile Paralysis, the Heart Association, and the Cancer Society. While they support certain local services and local educational programs, their primary emphasis has been on the financial support of medical research. For this reason, and because they have become organizational behemoths, fund-raising is central to their existence. Competition among them has become sharp. New organizations with similar objectives, in mental health, in cerebral palsy, in muscular dystrophy, have entered the field on the same basis. These organizations were in competition also with the local Community Chest agencies for the voluntary welfare dollar. In many larger communities, businessmen, most often the target of these appeals, promoted the creation of United Fund appeals. It was hoped that there would be but one major appeal a year, which would then be distributed by a citizens' budget committee to the local and national agencies participating. While this distribution presumably was to be made on the basis of the need which each participating agency filled in the community, the distribution was in fact very often made partly on the basis of the fund-raising potential each organization seemed to command.

There are many indications that the United Fund concept is failing. Professional fund-raisers insist that the United Funds have reached a ceiling in the amount of money they can extract from the members of their communities in "one big give." Many of them are certain that individual drives would amass a greater total. The large national health agencies are generally in agreement and are uneasy when they are tied down to United Fund drives. In 1958 the American Cancer Society ordered all of its local chapters to leave United Funds and mount their own campaigns. The American Heart Association has attempted to persuade its local affiliates to do the same.

A chaotic future for community welfare fund-raising seems imminent because of the increasing budget of these national health agencies and because the welfare donations of the community, with or without United Funds, seem to have reached an upper limit.

ADAPTATION 24 513

Following is, in abridged form, what staff writer Marguerite Shepard of the *St. Louis Globe-Democrat* said about the problem in a series of articles, "The Battle for Health . . . and Dollars." In the course of stressing the advantages of United Fund drives and pointing up the comparatively high costs of independent drives, this series took a long look at the national health agencies.]

Many millions of sick people could be helped if, nationally, we would distribute our health charity dollars with a little more generosity—and a lot more thought.

And research for cures or remedies could be speeded up if more of our voluntary health agencies could get the money they need—and cut their fund-raising costs.

These facts stand out in a survey this newspaper made of eight national agencies fighting the big killing and crippling diseases: The American Heart Association, the American Cancer Society, the National Tuberculosis Association, the National Foundation for Infantile Paralysis, the United Cerebral Palsy Association, the Muscular Dystrophy Association of America, the National Association for Mental Health, and the Arthritis and Rheumatism Foundation.

The diseases they fight reach into nearly every home in the land.

Compare what the voluntary health agencies were able to raise nationally in 1954 with the numbers of victims:

National Foundation for Infantile Paralysis—$70 million, 100 thousand victims.

National Tuberculosis Association—$25 million, 1 million victims.

American Cancer Society—$22 million, 750 thousand victims.

American Heart Association—$11 million, 10 million victims.

United Cerebral Palsy Association—$8 million, 550 thousand victims.

Muscular Dystrophy Association of America—$4 million, 200 thousand victims.

Arthritis and Rheumatism Foundation—$2 million, 11 million victims.

Notice that their money-raising ability has practically no relation to the size of their problem. The giants of the killers and cripplers are the midgets of the money-raisers.

For example, the Heart Association, dealing with the biggest killer, gets the crumbs of the public's health charity donations.

The answer seems to be that the success of charity drives depends upon how many people they reach, which in turn depends on how much noise they make, how well they get their story over, and, as a result, how many volunteer workers they get.

Far more children are crippled in this country by heart-damaging rheumatic fever than by polio. There are estimated to be at least half a million children with rheumatic fever or its aftereffects. Last year polio hit less than 30,000 persons. Half of all cases recovered completely; only about one-seventh are left with lasting aftereffects. Yet, year in and year out, polio raises several times as much money as heart. Why the disparity between what we give to fight our biggest killer and what we give to fight our smallest killer? Both depend mainly on personal solicitation, on volunteers ringing doorbells.

In 1955 the Mothers' March on Polio had 40,000 parents ringing doorbells all over the city in St. Louis County. Heart Sunday had 7,000 volunteers ringing doorbells in some sections only, because there weren't enough to cover the city and county.

HEART

Twenty-five cents of every Heart dollar goes to the American Heart Association, 75 cents stays in the community where it was raised. This is the way the American Heart Association says the Heart dollar was spent last year: fund-raising, 14.5 cents; administration, organization, and development, 12.3 cents; public education, 12.2 cents; professional education, 8.3 cents; community service (heart clinics, etc.), 14.6 cents; research, 38.1 cents.

Nationally, the American Heart Association's biggest expenditure is for research. Since its first national drive in 1949, it has put more than $13 million into research. The major source of heart research, however, is the federal government. In the current fiscal year the U.S. National Heart Institute is spending over $13 million on heart research. That's a total from the government and the American Heart Association of less than $18 million a year on cardiovascular research. Americans spend six times that much on chewing gum.

CANCER

Cancer is our most dread disease, yet the American Cancer Society nationally is suffering from undernourishment. Research for better cancer detection, better remedies, looks brighter than in any other major disease field. Yet last year the American Cancer Society, which puts more money into research than any other voluntary health agency, had to turn down one out of every three scientists' requests for research money.

The public supports the National Foundation for Infantile Paralysis two or three times as well as it supports the American Cancer Society. But if we compare the death tolls for 1954, an epidemic year for polio, we find that cancer killed 237,000 and polio less than 2,000.

Eyeing polio's huge money-raising success, the American Cancer Society is withdrawing from the United Funds and Community Chests, forbidding further participation and planning a lot of drum-beating of its own.

Here is the way the Cancer dollar was spent nationally and locally last year: fund-raising, 8.9 cents; administration, 7.1 cents; public education, 22.3 cents; professional education, 2.2 cents; patient service, 20.9 cents; research, 26.3 cents; balance to start next year, 12.3 cents.

Roughly $50 million is being spent in the United States this year on cancer research from all sources. The National Cancer Institute of the federal government again contributes the largest single amount of this total—over $15 million. The American Cancer Society has spent something over $6 million in the past year on research. Another branch of the federal government, the Atomic Energy Commission, has spent almost $3 million. The rest comes from private foundations, medical schools, and from industry, especially the drug industry.

POLIO

The National Foundation for Infantile Paralysis sells the polio fight the way a soap company sells soap. Its promotion has been so highly successful that most people honestly think polio is one of our major killers and cripplers and that it is the main disease threat to our children. Neither is true.

Yet overemphasis, even scare techniques, have paid off. The Polio Foundation got the money—some $400 million since its start in 1938. It has a polio vaccine.

A vaccine is a good thing to have. So is a bulletproof vest. And the chances of the average person needing the polio vaccine are no greater than of his needing a bulletproof vest. Statistically, more than three times as many people in this country die of homicide as die of polio. Each year heart disease, cancer, rheumatism, rheumatoid arthritis, cerebral palsy, and mental illness kill or cripple—each of them—more children than polio does. Yet we give the lion's share of our health charity dollars to polio.

Yes, we have a polio vaccine. Millions of parents can be thankful. But the Polio Foundation has spent far more on fund-raising than on research. In all its eighteen years of existence, the Polio Foundation has spent only $25 million on research. In the last two years alone it spent half that much on fund-raising.

The Polio Foundation's national annual report puts its fund-raising cost in a little, inconspicuous footnote, shows a sliced-up-pie picture of how its dollar is spent, and doesn't bother to include fund-raising in that picture at all. In 1954 the polio gross, the footnote says, was $67 million, and the net was $60 million. The footnote tells you that that amounts to fund-raising costs of 10.6 per cent—and lets you subtract to get costs of $7 million.

The Polio Foundation has made a soft place in most people's hearts because it takes care of polio patients. It is the only voluntary health agency that actually pays patients' bills. You don't have to take a pauper's oath to get your bills paid either. That's nice. But who takes care of the cancer patients? The heart patients? Who pays the relatively high price for new drugs for arthritis?

The American Cancer Society gives indirect help in supporting cancer clinics and supplying free dressings, but if it undertook to pay all cancer patients' bills in this country it would have a bill of $300 million a year to pay. Polio has so few patients affected and gets so much money that it can afford to pay all or part of the patients' hospital, doctor, nurse, drug, and equipment bills.

THE PROBLEM

Nothing is so irresistible as success, and many of the other voluntary health agencies are trying to follow the Polio Foundation's successful formula. Major ingredients of that formula seem to be the following. (1) Go it alone. Polio has never allowed itself to get into any federation. It has even been known to turn down money given to the United Fund that had been earmarked by givers for polio. (2) Beat the drums; sound cymbals; make everybody polio-conscious—even if you scare them half to death. Use a circus-ballyhoo technique in the process.

Last fall St. Louis set about ending the one-after-another charity drives by wrapping them up in one package. We had our first United Fund, "One Gift for All," campaign. It was a huge success, raising some $8,260,000, which was more than its goal. So what happened? The drive was not even over before, in November, we were asked to give to Muscular Dystrophy. In December we were asked to give to Tuberculosis. In January we were asked to give to Polio. In February we were being asked to give to Heart. In March there was a letup. March used to be Red Cross month. Now Red Cross is in the United Fund. In April we'll be asked to give to Cancer. In May it will be Mental Health Week. In May there would have been Cerebral Palsy asking, but Cerebral Palsy joined the United Fund last year. It's a gift nearly every month we're being asked for. Their causes are all good in varying degrees, but our health charity dollars are being given in proportion to noise, not need. United Fund asked them all to join, except for two. Mental Health was not asked, since it has no local chapter. TB was not asked, since it campaigns by mail and saves thousands of volunteers' time by doing so. Heart, Cancer, Muscular Dystrophy, and Polio all said no; only Cerebral Palsy said yes.

If we get four or six or eight shock appeals a year of the type Polio puts on, will we have any money left for other charities? Or will so many appeals make us callous and indifferent?

The need is great. Our health charity dollars distributed a little more generously and a lot more thoughtfully could step up the battle against disease, but it looks as though there will have to be one of two changes made. Either Americans are going to have to change their giving habits—giving where the need is greatest, not just where the yelling is loudest—or the national agencies are going to have to change their getting tactics. It will take one or the other.

POLITICAL PANACEAS AND THE AGED

adaptation 25

Abridged and adapted from John J. Corson and John W. McConnell, Economic Needs of Older People *(New York: Twentieth Century Fund, 1956), Chapter 5. Published in this form by permission of the Twentieth Century Fund.*

[The aged are an increasing segment of our population and one which tends to be "underprivileged." In the last several decades a number of organizations for and of the aged have sprung up, especially in California. These organizations have concentrated on securing increased public assistance for the aged, and several are briefly described below. The following discussion raises the question of the possible political potential of these or similar organizations of the aged.]

The political movement for old age security has sometimes been traced to the creation in 1907 of a Massachusetts commission to study old age pensions and insurance. About the same time, the first federal bill was introduced. This bill would have enlisted all the old persons in an "old home guard" and pensioned them as members of the military establishment. This method sought to avoid the possibility that a forthright pension bill would be declared unconstitutional. Old age pensions have been the subject of political controversy ever since and have even been the motivation of distinctive political movements. The increasing number of the aged has of course been the fuel to feed these political movements. The drafts which have fanned this fire are the decline in job opportunities for the aged, the increasing difficulty of saving for the future, and the inability of a typical urban family to support its dependent members.

In 1930 twelve states and Alaska had old age pension or relief statutes, but few of these had actually paid pensions. By 1934 the total number of states that had old age pension statutes on the books was twenty-eight. However, most of these state measures left the establishment of old age pensions to the option of their counties, and both state and county funds ran low in hard times. The majority of the laws provided for payment of pensions of a specific, uniform amount and only after the aged person had reached 70. More than half of all persons receiving pensions were in New York State.

THE TOWNSEND PLAN

At about this time Dr. Francis E. Townsend, a retired physician who was earning his living as a real estate agent in Long Beach, California, became interested in the cause of the aged. He claims to have looked out of his window one morning to see three old women picking scraps from garbage cans while he could also see the store windows filled with luxury foods. He was enraged and vowed to devote himself to relieving the problems of the aged. His efforts had marked influence.

The Townsend Plan consisted of three essentials. First, it proposed that all citizens of the United States 60 years or over should receive a monthly pension of $200. Second, every recipient of the monthly pension would be required under oath (a) not to engage in labor, business, or profession for gain and (b) to spend each monthly payment within the boundaries of the United States within 30 days. A third of the funds required to pay these pensions was to be raised by a 10 per cent tax on every business transaction. Together it was claimed that these provisions would accomplish two ends: (a) relieve suffering among all the aged and (b) restore national prosperity without inflation, provide immediate employment for all, reduce crime, reduce taxes, and balance the budget.

Dr. Townsend and a former colleague in the real estate business rented a small office in Long Beach, hired a stenographer, and began sending out leaflets to lists of names they obtained from various sources. Within a few weeks they were receiving 100 to 200 replies a day, most of them containing a membership fee of 25 cents for one year. A pamphlet was mailed out to new members urging them to form Townsend Clubs in their neighborhoods, to enlist members, and to have them send in their membership fees.

The political results of these efforts were first manifested in California but soon appeared in Congress. At the first convention of the Townsend Clubs in October, 1935, Dr. Townsend declared: "This is the greatest political convention ever held under the stars and stripes, although we care not for partisan politics . . . . We have become an avalanche of political power that no derision, no ridicule, or no conspiracy of silence can stem."

As early as 1935 Dr. Townsend and his associates declared that more than sixty members of Congress supported his pension proposals. Congressman McGroarty of California, a leader among these supporters, insisted, after claiming 20 million signatures on petitions for the Townsend Pension Plan:

"Congress is its own lobby on this question. The members will not dare oppose what their constituents back home want." It is felt that the growing strength of the Townsend movement had an effect upon the provisions for the maintenance of the aged incorporated into the Social Security Act. The Townsend movement probably reached its peak strength in 1935–38. Since then the power of the Townsendites has waned as jobs have increased, but the organization has continued and has exerted some influence. In 1950 it listed more than a score of lobbyists in the *Congressional Register.*

Economists challenge the grandiose claims of the Townsendites on the basis of these objections: (1) the incidence of a transactions tax is capricious and would burden excessively those taxpayers least able to pay; (2) the transactions tax could not be expected to yield the sums estimated or the amounts needed to pay the promised pension of $200 a month; (3) such a plan would be both difficult and costly to administer; (4) since there would be no relation of the increased spending to the available supply of goods, inflation would result; and (5) the functioning of this revolving pension plan might accentuate rather than reduce fluctuations of the economic cycle.

OTHER POLITICAL PANACEAS

The success of the Townsend movement led other advocates of pensions to establish their own pension movements. A few were essentially splinter groups of the Townsendites. Some of these became national in scope and urged amendments to federal old age and survivors insurance. Others were state groups.

Typical of those organizations which sought revision of old age and survivors insurance was the General Welfare Federation of America. This group was led by Arthur L. Johnson, once a staff member of the California State Department of Labor and subsequently an associate of the Townsend movement. Johnson's movement was essentially designed to raise minimum benefit payments under the Social Security Act, lower ages at which workers might retire, and change the financial structure of the old age insurance plan which already existed.

Perhaps the most colorful of the many plans which sprang up was the "Ham 'n' Eggs Plan," more formally known as the California Pension Plan, which flourished in California in 1937 and 1938. The authors of this plan proposed that California pay $30 every Thursday to every citizen of the state 50 years of age or older who was neither employed nor an employer. These payments were to be made in the form of $31 warrants. On the back of each warrant 52 squares were to be printed, dated one week apart. The first were to be dated seven days from the day of issuance; the state was to print a special 2-cent stamp which would sell for cash. These warrants were to be legal tender, spent by beneficiaries for whatever they chose to purchase;

to be negotiable, however, the warrant had to be stamped "up-to-date." That is, the holder must have purchased for cash the requisite number of 2-cent stamps to be placed on the back of the warrant each week.

Through the sale of stamps the state would receive a sum equal to or in excess of the value of the warrants issued. The beneficiaries would gain most by spending warrants promptly and hence passing the obligation for purchasing stamps on the back of each warrant to the next holder. The authors insisted that the rapid movement of these warrants (rapid because of the necessity to place a stamp on each warrant each week) would greatly stimulate business activity.

The Ham 'n' Eggs Plan attracted a considerable following in California. It became a major issue in the 1938 contest for the United States Senate between William G. McAdoo and Sheridan Downey. Downey, favoring Ham 'n' Eggs, won the nomination over Senator McAdoo, but the Ham 'n' Eggs proposals faded into oblivion when business, banking, and other conservative interests brought about its defeat in a special referendum election in California in 1938.

CHARACTERISTICS OF THE PROPOSED PANACEAS

The Ham 'n' Eggs Plan illustrates several characteristics common to many pension plans which have appeared since 1935.

The first hallmark is identification of the plan with some colorful personality. The Townsend movement revolved around Dr. Francis E. Townsend. The General Welfare Federation Plan was personified by Arthur L. Johnson. The Ham 'n' Eggs Plan was the joint product of a small group of political promoters led by Roy G. Owens. In considerable degree the success of each plan reflected the zeal and inspirational qualities of these men.

A second characteristic is the avowed objective of raising the general level of economic activity in the community. For example, Dr. Townsend and his colleagues argued that, by paying pensions to all the aged, the government would create purchasing power to stimulate business activity and enhance general prosperity. Reputable economists effectively discounted these claims, but the political strength of each movement was attributable in considerable part to these promises of prosperity for all.

Third, each movement appealed to a similar segment of the population. While older people predominated, this segment also included younger people and was made up chiefly of individuals in the lower-middle income groups. One writer has attempted to draw a composite portrait of a typical follower of these movements:

Mr. X is over 60; he has a wife about the same age. They have grown children, probably married and with children of their own. Most likely Mr. X is a farmer, small-town storekeeper, or mechanic. He has been thrifty and industrious all his life, but the depression caught him at a bad age. He lost his job, or his home, or his savings, or all of them, and he did not have the strength or the wit of a younger man to regain them .... Mr. X grew up in an era when country people were devoutly religious, and he and his wife are regular churchgoers and readers of the Bible. All his life he has been accustomed to the Biblical picture of an honorable and venerable old age. He has looked forward to his declining years as a period in which he would be one of the elders of the community .... Now he has suffered cruel disillusionment. He has the aches and the infirmities common to all old people—he finds himself poor, lonely, friendless and haunted by the specter of insecurity for himself and his family.[1]

Fourth, these movements have substantial political strength. Raymond Clapper wrote in 1938:

Probably it is no exaggeration to say that now the old folks constitute the most powerful bloc of voters and the group most feared by politicians. Time was when politicians out canvassing for votes used to kiss the babies. Now they don't waste their time on the voteless infants but lavish their campaigning affections on the old folks who vote, [who] are organized, [and who] know their power, and they are not hesitant about using it. Politicians have learned, some of them to their sorrow, that the old folks cannot be ignored with safety. Whatever they ask will be promised, if not granted.[2]

CONTINUED POLITICAL PRESSURES

Political pressures of specially organized groups of older people have continued to be felt in the states. These pressures are typically designed to obtain pensions which would supplement the benefits of old age and survivors insurance. For example, in California in 1948 a Citizens' Committee for old age pensions proposed that:

1. Every aged person in need receive $75 a month.

2. In determining whether an individual is in need, the state shall not consider the ownership of a home assessed for $3,500 or less, the ownership of specified personal property, or the ownership of a life-insurance policy with value of $1,000 or less.

3. Relatives of needy aged persons should be relieved of the responsibility for contributing to their support.

4. These pension payments should have a first claim on any moneys in the state treasury, with priority over support of such essential services as highways, schools, mental hospitals, prisons, and the like.

5. The age limit should be lowered to 60.

In the campaign that preceded the referendum in 1948, leaders of this

---

[1] Russell Porter, *New York Times Magazine*, February 5, 1939, as quoted in H. Cantril, *The Psychology of Social Movements* (New York: John Wiley & Sons, Inc., 1941), p. 191.
[2] Raymond Clapper, "Middle Age Money-Go-Round," *Survey-Graphic*, November, 1938.

Citizens' Committee vigorously publicized their proposals by newspaper, radio, and public meetings. There was no substantial effort to defeat the proposed amendment, and to the surprise of many Californians, this constitutional measure was adopted.

The inevitable result was a sharp increase in payments. The average payment to a recipient of old age assistance in October, 1948, a month before the referendum, was $61.25; in January, 1949, the second month after the referendum, it was $70.07. Simultaneously, the number of individuals receiving assistance increased by 3.8 per cent.

In 1949, realizing the increased costs of the program, the citizens of California repealed the section of the state constitution which liberalized pensions. The repeal raised the pension age to 65, placed some responsibility for the care of the aged on relatives, and established more stringent property and insurance qualifications.

[Not only financial but political considerations as well played an important role in repeal of the amendment. Repeal was greatly expedited by the feeling on the part of many Californians that they had been victimized by the adroit techniques of "pension politicians."—G. J. S. and E. R.]

THE LONG VIEW

In broadest terms it is clear that the increase in numbers of the aged, the handicaps suffered by members of this group, and the extent of need among them have in the past created and will create in the future constant political efforts to insure more liberal support for the aged who can no longer work and who lack resources of their own.

These political pressures will have the support of the majority of the ever-increasing number of old people, supplemented by many children and other relatives of the aged. This pressure group will include many persons who are approaching the retirement age and are becoming aware of the financial uncertainties they face as well as some of the economically insecure of any age who sympathize with the plight of the dependent aged and are concerned with their welfare.

Will this consolidated pressure influence action on a variety of public issues rather than the issue of pensions alone? This question is of prime significance to the country's future. The aged may vote as others in their economic class rather than as old people. Their political cohesiveness has not yet been demonstrated. Organizations of the aged, formed to work for their financial security, usually have devoted their entire energies to the one cause. So far, the evidence suggests that the political efforts of the aged will be focused only on attempts to better their own economic welfare; but their number is growing steadily, and, if they choose to turn their strength to other objectives, they may exercise substantial influence.

MENTAL HEALTH AREAS THAT PROMISE PROGRESS

Abridged and adapted from Paul V. Lemkau, M.D., "Toward Mental Health Areas That Promise Progress," Mental Hygiene, **36** *(April, 1952), 197–209. Published in this form by permission of the author and the National Association for Mental Health.*

[Many psychiatrists believe that, if significant progress in overcoming mental illness is to be made, it must be made in the area of prevention. As a consequence they emphasize the need for mental hygiene, that is, for knowledge and practice that will promote mental health and prevent the onset of mental illness. Sometimes this emphasis on the positive aspects of mental health rather than on the negative aspects of mental illness is little more than a pious hope. The following discussion points to three areas of knowledge upon which current efforts to promote mental health can be soundly based.]

Public health mental hygiene is the application of scientific knowledge about mental health and mental illness in the lives of the population. Unfortunately, mental illnesses have been associated with mystico-religious fantasies for so long that there is a tendency, in efforts toward the promotion of mental health, to borrow the starry-eyed enthusiasm of the fanatic reformer. In such a situation—and it is all too common—the enthusiast is likely to mount his steed of publicity and so-called "public education" and ride off at full speed. In so doing, he frequently wanders away from the narrow path of scientific knowledge and sets off across unmapped country, finally falling when some simple question, usually put forth by a harassed mother, looms up as insuperable because the knowledge has been left behind. Enthusiasm for a good cause will not take the place of scientific knowledge. To use the psychiatric jargon, there must be "content" as well as "affect," knowledge as well as enthusiasm, if progress is to be made in mental hygiene. It will be the purpose of this paper to set up three categories or axes of knowledge about human personality development and functioning, around which the available facts may be oriented.

THE AXIS OF DEVELOPMENT

The building of the human personality is no haphazard, unpredictable series of chance occurrences; it is an orderly succession of events, each dependent upon the preceding ones. If one studies an individual carefully, so that his present status is known, one can fairly well predict what will be happening to his development in the near future, barring accidents, of course. In the matter of rate of growth, for example, it can be said that an infant growing at the rate of twenty-two pounds per year will be growing at about one-seventh that rate at age three and around half that rate during the pubescent growth spurt. It can be predicted that the infant who holds up his head at six weeks and crawls at eight months will be walking within a few months of the time he is a year old. Depending upon hereditary and nutritional factors, it can be predicted that the girl will have her pubescent growth spurt about two years ahead of the male of the same chronological age. The delineation of the succession of events that takes place in the development of the human being in these anatomical and physiological spheres has been the life-work of many investigators, but there are many more facts of human biology that are yet unknown.

For example, there is a progression of behavior patterns which is predictable for most children; the departure from the progression in the direction either of delay or of acceleration is a signal to examine more carefully the mental health of the child. Not all of the events of the behavior sequence yield satisfaction to the parent; some are disturbing to the parent who is not aware that they are coming. Spock has pointed out that many parents enjoy their children until their second year but then are appalled by their "badness."

There is a very nice sequence in the film, *Preface to a Life*, that demonstrates this point. The baby has just learned to walk and is anxious to try out his new skill. His mother, partly in sorrow and partly in anger, complains that he is no longer satisfied to sit on her lap—he is always self-assertive. This is a phase of development that is predictable; it is an evidence of growth, and it should be a source of satisfaction to the mother that her child may be seen to be taking the first steps toward a healthy adult independence, and not a source of pique that he is more interested at the moment in the world of grass and leaves and things to put into his mouth than he is in his mother. Is it Shakespeare who said, "Parting is such sweet sorrow"? To the unprepared mother, the budding independence is likely to be sorrow with anger, not sweetness.

There are many other examples. There is a period in which the average child will tend to answer "No" to almost every request; this is known as the period of negativism, and it is predictable. There is the independence-dependence struggle in adolescence; it is predictable. There is the issue of changes of interests that go with the pubescent growth spurt; although these are predictable, they are rarely anticipated, and, for some, they are productive of stresses and strains.

It is worth pointing out that changes in adult life are also predictable within limits. There is a sequence of behavior, both apparent and within the woman's feeling and thinking, when she goes through a pregnancy. There is the predictable stress on parent and child when the children leave the family home as more or less mature adults. There is the predictable slowing of function and restriction of range of interests as the person approaches old age, a restriction that is probably more severe when unexpected and unprepared for than when foreseen and offset by the cultivation of what Meyer called "resting points of satisfaction."

Imagine yourself sitting in a cottage on the shores of Lake Michigan during your vacation when it is very hot. The doors and windows are, of course, open and there is a nice breeze blowing. You are comfortably ensconced in a wicker chair, your feet on the window sill, your back to the door, absorbed in a good detective story. Behind you the breeze catches the door, and slowly it begins to close. It speeds up gradually until, by the time it reaches the jamb, it is going very fast. It is stopped suddenly, there is a loud "bang!" and the cottage shakes. You jump and start and for a moment are puzzled, anxious, or confused. Then things become clear as you figure out what has happened; you open the door and find a wedge or a brick to hold it open.

But now suppose you had been facing the door, had noted the rising breeze, and had glanced at the door and noticed that the wedge wasn't under it. It being vacation time, you, of course, did nothing about it, but the thought registered that the breeze might slam the door. Then you watched it start to move, and with scientific detachment you watched the speedup and heard the slam. But you didn't jump; you were not anxious or confused; something predictable and expected, merely, had happened.

This long dissertation on slamming doors and the reaction to them has an application in mental hygiene in public health that is probably already clear to you. Julius Levy gave it a very good name back in the nineteen-thirties; he called it "anticipatory guidance." The thesis is very simple: many types of behavior that give rise to stresses in the parent-child relationship are predictable. If expected and anticipated as evidences of satisfactory growth and development, they are more easily tolerated and impose less severe stress on all concerned. It is quite clear that public health personnel—reaching as they do a significant proportion of the population in pregnancy, in child-health clinics, in school health programs, in X-ray surveys, in cancer-detection programs, and, most recently, in polyphasic screening situations—have an opportunity to use the facts of physical, physiological, and psychological development as an axis for progress in the promotion of mental health.

THE AXIS OF EPIDEMIOLOGICAL STUDY

The second axis for progress has to do with the study of the epidemiology of mental illnesses. Modern epidemiology has, among others, two main purposes. The first of these is to furnish answers to questions concerning how much medical care is needed for a population. But epidemiological studies should produce more than data essential for planning; they should also produce information about the causes of illness or, at least, about the factors associated with the appearance of mental health or disease. It is a cliché that factors that produce health are rarely studied; usually these are interpreted from data on factors that produce ill health.

Some mental health research, however, is being done. The long-term studies of development, both physical and of the personality, made by Washburn, Gesell, Sontag, and others are contributions in this direction. Baldwin has been able to make some very interesting predictions about the kind of children that will be produced by certain kinds of parents. Lewin and his co-workers were able to show the short-term effects on behavior of certain kinds of leadership. The field of industrial psychiatry has contributed rather exact knowledge as to what morale and competition can do in affecting production. Military psychiatry has demonstrated that the quality of leadership is of the greatest importance in maintaining the mental health of troops in the field. Conversely, both military and industrial psychiatry as well as less extensive studies of schoolteachers and their effects on children have shown that defective leadership can lead quite directly to high rates of mental illness and maladjustment.

Many more and better-controlled studies are needed, but epidemiological studies of this type are rapidly expanding our knowledge and are pointing out at what points and, to a less extent, at what ages preventive efforts may be productive of measurable results. Thus far, controlled experiments showing that prophylactic efforts actually prevent the appearance of illness are extremely few. Methods for conducting such studies are rapidly improving, however, and there is reason to hope that, before too much time has passed, we will be able to judge the value of prophylactic efforts on a basis other than subjective conviction and belief, the basis on which most of us must now operate.

Epidemiological studies have given other types of information. They have disposed of the old notion that neurotic illness is more prevalent among the wealthy than among the poor, and they have shown that the various types of illness are not identically distributed in all social groups. The best of such studies have been done by sociologists in Chicago and have proved repeatable in other areas of the country. Although the ultimate etiological problem has not yet been solved, it is known that broken homes produce an inordinate number of maladjusted and ill people. Some illnesses studied, such as psychotic depressions, showed remarkable differences in incidence between the sexes; this points to the need for study of differences in physiology or in the cultural position of the sexes to account for them.

The axis of epidemiology is one along which we may expect progress in a very active field, though it is one which psychiatrists generally are a little afraid of, probably because they fear that the individual patient, his problems, and his treatment will be lost in the maze of statistical calculations. I believe this to be a groundless fear; there is no reason to believe that patients with cholera suffered because Snow found out about the infamous Broad Street Pump.

THE AXIS OF HUMAN INTERRELATIONSHIPS

Two groups of girls sit in two identical rooms before bins of screws, pieces of metal, and slabs of insulation and combine these pieces to make contact plugs for telephone switchboards. As teams, they produce at a pretty regular rate. It is explained to them that a study is to be made to determine the best possible working conditions for them in terms of light, rest periods, and breaks for a little lunch. The experiment begins with varying the amount of light at the bench. When light is increased, production goes up—in both the experimental and the control group. Then the amount of light is lowered until it is barely possible to see to put the parts together; the intensity is about that of moonlight. Production rises. (Some wag points out that this was to have been expected, since production in humans so frequently takes place in moonlight.) But production also rose in the group in which the light intensity had not been changed. There were many more such experiments, and they led inevitably to the conclusion that the physical properties of the work situation did not completely determine the productivity of workers.

Three clubs of adolescent boys have three leaders, each of whom is able to lead them by three different techniques—autocratically, in a laissez-faire manner, and by the democratic process. Each leader exposes the groups to different types of leadership, and it is regularly found that the laissez-faire type brings destructive and pointless play, the autocratic method leads to productivity that stops the moment the leader is gone and is then followed by destructive play, while the democratic type of leadership leads to constructive play which continues for a considerable while after the leader leaves the group.

Two companies of soldiers in training under the same conditions are studied carefully, and their sick-call rates, absences without leave, and actions calling for discipline are recorded. It is found that one company has significantly fewer of these interruptions in its training and that, furthermore, the training scores in this company are higher than in the other. The company with the high training scores and few interruptions of the training schedule is one in which the officers have received special instruction in understanding the emotional reactions of the soldier and the soldiers themselves have had a short series of lectures on the common emotions of fear, homesickness, and reactions to authority.

These three experiments and many others show how important the factors of group feeling or morale are in the successful functioning of human beings. They are cited as representative of the kinds of thinking and experimentation that have established the axis of human interrelationships as an axis for progress in mental hygiene. Such experiments can discover techniques applicable to groups that will make them better teams and, in that way, also make their members more productive. These findings teach what "status" means to the workman and what happens to the productivity of the reacting human being under different situations of tension or comfort in human relationships.

SUMMARY

We have discussed three axes for future progress in mental hygiene: the axis of development, the axis of epidemiological study, and the axis of human relationships.

In the discussion of the development of the personality, the burden of the argument was that knowledge of what is likely to happen is insulation against useless and damaging anxiety. There are enough very real and pressing anxieties which cannot be foreseen. To allow the mother to come suddenly upon predictable anxiety-provoking reactions, such as the period of negativism, is a useless waste of human emotion and opens the opportunity for rifts between parent and child that may be detrimental. In the same way that knowledge can be helpful to parents in rearing the young child, it can be helpful to the child himself as he matures. To leave adolescents in ignorance of the biological changes of puberty is worse than neutral; it is harmful, and represents an inexcusable disuse of the predictive values in knowledge of development.

The second axis had to do with the epidemiology of mental health and mental illness. This has two values. First, it is essential for the planning of medical care. Second, it may in the future help to solve some of the perplexing problems of causation in diseases believed to be the product of multiple etiological factors.

The final axis for progress is the study of human interrelationships in all their fascinating scope—from "what makes the nations rage so furiously together and why do the people follow a vain thing," to what it is in the situation that brings that first heart-warming smile of recognition by the new baby of his new mother, who is so anxious and so eager for his approval, or the wonderment of the young student nurse who has had her first success in helping a new mother deal with her anxieties and fears about her child's feeding difficulties.

ALCOHOLISM AND GROUP THERAPY: ALCOHOLICS ANONYMOUS

adaptation 27

Abridged and adapted from Robert F. Bales, "Social Therapy for a Social Disorder—Compulsive Drinking," Journal of Social Issues, I (December, 1945), 1–9. Published in this form by permission of the author and the Journal of Social Issues.

[Alcoholism appears to be increasing in the United States. Psychiatric treatment, though perhaps of some help in individual cases, is not always successful; in any case it is not a practicable answer to widespread alcoholism. Although there is no reliable evidence, many claim that Alcoholics Anonymous has been remarkably successful in freeing its members of the compulsion to drink. In the following discussion, the author attributes the effectiveness of AA to its group approach to the problem of the alcoholic.]

The most convincing present evidence that a group approach to the re-education of the compulsive drinker works on a large scale with an effectiveness and efficiency hardly approached by any other means of therapy is provided by Alcoholics Anonymous. This movement started with two compulsive drinkers searching for a way to keep sober, in Akron, Ohio, in 1935, and now has something over fourteen thousand members, all ex-alcoholics, with groups in practically all of the large cities of the United States. This organization can certainly be said to have had spectacular success, even though various complications make any exact evaluation of their success in comparison with other methods quite difficult.

The new candidate for Alcoholics Anonymous finds that the group is made up exclusively of others who have been exactly in his own situation. He finds that they have schemed and planned and struggled and stolen to keep their supply of alcohol, just as he has. They have felt the same self-justification, inarticulate rage, and aggression. They have drunk their way into and out of every possible jam and, as a group, know every in and out of the life of the compulsive drinker.

That the members do know and understand the compulsive drinker who comes out in the group meetings, which are given over chiefly to short narratives by the members of their drinking experiences, humorous and tragic, of their final realization that their attempt to adjust through drinking was hopeless, and of the way in which they were able to stop. It is customary for a new member to qualify himself as a genuine alcoholic by relating events from his drinking experience which undeniably identify him with the other members who know and recognize all the signs. The new candidate in such a group intuitively recognizes that he is among friends and that when they speak of their experiences they speak of his own. They talk the same language. They feel as he feels. They do not condemn him. There is nothing to fight against.

The usual situation is here completely reversed; the alcoholic obtains recognition and response through the admission of thoughts and activities which, before, he had been desperately trying to hide, even from himself. In the course of time he opens out, and his experience becomes a part of the group experience. What he had thought were personal drinking secrets, monstrously invented and indulged in by himself alone, become trade secrets, and, humorously or dramatically told, they add to his effectiveness and sense of belonging. He becomes aware of habits of thought and feeling in himself which heretofore had been repressed and compulsively active. He undergoes a personal emotional catharsis, partly through the group meetings, partly through particular confidants he discovers in the group, and partly through his attempts to make amends to friends and associates for wrongs he feels he has done them in the course of his drinking career. The "Twelve Steps," which comprise a condensed statement of the therapeutic program and give it a religious rationale, take care of these various aspects in a systematic way. Although the program is admirably set forth in these twelve steps and individuals have been known to achieve sobriety through "The Book" alone, without benefit of group contact, there is little reason to doubt that getting across the basic ideas in the personal and group setting is vastly more effective for the majority.

It seems reasonable to assume that ideas which come to the individual as convictions held by an organized group of which he feels irrevocably a part come to him with a greater clarity and intensity than information which comes to him in printed form or as advice from a doctor or professional worker. A great many alcoholics, in fact, have a standing grudge against all professional workers, whom they tend to distrust and suspect of a lack of real and sympathetic understanding at best or of outright commercialism at the worst. It is a striking fact that an alcoholic will return to the doctor or social worker after a few meetings of Alcoholics Anonymous and will repeat to him with enthusiasm and conviction ideas of distinct therapeutic value which the professional worker had been unable to get over in a considerably longer time.

Many compulsive drinkers with long drinking careers and innumerable contacts with doctors come to recognize and emotionally accept for the first time as members of Alcoholics Anonymous the fact that they *are* alcoholics—that they cannot take even one drink without continuing on a spree and that their only hope is absolute and complete abstinence. They learn that it is the *first* drink which they must avoid. They learn to detect and recognize their "screwey alcoholic thinking" for what it is, namely, the first stirring fantasy which leads to the full-fledged craving and the fatal first drink. They learn that they must live in a world in which there is constant opportunity and encouragement to drink and yet be sufficiently armed within themselves to say "no" without feeling resentment that others can drink and get away with it. These ideas and many others are constantly reiterated, infinitely varied in form and detail, in the context of impressive personal experience.

It is a fact which continues to provoke a sort of wonder and awe among the members and others who have seen the process actually at work that in the course of participation in Alcoholics Anonymous *the craving disappears.* "I did not leave alcohol—alcohol left me," is one phrase which the members use to express this phenomenal fact. The impressiveness of this fact is one of the concrete bases for the belief of the members in "a Power greater than self." Belief in such a Power, stated in these very general terms, is gradually suggested to the candidate and gives the group a basically religious character.

The enthusiasm of the members is convincing evidence that the association gives them satisfactions and gratifications which they had previously been unable to attain. Membership and acceptance in the group alone provides a number of these satisfactions, but the action program gives still further opportunities for molding and confirming new, nonalcoholic modes of satisfaction for common human goals. The member is urged to work with other alcoholics and give them the opportunity to try the program for themselves. He has, in his own experience, the most effective possible kit of tools for this activity. No matter how ineffective he has been in other respects in the past, he has a good chance to succeed at this, since the number of alcoholics is very great, and some of those to whom he talks are bound to be receptive to the proper approach, as he was. He knows his job, where to put in the entering wedge, what language to use, how far to go, what reaction to expect, and how to deal with it, for in their experience and patterns of thought and feeling regarding drinking, alcoholics are very much alike.

In working to put over the new ideas which have enabled him to become sober, the member identifies himself still more strongly with the group. He confirms by repetition the effects it has had upon him. And in so doing, he feels a new sense of power, adequacy, and authority. His former position is reversed; whereas before he was the "child," the inferior and defensive "bad boy," or the "patient," he now is the wise and benevolent "father" or "mother," the mature adult who has made good in the face of handicaps. He is "the doctor." He is consulted and depended upon by others in the group. His opinions and explanations are respected. Now he is the teacher instead of the pupil.

The leaders of the group become the principal links with the larger community and are active in it, both in a general way and in ways which draw upon community resources for the benefit of alcoholics. The bridge back to the parent social body, with the various aids it can offer, is completed. A series of intermediate roles is thus established, bridging the gap between the position of the isolated and rebellious compulsive drinker and the position of a full-fledged, responsible member of the larger community. The alcoholic, even when not an explicit leader of the group, can pass from one to the other of these intermediate roles with relative ease. Although the ex-alcoholic will probably always want and need to retain his membership and activity in the group, since the old thought and feeling patterns lie constantly in wait within him, he is no longer an outcast but a full-fledged member of the larger community, participating in a way he would never have thought possible in his drinking days. He has finally found a bridge back to the parent social body.

Perhaps it might be said that re-education in the larger sense always involves a reintegration of the individual with the parent social body and its common life, its institutions, its ways of thinking, its valued symbols, its particular and exclusive practices. Permanent belongingness in an organized, locally rooted social system is the only concrete matrix capable of grasping and involving the whole motivation of the man, his whole emotional and active life, as well as his intellectual processes. Consequently, this sort of matrix is ultimately the most effective setting for the re-educational process. All other settings are partial and less effective. The most effective educative agencies—those in which the primary, formative socialization takes place (the family of orientation, friendship groups, the religious body)—all tend precisely toward this pattern, with a tendency to maximize solidarity, permanency, local and territorial segregation, common life and common rituals, and unlimited obligations of members to one another. The effectiveness of particular agencies in the educative process is closely related to the degree that they realize and embody this all-inclusive grasp on the individual.

Alcoholics Anonymous does not incorporate all of the elements mentioned, but it distinctly tends toward this pattern. It probably goes about as far in this direction as is easily compatible with our large institutional system. It certainly does go far enough to be remarkably effective in a task of re-education which has proved notably refractory to other, more superficial approaches. It is for this reason that it may provide concrete suggestions for other re-educative programs (e.g., racial prejudice, autocratic behavior) which are meant to modify individuals extensively but must still fit into the context of the larger social system and complement its activities.

SUGGESTIONS FOR FURTHER READING

Floyd A. Bond et al., *Our Needy Aged* (New York: Henry Holt & Co., Inc., 1954).

Helen I. Clark, *Social Legislation* (New York: Appleton-Century-Crofts, Inc., 1957).

Paul de Kruif, *Kaiser Wakes the Doctors* (New York: Harcourt, Brace & Co., 1943).

Albert Deutsch, *The Mentally Ill in America* (New York: Columbia University Press, 1949).

Herbert Goldhamer and Andrew W. Marshall, *Psychosis and Civilization* (Glencoe, Ill.: The Free Press, 1953).

August B. Hollingshead and Fredrick C. Redlich, *Social Class and Mental Illness: A Community Study* (New York: John Wiley & Sons, Inc., 1958).

James Howard Means, *Doctors, People and Government* (Boston: Little, Brown & Co., 1953).

Frank A. Pinner, Paul Jacobs, and Philip Selznick, *Old Age and Political Behavior: A Case Study* (Berkeley: University of California Press, 1959).

Arnold M. Rose (ed.), *Mental Health and Mental Disorder* (New York: W. W. Norton & Co., 1955).

Louis Goldman; Rapho-Guillumette

CHAPTER 11

The Individual and Society

Out of a study of social problems, and of related community problems, there comes at least one firm conclusion: social problems are not accidents or the result of whims or sheer human willfulness. They are, rather, symptoms of the essential nature of a society, its pattern of social relationships, and its aspirations. In this light, several related characteristics of our changing society emerge:

1. The traditional mechanisms of society have tended to lose some of their control over the individual. The individual has been thrust from his traditional orbits by the centrifugal forces of modern history. The family is not as powerful an instrument of social control as it was; nor is the local community.

Delinquency, for example, is partly an expression of this relative loss of control. So is the increasing failure of families to take responsibility for their dependent members and the pervasive attempt to put a "rearing" as well as an "educating" burden on the school system.

2. The individual is relating to larger and less personal rather than more intimate mechanisms of society. As the influence of family and neighborhood becomes less binding, the influence of the larger community and the

mass media becomes more significant. The institutions to which people relate are less personal and require less direct participation on the part of the individual. The dependent person has to deal not with the family, very often not even with the local community, but often with the federal government. More and more of the business of everyday life is transacted between strangers under rules that are depersonalized. This creates a sense of isolation and alienation from society.

3. Aspirations have risen and broadened in scope. Satisfaction with traditional social or economic status has broken down under the impact of recent developments in society. There is the knowledge that science and industry have created the possibility of material plenty for all. There is no longer the feeling that these material benefits, and other benefits, should be restricted to a few by traditional class or caste distinctions. The philosophy of democracy and egalitarianism is relatively old but is perhaps only now coming into its own as an accompaniment to the general weakening of traditional relationships.

The rise of intergroup prejudice as an active social problem is a symptom of this universal rise of aspirations. Delinquency is often an expression of dissatisfaction with traditional modes of life. The schools have been redesigned to perform an egalitarian function.

These related characteristics of our society manifest themselves not only in those conflicts and difficulties that we call "social problems" but in almost every aspect of the individual's relation to society.

GOVERNMENT AND THE INDIVIDUAL

Because of the gradual centralization of government, the seat of important decisions has moved steadily from local to state to federal levels, and even to international levels. The individual is not only physically farther away from the center of government but his relation to it is less direct and personal because government "belongs" to so many more people. The individual shares with more and more people the "representative" whom he chooses to vote *for* him on public issues. And the most important decisions are increasingly made by a national representative whom the individual shares with all the people and who does his "representing" the farthest distance away.

In addition, the governmental problems of modern society are increasingly complex, often requiring a wealth of information and technical knowledge which are not only outside the ken of the average citizen but have forced the representatives themselves to specialize in certain areas and seek advice in others. This emphasis on the expert has increased the individual's sense of distance from his governmental process.

The national government's foreign policy epitomizes this development.

GOVERNMENT AND THE INDIVIDUAL

In recent years foreign policy has become an ever more critical function of government. Yet it is the area of government in which the average citizen has probably the least competence and which, more than any other function of government, the citizenry must delegate to its government on trust. There is information which the government must keep secret from other governments and must therefore keep secret from the citizenry at large. There are secret agreements which all governments have to make in certain complex situations and which cannot be divulged, at the time they are made, to the citizenry at large. Now there is the United Nations, with which the average citizen feels less in touch than with his own government. Decisions are being made about which the individual knows little and over which he feels he has little control—decisions made by people he doesn't know at meetings he can't attend.

The apathy of the American citizen toward political affairs is often attributed to this increasing sense of distance. The citizen often feels more like a helpless spectator than a direct participant in daily political affairs. "What can I do?" is a typical attitude.

The formal instruments of opinion-molding have also become larger in many respects. In 1909 there was approximately one newspaper in this country for every 35,000 people; in 1957 the figure was closer to one newspaper

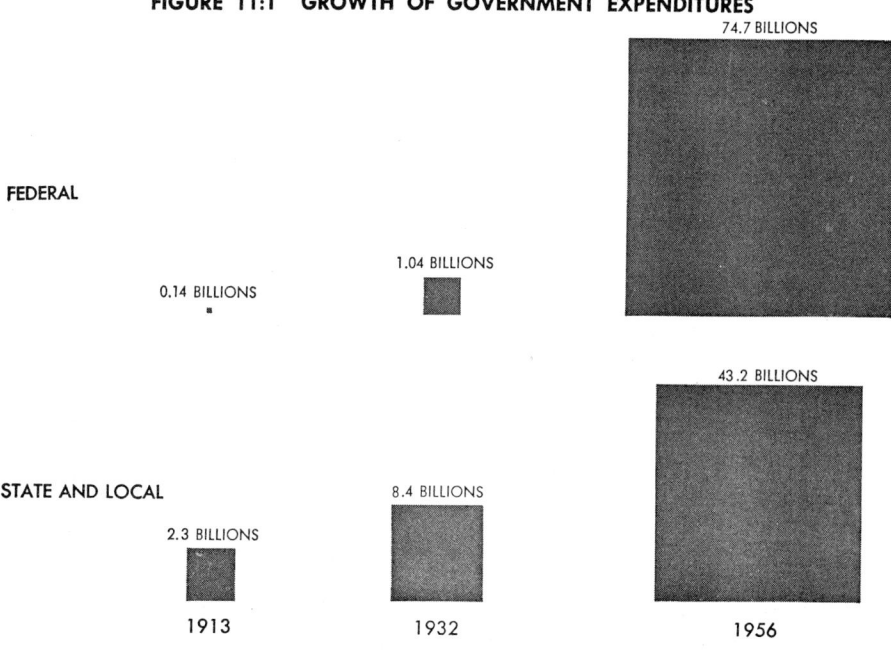

FIGURE 11:1 GROWTH OF GOVERNMENT EXPENDITURES

Source: U.S. Bureau of the Census, *Statistical Abstract of the United States, 1958* (Washington, D.C.: U.S. Government Printing Office, 1958), p. 407.

for every 95,000 people. The newspaper business has become big business, with an increasing number of mergers and an increasing number of cities with only one newspaper. National journals of news interpretation have gained wider circulation. And, of course, radio and television are primarily national phenomena, with relatively few local or regional broadcasts. It is a common fear that the citizen's nonparticipant posture toward daily governmental affairs is abetted by "mass" opinion-molding.

Moreover, the rising levels of aspiration have themselves helped create this sense of distance and nonparticipation by adding impetus to the centralization of government power. Dependency has become increasingly the concern of the federal government. The concept of dependency has been gradually redefined to mean not just unemployability or abject indigence but the maintenance of certain minimal standards of living, constantly revised upwards; it has also come to mean a sense of security that these standards will continue to prevail. Local units of government are not equipped to deal with this concept of dependency, partly because of lack of funds, partly because of the need to equalize standards across the nation. For the same reasons, public school systems, heavily burdened with the responsibility for meeting these new aspirations, have tended to seek help from larger units of government. The growth of big government is obviously not an

FIGURE 11:2 PUBLIC EMPLOYES, BY TYPE OF GOVERNMENT, APRIL, 1957

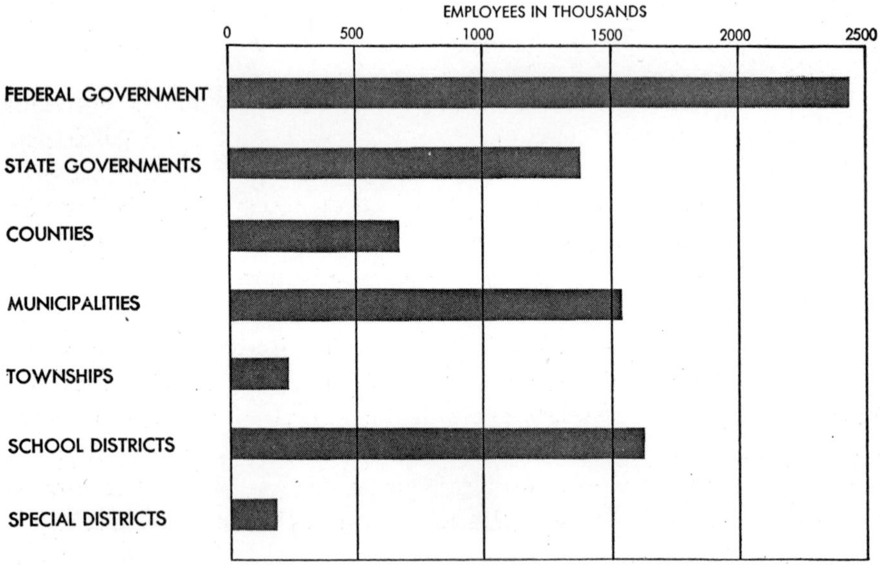

Source: U.S. Bureau of the Census, *U.S. Census of Governments: 1957*, Vol. II, No. 1 (Washington, D.C.: U.S. Government Printing Office, 1958), p. 2.

Owen; Black Star

The Union Dispatcher: Workmen at a union headquarters in San Diego, California, waiting for jobs. The union apparatus is an intermediary between workers and employers.

ideological whim but rather the outgrowth of many of the basic forces which are operating in our society today.

THE INDIVIDUAL AND HIS WORK

In making his living as well as in running his government, the individual has found himself relating to larger units—less personal, less participant, and apparently more "distant." The mass movement from farm life is the most obvious case in point. In 1820 over 70 per cent of all gainfully employed workers were occupied on farms; today, little more than 10 per cent are so employed.[1] And, like government, urban business became big business. Approximately the same number of manufacturing firms were employing about three times as many workers in 1949 as in 1899, according to U.S. Census Bureau estimates.[2] Mass-production methods and automatic machinery changed the relationship of the worker to both his employers and the product of his labors. He was further "removed" from his employers as a result of the sheer size of the working force. He was also further removed from the end product of his labors as a result of the job specialization in-

---

[1] U.S. Bureau of the Census, *Statistical Abstract of the United States, 1957* (Washington, D.C.: U.S. Government Printing Office, 1957), pp. 195, 199.

[2] *Ibid.*, p. 783.

volved in the assembly-line process. Even the service industries, which sprang up to meet the new standards of living and to fill the employment gap created by manufacturing automation, became big industries.

The laboring force, partly to meet these new conditions of mass employment, created an intermediary agency, the labor union, to bargain with their "distant" employers. Under the impact of the depression, labor unions grew from a total membership of less than 3 million in 1933 to over 8 million in 1940; and they continued to grow, to close to 20 million by 1957. The unions themselves consolidated into larger unions, and this trend was climaxed in 1957 by the amalgamation of the American Federation of Labor and the Congress of Industrial Organizations.

Accompanying the growth of large business and large unions was the phenomenon of bureaucracy, a symptom of large government as well. Now the large-scale unions as well as the large-scale employer had many hired specialists and underlings as well as an apparatus of impersonal rules and procedures between themselves and the rank-and-file workers. In many cases the worker began to feel as distant and nonparticipating toward his union as he did toward his employer and his government. Union leaders have claimed that the alleged evils of big unionism weigh little against the measure of dignity, stature, and material gain which the unions have brought

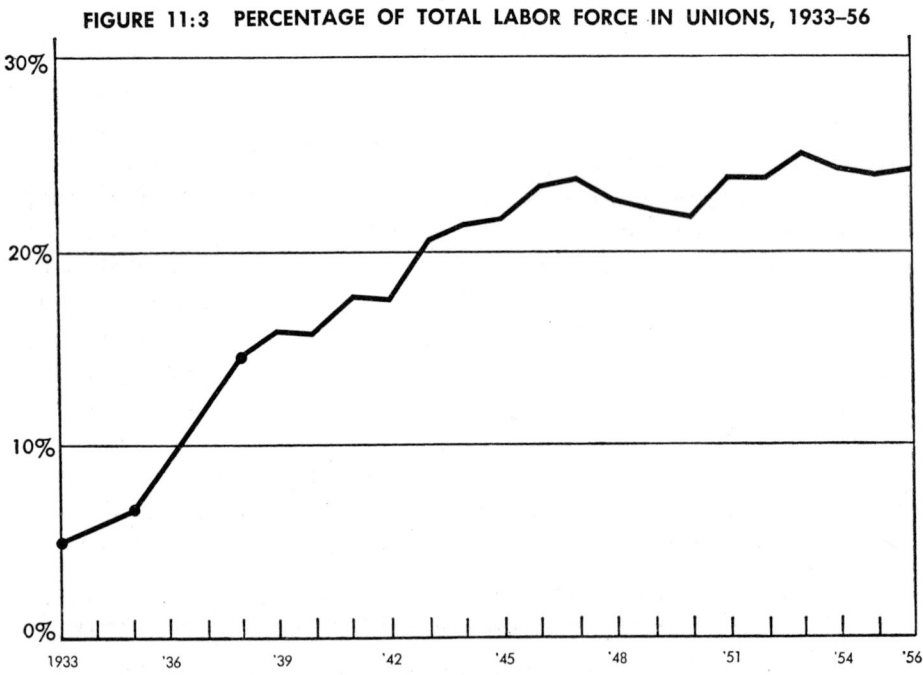

FIGURE 11:3   PERCENTAGE OF TOTAL LABOR FORCE IN UNIONS, 1933–56

Source: U.S. Bureau of the Census, *Statistical Abstract of the United States, 1958* (Washington, D.C.: U.S. Government Printing Office, 1958), p. 236.

their members in the last twenty-five years. They point to the relatively helpless and dependent condition of workers in big business before the advent of big unions. The descriptive fact remains, however, that the working life of the individual has tended to become more compartmentalized and more depersonalized on all levels.

THE INDIVIDUAL AND HIS LEISURE

Traditional patterns of leisure-time activity have also changed in accordance with the changing characteristics of society. The outward movement here is from family, neighborhood, and church activities to mass media. Obviously, the members of an urban family are no longer as dependent on one another for entertainment as was the case in the isolated farm family. The general feeling of social isolation which is engendered in the metropolitan center was epitomized by one woman, who, when asked what she missed most during a newspaper strike in New York city, said:

> I like the *Daily News*. It's called a scandal sheet, but I like it. It was the first paper I bought when I came to New York. When you live in a small town and read the paper, you know everybody who's mentioned in the paper. The *News* is the closest thing to them. The pictures are interesting, and it makes up for the lack of knowing people .... You get used to certain people; they become part of your family, like Dorothy Kilgallen .... [3]

It has been suggested that television has moved into this social vacuum and has, moreover, enlarged it. At the beginning of 1957, about 80 per cent of the homes of the nation were equipped with television sets, and it is only a matter of time before the figure approaches saturation. The average adult who has a television set spends over 18 hours a week watching it. The hope has been expressed that television might serve to bring the family back together again in its leisure pursuits. However, one study indicated that in only about one out of ten families does any substantial amount of talking take place while the set is on, and it concluded: "It appears that the increased family contact brought about by television is not social except in the most limited sense, that of being in the same room with other people." [4]

One effect of television, according to many observers, has been to emphasize the role of the individual as spectator rather than participant. In the words of one critic: "Because the world is brought into our homes, we do not have to explore it." [5] Allied to this has been the fear that personal taste

---

[3] Quoted in Bernard Berelson, "What 'Missing the Newspaper' Means," in Wilbur Schramm (ed.), *The Process and Effects of Mass Communication* (Urbana: University of Illinois Press, 1954), p. 43.

[4] Elinor B. MacComby, "Television: Its Impact on School Children," *Public Opinion Quarterly*, 15 (Fall, 1951), p. 444.

[5] Guenther Anders, "The Phantom World of Television," *Dissent*, 3 (1956), 14–24.

in recreational pursuits is increasingly molded by the larger instruments of society, such as the mass media, rather than by the more intimate influences of home and region. Since the mass media, by definition, must appeal to mass audiences, they tend to seek common denominators of appeal in their programing. The practical result of common-denominator programing is avoidance of any presentation which might offend or fail to interest any sizable segment of the total audience. The inevitable result is a general leveling-downward of program content by intellectual or artistic standards. The entertainment tends to be anesthetic rather than creative in nature. It serves only to distract, to fill time, rather than to stimulate the individual to any greater use of his own mental or physical capacities. If this is true, then it is on yet another level that the individual in our society is being subjected to larger and more impersonal forces.

AN EVALUATION: THE LOSS OF INDIVIDUALITY

One of the gloomy propositions implicit in this recital of the characteristics of modern society is that the individual is being destroyed. It is sometimes taken as axiomatic that if the institutions and mechanisms of society are becoming larger, the significance of the individual is dwindling. This is an overfacile assumption.

Usually cast as an archvillain in the alleged destruction of the individual are the mass media of communication. Evidence does not point, however, to the fact that the mass media have taken over, or have the capacity to take over, as the prime means of social control. Studies on intergroup attitudes and other attitudes related to deep-seated individual values indicate that, while the mass media are not without long-range effect, neither can they automatically machine-tool attitudes. One intensive study of opinion-making in Erie County, Ohio, during a political season indicated that seven months of mass-media campaign propaganda had only served to reinforce the original intention of the majority of those interviewed; only about five per cent had been converted. At least 10 per cent more people were involved in political discussions than listened to a major speech or read about the campaign in a newspaper. Furthermore, those who were already committed to a political attitude were those who tended to subject themselves most often to the mass-media presentations. Those who were less committed were more likely to receive most of their political education in group discussions.[6]

An evaluation of the effect of mass media on political opinion must also consider whether a state of monopoly exists for any one viewpoint. Radio and television in this country have been scrupulously governed by the con-

---

[6] Paul F. Lazarsfeld, Bernard Berelson, and Hazel Gaudet, *The People's Choice* (New York: Columbia University Press, 1944).

Post-Dispatch Pictures; Black Star

Sidewalk Politics: This candidate for the U.S. Senate speaks to a minute fraction of his electorate. While using the mass media as much as possible, most political candidates still believe that there is no substitute for face-to-face contacts with the voters.

cept that opposing political viewpoints must be given equal time and that the media themselves must remain "above the battle." There has even been criticism that radio and television stations and networks have failed to stimulate mature political thinking in the public, just because they have so timidly avoided any suggestion of an editorial or partisan tone in their political programing. The newspapers have not been so constrained, but there is serious question as to the effectiveness of their attempts to influence public opinion on the larger issues. Mott analyzed the partisan content of newspapers in presidential elections from 1792 to 1940 and concluded that there seems to be no correlation, positive or negative, between the support of a majority of newspapers during a campaign and success at the polls.[7]

The simple fact is that a mass audience is not necessarily an undifferentiated audience. Fifty million people may happen to hear a political speech at the same time, but they are still fifty million distinct people. Evidence indicates that these people would probably be more susceptible to the same political thoughts if they were expressed by a hundred local speakers on a hundred local television stations to smaller audiences. The possibility of

[7] Cited by Joseph T. Klapper, "Mass Media and Persuasion," in *The Process and Effects of Mass Communication,* p. 291 (see n. 3, above).

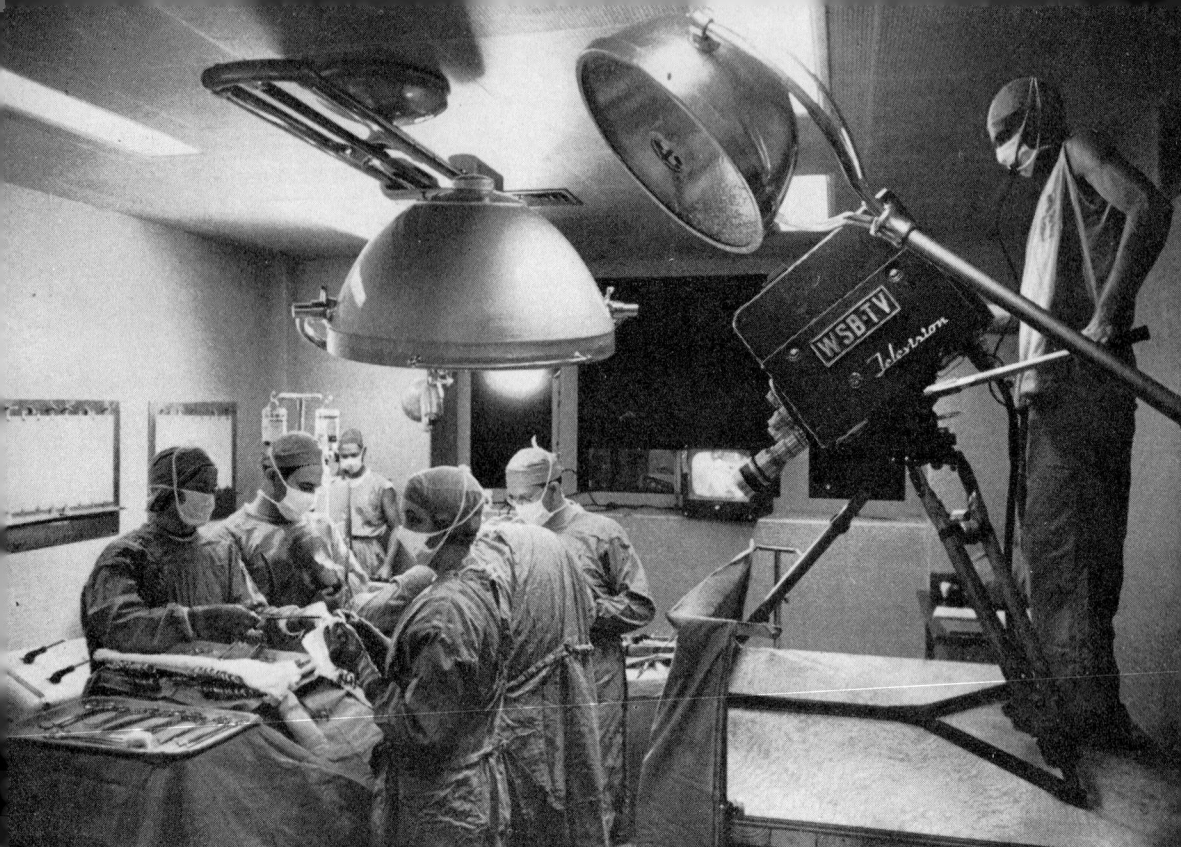

J. Leviton; Black Star

The Spectator: Television has the potential to allow every individual to inspect the world without leaving his living room.

manipulating the individual is probably at its highest point at the traditional town meeting and at its lowest point in the use of a national television network. It is at the town meeting that the individual may be *least* free to form and express his individual opinions because he is subject to more personal pressures and traditional ties. It is at the town meeting that he is most likely to be swayed by the personal power of suasion that some local leader may wield rather than by an objective evaluation of the issues.

The fear that our society may be turning into a monolithic cultural wasteland because of the mass media may also be partly an expression of nostalgia for a condition that never really existed. The artistic standards of the mass media may generally be low and "anesthetic," but there is no evidence that these low standards are a by-product of the size of modern society's institutions of communication. In some instances, the converse is indicated. At the turn of the century, opera music was enjoyed by only a handful of people. A single radio broadcast of the Metropolitan Opera today has an audience of 15 million. The same comparison might be made of the numbers of people who have had the opportunity to see a topnotch performance of a Shakespeare play or a ballet or to hear an informed discussion of books or world affairs. These are opportunities that were not provided by the "well-knit" family of a half-century ago, or the "stable" neighborhoods and communities in which they lived. It may indeed be deplored that the mass media have not done more to deliberately lift the cultural levels of society, but the blame cannot be laid at the door of the mass media without reference to the influence of home and school. Indeed, the mass media often provide a means for the individual to escape from the cultural level which surrounds him, and in this way they *free* him as an individual. The relative loss of social control through the weakening of the traditional institutions of society encourages rather than discourages individuation, defined by Ross as the "pulverising of social lumps."

The hazards that reside in our society for overwhelming the individual cannot be ignored. On the other hand, neither can the forces within the same society that operate toward the liberation of the individual be overlooked.

AN EVALUATION: LOSS OF SOCIAL ORGANIZATION

The power of the large institutions of modern society to overwhelm the individual is limited by the very fact that they are unable to fill the place of the more intimate and personal relationships which mark traditional group life. However, another one of the gloomy implications to be found in a listing of the characteristics of modern society is that traditional group life is disappearing, and nothing is taking its place. Dwight Macdonald has commented: "The masses are in historical time what a crowd is in space: a large quantity of people unable to express themselves as human beings because they are related to one another neither in rituals nor as members of a community—indeed they are not related *to each other* at all, but only to something distant, abstract, nonhuman." [8]

One of the observations of sociologists is that there *has* been a weakening of traditional group ties, of social organization. The orderly transmission of social values has been disrupted, and therefore social order itself has been affected. Delinquency is often an expression of this phenomenon. Presumably another effect has been a rise in the level of alienation: the feeling on the part of the individual that he is not significantly related to other human beings or human traditions but, if at all, to something "distant, abstract." There is a sense of rootlessness, of nonparticipation, of being another stranger in "the lonely crowd." This tendency accompanies and accentuates the loss of commitment to traditional social values.

However, the proposition of social disorganization is often overstated. Social organization is not so fragile as is sometimes suggested. Perhaps it would

[8] Dwight Macdonald, "A Theory of Mass Culture," in Bernard Rosenberg and David Manning White (eds.), *Mass Culture* (Glencoe, Ill.: The Free Press, 1957), p. 69.

be more accurate to refer to this era as one of social reorganization rather than social disorganization. For example, some of the functions of the family and some of its traditional relationships may be changing, but this does not decree the disappearance of the family as a meaningful social unit. It is to be sure a smaller unit, typically including only immediate members. It is no longer a productive economic unit. Its adult and older-child members do not spend as much time together. Some of its traditional influence is presumably lost as a consequence. But the new aspirations of family members must also be taken into account along with the family's partial loss of function. Wife and children aspire to new levels of independence and democratic relationship. They have new opportunities for achieving greater independence. Cohesive family life must be based on more genuine conditions of companionship and leadership. Children must be raised and family life conducted in light of this need. The preoccupation of parents in recent years with parent-child relationships has taken many a crude turn, with much oversimplification of psychological theory; but the preoccupation itself is an indication that more and more parents are prepared to face the new realities of family life. In the meantime, there is much confusion and even panic. The family is still an integral part of the total social scene, reflecting its general weaknesses and conflicts.

Some of the functions of the neighborhood may be irretrievably lost. But new associations are forming; ours has increasingly become a society of voluntary associations and organizations among adults and adolescents. The "return to the church" has been interpreted in part as another index of the felt need for group identification. So has the movement to suburbia.

On another level, the individual is seeking new means of participating directly in the decisions of his government. He is forming and joining voluntary citizens' associations concerned with influencing public policy in matters of foreign affairs, tax rates, health facilities, civil rights, and the entire range of important public affairs. These are, ideally, citizens' pressure groups, an important development in the democratic process, in which the individual can have a role of direct and continuing participation. These developments sometimes take the form of artificial and futile attempts to place a façade of social organization before an increasingly empty pattern of relationships, but they also often represent fumbling efforts to meet the realistic needs of modern society and the new aspirations of its people.

This is clearly a period of social dislocation. The social problems thereby created cannot be minimized. They are first of all to be recognized as symptoms of this dislocation. The symptoms themselves must be mitigated because they involve human suffering and disorder. They will resist total solution as long as the basic dislocations persist, and efforts at mitigation will be most effective and least frustrating in the light of this understanding.

Perhaps one way of approaching and gaining insight into these dislocations is through treating their symptoms. In any case, these basic dislocations are not to be taken as uniformly evil or retrograde with respect to individual self-fulfillment and democratic social order. Though these dislocations bring with them grave problems which must be dealt with, they are nevertheless the possible harbingers of a more mature, more flexible, and more universally rewarding social order.

PARTICIPATION AND MASS APATHY IN ASSOCIATIONS — adaptation 28

Abridged and adapted from Bernard Barber, "Participation and Mass Apathy in Associations," in Alvin W. Gouldner (ed.), Studies in Leadership (New York: Harper & Bros., 1950), pp. 477–504. Published in this form by permission of the author and the publisher.

[Many people have expressed concern about the "mass apathy" of the American people. They feel that, since we are a democracy, the average citizen ought to participate far more actively than he does in the affairs of his society. As things are, most people limit their political participation to an occasional vote. In this way the power that ought to reside in the people becomes concentrated in the hands of bosses and political machines.

The following discussion focuses attention on membership participation in voluntary associations, particularly in trade-unions. The author concludes that the nature of the voluntary association and its role in present-day society tend to discourage membership participation. Even in organizations that want to be democratic there is a strong tendency for minority control to emerge. He believes that responsible participation can be increased only if we have a realistic understanding of the factors that work to discourage it.]

THE VOLUNTARY ASSOCIATION IN AMERICA

America has been called a nation of joiners. After his visit to America in 1831, de Tocqueville wrote: "In no country in the world has the principle of association been more successfully used, or applied to a greater multitude of objects, than in America. Americans of all ages, all conditions, and all dispositions constantly form associations." Americans continue to get things done through the voluntary association. They form occupational, interest, and pressure groups of all sorts—committees, unions, chambers of commerce, service clubs, welfare organizations, recreational societies, veterans' and women's groups—and they form them consciously and voluntarily. Paradoxically, we are great joiners largely because we are great individualists. Americans pursue their own interests, but they join with others to pursue them better.

Voluntary associations can become so important as to lose their voluntary character. The increasing control by trade-unions over jobs, for example, has considerably altered the degree to which union membership is a matter of genuine choice, while doctors have discovered that local medical associations are often able to control access to hospitals.

The sheer number of voluntary associations is a striking fact in American life. A 1945 report on Boulder, Colorado, stated that this city of 12,000 had 245 associations. A study made in the thirties found that one American city of 17,000 had 357 associations. On the other hand, many Americans belong to no associations at all. One study found that, leaving church membership aside, a majority of people in New York City had no organizational affiliations.

MINORITY CONTROL

Most voluntary associations in the United States are organized democratically; through elections, they provide for membership participation and rule. In practice, however, they are usually run and controlled by a minority.

This is not the result of conspiracy and chicanery. A study of fraternal organizations concluded the following: "Though fraternal organizations are subject to democratic control, it appears that the actual formation of policy . . . is largely the function of a few interested individuals, with the great bulk of the membership acquiescing so long as these policies do not interfere with their private lives." Most studies have shown that even militantly democratic organizations find it almost impossible to gain the attendance and participation of their memberships. More than most other associations, the Consumer Co-operative Movement stresses the desirability of equal and active participation by all members. Nevertheless, it too is faced with indifference on the part of most.

VOLUNTARY ASSOCIATIONS AS INSTRUMENTS

Why is it that Americans are great joiners but poor participators in voluntary associations? Perhaps most basic is the fact that voluntary associations have a merely instrumental value for most people. Members are interested in the goals of the association but not in the association itself. They want to participate in the benefits secured by the association but not in the activities required to secure them.

Membership in a voluntary association can be contrasted with membership in a family or occupational community. The benefits of family life cannot be separated from participation in family activities; nor can the rewards of work be obtained apart from doing the job. In the case of voluntary associations, however, membership can be merely formal—a matter of paying dues—for it is quite possible for a small, active minority to achieve the goals of the association without membership participation. The consensus among observers is that whether they are workers, farmers, or businessmen, the membership of most organizations do not want self-government. Leaders are conceived of as getting paid to run the organization, and members are satisfied as long as the association protects their interests.

LEADERSHIP AS SKILL

Quite apart from lack of membership attendance and participation, there is a tendency in voluntary associations for a stable leadership to emerge, quite separate and distinct from the rank and file. This is true even when an association is organized democratically, the leadership is not corrupt, and the members are not wholly indifferent.

Leadership entails special skills—such as making speeches or being a good administrator—and a special kind of knowledge, such as familiarity with the association, its history, its policy, and the people and agencies with which it has to deal. Theoretically, many people are capable of acquiring the requisite skills and knowledge; but, in practice, some already have them and most others do not.

Leadership is likely to devolve upon those who have already learned to exercise it. Indeed, if membership participation is minimal, as it usually is in voluntary associations, some minority will be forced to take over the decision-making if the organization is to survive and achieve its aims.

Although rotation of leadership is consonant with democratic ideals, stability and continuity of leadership are important factors in developing the strength and effectiveness of an organization. Whether it be a trade-union, a medical association, or a veterans' group, it may take decades for a voluntary association to gain enough political influence to affect national policy. As a result, there is a tendency not to jeopardize hard-won gains by electing new officials but to continue to place in office those who are already established, recognized, and effective leaders.

LEADERSHIP AS A CAREER

Many voluntary associations are large, exist on a nation-wide scale, and require full-time leadership. Elected officers have no choice but to leave their old occupations and become employees of the association. Being an official of a voluntary association becomes a new occupation and a new career; and, like any other careerist, the paid executive of a voluntary association becomes interested in protecting his job. He will try to prolong his stay in office, especially when this brings him more money, more status, and more power than he formerly had. Moreover, the longer he remains an official, the more his old skills atrophy and opportunities for returning to his former occupation diminish.

The need of many voluntary associations for full-time, paid officials has increased their divergence from democratic practice. By providing for elections, voluntary associations continue to conform to democratic ideals; in practice, however, one or a number of officials are automatically re-elected year after year. This is the usual case in trade-unions, although it occurs also in other associations. In the American Medical Association the president, president-elect, and vice-president enjoy, as a rule, only a relatively short tenure, but the secretary and the treasurer are re-elected time after time. In many cases, long-tenure elected officials become centers of power and are able to stifle opposition and criticism. One secretary of the American Medical Association held his office for decades. Since he was also editor of the Association's journal, views opposing official policy had little chance of being expressed in writing.

TRADE-UNIONS

The large trade-unions in the United States are similar in democratic values and organizational structure to other large democratic associations. They also exhibit the same discrepancy between democratic values and actual practice as other associations. However, many people feel that undemocratic practices in trade-unions are not only more reprehensible but also more extreme than in other associations. Part of this criticism can be traced to the fact that trade-unions have a special connection with the democratic tradition. They represent the "common man," the "underdog." Hence, trade-unions appear especially hypocritical when they fail to observe democratic practices within their own ranks.

It appears to be the case, moreover, that the pattern of office-holding by executives in trade-unions is one of exceedingly long tenure, even of lifetime tenure; such length of tenure is apparently uncommon in other democratic associations. This pattern, though often regarded as a sign of corruption on the part of trade-union leaders, is a result of the special position they occupy in the job market.

The trade-union movement has provided an important channel of mobility for the working-class American. One study of the social origins of trade-union leaders encompassed 50 per cent of the presidents and secretaries of the AFL and CIO national and international unions and the same proportion of presidents and secretaries of the state federations of these two "houses of labor" (now consolidated into one). About 60 per cent of this sample were the sons of skilled laborers. Twenty-two per cent had gone to college, but the rest had gone only to grammar and high school. The typical career pattern was for these men to start as workers, become officials of a local, and gradually work up to the top of a national or international union or state federation. Even by middle-class standards, their salaries were definitely good.

Thus, trade-union leaders as a group have risen to enviable positions, especially in relation to those with similar origins and education. Their general social status is good, their opportunities to further the advance of their children great, and their effective influence on affairs large. Theirs is a situation which most Americans would like; they are successful men. And yet—and this is what is peculiar about their situation—they can, in general, maintain their position only by holding on to the *particular* positions they have. Career lines run pretty much within a given union. There is very little possibility of moving from an executive position in one union to another position of equal or higher status in another union. At best, an executive can move out of his own local union into the state and national federation. There is very little chance, moreover, that the trade-union leader can transfer his ability to other job markets. He has been pretty much shut out of government and business groups, partly because his very success may have rested on continual opposition to them. Thus the executive in the trade-union is locked up in the labor movement and is subjected to very great pressures to maintain his general social status and to preserve his success by any means available. It is often to the detriment of the practice of democracy in trade-unions that the "best means available" to the executive is to ensure himself permanent tenure. In the effort to guarantee his tenure, the executive may abandon much that is essential in democratic values.

CONCLUSION

Many factors contribute to the discrepancy between democratic values and democratic practices in voluntary associations. Most members are not interested in running the organization; they are glad to leave that to others. In addition, large voluntary associations require skillful leaders, continuity and stability of leadership, and full-time, paid officials. All these factors contribute to control by a small minority and the entrenchment of long-tenure officials. In trade-unions the difficulties are augmented because union executives are rarely able to move to other jobs of comparable income, status, and power. In order to maintain their social positions, they try to ensure re-election.

Because undemocratic practices tend to characterize voluntary associations, some people conclude that it is useless to believe in democracy. We believe, on the other hand, that democratic participation in voluntary associations can be enlarged, but only by understanding the factors that work against it.

---

adaptation 29   WORK AND ITS DISCONTENTS

Abridged and adapted from Daniel Bell, "Notes on Work," En-counter, 2 (June, 1954), 3–15. Published in this form by permission of the author and Encounter. *The author has dealt with the same subject in* Work and Its Discontents *(Boston: Beacon Press, 1956).*

[Many observers have commented on the alienation of the present-day worker from his work. Daniel Bell discusses below some of the human consequences as well as some of the social consequences of modern mass-production methods. He analyzes the way in which the size of the modern industrial enterprise, its emphasis on efficiency, and the need for management planning and co-ordination have all served to atomize and depersonalize the worker. The author also raises the question of whether contemporary emphasis on "human relations" and on leisure can be adequate compensation for a loss of satisfaction in work.]

Contemporary industrial enterprise sets up three peculiar logics: the logic of size, the logic of functional efficiency, and the logic of hierarchy. Each of the three imposes a set of constraints on the worker with which he is forced to wrestle every day. These are the daily facts of his existence.

THE LOGIC OF SIZE

For the man whose working day is from 8:00 A.M. to 5:00 P.M., the morning often begins long before the time he has to be at his place of work. After a hasty wash and a quick breakfast, he is off in his car or on the streetcar or bus or subway; often he may have to spend an hour or more in getting to the plant. There seems to be a law, as Bertrand Russell has noted, that improvements in transportation do not cut down the traveling time but merely increase the area over which people are compelled to travel.

The engineer believes that concentration is technologically efficient; under one roof there can be brought together the source of power, the raw materials, the parts and assembly. So we find such huge megaliths as the sprawling shed at the Ford plant at Willow Run, spanning an area two-

Wide World Photos

On Wheels: Automobiles pour into Los Angeles on the Pasadena freeway. In metropolitan life, people have to travel great distances between the places where they work, where they live, and where they play.

thirds of a mile long and a quarter of a mile wide, or such roofed-over, mile-long pavements as the Boeing plant in Wichita, Kansas.

Much of this thinking about the advantages of size was conditioned by the early problems of the limited amount of power available through the use of steam. For this reason, the engineer tended to crowd as many productive units as possible on the same shaft, or within the range of steam pressure that could be reached by pipes without excessive condensation losses. These considerations led, too, to the bunching of workers in the layout of work, since the machines had to be located along a straight-line shafting.

The introduction of electric power and electric motors allowed a new flexibility; and within the plant, newer work-flow designs often do avoid the antiquated straight-line shafts and aisles of the older factory. Yet the size of the factory remains unchallenged. But the question can be posed: Which is it cheaper to transport, living men twice a day, or materials and mechanical parts twice a week? As Percival and Paul Goodman so pertinently note: "The time of life of a piece of metal is not consumed while it waits for its truck; a piece of metal does not mind being compressed like a sardine." What the Goodmans propose is production in "bits and pieces" rather than on an integrated assembly; yet the question is rarely considered, for few industries pay directly for their workers' travel time. Calculations in terms of market costs do not force the enterprise to take into account such things as the time used up in going to and from work or the costs of roads and other transport to the factory site, which are paid for by the whole community out of taxes.

THE LOGIC OF EFFICIENCY

One of the prophets of modern work was Frederick W. Taylor (1856–1915), and the stop watch was his bible. If any such social upheaval can ever be attributed to one man, the logic of efficiency as a mode of life is due to him. With "scientific management" as enunciated by Taylor, and with the assembly line as refined by Henry Ford, we pass far beyond the old division of labor; we go into the division of time itself.

The significance of Taylorism lies in its attempt to enact a social physics. Once work was scientifically plotted, Taylor felt, there could be no disputes about how hard one should work or how much pay one should receive for labor. "As reasonably might we insist on bargaining about the time and place of the rising and setting sun," he once said.

Scientific management in essence is simply the systematic analysis and breakdown of work into its smallest mechanical components and the rearrangement of these elements into the most efficient combination. Taylor achieved fame in 1899 when he took a Dutchman named Schmidt and taught him to shovel forty-seven tons instead of twelve and a half tons of

Roland Patterson; Black Star

The Assembly Line: In this General Motors plant, each man performs his particular task as each automobile body is fitted to its chassis.

pig iron a day. Every detail of the man's job was specified; the size of the shovel, the bite into the pile, the weight of the scoop, the distance to walk, the arc of the swing, and the rest periods that Schmidt should take. By systematically varying each factor, Taylor got the optimum barrow load. But Taylor knew, too, what such a mechanical regimen would do to a man or, rather, what sort of man could fit into this strait jacket. "One of the very first requirements for a man who is fit to handle pig iron as a regular occupation," he wrote, "is that he shall be so stupid and so phlegmatic that he more nearly resembles an ox than any other type."

The logic of Taylorism was obvious; each man's work could be measured by itself; the time in which an operation could be performed could "without bargaining" be established as an impersonal "standard time"; pay could then be computed on the basis of the amount of work done and the time taken to do it.

In the modern economy, shadings of time are so important that a large company like General Motors contracts with its workers on a six-minute basis. For purposes of payroll calculations, General Motors divides the hour into ten six-minute periods, and, except for the daily three-hour minimum "call-in pay" (paid whenever the worker is called in to work), the G.M. worker is paid by the number of tenths of an hour he works.

THE LOGIC OF HIERARCHY

The fragmentation of work, although atomizing the workers, has also created a dependency and a hierarchy, for inherent in the division of labor is what Marx called "the iron law of proportionality." Thus, in the manufacturing process, the relations between numbers of workers are determined by the requirements of the different technological procedures. Marx cited an example in type manufacture; one founder could cast 2,000 type an hour, the breaker could break up 4,000, and the polisher could finish 8,000 in the same time; thus, to keep one polisher busy, the enterprise needed two breakers and four founders, and units were hired or discharged, therefore, in multiples of seven. Successively, in many other operations, notably on the assembly line, similar inflexible ratios become established, and the expansion and contraction of work is in terms of multiples of those ratios. But such dependency presupposes co-ordination and its concomitant, the multiplication of supervisory hierarchies.

The logic of hierarchy, the third of the logics created by modern industry, is thus not merely the sociological fact of increased supervision, which every complex enterprise demands; it is a peculiarly technological imperative. In a simple division of labor, for example, the worker has a large measure of control over his own working conditions, i.e., cleaning and repairing machines, the setup and make-ready, obtaining his own materials, etc. Under a complex division of labor, these pass out of his control, and he must rely on management to see that they are properly done. This dependence extends along the entire process of production. As a result, modern industry has had to devise an entire new superstructure which organizes and directs production. This superstructure draws in all possible brain work away from the shop; everything is centered in the planning and schedule and design departments. And in this new hierarchy there stands the technical employee, a figure known neither to the handicrafts nor to industry in its infancy. With the increasing growth of large factories and the development of automatic processes, the engineer and the technician ("the semiskilled engineer") assume an increasingly important role.

These three logics of size, time, and hierarchy converge in that great achievement of industrial technology, the assembly line—the long parallel lines require huge shed-space; the detailed breakdown of work imposes a set of mechanically paced and specified motions; and the degree of co-ordination creates new social hierarchies.

THE HUMAN-RELATIONS EMPHASIS

By and large, the sociologist and the engineer have written off any effort to readjust the work process; the worker, like the mythical figure of Ixion, is chained forever to the endlessly revolving wheel. But the spectacle has its unnerving aspect, and the sense of dehumanization is oppressive, even to engineers. Industry has learned, moreover, that production actually suffers when only the mechanical-engineering aspects of production are considered. Hence the growing vogue in recent years of "human relations." "[The] satisfactions of craftsmanship are gone, and we can never call them back," writes the Cornell sociologist, William F. Whyte. "If these were the only satisfactions men could get out of their immediate work, their work would certainly be a barren experience. There are other important satisfactions today: the satisfactions of human association and the satisfactions of solving technical and human problems of work."

The source of this interest in "human relations" was the famous experiment at the Hawthorne Works of the Western Electric Company in Chicago, perhaps the most painstaking experiment in the history of the social sciences. The first question studied concerned the relationship of fatigue to output. A group of five girls was subjected to exhaustive study; the methods were most meticulous in regard to scientific procedure and control. A series of possible variables affecting production were listed, e.g., amount of heat and degree of light, and for a period of thirteen weeks at a time one factor was changed while all others were constant. "A skilled statistician," Roethlisberger reports, "spent several years trying to relate variations in the physical circumstances of these five operators. For example, he correlated the hours that each girl spent in bed the night before with variations in output the following day. Inasmuch as some people said the effect of being out late one night was not felt the following day but the day after that, he correlated variations in output with the amount of rest the operators had had two nights before . . . . The attempt to relate changes in physical circumstances to variations in output resulted in not a single correlation of enough statistical significance to be recognized by any competent statistician as having any meaning."

However, in Period XII of the experiment, the girls were returned to a bread-and-water diet, so to speak—i.e., to a forty-eight hour week without rest breaks, lunches, etc.—yet output kept rising! It then became clear that the workers were responding, not to any of the physiological or physical variables, but to the interest and attention centered on them! The experiment itself, not any outside factor, was the missing link, the unknown determinant. This led to the second phase of the Hawthorne experiment: the introduction of ambulatory confessors, or walking counselors, ready at any moment to stop and listen to a harassed worker air his woes though usually not prepared to do anything about them. The effect on production was, apparently, good.

"COMMUNICATION" AND "PARTICIPATION"

While human relations, as a result of the tremendous publicity given to the Hawthorne findings, became a great vogue, personnel counseling in a broader sense has never spread widely, even within the Bell Telephone System, where it originated. The reason, in large measure, is that management itself has not fully understood its operation. There seemed to be no tangible "payoff" in diminished cost or increased production that management could point to; moreover, it seemed to some to represent too much "coddling." And the sociologist, in this instance, has taxed the manager for not fully appreciating the benefits of what Huxley called "advanced emotional engineering."

If counseling has not been widely adopted, "communication and participation" has become a great management fad. In theory, communication is supposed to open a two-way street whereby those down the line can talk back to those above and thus participate in the enterprise. In few instances have such systems become operative. In most cases "communication" consists simply of employee newsletters or of "chain-of-command" conferences, in which vice-presidents meet with managers, managers with supervisors, supervisors with foremen, and in which the opinions of top management are transmitted. In some cases, the system operates with a characteristic Madison Avenue twist. At Westinghouse, for example, company messages were recorded on tape, and by dialing on the interplant telephone system one could listen to the instructions given to the hundreds of top supervisors. The dial number ostensibly was a secret confined to 1,200 supervisory employees. In practice, it was secret in name only, since supervisors were instructed to "leak" the number "confidentially" to various employees; and these men, gleeful at knowing a secret, quickly spread the information to tens of others. The result was that thousands of workers eagerly rushed to listen to pep talks which at other times they might have received with utter indifference.

There are two points to be noted in the vogue of human relations. One is that, in the evident concern with understanding, communication, and participation, we find a change in the outlook of management, parallel to that in the culture as a whole, from authority to manipulation as a means of exercising dominion. The ends of the enterprise remain, but the methods have shifted; the older modes of overt coercion are now replaced by psychological persuasion. The tough, brutal foreman, raucously giving orders, gives way to the mellow-voiced, psychology-oriented supervisor. The worker doubtless regards this change as an improvement, and his sense of constraint is correspondingly assuaged. In industrial relations, as in large areas of American society, accommodation of a sort has replaced conflict.

The second point is that this approach in terms of human relations has become a substitute for thinking about the work process itself. All satisfactions are now extracurricular: in the fellowship of a group, in aspirations for promotion, in leisure pursuits, etc. The rising standard of living has been coupled with the idea of an increase in leisure. Work is irksome; but, if it cannot be evaded, it can be reduced. In the old days, the shadings between work and leisure were not so easy to distinguish. In modern life, the ideal is to minimize the unpleasant aspects of work as much as possible by pleasant distractions (wall colors, music, rest periods) and to hasten away from the factory as quickly as possible, uncontaminated by work and unimpaired by its arduousness. A gleaming two-page ad in *Life* magazine shows a beautiful Lincoln car in the patio–living room of an elegantly simple house, and the ad proclaims: "Your home has walls of glass. Your kitchen is an engineering miracle. Your clothes and your furniture are beautifully functional. *You work easily: play hard . . . .*"

STATUS BOOTSTRAP

This essay has talked, by and large, about "the" factory worker and the constraints imposed upon him. Certainly any of the large-scale generalizations that have been made become fuzzy if matched against the complex reality. And factory work, after all, is only a small percentage of the work done in the United States. Different occupational groups have their own work problems. A skilled worker may find his job monotonous and a chambermaid in a bustling metropolitan hotel may not. Nothing may be more deadly, perhaps, than the isolated, hermetic life of the bank teller in his cage or the elevator operator in his sealed jack-in-the-box. Longshoremen swear by their occupation, gaining satisfactions in the free use of muscle and the varieties of excitement on a big-city pier, while scorning those who are tied down to the bench or lathe. Musicians, typographers, miners, seamen, loggers, construction workers, all have their special cast of work. Yet the factory is archetypal because its rhythms, in subtle fashion, affect the general character of work the way a dye suffuses into a cloth. Coal mining, once spoken of as "underground farming," now—with the mechanization of cutting and conveying—takes on much of the routinization of factory work. In offices, the installation of high-speed calculators, tabulators, and billing machines tends to turn the white-collar workers into mechanically paced drones. The spread of mechanization into "materials handling" (e.g., supermarkets) introduces mechanical rhythms into the distributive sector of the economy.

These changes accentuate, too, the tendencies to the evasion of work which are so characteristic of the American factory worker today. The worker becomes bored, absent-minded, accident-prone, and hostile, or he retreats from reality, engulfed in a myriad of obsessive reveries. The big lure among workers remains the hope of running one's own business, of "being one's own boss." "The possibility of leaving the shop forms a staple topic of conversation on the job," states one observer who worked in a plant. Two California sociologists, Reinhard Bendix and S. M. Lipset, report that "the majority of every occupational category has had the goal of 'going into business' at some time. This aspiration has been even greater among manual workers than among the white-collar group. It is our guess," they conclude, "that the creed of the 'individual enterprise' has become by and large a working-class preoccupation. Though it may have animated both working class and middle class in the past, it is no longer a middle-class ideal today. Instead, people in the middle class aspire to become professional and, as a second choice, upper white-collar workers." Of course, few of those who think of it as a goal actually try to go into business—"but here again the manual workers report much more such effort than the white-collar group."

How realistic are these aspirations? We know that the labor force of the American economy is being transformed. Colin Clark, in his *Conditions of Economic Progress,* long ago pointed out that, as incomes rose and the quantity and quality of goods produced increased, large sections of the economy would shift to service and other "tertiary" occupations. Since 1910, the proportion of farmers, farm-owners, and unskilled workers in the labor force has decreased sharply; skilled workers have held their own; service workers have increased slightly; professional persons have moved up from 4.4 to 7.5 per cent and proprietors and managers from 6.5 to 8.8 per cent of the work force in this period. The largest increases have come in the categories of semiskilled labor and clerks and sales. The semiskilled group has increased from 14.7 per cent in 1910 to 22.4 per cent in 1950; the white-collar worker, from 10.2 to 20.2 per cent.

Certainly, the expansion of the American economy has opened the way for new careers; and the expanding occupations are on the whole located outside the factory. But fascination with these rates of growth should not mislead us into failing to consider the limited number of such positions available or the question whether, apart from the increase in the number of places, the possibility of "getting ahead" is real or chimerical. In the United States, social mobility is a matter *between* generations; it is the children who may get ahead, in comparison with the father. The father reaches one point and usually rests there. The study of occupational mobility by Bendix and Lipset showed that individuals held an average of 4.8 jobs over a 25-year period. But despite this high degree of circulation, between those who work with their hands and those who do not there is relatively little shifting. This is perhaps the most fundamental cleavage in American society. All those who work with their hands have spent 80 per cent of their working lives in manual occupations; all who do not work with their hands have spent 75 per cent of their working lives in nonmanual occupations.

In compensation, there is a considerable, and sometimes pathetic, effort to lift one's occupation by its own bootstraps. The effort to "professionalize" work has become the major means of giving one's job an honorific quality which the nature of the work itself denies. So the garage becomes the "lubritorium"; individuals do not say "I am selling skillets" but "I am in selling"; the janitor becomes the "superintendent," the hospital superintendent the "administrator," the secretary the "executive assistant," etc.

The most significant form taken by the flight from work is the desperate drive for leisure. The engineer, the executive, and the professional get wholly absorbed in work; the worker saves his energy for his leisure. Edward Bellamy, in his *Looking Backward,* foresaw a state wherein an individual spent twenty to twenty-five years of his life in a drudging routine for a few hours a day and then was free to pursue his own desires. Here in the United States, in mid-twentieth century, Bellamy's vision is in a curious fashion being realized. The average work week has been reduced from 70.6 hours (1850) to an average of 40.8 (1950). The two-day week-end is now standard in American life, and the seven-hour workday is at the threshold. What workers have been denied in work, they now seek to recapture in leisure. Over the past decade there has been a fantastic mushrooming of arts and crafts hobbies, of photography, home woodworking shops with power-driven tools, ceramics, "hi-fi" (high-fidelity) electronics, radio "hams," etc. America has seen the multiplication of the "amateur" on a scale unknown in previous history. And while this is a positive good, it has been achieved at a high cost indeed—the loss of satisfaction in work.

NO MORE WORK?

All this fretting and worrying and moralizing, however, may yet turn out to be academic. For we stand today on the verge of a second industrial revolution. While the assembly line tended to grip the worker bodily to the rhythm of the line, a vast development of electric motors and semiautomatic controls now has created a new situation. The development of the continuous flow has now eliminated the worker almost completely. On its present scale and complexity, the continuous-flow innovation dates back only to 1939, when Standard Oil of New Jersey and M. W. Kellog Co. erected the first of the oil industry's great fluid-catalytic crackers. In these new plants, the raw material—fluid or gas—flows continuously in at one end, passes through intricate stages, and debouches in a twenty-four hour stream of products at the other. The whole plant is run from central control rooms, with but a few men at the automatic control instruments, while mobile maintenance crews take care of any breakdown. The new Ford engine plant in Cleveland, opened in 1952, provides a continuous operation from the original flow of sand and the casting of molds to the flow of molten iron and the shaking-out of fully cast engine blocks, with almost no human hands touching the operation. Thus foundry work, the grimiest of tasks, gives way to the machine.

In this second industrial revolution there arises a new concept of work, of man as creator and regulator of delicate and precise machines. Some have hailed this "royal road" of technology as leading to the elimination of the semiskilled worker and the birth of a new class of artisans. Others see man as being further reduced in significance, standing completely outside his work and having no personal relation to it. Work, said Freud, is the chief means of binding an individual to reality. What will happen when not only the worker but work itself is displaced by the machine?

---

adaptation 30   *THE ALIENATED INDIVIDUAL*

Abridged and adapted from Rollo May, "A Psychologist Looks at Mental Health in Today's World," Mental Hygiene, 38 (January, 1954), 1–11. Published in this form by permission of the author and the National Association for Mental Health.

[A persistent theme in much speculation concerning the plight of modern man is that of alienation. It is claimed that industrialization and urbanization have placed a heavy psychological burden upon the individual by giving him the sense of being isolated and alone, a stranger among other strangers. In the following discussion, the psychologist, Rollo May, characterizes modern man as alienated from nature, himself, his fellow-men, and the meaning of life.]

There are several areas in which modern man is an alien in his world and so suffers anxiety and isolation. First, *modern man has become alienated from nature*. We see this most clearly in his alienation from his body. In the latter part of the nineteenth and early part of the twentieth centuries, people regarded their physical natures as the enemy. Freud pointed out classically how people in Victorian society repressed sexual instincts, the goal being to fight one's physical nature as if one's body were an outlaw to be held continually at gunpoint. We would all now agree that such alienation from one's body is harmful to both physical and mental health.

But it is just as true, though less obvious to many people, that the later gospel of release of libido also presupposes that the body is alien. Both methods use bodily nature as a machine, as if the body were an object to be manipulated. Many sophisticated people in our day know the rules of the body, the methods of sex and of birth control, and would be horrified if you accused them of repression of instincts; but their problem is often that they cannot feel—that sexual activity is so often empty and mechanical; and when we look below those symptoms, we discover that very often these people, too, live as though they were alienated from their bodies. The rules of bodily health, then, are not ways simply of manipulating and controlling one's physical nature but are rather ways of recovering one's strength, zest, and joyful experience of the physical aspects of life.

Modern man has also become alienated from nature in another sense. He has tended to lose the experience of closeness to the earth, the grass and trees, and other forms of physical nature. We have so well succeeded in controlling and manipulating physical nature for the sake of industrial progress that we have all but forgotten that our own organic roots are also in the earth and the natural elements. In a city like New York we live with a wall of concrete separating us from the earth and an almost as impenetrable wall of smog between us and the sky. Our roots are in nature; and when people have lost their feeling for the earth and the sky, something of the wholeness of the person is lost likewise.

Second, we observe that people in emotional difficulty have become *alienated from themselves*. This is shown chiefly in the fact that they have lost the sense of their own worth and do not accept themselves. They have clung to external proofs of their worth as selves—winning good grades in school, making a profitable marriage, keeping ahead of the Joneses, and so on. The upshot of this emphasis on self-esteem, in living up to what others expect, is that one does not really have a basic self-esteem at all. Actually, one's own real feelings, aims, and beliefs have been lost in the squirrel-cage whirl of living up to others' expectations, and one has become alienated from one's own self.

This has much to do with the fact that so many people feel lonely and isolated. Precisely because they are so dependent on the expectations of others, they have lost their real relation with themselves. Hence, no matter how much time they spend in social relationships or running along with the crowd, they still feel empty and isolated. They are the "lonely crowd," as David Riesman puts it. And then they redouble their efforts to become merged with the crowd in the vain hope of getting over their loneliness. As André Gide pithily remarks: "Most people are so afraid of finding themselves alone that they never find themselves at all." What is needed may be called self-acceptance or self-love or belief in oneself or what not; but however one names it, it boils down to the basic experience that one is a self in one's own right and that this self is worthy and to be esteemed. This esteem is a prerequisite to having esteem for other people. It is the healthy kind of self-love that is a prerequisite to loving others.

A third characteristic of modern people in emotional difficulties is that they have become *alienated from their fellow-men*. They have lost the experience of *community*. One of the odd things about our society is that there are so many words bandied about in newspapers and over the radio and television with so little real communication. There is so much social activity with so little real interchange of human emotions and experience among people. It is almost as though the chief rule for success in social life were to keep one's chatter meaningless and to cover up rather than reveal one's deepest and sincerest feelings. This means, of course, that people really are afraid of one another. The continuous talk is like a filibuster—its purpose is to prevent the real issues from coming to the fore.

In helping people in our society overcome alienation from one another, an important point is that they be able to experience themselves as *contributing* persons in the community. If in the Middle Ages I had been a maker of shoes and you bought a pair, I would have felt a deep and simple satisfaction every morning when you walked by my shop wearing the shoes that I had made for you. But in our days, most workers rarely see the persons who benefit from their labor. One of the tragedies of modern society is that this simple satisfaction of producing something of value for the community becomes diluted until it is almost nonexistent. Then we place the value not on what we produce but on what price it brings.

Certainly we are not suggesting turning the clock back to the Middle Ages, but we are issuing the challenge that work be seen again in its value for the community. We need to recover the sense of the dignity of work and the experience of our being interdependent, one upon the other, in our work. Furthermore, the growing amount of leisure time that modern technological progress affords gives us a new opportunity, which men in previous centuries did not have, to establish bonds of fellowship in community services as well as in hobbies and play. I am not suggesting that we construct meaningless activities in the community as if the goal were the mere routine of "busyness" for everybody. Our task, rather, is to look below the external motions of work in community life to a point where we see the relation of our work to the community. It is important to understand that everyone has a constructive role to play in his work and in his relations with his fellow-men.

Finally, modern man has become *alienated from the meaning of his life.* Man is the mammal who, through his power of self-awareness, can devote himself to freedom through beauty and love. Thus his security in distraught times can rest on beliefs more enduring than the threats of the moment. The fully integrated human being is a man who is so firm in knowing what he believes in that the crises and threats of the moment—even the extreme threat, death—can be met courageously. We can overcome insecurity and crises only to the extent that our belief in our values is stronger than these threats.

In overcoming our alienation from the meaning of our lives, the ethical wisdom of human history comes centrally into the picture. This does not mean ethics in the dogmatic sense of telling someone what he should believe or how he should act. Indeed, the kind of psychiatry and psychology of several decades ago that tried to divorce itself from ethics actually turned out to be the most dogmatic of all. These were the psychiatrists and psychologists who accepted uncritically the unconscious values of the culture, such as "adjustment" to society, success, and so on. We cannot avoid assuming values in any case, so we might as well endeavor to do it consciously, by free choice, and thus make sure that our values are the ones that we really want to believe in.

There are in our Hebrew-Christian tradition, for example, the beliefs that every man is to be respected regardless of color or race; that love is better than hate; that freedom for the individual person is a goal always to be striven for. It is by no means self-evident that these values are given in the structure of the world, despite the admirable faith of our forefathers. It is not easy to believe in real freedom for the individual personality, respect for every man's conscience, and real individual responsibility, in an age like ours. It is necessary that we come to our own convictions about these values; otherwise we shall not have enough confidence to stand by them when they are threatened.

adaptation 31   SOCIETY AS THE PATIENT

> *Abridged and adapted from Lawrence K. Frank, "Society as the Patient,"* American Journal of Sociology, *42 (1936–37), 335–44. Published in this form by permission of the* American Journal of Sociology.

[The following discussion throws doubt upon the long-range value of psychiatric treatment of the individual. The author asserts that the emotional disorders of individuals are but the symptoms of a sick society. According to this view, mental illness is one of the inevitable products of the social disorganization of present-day society.]

The disintegration of our traditional culture, with the decay of the ideas, conceptions, and beliefs upon which our social and individual lives were organized, brings us face to face with the problem of treating society, since individual therapy or punishment no longer has any value beyond mere alleviation of our symptoms.

The conception of a sick society in need of treatment has many advantages for diagnosis of our individual and social difficulties and for constructive therapy, although we may find it necessary to prescribe a long period of preparation before the patient will be ready for the remedies indicated. Perhaps the most immediate gain from adopting this conception is the simplification it brings. Instead of thinking in terms of the multiplicity of so-called social problems, each demanding special attention and a different remedy, we can view all of them as different symptoms of the same disease. That would be a real gain, even if we cannot entirely agree upon the exact nature of the disease. If, for example, we could regard crime, mental disorders, family disorganization, juvenile delinquency, prostitution, and sex offenses as evidence, not of individual wickedness, incompetence, perversity, or pathology, but as human reactions to cultural disintegration, a forward step would be taken. At present we cherish a belief in a normal, intact society against which we see these criminals, these psychopaths, these warring husbands and wives, these recalcitrant adolescents, these shameless prostitutes and vicious sex offenders as so many rebels, who threaten society and so must be punished, disciplined, or otherwise individually treated. This assumption of individual depravity or perversity gives us a comfortable feeling that all is well socially, but that certain individuals are outrageously violating the laws and customs that all decent people uphold.

It is indeed interesting to see how this conception of a social norm, with individuals as violators and frustraters of normality, runs through so much of our thinking. In political life we cherish a fond belief in the essential soundness and efficacy of representative government. The cumulative evidence of social injustice, of corruption in office, of legislative "deals" and intrigues—the whole slimy trail of graft and misfeasance—is treated as the vicious practices of dishonest politicians. We save our belief in democracy and in our representative political organization by imputing all their faults and shortcomings to individual malefactors. The remedy for political chicane is then viewed as investigation and prosecution: "Turn the rascals out."

In our economic affairs we follow a similar practice. Rugged individualism, free enterprise, the money and credit economy, the price system, with its supposed free play of economic forces and the law of supply and demand—all these are considered as naturally sound, effective economic practices based upon the very nature of society; if perverse and selfish individuals did not interfere with these natural forces, frustrate competition, and break these laws, we should have no economic troubles. When our industry and banking and commerce are crippled or paralyzed, we begin to look for the guilty persons who have interfered with normality. Some blame the stifling of competition, while others aim their accusations against this or that individual or organized group of individuals whose conduct is deemed to be uneconomic and therefore responsible for our trouble. The confusion over the nature and perpetrators of these economic misdeeds provides occasion for vivacious, sometimes vituperative, argument, but we generally agree that the trouble comes from individual misdeeds that must be curbed by more laws, more regulation, and more severe punishment.

Likewise, in family life, difficulties are similarly treated in terms of individual wickedness and guilt, to be corrected by severe moral instruction and legal adjudication on a semicriminal basis, as in divorce. Similarly, the admitted inadequacy of the courts, both civil and criminal, is blamed upon individuals—corrupt judges, unprincipled shysters, and unethical practitioners—whose disloyalty to their high duty has stained the bright garments of Justice and prevented honest administration of the laws.

When we regard the Western European culture that has emerged from an almost incredible background of conflict and confusion and mixture of peoples and see that for centuries it has not been unified either in ideas and beliefs or in socially approved practices, we can begin to understand the etiology of the sickness of our society. Our culture has no unanimity of individual or social aims, no generally accepted sanctions, and no common patterns of ideas or conduct. All our basic ideas, conceptions, and beliefs have been in process of revision for the past three hundred years or more, beginning with the displacement of the older notions of the universe and man's place therein and going on now to the supersedure of the traditional animistic, voluntaristic conceptions of human nature and conduct and man's relation to his society that were associated with these earlier cosmologies.

If we bear in mind this culture disintegration, then our so-called "social problems" and the seeming perversity of individuals become intelligible. They are to be viewed as arising from the frantic efforts of individuals, lacking any sure direction and sanctions or guiding conception of life, to find some way of protecting themselves, or of merely existing on any terms they can manage, in a society being remade by technology. Having no strong loyalties and no consistent values or realizable ideals to cherish, the individual's conduct is naturally conflicting, confused, neurotic, and antisocial, if that term has any meaning in the absence of an established community purpose and ideal. The more skillful contrive to profit from the social confusion and their own lack of scruples, while others evade or break laws, become mentally disordered or diseased, or otherwise violate the older codes of conduct, damaging themselves and those whose lives they touch.

Instead of clinging to the traditional conceptions of individual autonomy and moral responsibility that were dependent upon a coherent culture for their effective operation, we must begin to think in terms of individuals caught in a social confusion wherein individual conduct and ethics are no longer socially tolerable. The individual, instead of seeking his own personal salvation and security, must recognize his almost complete dependence upon the group life and see his only hope in and through cultural reorganization. The tradition of individual striving that was ushered in by the Renaissance has been the very process of this cultural disintegration, for the individual, in striving to be an individual, has broken down the inherited culture of common, shared beliefs and activities. Now that this necessary cultural disintegration has been accomplished, almost to the point of unbearable confusion, we must face the task of constructing a new culture, with new goals, new beliefs, and new patterns and sanctions but predicated upon the enduring human values that must be continually restated and given renewed expression.

---

adaptation 32 COMMENT ON "SOCIETY AS THE PATIENT"

Abridged and adapted from L. Guy Brown, "Society as the Patient—A Communication," American Journal of Sociology, *42 (1936–37), 717–18. Published in this form by permission of the* American Journal of Sociology.

[The following is a comment on and criticism of "Society as the Patient," which was summarized in the preceding Adaptation. It stresses the interaction of the individual and society, the uniqueness of individual experience, and the therapeutic goal of providing the individual with an adequate conception of his relation to society.**]**

Doubtless most sociologists would readily agree with Mr. Lawrence K. Frank that society is sick. However, when society is sick, human nature is equally sick. Consequently, the "social physician" will not gain anything by dismissing the individual as the patient and turning to society with his therapeutic measures. Long ago Cooley pointed out that the individual and society do not exist as separate entities. They are inextricably interrelated. Society is a reality only as the objective aspect of human nature. The point of departure is not the individual or society, but the interactive relationship between the two.

Individual therapy will always have its place. Each individual has his own unique experience, and occasionally one becomes a social variant in a cultural milieu that is not considered a sick society. A black sheep appears in a so-called "good" home where all others are well adjusted. The "social physician" notes that the culture in the home is not sick. If he is a modern social psychologist, he knows that the organic basis of the human nature of the black sheep was undefined at birth; therefore heredity is not the explanation. He is aware that heredity per se and environment per se do not hold the explanation of the adjustment of this individual. He knows that the explanation lies in the unique experience of the individual, which is different from the experiences of all other members of the household. The approach is through the individual who needs a new definition of the situation and a new conception of his role in the group.

In a culture that is not regarded as "sick," one nevertheless finds mental ill health, the problem child, the psychopathic personality, and the delinquent. In such an instance one does not think of "society as the patient" or talk about individual perversity or congenitally predetermined behavior but studies the unique experience of the individual for an explanation. If there is an interest in treatment, the student of this situation seeks to redefine the individual to himself and to give him a new definition of his social heritage and a new conception of his role in relation to his cultural milieu. In most cases the "social physician" must start with the interactive relationship between human nature and society if he wishes to achieve a better society. Social organization cannot transcend the quality of human nature. There will be an occasional need for individual treatment, but a well society will be an actuality only when the whole situation is considered, with human nature and the social order regarded as aspects of a totality.

This point of view does not assume individual depravity or perversity apart from social disorganization. It does not regard society as normal, with individuals in rebellion against it. There is no place here for the "time-honored beliefs in human volition and responsibility" of which Mr. Frank speaks. This point of view emphasizes the idea that when culture is "sick" and in need of treatment, human nature is also "sick" and in need of treatment. One aspect of the totality cannot be sick apart from the other, and one cannot be cured (changed) apart from the other. The social scientist who tries to isolate "society as the patient" and deal with it will find himself confronted with as many difficulties as those who have tried to salvage individuals while ignoring the social order.

SUGGESTIONS FOR FURTHER READING

Reinhard Bendix and S. M. Lipset (eds.), *Class, Status and Power* (Glencoe, Ill.: The Free Press, 1953).

George L. Bird and Frederick E. Merwin, *The Press and Society* (New York: Prentice-Hall, Inc., 1951).

Morris L. Ernst, *The First Freedom* (New York: The Macmillan Co., 1946).

Erich Fromm, *The Sane Society* (New York: Rinehart & Co., 1955).

Floyd Hunter, *Community Power Structure* (Chapel Hill: University of North Carolina Press, 1953).

Samuel Lubell, *The Future of American Politics* (New York: Harper & Bros., 1952).

C. Wright Mills, *White Collar* (New York: Oxford University Press, 1951).

José Ortega y Gasset, *The Revolt of the Masses* (New York: W. W. Norton & Co., Inc., 1932).

David Riesman, in collaboration with Reuel Denney and Nathan Glazer, *The Lonely Crowd* (New Haven: Yale University Press, 1950).

Bernard Rosenberg and David Manning White (eds.), *Mass Culture* (Glencoe, Ill.: The Free Press and The Falcon's Wing Press, 1957).

Wilbur Schramm, *Responsibility in Mass Communication* (New York: Harper & Bros., 1957).

Charles A. Siepman, *Radio, Television and Society* (New York: Oxford University Press, 1950).

William H. Whyte, Jr., *The Organization Man* (New York: Simon & Schuster, 1956).

Indexes

Name Index

Ackerman, N. W., 235, 404, 410
Adorno, T. W., 211, 236
Aichhorn, A., 87
Allport, F. H., 213
Allport, G. W., 174, 214, 215, 218, 236
Anders, G., 541
Anderson, O. W., 477
Anshen, R. N., 410
Ashmore, H. S., 196, 198, 236

Baird, J. H., 490
Bales, R. F., 529
Barber, B., 547
Barden, G. A., 429
Barnhart, E. C., 236
Bartlett, F. P., 452
Beard, B. B., 114
Bell, D., 552
Bell, H. M., 372
Bell, M., 102
Bellamy, E., 561
Belth, N. C., 247
Bendix, R., 560, 561, 570
Berelson, B., 264, 266, 541, 542
Berger, N., 236
Bernard, W. S., 322, 334, 353
Bestor, A. E., 413, 458
Bettelheim, B., 87, 211, 220
Biddle, F. B., 454
Bilbo, T. G., 192
Bird, G. L., 570
Black, H. L., 440
Blaine, D., 490
Blake, R., 214
Bloch, H. A., 29, 170
Blumer, H. S., 50
Bond, F. A., 533
Braverman, H., 247
Bredemeier, H. C., 29
Bronner, A. F., 41, 56, 58, 99
Broom, L., 29
Brower, W. E., 452
Brown, L. G., 568
Bryce, J., 173

Bryson, L., 222
Bugelski, R., 211
Burgess, E. W., 102, 355, 410
Burton, H. H., 466

Cabot, R., 97, 116
Cantril, H., 258, 521
Casassa, C. S., 455
Childs, J. L., 422, 423
Clapper, R., 521
Clark, B., 287 ff.
Clark, C., 560
Clark, H. E., 181
Clark, H. I., 533
Clark, K. B., 236
Clark, R. E., 170
Clark, T. C., 454
Clark, W., 287 ff.
Cohen, A. K., 87
Cohen, F. S., 222
Cohen, M. R., 222
Collins, L., 292
Collins, M. E., 279
Conant, J. B., 422
Cooley, C. H., 569
Corson, J. J., 517
Cosulich, G., 32
Coughlin, C. E., 206, 455
Crawford, P. L., 87
Cressey, D. R., 99, 170
Cushing, R. J., 173

Davie, M. R., 353
Davis, J. A., 246
Davis, K., 29, 374, 380
Dawson, J. M., 425
de Kruif, P., 483, 533
Dean, J. P., 205
Denney, R., 570
Dennis, W., 214
Deutsch, A., 111, 533
Deutsch, M., 279
Dewey, J., 434, 468
Dewhurst, J. F., 13, 96

Dilling, E., 455
Divine, G. B., 289
Dollard, J., 211, 236
Douglass, H., 468
Downey, S., 520
Dumpson, J. R., 87, 122
Dunning, C. E., 56, 95

Edman, M., 292
Eisenhower, D. D., 173, 207, 253, 295, 340, 471
Eisenstein, V. W., 397
Ellingston, J. R., 87
Ernst, M. L., 570

Fairchild, H. P., 344, 353
Faris, R. E., 29
Faubus, O., 253
Feldman, J. J., 477
Finkelstein, L., 222
Fisher, J., 212
Folsom, J. K., 356, 410
Ford, H., 206, 554
Frank, L. K., 566, 569
Frankfurter, F., 455, 464, 466
Franklin, B., 314
Frazier, E. F., 236
Frenkel-Brunswik, E., 212
Freud, S., 402, 562, 563
Friedlander, K., 88
Fromm, E., 570

Gaudet, H., 266, 542
George, W. F., 335
Gerbner, G., 456
Gide, A., 564
Ginzberg, E., 190, 236
Glazer, N., 570
Glick, P. C., 375
Glueck, E., 41, 43, 56, 58, 59, 71, 73, 74, 75, 77, 79, 80, 81, 88, 98, 101, 111, 112, 114, 380
Glueck, S., 41, 43, 56, 58, 59, 71, 73, 74, 75, 77, 79, 80, 81, 88, 98, 101, 111, 112, 114, 380
Goddard, H. H., 41
Goldhamer, H., 495, 533
Goldsen, R. K., 236
Goode, W. J., 367, 369, 375
Goodman, Paul, 554
Goodman, Percival, 554
Goring, C., 41
Goslin, W. E., 451 ff.
Gouldner, A. W., 547
Guterman, N., 236

Hallburg, R. E., 452
Handlin, O., 353
Harris, W. T., 421
Hartl, E. H., 41
Hartley, E. L., 29
Hartshorne, H., 92
Hatt, P. K., 29
Hauser, P. M., 50
Havighurst, R. J., 468
Hawkes, A., 452
Healy, W., 41, 56, 58, 99, 111
Higham, J., 353
Hightower, P. R., 92
Hill, C. M., 468
Himes, J. S., 29
Hitler, A., 177, 206
Hochwald, R. E., 421
Hodgkiss, M., 58
Hollingshead, A. B., 367, 368, 533
Hook, S., 468
Hoover, J. E., 337
Horowitz, E., 214
Hovland, C., 267, 268
Hunter, F., 570
Huxley, A., 558

Jackson, R. H., 440, 466
Jacobs, P., 533
Jahoda, M., 235
Janowitz, M., 211, 220
Janowsky, O. J., 204
Jefferson, M., 288
Jerome, H. W., 333
Johnson, A. L., 519, 520
Johnston, E., 174
Julian, P., 181

Kagan, H. E., 261, 262
Kahn, A. J., 88
Kefauver, E., 170
Kelley, C., 50
Kephart, W. M., 363
Kilgallen, D., 541
Kirkpatrick, C., 367, 369, 410
Klapper, J. T., 266, 543
Koenig, S., 170
Kolb, W. L., 29
Konvitz, M. R., 353
Kroeger, L. J., 454
Kvaraceus, W. C., 88

Lander, B., 52, 62
Landis, J. T., 370, 410
Landis, M. G., 410
Landis, P. H., 410

NAME INDEX

Lasker, B., 219
Lazarsfeld, P. F., 266, 542
Lee, A. M., 206, 236
Lees, H., 286
Lemkau, P. V., 523
Levy, J., 525
Levy, M. J., 29
Lewin, K., 526
Lincoln, A., 175, 243
Linton, R., 347
Lipset, S. M., 560, 561, 570
Locke, H. J., 355, 410
Loeb, M. B., 468
Lohman, J. D., 102
Lombroso, C., 40, 41
Lowenthal, L., 236
Lubell, S., 570
Lumsdaine, A. A., 267, 268

McAdoo, W. G., 520
MacComby, E. B., 541
McConnell, J. W., 517
MacCormick, A. H., 114
McDermott, E., 41
McDermott, J., 288, 290
McDonagh, E. C., 29
MacDonald, D., 545
McGarry, A., 288, 290
McGinnis, R., 410
McGroarty, J. S., 518
McIntyre, J. F., 340
MacIver, R. M., 222
McKay, H. D., 51, 56, 58, 88
McKeon, R., 222
McMahan, C. A., 29
Malamud, D. I., 87
Marshall, A. W., 87, 495, 533
Martin, J. B., 170
Marx, K., 556
Matson, F. W., 236
May, M. A., 92
May, R., 562, 563
Means, J. H., 533
Meany, G., 173
Melby, E. O., 468
Merrill, M. A., 41, 42, 59, 60
Merton, R. K., 175
Merwin, F. E., 570
Mihanovich, C. S., 400
Miller, N. E., 211
Mills, C. W., 236, 570
Monahan, T. P., 363
Montagu, M. F., 397
Mooney, E., 340
Morse, N. C., 213

Mott, F. L., 543
Murphy, F. J., 40
Mursell, G. R., 92
Myrdal, G., 185, 226, 227, 235

Newcomb, T. M., 29
Newell, H. W., 127
Nordskog, J. E., 29
Nye, F. I., 88

Ohlin, L. E., 158
Ortega y Gasset, J., 570
Owens, R. G., 520
Oxnam, G. B., 173

Padelford, M., 452
Park, R. E., 339
Peters, C. A., 483
Pfeffer, L., 468
Pinner, F. A., 533
Poliakov, L., 202
Porter, R., 521
Poston, R. W., 29
Powers, E., 97, 116
Prescott, D., 456
Puner, M., 468

Reckless, W. C., 170
Redl, F., 88
Redlich, F. C., 533
Reed, E. F., 94
Reiss, A. J., 29
Riesman, D., 564, 570
Riis, R. W., 48
Roethlisberger, F. J., 557
Roosevelt, E., 429
Roosevelt, F. D., 206, 246
Roper, E., 205, 212
Rose, A. M., 236, 533
Rosenberg, B., 545, 570
Russell, B., 223
Rutledge, W. B., 466

Sanford, R. N., 212
Schermer, G., 288, 289
Schermerhorn, R. A., 353
Schifferes, J. J., 479
Schramm, W., 264, 541, 570
Schroeder, C. W., 367
Schuessler, K. F., 154
Schuyler, G. S., 312
Schwartz, J., 452, 454
Scott, C. W., 468
Seidman, J. M., 410
Selznick, P., 29, 533

Senior, C., 236
Senn, M. A., 450, 451
Shanas, E., 56, 95
Shaw, C. R., 51, 56, 58, 88, 102
Sheffield, F. D., 267, 268
Sheldon, W. H., 41
Shepard, M., 511, 513
Shirley, M. M., 40
Siepman, C. A., 570
Simpson, G. E., 236
Sinclair, U., 451
Skaife, R. A., 413
Sklare, M., 236
Slawson, J., 206
Smith, G. L., 455
Smith, T. L., 29
Sorokin, P. A., 355
Spoerl, D. T., 263
Stauffer, S. A., 250
Stevenson, A., 143, 144
Sutherland, E. H., 44, 99, 136, 145, 146, 147, 168, 170
Swanson, G. E., 29

Tannenbaum, F., 170
Tappan, P. W., 88, 146, 166
Taylor, F. W., 554, 556
ten Broek, J., 236
Tertulian, Q. S., 182
Thomas, J. L., 371, 400
Tocqueville, A. de, 547
Thrasher, F., 95
Till, E., 303
Townsend, F. E., 518 ff.
Trager, H. G., 236
Truman, H. S., 207, 249, 311, 336, 340, 342, 425

Tunney, G., 455
Turck, F. B., 511

Van Vechten, C. C., 338
Vandenberg, A. H., 455
Vedder, C. B., 88, 170
Vincent, M. J., 29

Wainwright, J. M., 455
Wallin, P., 410
Waring, T. R., 300
Warner, W. L., 468
Warren, E., 304
Warren, R. L., 29
Wattenberg, W. W., 42
Weaver, R. C., 194
Wells, F., 452, 455
White, D. M., 545, 570
White, L. C., 353
Whyte, W. F., 88, 557
Whyte, W. H., 570
Williams, R., 205
Wilson, L., 29
Wilson, W., 336
Winch, R. F., 410
Wineman, D., 88
Wirth, L., 347
Witmer, H. L., 40, 58, 116
Woodward, C. V., 236
Wopschall, M., 456

Yarrow, M. R., 236
Yinger, J. M., 236

Zimmerman, C. C., 355, 410
Zoll, A. A., 454, 455

Subject Index

Academic freedom, 435–37
Adolescence
  in contemporary society, 388–91
  personality during, 404–9
Alcoholics Anonymous, 529–32
Alcoholism, 494
  group therapy for, 529–32
American Association of University Professors, 435
American Cancer Society, 479, 480, 512–17
American Federation of Labor, 272, 317, 340
American Federation of Teachers, 435
American Heart Association, 479, 480, 512–17
American Jewish Committee, 240, 241, 261
American Jewish Congress, 240, 247, 248
American Legion, 318, 455
American Medical Association, 484, 550
American Protective Association, 317
American Psychiatric Association, 499
Anti-Defamation League, 240, 259, 260, 261
Area projects, as delinquency remedy, 102
Area theory
  of delinquency, 51–55
    criticized, 64–65, 71–72
Arthritis and Rheumatism Foundation, 513–17
Associations
  apathy in, 547–52
  to combat prejudice, 239–41
  and community organization, 268–76
  differences among, 276
  among Negroes, 230–31, 234–35
  to remedy social problems, 24–25
  and social values, 22
Attitudes
  integrated housing and changes in, 279–86
  mass media and changes in, 263–68
  prejudiced, 180–84
Authoritarian personality, prejudice related to, 211–13

Big Brother program
  as delinquency remedy, 96–97
  experiment in, 116–22
Blue Cross Plan, 483–84
Blue Shield Plan, 484
Boys' clubs, as delinquency remedy, 93–96
Brown v. Board of Education, 304–8
Bureau of Intercultural Education, 261

Cambridge-Somerville Youth Study, 97, 116–21
Causal theories
  and remedies, 23–24
  of social problems, 9–23
Central Harlem Street Clubs Project, 122–27
Chicago Area Project, 102
Child guidance, as delinquency remedy, 97–100
Church World Service, 330
Civil liberties, defined, 241
Civil rights
  defined, 241
  of Negroes violated, 191–92
Cloture rule, 241
Communist Party
  and academic freedom, 435–36
  and civil rights, 273
  and immigration, 337–38
Community Chests, 511–17
Community organization
  aims of, 269–70
  defined in relation to social problems, 261–63, 268–69
  as delinquency remedy, 53–55, 102–4
  key forces in, 270–76
  and prejudice, 268–76
  and race riots, 286–92
Congress of Industrial Organizations, 272, 340
Congress of Racial Equality (CORE), 240
Constitution, United States
  civil rights amendments to, 244

577

Constitution, United States—*continued*
    and prejudice, 242–45
    First Amendment to, 464–68
Correctional institutions, for delinquents, 111–13
Crime, 135–70
    defined, 137
    gambling and, 140–45
    heredity as cause of, 40–42
    imprisonment for, 155–56
    Kefauver Committee on, 140, 141, 142, 143
    kinds of, 135–37
    major, 137–38
    narcotics and, 148
    nature of problem of, 148–50
    among Negroes, 231–33
    organized, 140–45
    predatory, 137
    prevention of, 148–57
    punishment for, 153–57
    "service," 140–45
    sex, 147–48
        fallacies concerning, 166–70
    white-collar, 145–47

Defamation
    of Jews, 206–7
    nature of, 180
    of Negroes, 199–200
Delinquency, 31–133
    area theory of, 51–55
        criticized, 64–65, 71–72
    causes of, 40–48, 60–62
    defined, 33–34, 60
    differential-association theory of, 44–45
    early detection of, 86–87, 100–101
    as family failure, 57–60
    gangs as source of, 44–45, 56–57
    group work as remedy for, 93–96
    hidden, 39–40
    legal concept of, 31–36
    mass media and, 49–51
    among Negro youth, 66–67, 69–70
    personality factors in, 42–44, 83–84
    poverty as cause of, 55–56, 65–66
    and religion, 81, 91–92
    remedies for, 93–133
    risk conditions of, 48–60
    social disorganization and, 45–48, 51–55
    statistics of, 37–40
Delinquents
    arrest of, 104–5
    correctional institutions for, 111–13
    detention of, 105–6

Delinquents—*continued*
    intelligence of, 41–42, 82–83
    juvenile court treatment of, 106–11
    kinds of, 60
    personality of, 42–44, 83–84
    probation for, 114–15
Democracy
    and prejudice, 175–76
    schools in relation to, 414–15
Dependency, 471–533
    of the aged, 502–11
    changing concept of, 472–75
    of the mentally ill, 488–502
    of the physically disabled, 476–88
Desegregation
    in the armed forces, 243–45, 249–51
    in public housing, 257, 279–86
    in schools, 251–57
    a southern view of, 300–304
Differential association, delinquency as caused by, 44–45
Discrimination
    against Catholics, 205
    defined, 177
    in education, 196–98, 204–5, 247, 251–57
    in employment, 192–96, 245–46
    in housing, 198–99, 248–49, 257, 286–92
    against Jews, 203–6
    laws against, 241–58
    against Negroes, 191–99
    in public places, 199, 247–48
Divorce, 360–83
    a Catholic view of, 400–403
    causes of, 381–83
    children and, 378–81
    among college women, 368–70
    and delinquency, 58–59, 78, 380–81
    and desertion, 377–78
    group factors in, 382–83
    among Negroes, 368–70, 371–73
    rate of, 361–66, 373–74
        and death rate, 376–77
        for educational levels, 368–70
        for income levels, 366–68
        during World War II, 373–74
    religion and, 370–71
    and remarriage, 374–76

Education
    defined in relation to social problems, 261
    direct and indirect, 261–62, 292–300
    discrimination in, 196–98, 204–5, **247**, 251–57
        against Catholics, 205

SUBJECT INDEX

Education—*continued*
    against Jews, 204–5
    against Negroes, 196–98, 251–57
    intellectual and participant, 262, 292–300
    life-adjustment, 431–34
    nature of contemporary, 417–18, 430–35
    and prejudice, 261–68, 292–300
    and remedying social problems, 26
    traditionalist view of, 433–34
    see also Schools
Employment
    discrimination in
        against aged, 505–7
        against Jews, 203–4
        against Negroes, 192–96
Ethnocentrism, 181
Everson v. Board of Education
    excerpts from, 464–68
    summarized, 427
Experience tables, 163–66

Fair employment practice laws, 245–46
Family, 355–410
    changes in, 355–60
    and the child, 383–91
    and delinquency, 57–60, 73–80, 380–81
    and dependency, 472
    loss of functions of, 384–91
    meeting the problem of, 391–97
    nature of problem of, 355–60
    Negro, 69–70, 227–28, 371–73
    and old age, 504
    prejudice as rooted in, 219–20
    as a risk factor, 23
    socialization role of, 383–84
    theories of contemporary, 355–60
Frustration-aggression theories, 210–11

Gambling
    prevention of illegal, 150–51
    and "service" crime, 140–45
Gangs
    delinquent, 44–45, 56–57
        redirection of, 101–2, 122–27
Government, big, 536–39
Group differences, nature of, 186–88
Group work, as delinquency remedy, 93–96

Ham 'n' Eggs Plan, 519–20
Heredity, delinquency as caused by, 40–42
Housing
    discrimination in, 198–99, 205, 248–49, 257, 286–92

Ideology, and prejudice, 183–84
Illinois Juvenile Court Act, 32

Immigrant adjustment
    aids to, 330–32
    economic, 332–35
    political, 335–38
    social, 338–39
    stages of, 327–28, 347–53
    theories of
        Americanization, 330
        cultural pluralism, 330
        melting-pot, 329
Immigration, 311–53
    history of, 313–26
    meeting the problem of, 339–42
    nature of problem of, 312–13
    "new," 316–18
    nonquota, 321–24, 325–26
    "old," 315–16
    prejudice and control of, 340–44
    quota, 318–21, 324–25
    restriction of, 317–26
        defended, 344–47
    security emphasis in control of, 326, 339–42
Immigration and Nationality Act, 324–26
Individual
    alienation of, 562–65
    in contemporary society, 536–42
    prejudice and the, 175–76
Individuality, loss of, 542–45
Ingrouping, prejudice in relation to, 214–16, 222–26
Insurance
    vs. dole, 475–76
    medical, 483–85
    old age, 507–10
Integration
    in the armed forces, 249–51
    in public housing, 257, 279–86
    in schools, 251–57
    a southern view of, 300–304
    Supreme Court decision on, 304–8
Intelligence, of delinquents, 41–42, 80, 82–83
Interposition, doctrine of, 242

Jews
    defamation of, 206–7
    discrimination against, 203–6
    history of, 200–203
Judge Baker Guidance Center, 98, 99
Juvenile Court Act, Standard, 105, 110
Juvenile courts, 106–11

Kefauver Committee, 140, 141, 143, 144
Knights of Labor, 317

Ku Klux Klan, 189, 256, 279, 296, 317, 425

Law
  and prejudice, 241–58, 277–79
  and remedying social problems, 25
Learning
  and delinquency, 44–45
  of prejudice, 213–14
Leisure, in contemporary society, 541–42
Lynching, 191

McCarran-Walter Act, 324–26, 337–38
McLaurin v. *Oklahoma State Regents,* 306, 307
Marital relations, and delinquency, 58–60, 73–78, 380–81
Mass media
  and attitude changes, 263–68
  delinquency as influenced by, 49–50
  leisure and the, 541–42, 544–45
  and prejudice, 216, 263–68
  public opinion as formed by, 542–43
Mass production, consequences of, 552–62
Medical plans, 483–85
Medical problems, 476–88
  of the aged, 510
Mental illness, 488–502
  neurosis, 492–93
  personality disorders, 493
  psychosis, 491–92
  social disorganization as source of, 566–70
Mental retardation
  nature of, 489–90
  treatment of, 496–97
Metropolitan area, defined, 11
Minority groups
  assimilation of, 344–47, 347–53
  assimilationist, 350–51
  militant, 352
  pluralistic, 349–50
  secessionist, 351–52
  see also Jews *and* Negroes, American
Muscular Dystrophy Association, 513–17

Narcotics
  and crime, 148
  remedies for problem of, 152–53
National Association for the Advancement of Colored People, 234, 240, 247, 248, 256, 257
National Association for Retarded Children, 497
National Cancer Institute, 515
National Catholic Resettlement Council, 330

National Catholic Welfare Council, 340, 421
National Conference of Christians and Jews, 240, 241, 261
National Council on American Education, 454–55
National Education Association, 431, 435, 440
National Episcopal Council, 340
National Foundation for Infantile Paralysis, 480, 512–17
National Grange, 318
National Institute of Mental Health, 497
National Lutheran Council, 340
National Origins Quota System, 318–21, 324
National Tuberculosis Association, 513–17
National Urban League, 240, 259, 260
Negroes, American
  culture of, 226–35
  crime among, 231–33
  delinquency among, 63–71
  family life, 69–70, 227–28, 371–73
  fraternal organizations among, 230–31
  history of, 188–91
  leadership among, 233–35
  religion among, 228–30
Neighborhood
  delinquency as influenced by, 102–4
  as a risk factor, 20–22
Neurosis, 492–93

Old age
  dependency of, 502–5
  meeting the problem of, 505–11
  pensions during, 507–9, 517–22

Parent-Teacher Association, 442
Parole
  in criminal cases, 156–57
  predicting success of, 158–66
Peer group
  delinquency as product of, 44–45, 56–57
  as a risk factor, 22
  socialization by, 387–91
Pension plans, old age, 507–10, 517–22
Permanente Plan, 484
Personality
  of adolescent, 404–9
  authoritarian, 211–13
  delinquent, 42–44, 83–84
  disorders, 493
  and prejudice, 210–13
  and social problems, 17–18
Physical disability, 476–88

SUBJECT INDEX

Physicians, shortage of, 480–82
Plessy v. *Ferguson,* 196, 305, 306, 308
Political tensions, and prejudice, 220–21
Poverty
   delinquency as related to, 55–56, 65–66
   prejudice as related to, 220–21
Prejudice, 173–308
   associations to combat, 204–41
   authoritarian personality as prone to, 211–13
   causes of, 209–22
   and community organization, 268–76
   community patterns of, 216–18, 222
   defined, 174–75
   democratic values and, 175–76
   economic factors in, 220–21
   education as remedy for, 261–68, 292–300
   effects of, 184–86
   family as transmitter of, 219–20
   frustration-aggression theory of, 210–11
   group differences and, 186–88
   ingrouping as related to, 214–15, 222–26
   against Jews, 203–7
   and law, 241–58, 277–79
   as learned, 213–14, 222
   mass media as influencing, 263–68
   against Negroes, 188–200
   political factors in, 220–21
   risk conditions of, 215–21
   and the schools, 261–62, 292–300
   states' rights and, 242–43
President's Commission on Higher Education, 204
Prisons, 155–56
Probation
   in criminal cases, 156–57
   in delinquency cases, 114–15
Protestants and Other Americans United for Separation of Church and State, 425
Protocols of the Elders of Zion, 206
Psychiatric treatment
   of children, 127–33
   of delinquents, 97–100
Psychoses, 491–92
Punishment, of crime, 153–57

Race riots, 191
   community organization to prevent, 286–92
Recreation, delinquency and facilities for, 53–56, 93–96
Reed-Johnson Act, 318
Religion
   among American Negroes, 228–30

Religion—*continued*
   and delinquency, 91–92
   and divorce, 370–71
   in the schools, 415, 416, 418–20, 437–40
Risk conditions
   nature of, 19–23

Scapegoating, 182–83
Schools, 413–69
   academic freedom in the, 435–37
   criticisms of, 413–14
   curriculum issues in the, 429–34
   delinquency detection in, 100–101
   delinquent behavior in, 80–81
   financial problems of, 446–50
   history of American, 416–21, 429–30
   parochial, 421–29, 464–68
   pedagogical issues in the, 434–35
   and prejudice, 261–63, 292–300
   religion in, 415, 416, 418–20, 437–40
   social issues and the, 414–16
   staffing problems of the, 443–46
   subversion in the, 436–37
   see also Education
Segregation
   in education, 251–57, 304–8
   laws against, 241–58
   in public housing, 257
   effects of, 279–86
   a southern view of, 300–304
   Supreme Court decision on, 304–8
   in transportation, 248
Slums, delinquency as product of, 55–56, 64–66
Social change
   and the schools, 415–16
   and social problems, 10–14, 535–42
Social disorganization
   and area theory, 51–55
   delinquency as caused by, 45–48, 62–71
   home-ownership as index to, 68–69
   and mental illness, 566–70
   nature of, 14–17
   and social reorganization, 545–47
   and value conflict, 46–47
Social problems
   causal factors in, 9–23
   the citizen's role in remedying, 24–28
   definition of, 4
   measurement of, 6–9
   psychological factors in, 17–18
   risk conditions of, 19–23
   social disorganization as a factor in, 14–17

Socialization
  by the family, 383–84
  by the peer group, 387–91
  by the school, 386–87
Society
  as delinquent, 48–49
  moral reform of, 91–92
  and prejudice, 216–19
  and "service" crime, 144–45
  and white-collar crime, 147
Southern Regional Council, 241
States' rights, 242–43
Stereotypes, 181–82
Street society, delinquency as product of, 55
Subversion, in the schools, 435–37
Sweatt v. *Painter,* 306, 307

Townsend Plan, 518–19

Unions
  bureaucratization of, 540–41
  leadership problems of, 550–51
  and prejudice, 272
United Cerebral Palsy Association, 513–17
United fund appeals, 512–17
United Service for New Americans, 330
Urbanization, as a factor in social problems, 10–14

Value conflict
  delinquency as related to, 46–47
  in education, 416

Wetbacks, 323–24
White House Conference on Education, 441, 442–43, 445–46, 449–50
Widows, 376–77
Work, in contemporary society, 539–41, 552–62

REC'D OCT 17 1985